SOVEREIGNTY

For over 100 years the *Proceedings of the British Academy* series has provided a unique record of British scholarship in the humanities and social sciences. These themed volumes drive scholarship forward and are landmarks in their field. For more information about the series and guidance on submitting a proposal for publication, please visit www.thebritishacademy.ac.uk/proceedings

PROCEEDINGS OF THE BRITISH ACADEMY · 253

SOVEREIGNTY

A GLOBAL PERSPECTIVE

Edited by
CHRISTOPHER SMITH

Published for THE BRITISH ACADEMY
by OXFORD UNIVERSITY PRESS

Oxford University Press, Great Clarendon Street, Oxford OX2 6DP

© The British Academy 2022

Database right The British Academy (maker)

First edition published in 2022

All rights reserved. No part of this publication may be reproduced, stored in a retrieval system, or transmitted, in any form or by any means, without the prior permission in writing of the British Academy, or as expressly permitted by law, by licence or under terms agreed with the appropriate reprographics rights organisation. Enquiries concerning reproduction outside the scope of the above should be sent to the Publications Department, The British Academy, 10–11 Carlton House Terrace, London SW1Y 5AH

You must not circulate this book in any other form and you must impose this same condition on any acquirer

British Library Cataloguing in Publication Data
Data available

Library of Congress Cataloging in Publication Data
Data available

Typeset by Newgen Publishing UK
Printed in Great Britain by TJ Books Ltd, Padstow, Cornwall

ISBN 978-0-19-726712-7
ISSN 0068-1202

Contents

List of Figures	vii
Notes on Contributors	viii
Acknowledgements	xiii

General Introduction   1
CHRISTOPHER SMITH

Part I Ancient Sovereignty   13

1. On the Usability of the Concept of 'Sovereignty' for the Ancient World   15
   CHRISTOPH LUNDGREEN

2. *Actiones Populares*, Popular Sovereignty, and the People   38
   VALENTINA ARENA

3. Between Sovereignty and Non-Sovereignty: The *maiestas populi Romani* and Foundational Authority in the Roman Republic   58
   DEAN HAMMER

4. The Invention of Imperial Sovereignty   78
   RICHARD ALSTON

5. Forms and Narratives of Sovereignty in Early Imperial China: Beyond Heaven's Mandate, All-Under-Heaven, and So Forth   99
   LUKE HABBERSTAD

Part II Imperial Sovereignty   121

6. Thinking with Sovereignty in Australia   123
   JOANNA CRUICKSHANK, JULIE EVANS, ANN GENOVESE,
   CRYSTAL MCKINNON, AND SHAUN MCVEIGH

7. Scalar, Spectacular, and Subaltern Sovereignty: Colonial Autocracy, Democracy, and Interwar India   147
   STEPHEN LEGG

Part III Sovereign Technologies — **169**

8 Chinese World Order, Sovereignty, and International Practice — 171
CATHERINE JONES AND CHI ZHANG

9 The Institution of Sovereignty in Central Asia — 189
FILIPPO COSTA BURANELLI

10 Contested Privatisation: On the State of Monetary Sovereignty in the Euro Zone — 210
AARON SAHR AND CAROLIN MÜLLER

11 Three Conceptions of Sovereignty in Contemporary Investment Law — 235
TAYLOR ST JOHN

Part IV Sovereignty on the Edge — **255**

12 El Niño, Cholera, and the Productive Uncertainties of Water in Nairobi — 259
JOOST FONTEIN

13 Hosts and Higher Powers: Asylum Requests and Sovereignty — 282
ELENA ISAYEV

14 'The Definite Is the Shadow and not the Owner': Hannah Arendt in the Shadows of Sovereignty — 307
LYNDSEY STONEBRIDGE

15 Resonant Sovereignty? The Challenge of Social Acceleration – and the Prospect of an Alternative Conception — 323
HARTMUT ROSA

Index — 343

List of Figures

7.1	Historical maps of India, 1765 and 1805	152
7.2	Political divisions of the Indian Empire	153

Notes on Contributors

Richard Alston is Professor of Roman History in the Classics Department, Royal Holloway, University of London. Much of his work ranges across the economic, social, and intellectual history of the Roman period and the reception of that history in 19th- and 20th-century social thought. His most recent relevant work explores issues of political power through readings of Tacitus in conjunction with various modern political philosophers or has concerned itself with the transformations in political systems that came with the Augustan monarchy.

Valentina Arena is Professor of Ancient History at University College London. Her work focuses on the history of ancient ideas and ancient political thought as well as the wider intellectual landscape of the Roman Republic. She is the author of *Libertas and the Practice of Politics in the Late Roman Republic* (2012) and has edited and co-edited volumes on ancient political culture (*Ancient Liberty and Modern Perspectives*, 2020; *A Companion to Roman Political Culture*, 2021) and Varro and the antiquarian tradition (*Varronian Moments*, 2017; *Reconstructing the Roman Republic: Varro and Imperial Authors*, 2018). She is currently the Principal Investigator of the European Research Council-funded research project 'Ordering, Constructing, Empowering: Fragments of the Roman Republican Antiquarians'.

Filippo Costa Buranelli is Senior Lecturer in International Relations at the University of St Andrews and is currently Chair of the English School section at the International Studies Association. His interests include International Relations theory, international history, global governance, Eurasian politics, and regionalism. His research has been published in *Millennium: Journal of International Studies*, *International Studies Quarterly*, *International Politics*, *Geopolitics*, *International Relations*, and *Global Discourse*, among other outlets. His co-authored work on the history and evolution of regionalism has been recently included in the *Oxford Research Encyclopaedia of International Studies*.

Joanna Cruickshank is Senior Lecturer in History at Deakin University, Melbourne. She researches the history of Christianity in colonial Australia and the British Empire, with a particular focus on the relationship between race and religion. She is currently a Chief Investigator on an Australian Research Council-funded Discovery Indigenous project, titled 'Indigenous Leaders: Lawful Relations from Encounter to Treaty'. Her recent publications include 'Religious Freedom in "the Most Godless Nation under Heaven"' (*History Australia*, 2021) and *White Women, Aboriginal Missions and Australian Settler Governments* (Brill, 2019, co-authored with Patricia Grimshaw).

Julie Evans is Principal Fellow at the Melbourne Law School and School of Social & Political Sciences, University of Melbourne. Her work explores the significance of western law's relation to Indigenous peoples from the late 15th century to the present with a view to fostering more lawful ways forward. Her books include *Keeping Hold of Justice: Encounters Between Law and Colonialism* (University of Michigan Press, 2020, co-authors Jennifer Balint, Mark McMillan, and Nesam McMillan); *Sovereignty: Frontiers of Possibility* (University of Hawaii Press, 2013, co-editors Ann Genovese, Alexander Reilly, and Patrick Wolfe) and *Edward, Eyre, Race, and Colonial Governance* (Otago University Press, 2005).

Joost Fontein is Professor of Anthropology at the University of Johannesburg and former Director of the British Institute in Eastern Africa (Nairobi). His books include *The Silence of Great Zimbabwe: Contested Landscapes and the Power of Heritage* (UCL Press, 2006), *Remaking Mutirikwi: Landscape, Water & Belonging in Southern Zimbabwe* (James Currey, 2015), and *The Politics of the Dead in Zimbabwe 2000–2020: Bones, Rumours & Spirits* (James Currey, 2022). His more recent research has focused on emergence, materiality, and becoming in urban contexts, as part of a large multi-authored, collaborative project between scholars and artists that he co-initiated, entitled 'Nairobi Becoming'. He has co-curated various exhibitions, and he is a founding member of the Bones Collective Research Group, and co-founder of *Critical African Studies*.

Ann Genovese is Professor of Law at the Melbourne Law School. As an Australian historian, and a jurisprudent, she researches: the relationship between Law and History as disciplines and practices; the nature of legal archives and the responsibilities of custodians and writers towards them; and the sources, forms, and techniques necessary to show how Australian people have lived with their law. Ann's publications include *Sovereignty: Frontiers of Possibility* (with Julie Evans, Patrick Wolfe, and Alexander Reilly) (UHP, 2013) and *Australian Critical Decisions: Remembering the Koowarta and Tasmanian Dams Cases* (Routledge, 2017).

Luke Habberstad is Associate Professor of Early Chinese Literature and Religion at the University of Oregon, with research interests in the early Chinese empires, ritual, court culture and politics, and excavated texts. He is the author of *Forming the Early Chinese Court: Rituals, Spaces, Roles* (UW Press, 2017) and articles in *Early China*, *Journal of the Economic and Social History of the Orient*, and *Oriens Extremus*. Currently, he is researching and writing a book on hydraulic engineering and political culture in late Warring States and early imperial China.

Dean Hammer is the John W. Wetzel Professor of Classics and Professor of Government at Franklin and Marshall College (USA). He has written numerous articles on Greek and Roman politics, as well as on contemporary political theory. He is the author of *The Puritan Tradition* (Lang, 1998), *The Iliad as Politics: The Performance of Political Thought* (University of Oklahoma Press, 2002), *Roman*

Political Thought and the Modern Theoretical Imagination (University of Oklahoma Press, 2008) and *Roman Political Thought: From Cicero to Augustine* (Cambridge University Press, 2014), and is the editor of *A Companion to Greek Democracy and the Roman Republic* (Wiley-Blackwell, 2015).

Elena Isayev is a historian and practitioner focusing on migration, hospitality, and displacement, which she has written about in *Migration Mobility and Place in Ancient Italy* (Cambridge University Press, 2017), for the Red Cross, and in editing *Displacement and the Humanities* with Evan Jewell (*Humanities* 2018–21). She works with colleagues in Palestine, with 'Campus in Camps' and 'Decolonising Architecture', is co-founder of *AlMaisha*, a communal learning environment employing hospitality as a radical political act, and is part of the UNDRR/ICCROM expert panel on indigenous knowledges for disaster risk reduction. Currently leading 'Imagining Futures through Un/Archived Pasts' (AHRC, GCRF Network+), she is Professor of Ancient History and Place at the University of Exeter.

Catherine Jones is a lecturer in International Relations at the University of St Andrews. Her research focuses on China's interaction and contribution to international norms and their implementation. Her work on Sino-DPRK relations was funded by the Korea Foundation through their Next Generation of Scholars award in 2017–18. Since 2018, she has a research project exploring East Asian cooperation and coordination in the areas of humanitarian assistance and disaster relief. She teaches on Northeast Asian international relations and the politics and development of Southeast Asia. Her publications have appeared in *The Pacific Review*, *Pacific Focus*, and *International Politics*, and her first monograph, *China's Challenge to Liberal Norms*, was published by Palgrave in 2018.

Stephen Legg is Professor of Historical Geography at the University of Nottingham, where he has taught since 2006, having completed his degree, his doctorate, and a Junior Research Fellowship at the University of Cambridge. His research focuses on interwar India as situated within the context of late colonial imperialism and modern internationalism. He is the author of *Spaces of Colonialism: Delhi's Urban Governmentalities* (Blackwell, 2007), *Prostitution and the Ends of Empire: Scale, Governmentalities and Interwar India* (Duke University Press, 2014), and *Round Table Conference Geographies: Constituting Colonial India in Interwar London* (Cambridge University Press, 2022). Since 2020 he has served as an editor of the *Journal of Historical Geography*.

Christoph Lundgreen is Professor of Ancient History in Dresden, holds a Magister Artium from Humboldt Universität zu Berlin, a PhD from Technische Universität Dresden, and a Diplôme national de docteur from ÉPHÉ-Sorbonne, Paris. He has been awarded numerous grants and fellowships, including a Feodor Lynen research scholarship from the Alexander von Humboldt Foundation and the Heinz Maier-Leibnitz Prize. He was a Visiting Scholar in Stanford, Rome, and Pisa, as well as

Fellow in Hellenic Studies at the CHS, Harvard. In 2016, he was elected to the Junge Akademie at the Berlin-Brandenburg Academy of Sciences and Humanities and the German National Academy of Sciences Leopoldina, and in 2019 he was awarded the Heisenberg fellowship of the DFG. He is currently working on a monograph on *Dimensions of Staatlichkeit in the Early Greek World*, as well as on a project titled 'Populism in Antiquity'.

Crystal McKinnon is a Yamatji woman who lives and works on Kulin Nations country. She is a historian and a critical Indigenous studies scholar, who is currently working at RMIT as a Vice Chancellor's Indigenous Research Fellow in the Social and Global Studies Centre. McKinnon's research work has looked at concepts of Indigenous sovereignty, justice and law, and Indigenous social movements, resistance and protest through the use of the creative arts, including music and literature. She is currently lead Chief Investigator on an Australian Research Council-funded Discovery Indigenous project, titled 'Indigenous Leaders: Lawful Relations from Encounter to Treaty'. Her publications include 'The Lives Behind the Statistics' (*Australian Feminist Law Journal*, 2020) and (as co-editor) *History, Power and Text* (UTS, 2014).

Shaun McVeigh is British-Australian academic. He is concurrently a Professor at the Melbourne Law School, University of Melbourne, and the Kent Law School, University of Kent. His recent research investigates questions of public authority, conduct of lawful relations and ethics in Australia through the disciplines of jurisprudence and jurisography. He is currently a Chief Investigator on an Australian Research Council-funded Discovery Indigenous project, titled 'Indigenous Leaders: Lawful Relations from Encounter to Treaty'. His publications include *Jurisdiction* (Routledge, 2012, co-written with Shaunnagh Dorsett).

Carolin Müller is a research associate at the Hamburg Institute for Social Research and a member of the research group on monetary sovereignty. Her research interests include theories of international political economy and financial sociology, as well as sovereign debt and the politics of financial and sovereign debt crises. Her dissertation project focuses on the transformations of sovereign creditworthiness in the euro zone

Hartmut Rosa got his PhD from Humboldt University, Berlin in 1997. He is director of the Max-Weber-Center at Erfurt University and Chair of Sociology and Social Theory at Friedrich Schiller University, Jena, Germany. He was a visiting professor at the New School for Social Research in New York from 2001 to 2006 and at the FMSH/EHESS in Paris. From 2008 to 2018, he co-edited the international journal *Time&Society*. His publications include *Alienation and Acceleration* (NSU Press, 2007), *Social Acceleration: A New Theory of Modernity* (Columbia University Press, 2013), *Resonance. A Sociology of Our Relationship to the World* (Polity Press, 2019), and *The Uncontrollability of the World* (Polity Press 2020).

Aaron Sahr, economic sociologist, is visiting professor at Leuphana University Lüneburg and head of the research group on monetary sovereignty at the Hamburg Institute for Social Research. His research interests include the sociology of money, banking and economic theory, the history of capitalism, inequality, and social ontology.

Christopher Smith is Professor of Ancient History at the University of St Andrews. He has also served as Director of the British School at Rome and is currently Executive Chair of the Arts and Humanities Research Council. His books include *Early Rome and Latium: Economy and Society c1000 to 500 BC* and *The Roman Clan: The* Gens *from Ancient Ideology to Modern Anthropology*. His research interests include the development of early Rome and the notion of Roman kingship which developed over time.

Taylor St John is Lecturer in International Relations at the University of St Andrews. She researches the history and politics of investment law. Her monograph, *The Rise of Investor–State Arbitration: Politics, Law, and Unintended Consequences*, was published by Oxford University Press in 2018. Subsequently she has published on contemporary negotiations to reform investment law. She has been a Postdoctoral Research Fellow at PluriCourts, University of Oslo and a Fellow in International Political Economy at the London School of Economics. She received her DPhil from the University of Oxford.

Lyndsey Stonebridge is Interdisciplinary Professor of Humanities and Human Rights at the University of Birmingham, UK. Her recent books include *Placeless People: Rights, Writing, and Refugees* (Oxford University Press, 2018), winner of the Modernist Studies Association Best Book Prize, 2019, and *The Judicial Imagination: Writing after Nuremberg* (Edinburgh University Press, 2011), winner of the British Academy Rose Mary Crawshay Prize, 2014. Her collection of essays, *Writing and Righting: Literature in the Age of Human Rights*, was published in 2020 by Oxford University Press. Other books include *The Destructive Element* (Routledge, 1998), *Reading Melanie Klein* (with John Phillips, Routledge, 1998), *The Writing of Anxiety* (Palgrave Macmillan, 2007), and *British Fiction after Modernism* (with Marina MacKay, Palgrave Macmillan, 2007). She is currently writing a book on the relevance of Hannah Arendt for our times.

Chi Zhang is a British Academy Postdoctoral Fellow at the University of St Andrews and an Associate Member of the Handa Centre for the Study of Terrorism and Political Violence. Her areas of research interest fall broadly within security studies, constructivism, and Chinese political philosophy. She holds a PhD in Politics and International Studies from the University of Leeds, and a master's degree in South Asian Area Studies from the School of Oriental and African Studies. She published extensively in *Terrorism and Political Violence*, *Studies in Conflict & Terrorism*, *Politics and Religion*, and *Asian Security*.

Acknowledgements

THIS VOLUME ARISES from the annual conference of the St Andrews Institute for Legal and Constitutional Research, held on 29–30 April 2019, which was sponsored by the British Academy with a conference grant and by the Academia Europaea from the Curien Fund, as well as by the University of St Andrews, to all of whom I am extremely grateful. I am also indebted to the Leverhulme Trust for a Major Research Fellowship, 2017–20, during which this conference was formulated and took place.

John Hudson, Tony Lang, and Jason König of the Schools of History, International Relations and Classics, respectively, at the University of St Andrews offered generous support, and John Hudson in particular shouldered much of the burden of local administration together with Fiona Swift from the School of Classics. At the conference itself, Ingrid Ivarsen and James Crooks were especially helpful. I am also grateful to many individuals from IT support services and other parts of St Andrews for assistance during the event.

Several other colleagues attended the conference or supported the event in various ways: Riccardo Alcaro, Kanad Bagchi, Pamela Edwards, Joanna Empson, John Ferguson, Jim Gallagher, Knud Haakonsen, Benjamin Holland, Caroline Humfress, Konrad Lawson, Amy Russell, Leila Sansour, Mark Somos, Ian Taylor†, Ali Watson, Richard Whatmore, and John Wilson.

John Robertson was a tower of support throughout the whole process.

From the British Academy I would like to thank Johanna Empson and Portia Taylor and from the Academia Europaea, David Coates, and Juliet Davies. I am immensely grateful to Joshua Hey for support in the editing process.

The conference was opened by Professor Sally Mapstone, Principal and Vice-Chancellor of the University of St Andrews, and by Cabinet Secretary Fiona Hyslop, MSP, who generously supported the idea from its inception.

General Introduction

CHRISTOPHER SMITH

SOVEREIGNTY HAS BEEN much in the news and in the public discourse for the past few years. It was frequently mentioned in the run up to the Brexit referendum in June 2016. In an attempt to outline the distinctiveness of the UK's approach after the result, Prime Minister Theresa May contrasted British and European attitudes to 'pooling' sovereignty. A moment in the Brexit parliamentary debates which was hailed as a sign of our functioning democracy was when an Etonian and a Wykehamist debated the role of the English Civil War in settling the relationship between executive authority and parliamentary sovereignty. Prime Minister Boris Johnson declared that the UK had 'recaptured' its sovereignty after the departure from the European Union, and the Democratic Unionist Party have complained that the Northern Ireland Protocol which emerged has curtailed Northern Ireland's and, by extension, the United Kingdom's sovereignty. Over much of the same time period, the head of the European Central Bank, Mario Draghi, recommended pooling sovereignty, whilst the Greek government claimed that their sovereignty had been usurped by that very body, and we are now discussing sovereign debt in Europe again after the 2010 crisis has been followed by the post-COVID-19 economic challenges. US President Trump used the concept 21 times in his first speech to the United Nations. President Biden committed himself at the outset of his term to tribal sovereignty and self-governance for the Tribal Nations, to Ukraine's sovereignty and territorial integrity, and provoked China to declare its determination to protect its national sovereignty in a row over Taiwan. The desire to be in control of one's destiny in regard to the pandemic has led to the notion of vaccine sovereignty, which is playing out as an aspiration as well as a stimulus to highly defensive economic and political decision-making and rows over contracts. And as the finishing touches were put to this introduction, Russian tanks, troops, and bombs are bringing war to Ukraine, violating a sovereignty which President Putin does not recognise.

Why is it that sovereignty is, if not the central topic of our time, a topic around which cluster an unusually large number of key debates? Not so long ago, there were serious questions raised over the extent to which sovereignty had any part of play in a 21st-century, globalising, ever smaller world, one where systemic shocks rippled with astonishing speed across digitised banking systems, where space age military weaponry rendered territoriality void, and where the multiple challenges of the Anthropocene demanded global approaches to climate change, population movement, and disease. It is, on the face of it, ironic that at precisely the time when an airborne virus has spread exponentially fast across continents, we see an uptick in attempts to erect the sturdy defences of sovereign power. Are we hammering shut the door after the horses have bolted? Did we forget tried and trusted mechanisms of rational self-protection, or are we reverting to an outdated symbol? This volume represents an attempt to address some of these questions, by focusing on the contingency of sovereignty and on its historical situatedness.

My own interest in sovereignty starts with the notion of a sovereign, and specifically a very early example, the Roman kings, those misty early figures such as Romulus and Numa and Tarquin the Proud, who give the underpinnings of the earliest history of the city, and were repeatedly reflected upon over time. Whether any of these kings actually existed is a moot point, but the Romans believed they did, and they wrote narratives of kingly behaviour both good and bad, which were absorbed into the bloodstream of classical western political philosophy, along with the kings of the Bible, from John of Salisbury to Machiavelli, and I would argue beyond.

In particular, the Roman king could be figured as a sort of father to the people, a *paterfamilias*, whose capacity over life and death, and in particular over the ability to exclude someone from the community, to make them *sacer*, offered two stories about what a sovereign looked like, which became transmuted in various ways. The possibility that sovereignty has a real prehistory is explored in this volume by Arena, Hammer, Alston, and Lundgreen, and in a rather different way by Isayev; but the stories of antiquity also furnished modernity with helpful metaphors.

The story of the *paterfamilias* was brilliantly revealed by Mary Nyquist (2015) as constitutive of a range of arguments over anti-tyranny, slavery, and revolution in early modern thought. The avoidance of slavery, and the justifiable limits to which an individual or a state could go in defending liberty, are debated through stories such as Tarquin's impiety towards his father-in-law (and worse his wife, who runs over her father in her chariot) and Brutus' discovery that his sons are plotting against the state and his subsequent ordering of their execution. The power of sovereignty derives from a family affair. This quasi-domestication and internalisation of the rule of law is part of the long-running trope of the state as a simulacrum of the patriarchal family, which was comforting to some, less so to others.

In more modern times, the power of the sovereign became cast more negatively as the capacity to reduce a human to nothing more than bare life, to render them *sacer*, to put them beyond the pale of human existence (Alston and Stonebridge, this volume). Agamben's (1998) *Homo Sacer* actually bears a rather slight relationship to antiquity, but the idea has been immensely significant; it seems so perfectly to define the plight of those who have fallen or are placed beyond borders, outside states. But the capacity to declare something *sacer* is as close to something real about the ancient powers of the Roman kings as we have. The connection arises from the coexistence on an inscription from the 6th century BCE in the Roman forum of the words king, and *sacer*, and a plausible reference to assembly. The king and the people and the excluded world circle tantalisingly on a piece of stone which stood for centuries in Rome's assembly place, possibly incomprehensible for most of that time, and found in 1899 by Giacomo Boni, around the time he was visited by James George Frazer (he of *The Golden Bough*) and just before Freud finally faced the city that terrified him. The Black Stone in time becomes the Black Box of Michel Serres' extraordinary reinvention of human history, which reaches through to Bruno Latour's worries about modernity and then back to Bergsonian problems about time, and then to Assman and the notion of memory.[1]

Much of this writing and rewriting of our beginnings is highly fictional, and the usual account was that it was also irrelevant, because the critical move from a sovereign to sovereignty rendered the old story irrelevant. But that depends on another myth, the myth of the sovereign state, whose specific characteristics come into being, or are disclosed, as the product of early modernity but at the same time as something of ineluctable logic. The less convinced we are about our kings, however, perhaps the less convinced we should be about the abstraction of their power. And from that doubt, in large part, this conference was inspired.

Sovereignty has been a much-used term in political discourse since Bodin, but it has also been noted that it has been more often used than explained, more frequently drawn into debate than analysed. There is something evasive about the nature of sovereignty, which is only partially concealed by the highly definitive way in which it is sometimes used. Hence, in one of the most recent discussions, Bourke & Skinner (2016: 1) write that '[p]opular sovereignty is a key component of modern political thinking, yet a history of the concept has not previously been attempted'. Their volume shows at every stage how this particular phenomenon of sovereignty is less unitary and more debated than one might suppose, an argument further supported by Arena's chapter here.

Moreover, especially in literature which has emphasised the supposed weakness of the modern nation-state in the face of globalisation, sovereignty has been regarded as lagging behind transnational developments, and there is a substantial literature on the problems of sovereignty as a conceptual framework or as a political tool (Barbour & Pavlich 2009; Love 2009; explored especially by Jones & Zhang and Costa Buranelli in the context of states manipulating western notions of sovereignty in search of competitive advantage). For a brief moment, just as Fukuyama announced history was over, so scholars – recognising that first our accounts of sovereignty were perhaps a lot more contingent than we had allowed for, second that the worst face of sovereignty arguments, what came to be called sovereigntism

---

[1] Favaretto & Pilutti Namer (2016) on Boni; Frazer (1911–15); Timpanaro (1984) on Freud; Serres (2015); Serres & Latour (1995).

in the Quebec independence debates, shaded into an ugly nationalism, and third that our challenges and perhaps some of our solutions were larger than the nation-state – started to wonder if the concept made any sense any more.

Thus a simple evolutionary model which moves from some original point of the emergence of the concept either as a theoretical framework, or as an actual phenomenon of political action (i.e. as description or performance), through absolutism to popular sovereignty to the sovereignty of the nation-state to a contemporary 'fuzzy', attenuated or redundant existence is highly problematic.[2] Each step of this path is insecure, as indeed is the idea that there is a single developmental line which is relevant beyond the specific historical circumstances of Europe.

At the same time, there have been significant attempts to restore the notion of sovereignty, such as Tuck (2016; cf. Loughlin 2016), and insofar as sovereignty exists to resolve a problem, that is the locus of the legitimacy of authority and law-making, it is clear that the problem will remain even if sovereignty as a concept were to be jettisoned (Stanton 2016).

This then leads to the philosophical challenge: what kind of concept is sovereignty? What would be lost if we stopped using it? These questions are not new, and the methodological framework in which they have been located is itself fragmented. As suggested by Koskenniemi (2010), the variety of approaches to sovereignty through law, history, politics, international relations, and globalisation studies do not end up resolving the paradox of sovereignty but merely reveal further incompatibilities in its performance.

We wish to start from Koskenniemi's (2010) observation that sovereignty fundamentally has to do with a conversation about power. Arguably, sovereignty takes this further by positing a notion of ultimate authority, though that remains a claim, an assertion which is itself embedded in a discourse of power. It proves difficult to locate this highest authority, but the volume is full of claims to hold or find the location of such ultimate resort. Whether one regards sovereignty as organised hypocrisy (Krasner 1999), a state of exceptionality (Schmitt 1985; Agamben 1998; Negri 2010), a necessary moderating principle within the dialectic relationship between constitution and revolution (Stanton 2016), or an idea which is in need of a revision, it is difficult to avoid the conclusion that sovereignty still matters, whether rhetorically, conceptually, or potentially as a positive project for the future.

Wittgenstein (1953: §115) said 'a picture held us captive. And we could not get outside of it, for it lay in our language, and language seemed to repeat it to us inexorably'. This applies, we argue, to the case of sovereignty; it lies in our language and we are having difficulty thinking outide it. As Havercroft (2011: 1) has elaborated Wittgenstein's phrase, '[a] picture holds the study of politics captive. It is a picture of politics organized into sovereign states'.

---

[2] See Monsutti (2012) for fuzziness; MacCormick (2010) and Praet (2010) for some post-sovereign scenarios; cf. Kalmo & Skinner (2010); Bourke & Skinner (2016).

Yet what countless studies have shown is that sovereignty is not one thing, and it is not timeless and it is not perfect; it is multifarious, highly contingent, and always at best an argument. It can be an argument about a person, a place, a corporation, a state, a combination of states (well-illustrated by the examples of India and Australia discussed here by Cruickshank *et al.* and Legg). It is now no longer only a subject for a small group of historically minded political scientists. For good or ill it belongs to the discourse of international law and the plight of the dispossessed, to the global banker and the working-class white voter, to the ecological campaigner and the cartographer. And it may even be allowed to Indigenous peoples who have been denied access to or knowledge of the concept; indeed, much of our argument implies that we have an obligation to recover the concept of sovereignty which was deployed by those against whom western sovereignty was weaponised specifically to deny their own intellectual values and accounts. In other words, one can find something which looks like one or other definition of sovereignty in many times and places, but we often see the claim to have 'real' sovereignty used offensively.

It makes no sense to say that sovereignty does not matter any more, because it clearly matters hugely to a great number of people, notably those who feel their rights to self-determination are threatened, but hardly any of them agree on how or why. Yet the notion of ultimacy, of the need to decide, for instance in Schmitt's (1985: 5) brilliant invention of the declaration of the exception, is seductive even when terribly misleading.

This volume was conceived not in the hope that we might resolve the muddle into a brilliant single solution, but rather that we might be more precise about the reason why sovereignty is as imprecise and as mythical and somehow ubiquitous as my early Roman kings. Our contention is that we might try to do this by looking for alternative genealogies and placing the concept in a broad international framework including contemporary global challenges such as the role of supranational military forces, financial regulation and human rights, with a specific focus on migration and environmentalism, and by contextualising it within the framework of critical theory.

Like power, sovereignty is a capacity, and as such it is not something we can lightly deny to people who have never had it because we have got past it; one of the most powerful moments at the conference came when Leila Sansour, founder and CEO of Open Bethlehem, showed a picture of the absurdly complex walled-in powerlessness of modern Bethlehem and said 'this is what it looks like to live without sovereignty'. The notion of sovereignty as a terrifying absence is also visible in the accounts by Isayev and Stonebridge of the (non-)place of refugees. Nation-states, however, are simply not the only entities with real ultimacy, as we have seen time and again in moments of natural disaster, financial collapse, or wanton despotism; Fontein's exploration of alternative sovereignties in the face of natural disaster is an example. And the latter is much aided by the notion of sovereigntism, the retreat behind borders which in so many places has turned out to be rather porous if not hopelessly ineffectual against overwhelming force. It is not at all surprising that the first story of the invincible border is Remus' demonstration that the Roman border did not work.

This does, however, neatly take us to the performative aspect of sovereignty. Zvi Ben-Dor Benite, Stefanos Geroulanos, and Nicole Jerr's recent edited volume *The Scaffolding of Sovereignty* (2017) insists that we take fuller account of the way sovereignty is performed and staged. Their starting point is very similar to mine, the contingency and imprecision of sovereignty, its potential harmfulness, its potentially poisoned promise, and their move to argue that the place we should look is the process of shoring up the rickety and fake staging, the smoke and mirror effects which aim at excluding too close an awareness of how artificial it all is. Sovereignty in the realm of aesthetics is their goal, and it is present in a number of chapter present in this volume, most obviously Legg's account of British displays of sovereignty in India.

An aesthetic of sovereignty helpfully reminds us that the concept is essentially about persuasion. The aesthetics of architecture can extend to the architecture of a wall which imposes an idea of sovereignty whilst radically dehumanising those beyond it, as for instance in John Lanchester's (2018) recent ecological apocalyptic novel *The Wall*, but the realities of law and the minutiae of process, the stuff of the archive, also need to be understood, I think, as part of a pathology of modernity. Wendy Brown (2010: 132) has worried precisely in the context of borders about sovereignty as what Freud calls an illusion powered by a myth. This implies that like religion, which was the subject of Freud's argument, sovereignty is not going anywhere, but perhaps also that pointing out the fact that it is all greasepaint and fustian is not quite enough. The reason sovereignty is so ubiquitous is that it stands for a set of desires which require analysis if they are not to become fetishised ends in themselves.

The focus of this volume therefore aims directly at the problem of the future of sovereignty; and this is explicit in St John's account of international arbitration, Isayev's discussion of sovereignty and asylum, and Rosa's epilogue on sovereignty and resonance. By putting sovereignty as a problem at the heart of our discussions, we hope to be able to see what it is that it is standing for, and why our desire to have ultimacy needs to be reassessed in the light of a new kind of politics more suited to our times. Can we find less problematic models of sovereignty, or more successful alternatives to sovereignty, for the contemporary period and in a global perspective?

One way of approaching this is to disrupt the standard genealogy of sovereignty, and here we take our lead from Bourke and Skinner's (2016) genealogy of popular sovereignty. Our argument will be that once one allows sovereignty to be conceptually operational before the early modern period, then other case studies of non-popular sovereignty become relevant, most obviously the two more or less contemporary empires of Rome and Han China (for the latter, see Habberstad, this volume). Moreover, the inevitable focus of debates around periods of intense crisis – the English Civil War, the French Revolution, the emergence of totalitarianism, to give three examples – distracts from the operation of power and authority in other times and places, where the dualism between sole ruler and people may be less relevant, and where the exercise of power may be straightforwardly mapped onto monarch, people, or nation-state.

Moreover, there is a challenging issue over the notion of sovereignty in the context of powerful populist leaders, who may claim popular support but may not really have popular sovereignty in mind. A concentration of power in the executive (which the federal structure of revolutionary America attempted, unsuccessfully, to avoid) brings into focus problems of government (Loughlin 2016) and of uniquely challenging interstices where traditional models will not work. For instance, it has been argued by Ong (2006; 2012) that models of graduated sovereignty better describe the world of globalised finance and (de-)regulation (cf. Holden 2017; Sahr and Müller, this volume; St John, this volume).

Another approach is pragmatic. Both the plethora of projects around sovereignty and the centrality of the subject to both national and international discourse invite debate, but thus far most of that debate has been genealogical, problematising, or descriptive – that is to say that the debate has demonstrated the fragility and incoherence of sovereignty, without being able to remove it from our discourse, or replace it. It would appear that we need sovereignty, even if we do not always like the way it is working, actively or rhetorically.

The challenge therefore is to move from the critical analysis of the frailty of sovereignty to a discussion of what we need sovereignty to do at various levels, local to international, and what sort of definition or description would best answer those needs. To be concrete, what are the ways in which we can describe sovereignty such that its supposedly indivisible nature is not an obstacle in an interdependent world, and that permits the coexistence of sovereignty and governance in a world of increasingly technical regulation? How can sovereignty be rescued from a description whereby it restricts rather than enables international conversations?

Koskenniemi (2010) has already pointed to the challenge of aligning deconstructive readings of sovereignty with actual conflict. An obvious example of the move towards shared goals of defence would be the recent development of PESCO (Permanent Structured Cooperation) at the EU level, but equally obvious are examples where local levels of perceived sovereignty are at the heart of crises over whether to intervene in crises such as in Syria or territorial ones such as the now tragically relevant conflict between Russia and Ukraine (Stoler 2006). What definitions of sovereignty are needed in conflict situations?

In the tension leading to and during military conflict, human rights are often a casualty; but human rights are at stake in broader conversations where sovereignty plays a problematic role (Macklem 2015). These include large-scale migration phenomena, issues over land ownership and land use, and climate change (see Fontein, Isayev and St John in this volume). One significant issue is accountability; if sovereignty defines accountability, where do we place the sovereign in issues such as the spoliation of the Amazonian rainforests (see e.g. Wapner 2002)? And what impact do international agreements such as the Paris Climate Change Accord have on sovereignty – do they strengthen, weaken, displace, or conceal accountability?

Whilst human rights often appear to be the most urgent and challenging issue, our interdependence also requires agreement on a huge range of individual areas of regulation. The process of the UK separating from the EU has shown the extent to which international regulation has expanded, and the debate remains sharp as to whether this represents a step forward or a diminution of sovereign control – and the whole area of regulation is one of the most significant elements of the globalisation debate.

It is interesting to note that the 2008/9 banking crisis has led to reconsiderations of the notion of sovereignty within the context of finance. For instance, the proposal by leading think-tank Bruegel specifically seeks to break what has been a consistent linkage between banks and sovereign debt through a European Sovereign Debt Restructuring Mechanism (Gianviti *et al.* 2010; Sahr and Müller, this volume). This reflects a broader issue; trade, flows of capital, and expected standards often transcend national borders, yet are often drawn into arguments over the diminution of the sovereign right to be free from the legislation of others. There is a radical insolubility here in that it is likely to be unclear in any given crisis, both immediately and over time, whether the predominance of blame lies with the absence of freedom from general yet onerous legislative requirements or the failure to implement more stringent regulation across wider areas; and there is a further insolubility in that the pragmatic difficulty of including everyone in a single framework implies that at some point borders will be drawn. Any optimistic claim of placing sovereignty at the very highest level of global governance is likely to meet this obstacle.

The key question therefore must be how to reconcile the inevitability and undeniable desirability of international governance with national sovereignty. How can we describe sovereignty in such a way as to tolerate conditions of cooperation and interdependence? This group of ideas then initiate the following thoughts:

1   One solution to our conundrum is to place sovereignty to one side of some key debates. If sovereignty owns but a part of the field of politics, this leaves the opportunity to confine sovereignty to areas of specific utility. Once that is permitted, it seems that sovereignty is already not only capable of being applied differently at different levels, but that at each particular level, government and accountability may be distinctively defined and applied. Sovereignty can be glossed as 'sovereignty-to' or 'sovereignty-over' with the relevant degree of derogation, accountability and limitation in law.

2   The idea of 'bundles of rights' as applied to sovereignty was proposed by Taylor (1997) and is congruent with this approach. In essence, the idea (derived from property law) is of bundled rights, where individual sticks can be passed over in certain circumstances without loss of the capacity to exercise the other rights. Taylor's additional step is to allow that non-state actors can receive some of these 'sticks' because they do not thereby become states.

3   The obvious challenge is where and how to move sovereignty to a higher supranational level, or to non-sovereign bodies; what remains at the traditional popular/nation-state level of sovereignty; and where accountability lies.

4   If, as stated above, theories of sovereignty vary so much precisely because they seek in specific circumstances to reconcile power and the desire for limit or accountability, to create a dialogic relationship in which the balance is held between constitution and revolution, and however rhetorically or hypocritically to construct a model of consent, it might be asked why at this stage the notion of sovereignty is in such crisis. One answer might lie in the notion of acceleration or, in other words, the sense that the modern world is moving so fast that there is a 'desynchronisation' of systems that disrupts the dream of dynamic stability and threatens to destroy the fabric of society and the planet itself (Rosa 2013). Many of the symptoms of the 'problem' of sovereignty (loss of control on the one hand, the failure to keep up with challenges facing the planet on the other) can be described precisely as 'desynchronicities' threatening a model which is almost by definition always intended to create an answer to forces of destabilisation.

5   Therefore, the larger framework with which the volume concludes is precisely to deploy the sociological theory developed as a response to acceleration, that of resonance (Rosa 2019; this volume). This attempts to develop a critical theory which places emphasis on responsive, transformative, non-instrumental relationships between individuals and their environments. The problem is defined as alienation in the mode of existence, the mode or form of our orientation towards the world, and whilst this can be set at the level of our absence of personal fulfilment, it can be scaled to a failure of resonance with our relationships towards the destitute or the natural world.

6   The argument is then that sovereignty should be a condition of the kind of government that can protect citizens and promote their liberty, but that implies that sovereignty is simply an instrument of human thriving, and that in a complex world, it should be regarded as a bundled concept where elements can be given up or transferred, and that the criteria for our judgement calls should be in line with a conception of resonance in its fullest sense, which includes a capacity to listen to and respond to different and dissonant views.

The chapters in this volume range from antiquity to the present, from China to Australia to Africa and beyond. Each section has its own introduction to give focus. The timescale and geographical extent are deliberately wide, and the notions of sovereignty canvassed – popular, national, mythical, technical – are intended to denote the non-unitary nature of the concept, and the disparate and contextualised work which sovereignty does. Despite their pervasive shadow, the absence of specific focus on the classic texts of sovereignty, from Bodin through Hobbes to Locke, is a deliberate attempt to differentiate our account from those which depend on a specific moment of 'invention' that is thereafter canonical. Instead, we argue that versions of sovereignty can be located in very different times and places, and some are less benign than others.

Sovereignty is a concept whose aggregative and expansive demands need to be constrained and guarded against. If we allow it to be unexamined and ill-defined, it can escape its historical and philosophical limits and do great damage. If we prefer an offensive mode of sovereignty to its more defensive potential to define and delimit the power of one over another, and to underpin the essence of respect for others even to the extent of self-diminution in favour of a greater good, we lay the most vulnerable open to even greater harm. This volume cannot by itself redeem a concept which has been so misused, or resolve its fundamental ambiguities, but by drawing attention to them we seek to point the way to a more thoughtful approach.

References

Agamben, G. (1998), *Homo Sacer: Sovereign Power and Bare Life* (Stanford, Stanford University Press).
Barbour, C. & Pavlich, G. (eds) (2009), *After Sovereignty: On the Question of Political Beginnings* (London, Routledge).
Ben-Dor Benite, Z., Geroulanos, S., & Jerr, N. (eds) (2017), *The Scaffolding of Sovereignty* (New York, Columbia University Press).
Bourke, R. & Skinner, Q. (eds) (2016), *Popular Sovereignty in Historical Perspective* (Cambridge, Cambridge University Press).
Brown, W. (2010), *Walled States, Waning Sovereignty* (Cambridge MA, MIT Press).
Favaretto, I. & Pilutti Namer, M. (eds) (2016), *Tra Roma e Venezia: la cultura dell'antico nell'Italia dell'Unità. Giacomo Boni e i contesti* (Venice, Istituto Veneto di Scienze, Lettere ed Arti).
Frazer, J.G. (1911–15), *The Golden Bough: A Study in Magic and Religion* (London, Macmillan and Co.).
Gianviti, F., Krueger, A.O., Pisani-Ferry, J., Sapir, A., & von Hagen, J. (2010), *A European Mechanism for Sovereign Debt Crisis Resolution* (Brussels, Bruegel).
Havercroft, J. (2011), *Captives of Sovereignty* (Cambridge, Cambridge University Press).
Holden, C. (2017), 'Graduated Sovereignty and Global Governance Gaps: Special Economic Zones and the Illicit Trade in Tobacco Products', *Political Geography*, 59: 72–81.
Kalmo, H. & Skinner, Q. (eds) (2010), *Sovereignty in Fragments: The Past, Present and Future of a Contested Concept* (Cambridge, Cambridge University Press).
Koskenniemi, M. (2010), 'Conclusion: Vocabularies of Sovereignty – The Powers of a Paradox', in Kalmo & Skinner (2010), 222–41.
Krasner, S.D. (1999), *Sovereignty: Organized Hypocrisy* (Princeton, Princeton University Press).
Lanchester, J. (2018), *The Wall* (London, Faber & Faber).
Loughlin, M. (2016), 'Active, Passive, or Dead? Sovereignty', rev. Tuck 2016, *London Review of Books*, 16 June 2016.
Love, M.C. (2009), *Beyond Sovereignty: Issues for a Global Agenda* (Boston, Wadsworth).
MacCormick, N. (2010), 'Sovereignty and After', in Kalmo & Skinner (2010), 151–68.
Macklem, P. (2015), *The Sovereignty of Human Rights* (Oxford, Oxford University Press).
Monsutti, A. (2012), 'Fuzzy Sovereignty: Rural Reconstruction in Afghanistan, between Democracy Promotion and Power Games', *Comparative Studies in Society and History*, 54.3: 563–91.
Negri, A. (2010), 'Sovereignty between Government, Governance and Acceptance', in Kalmo & Skinner (2010), 205–21.
Nyquist, M. (2015), *Arbitrary Rule: Slavery, Tyranny, and the Power of Life and Death* (Chicago, Chicago University Press).

Ong, A. (2006), *Neoliberalism as Exception: Mutations in Citizenship and Sovereignty* (Durham NC, Duke University Press).
Ong, A. (2012), 'Powers of Sovereignty: State, People, Wealth, Life,' *Focaal: Journal of Global and Historical Anthropology*, 62: 24–35.
Praet, P. (2010), 'Prolegomena to the Post-Sovereign *Rechtsstaat*', in Kalmo & Skinner (2010), 169–85.
Rosa, H. (2013), *Social Acceleration: A New Theory of Modernity* (New York, Columbia University Press).
Rosa, H. (2019), *Resonance: A Sociology of Our Relationship to the World* (Cambridge, Polity Press).
Schmitt, C. (1985), *Political Theology: Four Chapters on the Concept of Sovereignty* (Chicago, Chicago University Press).
Serres, M. (2015), *Rome: The Book of Foundations*, trans. R. Burks (London, Bloomsbury).
Serres, M. & Latour, B. (1995), *Conversations on Science, Culture, and Time*, trans. R. Lapidus (Ann Arbor, University of Michigan Press).
Stanton, T. (2016), 'Popular Sovereignty in an Age of Mass Democracy: Politics, Parliament and Parties in Weber, Kelsen, Schmitt and Beyond', in Bourke & Skinner (2016), 320–58.
Stoler, A.L. (2006), 'On Degrees of Imperial Sovereignty', *Public Culture*, 18.1: 125–46.
Taylor, C.R. (1997), 'A Modest Proposal: Statehood and Sovereignty in a Global Age', *University of Pennsylvania Journal of International Economic Law*, 18: 745–809.
Timpanaro, S. (1984), 'Freud's Roman Phobia', *New Left Review*, 147 (September–October): 4–31.
Tuck, R. (2016), *The Sleeping Sovereign: The Invention of Modern Democracy* (Cambridge, Cambridge University Press).
Wapner, P. (2002), 'The Sovereignty of Nature? Environmental Protection in a Postmodern Age', *International Studies Quarterly*, 46.2: 167–87.
Wittgenstein, L. (1953), *Philosophical Investigations*, trans. E. Anscombe (Oxford, Basil Blackwell).

Part I

Ancient Sovereignty

Introduction

THE FIVE CHAPTERS in this section offer a connected range of arguments which challenge the modern supremacy of the notion. The Roman example bulks large because the language of 'modern' sovereignty draws so evidently on Roman legal traditions and their evolution. What these chapters reveal, however, is a more complex story.

On the whole sovereignty is not widely used as a concept for antiquity, partly because of the notion that it is only pertinent to the modern period. However, these chapters show that aspects of sovereignty are valid in antiquity, and that the various aspects which are drawn upon highlight the fact that modern sovereignty is variously conceived and practised. In other words, comparison with antiquity shows modern sovereignty to be neither uniform nor unprecedented.

As Lundgreen shows in his wide-ranging chapter, to understand the way that sovereignty in this more fragile sense worked and evolved, one has also to think about (in Lundgreen's formulation) different attributes of 'Staatlichkeit', both the arrival at a density of public capacity (what Lundgreen calls stateness) and the external recognition normally applied to statehood. (It is helpful to read this chapter alongside Isayev's later use of Greek tragedy to inform notions of responsibility and obligation to outsiders.) One approach could be to deny that the markers of internal authority and external recognition amount to a sufficient level as to justify the appellations of sovereignty or stateness, but the underpinning question is whether these are ever achieved in their fullness or always on a spectrum; if the latter, we see approximations to a more or less clearly defined ideal, or the effective and functional possession of some but not necessarily all aspects of any given definition.

Arena approaches the notion of popular sovereignty and extracts the existence of some notion of the *populus* as having agency from a particular legal practice whereby any Roman citizen could act in defence of the *res publicae* (understood as their own property). This basic idea of the *populus* as a fictive person at such an early stage then underpins the idea of how one of its attributes could be its grandeur, or *maiestas*. This is the theme of Hammer's argument, that in time *maiestas* comes to have some of the attributes one might attribute to an independent notion of sovereignty, independent that is from a sovereign.

These two chapters therefore argue for two aspects of developed modern notions of sovereignty existing already in antiquity in some form, the notion of power deriving from the people and the idea of the abstraction of a notion of sovereignty from any individual. Alston looks in detail at the passage to the principate, the period in which an emperor helds sway, which Arena and Hammer both allude to. Arguably the weakness of these notions as defences of popular or non-personal sovereignty, and the forceful strength of Augustus' intervention, rest in his ability to create an institution in which a claim of popular support was combined with the transfer of the notion of *maiestas* to his own person. Alston's use of contemporary theory from Foucault to Agamben and Rancière focuses attention on the biopolitical aspect, 'the perceived dependence of the normal and everyday on the sovereign', including life and death, but also models for behaviour and sociability. The accumulation of communicative resource in the emperor and his family is key here, part of the scaffolding of sovereignty already discussed.

This more contingent view is supported by Habberstad's account of a different ancient example, from China. The notion of a 'mandate from Heaven' is interesting in that it is also a fictive but effective harnessing of religious power to strengthen the biopolitical aspects of the emperor's enormous power. However, Habberstad is also able to show that the concept was not stable, but rather fluctuated over time, and that it was revived in the guise of continuity. What follows is the sense that the abstraction of sovereignty as a concept hallowed by time is neither unique to the west nor a stable fact, but rather it is a rhetorical ploy, a mechanism of self-perpetuation.

It is of course no surprise to discover that sovereignty does not exist but is consistently reinvented. The chapters in this section, however, with their persistent explicit or implicit reference forward to the debates of the 16th and 17th centuries, undermine any notion that sovereignty is essentially modern. The tension between its normative conceptual capacity and its rhetorical function in the service of violence and power looks forward to both 19th-century reuse and more modern rethinking of sovereignty, for instance in China again (Jones and Zhang, this volume) and in central Asia (Costa Buranelli).

1

On the Usability of the Concept of 'Sovereignty' for the Ancient World

CHRISTOPH LUNDGREEN

Prologue

CORINTH, BETWEEN THE 7th and 6th centuries BCE, saw the prosperous rule of Periander. Doric temples and public buildings, a flourishing trade and Corinthian pottery, colonies and conquests are all attributed to the tyrant, who has sometimes even been counted as one of the Seven Sages. Only in his private relations was Periander less successful. Herodotus tells of Periander having, by accident or in rage, killed his wife, Melissa. When their son, Lykophron, found out and mourningly refused to ever speak with his father again, Periander angrily told him to leave the palace and instructed his herald publicly proclaim: 'that whoever sheltered the boy in his house or spoke to him, would owe a fine to Apollo'. Consequently, his son walked around lonely, hungry, and desperate, until Periander took pity on him; he asked his son whether he would not prefer to come back, accept his authority, and continue to live in the palace as the son of the ruler. Herodotus then tells of Lykophron answering that now he, Periander, would owe the money to the temple since he had just spoken to him, whereupon Periander banished his son to Kerkyra.[1]

Questions, problems, premises

This is not the place to delve into details about Periander's rule nor his family. Let us think, however, where, how, and if one could apply at any point the notion of sovereignty to this story. Many questions come to mind; for instance, should we regard Corinth, due to its infrastructural projects, colonies, and conquests, as a

---

[1] The story, to which we will return, is reported by Herodotus 3.50–3; the quotations follow the translation by Godley (Loeb). For Periander's rule, see Schmitz (2010: 37–45).

sovereign entity? Should we regard Periander as a sovereign ruler? Would it be important, for that matter, to know whether he did pay money to the temple of Apollo? Moreover, are the statements regarding the island of Corinth and its ruler, Periander, linked or independent of each other? And what would be the implication of applying 'sovereignty' at any specific point to this story? Behind this last question lurks the widely held assumption that one should not apply the notion of sovereignty to an ancient or pre-modern time,[2] since the term was coined much later, together with – and, indeed, for – the modern state,[3] with which we must therefore deal with in this chapter, too. Any meaningful responses to the claim of modernity can only consist in a careful reconstruction of different notions of sovereignty, for which no simple definitions exist.[4]

In the next section, a brief overview will be provided of versions and variants of sovereignty, in order to argue that we should not try in vain to find the one true definition but, instead, appreciate that this gemstone of political theory has many different aspects and is multifaceted. It is the use of specific facets of the term that has, in my view, a greater potential than an attempt to apply one large definition of sovereignty, especially since there are so many to choose from. 'Usability', furthermore, is not in itself a sufficient concept. Whereas one is, of course, free to 'use' whatever term one likes, there are two general rules to keep in mind. First, one should avoid confusion. Second, and more interesting, one should question how fruitful the terminology is. The first precept ranges from the mere avoidance of private language, in the sense of Wittgenstein, to an insistence on making one's own benchmarks and values explicit, in the sense of Weber; it also comprises knowledge of academic traditions as well as the history of the concept.[5] The second precept looks at the heuristic value and explanatory power of any chosen terminology. Are the terms used more selectively than others, in order to highlight differences? Or are they 'key-concepts', opening new perspectives thanks to their semantic, maybe

---

[2] To give but a few examples, Schuller (1993), in an article entitled 'Polis as State', emphasises sovereignty as the criterion for drawing a distinction between the 'modern' and the 'pre-modern' state. Hansen (1995: xi) states that while one could use without any problem the terms city-state for *polis*, constitution for *politeia*, and democracy for *demokratía* (which is doubtful), the term sovereignty should be avoided. Hansen (2006) has modified his vision:
> A new fluent concept of state is developing, one in which sovereignty and independence are concepts that have to be either redefined or dissociated from the concept of state. A new parallel between the concepts of *polis* and state is emerging, one which did not exist a few decades ago, but one which might be of importance in our re-evaluation of the concept of state in the years to come. (65)

The dominant tradition, however, remains sceptical, as represented by Christian Meier, with explicit reference to Carl Schmitt. See Lundgreen (2014a: 22–3).
[3] Koselleck (1990: 1). Berent (2000) constitutes a good example for the inherent difficulties for discussion of the notion of sovereignty for the (in his view) stateless Greek *polis*.
[4] Different aspects of sovereignty as an ambiguous and contested concept are discussed, for instance, in Kalmo & Skinner (2010), whose introduction is particularly recommended.
[5] Weber (1904: 156–7 and 181); as for the historical change of the content of the term, Koselleck (1990) remains fundamental.

even metaphoric, content?[6] Simply put, for our case, the question is: what do we gain by using the term 'sovereignty' when referring to ancient institutions or phenomena?[7] If this last criterion is not met, then historians merely play around with labels and get, as their 'results', a repetition of their starting definitions.[8] This will become all the more apparent when we look at some variants of sovereignty both in political thought as well as in current, interdisciplinary approaches.

Notions of sovereignty

Following Dieter Grimm, legal scholar and former judge on the German constitutional court, 'sovereignty' not only varies throughout the ages and with national traditions but was (and is) a concept that is in itself nearly always disputed, developed with certain aims in mind, and thus oscillating between normative and descriptive elements, which have rarely ever all been fulfilled, let alone at all times. Nevertheless, Grimm (2009) distinguishes three stages. First, there is the medieval (i.e. pre-Bodin) notion of sovereignty, already with the idea of 'final and binding decision making' at its centre, though in a relative sense only, that is valid within certain areas and fields, in a normative framework, which was itself not at anyone's disposal. Sovereignty was thus about finding or applying the law, not about making it. It would be precisely this missing legislative competence that was then added by Bodin, writing himself inter alia against any notion of a right of resistance. But even the 'Bodin-sovereign' remained in harmony with 'loix qui concernent l'estat du Royaume' as well as 'loy de Dieu & de nature'. The Sovereign was thus above 'the laws' but not 'the law', so to speak (Quaritsch 1986: 51–4, also for the quotations). The more important point in the conception, however, was that all intermediate powers of others, that is, the former so-called 'relative sovereign' rulers of smaller territories, were dissolved. The only public power left in place was the newly established state authority, thus rendering sovereignty both more abstract and absolute, as well as creating an intricate link with the notion of 'state', which itself changed (or better: developed) exactly due to Bodin's notion of an

---

[6] Schuppert (2010: 115–36) for the important role of semantics and (2007: 265) for sovereignty as a *Schlüsselbegriff*. See also Flaig (2019: 39–40) with recourse to Cassirer for 'state' as a *Funkionsbegriff*; similarly, one could, once again, cite Weber (1904: 208–9) for terms being a means to an end, not vice versa. My approach differs therefore from any attempt to establish sovereignty as a concept deriving from ancient political thought; see, for instance, Lane (2014).

[7] Similarly, regarding sovereignty and the EU, Walker (2003: 4).

[8] With this caveat I find myself in agreement with John K. Davies, whose article (1994) offers such strong arguments for the 'non-usability of the concept of "sovereignty" in an ancient Greek context' that I borrowed part of his title for this paper notwithstanding its different outcome, due not only to my slightly greater optimism around the conscious use of analytical categories but also the discussions of sovereignty in the last 20 years.

inseparable sovereignty, marking the beginning of territorial authority rather than personal authority; this has, in turn, become a precondition of international law.[9]

Continuing this painting with very broad strokes, the post-Bodin world is marked by various further stages and developments: by Thomas Hobbes and the distinction between the *persona ficta* of the state and the individual persona of the ruler; by John Locke and his ideas regarding the object/aim of the state – such as liberty – with the suggestion that this presents a possible constraint on the idea of sovereignty; by Jean-Jacques Rousseau and the idea of sovereign people both before and after some sort of social contract; and, finally, by the constitutions of the United States, Poland, and France at the end of the 18th century. When through this process the idea of 'popular sovereignty' was formulated, it had to be equated with either the 'nation' or the 'state',[10] interpreted by working with the concepts of delegation and representation,[11] or by applying the neat distinction between 'pouvoir constituant' and 'pouvoir constitué' by Sieyès,[12] from which it follows that sovereignty is hidden or merely latent within constitutions, only visible either in the very the act of creating the (or a new) constitution or, according to Carl Schmitt, in so-called emergency situations.[13] Regardless of whether or not we are left within constitutions with only 'competences' but no sovereignty, when viewed from the outside there also arises the question to what extent self-binding treaties and commitments are indicators of sovereignty, or the very opposite.[14] Conceptually, the establishment of international and supranational institutions, from the International Criminal Court (ICC) to the Tribunal Arbitral du Sport (TAS), as well as the phenomena of failing or failed states, have all been met by scholars in the last 20 years both with resigned comments about 'the end of sovereignty'[15] as well as creative

---

[9] UN Charter, Art. 2.1: 'The Organisation is based on the principle of the sovereign equality of all its Members.'

[10] A specific German element, it seems, is the possible separation of state and sovereignty. According to Georg Jellinek (1914), sovereignty is not the core of a state, just one quality; one can therefore speak of states, defined by their monopoly of state authority (*Staatsgewalt*), which are not sovereign (but part of the Deutsches Reich after 1871); Nettl (1968: 566–72) and Möllers (2008: 15–22).

[11] Next to the classic studies of Pitkin (1967) and Manin (1997), I find Urbinati (2006) to be of particular interest for the complex relations between democracy, representation, and sovereignty.

[12] Sieyès (1789: 120): 'Dans chaque partie, la constitution n'est pas l'ouvrage du pouvoir constitué, mais du pouvoir constituant.'

[13] Schmitt (1922: 13): 'Souverän ist, wer über den Ausnahmezustand entscheidet', who himself, however, immediately marks the inherent tension with any notion of constitution; see also Alston, this volume.

[14] Also, the assumed 'sovereign equality' of members in the United Nations, with, for example, its ban on external interventions, is in constant tension with human rights and other ideas of the Preamble, as well as Articles 1 and 139 of the UN Charter.

[15] See, for example, MacCormick (1999) or Loick (2012); further examples are cited in Schuppert (2007) and Bach (2013); for ancient history, see Ando (2017: 7): 'Sovereigntism is dead'; similar is Stollberg-Rilinger (2005: 13). Such positions are, however, not new: see Nettl (1968: 560) and already in 1914, Norman Angel in *The Foundation of International Polity* (quoted in Skinner 2012: 80).

talk about degrees of sovereignty, multi-level sovereignty, or sovereignty which is shared, pooled, or split.[16]

Semantically, the last examples illustrate the great distance from today's world to the conceptions of Bodin or Hobbes. And it becomes evident that the question itself of whether one can or cannot apply 'the' notion of sovereignty to the ancient world is flawed, as it does not specify which version of sovereignty is meant and there is the risk of circular arguments, given, for instance, Bodin's consideration of Roman political thought (Straumann 2016: 278–302). In order to establish common features – or, perhaps, core elements – of all (or most) variants, a brief look at the systematic approach by Stephen Krasner, American political scientist and policy advisor, is helpful.[17] Krasner, labelling sovereignty an 'organized hypocrisy', differentiates four aspects of sovereignty. The first is called 'Domestic Sovereignty', by which is meant the position of *authority* within the state, be it an individual ruler or an institution. The second aspect is called 'Interdependence Sovereignty', which focuses on the actual *control* of borders, that is, the flow of capital, goods, and people. Next is 'International Legal Sovereignty', which refers to the recognition of a political entity by others, that is, within the system of states, comprising diplomatic immunities, and through membership in organisations such as the United Nations. Lastly, there is the so-called 'Westphalian-cum-Vattelian Sovereignty', describing a completely autonomous territoriality with no external actors. Krasner's quadripartition can be ordered in two distinct ways, both of which facilitate further discussion. On the one hand, both domestic and international legal sovereignty apply the notion of authority, whereas the other two forms of sovereignty operate through the idea of factual control. The first juxtaposition thus follows the classic legal(istic?) notion of sovereignty, while the second complements it with notions of power that, for some, already considerably stretch the concept of sovereignty.[18] On the other hand, Krasner's terminology for domestic sovereignty underlines the important distinction between sovereignty (in whatever specific form) within a given entity and of a given entity, for which there seems to be widespread agreement across academic disciplines.[19] Taking both lines into account, let us now turn our attention towards

---

[16] Glenn (2013: 12, 104, 137 n. 62 [referring to *The Economist* 15.09.2012, 51, writing about 'more sovereignty' for Kosovo] 259–90); Schuppert (2007: 259) for 'Souveränität als Mehrebenenbegriff' and Delmas-Marty (2006: 29) for 'dilution de la souveraineté' not yet transformed into a real 'souveraineté partagée'; see also Krasner (2005) proposing the acceptance of shared sovereignty as a possible way to further democracy and wellbeing. Further variants are discussed by Walker (2003), who proposes the concept of 'late sovereignty', thereby marking the 'continuity' of the concept as well as the 'distinctive new phase' (19).

[17] For the following, see Krasner (1999: 9–25) and (2016). In the latter nothing is said anymore about 'interdependence sovereignty', and the 'Westphalian' version is termed 'Westphalian/Vattelian'. See also Isayev, this volume.

[18] Walker (2003: 6–9), writing against 'fallacies of description and abstraction' (9) and defining sovereignty primarily as a 'speech act' (6) and 'general ordering claim' (7); similar Biersteker & Weber (1996).

[19] Jackson & Rosberg (1982) distinguish between 'juridical and empirical statehood' for states in Africa; later, Jackson (1990) used 'negative sovereignty' for the outer recognition and 'positive sovereignty' for

the ancient world to discuss three different aspects of sovereignty and, within each category, different facets of the concept. The first two aspects of sovereignty will focus on its legal implications, regarding both the entity as a whole ('external sovereignty') and considering the entity from within ('internal sovereignty'). The third aspect tries to include an element of actual capacity, taking into account even more the notion of the 'state', with which any notion of sovereignty remains strongly entangled.[20]

The sovereignty of an entity

External sovereignty brings us back both to Corinth in the 6th century BCE as well as the intricate link between sovereignty and state in the sense of statehood. This chapter does, however, propose that one can avoid exactly this debate (and ballast) by focusing only on certain facets within external sovereignty. As soon as the historical link between external sovereignty and the state is decoupled, then the simple facet of 'mutual recognition of an entity by another entity as being similar' becomes apparent as both a core element of external sovereignty and as a heuristic tool and analytical concept. It is heuristic because it is a relative category, a specific attribution, not a timeless quality; it is analytical because it is not about Rome or Athens being 'sovereign' entities in a (howsoever defined) modern way, but about whether political entities in the ancient world treated other political entities in a way that resembles this idea of mutual recognition. Given the abundant ancient evidence of treaties, diplomatic missions and ambassadors, from Homeric heroes to the Roman fetial law, it seems difficult to disregard this notion of sovereignty for the ancient world. This is especially true, since the distinction between the legal or nominal status of entities and the huge differences in power amongst them is nicely captured exactly in the notion of sovereignty. A classic example is the famous Melian Dialogue, in which Thucydides presents the Athenians as blatantly disregarding Melos' wish to remain neutral (and thereby independent) by recourse to brute force and power (Thuc. 5.89–113). A different perspective is to be found in Herodotus' story of the Persian embassy demanding earth and water from Athens

---

internal capabilities; Schneckener (2004: 511) differentiates between '*de iure* and *de facto* sovereignty'. In ancient history, John Davies (1994: 55) defined 'sovereignty Type A' as the 'absence of constraint or obligation upon a political entity' and 'sovereignty Type B' as 'power within the state'. Meanwhile, Lane (2014: 289–90), somewhat traditionally, uses 'outer sovereignty' for the political might of Roman emperors but 'inner sovereignty' to mean 'the control of one's self'.

[20] This chapter is thus not concerned with the notion of sovereignty in relation to religion or the sacred nor, for instance, is it concerned with sovereignty and sexuality or its relation with gender, for which see Yelle (2018) or Manow (2011), respectively. That is not to say that the power of discourse and agenda setting should be disregarded; see for instance Ober (1989/1996: 120–1) regarding the power of the *demos* in Athens to assign political meanings and control the processes of signification.

and Sparta.[21] The very act of demanding this symbolic submission to the King of Kings implies in turn Spartan and Athenian nominal independence, at least from a Persian point of view; this is regardless of both our modern concepts, as well as any possible differences within the Greek world between 'cités souveraines' and 'cités sans souveraineté', both of which were encompassed in the notion of *polis*.[22]

The last example already shows that the higher precision of the analytical language of 'sovereignty as an attribution by others' (or a claim against others) was not always present in ancient terminology.[23] In addition, further benefits can be seen precisely in cases where the use of the term presents itself as somewhat problematic. The focus on communication and discourse, for example, only underlines the interesting ways in which rhetoric was used to camouflage differences in power. It highlights, too, how much the idea of mutual recognition was necessary even for matters of conquest, as Ando (2008) has shown for the Roman Empire by highlighting the intricate ways in which first the senate, then later the emperor in Rome, dealt with foreign powers both outside their boundaries and within the Empire, by applying a notion of sovereignty to other political entities for the purposes of diplomacy (or, indeed, war) without doubting their own supremacy.[24] Far from a system of equal entities, we are thus faced with problems of sovereignty within the context of superpowers or empires, very much resembling contemporary problems related to the conceptualisation of global empires within a world of states.[25] Another aspect of this discussion concerns the difficult parallels between sovereignty and ancient political thought. For instance, John Davies argued against the notion of sovereignty in Greek by pointing out that only a specific combination of *eleutheria* and *autonomia* would have come close to describing our modern notion of sovereignty. He also stressed that:

> the commonality within the Greek linguistic/cultural *koine* of ideas, values and institutions was too great, and the interlocking of nominally separate polities was too intricate, to allow the emergence of habits of behaviour so different and so independent of each other that they could generate the full-blown sovereignty which the word and the theory require us to be looking for. (Davies 1994: 61–2)

In both cases, however, different facets (instead of any 'full-blown theory') could help to sharpen our understanding of ancient phenomena, be it Krasner's

---

[21] Vgl. Hdt. 6.48f. esp., 7.133.1; Aristot. *Rhet.* 1399b; Kuhrt (1988) and Nenci (1998: 215–16): 'si tratta di una richiesta di riconoscimento formale dell'autorità persiana', but no 'atto di sottomissione vero e proprio'.
[22] Giovannini (2007) and see already Gschnitzer (1958) for 'Abhängige Orte' in the Greek world.
[23] Davies (1994: 56–62) offers particularly convincing arguments against any Greek terminology for 'sovereignty'.
[24] Furthermore, see Snowdon (2014) for the reciprocal but asymmetric communication between Rome and cities in the east.
[25] See Münkler (2005: 16–21) for the difference between states and empires by pointing out the difference between many states with clear borders and one empire with a fluid sphere of influence; he also (30–2) uses the cited example of Melos to show a specific 'imperial-logic', where neutrality is no option.

'Interdependence Sovereignty' as a cipher for 'real' independence or recently formulated ideas of multi-level sovereignty for the different dimensions of *demes*, *poleis* or leagues, as enumerated by Davies. The simple definition 'of mutual, if not equal, recognition', is in all cases not only applicable to the ancient word but actually facilitates a comparability of phenomena from Greek federations to the 'independent' cities within the Roman Empire with each other as well as later and modern phenomena. Whether or not one should go yet another step further by invoking concepts of international law or statehood for antiquity is a different matter;[26] to exclude, however, the notion of external sovereignty for any pre-Bodin phenomena seems unconvincing and could well be a missed opportunity.

Sovereignty within an entity

A different aspect of sovereignty concerns internal or domestic sovereignty, that is, sovereignty within any given entity regardless of its 'status' from the point of view of others. A classic take on this question for historians, as well as political scientists, is the search for the decisive political institution with the competence for final and binding decision-making, trumping all others in cases of conflict. This could be examined for any single ruler, like our tyrant Periander from the prologue or for a Roman emperor,[27] and the popular assemblies in both Athens and Rome have been discussed in this vein, too. While plausible for Athens, the notion of sovereign assemblies (let alone sovereign people) in Rome is more difficult to maintain and, thus, more interesting to pursue. On the one hand, it is a valid statement to claim that whatever the assemblies voted for became law, no matter whether or not, for example, the senate approved. Also, while the tribunes of the plebs could veto any proposal, they could not block a decision taken by the people. In this vein, it is possible talk about sovereign assemblies.[28] On the other hand, the assemblies could only answer a question brought before them by a magistrate, they had no initiative, and any magistrate convening them faced possible obstruction from colleagues, the previously mentioned tribunes, or religious experts, no matter how popular his proposal was (Nicolet 1976: 289–90). Given this dependency of the still decisive assemblies, Hurlet (2012: 36) has spoken fittingly of a 'souveraineté formelle des comices'.

---

[26] For a discussion of international law, see the brief remarks by Baltrusch (2008) as well as by Butkevych (2003). Regarding aspects of territoriality, see Lundgreen (2014a: 36–7) for possibilities as well as difficulties in applying, for instance, Jellinek's idea of *Staatsgebiet*; it is, however, interesting to note that the Romans structured their relations to foreigners 'as though each party to the negotiation were not only sovereign, but territorially defined' (thus, Ando 2008: 507), whereas nowadays some speak of 'autonomy without territorial exclusivity' (thus, in the context of the EU, Walker 2003: 23).

[27] See in addition, for the Hellenistic monarchs, the brief remarks by Mileta (2008: 72–3).

[28] This line starts with Mommsen, who, differently to others, distinguishes between his legal and historical notion of it; see Jehne (2005: 134–42), with further references.

Yet another take on this question was put forward by Christian Meier, pointing to the inherent, if not explicit, limits of what the assemblies simply could and could not change. They could not (at least did not), for instance, change the existence (and competencies) of the magistrates or the senate, or their own structure.[29] Even if one could argue that the 'constitutional amendments' we do see in the Roman Republic, from the increase in the number of praetors to the new rules regarding the voting process, always had the form of a *lex* approved by an assembly, Meier's argument as to inherent limits still seems valid. Its validity applies not only on the abstract notion of matters that are 'unthinkable' in every society, but especially regarding the evolved Roman normative order, where the precise relationship between *mos*, *ius*, and *lex* remains difficult to entangle.[30] This might not be surprising in a world where political entities increasingly came to regulate matters that had hitherto been in the realm of custom and/or family business. In this line, Sophocles' *Antigone* can be read as the classic reflection on possible limits for legislation – regardless of whether originating from a single ruler, as in the play, or the Athenian *ekklesia*, as in the times of its performance.[31] Even if Antigone's remarks are mostly (if unconvincingly) read regarding a higher divine order (and would be thus somewhat in line with Bodin's notion of moral and religious limits), already this discourse clearly points to the question of limits of sovereignty in the political realm.[32] That is not to say anything about the institutional adjustments in Athens after the (brief) oligarchic coup in 411 and the restoration of democracy in 403, creating a clear hierarchy between *nomoi* and *psephismata*, as well as safeguards against constitutional changes through both the *graphe paranomon* and the body of *nomothetai*.[33]

Apparently, just as the 'state' in the sense of statehood lurked in the background of external sovereignty, for internal sovereignty the 'state' in the sense of constitution becomes relevant, both in terms of a state being a necessary precondition for a constitution, as well as in the very different notion that precisely within a constitution the search for a sovereign institution becomes pointless,

---

[29] Meier (1997: 119) or (similarly) Badian (1984: 399). Mommsen (1887–8: 362) solved this dilemma by stating that 'die Gemeinde wohl Unrecht thun kann, aber niemals Unrecht thut'.

[30] For the latter, see Lundgreen (2017), with further references; for what is 'unthinkable', cf. Daube (1973) or Bloch (1992). The question regarding the limits of any Kompetenz-Kompetenz remains, however, pertinent in all times.

[31] Lundgreen (2019a); for the unlimited competences in 5th-century Athens, see Lanni (2010). Already Aristotle (Pol. IV, 1292 a11–17) remarked on the risk that the people, who – if taken together – could represent a single-ruler and might rule in a despotic way if not constrained by laws.

[32] For Bodin, see Quaritsch (1986: 51–4); for *Antigone*, see Cerri (1982) and Lundgreen (2019a). The tragedy, in turn, is evoked in modern debates as a point of reference for 'the law' being more important than mere laws; see various (newspaper) essays by the former president of the constitutional court of Italy and legal scholar, Gustavo Zagrebelsky.

[33] Hansen (1995: 167–83); in addition, see Yunis (1988) for the intricate interplay between law and politics and Schwartzberg (2004) arguing for entrenchment clauses (already from the 5th century) as being of greater symbolic importance to the Athenians themselves, as well as their allies, than a really effective self-binding mechanism. Regarding the German *Grundgesetz*, Dreier (2009) offers an insightful account for both the claim of eternal validity and the provision for changes.

because all constitutional organs are dependent on the normative order as such, particularly in systems with checks and balances and/or a separation of powers.[34] Such discussions have to be kept in mind, when applying – justly, I think – the term constitution for the ancient world, too.[35] When applied to Rome, one could follow a Polybian approach with a mixed constitution (and hence no sovereign institution), or interpret the interaction of magistrates and assemblies concerning legislation as the interplay of non-dependent, and thus sovereign, institutions.[36] Each approach differs considerably from attempts to single out just one decisive institution, as discussed above. Such difficulties, are, however, only confirmed by my own findings, that no rule of recognition in the sense of H.L.A. Hart can be established for the Roman Republic. This is due to the fact that even the last and binding decision of an assembly could be revoked if, first, religious experts agreed on a religious fault and, second, if the senate would declare their decision as valid for the political realm as well. This new decision by the senate, however, could have then been challenged and trumped again by the assembly, leading to a loop of possible objections.[37] In the end, in Rome, decisions were primarily political, and ad hoc *consensus* proved more important than constitutional concerns or abstract notions of normative orders (Lundgreen 2014b). Still, given the inherent flexibility between norms and deviance, rules and exceptions, it is also difficult (and unhelpful, I think) to apply Carl Schmitt's famous dictum, 'sovereign is he who decides on the exception', which is nevertheless sometimes brought into context with the (for Rome, equally famous) *Senatus Consultum Ultimum*. This so-called emergency decree, however, did not have any more legal implication than other

---

[34] A constitution may solve the problem with sovereignty only by creating a new one of interpretation (see Stolleis 2009 or Vorländer 2000), especially since there are often more than one, and conflicting, notions 'as to where ultimate, unchallengeable normative power is to be placed'; thus, Leff (1979: 1245). In addition, Davies (1994: 60) asks how one should envision for the ancient *polis* the modern distinction between state and society. The question remains disputed, notwithstanding clear evidence for both the abstract notion of 'the people' as well as the differences between private citizens and magistrates; see (for Athens) Ober (1989/1996) or Anderson (2009).

[35] Against the exclusive use of 'Verfassung' for modernity, see Dreier (2010). See also Pani (2010: 3–18), who distinguishes between 'costituzione' (in the sense of second-order norms, readily visible also in antiquity) and 'costituzionalismo' (referring to modern states with constitutions providing limits on their powers).

[36] These alternatives follow Nippel's (1980: 293) remarks regarding the difference of a mixed constitution on the one hand and a separation of powers on the other, in the context of English political thought of the 18th century. Every search for a locus of sovereignty becomes obsolete, however, if one considers sovereignty (as well as political power) in the wake of Arendt as 'relational' (Loughlin 2003: 68–71) or as outside the system; von Lübtow (1955: 475): 'Souverän ist allein der *populus Romanus*, die Volkseinheit, bestehend aus Senat, Magistratur und den Bürgern der jetzigen, früheren und künftigen Generationen'; see further below.

[37] Lundgreen (2011: 257–85) as well as (2001: 39–41) with regard to the rule of recognition developed in Hart (1994). Importantly, this is no Roman particularity, for there were comparable constitutional troubles in South Africa in 1954; Hart (1994: 122). It is, therefore, no argument as such against the notion of a constitution due to the existence of a certain hierarchy of norms, as argued for by Straumann (2016).

senatus consulta and is therefore not easily comparable to Schmitt's dictum or with other modern ideas on the state of exception.[38]

Notwithstanding everything said above, this chapter still maintains that the notion of sovereignty is not applied in vain to the Roman Republic. For instance, the peculiar role of the *comitia* as 'decisive but dependent' only becomes visible in such a manner thanks to the aforementioned discussion. The concept of sovereignty can thus lead to more precise results in describing the nature of the political system in the Roman Republic, precisely because of the problems in using it. An example of the key-concept above is the formulation of Christian Meier (1997), who, despite his reluctance to use the term sovereignty due to its conceptual proximity to the modern states, describes the tension within Roman institutions as follows: 'Wenn nicht so viel Falsches dabei mitschwingen würde, könnte man sagen: gegen die Rechtssouveränität konnte ein Anspruch auf Volkssouveränität gesetzt werden' (126). In a similar vein, Martin Ostwald has contrasted the important role of the Athenian *ekklesia* in the 5th century with the rising importance of law courts, charged amongst other things with the possibility of judicial review in Athens in the 4th century (see p. 23, notes 31, 32 and 33), leading to the title of his book: *From Popular Sovereignty to the Sovereignty of Law*.[39] One can criticise his lack of definition of sovereignty, but his focus on the facet of the most decisive institution helps to underline the historical development,[40] regardless of the fact that Athens, both in 5th as well as the 4th centuries, could very well be presented as being in accordance with what one could call 'popular sovereignty'. Similarly, Valentina Arena (2016) has contrasted under the heading of popular sovereignty the changing Ciceronian conceptions from a 'real mixed constitution' in *de re publica* to the idea of an 'aristocracy with only formal approval of the people' in *de legibus* (95). As much as this chapter agrees on this description of Cicero's political thought regarding the diminishing role of the people (see further Lundgreen 2020b), any use of 'popular sovereignty' for Rome has to deal not just with the mere 'formal sovereignty' of the assemblies (discussed above), but also the actual opportunities

---

[38] For the *Senatus Consultum Ultimum*, see Lundgreen (2015) for further references as well as now the papers in Buongiorno (2020). Yet another strand of the debate concerns works by Giorgio Agamben; for his take on Rome, see Lowrie (2007); Lundgreen (2009); Alston this volume. According to Mommsen (1907: 147), the mere idea of the completion of a task (or overcoming a state of emergency) even allows us to understand the extra-ordinary offices with *potestas rei publicae constituenda*, which hold no limits neither of scope nor of time (like the *decemviri* or the triumvirate after Caesar's death) as ephemeral powers only.

[39] Ostwald (1986); see xix: 'THE purpose of this book is to trace the growth of popular power in ancient Athens to the point at which it became popular sovereignty, to investigate the challenges popular sovereignty had to face, and to show how a principle of the sovereignty of law emerged from these challenges.'

[40] Ostwald (1986: xx) states: 'we do not pretend here to make a contribution to the theory of sovereignty, which has vexed political scientists, but rather use the term in a hierarchical sense, similar to that in which Aristotle speaks of τὸ κύριον to express the element in a society or in an institution that is decisive in authenticating its character.'

of 'the people'.⁴¹ Again, for Rome and Athens, and in our time, the question is whether one understands popular sovereignty as an active force within systems (leading possibly to a democratic character) or as an force outside of it, as a point of reference and legitimising the order as such.⁴² In the latter option, even the sovereignty of the Roman emperor could be seen as ultimately depending on, or at least deriving from, the people.⁴³ With all this in mind, it seems very apt to speak of the *maiestas populi Romani* as a foundational authority, as Dean Hammer proposes in this volume, thereby taking into account both the somewhat mystical content inherent in the sovereign act of creating (and perpetually defining) an order, as well as the latent potential of it being a point of reference in political controversies.⁴⁴

Continuing with the (smaller) facet of law-giving competencies, after all, according to Bodin, the 'point principal de la maiesté souveraine' (Quaritsch 1986: 46), further aspects can be examined. For instance, possible parallels between what we call the rise of the state and the rise of the *polis* – without, again, implying a specific concept of state, but still highlighting the difference between 'found' norms versus 'made' norms. Whereas the role of the Homeric *basileis* to uphold *dike* and *themis* could be brought into a crude analogy with pre-Bodin ideas of administering law and justice, we encounter from the very early inscriptions onwards a very clear notion not only of upholding the law but of actually making and creating norms by, in, and for Greek communities.⁴⁵ Finally, the aspects of a self-bound sovereign may even help to shed new light on some hitherto overlooked episodes. Let us remember

---

⁴¹ See here Jehne (2005: 159) and (2013) for the limits (from personal wealth to confined spaces in Rome) of participation, as well as (2014), which proposes that this phenomenon has never been seen as problematic, since every group of citizens could be transformed into the *populus Romanus* and act not only on behalf *of* it but, also, *as* it.

⁴² See an often-cited passage from Ober (1989/1996: 121), regarding Athens: 'The concept of sovereignty can unsuccessfully be applied to democracy only by replacing the idea of "sovereignty as located in institutions" with "sovereignty as the ability to change institutions".' Consequently, Ober (1989: 299–304) argues that the 'philosophical and constitutional contradiction between sovereign laws and sovereign popular will' (299–300) was well tolerated and maintained in practice. Regarding 'popular sovereignty', the articles in Bourke & Skinner (2016) and Kelly (2017) provide a good overview. Any notion of sovereignty within the system, however, would still leave room for the question of whether or not the boule in Athens or the senate in Rome should be regarded as the most powerful political institutions, even if not 'sovereign'.

⁴³ For a brief discussion of the relevant passages from the *Digest* and the famous *lex de imperio Vespasiani* from 69 CE, see Straumann (2016: 246–7). For Lane (2014: 290), this is the historical starting point of sovereignty: 'The idea of Sovereignty marks the point at which the powers that still in Roman law theoretically emanated from the people were put, in practice, largely beyond the reach of their control.'

⁴⁴ Hammer, this volume. A conceptually comparable approach regarding the notion of 'Geltungsgeschichten' (as well as the idea of stability, not despite, but because of, conflicting principles) was offered by the Sonderforschungsbereich 537 in Dresden; for example, the articles in Melville & Vorländer (2002).

⁴⁵ Compare, for example, Hom Il. 16.541–2; Od. 2.230–4; Od. 19.109–14; or Hes. erg. 224–37 (together with Cairns 2015) with the world of inscriptions, which is analysed amongst others by Hölkeskamp (1994; 2003). The starting point is procedural law concerning the Kosmos around 650 from Dreros (ML2 = Nomima I.81 = Gagarin/Perlman Dr.1), with its famous beginning: ἔϝαδε | πόλι·.

the story of Periander, addressing his son after he himself had forbidden anyone from talking to him. Regardless of any (unlikely) historical truth, the interesting question is whether or not Periander did pay the money to temple, that is, whether he was bound as a person by his edict as tyrant, publicly proclaimed by a herald (κήρυγμα ἐποιήσατο). As far as I know, this question has never been asked,[46] which is somewhat surprising given a wide acknowledgement of Herodotus' interest in the political debates of his own time and indeed his famous debate between the three Persian nobles about the virtues and disadvantages regarding the rule of one, few, or many, just 30 paragraphs later.[47] Not only because later discussions between Roman jurists about the emperor as *legibus solutus* provided a point of reference for Bodin himself,[48] but with the debate in the year 427 about the fate of Mytilene, where the decision to kill everyone was taken on one day and revoked on the next,[49] in mind, one could at least speculate whether Herodotus' story about Periander contained some reflections on contemporary discussions regarding the self-engagement of the Athenian *ekklesia* being somewhat bound by its own decisions, or open to constant revision.

The state as a manager – not as a monopolist

Both aspects discussed so far, external and internal sovereignty, have had their focus on sovereignty primarily as a legal category. For some scholars, however, sovereignty cannot be envisioned without any actual ability to enforce its own claims both externally and internally.[50] Hence, we have the alleged crisis of the modern state, being constricted between international and supranational actors on the one hand and powerful private actors on the other. Even if this chapter shall maintain at the end that this aspect is more relevant to the notion of 'state' (in terms of pervading a given society or 'density of stateness') than to sovereignty as such (if there is any 'as such'), it is worthwhile exploring the following 'governance

---

[46] So far, the story has been studied mostly as a classic example of a father–son conflict; Vernant (1982); further references in Schmitz (2010: 36).
[47] Hdt. 3.80–3. For this (Greek) debate, see Bleicken (1979); Meier (1983: 489); Asheri & Medaglia (1990: 472). For Herodotus' interest in the politics of his time, see Raaflaub (2002).
[48] Interestingly enough, Bodin regarded Augustus, for whom – in the context of his own marriage-laws – the idea of *princeps legibus solutus* was coined, only as a 'chef de la Republique' and not a 'prince souverain', since he had to be declared *legibus solutus* by laws and was thus dependent on them; Behrends (2007/2013: 510).
[49] Thuc. 3.36–49; see Flaig (2013: 316–24), for further references.
[50] See Krasner's categories above as well as the 'positive sovereignty' for actual capabilities of states by Jackson (1990). See further Münkler & Straßenberger (2016: 123–4), who also point to the emerging modern nation-state thanks to both a monopoly on military capacity as well as civil servants (141–5). I have tried (in Lundgreen 2020a) to distinguish the classic account of emerging states through a 'competition for the monopoly apparatus' as described by Nobert Elias (1997: 151–68) from the governance approach discussed in the following pages.

perspective', both in regard to the ancient world as well as in order to tackle, from yet another angle, the previously discussed problem of ever-differing notions of the state that always exist in the background while investigating sovereignty.

My starting point is an article by the political scientists Philipp Genschel & Bernhard Zangl (2008), who review the gradual, uneven, and discontinuous process of the establishment of modern nation-states in Europe from the 17th century onwards.[51] This involved states taking over the decision-making competence of other institutions – such as the church, aristocracy, guilds, and municipalities – replacing mercenary armies, and setting up tax administrations and public services, until unprecedented heights of political concentration were reached at the end of the 20th century. In turn, a contrary process of development is discussed, marked by a rising importance of both international actors, like the European Union, and transnational actors (from the World Health Organization to non-governmental organisations), plus, a decentralisation and privatisation of the economy. According to Genschel and Zangl, however, this development does not deprive the state of its quality of being a state, because the state still has to provide complimentary resources to each of these new actors. For instance, international actors need organisational support for their decisions, private actors need decisions and rules before they can operate, and transnational actors usually require both. All three groups, moreover, need and get complimentary legitimacy if acting (on whatever base) together with the state. The state therefore has not vanished, but has changed its role, hence their title: 'Transformations of the State – from Monopolist to Manager of Political Authority'.

Regardless of whether that is an adequate description of our contemporary situation, the tripartition of decision-making competence, organisational capacity, and legitimatory power has analytical potential for the ancient world, too.[52] That is true even if the perspective is somewhat turned upside-down, since we are not dealing with a state becoming less of a monopolist but with political entities coming into existence. But 'monopolist' is a difficult term anyhow; whereas sovereignty can be understood as the highest power, rarely has a state had all the power or done everything on its own.[53] With this in mind, however, the approach changes: just as the question 'who else governs?'[54] brings governance-actors like churches, guilds, and clans into the picture today (without excluding the political government), it also allows us for the Greek world to investigate governance-actors and governance-services as diverse as sanctuaries for water-supply and irrigation (Panessa 1983); amphiktyonies for common cults between neighbouring *poleis* (Funke 2013); or, more classically, families involved in dispute resolution, from Homer's shield

---

[51] Similar: Genschel & Zangl (2014). Their work is based upon Tilly (1999); Reinhard (2002); and others.

[52] All that follows is further explored in Lundgreen (2019a).

[53] Fittingly, Tilly (1999: 1) thus defined the state as having 'priority in some respects over all other organisations'.

[54] See Burris *et al.* (2008: 19) and Schuppert (2006) for state-actor and non-state-actor governance.

of Achilles to 4th-century law courts in Athens.[55] In all matters, the relationship between different governance-actors can be characterised by competition as well as cooperation and by hierarchy as well as mutual understanding.[56] The way of working together, of co-producing governance, is clearly visible in the way that norms were centrally decided upon but then enforced in a dispersed manner by individuals, sometimes encouraged by a share of a fine.[57] If decentralised enforcement of norms is neither new nor surprising, but most likely the pre-modern default,[58] then cases where the Greek *polis* did play a more active role are all the more highlighted. A survey of inscriptions edited by Koerner (1993) and van Effenterre & Ruzé (1994–5) elucidates two such areas: the allocation of land and burial rites. Very close to modern ideas of governance, a 5th-century inscription from Gortyn, for instance, first restates the family duty of purifying a house following a death; second, it outlines that, if necessary, a judge would come in order to do so, but would then also deduct double the amount he receives from the inheritance.[59] The *polis* here clearly comprises all mentioned governance functions, not only decision-making competence and legitimatory power, but also organisational competence, which included charging for the service (see Isayev, this volume, for the *polis* and hospitality).

Any such reconstruction of co-produced governance also highlights how the interplay of governance-actors is best understood as a zero-sum game. That is true insofar as everything decided upon by the one actor is not decided by another; what is punished, for example, by families is not punished by the state, and vice versa.[60] Conflicts and conflicting assertions of the right to decide should therefore not be surprising. In order not to evoke again Sophocles' *Antigone*, let us look at the *pater familias* in Rome and his changing position from the early Roman Republic to the Principate. Being the head of his household, with 'sovereign' competences regarding its members, including the infamous *ius vitae necisque*, the *patria potestas* became severely diminished when Augustus made the families open their books in order to set a tax on inheritance, put a limitation on the power of freeing slaves (and thus creating, eventually, new citizens) and started treating adultery as

---

[55] For dispute resolution regarding homicides, see Heitsch (1984); Gagarin (1986), Phillips (2008).
[56] See Beisheim *et al.* (2011: 258), for the three modi 'hierarchisch, kooperativ oder kompetitiv'; see further Zürcher (2007: 14–15) for the 'Ko-Produktion von Staatlichkeit'.
[57] An example other than dispute resolution is the regulation against pollution of a road in Paris from around 475/450 (IG XII 5.107 = Koerner 57). For the phenomenon of 'Popularklage', see already Ziebarth (1897); further Rubinstein (2003) for 'volunteer prosecutors'.
[58] See Crone (2015: 54–5) for such a 'pre-modern default'.
[59] See I Cret. IV 76 = Gagarin/Perlman G76; furthermore, see Frisone (2000: 31–5).
[60] See already Finley (1954/2002: 74) in regard to the prominent role of the *oikoi* in his *World of Odysseus*: 'Historically there is an inverse relationship between the extension of the notion of crime as an act of public malfeasance and the authority of the kinship group. ... The growth of the idea of crime, and of criminal law, could almost be written as the history of the chipping away of that early state of family omnipotence.'

a public crime.⁶¹ All of these measures enabled political power to penetrate spheres that were formerly regulated and organised by the *patres*, thus enlarging the public sphere at their expense. With no direct link to either the status of the Imperium Romanum nor the political position of the *princeps*, it certainly was a major step for a more intense 'state' and thus perhaps a form of sovereignty, too.

What is best called sovereignty? And what is best described otherwise?

The last aspect, both regarding the notion of governance in general as well as the particular shift from family rights and duties to a newly (and thereby) created public sphere, both in the Greek world and Augustan Rome, is, in the view of this chapter, best treated under the heading of 'state' instead of sovereignty. 'State' in this case is intended neither in the sense of statehood nor constitution, but in the sense of permeating the social order, for which I propose the term 'stateness' (based on Lundgreen 2019a). Sovereignty is thus preserved for a more selective use as an analytical tool, also taking into account thereby its history as a predominantly legal concept (and leaving it distinct from, for instance, 'power'). Others may differ, but, as was stressed in the beginning of this chapter, there is no absolute truth to find or defend; rather, it is about the fruitful application of terminology while consciously evading misunderstanding. For the latter, this chapter decided to treat different aspects separately; for the former it discussed various facets that can, without the ballast of all-comprising definitions, emphasise a difference, highlight something hitherto overlooked, or remind us of the puzzling tensions that are inherent in political systems and which may be better endured than solved. Given the long story (and still ongoing developments) of the term sovereignty and its many different (and partly contested) notions, a rejection of the term for the ancient world is in any case not persuasive. This is all the more true when 'wrong questions' sometimes lead to new results, or, to put it differently, when no answer regarding Periander could ever be as intriguing as the questions in all their variety.⁶²

---

⁶¹ For the *lex <Iulia de> vicesima hereditarium*, see Moreau (2007). For manumissions, see Mouritsen (2011: 80–92). For Augustan marriage regulations (judged as a harsh limitation of freedom by Tac. Ann. 3.28), see Mette-Dittmann (1991); Fayer (2005); Eck (2016). The rendering of private deviance into a *crimen publicum* reminds us of Finley, quoted in the previous note. For the role of the *patres*, sometimes understood as a 'state-countering institution' (thus Eder 1990: 18; Pani 2007: 322), see Martin (2002) and Linke (2014). My idea of the described change in the governance-balance under Augustus is further developed in Lundgreen (2019b: 124–8).

⁶² For critical comments and questions, I owe thanks to Florian Meinel and, above all, Christopher Smith, who is also responsible for both the exceptionally inspiring atmosphere at the conference and most wonderful days in St Andrews.

References

Anderson, G. (2009), 'The Personality of the Greek State', *Journal of Hellenic Studies*, 129: 1–22.
Ando, C. (2008), 'Aliens, Ambassadors, and the Integrity of the Empire', *Law and History Review*, 26: 491–519.
Ando, C. (2017), 'Introduction: States and State Power in Antiquity', in C. Ando & S. Richardson (eds), *Ancient States and Infrastructural Power: Europe, Asia, and America* (Philadelphia, University of Pennsylvania Press), 1–16.
Arena, V. (2016), 'Popular Sovereignty in the Late Roman Republic', in Bourke & Skinner (2016), 73–95.
Asheri, D. & Medaglia, S.M. (eds) (1990), *Erodoto. Le Storie, Libro III: La Persia* (Milan, Fondazione Lorenzo Valla).
Bach, M. (ed.) (2013), *Der entmachtete Leviathan. Löst sich der souveräne Staat auf?* (Baden-Baden, Nomos-Verlag).
Badian, E. (1984), 'Hegemony and Independence: Prolegomena to a Study of the Relations of Rome and the Hellenistic States in the Second Century BC', in J. Haramatta (ed.), *Actes du VII Congrès de la Féderation Internationale des Associations d'Études classiques I* (Budapest, Akadémiai Kiadó), 397–414.
Baltrusch, E. (2008), *Außenpolitik, Bünde und Reichsbildung in der Antike* (Munich, Oldenbourg).
Behrends, O. (2007/2013), '*Princeps Legibus Solutus*', in O. Behrends, *Zur Römischen Verfassung. Ausgewählte Schriften*, ed. M. Avenarius & C. Möller (Göttingen, Wallstein), 493–512.
Beisheim, M., Börzel, T.A., Genschel, P., & Zangl, B. (2011), 'Governance jenseits des Staates. Das Zusammenspiel staatlicher und nicht-staatlicher Governance', in M. Beisheim, T.A. Börzel, P. Genschel, & B. Zangl (eds), *Wozu Staat? Governance in Räumen begrenzter und konsolidierter Staatlichkeit* (Baden-Baden, Nomos), 251–66.
Berent, M. (2000), 'Sovereignty: Ancient and Modern', *Polis: The Journal for Ancient and Roman Political Thought*, 17: 1–34.
Biersteker, T.J. & Weber, C. (1996), 'The Social Construction of State Sovereignty', in T.J. Biersteker & C. Weber (eds), *State Sovereignty as Social Construct* (Cambridge, Cambridge University Press), 1–21.
Bleicken, J. (1979), 'Zur Entstehung der Verfassungstypologie im 5. Jahrhundert v. Chr. (Monarchie, Aristokratie, Demokratie)', *Historia*, 28: 148–72.
Bloch, M. (1992), 'What Goes Without Saying: The Conceptualization of Zafimaniry Society', in A. Kuper (ed.), *Conceptualizing Society* (London & New York, Routledge), 127–46.
Bourke, R. & Skinner, Q. (eds) (2016), *Popular Sovereignty in Historical Perspective* (Cambridge, Cambridge University Press).
Buongiorno, P. (ed.) (2020), *'Senatus consultum ultimum' e stato di eccezione* (Stuttgart, Franz Steiner Verlag).
Burris, S., Kempa, M., & Shearing, C. (2008), 'Changes in Governance: A Cross Disciplinary Review of Current Scholarship', *Akron Law Review*, 41: 1–66.
Butkevych, O.V. (2003), 'History of Ancient International Law: Challenges and Prospects', *Journal of the History of International Law*, 5: 189–236.
Cairns, D. (2015), 'The First Odysseus: Iliad, Odyssey, and the Ideology of Kingship', *Gaia*, 18: 51–66.

Cerri, G. (1982), 'Ideologia funeraria nell'Antigone di Sofocle', in G. Gnoli & J.-P. Vernant (eds), *La mort, les morts dans les sociétés anciennes* (Cambridge & Paris, Cambridge University Press & Éditions de la Maison des sciences de l'homme), 121–31.

Crone, P. (2015), *Pre-Industrial Societies: Anatomy of the Pre-Modern World* (London, Oneworld Publications).

Daube, D. (1973), 'Das Selbstverständliche in der Rechtsgeschichte', *Zeitschrift der Savigny-Stiftung für Rechtsgeschichte. Romanistische Abteilung*, 90: 1–13.

Davies, J.K. (1994), 'On the Non-Usability of the Concept of "Sovereignty" in an Ancient Greek Context', in L. Aigner-Foresti, A. Barzanò, C. Bearzot, L. Prandi, & G. Zecchini (eds), *Federazioni e federalismo nell'Europa antica* (Milan, Vita e Pensiero), 51–65.

Delmas-Marty, M. (2006), *Les forces imaginantes du droit*, ii: *Le pluralisme ordonne* (Paris, Seuil).

Dreier, H. (2009), *Gilt das Grundgesetz ewig? Fünf Kapitel zum modernen Verfassungsstaat* (Munich, Carl-Friedrich-von-Siemens-Stiftung).

Dreier, H. (2010), 'Verfassung', in H.-J. Sandkühler (ed.), *Enzyklopädie Philosophie*, iii (Hamburg, Meiner), 2867–75.

Eck, W. (2016), 'Die augusteische Ehegesetzgebung und ihre Zielsetzung. Die lex Iulia de maritandis ordinibus, die lex Papiria Poppaea und ein commentarius des Jahres 5 n.Chr. als Grundlage der lex Papia Poppaea', *Maia: Rivista di letterature classiche*, 68.2: 282–99.

Eder, W. (1990), 'Der Bürger und sein Staat – Der Staat und seine Bürger. Eine Einführung zum Thema Staat und Staatlichkeit in der frühen römischen Republik', in W. Eder (ed.), *Staat und Staatlichkeit in der frühen römischen Republik* (Stuttgart, Franz Steiner Verlag), 12–32.

Effenterre, H. van & Ruzé, F. (1994–5), *Nomima. Receuil d'inscriptions politiques et juridiques de l'archaisme grec* (Rome, École Française de Rome).

Elias, N. (1997), *Über den Prozeß der Zivilisation. Soziogenetische und psychogenetische Untersuchungen. Zweiter Band, Wandlungen der Gesellschaft, Entwurf zu einer Theorie der Zivilisation* (Frankfurt am Main, Suhrkamp).

Fayer, C. (2005), *La familia romana. Aspetti giuridici ed antiquari. Concubinato Divorzio Adulterio* (Rome, L'Erma di Bretschneider).

Finley, M.I. (1954/2002), *The World of Odysseus*, with introduction by B. Knox (New York, Viking Press).

Flaig, E. (2013), *Die Mehrheitsentscheidung. Entstehung und kulturelle Dynamik* (Paderborn and others, Schönigh).

Flaig, E. (2019), *Den Kaiser herausfordern. Die Usurpation im Römischen Reich*, 2nd edn (Frankfurt am Main & New York, Campus Verlag).

Frisone, F. (2000), *Leggi e regolamenti funerari nel mondo greco*, I: *Le fonti epigrafiche* (Lecce, Congedo Editore).

Funke, P. (2013), 'Greek Amphiktyonies: An Experiment in Transregional Governance', in H. Beck (ed.), *A Companion to Ancient Greek Government* (Malden MA, Wiley-Blackwell), 451–65.

Gagarin, M. (1986), *Early Greek Law* (Berkeley, University of California Press).

Genschel, P. & Zangl, B. (2008), 'Metamorphosen des Staates – vom Herrschaftsmonopolisten zum Herrschaftsmanager', *Leviathan*, 36: 430–54.

Genschel, P. & Zangl, B. (2014), 'State Transformation in OECD Countries', *Annual Review of Political Science*, 17: 337–54.

Giovannini, A. (2007), *Les relations entre États dans la Grèce antique du temps d'Homère à l'intervention romaine (ca. 700–200 av. J.-C.)* (Stuttgart, Franz Steiner Verlag).

Glenn, H.P. (2013), *The Cosmopolitan State* (Oxford, Oxford University Press).
Gschnitzer, F. (1958), *Abhängige Orte im Griechischen Altertum* (Munich, Beck).
Grimm, D. (2009), *Souveränität. Herkunft und Zukunft eines Schlüsselbegriffs* (Berlin, Berlin University Press).
Hansen, M.H. (1995), *Die Athenische Demokratie im Zeitalter des Demosthenes. Struktur, Prinzipien und Selbstverständnis* (Berlin, Akademie Verlag).
Hansen, M.H. (2006), *Polis: An Introduction to the Ancient Greek City-State* (Oxford, Oxford University Press).
Hart, H.L.A. (1994), *The Concept of Law*, 2nd edn (Oxford, Oxford University Press).
Heitsch, E. (1984), *Aidesis im attischen Strafrecht* (Mainz, Franz Steiner Verlag).
Hölkeskamp, K.-J. (1994), 'Tempel, Agora, Alphabet. Die Entstehungsbedingungen von Gesetzgebung in der archaischen Polis', in H.-J. Gehrke (ed.), *Rechtskodifizierung und soziale Normen im interkulturellen Vergleich* (Tübingen, Gunter Narr Verlag), 135–46.
Hölkeskamp, K.-J. (2003), 'Institutionalisierung durch Verortung. Die Entstehung der Öffentlichkeit im frühen Griechenland', in K.-J. Hölkeskamp, J. Rüsen, E. Stein-Hölkeskamp, & H.T. Grütter (eds), *Sinn (in) der Antike. Orientierungssysteme, Leitbilder und Wertkonzepte im Altertum* (Mainz, Verlag Philipp von Zabern), 81–104.
Hurlet, F. (2012), 'Démocratie à Rome? Quelle Démocratie? En relisant Millar (et Hölkeskamp)', in S. Benoist (ed.), *Rome: A City and its Empire in Perspective. The Impact of the Roman World through Fergus Millar's Research* (Leiden & Boston, Brill), 19–43.
Jackson, R.H. (1990), *Quasi-States: Sovereignty, International Relations and the Third World* (New York, Cambridge University Press).
Jackson, R.H. & Rosberg, C.G. (1982), 'Why Africa's Weak States Persist: The Empirical and the Juridical in Statehood', *World Politics*, 35: 1–24.
Jehne, M. (2005), 'Die Volksversammlungen in Mommsens Staatsrecht', in W. Nippel & B. Seidensticker (eds), *Theodor Mommsens langer Schatten. Das römische Staatsrecht als bleibende Herausforderung für die Forschung* (Hildesheim, Zurich & New York, Georg Olms Verlag), 131–60.
Jehne, M. (2013), 'Politische Partizipation in der römischen Republik', in H. Reinau & J. von Ungern-Sternberg (eds), *Politische Partizipation. Idee und Wirklichkeit von der Antike bis in die Gegenwart* (Berlin & Boston, De Gruyter), 103–44.
Jehne, M. (2014), 'Das Volk als Institution und diskursive Bezugsgröße in der römischen Republik', in C. Lundgreen (ed.), *Staatlichkeit in Rom? Diskurse und Praxis (in) der römischen Republik* (Stuttgart, Franz Steiner Verlag), 117–37.
Jellinek, G. (1914), *Allgemeine Staatsrechtslehre*, 3rd edn (Berlin, Häring).
Kalmo, H. & Skinner, Q. (eds) (2010), *Sovereignty in Fragments: The Past, Present and Future of a Contested Concept* (Oxford, Cambridge University Press).
Kelly, D. (2017), 'Populism and the History of Popular Sovereignty', in C. Rovira Kaltwasser, P. Taggart, P. Ochoa Espejo, & P. Ostiguy (eds), *The Oxford Handbook of Populism* (Oxford, Oxford University Press), 511–34.
Koerner, R. (1993), *Inschriftliche Gesetzestexte der frühen griechischen Polis. Aus dem Nachlaß von Reinhard Koerner*, ed. K. Hallof (Cologne, Weimar & Vienna, Böhlau).
Koselleck, R. (1990), 'Staat und Souveränität', in O. Brunner, W. Conze, & R. Koselleck (eds), *Geschichtliche Grundbegriffe. Historisches Lexikon zur politisch-sozialen Sprache in Deutschland*, vi (Stuttgart, Klett-Cotta Verlag), 1–68.
Krasner, S.D. (1999), *Sovereignty: Organized Hypocrisy* (Princeton, Princeton University Press).
Krasner, S.D. (2005), 'The Case for Shared Sovereignty', *Journal of Democracy*, 16: 69–83.

Krasner, S.D. (2016), 'The Persistence of State Sovereignty', in O. Fioretos, T.G. Falleti, & A. Sheingate (eds), *The Oxford Handbook of Historical Institutionalism* (Oxford, Oxford University Press), 521–37.

Kuhrt, A. (1988), 'Earth and Water', in A. Kuhrt & H. Sancisi-Weerdenburg (eds), *Achaemenid History*, iii: *Method and Theory* (Leiden, Nederlands Instituut voor het Nabije Oosten), 87–99.

Lane, M. (2014), *The Birth of Politics: Eight Greek and Roman Political Ideas and Why They Matter* (Princeton & Oxford, Princeton University Press).

Lanni, A. (2010), 'Judicial Review and the Athenian Constitution', in *Démocratie Athénienne – Démocratie Moderne: Tradition et Influences* (Geneva, Fondation Hardt), 235–76.

Leff, A.A. (1979), 'Unspeakable Ethics, Unnatural Law', *Duke Law Journal*, 6: 1229–49.

Linke, B. (2014), 'Die Väter und der Staat. Die Grundlagen der aggressiven Subidiarität in der römischen Gesellschaft', in C. Lundgreen (ed.), *Staatlichkeit in Rom? Diskurse und Praxis (in) der römischen Republik* (Stuttgart, Franz Steiner Verlag), 65–90.

Loick, D. (2012), *Kritik der Souveränität* (Frankfurt am Main, Campus Verlag).

Loughlin, M. (2003), 'Ten Tenets of Sovereignty', in N. Walker (ed.), *Sovereignty in Transition: Essays in European Law* (Portland, Hart), 55–86.

Lowrie, M. (2007), 'Sovereignty before the Law: Agamben and the Roman Republic', *Law and Humanities*, 1: 31–55.

Lübtow, U. von (1955), *Das römische Volk. Sein Staat und sein Recht* (Frankfurt am Main, Klostermann Verlag).

Lundgreen, C. (2009), '*Qua lege, quo iure?* Die Ausnahme in der Römischen Republik und ihre Rezeption bei Carl Schmitt und Giorgio Agamben', in G. Kamecke, B. Klein, & J. Müller (eds), *Antike als Konzept. Lesarten in Kunst, Literatur und Politik* (Berlin, Lukas-Verlag für Kunst- und Geistesgeschichte), 55–67.

Lundgreen, C. (2011), *Regelkonflikte in der römischen Republik. Geltung und Gewichtung von Normen in politischen Entscheidungsprozessen* (Stuttgart, Franz Steiner Verlag).

Lundgreen, C. (2014a), 'Staatsdiskurse in Rom? Staatlichkeit als analytische Kategorie für die römische Republik', in C. Lundgreen (ed.), *Staatlichkeit in Rom? Diskurse und Praxis (in) der römischen Republik* (Stuttgart, Franz Steiner Verlag), 15–61.

Lundgreen, C. (2014b), 'Gesetze und ihre Geltung: leges und konkurrierende Normen in der römischen Republik', in U. Walter (ed.), *Gesetzgebung und politische Kultur in der römischen Republik* (Heidelberg, Verlag Antike), 108–67.

Lundgreen, C. (2015), '*Senatus Consultum Ultimum*', in R.S. Bagnall & K. Brodersen, *The Encyclopedia of Ancient History* (Malden MA, Wiley).

Lundgreen, C. (2017), 'Norme, loi, règle, coutume, tradition: terminologie antique et perspectives modernes', in T. Itgenshorst & P. Le Doze (eds), *Les fabriques de la norme sous la République romaine et le Haut-Empire* (Bordeaux, Ausonius), 17–33.

Lundgreen, C. (2019a), *Staatlichkeit in der frühen griechischen Antike* (Habilitationsschrift im Rahmen des Habilitationsverfahrens an der Philosophischen Fakultät der Technischen Universität Dresden).

Lundgreen, C. (2019b), 'Statualità e Principato augusteo', *Politica Antica*, 9: 99–139.

Lundgreen, C. (2020a), 'Schlüsselmonopole oder Governance-Funktionen? Alternative Annäherungen an Staatlichkeit in der griechischen Archaik', in J. Meister & G. Seelentag (eds), *Konkurrenz und Institutionalisierung in der griechischen Archaik* (Stuttgart, Steiner Verlag), 157–92.

Lundgreen, C. (2020b), '*Consul popularis* ou populiste moderne? La différence entre le bien, la volonté et la décision du peuple dans la rhétorique cicéronienne', *Cahiers Glotz*, 31: 287–318.

MacCormick, N. (1999), *Questioning Sovereignty: Law, State and Nation in the European Commonwealth* (Oxford, Oxford University Press).
Manin, B. (1997), *The Principles of Representative Government* (Cambridge, Cambridge University Press).
Manow, P. (2011), *Politische Ursprungsphantasien. Der Leviathan und sein Erbe* (Konstanz, Konstanz University Press).
Martin, J. (2002), 'Formen sozialer Kontrolle im republikanischen Rom', in D. Cohen & E. Müller-Luckner (eds), *Demokratie, Recht und soziale Kontrolle im klassischen Athen* (Munich, Oldenbourg), 155–72.
Meier, C. (1983), *Die Entstehung des Politischen bei den Griechen* (Frankfurt am Main, Suhrkamp).
Meier, C. (1997), *Res publica amissa. Eine Studie zu Verfassung und Geschichte der späten römischen Republik*, 3rd edn (Frankfurt am Main, Suhrkamp).
Melville, G. & Vorländer, H. (eds) (2002), *Geltungsgeschichten. Über die Stabilisierung und Legitimierung institutioneller Ordnungen* (Cologne and others, Böhlau).
Mette-Dittmann, A. (1991), *Die Ehegesetze des Augustus. Eine Untersuchung im Rahmen der Gesellschaftspolitik des Princeps* (Stuttgart, Franz Steiner Verlag).
Mileta, C. (2008), *Der König und sein Land. Untersuchungen zur Herrschaft der hellenistischen Monarchen über das königliche Gebiet Kleinasiens und seine Bevölkerung* (Berlin, Akademie-Verlag).
Möllers, C. (2008), *Der vermisste Leviathan. Staatstheorie in der Bundesrepublik* (Frankfurt am Main, Mohr Siebeck).
Mommsen, T. (1887–8), *Römisches Staatsrecht*, 3rd edn (Leipzig, Hirzel).
Mommsen, T. (1907), *Abriß des römischen Staatsrechts*, 2nd edn (Leipzig, Duncker und Humblot).
Moreau, P. (2007), 'Loi Iulia de maritandis ordinibus', in *Lepor. Leges Populi Romani*, sous la dir. de Jean-Louis Ferrary et de Philippe Moreau, www.cn-telma.fr/lepor/notice449/.
Mouritsen, H. (2011), *The Freedman in the Roman World* (Cambridge, Cambridge University Press).
Münkler, H. (2005), *Imperien. Die Logik der Weltherrschaft – vom Alten Rom bis zu den Vereinigten Staaten* (Berlin, Rowohlt).
Münkler, H. & Straßenberger, G. (2016), *Politische Theorie und Ideengeschichte. Eine Einführung* (Munich, Beck).
Nenci, G. (ed.) (1998), *Erodoto. Le Storie*, vi: *La battaglia di Maratona* (Milan, Fondazione Lorenzo Valla).
Nettl, J.P. (1968), 'The State as a Conceptual Variant', *World Politics*, 20: 559–92.
Nicolet, C. (1976), *Le métier de citoyen dans la Rome républicaine* (Paris, Gallimard).
Nippel, W. (1980), *Mischverfassungstheorie und Verfassungsrealität in Antike und Frn Vereinigte* (Stuttgart, Klett-Cotta).
Ober, J. (1989), *Mass and Elite in Democratic Athens: Rhetoric, Ideology, and the Power of the People* (Princeton, Princeton University Press).
Ober, J. (1989/1996), 'The Nature of Athenian Democracy', in *The Athenian Revolution: Essays on Ancient Greek Democracy and Political Theory* (Princeton, Princeton University Press), 107–22.
Ostwald, M. (1986), *From Popular Sovereignty to the Sovereignty of Law: Law, Society, and Politics in Fifth-Century Athens* (Berkeley, University of California Press).
Panessa, G. (1983), 'Le risorse idriche dei santuari greci nei loro aspetti giuridici ed economici', *Annali della Scuola Normale Superiore di Pisa (Lettere e Filosofia, Serie III)*, 13: 359–87.

Pani, M. (2007), 'Forme di individualismo antico', in P. Desideri, M. Moggi, & M. Pani (eds), *Antidoron. Studi in onore di Barbara Scardigli Forster* (Pisa, Edizioni ETS), 317–40.

Pani, M. (2010), *Il costituzionalismo di Roma antica* (Rome & Bari, Edizioni Laterza).

Phillips, D.D. (2008), *Avengers of Blood: Homicide in Athenian Law and Custom from Draco to Demosthenes* (Stuttgart, Franz Steiner Verlag).

Pitkin, H.F. (1967), *The Concept of Representation* (Berkeley, University of California Press).

Quaritsch, H. (1986), *Souveränität. Entstehung und Entwicklung des Begriffs in Frankreich und Deutschland vom 13. Jahrhundert bis 1806* (Berlin, Duncker & Humblot).

Raaflaub, K.A. (2002), 'Philosophy, Science, Politics: Herodotus and the Intellectual Trends of his Time', in E.J. Bakker, I.F.J. Jong, & H. van Wees (eds), *Brill's Companion to Herodotus* (Leiden, Brill), 149–86.

Reinhard, W. (2002), *Geschichte der Staatsgewalt. Eine vergleichende Verfassungsgeschichte Europas von den Anfängen bis zur Gegenwart* (Munich, Beck).

Rubinstein, L. (2003), 'Volunteer Prosecutors in the Greek World', *Dike*, 6: 87–113.

Schmitt, C. (1922), *Politische Theologie. Vier Kapitel zur Lehre von der Souveränität* (Berlin, Duncker und Humblot).

Schmitz, W. (2010), 'Kypselos und Periandros. Moderne Despoten oder Wohltäter der Stadt?', in B. Linke, M. Meier, & M. Strohtmann (eds), *Zwischen Monarchie und Republik. Gesellschaftliche Stabilisierungsleistungen und politische Transformationspotentiale in den antiken Stadtstaaten* (Stuttgart, Franz Steiner Verlag), 19–49.

Schneckener, U. (2004), 'Fragile Staaten als Problem der internationalen Politik', *Nord-Süd aktuell*, 18: 510–24.

Schuller, W. (1993), 'Die Polis als Staat', in M.H. Hansen (ed.), *The Ancient Greek City-State* (Copenhagen, Munksgaard), 106–28.

Schuppert, G.F. (2006), 'The Changing Role of the State Reflected in the Growing Importance of Non-State Actors', in G.F. Schuppert (ed.), *Global Governance and the Role of Non-State-Actors* (Baden-Baden, Nomos), 203–44.

Schuppert, G.F. (2007), 'Souveränität – überholter Begriff, wandlungsfähiges Konzept oder "born 1576, but still going strong"?', in T. Stein, H. Buchstein, & C. Offe (eds), *Souveränität, Recht, Moral. Die Grundlagen politischer Gemeinschaften* (Frankfurt & New York, Campus Verlag), 251–69.

Schuppert, G.F. (2010), *Staat als Prozess. Eine staatstheoretische Skizze in sieben Aufzügen* (Frankfurt & New York, Campus Verlag).

Schwartzberg, M. (2004), 'Athenian Democracy and Legal Change', *American Political Science Review*, 98: 311–25.

Sieyès, A. (1789), *Qu'est-ce que le tiers état? Nouvelle edition précédée d'un entretien inédit avec Annie Jourdan* (Paris, Flammarion).

Skinner, Q. (2012), *Die drei Körper des Staates* (Göttingen, Wallstein).

Snowdon, M. (2014), 'Res Publica, Provinciae und Imperium Romanum: Die Kommunikation zwischen den Römern und den Städten des Ostens', in C. Lundgreen (ed.), *Staatlichkeit in Rom? Diskurse und Praxis (in) der römsichen Republik* (Stuttgart, Franz Steiner Verlag), 163–84.

Stollberg-Rilinger, B. (2005), 'Was heißt Kulturgeschichte des Politischen? Einleitung', in B. Stollberg-Rilinger (ed.), *Was heißt Kulturgeschichte des Politischen?* (Berlin, Duncker & Humblot), 9–24.

Stolleis, M. (2009), 'Die Legitimation von Recht und Gesetz durch Gott, Tradition, Wille, Natur, Vernunft und Verfassung', in M. Avenarius, R. Meyer-Pritzl, & C. Möller (eds), *Ars Iuris: Festschrift für Okko Behrends* (Göttingen, Wallstein), 533–46.

Straumann, B. (2016), *Crisis and Constitutionalism: Roman Political Thought from the Fall of the Republic to the Age of Revolution* (Oxford, Oxford University Press).
Tilly, C. (1999), *Coercion, Capital, and European States, AD 990–1990* (Cambridge MA & Oxford, Blackwell).
Urbinati, N. (2006), *Representative Democracy: Principles and Genealogy* (Chicago, University of Chicago Press).
Vernant, J.-P. (1982), 'From Oedipus to Periander: Lameness, Tyranny, Incest in Legend and History', *Arethusa*, 15: 19–38.
Vorländer, H. (2000), 'Die Suprematie der Verfassung. Über das Spannungsverhältnis von Demokratie und Konstitutionalismus', in W. Leidhold (ed.), *Politik und Politeia. Formen und Probleme politischer Ordnung* (Würzburg, Königshausen und Neumann), 373–83.
Walker, N. (2003), 'Late Sovereignty in the European Union', in N. Walker (ed.), *Sovereignty in Transition* (Oxford & Portland, Hart), 3–32.
Weber, M. (1904), 'Die "Objektivität" sozialwissenschaftlicher und sozialpolitischer Erkenntnis', in M. Weber, *Gesammelte Aufsätze zur Wissenschaftslehre*, ed. J. Winckelmann (Tübingen, Mohr Siebeck) ^{4}1973, 146–214 [urspr. *Archiv für Sozialwissenschaft und Sozialpolitik* 19: 22–87].
Yelle, R.A. (2018), *Sovereignty and the Sacred: Secularism and the Political Economy of Religion* (Chicago, University of Chicago Press).
Yunis, H. (1988), 'Law, Politics, and the *Graphe Paranomon* in Fourth-Century Athens', *Greek, Roman and Byzantine Studies*, 29: 361–82.
Ziebarth, E. (1897), 'Popularklagen mit Deleatorenpraemien nach Griechischem Recht', *Hermes*, 32: 609–28.
Zürcher, C. (2007), 'When Governance Meets Troubled State', in M. Beisheim & G.F. Schuppert (eds), *Staatszerfall und Governance* (Baden-Baden, Nomos), 11–27.

2

Actiones Populares, Popular Sovereignty, and the People

VALENTINA ARENA*

Introduction

NO MODERN SCHOLAR nor ancient author seems to dispute that in the Roman Republic, sovereignty, understood as the ultimate authority within the political community, resided in the people. It was the people who, gathered in assembly, passed the laws that regulated the life of the polity and elected the magistrates who administered its daily affairs. By the 1st century BCE, laws were conceptualised and referred to, even by politicians like Cicero, as *iussa populi*, the orders of the Roman people, and so powerful was this understanding that in the 2nd century CE a Roman jurist could state that 'the laws are binding on us only because they have been accepted by the judgment of the people'.[1]

However, this claim is often followed by the correct observation that, despite the Roman ideological construct that places sovereignty with the people, Roman political language seems to lack a term that expresses properly this notion, and the closest to it that Latin can offer is the expression *maiestas populi Romani* (Hellegouarc'h 1963: 314–20; d'Aloja 2011; Hammer, this volume). As Ferrary (1983) observed, Saturninus had, at the turn of the 1st century BCE (103 or 100 BCE), with the passage of the *lex Appuleia de maiestate minuta*, introduced to the realm of domestic politics the notion of the *maiestas populi Romani*, which in the 2nd century had pertained to the world of international relations. Thus, an expression, which had previously indicated the superiority of Roman people against other populations, came to signify, in the words of politicians who posed to pursue

---

* Al mio babbo.
I would like to thank Georgy Kantor, Claudia Moatti, Antonino Pittá, and Christopher Smith for stimulating comments and interesting discussions on issues raised by this paper.
[1] *Dig.* 1.3.32. For sources and discussion, see Arena (2012: 63); Straumann (2016: 37).

a popular agenda, the superiority of the popular assembly over magistrates and senate, and, in the words of their opponents, a wider and, to a certain extent, vaguer notion of the dignity (*dignitas*) and the grandeur (*amplitudo civitatis*) of the Roman people and of the *res publica*.[2] An important point to observe is that in the political debates of the late Republic this sematic shift of the *maiestas populi Romani* did not only involve the notion of *maiestas*, but also, and perhaps more revealingly, the idea of *populus*. Whilst, in the first case, this was conceptualised as the unity of the Roman people resulting from their gathering in assembly either by tribes or by *centuriae* to express their political will, either to elect magistrates or to pass legislation, in the second case, the *populus Romanus* was thought about as a single abstract entity.

It remains true that the idea of popular sovereignty, either as de facto manifested in the pivotal role of the popular assemblies in Republican political life and articulated in the conceptualisation of laws as popular orders or conceptualised in the (rather vague) notion of the majesty (or greatness) of the Roman people, was consistently based on the premise of an understanding the people as a unity. Whilst from an institutional perspective people gathered in assembly were considered as expressing the will of the Roman people, the notion of the *maiestas populi Romani* referred to the unitary identity of the abstract idea of the Roman people.

Scholarly debate has so far focused on two main points: first, the dichotomy between the notion of popular sovereignty as performed in popular assemblies and the actual exercise of this ultimate authority by the people of Rome; second, the existing relation between the Roman people who met in the assemblies and the abstract notion of *populus Romanus*. These two issues are different permutations of the same problem and have at their core the question concerning the relation between the world of ideas and the practice of politics. These have occupied a prominent role in the lively discussion of the nature of the Roman Republican system initiated about 30 years ago by Fergus Millar,[3] and lay at the basis of the difficulty of mapping the Roman understanding of the idea of popular sovereignty onto its modern conception (in itself, incidentally, a very contested notion) and the ensuing discussion about the validity of the application of the term sovereignty to the ancient world.

However, a rival, and only partially convergent, understanding of popular sovereignty was developed in Rome during the mid-Republic and, alongside these ways of thinking about popular sovereignty, almost like a historical relic, carried on into the Empire. According to this notion, the Roman people were sovereign as each and everyone had the ultimate authority to dispose of what was theirs according to

---

[2] Arena (2012: 132–7). For the etymology of *maiestas* from the comparative *maior* and the notion of relative superiority encapsulated by the idea of *maiestas*, see Thomas (1991). See also discussion in Moatti (2020: 129–35); Hammer, this volume.

[3] Millar (2002: 8): '"the real" Roman Republic ... represents a radical example of popular sovereignty untrammelled by constitutional safeguards'. For a review of this debate, see Arena & Prag (2022).

their wishes by taking direct responsibilities in regulating its uses and abuses. The term, perhaps, was not there, but the way in which they organised their communitarian life, their administration of the commonwealth, and the way in which they talked about it in their juridical works were expressions of an idea that is akin to the modern (or, at least, early modern) notion of popular sovereignty.[4]

The aim in what follows is twofold: first, the chapter will unveil this distinct understanding of popular sovereignty in ancient Rome by focusing on the *actiones populares*, legal proceedings that enabled any Roman citizen to act in defence of the *res publicae* and, more specifically, of their use. It will show that, although in Republican Rome a doctrine of popular sovereignty was not fully elaborated, there was a concept framed in juridical reasoning, which expressed the source of the ultimate authority of an extra-legal and extra-constitutional quality rather akin to what we have come to recognise and talk about as the notion of sovereignty.[5] Second, it will trace down the intellectual developments that contributed to the later elaboration of the notion of popular sovereignty as the ultimate authority that resided in the Roman citizen body as a whole.[6]

The *actiones populares*

From the 3rd century BCE, our sources seem to attest the existence of an interesting, although somewhat neglected, legal proceeding, the so-called *actiones populares*.[7] As Watson (1985: s.v. *actio popularis*) succinctly puts it, an *actio popularis* was 'a penal action which could be brought by any person to protect the public interest in certain circumstances. The penalty was often paid to the complainant'.[8]

The cases in which the Romans adopted the *actiones populares* were of various kinds and covered unlawful acts such as, for example, those that compromised the safe use of public and private streets, as when objects and liquids were thrown from a window onto the adjacent street;[9] those that prevented the safe and free use of *loca publica*, as when a citizen was prevented from enjoying free passage through those places;[10] those that tampered with public aqueducts or polluted the

---

[4] See Mackie (1992) about the relation between the absence of key political vocabularies from Roman political discourse and their actual articulation through not only close terms, but also 'the institutions and adjuncts of power'.

[5] For the notion of popular sovereignty in early modern thought see Lee (2016).

[6] For a discussion of these ideas in Cicero's and Livy's writings, see Schofield (2021: 46–59).

[7] Fadda (1894) sees an evolution in the institute of the *actiones populares*, which, in his opinion, began as part of the praetorian edict and prescribed the award of the damage to the individual who had brought forward the proceedings, but in the 1st century BCE came to be instituted by law and awarded the damage to the *aerarium*.

[8] On this legal proceeding, see most recently Riggsby (2016).

[9] The *actio de effusis vel deiectis* (*Dig.* 9.3.1pr and 5.5); the *actio de feris* (*Dig.* 21.1.41), the *actio de positis vel suspensis* (*Dig.* 9.3.5.6 and 7); the *actio de via publica* (*Dig.* 3.3.42pr).

[10] *Dig.* 21.1.40.1 and 42 (Ulp. 2 ad ed. aed. cur.).

waters of a river;[11] those that altered fraudulently the boundaries of a colony;[12] those that violated a sacred wood;[13] and those that desecrated sepulchres.[14] To provide a fuller view of the wide casuistry that could be covered, to these we should perhaps add those that infringed laws on gambling and usury by, for example, illegitimately charging someone,[15] and those that fraudulently induced a minor to enter into a transaction, that is, in modern parlance, the circumvention of minors (Di Salvo 1979).

In the course of the Republic, the Roman juridical system declined the *actiones populares* in various articulations, whose historical development, exact nature, and potential for revival for the contemporary world are currently the subject of intense debate amongst scholars of Roman law.[16] There is, however, now a certain degree of consensus on the view that when an *actio popularis* was instituted by a *lex*, the beneficiary of the successful conviction would have been the *aerarium* of the *res publica*, as in this case the individual acted as representative, it is claimed, of the civic community, which, according to some scholars, had provided him with a mandate to rectify the misuse of the *res publicae*, the common goods. When, on the other hand, the *actio popularis* was instituted by praetorian *iurisdictio*, the individual actor, and not the *aerarium*, would have benefited from the proceeds of a possible victory, as he would have acted in his own name to protect his personal interest (and by extension, as we shall see, the interests of the community), which had been violated, acting however, crucially, not as a private individual but rather as a member of the community. Alongside the proceedings that the ancient sources explicitly describe as *actiones populares*, the Republican juridical system developed another procedure of legal action with no formal categorisation, which, despite being a *iudicium publicum* rather than a private action and not having the same monetary limits and involving the use of the *recuperatores*, shared with

---

[11] *Lex Quinctia de aquaeductis* (9 BCE), *FIRA*, Leges, 153; *Sc. de aquaeductibus* (12 BCE), ch. 127, *FIRA*, Leges, 280; *Lex rivi incerta*, *FIRA*, Negotia, 224 s.; Front., *De aquaed.*, 127. These were also protected by the *interdicta popularia*, such as those *de rivis* (*Dig.* 43.21); *de fonte* (*Dig.* 43.22); *de cloacis* (*Dig.* 43.23); *de rebus sacris* or *ne quid in loco publico vel itinere fiat* (Ulp. 68 ad ed. *Dig.* 43.8.2.34). On this see Di Porto (1994: 518ff.); Scevola (2012, vol. 2); Bannon (2017); and most recently Schiavon (2019: 160–1), with ample discussion of previous literature.

[12] *Lex Mamilia Roscia Peducaea Alliena Fabia* (*Lex Iulia agraria*, 59 BCE), ch. 4, *FIRA*, Leges, 139; *Lex Coloniae Genetivae Iuliae* (44 BCE), ch. 104, *FIRA*, Leges, 191; *Dig.* 47.21.3.

[13] *Lex luci Lucerina* (3rd cent. BCE?), *FIRA*, Negotia, 224; *Lex luci Spoletina* (3rd cent. BCE?), *FIRA*, Leges, 223.

[14] *Dig.* 47.12.3 pr. (Ulp. 25 ad ed.) and *Dig.* 11.7.2.2 (Ulp. 25 ad ed.). For an exhaustive list see Fadda (1894: 2ff.) and Albanese (1955: 39ff.). Most recently the excellent essay by Saccoccio (2011) also reviews those uncertain cases, and on this much of my analysis depends.

[15] These were connected to the *quadruplatores*: De Martino (1955); Rivière (1997); Russo Ruggeri (2001).

[16] See Halfmeier (2006); Saccoccio (2011); Settis (2012); Giagnorio (2012); Garofalo (2016), all also reviewing earlier contributions. As Saccoccio observes, following Casavola (1955), this legal institute, at the centre of scholarly attention in the 19th century, faded into the background for most of the last century, reflecting contemporary political preoccupations.

the *actiones populares* the important constitutive trait of being a proceeding for the benefit of the people (*populus*) (Crawford 1996: 21). Including *multam dicere* by a magistrate, *multam petere* by *qui volet* or a magistrate, and *multam irrogare* by a magistrate or by *qui volet*, they are, therefore, often considered by scholars conceptually homogenous to the *actiones populares* and analysed within the same group.[17] In what follows, I shall focus on those private proceedings to which the ancient sources refer as *actiones populares*, which initiated by a private person were understood for the benefit of the whole community.

Let us turn to the definition that the jurist Paulus gave of the *actiones populares* and that opens the last title in book 47 of the *Digest* where their general rules are listed (*Dig.* 47.23.1 (Paulus 8 ad ed.)): '*Eam popularem actionem dicimus, quae suum ius populi tuetur.*' Although very brief and, at first sight, of simple translation, this definition has been at the centre of great scholarly debate. This has been variably translated: 'we call popular an action that protects the right of the people as its own'; 'we call popular an action that protects what belongs to the people as his own'; or, with Scott (1932), more convincingly if we maintain the extant text, 'we call that a popular action which protects the rights of the party who brings it, as well as those of the people'.

The crux of the matter lies principally in the interpretation of the adjectives *popularis* and *suum*, as well as the syntagma *ius populi*. As far as the adjective *popularis* is concerned, this has been interpreted either as indicating the subject of the action, which can be initiated by anyone of the *populus* (*quivis ex populo*), or as the object of the action, that is an action that is brought *pro populo*, 'for the benefit of the people'. In the first reading, the adjective *popularis* is read as putting emphasis on the agent who initiates the *actio*; in the latter, it refers to the function of the *actio*, that is the readdressing and punishing of a wrong suffered by the community, the *populus* (see discussion in Casavola 1958; Saccoccio 2011; Giagnorio 2012).

The syntagma *ius populi* has been subjected to a similar polarity of interpretations: either a subjective genitive, which indicates that the subject who holds this right is the people (opening up, incidentally, the discussion of the existence of subjective rights in Rome), or an objective genitive, which refers to the sphere of competence of that right, in this reading this *ius* concerns the people.[18] Following this interpretation of the syntagma *ius populi*, Paulus' definition does not provide us with a clarification of who is the holder of the right and thereby its legitimate enactor to protect the common goods, but rather it refers to a right that concerns the interests of the people. In this reading, the focus is not on the authority that is

---

[17] See, for some examples, Gell. 10.6.2–4; Bremer 2, 284; the *lex Latina Tabulae Bantinae*, Law 7; the *Tabula Heracleensis*, Law 24, ll. 118–19. Contra Casavola (1958). See also Kaser (1968: 208).

[18] The interpretation of *ius populi* is connected to the question of the existence of subjective rights in Rome already in the Republican period. On this debate more in general, see Pugliese (1953); Villey (1957); Garnsey (2007). Of interest in this context also Orestano (1960) and Catalano (2001).

entitled to act legitimately, but rather on its function, the protection of people's interests.

Finally, the adjective *suum* has caused the greatest obstacle to the understanding of the text, to the extent that in the past some scholars have also considered the text interpolated. Maschke (1885: 234 n. 1), in fact, expunged it. Mommsen ([& Krueger] 1928: 840, n. 16) replaced it with '*sua vi*', and von Keller (1883: 477) and Colonieu (1888: 17, 45) with '*qua ius suum populus tuetur*' (the latter, however, does not seem to produce a great interpretative improvement on the text). Scholarly consensus, however, seems now to gather around accepting the authenticity of the preserved text.[19] In this case, the true interpretative crux lays in two issues: first, the interpretation of *populus* as indicating the whole community, or rather the *singuli cives*, who made up the people and were entitled singularly, as individual members of the community, to bring this action; second on the emphasis either on *suum ... populi*, what belongs to the people, or rather on *suum ius*, the right that, the text reinfornces, pertains to them. In my reading, as the discussion will show, an *actio* is *popularis*, as it can be initiated by any member of the civic community (subjective function), it protects the interest of the individual citizen who puts forward the claim and, by doing so, it protects also the interest of the people, understood as the plurality of its components, the citizens (objective genitive).[20]

A close examination of the cases covered by the *actiones populares* highlights two fundamental points: the first concerns who is entitled to initiate the proceeding; the second, its aim. As far as the first point is concerned, there are some cases where the right to initiate the action resides, in the first instance, in the person who has a direct and immediate interest in the violation, and only subsequently, almost in a subsidiary way, if the person entitled fails to do so and/or passes away, it falls in anybody else who wishes to do so (Saccoccio 2011: 727–8; Giagnorio 2012). Thus, for example, in the case of the *actio de sepulchro violato*, the person entitled to bring an action is the title holder of the tomb, and only in a case where he is dead is another party entitled to act (*Dig.* 47.12.3 (Ulp. 25 ad ed.); see also *Dig.* 47.12.6 (Ulp. 10 dig.)); similarly, in the case of the *actio de effusis vel deiectis*, only the wounded is allowed to initiate the *actio*, and only in case he dies without having had the opportunity to act, can another party, which in the first place should be either the heir or a relative, initiate proceedings. More generally, even when anyone is entitled to bring the action legitimately, the person who has a direct vested interest in the case should be preferred (*Dig.* 47.23.3.1; 9.3.3.5). Failing that, however, if this person is unable to do so, any citizen can bring the lawsuit, and if more than

---

[19] An exception to the current consensus is Danilovic (1974: 22). For a review, see Saccoccio (2011), on whom I rely here (given the lack of library access because of current restrictions).

[20] As Antonino Pittá suggested, it would also be possible to solve the redandance of *suum* and *populi* by intervening on the text and adding either *et* (the text would read *suum ius et populi*) or *sicut* (*suum ius sicut populi*).

one citizen wishes to do so, it is down to the praetor to adjudicate which person is entitled to do so.[21]

It follows that the actor who initiates the proceedings exercises his right to protect, in the first place, his private interest, which, preceding the interests of the other members of the community, legitimates his action. However, crucially, the function of his action remains not only beneficial to him, but also to the whole community, hence the ability recognised to any Roman citizen to bring forward the *actio*. It is the source of the action that has a private nature, not its objective (Casavola 1958: 15ff.). In this reading, therefore, the genitive of the syntagma *ius populi* of Paulus' definition should be read as referring to the object, understood as the protected interests, that is the interests of the *populus* as the sum of the individuals of the political community.

Contrary to the reading first put forward by von Savigny (1840: 131ff.) and fully elaborated by Mommsen (1905), according to which the individual citizen, *quivis ex populo*, acted as representative of the *populus*, as its *procurator*, in defence of its public safety and common interest, recent interpretations consider the individual citizen who initiates an *actio popularis* as acting in defence of his personal as well as public interest by virtue of being a member of the *populus*.[22] According to this reading, therefore, the citizen would be acting in the name of the people, not on its behalf. He would bring forward a private action as a member of the community, whose interest he administers in the first person, not as a delegate of this very community (which we today call a state). In other words, while according to Mommsen's interpretation, the individual citizen, *uti singulus*, acted in defence of the public interest, as if he had received a mandate to act on behalf of the community and, therefore, if successful, was entitled to enjoy personally the indemnity as compensation for having assumed this task on behalf of the community, in this interpretation, the individual does not act as representative of the commonwealth, but rather as its co-owner alongside the other *cives*. According to this interpretation, any citizen (*quivis ex populo*) is legitimated to initiate this action, as he is entitled to defend what belongs to him by virtue of his civic membership and not because he has received a mandate by the polity.

As the categories of cases in which the *actiones populares* are adopted show, the objective of this right was the protection of the ability to use freely and undisturbed those things that follow into the category of the *res in usu publico*. These *res*, which belong to the rather loose category of the *res publicae*, public properties, were neither strictly public nor private, but, along the same lines as the category of *loci publici* discussed by Labeo, each member of the civic community had equal right to use them. As the *Digest* attests, 'Labeo defines the term, "public place", as applying to such localities, houses, fields, highways, and roads as belong to the

---

[21] Paul. 1 ad ed. D. 47.23.2: *Si plures simul agant populari actione, praetor eligat idoneiorem.*
[22] This reading, first put forward by Bruns (1864) and then revised by Casavola (1958), is currently accepted by most scholars.

community at large'.[23] As Ulpian later specifies in the *titulus* preserved prior to Labeo's definition, 'public places are intended for the use of private persons, that is to say, as the property of the civic community (*civitas*), and not as belonging to any individual; and we have only as much right to their enjoyment as anyone of the people has to prevent their being interfered with' (*Dig.* 43.8.2.2 (Ulp. 68 ad ed.)).

The crucial point here is that the offence against the right of an individual, for the sake of argument, to walk through the streets of the city without fear of danger does not affect him as a private citizen but rather as a member of his community, the *civitas*, to which he belongs. If an accident takes place, this pertains in the first instance to the person to whom the incident happened, but then by extension also to anybody else who, as a member of the same community, could potentially incur the same problem by, following the chosen example, walking in the same street. It follows that the action should be brought first by the person who has been directly affected by it, but then, in case he is unable or unwilling to do so, by any other member of the community, as the offence has not been directed against that person as an individual, but rather as a member of the wider collectivity (Saccoccio 2011: 746–7). Holding, therefore, a very peculiar character, being, on the one hand, initiated by a private citizen and, on the other, pursuing a public objective, that is the protection of common interest, the *actiones populares* looked for retribution for the damages inflicted to the so-called 'generic interests'. These 'generic interests', which Scialoja was the first to call 'interessi pubblici diffusi', lie in an intermediary position between the public and the private sphere: although they belong to the individual members of the community, they do not coincide with them either.[24] Contrary to public interests, generic interests do not apply to the universality of the collectivity, but to any individual member of the community who could be harmed by their violation. 'Throwing things out of windows into a crowded street', as Riggsby notes 'or keeping lions, tigers and bears (popular offences) endanger the whole neighbourhood'.[25] If

> anything is thrown down or poured out from anywhere upon a place where persons are in the habit of passing or standing, I [the praetor] will grant an action against the party who lives there for twofold the amount of damage occasioned or done. ... No one will deny that this Edict of the Praetor is of the greatest advantage (*summa cum utilitate*), as it is for the public welfare (*publice utile est*) that persons should come and go over the roads without fear or danger.[26]

---

[23] *Dig.* 43.8.2.3 (Ulp. 68 ad ed.): *publici loci appellatio quemadmodum accipiatur, Labeo definit, ut et ad areas et ad insulas et ad agros et ad vias publicas itineraque publica pertineat*. For a full discussion of the *res in usu publico* in relation to the praetorian *interdicta*, see Schiavon (2019), who also traces down and delineates the distinction between these and the *res communes omnium*.

[24] Saccoccio (2011), also with reference to Scialoja at 725 n. 31; on 'interessi diffusi e collettivi', see also Trocker (1989).

[25] Riggsby (2016: 317), who also specifies that 'the justification for preventing "violation" of tombs is apparently religious, and so has collective implications (D.47.12.4)'.

[26] *Dig.* 9.3.1pr. (Ulp. ad ed. 23). Cf. *Dig.* 9.3.5.5, where it is referred to explicitly as an *actio popularis* that could be initiated by anyone, although the affected party or a relative would be preferable, and is carried out on the basis of what is *bonum et aequum*.

Even if the specific act might harm only a single member of the community, its threat looms conspicuously on all the others. These interests, which are not strictly private nor public, but have a close connection with both and gravitate in a sphere close to the public dimension, may be qualified as *populares*. Discussing the classification of the *sacra*, Festus reports Labeo stating that these should be divided in *sacra privata* and *sacra publica*, and that the latter, in turn, as attested in another passage, should be distinct from the *sacra popularia*.[27] The *sacra publica*, in his definition, were those celebrated on behalf of and for the people at public expenses, while the *sacra privata* were observed on behalf of and for the single individuals, their families and *gentes*. The *sacra popularia*, on the other hand, were distinct from them as they were celebrated by all Roman citizens, *omnes cives*, but were not associated to any familial structure. In this classification, the community was considered as composed by all citizens, understood in their individuality as members of the polity and not as members of familial and gentilician structures. It seems, therefore, that in Roman juridical thought there was indeed a category, qualified by the adjective *popularis*, which, although connected, was in opposition to *privatus* – as this would refer to the individual in his familial structures – and to *publicus* – as this would refer to the whole community.[28] As also attested in texts by Republican poets and playwrights, *popularis* could mean *civis*, member of the community, and articulated the relation between the individual and the collectivity.[29]

By initiating an *actio popularis*, the immediate scope of a citizen was not, as discussed in the context of a person who violated a tomb, the recovery of the property, but rather penalty and punishment (*Dig.* 29.2.20.5 (Ulp. 61 ad ed.); see also *Dig.* 47.12.10 (Papinianus 8 quaest.)). As Julian states in a similar context, the aim of this legal proceeding was the *ultio*, the punishment for the damning behaviour, which takes priority even over the legitimate right to initiate the action by the person whose property has been violated:

> The action for violating a sepulchre is, first of all, granted to him to whom the property belongs, and if he does not proceed, and someone else does, even though the owner may be absent on business for the commonwealth, the action should not be granted a second time against one who has paid the damages assessed. The condition of the person who was absent on business for the commonwealth cannot be held to have become worse, as this action does not so much concern his private affairs as it does the public vengeance.[30]

---

[27] Fest. s.v. *publica sacra* (Lindsay, 284): *publica sacra, quae publico sumptu pro populo fiunt, quaeque pro montibus, pagis, curis, sacellis; at privata, quae pro singulis hominibus, familiis, gentibus fiunt*; and s.v. *popularia sacra* (Lindsay, 298): *Popularia sacra sunt, ut ait Labeo, quae omnes cives faciunt, nec certis familiis adtributa sunt: Fornacalia, Parilia, Laralia, porca praecidania.* See discussion in Casavola (1958: 15–16).

[28] For further discussion on the distinction between *publicus* and *popularis* see Catalano (1974: 102ff.).

[29] Naev. *Pun.* 50 FPL4.H; Enn. *Ann.* 304 Sk. ; Plaut. *Poen.* 1039; *Aul.* 406; Ter. *Eun.* 1031; *Adelph.* 155 with discussion in Catalano (1974: 116ff.)

[30] *Dig.* 47.12.6 (Julianus, Digest, Book X): *sepulchri violati actio in primis datur ei, ad quem res pertinet. quo cessante si alius egerit, quamvis rei publicae causa afuerit dominus, non debebit ex integro*

Thus, the aim of these *actiones populares* was the application of a penalty/punishment (*ultio, poena, vindicta*), which could have been imposed by virtue of the legitimate exercise of a right held by each individual citizen to act in defence of his own interest. Crucially, however, by defending his own interest, the citizen who brought forward this action acted in defence of the interests of any other member of the community. Even if the person who was meant to initiate the action was unable to do so by virtue of a valid reason, he was not entitled to benefit from the result of the *ultio*, the punishment and restitution that goes with it. As this example clearly shows, in the *actiones populares* what is at stake is an interest that cannot be considered private but has rather almost a meta-individual nature (Saccoccio 2011: 742). The *actiones populares* acted as systems to punish the abuses of the properties the people shared in common, and thereby punished the violation of a *utilitas* that was individual as well as *communis*.

Although the jurists may seem not particularly focused on the identity of the person entitled to initiate proceedings, but rather on its aim of righting a wrong suffered by, implicitly, the whole community, it remains that the *actiones populares* were the juridical mechanism by which any Roman citizen (*quivis ex populo*) was entitled to manage directly the common property in the interest of the whole community. This proceeding embodies a notion of popular sovereignty that resided in the individual citizen who acted not as delegate of the community (let alone the state), but in his own name. This meant that the uncontested centre of public authority, which we often refer to as sovereignty, was each and every individual member of the *civitas*. His ultimate authority derived its legitimacy from his entitlement over its own *res*. As a member of the civic community, the Roman citizen had the right to use what he owned in common with the other fellow citizens.[31] His immediate scope was the infliction of the punishment for this violation, which, however, was understood within the wider framework of the infringement of the 'generic' – *populares*, one might say borrowing from Labeo – interests. The citizens, therefore, should not be understood as a distinct unitary entity, the entity that we call a 'state', but rather as the sum of its members. These interests occupied a sphere between the public and the private.

In essence, at the heart of the *actiones populares* was an action brought forward by an individual and not the community, where the individual perceived himself as wronged. However, the *privatus*, who brought forward the *actio*, did not act in the interest of 'the people' as its representative, whatever form this might have taken. Rather, he acted first in the name of his personal right to defend his own interest, which, in turn, was crucially perceived as equal in nature and status to the right of the other individual members of the community to defend that very interest.

---

adversus eum, qui litis aestimationem sustulerit, dari. nec potest videri deterior fieri condicio eius, qui rei publicae causa afuit, cum haec actio non ad rem familiarem eiusdem, magis ad ultionem pertineat.

[31] The juridical status of the *res publicae* is the subject of extensive scholarly debate (for a review, see Schiavon 2019: 11–144). My inclination is that there might have been a change in this regard from the early Republic to the classical period of the jurists.

Thus, the exercise of this right would have acted according to the same logic and by the same force as the right of any other member of the community. By protecting the *utilitas singulorum* and, therefore, the *utilitas publica*,[32] the *actiones populares* attest a strand of Roman juridical and political thinking that envisaged a pluralistic articulation of the ultimate public authority.

The *populus* and popular sovereignty

From a theoretical point of view, late Republican intellectuals, such as the polymath Varro and the jurist Alfenus Varus, operated an ideological innovation of the greatest importance for the later history of the notion of popular sovereignty: they united these pluralistic centres of authority that resided in *singuli cives*, in one, single, indivisible and eternal entity: the *populus*.

In his *de Lingua Latina*, discussing the usage of the language and the need to follow regularity (*analogia*), Varro states that:

> for some things belong to the people as a whole and others to individuals (*alia enim populi uniuersi, alia singulorum*), and of these what belongs to the orator and what belongs to the poet is not the same, because they do not have the same rights. Therefore, the people as a whole (*populus universus*) must use analogy in all words, and if it has acquired a wrong use, it must correct itself, whereas the orator must not use it in all words, because he cannot do so without offence, whereas the poet can leap across the lines with impunity. For the people is in its own power, and individuals are in the power of the people. Thus as everybody must correct his own usage if it is bad, so the people must correct its usage. I am not, as it were, the master of the people's usage, but the people is the master of mine. As the helmsman must obey reason, and each and everyone on the ship must obey the helmsman, so the people must obey reason, and we, the individuals, must obey the people (*populus enim in sua potestate, singuli in illius. Itaque ut suam quisque consuetudinem, si mala est, corrigere debet, sic populus suam. Ego populi consuetudinis non sum ut dominus, at ille meae est. Vt rationi optemperare debet gubernator, gubernatori unus quisque in naui, sic populus rationi, nos singuli populo*). Therefore, if you pay attention to every principle to which I shall refer in the matter of speaking, you will understand whether analogy is said to exist or whether it is said that it ought to be used; and likewise you will understand, if one ought to direct the usage of speaking towards analogy, that this is then said differently for the people than for the individual who is within the people (*tum dici id in populum aliter ac [inde omnibus dici] in eum qui sit in populo*).[33]

Discussing the linguistic practices that should be adopted, a topic perceived as of powerful political significance at the time, Varro importantly distinguishes the two main social actors: on the one hand, the people as a whole, the *populus universus*,

---

[32] On their relation, see Scevola (2012).
[33] Varro *Ling. Lat.* 9.5–6. The text is notoriously corrupted. Here I follow the reading of De Melo (2018: ad loc. with commentary and translation).

and, on the other, the individual language users, the *singuli*.[34] Crucially, these two groups should not follow the same rules. The people as a whole should follow the principle of regularity and correct itself if and where appropriate; the individual persons, amongst whom Varro singles out the orators and the poets who must adhere to different degrees (or even absence) of regularity, should follow the lead of the people. However, moving even further the conceptualisation of the *populus* as a unitary entity in explicit opposition to its individual constitutive members, Varro makes the striking innovation of articulating conceptually the people in personified terms. The *populus* is, in fact, assimilated to two persons: a *dominus*, that is a property owner, who holds *in sua potestate* the individual citizens (with the exception of the poets), who, following the juridical metaphor, are therefore his slaves, and a *gubernator*, the helmsman of a ship, whose crew members ought to obey.[35] The people should act as a distinct person, who is expected to correct its own usage of language, independently from the behaviour of its individual members (although they too are expected to correct their own usage if this is not accurate). Three important observations, therefore, emerge from this passage: first, the *singuli cives*, the individual citizens, are distinct from the people as a whole; second, the people in its unity is now conceptualised as one person, who behaves according to its own logic and should follow the principle of *ratio*; and third, its components should follow this unitary entity, which acts as their helmsman or, one might be tempted (albeit rather arbitrarily) to say, their 'sovereign'.

Belonging broadly to the same intellectual world, the jurist Alfenus Varus, student of the eminent Servius Sulpicius Rufus, who lived in the second half of the 1st century BCE and was, therefore, partly contemporary to Varro, articulated further the personification of the people. In his *Digest*, from which about 70 excerpts have been preserved in Justinian's compilation that goes by the same name, Alfenus Varus gives the following *responsum*:[36]

> The following case was suggested. Certain judges were appointed to hear the same action, some of them having been excused after it was tried, others were appointed in their stead; and the question arose whether the change of some individual judges left the case in the same condition, or placed it in a different one. I answered that not only one or two might be changed, but all of them as well, and that the action would continue to be the same that it was previously, and in fact this was not the only case in which it happened that though the parts were changed, still the thing itself was considered to be the same, but this occurred in many other instances (*neque in hoc solum evenire, ut partibus commutatis eadem res esse existimaretur, sed et in multis*

---

[34] Contra Varro *Ling. Lat.* 10.16, where the people is not an homogenous entity.
[35] On the political metaphor of the ship and its long history, see Brock (2013: 53–68). On the distinctively different use of this metaphor in Cicero's *post reditum* speeches (*Dom.* 24, 129, 137; *Sest.* 16, 25, 45, 46; *Pis.* 4, 9, 10, 20; *Sest.* 25), see Mebane (2018); for its use in Cicero's *de re publica*, see Zarecki (2014) and Schofield (2021: 87).
[36] Schiavone (2005: 232) considers Servius Sulpicius Rufus the original giver of this *responsum*, which, in his opinion, was then registered by his student Alfenus Varus. Cf. Fest. 462.25L that is based on the premise of Alfenus' positive *responsum* and may derive from Servius Sulpicius; see Bona (1964: 118ff.).

ceteris rebus). For a legion is considered to be the same, even though many of those belonging to it may have been killed, and others put in their places; and the people are deemed to be the same now as they were a hundred years ago, although not one of them may at present be living (*et populum eundem hoc tempore putari qui abhinc centum annis fuissent, cum ex illis nemo nunc viveret*), and also, where a ship has been so frequently repaired that not even a single plank remains which is not new, she is still considered to be the same ship. And if anyone should think that if its parts are changed, an article would become a different thing, the result would be that, according to this rule, we ourselves would not be the same persons that we were a year ago (*si quis putaret partibus commutatis aliam rem fieri, fore ut ex eius ratione nos ipsi non idem essemus qui abhinc anno fuissemus*), because, as the philosophers inform us, the very smallest particles of which we consist are daily detached from our bodies, and others from outside are being substituted for them. Therefore, where the outward appearance (*species*) of anything remains unaltered, the thing itself is considered to be the same (*quapropter cuius rei species eadem consisteret, rem quoque eandem esse existimari*).[37]

In his *responsum*, Afenus Varus answers a rather specific question, pertinent to his case at hand. The question concerns the identity of a *iudicium* when some of the appointed *iudices* had to be substituted by others.[38] To support his positive answer, Alfenus puts forward four analogous cases where the change of the parts does not affect the identity of the whole in question, be it a legion, the people, a ship or even our own person.[39] As long noted by scholars, Alfenus' reasoning is based on the premises of the Stoic division of the bodies: the unitary bodies (*sōmata hēnomena* or *corpora quae uno spiritu continentur*), such as, for example, human beings; bodies composed by coherent parts (*sōmata ek sunaptomēnōn* or *corpora ex cohaerentibus*), which are in contact with one another at the surface and do not undergo any change as a result of such juxtaposition, as in the case of ships; and bodies composed by distinct parts (*sōmata ek diestōtōn* or *corpora ex distantibus*), in which the change of one does not affect the change of the others, as in the case of the army, the people, and the flock.[40] The first two examples, the *legio* and the

---

[37] *Dig.* 5.1.76. Cf. *Dig.* 8.2.20.2 (Paul *ad Sab.* 15):
where a building from which water drips from the roof is removed in order that another of the same shape and nature may be erected there, the public welfare requires that the latter should be understood to be the same structure; for, otherwise, if a strict interpretation is made, the building afterwards erected on the ground will be a different one; and therefore when the original building is removed the usufruct will be lost, even though the site of a building is a portion of the same.

[38] On the private nature of this *iudicium*, the discussion about the *iudices*, either *recuperatores* or *centumviri*, and the identification of the actual issue at stake, see the excellent essay by Mantovani (2010), who reviews both the technical-juridical aspects as well as the philosophical ascendency of the *responsum*.

[39] The *iudicium* and the *iudices* do not fully correspond to the other cases, as technically the *iudices* are not parts of the *iudicium*, an attestation, according to Mantovani (2010: 14 n. 41) of the technical nature of Alfenus' reasoning.

[40] Chrysipp. *SVF* 2.302 (Sex. Emp. *Math.* 9. 78–82); *SVF* 2.124 (Plut. *Praec. Coniug.* 34); *SVF* 2.129 (Simpl. *in Cat.* 55E); *SVF* 3.38 (Sen. *epist.* 102.2). For the Stoic ascendancy, most recently Moatti (2018: 282–4). For review of past scholarship see Mantovani (2010: 15 n. 45), who, however, despite accepting the Stoic influence of the tripartite division of the *corpora*, emphasises the vast philosophical

populus, the two best suited to Alfenus' case, discuss *corpora ex distantibus*, that is bodies where the substitution of the parts (soldiers in the case of the *legio* and members of the people in the case of the *populus*) would not alter the bodies per se, the same *legio* and the same *populus* would continue to exist.[41] The crucial point for the present argument is that even if the *partes* change, the body will retain the same identity (*eadem res*), provided that its form, *species*, is not altered. It is, therefore, the notion of *species*, of Aristotelian origin, but forged by the socio-economic operational context of the jurists, that must remain the same, so that any entity may retain its own identity both in nature and throughout time. It follows that the people, the property owner in Varro's formulation, should be now conceived as distinct from its individual components and thereby also immutable and eternal.

Varro's and Alfenus Varus' attestations do not necessarily respond to the same conception of politics, and indeed it is possible to imagine that these two thinkers in the second half of the 1st century BCE held very different understandings of the commonwealth and its *loci* of power. However, what they clearly attest is that, in Roman political and juridical thought, alongside the notion of the people as the sum of *singuli cives*, an alternative, new, way to conceive the *populus* was elaborated. By the late Republic, this *populus* was no longer understood as a gathering of individual people, nor as in Cicero's famous formulation as a gathering of people united (*sociatus*) by the sharing of *ius* and *utilitas*, but rather as a person, a *dominus* or a *gubernator* according to Varro's analogies, whose identity remained unvaried throughout time and was eternal.[42] This notion of a unitary *populus* constituted a 'centralised' focus of authority, and a first, powerful, step towards the elaboration of medieval and early modern theories of sovereignty, where the sovereign was conceived as indivisible and with a unitary will.

From citizens to people

As Daniel Lee (2016: 10) has shown, the notion of an uncontested centre of public authority as developed in early modern times, and partly inherited by us, 'was regarded, by its adherents, as intrinsic to, and inseparable from, the concept of the

---

breath of Alfenus' *responsum* (which includes the influence of Aristotle, Democritus, and Epicurus as well as the Presocratics).

[41] The case of the ship was most probably an echo of the famous ship of Theseus, which had been preserved up to the 4th century BCE and had opened up the debate about the identity of the ship whose parts had been restored throughout the centuries: Plut. *Thes.* 23.

[42] Cic. *de rep.* 1.39 on which, most recently, Moatti (2018: 259–74) and Schofield (2021: 46–93). Cic. *de off.* 1.124 shows the same conceptual move, albeit in the opposite direction: here Cicero reminds that the magistrate should wear the *persona civitatis* (*se gerere personam civitatis*), that is a process of personification where the *civitas* is articulated as a distinct entity and the magistrate, called to act in its name, provides it with a bodily substance. See Orestano (1968: 185ff.); Catalano (1974); Lobrano (1996).

state and its authority'. This concept of the state was not elaborated in the Roman Republic, where, therefore, we do not find developed a *doctrine* of sovereignty, in any of its forms, including popular sovereignty. However, even if the Romans did not have such a doctrine, by the 1st century BCE they began to use in the context of domestic policies a notion often considered somehow akin to it, *maiestas populi Romani*. This idea, contested at the time, was based on the premise that the *populus Romanus* was somehow a united entity, in the first place the Roman people who gathered in assembly – and scholarly debate has focused on the extent to which this notion might resemble a modern idea of popular sovereignty.

However, focusing on the *actiones populares*, whose first attestations go back to the 3rd century BCE, has provided us with a window on a, thus far, hidden way to conceptualise sovereignty in Rome, that is a power held by the people and situated outside the realm of institutional politics, of an extra-legal and extra-constitutional quality. This power is anterior to and independent from public institutions and in particular popular assemblies, which, in principle, gathered the sum of the Roman people to pass legislation and elect magistrates, despite some well-known institutional (and social) limitations.[43] Its focus is on the individual person, who holds and exercises authority, before he gathers with the other citizens to compose an assembly, which, in turn, will empower and enable him to exercise institutionally this power in the context of a mixed constitution. As this ultimate source of authority lies in each individual citizen, it is possible to state that in the Roman Republic we find attestations, informed by juridical thinking, of a notion of pluralistic centres of authority. These centres, however, which might go back to Rome's gentilician structure, were not completely independent from one another. Rather, they operated within a *popularis* dimension, that is the sphere where an individual citizen acts in the shared realm of the community. In the course of the 1st century BCE, these individuals, who acted in defence of diffuse interests within this *popularis* context, came to be conceptually aggregated to become members of the same unitary system. Within the realm of juridical thinking and practice, a *lex* came to enable them to proceed in defence of the *res publicae*, making them act, according to the famous formulation by Mommsen, as *procuratores* of the Roman people. Philosophically, in the mid-50s in *de re publica* Cicero transformed them into a sum of people, united in civil partnership by a sharing of justice and interests. This was the first conceptual move that was required for a full elaboration of the notion of *maiestas populi Romani*. A decade later or so, Varro and, slightly later, Alfenus Varus took the further conceptual step on which the later theories of popular sovereignty depend. They conceptualised the Roman people no longer as the sum of the individual citizens, but rather as a unity, who could act as collective agent with an unchanging identity throughout time, an essential intellectual move for it to function as a permanent, unchanging, source of public authority. Only by virtue of this further elaboration, was it possible to conceptualise plausibly the

---

[43] The best modern treatment of the Roman institutional working remains Lintott (1999).

transferal of the sovereign powers from the people to the emperor, who could then, in principle, be authorised to speak and act in their name. By being conceptualised as a single person, as only individuals could be holders of rights, the corporate body of the people could be thought about as entrusting, transferring, or even alienating its right over the management of its own property, whilst the emperor could be thought about as superior to the person of the people, or, by the opposing argument, superior to the *singuli cives*, but inferior to the *potestas* of the people as a whole (Skinner 2018). For Ulpian, being able to state in the 3rd century CE that 'what pleases the princeps has the force of law, insofar as by the *lex regia* which is passed concerning his power, the people transfers to him and into him all its command and power' (*Dig.* 1.4.1pr), the ultimate source of all authority had to be thought as an individsible entity with a unitary will and personality.

The focus on the *actiones populares* has shown that in the Roman Republic, even in the absence of a modern idea of the state, it is possible to identify a concept of sovereignty articulated along juridical lines and expressed in terms of actionable rights and obligations. More strikingly, however, it also shows that in Republican Rome this concept of sovereignty, cast in terms of juridical reasoning, could not have been defined in any other way but as popular sovereignty. The fundamental reason why the people were thought about as holders of this ultimate power, the sovereign right of creating and empowering the institutions of the commonwealth (its assemblies in the first place, from which conceptually the magistrates and ultimately the senate derived), is because they were conceptualised and could also act as the property owners of such a commonwealth.

As Claudia Moatti has convincingly shown, the most encompassing meaning of *res publica* as 'the world of affairs about which the citizens have conflicts or debates, and about which they act in common', in the late Republic came to signify 'public property', a meaning which, she notes, had also been in place earlier.[44] By the 1st century BCE, to a Roman, *res publica* must have functioned, as Miriam Griffin (2013: 98) has observed, as a 'legal correlative of *res privata*', where rather than ownership of property by an individual, the ownership of property by the *populus* was at stake.[45] In Cicero's discussion of the legitimate *res publica*, this sense was emphasised by the list of the physical structures of the city, which under a tyrant did not belong to the *populus*, as in the case of Syracuse under the tyrant Dionysius, where none of the beautiful buildings, streets, harbours, porticoes, temples, and walls belonged to the people (Cic. *de rep.* 3.43; cf. 1.41).[46] As

---

[44] Moatti (2017: 36), further developed in Moatti (2018). Most interestingly, the expression *res publica populi Romani Quiritium* is found in the censors' prayers at the *lustratio*, the ceremony that took place after the census when people were registered on the basis of their property, assigned to a voting unit and enrolled in the army. Varro *Ling. Lat.* 6.86. Cf. Fest. 333L (Livius Andronicus).

[45] According to Thomas (2011: 423), material goods (*familia pecuniaque*) came to be unified under *res* in the 3rd century BCE.

[46] As Schofield (2021: 48) notes, Cicero's definition of *res publica* must have captured 'something fundamental in what Romans in general understood by *res publica*'.

shown by the *actiones populares*, the people's ownership of the *res publica* was not thought about as a metaphor; their exercise of the right to administer such a property was not tantamount to a notional right, but was rather a proper, actual, right to defend what was their own.[47] These legal proceedings, which were adopted also in the Empire, show in fact a direct engagement with the use and abuse of the physical reality of what belonged to the people in the defence of individual as well as communitarian, that is *popularis*, interests.

Contrary to common scholarly opinion, in Rome it is possible to identify a distinct way of conceptualising sovereignty that did not reside in the abstract notion of the *populus* as holder of *maiestas*, but rather in every single citizen, whose source of legitimacy resided in being conceived as the owner of the *res publica*.

References

Albanese, A.O. (1955), *L'azione popolare da Roma a noi* (Rome, Studio di ricerche giuridiche).
Arena, V. (2012), *Libertas and the Practice of Politics in the Late Roman Republic* (Cambridge, Cambridge University Press).
Arena, V. & Prag, J. (eds) (2022), *A Companion to Roman Republican Political Culture* (Hoboken NJ, John Wiley & Sons).
Bannon, C. (2017), 'Fresh Water in Roman Law: Rights and Policy', *Journal of Roman Studies*, 107: 60–89.
Bona, F. (1964), *Contributo allo studio della composizione del 'de verborum significatu' di Verrio Flacco* (Milan, Giuffré).
Brock, R. (2013), *Greek Political Imagery from Homer to Aristotle* (London & New York, Bloomsbury).
Bruns, K.G. (1864), 'Die römischen Popularklagen', *Zeitschrift der Savigny-Stiftung für Rechtsgeschichte*, 3: 341–415 (= Kleinere Schriften, I, 1882).
Casavola, F. (1955), 'Fadda e la dottrina delle azioni popolari', *Labeo*, 1: 131–40.
Casavola, F. (1958), *Studi sulle azioni popolari romane. Le 'actiones populares'* (Naples, Jovene).
Catalano, P. (1974), *Populus Romanus Quirites* (Turin, Giappichelli).
Catalano, P. (2001), 'Diritto, soggetti, oggetti: un contributo alla pulizia concettuale sulla base di D.1,1,12', in *'Iuris Vincula'. Studi in onore di M. Talamanca* (Naples, Jovene), 95–117.
Colonieu, V. (1888), *Les actions populaires en droit romain* (Paris).
Crawford, M.H. (ed.) (1996), *Roman Statutes* (London, Institute of Classical Studies).
d'Aloja, C. (2011), *Sensi e attribuzioni del concetto di maiestas* (Lecce, Edizioni Crifó).
Danilovic, J. (1974), 'Observations sur les "actiones populares"', in *Studi in onore di Giuseppe Grosso* (Turin, Giappichelli), VI, 15–43.
De Martino, F. (1955), 'I "quadruplatores" nel "Persa" di Plauto', *Labeo*, 1: 32–48.
De Melo, W.D.C. (2018), *Varro, de Lingua Latina: Introduction, Text, Translation, and Commentary* (Oxford, Oxford University Press).

---

[47] On property as metaphor, see Russell (2020: 555).

Di Porto, A. (1994), 'Interdetti popolari e tutela delle "res in usu publico". Linee di una indagine', in *Diritto e processo nella esperienza romana. Atti del Seminario torinese (4–5 dicembre 1991 in memoria di G. Provera)* (Naples, Jovene), 483–520 = in A. Di Porto (2013), *Res in usu publico e 'beni comuni'. Il nodo della tutela* (Turin, Giappichelli), 26–34.

Di Salvo, S. (1979), *'Lex Laetoria'. Minore età e crisi sociale tra il III e il II sec. a.C.* (Naples, Jovene).

Fadda, C. (1894), *L'azione popolare. Studio di diritto romano ed attuale* (Turin, UTET, repr. Rome, L'Erma di Bretschneider, 1972).

Ferrary, J.-L. (1983), 'Les origines de la loi de majesté à Rome', *Comptes rendus des séances de l'Académie des Inscriptions et Belles-Lettres*, 127.4: 556–72.

Garnsey, P. (2007), *Thinking about Property from Antiquity to the Age of Revolution* (Cambridge, Cambridge University Press)

Garofalo, L. (ed.) (2016), *I beni di interesse pubblico nell'esperienza giuridica romana*, 2 vols (Naples, Jovene).

Giagnorio, M. (2012), 'Brevi note in tema di azioni popolari', *Teoria e Storia del Diritto Privato*, 5: 2–87.

Griffin, M. (2013), 'Latin Philosophy and Roman Law', in V. Harte & M. Lane (eds), *Politeia in Greek and Roman Philosophy* (Cambridge, Cambridge University Press), 96–115 = (2018), *Philosophy and Politics at Rome: Collected Papers* (Oxford, Oxford University Press), 693–706.

Halfmeier, A. (2006), *Popularklagen im Privatrecht: Zugleich ein Beitrag zur Theorie der Verbandsklage* (Tübingen, Mohr Siebeck).

Hellegouarc'h, J. (1963), *Le vocabulaire latin des relations et des partis politiques sous la République* (Paris, les Belles Lettres).

Kaser, M. (1968), *Roman Private Law*, 2nd edn (London, Butterworths).

Lee, D. (2016), *Popular Sovereignty in Early Modern Constitutional Thought* (Oxford, Oxford University Press).

Lintott, A.W. (1999), *The Constitution of the Roman Republic* (Oxford, Clarendon Press).

Lobrano, G. (1996), *Res publica res populi. La legge e la limitazione del potere* (Turin, Giappichelli).

Mackie, N. (1992), '"Popularis" Ideology and Popular Politics at Rome in the First Century BC', *Rheinisches Museum für Philologie*, 135: 49–73.

Mantovani, D. (2010), 'Lessico dell'identità', in A. Corbino, M. Humbert & G. Negri (eds), *Homo, caput, persona. La costruzione giuridica dell'identità nell'esperienza romana dall'epoca di Plauto a Ulpiano* (Pavia, IUSS Press), 3–48.

Maschke, R. (1885), 'Zur Theorie und Geschichte der Popularklage. Erster Beitrag', *Zeitschrift der Savigny-Stiftung für Rechtsgeschichte Romanistische Abteilung*, 6: 226–41.

Mebane, J. (2018) 'Negotiating Exile: The Ship-of-State in Cicero's Post-Reditum Speeches', Paper at the 149 Annual Meeting of the Society of Classical Studies (Boston, 4–7 January 2018), accessed 30 May 2021, https://classicalstudies.org/annual-meeting/149/abstract/negotiating-exile-ship-state-cicero%E2%80%99s-post-reditum-speeches.

Millar, F. (2002), *The Roman Republic in Political Thought* (London, University Press of New England).

Moatti, C. (2017), '*Res publica, forma rei publicae*, and *SPQR*', *Bulletin of the Institute of Classical Studies*, 60: 34–48.

Moatti, C. (2018), *Res publica. Histoire romaine de la chose publique* (Paris, Fayard).

Moatti, C. (2020), 'The Notion of *res publica* and its Conflicting Meanings at the End of the Roman Republic', in C. Balmaceda (ed.), *Libertas and Res Publica in the Roman Republic: Ideas of Freedom and Roman Politics* (Leiden, Brill), 118–37.

Mommsen, T. (1905), *Gesammelte Schriften*, I, Juristische Schriften (Berlin, Weidmann) = T. Mommsen, (1855), *Die Stadtrechte der lateinische Gemeinde Salpensa und Malaca in der Provinz Baetica* (Leipzig, Hirzel)

Mommsen, T. & Krueger, P. (1928), *Corpus iuris civilis. Institutiones recognovit Paulus Krueger; Digesta recognovit Theodorus Mommsen*, i (Berlin, Weidmann).

Orestano, R. (1960), 'Diritti soggettivi e senza oggetto. Linee di una vicenda concettuale', *Jus*, 11: 78–95.

Orestano, R. (1968) *Il 'problema delle persone giuridiche' in diritto romano* (Turin, Giappichelli).

Pugliese, G. (1953), 'Res corporales e res incorporales e il problema del diritto soggettivo', in *Studi in onore di Vincenzo Arangio-Ruiz nel XLV del suo insegnamento* (Napoli, Jovene), III, 223–60.

Riggsby, A. (2016), 'Public and Private Criminal Law', in P. du Plessis, C. Ando & K. Tuori (eds), *The Oxford Handbook of Roman Law and Society* (Oxford, Oxford University Press), 310–23.

Rivière, Y. (1997), 'Les "quadruplatores": la répression du jeu, de l'usure et de quelque autres délits sous la République romaine', *Mélanges de l'École Française de Rome*, 109: 577–63.

Russell, A. (2020), 'The Economic World of the *populus Romanus*', *Journal of the History of International Law*, 22: 536–64.

Russo Ruggeri, C. (2001), 'Leggi sociali e "quadruplatores" nella Roma postannibalica', *Labeo*, 47: 349–83.

Saccoccio, A. (2011), 'Il modello delle azioni popolari romane tra diritti diffusi e "class actions"', in L. Garofalo (ed.), *'Actio in rem' e 'actio in personam'. In ricordo di Mario Talamanca* (Padua, Cedam), 713–77.

Scevola, R. (2012), *Utilitas publica*, 2 vols (Padua, Cedam).

Schiavon, A. (2019), 'Interdetti "de locis publicis" ed emersione della categoria delle res in usu publico' (PhD thesis, Università degli Studi di Trento).

Schiavone, A. (2005), *Ius. L'invenzione del diritto in Occidente* (Turin, Einaudi).

Schofield, M. (2021), *Cicero: Political Philosophy* (Oxford, Oxford University Press).

Scott, P. (ed.) (1932), *The Civil Law, including the Twelve Tables: The Institutes of Gaius, the Rules of Ulpian, the Opinions of Paulus, the Enactments of Justinian, and the Constitutions of Leo, Translated from the Original Latin, Edited, and Compared with All Accessible Systems of Jurisprudence Ancient and Modern* (Cincinnati, Central Trust Co.).

Settis, S. (2012), *Azione popolare. Cittadini per il bene comune* (Turin, Einaudi).

Skinner, Q. (2018), 'Classical Rhetoric and the Personation of the State' in Q. Skinner, *From Humanism to Hobbes: Studies in Rhetoric and Politics* (Cambridge, Cambridge University Press), 12–44.

Straumann, B. (2016), *Crisis and Constitutionalism: Roman Political Thought from the Fall of Rome to the Age of Revolution* (Oxford, Oxford University Press).

Thomas, Y. (1991), 'L'institution de la Majesté', *Revue de synthèse*, 112.3–4: 331–86.

Thomas, Y. (2011), *Les opérations du droit* (Paris, Éditions Gallimard et des Éditions du Seuil).

Trocker, N. (1989), 'Interessi collettivi e diffusi', in *Enciclopedia giuridica Treccani* (Rome, Istituto della Enciclopedia Italiana), xvii, 1–9.

Villey, M. (1957), *Leçons d'histoire de la philosophie du droit* (Paris, Libraire Dalloz).
von Keller, F.L. (1883), *Der römische Civilprozess und die Aktionen in summarischer Darstellung* (Leipzig, Bernh. Tauchnitz; repr. Aalen, 1966).
von Savigny, C.F. (1840), *System des römischen heutigen Rechts* (Berlin).
Watson, A. (ed.) (1985), *The Digest of Justian*, Latin text ed. Theodor Mommsen with the aid of Paul Krueger, English trans. ed. Alan Watson, 3 vols (Philadelphia, University of Pennsylvania Press).
Zarecki, J. (2014), *Cicero's Ideal Stateman in Theory and Practice* (London, Bloomsbury).

3

Between Sovereignty and Non-Sovereignty: The *maiestas populi Romani* and Foundational Authority in the Roman Republic

DEAN HAMMER[*]

Introduction

MY INTEREST IN this chapter is to modify how we understand the operation of sovereignty in discussions of the Roman Republic. The modification is important because of both the frequency with which the term is employed in discussions of the Republic and the often-uncritical range of its usages. One gets some indication of its limited explanatory or analytic value in a Roman context when sovereignty is used to denote everything from constitutional laws and procedures to the suspension of law, and from state domination to the expression of popular will. Sovereign authority, furthermore, is seen as residing variously in assemblies, a constitution, the people, consuls, and the senate.

To view the Roman Republic through the lens of sovereignty presents an immediate problem: the English word 'sovereign', from the Old French word 'soverain', does not appear until 1200 years after its fall. The term and concept are now invested with a history the Roman Republic never knew: a singular God, papal authority, feudal structures, secular struggles against imperial and papal authority, and the rise of the modern state. And the term itself does not admit of a single definition. For some, sovereignty refers to a will, whether of a collectivity or of a single individual, that orders or creates, but is not governed by another will (Bentham 1970 [1789];

---

[*] Earlier versions of this chapter were presented at the University of Wisconsin Political Theory Workshop, the UCLA Political Theory Workshop, and the Institute of Classical Studies Spring Seminar. All translations are my own unless otherwise noted. My thanks to Mikayla Bean for her research assistance and to Michael Kicey for his helpful comments.

Bodin 1992 [1576]: book 1, chapter 8, p. 11; Austin 1995); for others, sovereignty is embedded in law (rather than law being an expression of a sovereign's command) (Kelsen 1992; Habermas 1996: 486; Kant 1996 [1797]: sect. 49; Habermas and Rehg 2001; Hart 2012: 59, 95, 101–3); for still others, that sovereign will lies outside law in the power to decide (Schmitt 2008: 86, 268; Alston, this volume). The grip of sovereignty on our conception of power extends even to those who reject the applicability of the concept to ancient politics, leading those scholars to seek its opposite, contrasting the concentrated power associated with the state to the diffuse power of the people to govern themselves (Hinsley 1986: 37; Davies 1994: 60; Pettit 1996; 1997: 20, 27–8, 36, 283–4, 97–8; Skinner 2002a: 263; 2002b: 17; 2009: 346; Loughlin 2003: 57–9).

I position my argument between two contending claims. I depart from attempts to identify an absolute power to either will or decide since these notions associated with sovereignty do not map particularly well onto the complex and historically constituted gradations of power in the Republic. Simply put, we cannot read a modern notion of sovereignty into Roman politics (as Alston and Lundgreen, both this volume, also illustrate). The other view argues that sovereignty is a historically specific type of power that arises with the modern state. This latter approach, however, go too far both in generalising about the characteristics of ancient politics and in interpreting ancient politics as offering an alternative to the sovereign state, one in which the state is not conceptually distinct from the collection of citizens. I want to step outside the dichotomy of sovereignty and non-sovereignty, arguing for a notion of *foundational authority* that bears some similarities to, but is not identical with, sovereignty. I locate this authority in the *maiestas populi Romani*. Before developing its foundational aspects, I will lay out briefly how the *maiestas populi Romani* shares characteristics associated with aspects of sovereignty and non-sovereignty without being identifiable as either.

First, the *maiestas populi Romani* is not theorised as a definite concept. Rather, it is a semantic field that is associated with such terms as *imperium*, *potestas*, *dignitas*, *honor*, and *obsequium*, as well as emotions of awe and reverence.[1] Its meaning emerges through an ongoing series of contestations and interpretations that are remembered and transmitted through a range of social, religious, and political practices.

Second, the *maiestas populi Romani* embodies neither an absolute, indivisible, authoritative will nor a legal structure, but offers, instead, a regulative idea by which actions are authorised and obligations asserted. My approach is informed by Hannah Arendt, in her rethinking of sovereignty, when she argues that the perpetuity in and by which the act of constitutional foundation persists resides not in an 'identical will' but 'by an agreed purpose for which alone the promises are valid and binding', able to 'dispose of the future as though it were the present'.[2] Pavlos

---

[1] On *honor* and *obsequium*, see Kraus (1996: 123); Livy 6.6.8, 7.30.19.
[2] Arendt (1998: 245); see Stonebridge, this volume, for more on Arendt.

Eleftheriadis, too, in reconceptualising sovereignty, sees it as 'a public system of reasoning that is capable of guiding our actions and fixing our expectations about the actions of others' (Eleftheriadis 2010: 569). The *maiestas populi Romani*, as a form of foundational authority, is not an institution, a legal formulation, or a person. Rather, foundational authority emerges as a discursive framework within which the collectivity is imagined, laws and institutions created, political obligations defined, decisions made, and actions justified, and from which there is no appeal.

Third, the *maiestas populi Romani* brings together two ways of conceiving of the people: as the power of people assembled, engaging in concrete actions, and as an attribute or endowment of a fictive or abstract entity. The *maiestas populi Romani* is seen as endowed with perpetuity, indivisibility, and inviolability.

Finally, the *maiestas populi Romani* is not 'purely impersonal', as Skinner (1989: 125) characterises the 'agency' of the modern state, but combines aspects of both law and reverence that are retained from its early associations with the gods. That awe underlies the sense of inviolability by which the integrity of the *res publica* is protected from both external and internal threats.[3]

In developing the argument, I will explore: (1) the fictive aspects of *maiestas* that endow the entity with indivisibility and perpetuity; (2) an attendant notion of office in which authority rests on one's official relationship to the fictive entity; (3) the inviolable aspects of *maiestas* that are used to protect the integrity of the state against both external and internal threats; (4) efforts made to protect the framework; and (5) revisions to the authorising language of *maiestas* that accompany the end of the Republic.

Maiestas as fictive entity

At its etymological core, *maiestas* is associated with the divine, generally, and with supremacy attributed to Jupiter, specifically.[4] Although it is recognised that *maiestas* refers to the stature of the gods, to which reverence is owed, less appreciated is its connection to their regulative function. In the different aetiologies of *maiestas*, one sees a common theme of how *maiestas* joins the juridical with the magical. In Ovid's treatment (in a debate about the etymological origin of the month of May), *Maiestas* (born from *Reverentia* and *Honor*) emerges from the chaos of creation to serve as moderator of the whole world (Ov. *Fast.* 5.25). In Ovid's novel theogony, *Maiestas* is treated as a goddess who initially rules with

---

[3] See also Arena, this volume, for the importance of the *res publica*.
[4] Association with divine: Pollack (1908); Dumézil (1952); Drexler (1956: 196); Bauman (1967: 4–6). Ancient evidence includes Liv. Andron. *Trag.* (*Aeg.*) 12–13 [Warmington]) from the 3rd century BC; Quint. *Inst.* 3.7.7; Cic. *Div.* 1.38.82, 3.6.5; Ov. *Fast.* 5.25, 126; Ov. *Met.* 2.62, 937, 4.540; Virg. *Aen.* 12.820: descent from Saturn; Hor. *Carm.* 1.12–19; Macrob. *Sat.* 1.12.17: etymology of May derived from god, Maius, who is identified with Jupiter. Challenges to this association: Gundel (1963: 312–14); Thomas (1991: 338–41).

Saturn. In their interactions with *Maiestas*, the gods are portrayed as composing their expressions when looking at her (5.26–30). *Maiestas*, who does not wield weapons, ultimately must rely on Jupiter, who usurps Saturn, for protection from the giants. Suggestive of the joining of the divine with a regulative function, *Maiestas* assures the continuation of Jupiter's power (5.45–6) by establishing hierarchies so that 'greaterness' – whether towards the gods, parents, or political authorities (and one can add here 'the people') – is recognised (5.49–52). *Maiestas* is transmitted to Rome's founders, where she is worshipped by Romulus and Numa (5.47–8), enhancing the respect of rulers, *patres*, families, and the *triumphator* (5.49–52).[5] In its republican form, *maiestas* is located in the fictive entity of the *populus Romanus* and remains connected to Jupiter, who is seen as the protector and augmenter of the *res publica*. *Maiestas*, as Cicero notes at one point, could be understood as the *nomen* and power of the Roman people (Cic. *De part. orat.* 30.105: *Maiestas est in imperii atque in nominis populi Romani dignitate*).

Livy provides a republican story of the recognition of the *maiestas populi Romani* as the foundational authority of the Republic. After the battle of Veii, the once popular consul Publius Valerius faced growing suspicion that he was seeking kingship. He called an assembly and ordered the *fasces* lowered to acknowledge the superior *maiestas* and might of the people (*populi quam consulis maiestatem vimque maiorem*; Livy 2.7.7; also 2.57.3 on the *vis* of the Roman people; also Flor. 1.9.4). When Livy distinguishes between the power of the people's *maiestas* and their might, he locates the power in a divine element that, like Ovid's *Maiestas*, elicits, maybe even demands, recognition. It is worth noting that in this formulation, *maiestas* is not simply symbolic but joined (as it was with Jupiter) with *vis*, a power premised on the overwhelming numbers of the Roman people.

Maiestas does not simply describe a collection of citizens, or even a collection of citizens acting together. It is not the power of a crowd or an army. Livy's depiction of the relationship between *vis* and *maiestas* suggests how the *maiestas populi Romani* brings together two ways of conceiving of this authorising authority: as the power of people assembled, engaging in concrete actions, and as an attribute or endowment of a corporate entity that is abstracted from, but authorised by, the people. One sees in Sallust's recounting of Adherbal's appeal to protect the land that the Roman people had given, as well, a reference to a more abstract, perpetual aspect of the *maiestas populi Romani* that has a direct political tie to the past concrete actions of the people (Sal. *Jug.* 14.7–8: *Verum ego eis finibus eiectus sum quos maioribus meis populus Romanus dedit*).

I am not suggesting that the *res publica* functioned like the modern state in which there is the transfer of authority to a fictional, Hobbesian person. But the pervasive legalism that underlies almost every aspect of Roman collective life underscores a particular way of conceiving of the *res publica* as something different from the sum of individuals, as itself having a corporate existence or personality.

---

[5] Fantham (2006: 409) argues for a republican interpretation of the myth.

Notably, Cicero conceptualises the *res publica* as a *societas*: a partnership that is (in a sense) publicly owned and whose rights of ownership can be transferred or entrusted to a *procurator* (*Rep*. 1.25.39–42, 2.29.51; see Schofield 1995; Asmis 2004; Hammer 2014: 49–67). There is also a suggestive parallel between how the collective entity of the *res publica* operates and the institution of *condominium*, or joint ownership of property between *sui heredes* ('his heirs' or co-heirs). The institution of *condominium* has archaic roots that parallel the 'joint sovereignty' (*la sovranità commune*) of the magistrates (Bonfante 2006 [1919]: 276; also de Zulueta 1935: 24). The original provision, *societas ercto non cito*, or partnership of undivided inheritance, likely referred to the continuation of the household as it was before the death of the *paterfamilias*, 'except that there were now several persons who had equal right to perform independently the acts of administration previously performable only by the deceased or with his authority'.[6] The ancient consortium of *sui heredes* was likely the basis for the classical *societas omnium bonorum*, or a partnership of all assets, by which through contractual agreement the assets of the *socii* and future acquisitions were held in common. Ownership is changed from something seen as deriving from a pre-existing natural union (the family) to something artificial and constituted by law, though there are no differences in their legal effects (de Zulueta 1935: 20, 25, 30).

Cicero seems to play upon these legal notions when he connects the *maiestas* of the *populus Romanus* to property and inheritance in *De lege agraria*, asking if the people would not rather have the territory that belongs to the Roman people remain part of their *patrimonio*, rather than be divided up into private lots (*Leg. agr.* 2.29.79–80). That is, the power of *maiestas* lies in its indivisibility, that would be weakened once divided. Second, Cicero associates *maiestas* with having a say in the adjudication of that property. Thus, Cicero continually associates removing the control of these lands by the people to kingship and the abrogation of liberty (*Leg. agr.* 2.10.24–5; 2.11.29; 2.27.71). However much we may discount Cicero's argument as disingenuous, the language he employs parallels the Roman institution of *condominium*, or joint ownership. From this perspective, the *maiestas* of the people is connected to them functioning as a fictional entity in the absence of the political equivalent of a *paterfamilias*, a king, that is artificial and perpetual. We have other indications of the legal resonance of the term, as well, in Cicero's description of the *maiestas populi Romani* as the *nomen* of the Roman people. In his defence of Caecina, Cicero distinguishes between slaves and their *nomen* as a collectivity of the household (*familia*) (*Caec.* 20.57). In this case, the collectivity is a legal entity possessing certain rights, and the number of slaves does not change the status of that entity.

Thus far, I have provided some indications of how the *maiestas populi Romani* was conceived as a fictive entity, one that is consistent with Roman legal conceptions of partnerships and confirmed in Cicero's allusion to the *maiestas* of

---

[6] From Gaius 3, 154a, reproduced in de Zulueta (1934; 1935: 25).

the *populus Romanus* as a jointly owned inheritance, in this case connected to the adjudication of common property. We find in the language of both Sallust and Livy expressions of the *maiestas populi Romani* as a unitary body that is both indivisible and perpetual.

Office: representing *maiestas* without possessing it

A critical development in conceptualising the *maiestas populi Romani* as a corporate entity is its association with a notion of office. By office I mean that the authority of the person is seen as lying not in any personal attributes but in their official relationship to act on behalf of that entity. We can place this accountability against what we see in the Republic as the beginning of the construction of a *persona* assumed by the holder of an office that entails certain legal responsibilities. In its concrete significance, *persona* is the mask that an actor assumes in playing a part. However, the semantic field of the term is later extended to include not only a role or function a person may perform in a specific context (e.g. orations), but also to the possession of legal rights and obligations that are entailed by a position (Just. *Inst.* 1.3.pro.; Just. *Dig.*1.5.1; see Buckland 1921: 175). In one striking example, Cicero talks about how a magistrate wears the *persona* of the *civitas*, and his duty is 'to uphold its dignity and honour, to guard the laws, to apportion rights, and to remember that all this has been joined to him as a trust' (*Est igitur proprium munus magistratus intellegere se gerere personam civitatis debereque eius dignitatem et decus sustinere, servare leges, iura discribere, ea fidei suae commissa meminisse*; *Off.* 1.124). Similarly, in Cicero's use of *nomen*, he distinguishes between the actual owner of the property and the agent (*procurator*) who acts in the *nomen* of the owner. He is in a legal sense 'practically in the position of owner of all the property belonging to someone' and 'possesses the rights of another as his representative' (*Caec.* 57, trans. Grose Hodge 1927).

We are not going to find a modern, legal-rational notion of office associated with the *maiestas populi Romani*. There are instances in which *maiestas*, and the authority engendered by *maiestas*, is associated with qualities of individuals, like it is for the gods.[7] But in its republican form, the authority of *maiestas* is derived less from individual charisma, to draw on Weber's categories here, and more by virtue of its legal transferability. Just as there are individuals or groups who are sanctioned to act as proxies for a household or a *societas* by virtue of the transferability of ownership rights, so there are those who, without being formally or exclusively invested with *maiestas* themselves, are sanctioned to act on behalf of the

---

[7] I depart from Bauman (1967: 2), who argues that *maiestas* always depicts a relationship and not a quality. See, for examples, *maiestas* as attributes of individuals: Cic. *Rosc. Am.* 131 (Sulla); Livy 7.22.9, 7.40.8, 26.19.14, 28.35.6. Of groups, such as the nobility: Livy 5.41.8. Of the gods: Cic. *Div.* 1.38.82, 2.49.101, 2.51.105, 2.65.135.

maiestas populi Romani. In the transfer to a designated agent under the Republic, the authority and duty conferred by that position derive from a relation between the agent and the people that is distinct from any particular personal ties.[8] Individuals are made legally accountable to the *maiestas populi Romani*.

A range of individuals could represent the *maiestas* of the Roman people, including ambassadors (Livy 29.11.4), magistrates and commanders (Cic. *Pis.* 11.24; *Vat.* 9.22; *Balb.* 16.37), and soldiers (Caes. *BGall.* 7.17). Beginning in 103 or 100 BC with the passage of the *lex Appuleia de maiestate* under Saturninus, there are a series of attempts to both expand and formalise the specific actions associated with *maiestas*. The *lex Appuleia* established the crime of diminishing *maiestas* (initially encompassing, and in later laws replacing, *perduellio*) and possibly created a permanent court for trying *maiestas* cases (Chilton 1955: 73; Bauman 1967: 44–9; Harries 2007: 75). The law was aimed at holding consular and proconsular generals and other magistrates accountable for damaging the interests of the state through corruption or incompetence. The use of *maiestas* in a series of subsequent measures to authorise action against a variety of harms to the state suggests the malleability of the concept: Saturninus invokes *maiestas* to protect the tribunes with the aim of passing agrarian reform; Varius uses it against factions seen as aiding enemies in the Social War; and Sulla employs the idea as insurance against uprisings opposed to his power (Chilton 1955: 74; Bauman 1967: 79–81; Reinhold 1981; Ferrary 1983; Thomas 1991; Seager 2001). Critically, though, at no point during the Republic is *maiestas* ever conceived in any way other than in its relationship to the *populus Romanus*.

Entailed in the delegation of *maiestas* are not just legal obligations by the holder, but also recognition by others of that authority. That is Lentulus' point when he connects the violation of the *maiestas populi Romani* to the Rhodian treatment of him in his official capacity. Lentulus describes how he bore 'the indignity and the diminution to *maiestas*, not only of our right, but even now of the empire and people of Rome' (*indignitatem deminutionemque maiestatis non solum iuris nostri sed etiam imperi populique Romani*; *Fam.* 12.15.2). That is, the affront was to the authority he had on behalf of the *maiestas populi Romani*. Recognition is owed by virtue of an official position, not one's social status.

Further indicative of this notion of office, the authorising powers of *maiestas* and the recognition owed by others that attended one's official duties do not follow that person once outside that office. Caesar's words to Deiotarus, king of the client state of Armenia Minor, when the latter provides aid to Pompey, reveals how it is the responsibility of officials to know, in effect, who can act as an agent of the Roman people ([Caesar] *BAlex.* 68). When Deiotarus gives aid to Pompey, Caesar argues, he is acting against the legal authority of Rome. In the midst of tumultuous violence, Antonius is charged with *maiestas imminuta* for the territorial grants to Cleopatra. There was precedent for an *imperator* to both request aid from and adjust

---

[8] On the similarity of public office to a contract of mandate in civil law, see Watson (1961: 2–3).

territory for client states (Reinhold 1981: 101). But his criminality is established by declaring him a *privatus*, no longer acting in an official capacity on behalf of the state.

Inviolability

Thus far I have sought to identify how the *maiestas populi Romani* referred to a fictive entity by which the Roman Republic and the *populus Romanus* imagined themselves as both indivisible and perpetual. It is in the name of that fictive entity that officials were authorised to act and obligations were defined. But the *maiestas populi Romani* did not function in purely legal or impersonal terms. It is worth noting that few states are purely impersonal. Carl Schmitt (2005: 36) is probably correct in arguing that there remains something almost mythical that lies at the origins of states. There is certainly nothing rational, as Joseph Raz (1979: 233–49) has demonstrated, that can command a duty to obey. And despite Hans Kelsen's (1992) best efforts, there is no purely impersonal origin to a constitution. Yet, citizens pledge allegiance, swear loyalty, and die on a state's behalf. That allegiance depends on something affective, such as awe. *Maiestas* foregrounds that awe, certainly more than one encounters in the modern state. It is around the role of *maiestas* in modifying the *populus Romanus* that scholars differ. In one view, *maiestas* does not affect the meaning of the *populus Romanus*. Whatever religious associations there might have been with *maiestas* earlier, by the late Republic the *maiestas populi Romani* had evolved into a legal term (Gundel 1963: 319; Bauman 1967: 13; Ferrary 1983: 569–70; Arena 2012: 135, 139). In the second view, the juridical form of the corporate body of the *populus Romanus* is shrouded in, or inconsistent with, the murkiness of religious superstition (Badian 1969: 450; Mackie 1992: 89; Seager 2001: 153; Burton 2011: 275). The religiously charged language of *maiestas* enhances the authority of the *populus Romanus* by endowing the corporate body with inviolability. That inviolability functions to secure the integrity of the state against both external and internal threats by making the *maiestas populi Romani* the authority to which there was no appeal.

Inviolability and territorial integrity

The earliest extant attestations of the *maiestas populi Romani* appear in the context of international relations. Rulers of conquered territories were obligated to recognise and preserve the *maiestas populi Romani* (*maiestatem populi Romani conservanto*; Cic. *Balb.* 16.35, 17.38), and these territories were compelled to swear oaths in recognition of the *maiestas* of the Roman people.[9] The recognition does not

---

[9] Gundel (1963: 289–94); Reinhold (1981: 98, 100); Lewis and Reinhold (1990); Thomas (1991). See *Lex Gabinia Calpurnia de Insula Delo RS* 22.18–19, in Crawford (1996); Livy 38.11.2. Other *maiestas*

derive solely from its legal formulation but from its sacred element. Cicero gives us insight into the source of this inviolability in his defence of L. Cornelius Balbus. Looking to take advantage of the weakening partnership of Caesar, Pompey, and Crassus in 56 BC, opponents of the triumvirate were able to get a citizen of Gades to charge Balbus (also from Gades) with improperly receiving citizenship from Pompey in contravention of the sacrosanctity of a treaty between Rome and Gades. But Cicero turns the prosecution's argument on its head, arguing that the treaty is not sacrosanct since it was never ratified by the people (*Balb.* 15.34). As Cicero writes, in talking about treaties, 'For nothing can be sacrosanct unless it has been enacted through the People or the Commons' (*Sacrosanctum enim nihil potest esse, nisi quod per populum plebemve sanctum est*; *Balb.* 15.35, trans. Gardner). Cicero's verbal variation is striking: the contingent enactment or *sanctio*, which includes the authority of the senate, establishes the recognition of the *maiestas* of the people as inviolable, perpetual, and literally sacrosanct.[10] Without the enactment of the people, there can be no sacred public obligation (*quod publica religione sanciri potuit, id abest*; *Balb.* 15.35).

Once enacted, the treaty was to be venerated, like the divine quality attributed to *maiestas*. One sees that veneration, for example, in the worship by subject territories of the deified *Urbs Roma* (see Magie 1950: 1.106). Further suggestive of this republicanised majesty, one sees not just a veneration for, but also a beneficence of the *populus Romanus* that is associated with reverence for the gods (Cic. *Nat. D.* 2.30.77; Quint. *Inst.* 3.7.7). For example, Cicero describes the benefits that such worship of the majesty of the Roman people in turn brings (*Balb.* 16.37). *Maiestas* becomes a statement of the inviolability of Roman authority – the territory Hercules marked at the end of his labours, as Cicero exclaims – upheld in the name of the Roman people (*Balb.* 17.39).

Inviolability and treason

The external threat to the integrity of the *res publica* posed by states who acted against the *maiestas populi Romani* was extended analogously to internal threats posed by domestic actors. *Maiestas* crimes (technically, *maiestas minuta populi*

---

treaties were made with Gades in 206 and renewed in 78 (Cic. *Balb.* 16.35), the Aetolians in 189 (Livy 38.11.2; Polyb. 21.32), Rhodes in 165/4 and renewed in 51 (Bauman 1989: 220–2), possibly Cnidus in 28 (Täubler 1913: 451, though fragmentary and Täubler's reconstruction is disputed), and Mitylene in 25 (*IGR* 4.33, also fragmentary; Gundel 1963: 294).

[10] Note, as well, the performance of fetial rituals in solemnising a treaty (Livy 1.24.3, 9.5.1–5; implied in Cic. *II Verr.* 5.49 and Varro *Ling.* 5.86). See Watson (1993: 31–7); Rich (2011: 193–5). There are other suggestions of this relationship between the people and divinity. The *pomerium* was a boundary that was both sacred, protecting Rome from enemies, and civil, protecting citizens as a whole in their exercise of the highest authority from *imperium* (Drogula 2015: 49–56). Cicero, for example, suggests that the power of the people is second only to the immortal gods (Cic. *Rab. perd.* 2.5). In Gaius, one sees the ongoing association of *res sacra* with an action of the whole people (Gaius *Inst.* 2.5).

Romani) were seen as acts of malice or treason, aimed primarily at public officials rather than private individuals, against the foundation of the *res publica*.[11] This formulation is important, not least because it challenges Skinner's (1989: 124) contention that the emergence of the modern state transforms the idea of treason from crimes against the majesty of the king to crimes against an abstract entity that is separate from any individual.

It has been noted quite rightly that *maiestas* laws did not provide particularly precise legal guidance (Seager 2001: 150; Cic. *Fam.* 3.11.3; *De or.* 2.25.107–8, 2.39.164; *Part. or.* 30.105). The legal ambiguities arise in large part because of the religious aspects that remain a part of *maiestas*. These religious aspects are not accidental artifacts of earlier meanings of the term, nor do they rise to the legal specificity of *sacrilegium* as seen in the *Lex Julia peculatus*, but they convey a notion of inviolability that remains present in and gives force to the corporate aspects of agency (that a person can officially represent *maiestas* without possessing it). The Roman official occupies the same relationship to, and is required to uphold in the same way, the *maiestas populi Romani* as other states.

Seneca the Elder gives insight into the resonances of *maiestas* not easily captured in legal form. Seneca straddled the world of the Republic and the principate, composing his rhetorical exercises presumably from his prodigious memory as well as possibly from other written works and his own notes (Fairweather 1981: 38–42). In one declamation, he describes how Quinctius Flamininus as proconsul in 193 BC had a condemned criminal executed during a banquet at the request of a prostitute who said she had never seen a man beheaded (*Controv.* 9.2.pro.). He is accused of violating *maiestas*, though it is uncertain whether there was ever a prosecution. There are two noteworthy aspects of this rhetorical exercise. First, the charge is not that a criminal was executed, but that the proconsul degraded the position by acting at the behest of a prostitute rather than according to the procedures put in place to protect the *maiestas populi Romani* (9.2.2, 4, 8 [not ruled by law]). The authorised agent is engaged in actions that are unauthorised by the Roman people (thus violating the legal obligations of office) (see also 9.2.15). But the actions also pollute the religiously charged 'greaterness' of the corporate entity. Seneca the Elder describes a 'table defiled' (*contactam*) by blood (9.2.5), as well as a *victuma* or slaughtered sacrificial victim, emphasising the sacrilege by adding that it occurs before the gods (just as it occurs in the name of the *maiestas* of the people) (9.2.6). By granting to 'a whore' what was granted 'by the Roman people', Flamininus 'made a game out of the terror inspired by the empire of Rome' (9.2.3, 6, trans. Winterbottom 1974). A second note is that even if the reference to a legal violation

---

[11] *Rhet. Her.* 2.12.17, 4.25.35; Livy 1.26.5, 6.20.11–12; Just. *Dig.* 48.4.1.3 on punishment under the Twelve Tables for stirring up the enemy or delivering a citizen to the enemy, though likely not originally in the Tables (see *RS* 40, in Crawford 1996: 703). See Bauman (1967: 8) and Drexler (1956: 198) for the range of terms associated with the diminution of *maiestas*.

of *maiestas* is anachronistic, it is striking how it is read back into Roman history as a foundational principle of the Republic.

The persistence of the divine in *maiestas* crimes is further suggested by its overlapping meaning with earlier terms connoting sacred violations. For example, Cicero accuses Antonius of *parricidium* in besieging the loyal colony of Mutina by ignoring the *maiestas* – derived from the people – of the consul-elect, Decimus Brutus, who was trying to stop Antonius (*Phil.* 13.20). *Parricidium* is a rhetorically powerful word here, evoking the sacrilege of killing one's kin (now extended by analogy to killing one's *patria*).[12] It is not the only time we see *parricidium* associated with treason (*perduellio*). When Horatius kills his sister (for mourning for an enemy) during the regal period, an act of *parricidium*, he is charged with *perduellio* in Livy's account (1.26), but *parricidium* in other accounts (Festus s.v. *Sororium tigilium*; Dio. Hal. 3.22; Florus 1.1.3.6). *Perduellio* was a capital offence for actions deemed directly hostile to the state, such as aiding an enemy, that is then incorporated into *maiestas* laws (though the procedures associated with *perduellio* are recalled in 63 in the trial of Rabirius). Although we know little about either these laws or their procedures in early Rome, I agree with Alan Watson (1979: 436–7) that there is no reason to reject Livy's account. What I want to emphasise is that the blurring of *parricidium*, *perduellio*, and *maiestas* points to some commonality among them.

We get a further sense of this commonality when Cicero suggests that 'to betray one's country, to do violence to one's parents, to plunder a temple' (*patriam prodere, parentes violare, fana depeculari*) are similar acts of *peccatum* (transgression) (*Fin.* 3.9.32). What these different acts have in common is that they breach what is seen as some inviolable authority. The authority is inviolable because it is seen as fundamental to the social order. We can add the mention by Dionysius of Halicarnassus of impious actions of patrons and clients towards each other that was punishable as treason (*prodasia*) under a law of Romulus (Dion. Hal. *Ant. Rom.* 2.10). One can see in these laws the protection of the different social units that are seen as fundamental to Roman order: the *paterfamilias*, kin, patron-clients, the *res publica*, the *maiestas populi Romani*, and later the *princeps* and family. There are changes that emerge in their association with violations of the *maiestas populi Romani*: the foundational authority that is being threatened is that of the *populus Romanus*, and the crimes, though retaining the elements of majesty, are shed of some of the barbaric cruelty of sacral punishments. That is Cicero's point in arguing against the attempt to try Rabirius under the archaic procedures of *perduellio* (e.g. *Rab. perd.* 3.10).[13]

Although the religiously charged resonance of *maiestas* makes it difficult to define with legal precision, it differentiates the term conceptually from other types of violations. In Cicero's denunciation of Verres in his corruption and extortion

---

[12] See Cloud (1971) in his attempt to trace the complicated history of *parricidium*.
[13] Cloud (1971: 60, 62–5) argues that the primary purpose of the *lex Pompiea de parricidiis* was to substitute *interdictio* for the punishment of the *culleus* for the standing courts.

trial in 70 BC when he was governor of Sicily, Cicero recites a litany of *maiestas* violations, including removing statues that were monuments of Roman victory (*II Verr.* 1.11, 4.34.75–6, 4.36.79–80, 4.41.88). Cicero provides insight into the different charges that could have been brought: extortion for having robbed an ally; public embezzlement for having stolen what belonged to the Roman people; impiety (*scelus*) for having profaned a religious statue; cruelty for his treatment of their president, Sopater; or *maiestas* for having removed a monument of Rome's power, renown, and achievements.[14] That is, a charge of *maiestas* is meant to address the effect of an action on the aura of the whole, conceived as an indivisible unity. The diminution of that aura is seen as threatening the greaterness, and thus the authority, of the *populus Romanus*. It might seem trivial, but in a world in which power was communicated visually, the statue was a reminder of both Rome's power (and the terror it invoked) and its recognition of the loyalty of its allies (*II Verr.* 4.39.84; on terror, see Sen. *Controv.* 9.2.8), both central to maintaining security. To remove the reminder is to diminish the safety of Rome.

Protecting the framework

My interest in the previous sections was to suggest how *maiestas* introduces inviolability to the indivisibility and perpetuity of the *populus Romanus*. *Maiestas* is located in the people and requires some form of action either by the people or by an official who is authorised to act on behalf of, but who does not possess, *maiestas*. Once enacted, the action is inviolable and the source of that authorisation takes on a more abstract, fictional quality that is indivisible and perpetual, extending to protections from both external and internal threats. What I want to turn to now are efforts to, in effect, protect the framework. That becomes very difficult because the *maiestas populi Romani* is more a cultural than a legal code. Cicero, for example, distinguishes between the right of law (*iure legum*) and *maiestas imperii* (*Vat.* 9.22). And in his denunciation of Antonius, he draws the institutions and customs of ancestors into the semantic field of *maiestas*: 'Do those men know the form of the *res publica*, the laws of war, the *exempla* of our ancestors? Have they considered for what the *maiestas populi Romani* and the gravity of the senate require?' (*Norunt isti homines formam rei publicae, iura belli, exempla maiorum, cogitant quid populi Romani maiestas, quid senatus severitas postulet*; *Phil.* 5.25). The associations do not detract from *maiestas* but place it alongside other deeply felt and important cultural norms.

Norms are hard to question, in part because they frame the context in which discussions can even occur. And they are slippery. They can evolve while still appearing continuously recognisable. That is what gives such endurance to the *mos*

---

[14] *II Verr.* 4.41.88; also Cic. *Fam.* 3.11.2 on distinction between corruption and *maiestas* crimes.

maiorum.¹⁵ With the passage of the *maiestas* laws, though, debates arose about what it means to diminish the *maiestas populi Romani*. The rhetorical exercises in *Rhetorica ad Herennium*, written in the 80s BC, point to different ways in which *maiestas* could be diminished. One could understand *maiestas* by its constituent elements, namely elections and consular assemblies. Thus, 'He diminishes the *maiestas* of the state who destroys the *elements* constituting its greatness' (*Maiestatem is minuit qui ea tollit ex quibus rebus civitatis amplitudo constat*; 2.12.17). Or one could understand *maiestas* more abstractly, as referring collectively to the *civitas*. The speaker provides the alternate definition: 'He diminishes the *maiestas* of the state who inflicts damage upon its greatness' (*Maiestatem is minuit qui amplitudinem civitatis detrimento adficit*; *Rhet. Her.* 2.12.17, 4.25.35; also Cic. *De or.* 2.39.164). It is in keeping with the notion of the *maiestas populi Romani* as indivisible that *minuo* carries with it the meaning of dividing into pieces. That is, one can diminish the *maiestas populi Romani* by somehow lessening how one sees the collectivity (e.g. by taking monuments) as well as by dividing up that collectivity. I think that is the meaning Cicero employs in *De lege agraria* when suggesting that the *maiestas* of the Roman people will be diminished if they divide up their inheritance.

Valentina Arena, following Jean-Louis Ferrary, reads these definitional controversies as reflecting two ideological discourses that contended over the relationship between *maiestas* and the *populus Romanus*. One ties *maiestas* directly to the actions of the people in what Arena characterises as the 'direct exercise of popular sovereignty'; the second of these discourses, a more abstract version of *maiestas*, was aimed at 'the devolving of popular sovereignty upon magistrates' (Arena 2012: 135, 39; and further this volume; also Gundel 1963: 319; Ferrary 1983: 569–70). There is no doubt that the *maiestas* trials were ideologically charged, though opportunism likely figured in as much as ideology. The point I want to emphasise is that the abstractness that Arena sees as a dilution of the meaning of *maiestas* is not exclusive of the direct role of the people but structures the relationship of *maior–minor* from its beginnings. There does not seem to be any suggestion that the legal formalisation of the phrase is particularly surprising or breaks new conceptual ground. It is more evolutionary than revolutionary.

What the *lex maiestatis* attempts to do is give the greaterness of the Roman people legal protection. The authority derived from *maiestas* superceded private authority (Cic. *Inv.* 2.17.52). Particular positions were subordinate to, and given authority on behalf of, the *maiestas populi Romani*, and what officials could and could not do were designated increasingly by legally prescribed rules. The laws were used not only to hold officials accountable, but also to defend tribunician power. Thus, Antonius employs this more abstract version of *maiestas* precisely to argue for the proper functioning and role of the tribunes. Antonius develops his

---

¹⁵ See Hölkeskamp (2010), who attributes the power of the senate to their absence of formal (but abundance of informal) powers, and Arena (2015) for her discussion of the evolution of informal norms.

defence of a tribune, Norbanus, for violence against two tribunes attempting to stop the prosecution of Caepio, by associating *maiestas* not with a constituent element of the state – obstructing a tribune, for example – but with actions that promote (or diminish) a more abstract notion of the grandeur of the state. Antonius responds,

> His somewhat disorderly procedure in respect of Caepio involved no treason; the violence in question was aroused by the just indignation of the public and not by the action of the tribune; whereas the majesty of the Roman people, inasmuch as that means their greatness, was increased rather than diminished in the maintenance of its power and right.
>
> [*Non minuit maiestatem quod egit de Caepione turbulentius; populi enim Romani dolor iustus vim illam excitavit, non tribuni actio; maiestas autem, quoniam est magnitudo quaedam, populi Romani in eius potestate ac iure retinendo aucta est potius quam diminuta.*] (Cic. *Part. or.* 30.105, trans. Rackham 1942)

Cicero makes reference to Antonius' defence in *De oratore*, suggesting, 'If *maiestas* is the grandeur and dignity of the *civitas*, it was diminished by the one [Caepio] who delivered up to the enemy the Roman People, not by the one [Norbanus] who delivered the man that did it into the power of the Roman People' (*si maiestas est amplitudo ac dignitas civitatis, is eam minuit, qui exercitam hostibus populi Romani tradidit, non qui eum, qui id fecisset, populi Romani potestati tradidit*; *De or.* 2.164). That is, violence, including the overthrow of the kings and actions leading to establishing protections for the people, could be justified if it contributed to the health of the community (*saluti ... civitati*; Cic. *De or.* 2.199). Antonius makes a powerful and revealing claim that *maiestas* is not diminished when one was carrying out 'the will of the Roman people' (*voluntate populi Romani*; Cic. *Part. or.* 30.105; also Plut. *Ti. Gracch.* 5.2–4). I do not want to just pass by this formulation without noting its significance: in this case the *maiestas populi Romani* is not associated with a particular office or procedure but with action that carries out the intention or desire of the fictive person of the *civitas*. Plutarch provides some indication of the *populares* origin of the discursive strand that would justify Antonius' argument when he has Tiberius Gracchus say that 'if [a tribune] annuls the power of the people, he is no tribune at all' (Plut. *Ti. Gracch.* 5.3, trans. Perrin 1921).

We can understand the importance of the formulation of *maiestas* crimes, regardless of the definitions employed, as a way of controlling, or bringing back under control, the centrifugal forces of clientalism, corruption, and dynastic competition that privileged personal attachments over loyalty to the Roman state (see Drogula 2015: 292–6). It may well be the case that the heightened references to the *maiestas populi Romani* in the Republic are attempts to assert – or reassert – this once-agreed-upon foundational authority in the face of fragmenting loyalties. One can hear in Sallust's language the growing concern with unauthorised power that turns precisely on the distinction between the legitimate transfer and illegitimate theft of the *maiestas populi Romani*. Speaking to the people, Memmius condemns the willingness of corrupt members of the senate to sell the people's *maiestas* to the highest bidder in order to enhance their own wealth and power (*Jug.* 31.9). In this case, it is the betrayal of a treaty sanctified by the people for a bribe (*Jug.* 14.7, 25). Similarly, honours and triumphs – the latter involving (though the procedures could vary) senatorial and popular approval to allow the general *imperium* to lead his troops within the boundaries of the city (Beard 2009: 202) – no longer represent *maiestas* because they have not been entrusted by those who possess that *maiestas* (*Jug.* 31.19). Memmius makes clear what it means to undermine *maiestas*: it means that individuals are able to act with impunity in a way that recalls the monstrous liberty of the *reges* (*Jug.* 31.27; also 31.11–20). In the language of this framing authority, for the individual to appropriate *maiestas* from the collective amounts to an act of treason against the *maiestas populi Romani*, the foundation of the Republic.[16]

The end of the Republic

That is precisely the appropriation which happens. What accompanies the end of the Republic and the rise of the principate is the divestment of *maiestas* from the corporate entity of the *populus Romanus* and its incorporation into the personal authority of Caesar, first, and the *principes* who followed (see further, Alston, this volume). It does not occur by way of a legal transfer, as some have suggested, but as a discursive transformation in the foundational framework (Bauman 1967: 228; Lintott 1999: 40; Straumann 2016: 246–7). We can witness the beginning of the transformation when Caesar connects the *maiestas populi Romani* to his own *dignitas*.[17] *Dignitas* and *maiestas* are often related (e.g. Cic. *De or.* 2.39.164; *Part. or.* 30.105; *Balb.* 5.13; *Phil.* 3.4.13; *Dig.* 49.15.7.1) (Drexler 1956: 196), but that *dignitas* was in relationship to the *maiestas populi Romani* and the individual's fulfilment of public office, not to *dominatio* (Cic. *Att.* 7.11.1). We can recall how Lentulus connects the indignity of Rhodian actions toward him with his official capacity as an agent of the *maiestas populi Romani*. What one sees with Caesar in the face of charges that he had violated the *lex maiestatis* by leaving his province (as well as his massacre of two German tribes and his arrest of German envoys) is a subtle assimilation of *maiestas* to his own personal *dignitas*. For example, Caesar justifies the revenge for the *insignis calamitas* against the Tigurini on the basis of the public injury suffered by the Roman people, but adds that the revenge was also taken to compensate for 'private injuries' (Caes. *BGall.* 1.12; also *BCiv.* 1.7). The widening gap between Caesar's personal *dignitas* and the *maiestas* of the people can be seen in *BCiv.* 1.8 in calling for Caesar to postpone his *dignitas* on behalf of the state. It is not that Caesar failed to recognise the claims of the people's *maiestas* (e.g. *BGall.* 1.8, 7.17; *BCiv.* 1.7); rather, what was traditionally associated with the

---

[16] Mommsen (1899: 550–1) argues that attempts to establish kingship fell under the crime of *perduellio*.
[17] Bauman (1967: 121–2) argues for the connection as propaganda but not evidence of change in the technical definition of *maiestas*; Drexler (1956: 209–10) argues for a shift in the meaning of *maiestas*.

maiestas populi Romani becomes the justification for personal power rather than the basis for the official exercise of power (e.g. *BGall.* 8.6; 8.24; *BCiv.* 1.7).

There are other indications of Caesar's personal appropriation of the sacred aspects of *maiestas* as well. Caesar wore the clothes of the *triumphator* permanently (Cass. Dio 44.4; Beard 2009: 275–6), seemed to claim Jupiter's 'divine status for himself' in his triumph in 46 by having four white horses pull his chariot,[18] denied two tribunes their powers for their criticism of him (Cic. *Phil.* 13.31; Livy *Per.* 116; App. *B Civ.* 2.16.108, 2.17.122, 2.19.138; Vell. Pat. 2.68.4–5; Val. Max. 5.7.2; Suet. *Jul.* 79.1, 80.3; Cass. Dio 44.9.2–10.4, 46.49.2; Plut. *Caes.* 61.4–6; Plut. *Ant.* 12.4), and set in motion the possibility of deification by establishing a cult with a dedicated *flamen* (Steel 2013: 208). J. Rufus Fears (1981: 55) notes that coinage in 44 BC bears the image of Venus on one side and the head of Caesar instead of Jupiter on the other, usurping 'that place which, on the *denarii* and the *victoriati* of the great age of the *res publica*, had been held by the personification of the Roman People, Roma, and by the divine patron of the commonwealth, Jupiter'.

The importance of the foundational language of *maiestas* is borne out by the attention paid by the early principate to continuities between it and the *maiestas populi Romani*. Augustus was careful to retain its legal aspects, claiming to possess *maiestas* by way of magisterial office as an agent of the people (*Dig.* 48.4.1.1; Dio Cass. 53.17.3–10; Ando 2011: 101). He could retain the sacred associations of *maiestas* by way of the sacrosanctity associated with the tribunician power (*RG* 4.4). And he could draw on the legal fiction of the transferability of the *maiestas populi Romani* as ratifying his supremacy (e.g. *RG* 1.4, 8.1, 13, 21.3, 26.1, 27.1, 30.1, 32.3, 34.1, 35.1). That is the importance of Augustus' gesture, as disingenous as it may have been, of returning all the laws, provinces, and the army to the people and rejecting his own *hegemonia* in order to have his 'supremacy ratified by the senate and by the people' in 28–27 BC (Dio Cass. 53.12.1; also 53.7.3–4, 53.17.11–18.1, trans. Cary & Foster 1917). Subsequent *principes*, though appointed for life, would similarly hold a celebration every 10 years as if to renew this transfer as Augustus had done (Dio Cass. 53.16.2). Early on, Augustus cloaks his personal *maiestas* with the ancient trappings of the *ludi saeculares* in 17 BC, reciting an archaic prayer on behalf of the *maiestas* of the Roman people (*CIL* 32323.93: *vos quaeso precorque uti imperium maiestatemque p. R.*), but also including himself and his family (*CIL* 32323.98–9: *harum rerum ergo macte hac agna femina | inmolanda estote fitote v[olente]s propitiae p. R. Quiritibus, XVvirum collegio, mihi, domo, familiae*).

But beneath these gestures is a more fundamental transformation in the authorising framework (see Hammer 2021). The inviolability of a fictive entity, the *populus Romanus*, is now relocated in the inviolability of a real individual. Moreover, the *princeps* does not possess inviolability because he is acting as an

---

[18] Cass. Dio 43.14.3; Beard (2009: 233). Compare to the outrage over Camillus' triumph in 396: Livy 5.23.5–6; Plut. *Cam.* 7.1; Cass. Dio 52.13.3. Whether the story is a new creation or not, it suggests that Caesar's actions departed from the republican authorising framework.

agent of that entity, as would have been the case in the Republic, but because he is endowed with a divine quality of supremacy inherited from Jupiter in perpetuity (*sacrosanctu[s in perp]etu<u>m*) (*RG* 10.1; also Cass. Dio 53.17.9; *Dig.* 48.4.1.1) that is to be recognised unconditionally by the people (Tac. *Ann.* 1.73; Suet. *Aug.* 25.2, 37; Val. Max. 2.10.praef.) and by other states (Aug. *RG* 25; Tac. *Ann.* 2.42; Dio Cass. 57.17.3–5).[19] If republican authority bears similarity to the joint ownership of property that arises with the death of the *paterfamilias*, then with Augustus that father returns, an image that Augustus exploits fully by envisioning the state as an extension of his family (*RG* 9.2, 15, 17, 18, 35.1; Ov. *Tr.* 4.4.13–15; Suet. *Aug.* 58.1–2; Dio Cass. 53.17.3). It is as though Augustus and subsequent *principes* reverse the legendary transfer of *maiestas* from the gods to the kings and then to the people, investing themselves with a much earlier version of *maiestas*. In this transformation we can appreciate in retrospect how *maiestas* framed and sustained the authority of the *populus Romanus* in the Republic.

References

Ando, C. (2011), *Law, Language, and Empire in the Roman Tradition* (Philadelphia, University of Pennsylvania Press).
Arena, V. (2012), *Libertas and the Practice of Politics in the Late Roman Republic* (Cambridge, Cambridge University Press).
Arena, V. (2015), 'Informal Norms, Values, and Social Control in the Roman Participatory Context', in D. Hammer (ed.), *A Companion to Greek Democracy and the Roman Republic* (Malden MA & Oxford, Wiley-Blackwell), 217–38.
Arendt, H. (1998), *The Human Condition* (Chicago, University of Chicago Press).
Asmis, E. (2004), 'The State as a Partnership: Cicero's Definition of *Res Publica* in His Work *On the State*', *History of Political Thought*, 25: 569–98.
Austin, J. (1995), *The Province of Jurisprudence Determined* (Cambridge, Cambridge University Press).
Badian, E. (1969), 'Quaestiones Variae', *Historia*, 18.4: 447–91.
Bauman, R.A. (1967), *The Crimen Maiestatis in the Roman Republic and Augustan Principate* (Johannesburg, Witwatersrand University Press).
Bauman, R.A. (1989), *Lawyers and Politics in the Early Roman Empire: A Study of Relations between the Roman Jurists and the Emperors from Augustus to Hadrian* (Munich, C.H. Beck).
Beard, M. (2009), *The Roman Triumph* (Cambridge MA, Belknap).
Bentham, J. (1970 [1789]), *Of Laws in General* (London, Athlone Press).
Bodin, J. (1992 [1576]), *On Sovereignty: Four Chapters from the Six Books of the Commonwealth* (Cambridge, Cambridge University Press).
Bonfante, P. (2006 [1919]), *Istituzione de diritto Romano* (Milan, Francesco Vallardi).
Buckland, W.W. (1921), *A Text-Book of Roman Law from Augustus to Justinian* (Cambridge, Cambridge University Press).

---

[19] I follow the text of Cooley (2009). See Dumézil (1952: 18) on the association with Jupiter.

Burton, P.J. (2011), *Friendship and Empire: Roman Diplomacy and Imperialism in the Middle Republic (353–146 BC)* (Cambridge, Cambridge University Press).
Cary, E. & Foster, B. (trans.) (1917), Dio Cassius's *Roman History, volume VI: Books 51–55* (Cambridge MA, Harvard University Press).
Chilton, C.W. (1955), 'The Roman Law of Treason under the Early Principate', *The Journal of Roman Studies*, 45: 73–81.
Cloud, J.D. (1971), 'I. *Parricidium*: From the *Lex Numae* to the *Lex Pómpela de Parricidiis*', *Zeitschrift der Savigny-Stiftung für Rechtsgeschichte: Romanistische Abteilung*, 88: 1–66.
Cooley, A. (ed. and trans.) (2009), *Res Gestae Divi Augusti: Text, Translation, and Commentary* (Cambridge, Cambridge University Press).
Crawford, M.H. (1996), *Roman Statutes* (London, Institute of Classical Studies, School of Advanced Study, University of London).
Davies, J. (1994), 'On the Non-Usability of the Concept of Sovereignty in an Ancient Greek Context', in L.A. Foresti, A. Barzanò, C. Bearzot, L. Prandi & G. Zecchini (eds), *Federazioni a federalismo nell'Europa antica* (Milan, Università cattolica del Sacro Cuore), 51–65.
de Zulueta, F. (1934), 'The New Fragments of Gaius (PSI 1182)', *The Journal of Roman Studies*, 24: 168–86.
de Zulueta, F. (1935), 'The New Fragments of Gaius. Part II: *Societas ercto non cito*', *The Journal of Roman Studies*, 25: 19–32.
Drexler, H. (1956), 'Maiestas', *Aevum*, 30: 195–212.
Drogula, F.K. (2015), *Commanders and Command in the Roman Republic and Early Empire* (Chapel Hill, The University of North Carolina Press).
Dumézil, G. (1952), 'Maiestas et gravitas: de quelques différences entre les Romains et les Austronésiens', *Revue de philologie, de littérature et d'histoire anciennes*, 26: 7–28.
Eleftheriadis, P. (2010), 'Law and Sovereignty', *Law and Philosophy*, 29: 535–69.
Fairweather, J. (1981), *Seneca the Elder* (Cambridge, Cambridge University Press).
Fantham, E. (2006), 'Ovid, Germanicus, and the Composition of the *Fasti*', in P.E. Knox (ed.), *Oxford Readings in Ovid* (Oxford, Oxford University Press), 373–414.
Fears, J.R. (1981), 'The Cult of Jupiter and Roman Imperial Ideology', in W. Haase (ed.), *Aufstieg und Niedergang der römischen Welt* (Berlin, Gruyter), 7–141.
Ferrary, J.-L. (1983), 'Les origines de la loi de majesté à Rome', *Comptes rendus des séances de l'Académie des Inscriptions et Belles-Lettres*, 127.4: 556–72.
Grose Hodge, H. (trans.) (1927), Cicero's *Pro Lege Manilia. Pro Caecina. Pro Cluentio. Pro Rabirio Perduellionis Reo* (Cambridge MA, Harvard University Press).
Gundel, H.G. (1963), 'Der Begriff Maiestas im politischen Denken der römischen Republik', *Historia*, 12: 283–320.
Habermas, J. (1996), *Between Facts and Norms: Contributions to a Discourse Theory of Law and Democracy* (Cambridge MA, MIT Press).
Habermas, J. & Rehg, W. (2001), 'Constitutional Democracy: A Paradoxical Union of Contradictory Principles?', *Political Theory*, 29: 766–81.
Hammer, D. (2014), *Roman Political Thought: From Cicero to Augustine* (Cambridge, Cambridge University Press).
Hammer, D. (2021), 'Reading Sovereignty in Augustus' *Res gestae*', in S. Achilleos & A. Balasopoulos (eds), *Reading Texts on Sovereignty: Textual Moments in the History of Political Thought* (London, Bloomsbury Academic), 33–40.
Harries, J. (2007), *Law and Crime in the Roman World* (Cambridge, Cambridge University Press).

Hart, H.L.A. (2012), *The Concept of Law* (Oxford, Oxford University Press).
Hinsley, F.H. (1986), *Sovereignty* (Cambridge, Cambridge University Press).
Hölkeskamp, K.-J. (2010), *Reconstructing the Roman Republic: An Ancient Political Culture and Modern Research* (Princeton, Princeton University Press).
Kant, I. (1996 [1797]), *The Metaphysics of Morals* (Cambridge, Cambridge University Press).
Kelsen, H. (1992), *Introduction to the Problems of Legal Theory* (Oxford, Clarendon Press).
Kraus, C.S. (1996), *Livy: Ab Urbe Condita* (Cambridge, Cambridge University Press).
Lewis, N. & Reinhold, M. (1990), *Roman Civilization: Selected Readings* (New York, Columbia University Press).
Lintott, A.W. (1999), *The Constitution of the Roman Republic* (Oxford, Clarendon Press).
Loughlin, M. (2003), 'Ten Tenets of Sovereignty', in N. Walker (ed.), *Sovereignty in Transition: Essays in European Law* (Portland, Hart), 55–86.
Mackie, N. (1992), 'Ovid and the Birth of *Maiestas*', in A. Powell (ed.), *Roman Poetry and Propaganda in the Age of Augustus* (London, Bristol Classical Press), 83–97.
Magie, D. (1950), *Roman Rule in Asia Minor, to the End of the Third Century after Christ*, 2 vols (Princeton, Princeton University Press).
Mommsen, T. (1899), *Römisches Strafrecht* (Leipzig, Duncker & Humblot).
Perrin, B. (trans.) (1921), Plutarch's *Lives, volume X: Agis and Cleomenes. Tiberius and Gaius Gracchus. Philopoemen and Flamininus* (Cambridge MA, Harvard University Press).
Pettit, P. (1996), 'Freedom as Antipower', *Ethics*, 106: 576–604.
Pettit, P. (1997), *Republicanism: A Theory of Freedom and Government* (Oxford, Clarendon Press).
Pollack, E. (1908), *Der Majestätsgedanke im römischen Recht: Eine Studie auf dem Gebiet des römischen Staatsrechts* (Leipzig, Veit & Comp.).
Rackham, H. (trans.) (1942), Cicero's *On the Orator: Book 3. On Fate. Stoic Paradoxes. Divisions of Oratory* (Cambridge MA: Harvard University Press).
Raz, J. (1979), *The Authority of Law: Essays on Law and Morality* (Oxford, Clarendon Press).
Reinhold, M. (1981), 'The Declaration of War against Cleopatra', *Classical Journal*, 77: 97–103.
Rich, J. (2011), 'The *Fetiales* and Roman International Relations', in J.H. Richardson & F. Santangelo (eds), *Priests and State in the Roman World* (Stuttgart, Franz Steiner Verlag), 187–242.
Schmitt, C. (2005), *Political Theology: Four Chapters on the Concept of Sovereignty* (Chicago, University of Chicago Press).
Schmitt, C. (2008), *Constitutional Theory* (Durham NC, Duke University Press).
Schofield, M. (1995), 'Cicero's Definition of *Res Publica*', in J.G.F. Powell (ed.), *Cicero the Philosopher* (Oxford, Clarendon Press), 63–83.
Seager, R. (2001), '*Maiestas* in the Late Republic: Some Observations', in A. Watson, J.W. Cairns, & O.F. Robinson (eds), *Critical Studies in Ancient Law, Comparative Law and Legal History: Essays in Honour of Alan Watson* (Oxford, Hart), 143–53.
Skinner, Q. (1989), 'The State', in T. Ball, J. Farr, & R. Hanson (eds), *Political Innovation and Conceptual Change* (Cambridge, Cambridge University Press), 90–131.
Skinner, Q. (2002a), 'A Third Concept of Liberty', *Proceedings of the British Academy*, 117: 237–68.
Skinner, Q. (2002b), *Visions of Politics*, vol. ii: *Renaissance Virtues* (Cambridge, Cambridge University Press).

Skinner, Q. (2009), 'A Genealogy of the Modern State', *Proceedings of the British Academy*, 162: 325–70.
Steel, C.E.W. (2013), *The End of the Roman Republic, 146 to 44 BC: Conquest and Crisis* (Edinburgh, Edinburgh University Press).
Straumann, B. (2016), *Crisis and Constitutionalism: Roman Political Thought from the Fall of the Republic to the Age of Revolution* (New York, Oxford University Press).
Täubler, E. (1913), *Imperium Romanum: Studien zur Entwicklungsgeschichte des römischen Reichs* (Leipzig, Teubner).
Thomas, Y. (1991), 'L'institution de la Majesté', *Revue de synthèse*, 112: 331–86.
Watson, A. (1961), *Contract of Mandate in Roman Law* (Oxford, Clarendon Press).
Watson, A. (1979), 'The Death of Horatia', *The Classical Quarterly*, 29: 436–47.
Watson, A. (1993), *International Law in Archaic Rome: War and Religion* (Baltimore, Johns Hopkins University Press).
Winterbottom, M. (trans.) (1974), Seneca the Elder's *Declamations, vol. 2: Controversiae, Books 7–10. Suasoriae. Fragments* (Cambridge MA, Harvard University Press).

4

The Invention of Imperial Sovereignty

RICHARD ALSTON

Introduction

THIS CHAPTER DISCUSSES the nature of sovereignty through a reconsideration of one of the oldest issues in Roman history: the transition from Republic to Empire. The crux of that question stems from the foundational claim of the Augustan regime to have restored the *res publica*, as expressed in his inscribed autobiography (*Res Gestae*) and contemporary calendars and coinage, which contrast with later ancient descriptions and a long historiographical tradition that has seen Augustus as the first Roman emperor.[1] Modern historiography has interpreted this paradox through the question of sovereignty. Mommsen (1887–8: vol. 3, part 1, 127–42; 300–68; vol. 3, part 2, 1030) argued that sovereignty remained with the *populus*, who delegated their power to the emperor.[2] If citizens remained ultimately sovereign and the institutions of the *res publica* continued to function, the Augustan regime could be cast as a continuation of the Republic.[3] This argument turns on the nature of sovereignty and, in particular, whether Augustan sovereignty was embedded in law. The evident transformation of political practice in the absence of a clear

---

[1] For republican restoration, see *Res Gestae* 34, *Fasti Praenestine* (13 January), perhaps with Ovid, *Fasti* 1.589–90, Velleius Paterculus 2.89, and an *aureus* of 28 BC (British Museum CM 1995.4–1,1; Blackburn Museum RNUM-063004) and a *cistophorus* of the same year: see publications in Sutherland (1970: 12–14); Rich & Williams (1999); Abdy & Harling (2005); Mantovani (2008). Dio 53.2–20; Tacitus *Annales* 1.1–5 and 3.28; Suetonius, *Augustus* 28; and Strabo, *Geography* 17.3.25 assert Augustus' monarchic status.

[2] See the discussions of Nippel (2015) and Winterling (2005). On Mommsen's intellectual legacy, see Jehne (2005). For more recent attempts to defend Mommsen's approach, see Sommer (2011) on legal aspects, and Peachin (2005) and Linderski (1990) on extra-legal aspects of the imperial position.

[3] Heuss (1974); Ferrary (2015). See Hammer, this volume, for the argument that the principate represents a distinctive shift. The argument for Republican continuity continues to be made; see Ando (2010), Veyne (2002) and Kaldellis (2015), though it requires an understanding of Republican *Staatsrecht* that incorporates traditions and practices (Jehne 2005; Arena 2015).

legal change has encouraged historians to distinguish between the everyday monarchic operation of politics and Republican constitutional practices. Sovereignty is located in the latter category as a theoretical concept of no everyday significance for Roman politics.[4] The most obvious modern parallel is that of British politics and its constitution.[5]

We find a very different approach in the major theorists of sovereignty, from Bodin onwards, who all drew heavily on Roman political history. The transitions between kingdom and Republic and Republic and Empire, and writers such as Cicero, Livy, Polybius, and Tacitus, provided the paradigms through which their political theory was developed. Nevertheless, as I shall argue in the next section, their notions of sovereignty laid claim to universal applicability. Sovereignty is understood as an ontological requirement for the formation of the political community. It is seen as 'theological', in that it exists externally to the frameworks of law and constitution, which in themselves depend on the foundational actions of the sovereign. Sovereignty has an inherent mythic quality that parallels the mythic origins of the polity (crown, people, nation). It might be transferred between different personae (citizens, nobles, monarch), and that transfer provides sovereignty with a history, but it is in itself a fixed element. This philosophical tradition identifies the holders of sovereignty through powers to extend or suspend law; to rule on exceptions to the law; to declare the state of emergency (or exception or siege); to define who is protected by the law (the citizen) and who is excluded from such protections (the non-citizen or enemy). The limitations on the sovereign are meagre since the sovereign retains the power to act beyond law.

My argument seeks to demythologise sovereignty by seeing it as an expression of the concentration of a nexus of social powers. I argue that 'sovereign' designates the holder of multiple sources of power rather than sovereignty being a power in itself. Paradoxically, this makes the sovereign a more useful analytical concept, since it comes to designate the social persona, such as an individual, institution, or mythic entity (people/nation), on whom there is a concentration of social and political power sufficient that the state and citizen depends critically on that persona.[6] 'Sovereignty' becomes a descriptive portmanteau term for the powers concentrated on the sovereign. It is not a representation of a 'last instance' power called into action in moments of extremity, but is quotidian in its relationship to

---

[4] Syme (1939: 3–7) rejected constitutionalism. Galinsky (1996: 6, 8–41, 56, 64, 77–9) sees the relational concept of *auctoritas* as empowering the regime sufficiently to render irrelevant constitutional concerns. Wallace-Hadrill (1997; 2005) sees the Augustan transformation as primarily affecting cultural norms. See also Wallace-Hadrill (2018: 37), Millar (1973) and Lacey (1974).

[5] See Merivale (1850–64: iii.552–3) for a 19th-century comparison and the recent discussion in Straumann (2011). One wonders whether recent political events in the UK would change these perceptions.

[6] Making sovereignty a descriptor of a concentration of powers that clearly existed in ancient societies rather than a power in itself answers the objections of Atkins (2018: 19), Hammer (this volume), Hoekstra (2016), and Lundgreen (this volume) to the use of 'sovereignty' in discussions of ancient politics since there is no term in Latin and Greek that is easily translated as sovereignty.

socio-political processes and shifting in its contours in conjunction with social and political structures.

In the third section, I discuss the paradigmatic instance of Augustan sovereignty. My historicist approach locates the imperial sovereign as emerging through the political processes of the triumvirate and Augustan age.[7] Augustus came to control the means of repression, the power to destroy citizens, the power to provide the means of life, and the cultural power to determine truth: Augustus decided the political order of things.[8] My argument is Tacitean in stressing the gradualness of the concentration of power in Augustus and the education of citizens in their subordination to the sovereign:

> When he had seduced the soldiers with gifts, the people with grain, and the rest with the sweetness of rest, little by little he rose up and drew into himself the functions of the senate, magistrates and law. ... Therefore, the situation of the city had been overturned. Nothing survived of the original and untarnished customs. All, deprived of equality, looked to the orders of the *princeps* with no worry for the present, while Augustus was strong and not old and sustained the (imperial) house in peace.
>
> [*ubi militem donis, populum annona, cunctos dulcedine otii pellexit, insurgere paulatim, munia senatus magistratuum legum in se trahere ... Igitur verso civitatis statu nihil usquam prisci et integri moris: omnes exuta aequalitate iussa principis aspectare, nulla in praesens formidine, dum Augustus aetate validus seque et domum in pacem sustentavit.*] (Tacitus, *Annales* 1.2–4)

Tacitus locates sovereign power within political and relational systems that operated to concentrate power on the imperial person. While contemporaries were sure of that power, they struggled to define and represent it. The roots of this power were diverse and not limited to a legal or magisterial system. The magisterial powers garnered by Augustus were a means of designating the sovereign. Augustan sovereignty was performed, normalised, and recognised. Such recognition does not presuppose legitimacy.[9] Ritualistic performance of subordination to the sovereign recognised an understanding of the sovereign's power and displayed individuals' and groups' loyalty to the sovereign.[10] The sovereign's concentration of multiple forms of social power made it dependent on a perceptible extension of power through multiple fields of what we might call civil society, and encouraged the sovereign to engage in social and cultural regulation so that its power became cultural, quotidian, and pervasive (Lowrie 2009: 279–98).

---

[7] The Augustan sovereign was new; though see the discussion of Caesar's power in Tuori (2016: 28–47); Hammer, this volume.

[8] I use the term in the sense that it was employed by Foucault (2002) to designate epistemological order.

[9] Contra Flaig (1992; 2011; 2015a; 2015b), Veyne (2002), and Rich (2015). Neither Cassius Dio in books 52 and 53 nor Tacitus, *Annales* 1.1–4, repeated in 3.28 and 4.32–3, hint at Augustan sovereignty depending on popular recognition. See n. 2 above.

[10] Such performances need not be sincere. See Bartsch (1994), Rudich (1993) and Wilkinson (2012). Fascist regimes have no difficulty generating consensus rituals. For an explicit modern comparison between imperial Rome and totalitarian regimes, see Rosenblitt (2012).

This historicist approach undermines legalistic and theological views of sovereignty. The final section critiques sovereignty. The emergence of a monopolistic *locus potestatis* (the people, the king) was an outcome of specific historical processes. Although it is appropriate to recognise that *locus* as sovereign, sovereignty itself operates mythically in presenting itself as *sine qua non* for political society and hence naturalising a concentration of power in that single *locus*. In any complex society, power is dispersed through a variety of social agents. The sovereign requires those social agents to recognise its power, and those agents have the theoretical capacity to withdraw that recognition. The sovereign is strengthened by the implication of those agents. Sovereign power erodes or incorporates powers external to it so as to establish an identification of society and sovereign. The sovereign disempowers the diverse multitude of citizens by enforcing their unity (*the* people; *the* nation).[11] *Dissensus* is repressed by raising the social costs of difference.[12] Yet, polities can function without a sovereign. Indeed, a singular sovereign entity is, as we can see in the Roman experience, incompatible with freedom.

Against theological sovereignty

In the epigraph to *Political Theology*, Carl Schmitt (1985 [1922]: 1) writes that 'Soverän ist, wer über den Ausnahmezustand entscheidet' ('sovereign is he who decides on the exception'). But sovereignty did not only apply in the exceptional moment. As Schmitt puts it, sovereignty is 'a general concept in the theory of the state, and not merely to a construct applied to any emergency decree of state of siege'.[13] The sovereign decision is always in play in guaranteeing, recognising, and enabling the law and in determining who is the citizen and who is the enemy and whether the laws are to be applied in the individual instance (Schmitt 1985 [1922]: 1–36). The judgement on the state of exception is, therefore, an everyday judgement.

Schmitt drew on Jean Bodin's *Les six livres de la République* (1576). Bodin invested his concept of sovereignty with a mythic quality: the presence of the sovereign distinguished a state from a community. Thus, the sovereign had either to pre-date or to be contemporaneous with the creation of the state. Consequently, the sovereign existed outside of and unconstrained by any legal framework (Bodin 1576: 1, 125, 147), which only came into being by and depended for its existence on the act of the sovereign (Schmitt 1985 [1922]: 13). The sovereign's ability to suspend the legal system placed the sovereign outside that system. Bodin and

---

[11] See Hardt & Negri (2004) for the destabilising effects of diversity.
[12] Rancière (2010; 2015). See also Rosa, this volume, for reference to Rancière's work.
[13] Schmitt (1985 [1922]: 1). 'State of siege' was employed as a technical term to refer to a moment in which the state faced an existential threat. See Lundgreen, this volume, for further reflections on Schmitt's famous formulation.

Schmitt's sovereign power was absolute and analogous to divine power in its 'miraculous' capacity to exceed the bounds of law and call law into being.[14] In Schmitt's (1985 [1922]: 47–9, 65) view, sovereignty is a pure political idea since it transcends any situation and particular socio-economic-cultural structures and is not shaped by those structures. Sovereignty is therefore an absolute concept (not having a history) and the sovereign a mythic figure who transcends historical circumstance. The conception is fascistic and quasi-religious (Preuss 1999).

Schmitt's emphasis on the sovereign decision allowed a sleight of hand. He attributed sovereignty to the mythic persona of the (German) people. But since the people are incapable of taking the decision, they need a guardian leader who becomes an epitome of the people. This Caesarist dictator became in effect sovereign through this quasi-religious identification and, in a borrowing from later Roman Republican history, took upon himself the capacity for the (re-)making of the state.[15]

Giorgio Agamben deploys this fascistic philosophy to critique the modern state. In his understanding, the sovereign is the person who can declare the state of exception and who can reduce the citizen to bare life. In both instances, law is suspended, across society in the state of exception and for the individual in the case of bare life. Thus, the sovereign exists beyond law (Agamben 2005: 2–35). Agamben (2005: 47–70) follows Bodin and Schmitt in seeing sovereignty as transcending historical circumstances. Consequently, the foundational quality of sovereignty which he detects in Roman practice can be seen in all (western) states irrespective of societal forms and constitutional arrangements.[16] Agamben (2005: 117–88) thus connects regimes as diverse as the Roman, the liberal, and the fascist in manifesting this foundational sovereignty. For opposed ideological reasons, Agamben and Schmitt consider sovereignty as separate from social context.

Agamben's treatment is a rejection of Foucault's dismissal of sovereignty: 'One of the most persistent features of Foucault's work is its decisive abandonment of the traditional approach to the problem of power, which is based on juridico-institutional models … in favour of an unprejudiced analysis of the concrete ways in which power penetrates subjects' very bodies and forms of life' (Agamben 1998: 5). While Foucault focused on the multiple interconnected systems of power that produce the citizen, which he named the biopolitical, Agamben (1998: 6) argues that the 'production of the biopolitical body is the original activity of the sovereign power' and claims that there is no citizen without the sovereign. Foucault (e.g. 1979a; 1979b: 88–9; 1994) had argued polemically for a decentring of the sovereign in political philosophy. But later, he connected the discourses and structures of

---

[14] Schmitt (1985 [1922]: 36). See discussion in Kalyvas (2000b); Lundgreen, this volume, for a fuller genealogical account.

[15] Schmitt (1921). See discussion in Kalyvas (2000a) and n. 19 for Roman parallels.

[16] Agamben draws many of his conceptions from Roman history. His 1998 *Homo Sacer* starts from a Roman religious-political status, while his 2005 *State of Exception* draws on the Roman concepts of *tumultus* and *iustitium*.

everyday power to the state through notions of the biopolitical and governmentality. Such mechanisms encompass sovereign authority within the multiple networks of power operative within societies. The state implicated those networks in its order through the guaranteeing of the function of those networks.[17]

Establishing a dialectic between the biopolitical and the sovereign inserts sovereignty within a historically specific set of relationships. If the power of the sovereign is made real in the act of exclusion from the rights and benefits of citizenship, sovereign power must depend on those rights and benefits and the degree to which those rights and benefits are controlled or perceived to be controlled by the sovereign. Agamben might stress the exclusionary operation of sovereign power, but as Bhatt (2017a) argues, the provision of the means for life also depends on the state in most complex societies. Sovereign power is made real not just in its capacity to declare the state of exception, but also in the perceived dependence of the normal and everyday on the sovereign.

Two central premises follow from relating sovereignty to the biopolitical. The first is to undermine any claim of sovereignty to be theological. It exists in dialectic with society, intermeshed with other forms of power. The second premise is that sovereign power is relational. It depends on a process of acceptance in which the citizens recognise the prerogatives of the sovereign and the sovereign recognises the citizen. Such a recognition is not neutral, but is rather determined by a political negotiation in which the *realia* of economic, cultural, institutional, and military power play their part. Further, recognition is in itself a social act which requires performance. Sovereign power cannot be notional, archaic, or latent, but is embedded in and fundamental to the everyday.

If we take the argument one step further, the dialectic with the biopolitical undermines the claim of sovereignty to be a power in and of itself. Rather, it can be seen as a portmanteau for other forms of power. The advantage of deconstructing sovereignty is to demythologise it as an aspect of political life so as to focus on the material aspects of power which underpin the position of any claimant to sovereignty. If we view the *res publica* as an agglomeration of social goods,[18] there is no a priori reason to attribute those social goods to a mythological origin or that those social goods should be managed at a single *locus potestatis*. If we see the sovereign as a singular *locus* of concentrated power, sovereignty ceases to be of philosophical interest. But the sovereign, as a persona who lays claim to or exercises a near monopoly of political power, becomes a more acute historical problem, since such a hegemonic position is not a *sine qua non* of state formation but a specific

---

[17] Foucault (2010; 2003: 29). See the discussion in Neal (2004). Agamben's (1995; 2003) critiques of Foucault came before the publication of most of Foucault's lectures in which he modified his position on sovereign power. See Alston (2017), with further references; Legg, this volume.

[18] On the *res publica* as property, see Cicero, *De officiis* 1.10.21, 1.39, 2.73; Cicero, *De rep.* 1.26.41. Caesar's contrary remark, Suetonius, *Julius Caesar* 77, seems to have been intentionally controversial. Recent accounts have followed Cicero in emphasising materiality: see Moatti (2018); Atkins (2018: 57); Hodgson (2016); Hammer (2017).

arrangement of power. Given the prevalence of sovereigns across a broad historical field, it seems that the attraction of powers to an already powerful persona is a normal dynamic: the powerful within a system act to extend and intensify their range of powers.

A sovereign is thus an outcome of historical processes within a state rather than a location of power necessary for the foundation and function of the state. Contrary to Schmitt, the sovereign does not inhabit a pure political sphere separated from the quotidian of social and economic powers, but a *locus* embedded in quotidian powers. The power of the sovereign is not defined by an absolute quality of sovereignty, but by the control of the biopolitical regime exercised by the sovereign, the extent to which that regime is necessary for the life of the citizen, and the repressive powers wielded by the sovereign. If sovereigns can be categorised following various broad characteristics, the processes of sovereign-formation are specific to particular sociological and historical circumstances. There is, however, no defining power that a sovereign institution must have, and it follows that those identified as sovereign may have different relations to the various biopolitical regimes. The sovereign is thus a fundamentally historical or sociological problem rather than a legal or philosophical issue.

In the next section, I consider the paradigmatic instance of the Augustan sovereign. I argue that Augustus was sovereign by any definition. That sovereign power was not the creation of a legal act or of a historical moment but followed from a progressive accumulation of powers both legal and extra-legal, which enabled Augustus to wield power so as to suspend legal protections summarily, to end the life of a citizen, and to provide the means of life for the citizens. Augustan sovereignty was thus embedded within the biopolitical regime.

The invention of the Augustan sovereign

The origins of Octavian as sovereign lie in his empowerment as *triumvir rei publicae constituendae* by the *lex Titia*. The office granted to Antony, Lepidus, and Octavian was limited by time and by its collegiality. It was likely analogous to those given to recent Roman dictators Sulla and Caesar.[19] The powers granted were probably ill-defined but entailed an ability to suspend law and civil protections

---

[19] See Straumann (2016: 57–88) on the paralells between the early and late Republican dictatorial offices. Traditionally, a stark difference is proposed between the early dictatorships and the Sullan and Caesarian. This difference is based on the limitation of the older office to a specific task and by time: see Cornell (2015) with a survey of the scholarship. Nevertheless, the Sullan office had a specific enabling purpose: his title appears on a fragmentary inscription *Corpus Inscriptionum Latinarum* VI 40951 = VI 31609 as *[L Cornelius L. f. Sulla] Felix d[ictator r(ei) p(ublicae)] co[nstituendae]*. Caesar's title likely followed that of Sulla, see *Corpus Inscriptionum Latinarum* I 2969 = *L'Année épigraphique* (1969/1970) 132, with discussion in Broughton (1986: 107–8). Caesar's controversial step was removing any time limitation on the office.

(allowing summary executions), military commands over extended *provincia*, and extensive powers in Rome and Italy. The first period of the triumvirate lapsed in January 37 and was renewed for a further five years (Appian, *Bellum Civile* 5.95; Dio 48.54). Octavian and Antony should have ceased to be *triumviri* at the end of December 33 BC.[20] If the triumvirate provided a framework for Octavian's power up until January 32 BC, his hegemony after that point was historically anomalous. I suggest that thereafter Octavian-Augustus' prominence allowed him to accumulate a variety of social and political powers that elevated him to the position of sovereign. No one of those powers or categories of power defined his position. Augustus exerted power within the law and beyond the law. Law, freedom, and the state were seen to depend on the person of the sovereign. Yet, a notion equivalent to sovereignty did not develop in Roman thought, and this absence accounts for the terminological vagueness in discussions of Augustus' position. In the summary account that follows, I begin with the foundational events of 28–27 BC, before focusing on a more thematic consideration of Augustan powers.

Vervaet (2010) and Rich (2012) argue that the triumvirate continued to the end of 28 BC (see also Bleicken 2015: 276–85). Yet the triumvirate *de iure* seems not to have applied after December 33, though Octavian appears to have behaved as if he held the same powers until January 28 BC. Dio (50.2) emphasises that Octavian was not in the senate on 1 January 32, the first moment at which the triumvirate should have lapsed. This may have encouraged the consuls in expressions of hostility to Octavian. But when Octavian appeared, he came with military support and sat with the consuls, as if a *triumvir*, suggesting that whatever the legal situation, there was no change in Octavian's material power between December 33 and January 32 BC.[21] The epigraphic evidence also points to the ending of his triumviral office: *ILS* 77 of 33 or 32 BC records Caesar as triumvir (Ermatinger 1993; Wardle 1995); *ILS* 79 (31 BC), 80 (29 BC), *AE* (1993) 1461 (29 BC), *ILS* 78 (28 BC), 81 (28 BC), and the victory inscription from Nikopolis (28 BC) (Murray & Petsas 1989) do not.[22] Suetonius (*Augustus* 27.1) and *Res Gestae* (7.1) record ten years of triumviral power. *Res Gestae* (34) also describes Octavian's power in 28 BC not as triumviral, but as resting on universal consent and extending over all things, which would seem a good description of a sovereign.

His actions of 28–27 become the more remarkable since they are represented as a laying aside of that complete control. Those years marked the end of the triumviral crisis (Lange 2009: 181). Dio's account (52.42–3; 53.1–2) of 28 BC attests a programme of restoration culminating in debates in the senate in January 27, which pretended a return of the *res publica* to the senate and people. All our sources (*Res Gestae* 34; Dio 52–3.21; Tacitus, *Annales* 3.28; Ovid, *Fasti* 1.589–90;

---

[20] See *Fasti Colotiani* for 43 BC for a concern over precise dating.
[21] See Bleicken (1990: 65–82) for a possible extension of Octavian's powers.
[22] Wardle (1995) suggests that the coinage is of limited help, though Antonian coinage may reference his triumviral powers after 33 BC.

the *Fasti Praenestini*; and Velleius Paterculus 2.89) are compatible with such an interpretation. Recent studies have downplayed the events of 28–27 BC, stressing the continuity in Octavian-Augustus' hegemony (Judge 1974; Lacey 1974; Rich & Williams 1999; Gruen 2005; Rich 2012; Bleicken 2015: 272–92). John Rich (2015) and Egon Flaig (2011) understand the senatorial debate of January 27 BC as a consensus ritual. Yet, contemporary reactions point to an importance that went beyond a performance of loyalty.[23] The association of Octavian with Romulus and the granting of the name Augustus suggest refoundation (Suetonius, *Augustus* 7.2, 28.2). The holding of a census and the repair of temples, and Octavian's declaration to have abided by the law in January 27, invoked the annual magistracies and subordination to the law that Livy (2.1) saw as central to the Republic.[24] The coinage references similar messages. A *cistophoros* of 28 BC proclaims the Imperator Caesar as *libertatis vindex* (defender of liberty) (Sutherland 1970: 12–14; Mattingly 1976: no. 691), the return of freedom being identified with Republicanism. The rule of law is celebrated in an *aureus* of the same year in which Octavian is seen personally restoring *leges et iura p. R.* ('laws and rights of the Roman people') (British Museum, CM: 1995,0401.1; Abdy & Harling 2005). This coin references a decree that Dio reports in 53.2.5 as coming into force in January 27 ending lawlessness and injustices (ἀνόμως καὶ ἀδίκως, a negative translation of *leges et iura*).

All this evidence points to a restoration of the political processes of the Republic after their suspension under the triumvirate and Octavian. Yet the freedom, the rights and the laws of the Roman people, and the return of the *res publica* are portrayed as concessions or personal benefactions of Octavian so that the Republic would seem to depend on his person. The voting of honours, notably the name, Augustus, a shield in the senate house proclaiming his virtues, and the decoration of his house with symbols of victory are responsive to those concessions and focused on his person.[25] Augustus' representation of his hegemony denies that he held any superior legal power after January 27 BC (*Res Gestae* 34), but that he guided the Roman state through his *auctoritas* (authority). His hegemony was located outside any legal framework in the exceptional moral qualities of his person (Galinsky 1996: 10–41, 80), reflecting an individualisation of power and relating that power to moral and social codes.[26]

---

[23] Turpin (1994) explains the reaction by postulating Octavian's rejection on 17 January of powers offered on 13 January, but this seems a convoluted explanation.

[24] Millar (1973) argues that the institutions of the *res publica* were maintained throughout the triumvirate, so that there was nothing to be restored in January 27. Yet, in Livy's account many of those institutions were present in the regal period, but 509 still saw a foundation of the free Republic.

[25] *Res Gestae* 34; Galinsky (1996: 80); *An. Ep.* 1952, 165. The shield is popular on Augustan coins; see, for examples, Mattingly (1976: nos 321, 336, 338–9, 354–5, 381–3, 405, 407–8); Sutherland (1984: nos 1, 35, 36a, 43a, 43b, 44, 52a, 79a, 79b, 89, 92, 95).

[26] As argued in slightly different ways by by Lowrie (2009: 279–98), Tuori (2016: 104–20), Crook (1996), and Peachin (2015).

Although Augustus devoted considerable attention to his assemblage of legal powers (*Res Gestae* 1–7, 34), there was no power, office or act that established his sovereignty.[27] Tacitus (*Annales* 3.56) identified *tribunicia potestas* (the power of the tribune) as the *vocabulum* (designation) of the highest office. Similarly, Dio (54.12 and 54.28) associated the highest power with *tribunicia potestas* and the funeral oration for Agrippa (*SB* 16 13033) stresses *tribunicia potestas* alongside provincial *imperium* (magisterial power) (compare Dio 55.9, 55.13, 56.28). Dio (54.10) identifies a grant of permanent consular power in 19 BC, but that is also presented primarily as an honour and is problematically absent from the *Res Gestae*.[28] Augustus wielded proconsular *imperium* within his provinces (Alföldy 2000; Richardson 2002). After 23 BC, he held *imperium maius* (superior magisterial power) (Dio 51.31.5). In Rome itself, where arguably the *res publica* was situated, Augustus had an ability to command troops, though the legal basis for that power is obscure, perhaps resting in a special extension of his provincial *imperium*.[29] Tacitus' use of *princeps* and *principatus* for 'emperor' and 'reign' seem designations rather than definitional.[30] Nothing that is awarded constitutes sovereign power, but the titles and offices designate that power.

In the Tacitus quotation above, Augustan power is related to the social goods he provided. Material benefits are listed in the *Res Gestae*. Chapter 15 focused on donations to the plebs, while 16–18 listed rewards for the soldiers and veterans and payments to the treasury. *Res Gestae* 17 gives the impression that the finances of Rome depended on Augustus' personal generosity. In *Res Gestae* 15 the distributions are described as being from the spoils of war, from his inheritance, or private. The donations show a personal care exercised by Augustus. The rewards from war point also to the benefits brought by Augustan supervision of the Empire. In addition to financial rewards, Augustus brought peace, security, and the collective status that came from possession of an Empire.[31]

The importance of these donations can be seen in the events of 24–19 BC.[32] Augustus celebrated his return from Gaul and Spain with a gift of 400 *sesterces* to each member of the plebs. The notice of the gift was delayed until he gained senatorial approval, a performance of deference on Augustus' part. The senate responded by freeing him from the compulsion of the laws and honouring young male family members (Dio 53.28). The following year, which was one of famine,

---

[27] See the discussion in Ferrary (2001).
[28] See the recent discussion in Dalla Rosa (2015) and Vervaet (2014: 265–70).
[29] On the political centrality of Rome, see Hodgson (2016).
[30] Cooley (2019) notes that *principatus* is not clearly attested in the sense of a reign until the Claudian period. See also Gruen (2005). But Tacitus (*Annales* 3.12) would seem to suggest a Tiberian usage. Suetonius (*Augustus* 28) has Augustus himself using the word *status* to describe the regime.
[31] On the advertised benefits of imperialism, see Alston (2013), with further references, and on peace, see Cornwell (2017).
[32] There are multiple discussions of these years which Syme (1939: 331–48) called 'a crisis in party and state'. See my summary account in Alston (2015: 247–71).

he distributed 12 rations of grain to the plebs (Dio 53.30–3; *Res Gestae* 15). In 22, faced with grain shortages, the people demonstrated against the senators and tried to have Augustus appointed as dictator, a position he refused.[33] The dictatorship would have been a permanent magisterial recognition of a power that was performed through this request and its refusal. The offer reflects a perception that only Augustus could provide, and his rapid success in alleviating the food crisis confirmed that perception.[34] Electoral support manifested in this period through the holding of one of the consular positions open for Augustus often *in absentia*, which he repeatedly refused to take up. In 19 BC, the senate celebrated his return from the East with further honours, including the Altar of Fortuna Redux, the *cura morum legumque* (care of customs and laws), and the attendance of lictors, as if he held magisterial power (Dio 54.6, 54.10; *Res Gestae* 6, 11–12; Suetonius, *Augustus* 27). His provision of social benefits translated directly into political power that allowed the further provision of benefits, such as to make it seem as though a significant proportion of the population depended on Augustan power.

If the Augustan regime could provide, it could also punish. Bodin (1576: 1) identified *maiestas* (majesty) as the Latin term for sovereignty. Hammer (this volume) shows that *maiestas* operated as a loose concept during the Republic, always associated with the *populus*. It could be paired with *imperium* but was evidently primarily a cultural or moral value.[35] Moatti (2018: 116–50) also argues that *maiestas* was relational during the Republic, reflecting social hierarchy, and a crime against *maiestas* was an offence against social order (Giovannini 2015: 15–17). Gradually, it came to be a crime against the sovereign on whom that social order depended. The emperor had the primary adjudication on this law (see Dio 56.27 and discussion in Eder 2005; Bauman 2013; Peachin 2015). Consequently, by the reign of Tiberius, *maiestas* prosecutions were identified with imperial tyranny (Richardson 1997). Bhatt (2017b) sees the enforcement of the law as performing state violence and sovereign power. She draws this perception from Tacitus' reading (*Annales* 3.25–8) of law not as an element of freedom (as in 28–27 BC and at the foundation of the Republic) but as the tool of tyranny. This transformation in the functions of law resulted from the historical experience of the imperial operation of law.[36]

That experience can be seen in several prominent suppressions of individuals across the Augustan and Tiberian periods: Cornelius Gallus, Agrippa Postumus, Ovid, and Decimus Silanus. Gallus' fault seems to have amounted to little more than gossip to which Augustus responded by breaking off his friendship (Dio 53.23; Suetonius, *Augustus* 66.2). But a lack of respect to Augustus was a threat to an order grounded in Augustus' moral status, and the senators were obliged to demonstrate

---

[33] Dio 54.1; *Res Gestae* 5 on two offers of the dictatorship.
[34] Dio 55.27 for famine leading to a questioning of Augustus' position.
[35] Cicero (*Pro Rab. Perd.* 20) claims that the emergency decree against Saturninus called on the consuls to act to 'preserve the *imperium populi Romani maiestasque*'.
[36] Cooley (2019) sees the age of Augustus as a gradual and transformatory process.

their loyalty to that order by issuing an instruction to a court to convict him. Law was invoked or invented to support Augustan hegemony, leading to the exclusion of the individual who had offended imperial status. Gallus' suicide followed. It mattered little that Augustus himself was not involved in prosecution, since the requirements of the regime determined the actions of the senators and the outcome of the case. Similarly, Tacitus' account (*Annales* 1.6) of the murder of Agrippa makes the crime the responsibility of the 'new principate' and is explained as a necessary act so that there be a single point of authority. Ovid's studiously vague crimes (*Tristia* 2.125–40) were condemned by no court or senatorial sanction, but by an edict of Augustus, who is described as acting personally as was worthy of the *princeps* (133–4). Ovid claims that Caesar granted him his life (127).[37] Tacitus (*Annales* 3.24) reports the return of Decimus Silanus from exile. On being thanked, Tiberius noted that his exile had no legal basis; it was merely at the will of Augustus. His return was evidently a concession by Tiberius. These instances demonstrated repeatedly that offences to the imperial person, real or perceived, required death or social exclusion and that the will of the emperor was enough to exile or lead to the death of the citizen. Such power parallels the imperial ability to spare the individual from the law, *clementia*, which Seneca (*de Clementia*) theorised as being central to the powers of the emperor and essential for the functioning of society.

Benjamin (1996) draws a distinction between mythic violence, which is controlled and contributory to order, and divine violence, which is revolutionary and sovereign. This distinction separates the everyday violence of the law from the exceptional foundational violence of sovereignty. Tacitus' narrative of imperial law interrelates these categories (Bhatt 2017b). Tiberian trials conform to the mythic category in that the violence and the narratives around the violence perform and reinforce imperial order through law. But the ever-present threat is of a failure of order and a consequent unleashing of the revolutionary violence of civil war unlimited by law or convention.[38] Arguably, violence existed on a spectrum, and it was a political judgement as to whether one regarded the violence exercised by the state as affirming order and law or as quasi-civil war.[39] The operation of law appears to have been concessionary (Lendon 2006), both in the Augustan restoration of law and in the emperors allowing legal process to take place rather than exercising their divine violence. Consequently, legal and mythic violence depended upon the extra-legal and revolutionary violence latent in the regime, and law became a function of the sovereign power, enhancing that power since the sovereign allowed its operation.

Augustan power was built into the aesthetics of Rome and performed through public rituals. These had the effect of educating the people into the ideological

---

[37] See discussion in Tuori (2016: 75–80).
[38] Alston (2021) argues that Germanicus' assertion of sovereign power on the German frontiers both depended on the threat of extreme violence and the ability of Germanicus to define friends and enemies.
[39] For the delicate negotiations of legal and imperial violence, see the discussions around the Piso episode in which the trial of Piso was a concession by the imperial family offended by his opposition to Germanicus; see Potter & Damon (1999).

systems of the regime that centred power on Augustus. Rome was the primary stage for these performances, in the celebrations of and monuments for Augustus' returns from campaigns, familial funerals, the grand festivals of 17 BC and 2 BC, the offering and rejection of honours, and the everyday performance of *obsequium* (compliance) that marked adherence to the emperor. The monumental transformation of Rome was in itself a representation of a *res publica* dependent on the sovereign.[40] Such rituals and representations were adopted in the provinces, which suggests a geographically more extensive conception of the political community and *res publica*.[41] The unification of the Roman people under imperial rule found metaphoric expression in the award of the title of *pater patriae* (father of the fatherland; *Res Gestae* 35; Dio 55.10.10; Suetonius, *Augustus* 58). This title represented the Roman state as a mythic family, structured under the authority of a single *pater*, as opposed to a coming together of citizens and many *patres* for mutual benefit in a hierarchically organised community.[42]

Across the Augustan era, we see a concentration of powers on Augustus. Those powers found mythic representation and were depicted as fundamental to the functioning of Roman society. The imperial sovereign thus came into being not as a theoretical construct, and hence there was no single term for sovereign, but as a clustering of powers, some embedded in law and some external to law.[43] That power was relational: it required the acceptance of citizens (and others). Recognition came through multiple public demonstrations of loyalty which were built into Rome's political aesthetics and required new communicative practices.[44] The experiences of civil violence and Augustan repression of dissent operated alongside the benefits provided to senators, soldiers, and plebs. The more the regime displayed its provision of social benefits and its disciplinary powers, the more persuasive the regime became. The experience of Augustan power educated the Roman people into their subordination to the sovereign.

The invention of the imperial sovereign was consequential on Octavian-Augustus acquiring vast political resources. Augustus was able to determine membership of and exclude individuals from the community. The sovereign was seen to provide the means for social reproduction, maintain law and tradition, and guarantee the security of the senate and people. He himself was beyond the reach of law and could act outside of law to protect the state or preserve the citizen (through

---

[40] See, from an extensive bibliography, Hodgson (2016) on Rome as *res publica*, Zanker (1990) on the transformation of Rome, and Wallace-Hadrill (2005) for the related transformation of epistemes.

[41] This becomes most obvious in honorific statues and cult, which were widely disseminated: see, for example, Rose (1997) and Price (1984). Ando (2000: 5–19) shows how the imperial political aesthetic extended to the provinces.

[42] Milnor (2008), Severy (2003), and Eder (2005) see the metaphor of family for the state as an Augustan innovation. Hammer (2017) argues that Republican Romans deployed the metaphor of the *societas*.

[43] Ando (2000: 28) sees the legalistic and cultural approaches as binary, but, as Hurlet (2007) argues, these elements must have coalesced around the person of the emperor.

[44] For Roman Republican politics as an aesthetic system, see Connolly (2015). On the transformation of communicative practices as a socio-political revolution, see Habermas (1991).

clementia). In the regime's representation, all depended on the sovereign. In this instance, sovereignty is not a quality inherent in the state, but is a representation of an extreme concentration of power in a single *locus*, so as to make that *locus* seemingly responsible for the maintenance of the social and political system and all the citizens therein. As Tacitus (*Annales* 1.4) puts it, *omnes exuta aequalitate iussa principis aspectare* ('all, stripped of equality, looked for the orders of the *princeps*').

Against sovereignty

In this concluding section, I explore the implications in political theory of the above historical analysis. Foucault's notion of the biopolitical undermines ideas of theological sovereignty. Foucault, however, did not consider the political dynamics that followed from his model. For that I turn to Antonio Gramsci and his consideration of the relationship of civil society and the state. The state was for him a centre of coercive power with which civil society was in some degree of conflict (Gramsci 1971: 245). Yet a dialectic relationship between state and civil society blurs the boundaries between the two. Civil society is identified in a multiplicity of 'private' organisations (Gramsci 1971: 262–5). It operates as a network of defences that sustain a particular hegemonic group in spite of incursions and catastrophes (such as economic failure).[45] The plurality of civil society rests on multiple locations of power which can never be isolated from the hegemonic structures but are at least quasi-autonomous. Such groups are resistant to political insurgents, though that resistance rests more in the complexity of the multiple social relations than in any prior ideological commitment to conservatism.

Gramsci's theorisation of fascism points to those private institutions being either broken by fascism, supplanted in one form or another, or incorporated into the hegemonic political entity. The state/party extends its reach so as to bring about a union of political and civil society which can be seen as the formation of a national society or a national culture which radically simplifies through appropriation of the institutions and structures of civil society.

Such unity is mythic, and no regime, ancient or modern, could ever achieve that level of domination, though it may aspire to do so. Mythic unity justifies the social and political exclusion of those identified as being outside or hostile to the unitary state-society. The totalitarian regime's drive towards a monopolisation of social power leads to the suppression of those cultural differences made treasonable in the politicisation of civil society.

---

[45] The power of civil society is a central element in Gramsci's explanation for the delayed revolution in the West and its success in Russia. See Gramsci (1971, 232–5) with commentary in Anderson (2017, 53–8). One may compare Althusser's notion of Ideological State Apparatus, first explored in 1970; see Althusser (2008; 2014).

The theorists of sovereignty discussed see the unitary state-society as being a natural or ontological characteristic of the state. Although such concentrations of power are historically familiar and may be a common dynamic in regimes, they are not universal and can be seen to come into being through specific historical processes.

Augustan sovereignty employed mythological reasoning to justify the emergence of the sovereign through the exceptionality of Augustus, the dependence of the *res publica* on that exceptionality, and the repeated performances of a unified community.[46] The invention of the sovereign led to the cultural manifestation of the sovereign's power and the appropriation of cultural resources, such as Roman history and mythology, to sustain the regime. The unification of culture and politics absorbs, incorporates, or destroys the plurality of locations of power, such as religious institutions, the family, and localised social units (*vici*) (Lott 2004) as well as major political institutions (the senate, assemblies, etc.). Regional variation was reduced in the spread of imperial cultural expression and values through Italy and beyond.[47]

In a drive for a unitary state, cultural values and behaviours come to be identified with the sovereign. Since the sovereign determines membership of the community and access to societal benefits through a recognition of a shared culture, locations of *dissensus* or of cultural difference are rendered precarious.[48] It becomes a social requirement to demonstrate loyalty and adherence to the cultural forms of the state.

In this reading, the mere presence of a sovereign persona becomes a source of repression, even if the sovereign is identified with a multiplicity of persons (the nation/the people). The extensive claims of the sovereign entity are dependent on a concentration of social and political powers which would make that sovereign claim real.[49] A sovereign is a product of a dynamic process of accretion of power which tends to the unification of culture (civil society) and politics (state) for which the sovereign seeks ideological justification. The notion of sovereignty as an essential characteristic of the state provides one means for that justification. It follows that freedom and the *res publica* require a rejection of sovereignty, and any sovereign, and an embracing of *dissensus* (Rancière 2010; 2015), diversity, and difference in a plural society committed to a multiplicity of locations of social power.

---

[46] See Moatti (2018) on the invention of the unitary state alongside the invention of imperial sovereignty.
[47] See Ando (2000), Torelli (1998), and Crawford (1996), though the Augustan period accelerated existing cultural processes.
[48] See Appadurai (2006) on how nationalist groups exclude those represented as different so as to enhance their claims on the state and its benefits.
[49] Lowrie (2007) argues for the inapplicability of Agamben's model of sovereignty to Republican Rome precisely because of this dispersal of power across society.

References

Abdy, R. & Harling, N. (2005), 'Two Important New Roman Coins', *Numismatic Chronicle*, 165: 175–8.
Agamben, G. (1995), *Homo Sacer. Il potere sovrano e la vita nuda* (Turin, Einaudi).
Agamben, G. (1998), *Homo Sacer: Sovereign Power and Bare Life*, trans. D. Heller-Roazen (Stanford, Stanford University Press).
Agamben, G. (2003), *Stato di eccezione* (Turin, Bollati Boringhieri).
Agamben, G. (2005), *State of Exception* (Chicago, University of Chicago Press).
Alföldy, G. (2000), 'Das neue Edikt des Augustus aus El Bierzo in Hispanien', *Zeitschrift für Papyrologie und Epigraphik*, 131: 177–205.
Alston, R. (2013), 'Augustan Imperialism', in D. Hoyos (ed.), *A Companion to Ancient Imperialism* (Leiden & Boston, Brill), 197–211.
Alston R. (2015), *Rome's Revolution: Death of the Republic and Birth of the Empire* (New York, Oxford University Press).
Alston, R. (2017), 'Foucault's Empire of the Free', in S. Bhatt & R. Alston (eds), *Foucault's Rome*, special edition of *Foucault Studies*, 22: 94–112.
Alston, R. (2021), 'Drawing Imperial Lines: Sovereignty and Tacitus' Germanicus', *Lexis*, 39.2: 413–44.
Althusser, L. (2008), 'Ideology and Ideological State Apparatuses (Notes Towards an Investigation)', in L. Althusser, *On Ideology* (London & New York, Verso), 1–60.
Althusser, L. (2014), *On the Reproduction of Capitalism: Ideology and Ideological State Apparatuses*, trans. and ed. G.M. Goshgarian (London & New York, Verso).
Anderson, P. (2017), *The Antinomies of Antonio Gramsci* (London & New York, Verso).
Ando, C. (2000), *Imperial Ideology and Provincial Loyalty in the Roman Empire* (Berkeley, University of California Press).
Ando, C. (2010), '"A Dwelling beyond Violence": On the Uses and Disadvantages of History for Contemporary Republicans', *History of Political Thought*, 31: 183–220.
Appadurai, A. (2006), *Fear of Small Numbers: An Essay on the Geography of Anger* (Durham NC, Duke University Press).
Arena, V. (2015), 'Informal Norms, Values, and Social Control in the Roman Participatory Context', in D. Hammer (ed.), *A Companion to Greek Democracy and the Roman Republic* (Chichester, Wiley-Blackwell), 217–38.
Atkins, J.W. (2018), *Roman Political Thought* (Cambridge, Cambridge University Press).
Bartsch, S. (1994), *Actors in the Audience: Theatricality and Doublespeak from Nero to Hadrian* (Cambridge MA, Harvard University Press).
Bauman, R.A. (2013), *The crimen maiestatis in the Roman Republic and the Augustan Principate* (Johannesburg, Witwatersrand University Press).
Benjamin, W. (1996), 'Critique of Violence', in W. Benjamin, *Selected Writings*, vol. i: *1913–1926*, ed. M. Bullock & M.W. Jennings (Cambridge MA & London, Belknapp Press), 236–52.
Bhatt, S. (2017a), 'The Augustan Principate and the Emergence of Biopolitics: A Comparative Historical Perspective', in S. Bhatt & R. Alston (eds), *Foucault's Rome*, special edition of *Foucault Studies*, 22: 72–93.
Bhatt, S (2017b), 'Useful Vices: Tacitus's Critique of Corruption', *Arethusa*, 50: 311–33.
Bleicken, J. (1990), *Zwischen Republik und Principat. Zum Charakter des zweiten Triumvirats* (Göttingen, VandenHoeck & Rupprecht).
Bleicken, J. (2015), *Augustus: The Biography*, trans. A. Bell (London, Allen Lane).
Bodin, J. (1576), *Les six livres de la République* (Paris, Jacques de Puy).

Broughton, T.R.S. (1986), *The Magistrates of the Roman Republic* (Atlanta, American Philological Association).
Connolly, J. (2015), *The Life of Roman Republicanism* (Princeton & Oxford, Princeton University Press).
Cooley, A.E. (2019), 'From the Augustan Principate to the Invention of the Age of Augustus', *Journal of Roman Studies*, 109: 71–87.
Cornell, T.J. (2015), 'Crisis and Deformation in the Roman Republic: The Example of the Dictatorship', in V. Gouschin & P.J. Rhodes (eds), *Deformations and Crises of Ancient Civil Communities* (Stuttgart, Franz Steiner), 101–25.
Cornwell, H. (2017), *Pax and the Politics of Peace: Republic to Principate* (Oxford, Oxford University Press).
Crawford, M. (1996), 'Italy and Rome from Sulla to Augustus', in A. Bowman, E. Champlin, & A. Lintott (eds), *Cambridge Ancient History*, vol. x: *The Augustan Empire, 43 BC–AD 69*, 2nd edn (Cambridge, Cambridge University Press), 414–33.
Crook, J.A. (1996), 'Political History, 30 B.C. to A.D. 14', in A.K. Bowman, A. Lintott, & E.J. Champlin (eds), *Cambridge Ancient History*, vol. x: *The Augustan Empire, 43 B.C.–A.D. 69*, 2nd edn (Cambridge, Cambridge University Press), 70–112.
Dalla Rosa, A. (2015), 'L'autocrate e il magistrate: l'attività di Augusto negli ambiti di competenza consolare', in J.-L. Ferrary & J. Scheid (eds), *Il princeps romano: autocrate o magistrato? Fattori giuridiche e fattori sociali del potere imperiale da Augusto a Commodo* (Pavia, IUSS Press), 555–85.
Eder, W. (2005), 'Augustus and the Power of Tradition' in K. Galinsky (ed.), *The Cambridge Companion to the Age of Augustus* (Cambridge, Cambridge University Press), 13–32.
Ermatinger, J. (1993), '*ILS* 77 and 78: The End of the Second Triumvirate', *Historia*, 42: 109–10.
Ferrary, J.-L. (2001), 'À propos des pouvoirs d'Auguste', *Cahiers du Centre G. Glotz*, 12: 101–54.
Ferrary, J.-L. (2015), 'Nature et périodisation du Principat, des juristes humanistes à Mommsen', in J.-L. Ferrary & J. Scheid (eds), *Il princeps romano: autocrate o magistrato? Fattori giuridiche e fattori sociali del potere imperiale da Augusto a Commodo* (Pavia: IUSS Press), 3–34.
Flaig, E. (1992), *Den Kaiser herausfodern. Die Usurpation im Römischen Reich* (Frankfurt: Campus).
Flaig, E. (2011), 'The Transition from Republic to Principate: Loss of Legitimacy, Revolution, and Acceptance', in J.P. Arnason and K.A. Raaflaub (eds), *The Roman Empire in Context: Historical and Comparative Perspectives* (Malden MA & Oxford, Blackwell), 67–84.
Flaig, E. (2015a), 'A Coerent Model to Understand the Roman Principate: "Acceptance" Instead of "Legitimacy" and the Problem of Usurpation', in J.-L. Ferrary and J. Scheid (eds), *Il princeps romano: autocrate o magistrato? Fattori giuridiche e fattori sociali del potere imperiale da Augusto a Commodo* (Pavia, IUSS Press), 81–100.
Flaig, E. (2015b), 'How the Emperor Nero Lost Acceptance in Rome', in B.C. Ewald & C.F. Noreña (eds), *The Emperor and Rome: Space, Representation, and Ritual* (Cambridge, Cambridge University Press), 275–88.
Foucault, M. (1979a), 'Truth and Power: An Interview with Michel Foucault', *Critique of Anthropology*, 4.13–14: 131–7.
Foucault, M. (1979b), *The Will to Knowledge: The History of Sexuality: An Introduction*, trans. R. Hurley (Harmondsworth, Penguin Books).

Foucault, M. (1994), 'L'oeil du pouvoir', in M. Foucault, *Dits et écrits 1954–1988, vol. iii: 1976–1979*, ed. D. Defert and F. Ewald (Paris, Gallimard), 190–207.
Foucault, M. (2002), *The Order of Things: An Archaeology of the Human Sciences* (London & New York, Routledge).
Foucault, M. (2003), *Society Must Be Defended (Lectures at the College de France, 1975–1976)*, ed. M. Bertani & A. Fontana, trans. D. Macey (New York, Picador).
Foucault, M. (2010), *The Government of the Self and Others: Lectures at the Collège de France, 1982–1983*, ed. Frédéric Gros, trans. G. Burchell (Basingstoke, Palgrave Macmillan).
Galinsky, K. (1996), *Augustan Culture: An Interpretative Introduction* (Princeton, Princeton University Press).
Giovannini, A. (2015), *Les institutions de la République romaine des origines à la mort d'Auguste* (*Schweizerische Beiträge zur Altertumswissenschaft* 42; Schweizerische Vereinigung für Altertumswissenschaft, Basel).
Gramsci, A. (1971), 'State and Civil Society', in Q. Hoare & G.N. Smith (eds), *Selections from the Prison Notebooks* (London, Lawrence & Wishart), 210–76.
Gruen, E.S. (2005), 'Augustus and the Making of the Principate', in K. Galinsky (ed.), *The Cambridge Companion to the Age of Augustus* (Cambridge, Cambridge University Press), 33–51.
Habermas, J. (1991), *The Structural Transformation of the Public Sphere: An Inquiry into a Category of Bourgeois Society*, trans. T. Burger & F. Lawrence (Cambridge MA, MIT Press).
Hammer, D. (2017), 'Foucault, Sovereignty and Governmentality in the Roman Republic', in S. Bhatt & R. Alston (eds), *Foucault's Rome*, special edition of *Foucault Studies*, 22: 49–71.
Hardt, M. & Negri, A. (2004), *Multitude: War and Democracy in the Age of Empire* (London, Penguin).
Heuss, A. (1974), 'Theodor Mommsen und die revolutionäre Struktur des römischen Kaisertums', *Aufstieg und Niedergang der römischen Welt*, series II, 1.1: 77–90.
Hodgson, L. (2016), *Res Publica and the Roman Republic* (Oxford, Oxford University Press).
Hoekstra, K. (2016), 'Athenian Democracy and Popular Tyranny', in R. Bourke & Q. Skinner (eds), *Popular Sovereignty in Historical Perspective* (Cambridge, Cambridge University Press), 15–51.
Hurlet, F. (2007), 'Une décennie de recherches sur Auguste. Bilan historiographique (1996–2006)', *Anabases*, 6: 187–218.
Jehne, M. (2005), 'Die Volkersammlungen in Mommsens Staatsrecht, oder: Mommsen als Gesertzgeber', in W. Nippel and B. Seidensticker (eds), *Theodor Mommsens langer Schatten: Das römische Staatsrecht als bleibende Herausforderung für die Forschung* (Hildesheim & New York, Olms), 131–60.
Judge, E.A. (1974), '"Res Publica restituta": A Modern Illusion?', in J.A.S. Evans (ed.), *Polis and Imperium: Studies in Honour of Edward Togo Salmon* (Toronto, Hakkert), 279–311.
Kaldellis, A. (2015), *The Byzantine Republic: People and Power in New Rome* (Cambridge MA, Harvard University Press).
Kalyvas, A. (2000a), 'Carl Schmitt and the Three Moments of Democracy', *Cardozo Law Review*, 21: 1525–65.
Kalyvas, A. (2000b), 'Hegemonic Sovereignty: Carl Schmitt, Antonio Gramsci and the Constituent Prince', *Journal of Political Ideologies*, 5: 343–76.

Lacey, W.K. (1974), 'Octavian in the Senate, January 27 BC', *Journal of Roman Studies*, 64: 176–84.
Lange, C.H. (2009), *Res Publica Constituta Actium, Apollo, and the Accomplishment of the Triumviral Assignment* (Boston MA, Brill).
Lendon, J.E. (2006), 'The Legitimacy of the Roman Emperor: Against Weberian Legitimacy and Imperial "Strategies of Legitimation"', in A. Kolb (ed.), *Herrschaftsstrukturen und Herrschaftspraxis: Konzepte, Prinzipien und Strategien der Administration im römischen Kaiserreich* (Berlin, Akademie), 53–63.
Linderski, J. (1990), 'Mommsen and Syme: Law and Power in the Principate of Augustus', in K.A. Raaflaub & M. Toher (eds), *Between Republic and Empire: Interpretations of Augustus and His Principate* (Berkeley, Los Angeles & Oxford, University of California Press), 42–53.
Lott, J.B. (2004), *The Neighborhoods of Augustan Rome* (Cambridge & New York, Cambridge University Press).
Lowrie, M. (2007), 'Sovereignty before the Law: Agamben and the Roman Republic', *Law and Humanities*, 1: 31–55.
Lowrie, M. (2009), *Writing, Performance, and Authority in Augustan Rome* (Oxford, Oxford University Press).
Mantovani, D. (2008), 'Leges et iura p(opuli) R(omani) restituit: principe e diritto in un aureo di Ottaviano', *Athenaeum*, 96: 5–54.
Mattingly, H. (1976), *Coins of the Roman Empire in the British Museum*, vol. i: *Augustus to Vitellius*, rev. edn (London, British Museum Publications).
Merivale, C. (1850–64), *History of the Romans under the Empire*, 7 vols (London, Longman).
Millar, F. (1973), 'Triumvirate and Principate', *Journal of Roman Studies*, 63: 50–67.
Milnor, K. (2008), *Gender, Domesticity, and the Age of Augustus* (Oxford, Oxford University Press).
Moatti, C. (2018), *Res publica: histoire romaine de la chose publique* (Paris, Fayard).
Mommsen, T. (1887–8), *Römisches Staatsrecht*, 3 vols, ed. K.J. Marquardt (Leipzig, S. Hirzel).
Murray, W.M. & Petsas, Ph.M. (1989), *Octavian's Campsite Memorial for the Actian War* (Philadelphia, The Johns Hopkins University Press).
Neal, A.W. (2004), 'Cutting Off the King's Head: Foucault's Society Must Be Defended and the Problem of Sovereignty', *Alternatives: Global, Local, Political*, 29: 373–98.
Nippel, W. (2015), 'The Structure and Legacy of Mommsen's Staatsrecht', in J.-L. Ferrary & J. Scheid (eds), *Il princeps romano: autocrate o magistrato? Fattori giuridiche e fattori sociali del potere imperiale da Augusto a Commodo* (Pavia, IUSS Press), 35–53.
Peachin, M. (2005), 'Mommsens Princeps', in W. Nippel & B. Seidensticker (eds), *Theodor Mommsens langer Schatten: Das römische Staatsrecht als bleibende Herausforderung für die Forschung* (Hildesheim & New York, Olms), 161–76.
Peachin, M (2015), 'Augustus' Emergent Judicial Powers, the "crimen maiestatis", and the Second Cyrene Edict', in J.-L. Ferrary & J. Scheid (eds), *Il princeps romano: autocrate o magistrato? Fattori giuridiche e fattori sociali del potere imperiale da Augusto a Commodo* (Pavia, IUSS), 497–553.
Potter, D.S. & Damon, C. (eds & trans.) (1999), 'The Senatus Consultum De Cn. Pisone Patre', *American Journal of Philology*, 120: 13–42.
Preuss, U.K. (1999), 'Political Order and Democracy: Carl Schmitt and His Influence', in C. Mouffe (ed.), *The Challenge of Carl Schmitt* (London and New York, Verso), 155–79.
Price, S.R.F. (1984), *Rituals and Power: The Roman Imperial Cult in Asia Minor* (Cambridge, Cambridge University Press).

Rancière, J. (2010), *Dissensus: On Politics and Aesthetics*, trans. S. Corcoran (London & New York, Continuum).
Rancière, J. (2015), 'Ten Theses on Politics', in J. Rancière, *Dissensus: On Politics and Aesthetics*, ed. and trans. S. Corcoran (London, New Delhi, New York, & Sydney, Bloomsbury), 35–52.
Rich, J.W. (2012), 'Making the Emergency Permanent: Auctoritas, Potestas and the Evolution of the Principate of Augustus', in Yann Rivière (ed.), *Des Réformes Augustéennes* (Rome, École française de Rome), 37–121.
Rich, J.W. (2015), 'Consensus Rituals and the Origins of the Principate', in J.-L. Ferrary and J. Scheid (eds), *Il princeps romano: autocrate o magistrato? Fattori giuridiche e fattori sociali del potere imperiale da Augusto a Commodo* (Pavia, IUSS Press), 101–38.
Rich, J.W. & Williams, J.H.C. (1999), '*Leges Et Ivra P. R. Restitvit*: A New Aureus of Octavian and the Settlement of 28–27 BC', *Numismatic Chronicle*, 159: 169–213.
Richardson, J.S. (1997), 'The Senate, the Courts, and the *SC de Cn. Pisone Patre*', *Classical Quarterly*, 47: 510–18.
Richardson, J.S. (2002), 'The New Augustan Edict from Northwest Spain', *Journal of Roman Archaeology*, 15: 411–15.
Rose, C.B. (1997), *Dynastic Commemoration and Imperial Portraiture in the Julio-Claudian Period* (Cambridge, Cambridge University Press).
Rosenblitt, A.J. (2012), 'Rome and North Korea: Totalitarian Questions', *Greece & Rome*, 59: 202–13.
Rudich, V. (1993), *Political Dissidence under Nero: The Price of Dissimulation* (London, Routledge).
Schmitt, C. (1921), *Die Diktatur von den Anfängen des modernen Souveränitätsgedankens bis zum proletarischen Klassenkampf* (Munich & Leipzig, Dunker und Humboldt).
Schmitt, C. (1985 [1922]), *Political Theology: Four Chapters on the Concept of Sovereignty*, trans. G. Schwab, foreword T.B. Strong (Chicago & London, University of Chicago Press).
Severy, B. (2003), *Augustus and the Family at the Birth of the Roman Empire* (Abingdon, Routledge).
Sommer, M. (2011), 'Empire of Glory: Weberian Paradigms and the Complexities of Authority in Imperial Rome', *Max Weber Studies*, 11.1: 155–91.
Straumann, B. (2011), 'Constitutional Thought in the Late Roman Republic', *History of Political Thought*, 32: 280–92.
Straumann, B. (2016), *Crisis and Constitutionalism: Roman Political Thought from the Fall of the Republic to the Age of Revolution* (New York, Oxford University Press).
Sutherland, C.H.V. (1970), *The Cistophori of Augustus* (London, Royal Numismatic Society).
Sutherland, C.H.V. (1984), *Roman Imperial Coinage* (London, Spink and Co.).
Syme, R. (1939), *The Roman Revolution* (Oxford, Clarendon Press).
Torelli, M. (1998), *Tota Italia: Essays in the Cultural Formation of Roman Italy* (Oxford, Clarendon Press).
Tuori, K. (2016), *Emperor of Law* (Oxford, Oxford University Press).
Turpin, W. (1994), 'Res Gestae 34.1 and the Settlement of 27 BC', *Classical Quarterly*, 44: 427–37.
Vervaet, F.J. (2010), 'The Secret History: The Official Position of *Imperator Caesar Divi filius* from 31 to 27 BCE', *Ancient Society*, 40: 79–152.
Vervaet, F.J. (2014), *The High Command in the Roman Republic: The Principle of the Summum imperium auspiciumque from 509 to 19 BCE* (Stuttgart, Franz Steiner).

Veyne, P. (2002), 'L'empereur, ses concitoyens et ses sujets', in H. Inglebert (ed.), *Idéologies et valeurs civiques dans le monde romain. Hommage à Claude Lepelley* (Paris, Picard), 49–64.

Wallace-Hadrill, A. (1997), '*Mutatio morum*: The Idea of a Cultural Revolution', in T. Habinek & A. Schiesaro (eds), *The Roman Cultural Revolution* (Cambridge, Cambridge University Press), 3–22.

Wallace-Hadrill, A. (2005), '*Mutatas Formas*: The Augustan Transformation of Roman Knowledge', in K. Galinsky (ed.), *The Cambridge Companion to the Age of Augustus* (Cambridge, Cambridge University Press), 55–84.

Wallace-Hadrill, A. (2018), *Augustan Rome* (London, Bloomsbury).

Wardle, D. (1995), '"ILS" 77: Nothing to Do with the End of the Second Triumvirate', *Historia*, 44: 496–7.

Wilkinson, S. (2012), *Republicanism during the Early Roman Empire* (London & New York, Continuum).

Winterling, A. (2005), 'Dyarchie in der römischen Kaisererzeit. Vorschlag zur Wiederaufnahme der Diskussion', in W. Nippel & B. Seidensticker (eds), *Theodor Mommsens langer Schatten: Das römische Staatsrecht als bleibende Herausforderung für die Forschung* (Hildesheim & New York, Olms), 177–98.

Zanker, P. (1990), *The Power of Images in the Age of Augustus* (Ann Arbor, University of Michigan Press).

5

Forms and Narratives of Sovereignty in Early Imperial China: Beyond Heaven's Mandate, All-Under-Heaven, and So Forth

LUKE HABBERSTAD

> The narrative bridges ... seem to me to be flimsy things, instrumentally constructed, spanning a watery chaos.
>
> Emily Fox Dixon (2003: 27)
>
> 先王見始終之變
> The early kings perceived the transformations of beginnings and endings.
>
> Sima Qian 司馬遷 (?145–?86 BCE)

Introduction

Debates about whether or not recent political and economic developments in the People's Republic of China (PRC) constitute a genuinely new 'model' capable of expanding outside the country's borders have lent new international visibility to topics in traditional Chinese politics that were previously only the domain of specialists.[1] Such discussions often invoke the 'Mandate of Heaven' (*Tian ming* 天命), a heaven-endowed right to rule over the territory 'All Under Heaven' (*Tian xia* 天下), as the singular justification for sovereign political power.[2] As the story goes, this idea supposedly operated at the very dawn of Chinese rulership, when the corrupt and benighted final king of the Shang 商 (c. 1250–c. 1050 BCE) lost

---

[1] For a critical overview of the 'Chinese model', see Dirlik (2012), who emphasises that such debates generally fail to situate the political and economic trajectory of the PRC in terms of its modern revolutionary history and the models provided by its East Asian neighbours.
[2] Essays in Wang (2017) discuss 'All-Under-Heaven' and its entry into debates about global politics.

the Mandate of Heaven, which transferred to a rival, the righteous ruler of the Zhou 周 (Western Zhou: c. 1045–771 BCE; Eastern: 770–256 BCE). This Zhou ruler eventually vanquished the Shang king and established his own 'dynasty', using the Mandate to legitimate his rule. Some writers have argued the narrative contrasts with the European tradition of the 'divine right of kings', insofar as it theoretically left space for 'moral criteria' in the determination of sovereign legitimacy (i.e. the bad Shang king lost the Mandate to the good Zhou ruler) (Fairbank 2006: 39). This interpretation, however, immediately raises at least two questions. First, was the 'Mandate of Heaven' narrative truly in place from such an early period, at the Zhou conquest? Second, is the presence of 'moral criteria', however defined, actually separable from the 'divine' or 'sacred'?[3]

That the answer to both questions is 'no' provides a starting point for this chapter. To preview the evidence and arguments presented below, recent scholarship has clarified that the Mandate of Heaven concept emerged only gradually, in fits and starts. The first evidence for the Mandate probably dates to no earlier than several centuries after the Zhou defeated the Shang, and the full Mandate narrative was not fixed and regularly cited until centuries after imperial unification in 221 BCE under the Qin 秦 (221–206 BCE). This more historically grounded narrative requires us to situate the Mandate of Heaven within a complex pre-imperial vocabulary of rulership, in which royal commands or 'mandates' (*ming* 命) circulated power and goods between gift-giving rulers and people who had committed acts of 'merit' (*gong* 功) benefiting the ruling household and the ancestral lineage. Such a *do ut des* style of rulership, which invoked the power of the ancestral spirits as much as their worldly descendants' achievements, was clearly evident when the First Emperor of Qin unified the empire in 221 BC. It was only towards the end of the 1st century BCE, during the final decades of the Western Han 西漢 (202 BC–9 CE), and more clearly during the subsequent Xin 新 (9–23) and Eastern Han 東漢 (25–220) periods,[4] that the Mandate of Heaven started to gain prominence as an alternative.

Scholars have described this shift as a transformation from a materialist, realpolitik basis of sovereign authority, dominant in the pre-imperial and Qin periods, to a sovereignty rooted in cosmic powers and patterns. In an influential essay, Michael Loewe summed up the change:

> At the outset of the Qin empire the right to rule needed no greater defence or explanation than that of successful conquest, achieved by force of arms; by the end of the Han empire a new dynasty was obliged to demonstrate that it had received Heaven's command to rule and Heaven's blessings in its undertakings. ... While the governors

---

[3] The classic refutation of the secular–sacred divide in early Chinese philosophy remains Fingarette (1972).

[4] 'Han' in this chapter refers solely to the institutions and officials of the Han dynasty government and ruling household. 'Han' did not become an ethnonym until centuries after the final Eastern Han emperor gave up his throne in 220 CE.

of Qin had been content to take material wealth and strength as the objective of their rule, by the third century AD it had become firmly established that a new dynasty could only claim support if it could show that its purpose lay in the unfolding of cosmic destiny.[5]

While this chapter confirms that the authority of Heaven and its Mandate (i.e. Loewe's 'command') did not become a primary concern until long after Qin's initial imperial settlement, it simultaneously emphasises that we cannot separate materialist and cosmic powers so neatly. 'Metahuman' forces, to borrow a term from David Graeber and Marshall Sahlins (2017: 2 and *passim*), are central to both of these ideas of sovereignty, which coexisted even into late Eastern Han. Throughout the early imperial period, people confronting the problems and traumas of forging a unified empire wrestled with parallel, sometimes contradictory narratives about the origin and transmission of imperial power. As is evident in the range of sources discussed below, attempts to resolve these contradictions were marked by semantic shifts in the vocabulary of rulership, recombination of different concepts and narratives, and concern about upsetting the various metahuman sources of power. While it is possible to cast the Mandate as a distinctly Chinese form of sovereignty, one that allowed officials to limit the emperor's power,[6] this chapter rather stresses commonalities between the Chinese case and other pre-modern empires, if not modern nations. As the final remarks will explore, attempts to move between political and metahuman realms in order to justify assertions of sovereign power, marked by unending questions about whether such transpositions can ever make sense, are evident in many claims of sovereignty.

'The Mandate' and mandates, charismatic power and merit: sources of metahuman authority before and after imperial unification

While this chapter emphasises that for much of the early imperial period the 'Mandate of Heaven' and its associated idea, 'All-Under-Heaven', were not dominant concepts, the pair did eventually form a central paradigm in notions of sovereignty and political legitimacy in later eras of Chinese history.[7] In their simplest terms, the concepts held that an entity called 'Heaven' (*tian* 天) endowed a king with a mandate to rule over an area called 'All-Under-Heaven'. He and his descendant rulers, all of them called 'Sons of Heaven' (*tian zi* 天子), maintained this

---

[5] Loewe (1994: 85). I have used pinyin romanisation in place of Wade–Giles in Loewe's original.
[6] For such an interpretation, common in the secondary literature, see Pines (2017).
[7] It was arguably not until the late imperial period, however, that the Mandate of Heaven became the most dominant narrative of political legitimacy. Buddhist notions of kingship were equally important prior to the Song period, and they maintained a diminished role even up to the collapse of the Qing empire in 1911. See Hughes (2021).

mandate only as long as they ruled with 'charismatic power' (*de* 德). A lack of this power caused the imminent loss of the mandate, often presaged by all manner of portents (sickness, famine, earthquakes, comets, and so forth). If the offending ruler did not mend his ways, the mandate would be transferred to some other, more worthy ruler, whose coming rise was often foretold by various auspicious omens, including mystical creatures emerging from the forest and magical texts coming out of rivers. This new ruler could then set up a ruling household (or 'dynasty') that would then rule 'All-Under-Heaven'. Of course, the founding ruler and his descendants also had to rule with virtuous power, or the whole cycle would start over again.

Even this brief and schematic outline shows that the theories raised as many questions as they answered. Was 'Heaven' a theistic deity or a cosmic concept? What duties had to be fulfilled in order to demonstrate charismatic rule, and how did those duties balance against each other? Were responsibilities for providing for the people, for instance, more or less important than maintaining sacrificial rites? What exactly qualified as a portent that reflected a ruler's virtuous power (or lack thereof) and the stability of his realm? Could systems or patterns be devised to predict the emergence of such portents? Did 'All-Under-Heaven' refer to the entire known world, a physical territory or social group contained within defined or definable boundaries, or a cultural sphere that did not precisely map onto political borders? The evident connection between these questions and all manner of problems (moral action, political economy, cosmic patterns, ritual obligations, etc.) perfectly exemplifies the inherently 'embedded' nature of sovereignty 'within particular constellations of ideas, aesthetics, and practices' that are by no means bound by the 'state', however defined.[8]

If a chapter of this length cannot hope to answer all these questions in detail, their sheer complexity suggests that we should not expect such an elaborate narrative to have been fully worked out and in place when Zhou vanquished Shang, *c.* 1050 BCE. Recent scholarship, based on archaeological evidence, shows that while the Zhou seem to have worshipped a deity called 'Heaven' from its early days, the Mandate of Heaven did not legitimise the Zhou conquest in real time. Rather, the first details of the full narrative began to emerge only centuries later, in the context of mid- and late Western Zhou ancestral ritual memorialising the Zhou founders. Martin Kern has recently pointed out that in Zhou bronze inscriptions the 'Mandate of Heaven' and terms associated with it (e.g. 'Son of Heaven', the high deity 'Lord' (*di* 帝), and Wen-Wu 文武, a binome referring to the founding Zhou kings Wen and Wu) are relatively rare from bronzes cast in early Western Zhou. They appear with

---

[8] Benite *et al.* (2017: 14). They consciously contrast their 'embedded' understanding of sovereignty with attempts to 'disentangle … the complex links between concepts, institutions, practices, and doctrines' advocated by Kalmo and Skinner (2010: 7). I agree that attempts to 'disentangle' tend to end up privileging government institutions and, in any case, are ultimately futile. For criticism of the 'state' as a category that does not helpfully illustrate the dynamics behind sovereignty and the legitimacy of rulers and ruling institutions, see Graeber and Sahlins (2017).

more regularity only in the final century of Western Zhou, when the royal court was already faltering and losing power. This period saw the reform and expansion of ritual ceremonies at the Zhou ancestral temple, with temple ceremonies 'evolv[ing] from close and intimate kinship sacrificial rites to rituals of broader socio-political representation' (Kern 2009: 152). The concept of the 'Mandate of Heaven', then, was always an idealised memory, invoked during ancestral ceremonies and designed to extol in retrospective and highly idealised terms the virtues of the Zhou founders. Rather than a theory of sovereign legitimacy operative at the founding of the dynasty, the 'Mandate' was a 'commemoration of origin', one that established 'the religious legitimacy of the entire dynasty, [and] created an ideal past as a parallel reality to an actual experience of loss and decay' (Kern 2009: 150).

In the late Western Zhou, the Mandate was thus primarily commemorative, designed to extol the halcyon days of founding hero kings in the context of ancestral ceremonies. It did not justify any conquest in real time or even explain cycles of political change and the toppling of dynasties; such elaborate theories would not achieve their fullest forms until many centuries later, during the final decades of Western Han (see below). This commemorative function of the Mandate and associated concepts directs our attention towards the context of ancestral rituals, which were central to pre-imperial politics. Important here is that the word 'mandate' (*ming* 命) in early bronze inscriptions is interchangeable with the word 'command' (*ling* 令). Both referred more often to official pronouncements conferred by rulers than they did to commands from Heaven. Many Zhou bronze inscriptions record what most scholars term 'investiture' or 'appointment' ceremonies. During these rituals, the Zhou king or a noble would bestow a *ming* or *ling* to a subordinate, thus endowing him with 'command' to serve in a position at court or to complete a military mission.[9] Alongside this command, the recipient of the *ming* received various material goods (sacrificial wine, court garments, horses, and so forth), many of which functioned as 'outward insignia', symbolising his newly conferred duties (Kane 1982–3: 17). After 'accepting' (*shou* 受) the appointment and accompanying goods, the recipient would cast a bronze vessel, commemorating equally his new charge and the actual performance of the appointment ceremony. The appointment ceremonies and the vessels produced to commemorate them explicitly invoked ancestral deities and ensured their lasting memory, since the bronzes would continue to be used in ancestral temples for sacrificial offerings. The 'command' thus initiated and in some sense financed the circulation of material goods, which at all levels of elite society were diverted and converted into sacrificial offerings. The practice linked together rulers, subordinate nobles, and ancestral spirits into a system of power and exchange that bound together elite Zhou society, and remained a powerful model into the early imperial period.[10]

---

[9] For a concise overview, see Kane (1982–3).
[10] For more details, see Cook (1997), Schaberg (2005), and Sterckx (2009).

'Charismatic power' (*de* 德), mentioned above as the quality rulers must possess in order to retain the 'Mandate', played a central role in this dynamic. Modern scholarly discussions of the 'Mandate', perhaps confused by the common translation of *de* as 'virtue', tend to conceive of *de* as an abstracted quality of moral goodness (i.e. if a ruler was not a good and virtuous king, he would lose the Mandate). In some bronze inscriptions as well as poems included in the *Odes*, however, the word clearly refers to gifts themselves or sometimes, as David Schaberg (2005: 28–9) has put it, a 'reputation for liberality' ascribed to the host of a ceremony or banquet. The dispensation and circulation of goods, then, was a virtual requirement for obtaining charismatic power, a fact that tallies with the paranomastic gloss, common in early texts, of *de* 德 ('charismatic power') as equivalent to *de* 得 ('obtain'). The word implies the existence of a debt or obligation, commonly felt after obtaining a gift or favour from somebody else. The possessor of 'charismatic power' is one who has elicited such feelings in others, since the 'felt force or compulsion, in the receiver of a favor, is psychologically transferred to the giver' (Nivison 1978–9: 53). Moreover, from pre-imperial through Han times, early texts inevitably paired the 'charismatic power' of kings with their ability to enact 'mutilating punishments' (*xing* 刑); in fact, *xingde* ('punishment and charismatic power') was practically a synonym of *shangfa* 賞罰 ('reward and punish'), with both terms commonly surfacing in discussions of the power and role of rulers.[11] Certainly, in the several centuries of warfare and competition between realms that preceded imperial unification in 221 BCE, contending rulers used this vocabulary to consolidate power and justify military campaigns.

It is no wonder, then, that when the King of Qin finally declared victory over all rival kings and established his unified empire in 221 BCE, he made no mention of a Mandate of Heaven. Rather, in calling court officials to debate changes to his official title and associated imperial nomenclature, he mentioned the punitive measures he had enacted and the support he had received from the ancestral spirits:

> 秦初并天下，令丞相、御史曰：「…寡人以眇眇之身，興兵誅暴亂，賴宗廟之靈，六王咸伏其辜，天下大定。今名號不更，無以稱成功，傳後世。其議帝號。」

> When the King of Qin first unified All-Under-Heaven, he issued an order to his Chancellor and Imperial Counselor, saying … 'With my insignificant person, I have mustered troops and punished violence and disorder. Due to the sacred power of our

---

[11] Traditionally, such ideas have been categorised as 'Legalist' in nature and put in opposition to 'Confucian' concepts. Though they still appear with regularity, the two categories have received extensive revisionist critique over the last two decades, with many scholars pointing out that neither category comprised a fixed school of thought supported by defined institutions and social groupings. For one analysis of early sovereignty that retains 'Legalist' and 'Confucian', but only as idealised concepts that can help illuminate philosophical debates, see Cheng (2011). Note also that the concepts *xingde* and *shangfa* are central concepts on charts, recovered from several late Warring States and Western Han tombs, whose design was organised according to numerical schemes that provided a template for divination, prediction, or even game play.

ancestral temple, the six kings have all admitted their guilt and All-Under-Heaven is broadly settled. Now, if titles do not change, we will have no way to mark the completion of this merit (*gong* 功) and pass it on to later generations. Debate the ruler's titles.'[12]

The term 'merit' (*gong*) here is significant, for in pre-imperial texts it regularly refers to the notable achievements (often, but not always, military victories) of rulers or their subordinates, which in theory could initiate the kinds of rewards given out in the investiture ceremonies described above. Indeed, establishing a clear link between merit and reward became a technique of government extolled in early texts.[13] In this case, the King of Qin claims, notwithstanding his use of the humilific phrase 'insignificant person', that indeed the merit came from his military actions. At the same time, he combines his individual achievement, in proportions that the statement leaves vague, with the support he received from the ancestral spirits (perhaps as partial recognition for his accumulated merit, though the passage does not make this point entirely clear). Subtly implied in his call to debate a new imperial nomenclature, then, was a question about how imperial unification in fact happened: through his own work, or through the power of longstanding institutions (e.g. the ancestral temple and the deities housed therein), or both?

In the response from the King of Qin's officials, and in his amendment to their suggestion, the answer seems to have been 'both', even though the rhetorical emphasis was on the newness and unprecedented nature of the King's individual accomplishment:

> 丞相綰、御史大夫劫、廷尉斯等皆曰：「昔者五帝地方千里，其外侯服夷服諸侯或朝或否，天子不能制。今陛下興義兵，誅殘賊，平定天下，海內為郡縣，法令由一統，自上古以來未嘗有，五帝所不及。臣等謹與博士議曰：『古有天皇，有地皇，有泰皇，泰皇最貴。』臣等昧死上尊號，王為『泰皇』。命為『制』，令為『詔』，天子自稱曰『朕』。」
>
> 王曰：「去『泰』，著『皇』，采上古『帝』位號，號曰『皇帝』。他如議。」
>
> 制曰：「可。」

The Chancellor, Imperial Counselor, and Superintendent of Trials all stated: 'In ancient times the Five Lords had lands one thousand *li* square in area. Among their

---

[12] *Shiji* 6.235–6. All translations are by the author.

[13] As the 'Wang zhi' 王制 (Royal Regulations) chapter of the *Xunzi* 荀子 (compiled *c.* late 3rd century BCE) put it: 'The judgements of the king are these: those without charismatic power are not esteemed; those without ability are not given office; those without merit are not rewarded; those who have committed no crime are not punished' (王者之論無德不貴，無能不官，無功不賞，無罪不罰; *Xunzi jian shi*, 106). Traditionally, the realm of Qin has been especially associated with this emphasis on military 'merit'. According to the *Shiji*, before imperial unification the Qin supposedly implemented a system that so tightly linked military 'merit' to the receipt of rank and gifts that even members of the ruling household could not remain in the Qin lineage registries, let alone receive an increase in rank, if they did not achieve 'merit' (see *Shiji* 68.2230). Many pre-imperial realms other than Qin, however, emphasised the accumulation of merit.

outer lords and subordinate foreigners and lords, some submitted to the annual court audience [in which they declared loyalty], but others did not. The Son of Heaven was unable to control them. Now, Your Majesty has raised righteous troops, punished the vicious and murderous, and pacified and settled All-Under-Heaven, making counties and commanderies out of all land within the seas, with laws and orders coming from a single thread. Since high antiquity this has never occurred; it is something that the Five Lords did not surpass. Your humble servants have carefully discussed the matter with the Academicians, who said: "In ancient times there were the Heavenly August (*tian huang* 天皇), Earthly August (*di huang* 地皇), and Supreme August (*tai huang* 泰皇), with the Supreme August most esteemed." Your humble servants on pain of death offer up these esteemed titles: Your royal highness shall become the "Supreme August". Your commands shall become "pronouncements" (*zhi* 制). Your orders shall become "edicts" (*zhao* 詔). The Son of Heaven shall call himself *zhen* 朕.'

The King of Qin said: 'Eliminate "Supreme" (*tai*) but use "August" (*huang*) and take the position and title of "Lord" (*di* 帝) from high antiquity, so the title shall be: "August Lord" [Emperor] (*huangdi* 皇帝). The rest shall be as you discussed.'

The pronouncement stated: 'Approved.'[14]

The final 'pronouncement' should raise eyebrows, since of course the Emperor (*huangdi*) who said 'approved' is precisely the same King of Qin who moments before had amended his advisors' suggestions. The passage thus portrays the establishment of a new sovereign power, the instantaneous transformation of King into Emperor. Such a move was necessary, both officials and king argued, because the Qin triumph represented a historical break, one that far surpassed the achievements of the hoary 'Five Lords', and thus required new forms of representation. At the same time, the Qin court worked within a vocabulary of rulership that had deep historical roots: note that the advisors referred to the First Emperor as 'Son of Heaven', a title that, as mentioned above, was rooted in the Zhou cult to Heaven. Moreover, while the title 'Emperor' (*huangdi*) was a new creation, it combined the appellations of mythical hero rulers from high antiquity (the 'August') with the high 'Lord' worshipped by Shang and Zhou rulers alike.

The passage thus reveals splits between the First Emperor of Qin's claims of newness and a deeper rhetoric of sovereignty that supported his entire project: while the former cast imperial unification as an entirely unprecedented achievement, the latter was still rooted in long-standing practices and concepts. These practices and concepts included the idea of the ruler as the giver of rewards and punishments, a notion of royal authority rooted in what the First Emperor called 'the sacred power of our ancestral temple' (*zongmiao zhi ling* 宗廟之靈), and an imperial vocabulary that, by referring to sage kings and the deity 'Lord', consciously called upon religious ideas and practices that were not particular to Qin but enjoyed an ancient imprimatur.[15]

---

[14] *Shiji* 6.235–6. Note that the Chinese includes the surnames of the officials who participated in the discussion, but for the sake of simplicity they are not included in the translation.

[15] After unification, these practices included worship of a range of deities at altars throughout the new empire. For a discussion of these state cults, which survived the collapse of Qin and continued to receive imperial support until the late Western Han, see Tian (2015).

The king and officials were thus trying to answer a series of questions. Was imperial unification entirely unprecedented, or based on older practices? Was it the result of individual achievement or an accumulation of support over the long-term, exemplified by the approval of the ancestral spirits? Were past titles sufficient to represent the accomplishment, or was some new recombination of vocabulary necessary? Even at the very inception of the empire, then, we see the possibility of different narratives about the origins of sovereign power and different claims about the extent to which unified empire constituted a break from the imperial past.[16] Claims of sovereign power were necessarily claims about history.

While the presence of narrative confusion and contradiction at a moment of potentially fundamental change is perhaps not surprising, at least two points are significant. First, whether understood as an unprecedented achievement or a continuation of past practices, none of these narratives were rooted solely in a concern with 'material wealth and strength', to refer back to Loewe's characterisation of Qin's objectives. The accumulation of merit, the support of the Qin ancestral temple, and a vocabulary of titles and rulership extending back to Zhou times all drew upon and referred to metahuman powers. This is, of course, not to deny the importance of wealth, but rather to emphasise that wealth and material goods were caught up in larger concepts of sovereignty that linked the ruler to different deities (ancestral or otherwise) and bound him and his subjects together in relations of exchange, debt, and obligation. Second, and relatedly, despite the persistence of these longstanding sources of power, the debate about titles also reveals a desire to move beyond them in order to mark a new historical period. As we will see in further detail in what follows, attempts to step back, compare, and transcend past practices continued to occur over the course of the early imperial era.

'Mandates', omens, and patterns: stories of sovereignty after unification

As many students of early imperial China have demonstrated, from a variety of perspectives, on almost every measure the collapse of Qin and the establishment of the Western Han did not bring any fundamental change to notions of sovereignty or the imperial administrative structure.[17] The Western Han court emphasised the 'merit' (*gong*) and 'charismatic power' (*de*) of the Han founder and his military supporters; used the same colour (black) and symbol (water) used by Qin to signify the dynasty; maintained many of the same cults, located at sites around the

---

[16] Needless to say, this question continues to generate debate among specialists. See, for example, the essays assembled in Pines *et al.* (2014).
[17] This fact is perhaps not surprising, since the Western Han founder, unlike the First Emperor of Qin, was a commoner with no royal pedigree and thus could not draw upon the ritual and administrative traditions of a ruling household.

empire, that had been supported by the Qin; used the same graded orders of merit and honour (*jue* 爵) that Qin gave to imperial subjects in order to reward service and to provide a framework for the dispersal of gifts; and continued to use the same administrative territories of commanderies and counties established by Qin (even if large portions of the Han empire had to be ceded as mostly autonomous kingdoms to military supporters of the Han founder and family). It was not until well over a century after the founding of the dynasty, by which time the Western Han court had consolidated power and eliminated major internal and external threats to its power, that Han officials managed to substantially alter the precedents established by the Qin.[18] The complicated historical trajectory of this process of reform, however, which eventually resulted in new bases for justifying imperial rule, was far from linear and cannot be characterised as following a fully consistent ideological programme.[19]

Nonetheless, it is entirely true that the end of the Western Han saw greater attention to the 'Mandate of Heaven', as well as greater concern about omens portending the downfall of the dynasty, which seemed increasingly possible given the ever more vicious political struggles that divided the Han court. Indeed, starting in the late Western Han, a widening variety of 'predictive writings' (*chenshu* 讖書) emerged that promised insight into the fate of the Han ruling household.[20] To take but one example, during the reign of Emperor Ai (Aidi 哀帝, r. 7–1 BCE), a man reported to the court that, on the basis of calendrical computations, the Han had entered a cyclical period of decline. By his estimation, it would therefore 'be appropriate for [the Han] to again receive the Mandate' (當再受命) after reforming the imperial calendar, the annual promulgation of which was one of the court's central responsibilities (*Hanshu* 11.340). Throughout the final years of Western Han, we see an increasing concern with such calendrical calculations and ever more promises to reveal the long-term cycles and 'regularities of Heaven' (*tian shu* 天數) that drove celestial and terrestrial changes, understood to be inextricably linked.[21] Such knowledge could be used to predict, understand, and perhaps even stave off or avoid political changes. It is no coincidence, then, that emperors and advisors during this period, especially Wang Mang 王莽 (46 BCE–23 CE), who founded the interregnum Xin ('New') dynasty, and Emperor Guangwu (Guangwudi 光武帝, r. 25–57 CE), the founding emperor of Eastern Han, all but openly solicited

---

[18] An early but still vitally important work that demonstrates this point is Loewe (1976). For an overview with relevant and more recent citations, see Nylan (2015).

[19] By illustrating the messy, unplanned nature of the decades-long process by which the imperial sacrifices were reformed, for instance, Tian (2015) shows in great detail that the old canard of a 'victory of Confucianism' at the Western Han court is not supported by the evidence.

[20] For overviews, each from different perspectives, see Espésset (2014) and Liu (2015).

[21] The articulation of such regularities is one of the main points of the 'Treatise on Pitchpipes and the Calendar' (Lü li zhi 律曆志) in the *Hanshu*. For discussions of calendrical systems, which became increasingly sophisticated starting in late Western Han, see Cullen (2001) and Liu (2015).

physical signs or 'tokens' (*fu* 符) that verified they had 'received the Mandate' (*shou ming*) and that Heaven's cycles favoured their political success.[22]

Indeed, often lost in discussions of the 'Mandate of Heaven' and the 'virtue' supposedly required by rulers who wished to maintain it is the fact that court debates and controversies in the late Western Han, Xin, and Eastern Han periods frequently focused on accurately identifying the cyclical patterns that determined political outcomes, irrespective of the achievements of the ruler. Perhaps the most famous articulation of this idea is an essay entitled *On the Mandate of Kings* (*Wang ming lun* 王命論), composed by an advisor and supporter of Emperor Guangwu as an attempt to justify the establishment of the Eastern Han and the renewal of the Liu 劉 ruling household after the Xin interregnum. Others have ably summed up the ideas in the essay (see Loewe 1994: 109–10), the importance of which can easily be overemphasised, as Grégoire Espésset (2014: 410 n. 77) has rightfully pointed out. Nonetheless, it is helpful to linger on it briefly, for the essay contrasts with the First Emperor of Qin's statement already discussed: *On The Mandate of Kings* roots the legitimacy of a ruling household not in 'the abilities of exceptional individuals', which as we saw above did play a partial role in the First Emperor's justification of his conquest, but rather in 'universal mechanisms' (Espésset 2014: 410; recalling Loewe's 'cosmic destiny'), including the Mandate of Heaven. At the same time, it still uses some of the same categories and concepts employed when the First Emperor changed imperial titles, showing that they were not entirely abandoned, but instead reformulated.

To take one specific example, *On the Mandate of Kings* pairs 'merit and charismatic power' (*gongde* 功德), concepts of rulership that figured in pre-imperial and Qin times, with the Heavenly cycles in vogue during the late Western Han, Xin, and Eastern Han. For instance, it reads:

> 帝王之祚，必有明聖顯懿之德，豐功厚利積絫之業，然後精誠通於神明，流澤加於生民，故能為鬼神所福饗，天下所歸往，未見運世無本，功德不紀，而得屈起在此位者也。

> It is the good fortune of lords and kings for it necessarily to be the case that upon possessing a charismatic power (*de*) of shining sagacity and exemplary worth, as well as a legacy of rich merit (*gong*) and generous benefits which have accumulated over time, their essence will truly penetrate to the gods of heaven and earth, and their flowing grace will extend to the people. They are thus able to be favored by the ghosts and spirits, and to receive the submission of All-Under-Heaven. Never has there been seen a person with no basis in the cycle of generations, or merit and charismatic power that has not been recorded, who has successfully risen up to this position.
>
> (*Hanshu* 100.4208)

---

[22] For a summary, see Espésset (2014: 396–401). The absorption of predictive writings, and related symbols and insignia (including 'tokens'), into Daoist religious practice during the late Eastern Han and post-Han periods receives thorough treatment in Seidel (1983).

The difference in tone and emphasis between this explanation of sovereign power and what we saw in the First Emperor's statement is striking. Of course, comparison of the two is no easy matter, since a representation of a court debate about imperial titles is hardly the same thing as an essay expressly written to formulate a theory of sovereignty supporting the newly established Eastern Han dynasty. Nonetheless, the passage contains nothing similar to the First Emperor's characterisation of his vanquished rivals as guilty parties whose infractions merited the punishment he so effectively meted out. Indeed, there is hardly anything about rivals here at all, aside from an implied contrast at the end between clearly lesser men who simply cannot compare to rulers whose obvious exemplarity and accumulated worth made their rise to the throne inevitable. As the essay famously goes on to state, the 'divine implements [of the ruler] (*shen qi* 神器) have their Mandate (*ming*) and cannot be sought by means of cleverness or strength' (*Hanshu* 100.4209). Attainment of the throne, the essay argues, is so predetermined by fate and timing that no amount of effort would seem to have any effect.

Nonetheless, the passage still uses the concepts of *de* ('charismatic power') and *gong* ('merit'), which as we saw above were so essential to rulership in the pre-imperial period, and which the First Emperor explicitly cited in order to justify his unification of the empire and creation of new imperial titles. The notion that the ruler rested at the centre of a network of exchange, reward, and punishment is thus very much present in *On the Mandate of Kings*. The difference, perhaps, is temporal: whereas the First Emperor's changed titles commemorated a specific, single act of meritorious achievement, *On the Mandate* emphasises the long-term accumulation or even the inheritance from previous generations of merit and charismatic power.[23] It is perhaps this temporal difference that has caused some scholars to continue translating *de* as 'virtue'. After all, statements such as this one from *On the Mandate* tend to depict the emperor not as an energetic agent directing the circulation of goods and favours, but rather as a quietist figure whose proper comportment ensures the continuation of the imperial inheritance (what, indeed, would it mean to inherit 'charisma'?).[24] Moreover, the two sources have rulers cashing in their merit for different things. The First Emperor's merit allows him to establish the empire and create a whole system of imperial nomenclature. *On the Mandate*, meanwhile, emphasises that accumulated merit and charisma allow the ruler to commune with the spirits. In both horizontal (i.e. temporal) and vertical (i.e. cosmic) terms, then, the essay transposes the same concepts of merit and charismatic power from the First Emperor's debate, as well as the power of the

---

[23] It is perhaps no coincidence, then, that starting in the 1st century BCE we see increasingly sophisticated attempts at the imperial court to establish timelines and calendars that extended back many centuries. See Cullen (2001).

[24] While a full discussion of the question must remain outside the bounds of this chapter, this possibility of cross-generational transfer and inheritance suggests that the concept of *de* confounds Weber's distinction between charismatic and traditional authority. Translating *de* as 'charismatic power' thus should not be understood as an endorsement of the Weberian typology.

ancestral spirits, into much broader frameworks justifying and explaining imperial rule. At the same time, instead of the tension seen in the debate between the individual merit of the First Emperor and the blessings of the ancestral deities, *On the Mandate of Kings* introduces a different tension between that which is determined by (a) stores of merit and charismatic power built up over time or inherited, and (b) celestial cycles.

New or old, individually achieved or accumulated over generations, rooted in ancestral spirits or Heavenly patterns: the fact that all of these different explanations drew upon the same language of *gong* ('merit') and *de* ('charismatic power' or 'virtue') suggests that Loewe's shift from 'material power' to 'cosmic destiny' over the course of the two Han dynasties was a change in degree, not necessarily in kind, even while rulers and officials endlessly debated how to resolve the tensions between different narratives of sovereignty. As a final illustration, let us turn to two statements written at roughly the same time, in the final decades of Eastern Han (again, after concerns about 'cosmic destiny' and the Mandate of Heaven had become more prominent). The first passage comes from *Solitary Decisions* (*Du duan* 獨斷; compiled *c.* 189 CE), a text composed by an official and advisor in the Eastern Han imperial capital that describes government titles and institutions. The passage in question sketches the origin of monarchical titles from high antiquity all the way to the Qin and finally to Han:

> 皇帝、皇、王后、帝皆君也。上古天子庖犧氏、神農氏稱皇。堯、舜稱帝。夏、殷、周稱王。秦承周末為漢驅除，自以德兼三皇，功包五帝，故并以為號。漢高祖受命，功德宜之，因而不改也。
>
> 'Emperor', 'August One', 'King', 'Queen', and 'Lord': these are all terms for rulers. In high antiquity the Sons of Heaven Baoxi and Shennong were called 'August' (*huang*). Later, Yao and Shun were called 'Lord'. During the Xia, Yin, and Zhou [rulers] were called 'King'. The Qin picked up the remnants of the Zhou and forged a path for the Han, believing on their own that their charismatic power (*de*) encompassed that of the 'Three Augusts' and their merit (*gong*) that of the 'Five Lords' (*wu di*). Therefore, they combined the two to make a title [i.e. *huangdi*, 'Emperor']. The founding emperor of the Han, Gaozu, received the Mandate. His merit and virtue matched that of the Qin, so he followed them and did not change [the title].
>
> (*Cai zhong lang wai ji juan si* 蔡中郎外集卷四, in Lau [1998], 79.14–16)

The author called upon his knowledge of the First Emperor's creation of titles in order to draw the Han into a larger narrative of sovereign power. Just like the First Emperor himself, at least as our source above represented him, the passage shows both change and continuity. The Qin sought to mark an achievement whose 'merit' (*gong*) and 'charismatic power' supposedly exceeded all the rulers of high antiquity.[25] The passage also emphasises, however, that all the different titles,

---

[25] Note that the story of the First Emperor's creation of the title 'Emperor' does mention the 'Three August Ones' (*san huang*) and the 'Five Lords' (*wu di*). However, in contrast to *Solitary Decisions*, it does not tightly link 'virtue' (*de*) to the 'Three August Ones' nor 'merit' to the 'Five Lords'.

including 'Emperor', referred to the same thing: a ruler. Moreover, the author clearly indicates the Han debt to Qin, since the latter 'picked up the remnants of the Zhou and forged a path for the Han', while noting that there was no need to create a new title for the ruler, since Han's *gong* and *de* were comparable to those of Qin. At the same time, by going out of its way to state that Gaozu, the founding emperor of Western Han, received the Mandate (without explaining precisely why or under what mechanism), the passage pointedly suggests that the Qin did not: note the implicit contrast between the Han's mandate and the Qin 'believing on their own' that they were comparable to match the legendary sage rulers. The author thus attempts to thread the needle between the new yet old nature of the Qin system, one to which the Han was entirely indebted, even while simultaneously emphasising that Han's receipt of the Mandate put it in a different and superior category that transcended the patterns established by the Qin.

An entirely different characterisation in form, substance, and tone can be found in a poem written by a late Eastern Han exegete and author, one who commanded some authority but still remained on the outskirts of power, his standing perhaps not helped by the severe tone evident in some of his extant writings.[26] These would include our chosen poem, entitled 'Rhapsody Criticising the World and Objecting to Evil' (Ci shi ji xie fu 刺世疾邪賦), which opens with a characterisation of different historical periods, starting with the same 'Five Lords' mentioned in the passage above from *Solitary Decisions*. Compared to *Solitary Decisions*, the 'Rhapsody' is entirely different, not only in its open condemnation of Qin and even Han, but also in its understanding of the process of historical change and the true, more nakedly materialistic interests that lay at the heart of imperial rule:

Ah, the Five Lords had different rites,	伊五帝之不同禮
And the Three Kings for their part had different music.	三王亦又不同樂
When regularities reach an apex they naturally transform,	數極自然變化
Wrong and right causes negate each other.	非是故相反駁
Virtuous (*de*) governing cannot save the world from foul chaos,	德政不能救世溷亂
So how could rewards and punishments possibly correct the times and clean the sullied?	賞罰豈足懲時清濁
The Springs and Autumns period saw the beginning of calamitous failure,	春秋時禍敗之始
While the Warring States period repeatedly increased its suffering and cruelty.	戰國愈復增其荼毒

---

[26] Cao Dehong described the author, Zhao Yi 趙壹 (*c.* 130–*c.* 185), as 'eccentric', and noted that the 'outcry against abuses and corruption at court' contained in his poem was 'rarely seen in the Han *fu* [rhapsodies]'. See 'Han *fu* 漢賦', in Keul *et al.* (2010: 325).

Qin and Han had no way to move beyond it,	秦漢無以相踰越
But in fact further increased its enmity and bitterness.	乃更加其怨酷
Rather than calculating a mandate to give life to the people,	寧計生民之命
They only profited themselves to their own satisfaction.	唯利己而自足

(*Hou Hanshu* 80b.2630)

Even if the 'Rhapsody' is extremely different in tone and style from the sources discussed earlier, it still played with the same concepts of sovereignty. Like *Solitary Decisions*, the poem presents both change and continuity, though in a rather idiosyncratic way, as demonstrated by the opening two couplets. The first emphasises change: the Five Lords and the Three Kings, mentioned in both the First Emperor's debate and *Solitary Decisions*, ruled one after the other in high antiquity, each with their own distinct set of institutions. The second couplet hints at a continuous cycle that might link all of these political transformations: note in particular the reference to 'regularities' (*shu* 數), which, as mentioned above, by late Western Han had become an important object of calculation by specialists at court who sought to link political changes to cosmic transformations.

The poem, however, goes on to disrupt any sense of cyclical change familiar from *On the Mandate of Kings*: transformation is fated, but it seems to rest entirely outside and separate from the world of *gong* and *de*. Indeed, the poem explicitly states that governance by virtue or charismatic power (*de*), rewards, and punishments are all hopelessly misguided strategies for righting the wrongs of the age, which in any case for the Qin and Han were already present during the pre-imperial era of the Springs and Autumns and Warring States periods. All we can do, it seems, is wait for the moment when things become so unbearably wrong that the course of history inevitably shifts. Contra the First Emperor's debate, *On the Mandate of Kings*, or *Solitary Decisions*, there is no salutary role for *gong* or *de* here, whether achieved suddenly or accumulated over time. Indeed, even human attempts to understand the rhythms of cosmic change come under criticism. Note here the sly reference at the poem's end to 'calculating' (*ji* 計), in this case a 'mandate for the people', rather than calculations of cosmic regularities that would foretell the downfall of the dynasty. As the poem's conclusion implies, the latter kind of reckonings add up to nothing more than self-serving figures cooked up for the benefit of rulers. Aside from naked self-interest, then, the poem seems to despair at finding any narrative that could once and for all ensure that everything made sense.

Surprisingly, then, at first glance the author appears to go one step further than Loewe's thesis, arguing that *all* rulers have only in fact been concerned with 'material wealth and strength', whether or not they tried to characterise their techniques of rulership as 'virtuous government', 'punishments and rewards', or the outcome of predetermined cycles. The question is not 'new or old?' or 'the outcome of merit or fated event?' but this: when will the cycle of selfish profit and material accumulation reach its logical endpoint, and begin again? The poem's extreme critique, surprisingly congruent with the most cynical assessments of our contemporary politics, thus verges on dismissing all discussion of the cosmic and moral dimensions of rule as little more than a façade designed to obscure base motivations. Verges on, that is, but does not quite take the final step. A plausible reading of the word 'regularities' in the poem would still retain that term's connection to cosmic cycles, but a sort of cycle that simply cannot be fathomed by human beings, who would be better served by focusing on more concrete and worldly measures for bettering human society. Even during the Han, such a position was not unprecedented and would have found prominent support in earlier philosophical writings.[27] Regardless, the fact that the poem was so radical, and the poet himself sidelined at court, shows that there were limits to this line of thinking. If the foregoing sources help us trace the emergence of ever more complex layers of narratives that attempted to break free from the contradictions and tensions necessarily built into claims of imperial power, the poem helps us understand that a full reduction of such claims to entirely human causes remained outside the realm of the possible.

Final remarks

The sources discussed in this chapter are selective but span a range of registers: a representation of a court debate; an essay on the nature of imperial sovereignty; a section from a sprawling treatise on government institutions; and a poem presenting a harsh assessment of rulers and their motivations. They hopefully manage to articulate the nature and persistence of debates about sovereign political power over the *longue durée* of early imperial Chinese history. It was not simply a question of the Mandate of Heaven, which does not have nearly as ancient an imprimatur as popular accounts would suggest. Nonetheless, it is undeniably true that the First Emperor of Qin and his successor rulers during the Western Han, Xin, and Eastern Han continued to work with old ideas, drawing on a vocabulary of rulership that extended back long before imperial unification. Over the course of the early imperial period, these concepts layered on top of each other, and throughout we see attempts to deal with the tensions and contradictions engendered by the process of creating new narratives of sovereign power.

Without recapitulating the entire discussion above, a review of some of our terms helps highlight some of these tensions. For instance, we saw the First Emperor emphasising the 'merit' (*gong*) that he had accumulated. This concept of merit came straight out of pre-imperial politics and government, in which merit was awarded by rulers to nobles for service rendered, often in the context of investiture ceremonies. The First Emperor, however, emphasised that his merit was so far

---

[27] The 'On Heaven' (*Tian lun* 天論) chapter of the *Xunzi* (*c*. 3rd century BCE) famously argued that the ways of Heaven, Earth, and Man were entirely separate, and that we waste far too much time fretting about cosmic portents and cycles, when in fact we should be devoting our energies to improving the lot of our fellow human beings.

beyond anything previously achieved or contemplated that an entirely new system of titles was required to mark the inauguration of a new system of government. It was effectively an attempt to break out of the political patterns and precedents that preceded him, even if he nonetheless recognised the enduring power of the deities housed in his ancestral temple. When we move to *On the Mandate of Kings*, written almost 250 years after the First Emperor assumed the imperial throne, 'merit' still makes an appearance. However, it is not a merit achieved by an individual ruler, but rather a merit that had been inherited over time, perhaps even from the ancestors. In this sense, *On the Mandate of Kings* attempts to resolve the contradiction introduced by the First Emperor's debate, since it blurs the line between merit achieved individually and merit passed down through the generations.

A similar shift can be seen in treatments of 'charismatic power' (*de*): in the pre-imperial world, it was tightly enmeshed in the politics of gift-giving and reciprocity that were the hallmark of the investiture ceremonies described above. The pre-imperial ruler's 'charismatic power', achieved by the generous dispensation of gifts in return for service rendered, paired with his ability to inflict punishments on wrongdoers. The First Emperor explicitly cited this punishment–reward mode of rulership when he called for the debate on titles, emphasising that his rivals deserved to be punished. *On the Mandate of Kings*, however, casts 'charismatic power' as a more abstracted quality that is inherited, and certainly has nothing to do with exerting strength or displaying largesse; perhaps it is this changed sense of *de* that has prompted so many scholars to translate the word as 'virtue'. Regardless, in *On the Mandate* the possession of *gong* and *de* alike are more a matter of fate and timing.

This emphasis on timing and fate only became more pronounced over the course of the late Western Han, Xin, and Eastern Han period, with the emergence of ever more complex schemes for calculating the 'regularities' (*shu*) that governed the rise and fall of dynasties, and thus by extension the receipt of the Mandate of Heaven. Indeed, it was the imbrication of this discussion of 'regularities' onto understandings of the 'Mandate' that helped shift the pre-imperial concept of 'mandates' from rulers to a cosmic sphere, with attempts to insert receipt and loss of the mandate into calculable cosmic cycles. Even a source such as *Solitary Decisions*, which did not engage in such calculations, still could not help but note that while the Han had received the Mandate, the Qin had acted presumptuously in assuming 'on its own' that it had attained the necessary conditions to found the empire. Even if the text did not interrogate the nature of the Mandate of Heaven itself, it did thereby imply that Han's receipt of the Mandate relied upon forces over which it did not have complete control. The final poem, meanwhile, while categorically rejecting the whole collection of concepts discussed above as so much window-dressing to obscure more base motivations, still left ambiguous the role of 'regularities' in dictating cycles of political change. In effect, the poem suggested that a world of cycles might determine patterns of transformation, but that such a world was beyond the ken of humankind.

In leaving this possibility open, even while yanking us out of the clouds and back into the world of material goods and desires, the poem opens up broader questions about the nature of sovereignty and its relationship to sacred and transcendental powers. Theorists have consistently argued, despite the ever-growing collection of sovereignties (legal, economic, contingent, 'mobile', and so forth) that populate academic studies, that all discussions of 'sovereignty' are necessarily based in Christian ideas, particularly a divine *creation ex nihilo* (creation out of nothing).[28] As Robert Yelle has explored in some detail, almost all of the problems and contradictions of sovereignty (e.g. its dialectical relationship to a legal order) can be traced to long-standing debates in Christian theology. At the same time, historical and anthropological evidence suggests that a desire to create an order founded on systems of exchange and value unsullied by established systems of monetary exchange, legal frameworks, political conventions, and other mundane considerations is fundamental to almost all religious movements and also many claims of political power (Yelle 2019). While the chaos and violence of states of exception perhaps lie at the foundation of many religions and polities, a variety of ritual techniques (sacrifice, Jubilee debt forgiveness, etc.) from many different times and spaces, though by no means foolproof, were designed to transpose this violence into terms and realms that were potentially less destructive. In Yelle's (2019: 8) words, then, the work of the 'sacred' constituted 'a dynamic interplay between a normative order and a drive to go beyond that order, either to escape or legitimate it'. Sovereign claims, whether we cast them in political or religious terms, are precisely this move between different orders, and we saw that repeatedly in the semantic shifts occurring in the sources discussed above, though perhaps most dramatically in the final poem's insistence that we redirect our attention away from the cosmos and back to the human world.[29]

What Yelle does not explore, however, is the fact that claims of sovereignty in any given culture never exist in a historical vacuum. Rather, they rest alongside each other, often rather uncomfortably; prior moves from one sphere to another never go unnoticed in later times, which struggle to explain past failures and anticipate future challenges. The narratives examined in this chapter illustrate such tensions. Even though they continued to advance claims that something 'new' was being established (note that the Xin Dynasty of Wang Mang literally means 'New Dynasty'), the old was never pushed too far in the background. The Qin, Western Han, Xin, and Eastern Han rulers presented rather different justifications for their rule, but the questions they grappled with did not change significantly. Moreover, despite their different answers and rhetorical emphases, when responding to the

---

[28] Carl Schmitt, of course, is the most prominent theorist to this effect, and debates about his ideas had a direct effect on work of Ernest Kantorowicz (see Geréby 2004). For general discussions, see Kahn (2011) and also Goldstone (2014), who evinces some exhaustion on the entire topic.

[29] For a helpful comparison, see Jan Assmann's (2008: 78–83) discussion of 'semantic transpositions' in ancient Egypt between the 'sociopolitical' and 'divine' spheres.

question of 'new or old?', rulers and advisors at the courts of the early Chinese empires usually ended up saying: a little bit of both.

The answer should sound familiar to citizens of modern nations. For instance, the United States (as a citizen and resident, my selection is admittedly not random) continually proclaims its newness with catchphrases like 'the American experiment'; it also continually calls upon its old myths, its quasi-deified (or for some strains of American Christianity, actually deified) Founding Fathers. The significance of the evidence and texts assembled above, then, is not so much that they reflect dynamics of sovereignty that radically contrast with those of the Christian (even if 'secular') west, though it is true that Chinese rulership does look different and calls upon different kinds of metahuman powers. Rather, the foregoing discussion helps illustrate that the old stories never entirely go away, even when new theories and answers layer on top of them. The recombination of narratives, the calling upon of old stories towards new purposes, is an abiding feature of all stories of sovereign power. It is this ongoing work of recombination, the continuing desire to somehow make it all make sense, that lies at the heart of constructing durable political institutions.

References

Assmann, J. (2008), *Of God and Gods: Egypt, Israel, and the Rise of Monotheism* (Madison, University of Wisconsin Press).
Benite, Z.B., Geroulanos, S. & Jerr, N. (2017), 'Editors' Introduction', in Z.B. Benite, S. Geroulanos & N. Jerr (eds), *The Scaffolding of Sovereignty: Global and Aesthetic Perspectives on the History of a Concept* (New York, Columbia University Press), 18–80.
Cheng, A. (2011), 'Virtue and Politics: Some Conceptions of Sovereignty in Ancient China', *Journal of Chinese Philosophy*, 38: 133–45.
Cook, C. (1997), 'Wealth and the Western Zhou', *Bulletin of the School of Oriental and African Studies*, 60.2: 123–94.
Cullen, C. (2001), 'The Birthday of the Old Man of Jiang County and Other Puzzles: Work in Progress on Liu Xin's "Canon of the Ages"', *Asia Major* (third series), 14.2: 27–60.
Dirlik, A. (2012), 'The Idea of a "Chinese Model": A Critical Discussion', *China Information*, 26.3: 278–301.
Dixon, E. (2003), 'Book of Days', *American Scholar*, 72.1: 17–32.
Espésset, G. (2014), 'Epiphanies of Sovereignty and the Rite of Jade Disc Immersion in Weft Narratives', *Early China*, 37: 393–443.
Fairbank, J.K. (2006), *China: A New History*, 2nd enlarged edn (Cambridge MA, Belknap Press).
Fingarette, H. (1972), *Confucius: The Secular as Sacred* (San Francisco, HarperCollins).
Geréby, G. (2004), 'Carl Schmitt and Erik Peterson on the Problem of Political Theology: A Footnote to Kantorowicz', in A. Al-Azmeh & J.M. Bak (eds), *Monotheistic Kingship: The Medieval Variants* (Budapest, Central European University Press), 31–88.
Goldstone, B. (2014), 'Life after Sovereignty', *History of the Present*, 4.1: 97–113.
Graeber, D. and Sahlins, M. (2017), *On Kings* (Chicago, Hau Books).
Hanshu 漢書. Compiled by Ban Gu 班固 32–92, Ban Zhao 班昭 45–ca. 116, *et al.* 12 vols. All refs to the punctuated edition. Edited by Yan Shigu 顏師古 (Beijing, Zhonghua shuju, 1962).

Hou Hanshu 後漢書. Compiled by Fan Ye 班固 32–92, 12 vols. All refs to the punctuated edition (Beijing, Zhonghua shuju, 1965).

Hughes, A. (2021), *Worldly Saviors and Imperial Authority in Medieval Chinese Buddhism* (Honololu, University of Hawaii Press).

Kahn, P. (2011), *Political Theology: Four New Chapters on the Concept of Sovereignty* (New York, Columbia University Press).

Kalmo, H. and Skinner, Q. (eds) (2010), *Sovereignty in Fragments: The Past, Present, and Future of a Contested Concept* (Cambridge, Cambridge University Press).

Kane, V.C. (1982–3), 'Aspects of Western Chou Appointment Inscriptions: The Charge, the Gifts, and the Response', *Early China*, 8: 14–23.

Kern, M. (2009), 'Bronze Inscriptions, the *Shijing* and the *Shangshu*: The Evolution of the Ancestral Sacrifice during the Western Zhou', in J. Lagerwey and M. Kalinowski (eds), *Early Chinese Religion, Part One: Shang through Han (1250 BC–220 AD)* (Leiden, Brill), 143–201.

Keul, I., Taiping Chang, & Knechtges, D. (2010), *Ancient and Medieval Chinese Literature: A Reference Guide, Part One* (Leiden, Brill).

Lau, D.C. (ed.) (1998), *Concordances to the Caizhong langji and Zhongjing* (Hong Kong, The Commercial Press).

Liu, T. (2015), 'Calendrical Computation Numbers and Han Dynasty Politics: A Study of Gu Yong's Three Troubles Theory', in M. Nylan and G. Vankeerberghen (eds), *Chang'an 26 BCE: An Augustan Age in China* (Seattle, University of Washington Press), 298–322.

Loewe, M. (1976), *Crisis and Conflict in Han China* (London, Allen & Unwin).

Loewe, M. (1994), 'The Authority of the Emperors of Ch'in and Han', in *Divination, Mythology, and Monarchy in Han China* (Cambridge, Cambridge University Press), 85–111.

Nivison, D. (1978–9), 'Royal "Virtue" in Shang Oracle Inscriptions', *Early China*, 4: 52–5.

Nylan, M. (2015), 'Introduction', in M. Nylan and G. Vankeerberghen (eds), *Chang'an 26 BCE: An Augustan Age in China* (Seattle: University of Washington Press), 3–52.

Pines, Y. (2017), 'Heaven, the Monarch, the People, and the Intellectuals in Traditional China', in Z.B. Benite, S. Geroulanos, & N. Jerr (eds), *The Scaffolding of Sovereignty: Global and Aesthetic Perspectives on the History of a Concept* (New York, Columbia University Press), 141–74.

Pines, Y., Von Falkenhausen, L., Shelach, G., & Yates, R.D.S. (eds) (2014), *Birth of an Empire: The State of Qin Revisited* (Berkeley, University of California Press).

Schaberg, D. (2005), 'Command and the Content of Tradition', in C. Lupke (ed.), *The Magnitude of Ming: Command, Allotment, and Fate in Chinese Culture* (Honolulu, University of Hawaii Press), 23–48.

Seidel, A. (1983), 'Imperial Treasures and Taoist Sacraments: Taoist Roots in the Apocrypha', in M. Strickmann (ed.), *Tantric and Taoist Studies in Honour of R.A. Stein*, ii (Brussels: Institut belge des Hautes Études Chinoises), 291–371.

Shiji 史記. Compiled by Sima Qian 司馬遷 et al. 12 vols. All refs to the punctuated edition (Beijing, Zhonghua shuju, 1972).

Sterckx, R. (2009), 'The Economics of Religion in Warring States and Early Imperial China', in J. Lagerwey and M. Kalinowski (eds), *Early Chinese Religion, Part One: Shang through Han (1250 BC–220 AD)* (Leiden, Brill), 839–80.

Tian, T. (2015), 'The Suburban Sacrifice Reforms and the Evolution of the Imperial Sacrifices', in M. Nylan and G. Vankeerberghen (eds), *Chang'an 26 BCE: An Augustan Age in China* (Seattle, University of Washington Press), 263–92.

Wang, B. (ed.) (2017), *Chinese Visions of World Order: Tianxia, Culture, and World Politics* (Durham NC, Duke University Press).

Xunzi jian shi 荀子簡釋, edited by Liang Qixiong 梁啟雄 (Beijing, Zhonghua Shuju, 1983).

Yelle, R. (2019), *Sovereignty and the Sacred: Secularism and the Political Economy of Religion* (Chicago, University of Chicago Press).

Part II

Imperial Sovereignty

Introduction

As has been noted, for instance by Lundgreen in Chapter 1, the established view of sovereignty emerges from an arc of thought from Bodin via Hobbes to Locke and Rousseau, and whilst it can be presented as a single and unitary story, it is far more complex, and we would argue reflects the contingent realities of war and internal strife. What sovereignty does do, however, is to provide a kind of charter for power and its exercise over others, and it does so especially effectively in the context of imperialism.

The two chapters in this section introduce two very different case studies in the global application of locally constructed ideological models. Cruickshank, Evans, Genovese, McKinnon, and McVeigh look at how the denial of Indigenous sovereignty in Australia was predicated on the exaltation of a legal tradition. Similar stories could be told elsewhere, for instance in New Zealand; local knowledge and traditions, often of great historical depth, were characterised as of no value or interest because they did not conform to pre-existing views of what constituted political thought and legal title. What follows is in some ways equally troubling; even in attempts to find redress, the Indigenous claims have to be framed within the normative context of a western legal tradition. There is a sort of 'knowledge sovereignty' here at work, in which what is precisely at stake is whose knowledge system is predominant. At the same time, the authors argue for a reorientation of non-Indigenous scholarship to rethink who the 'law people' are. When we come to look again at the Australian case in Isayev's reflections on contemporary arguments of over asylum, we will see again that the notion of territory can be deployed as a definitional tool to enshrine one set of values over another.

Legg's work on India has parallels in terms of the imposition of models of thought. Here, sovereignty is granted – acquired – but in such a way as to further the aims of the dominant power. Sovereignty is by no means absolute; rather it is the gift of a power that used it to reinforce its dominance. Thus sovereignty in India becomes almost self-negating; and that is part of the subaltern experience, a fractioned and divided experience which both legally and via the means of spectacle (a profoundly biopolitical exercise) is one of subordination.

The emergence of ways of granting but not granting sovereignty through the exercise of imperial power, underwritten by western hierarchies of thought and dominance, is now increasingly seen through a postcolonial lens. But deep in the exercise of these mindgames is a recognition that sovereignty is far from unitary. Rather it is a technique of domination. This section offers a glimpse of the complexity of imperial sovereignty in the 19th and early 20th centuries, before the next section brings this into the contemporary world.

6

Thinking with Sovereignty in Australia

JOANNA CRUICKSHANK, JULIE EVANS, ANN GENOVESE,
CRYSTAL MCKINNON, AND SHAUN MCVEIGH

> While the European idea of sovereignty was a concept alien to Nungas, the Europeans failed to comprehend or accept that First Nations' Sovereignty even existed. This is the unfinished business ... that must be addressed before we can consider entering into a dialogue.
> Irene Watson, Tanganekald, Meintagk and Boandik jurisprudent (2014: 152)

THIS CHAPTER IS written to explain something of the history of sovereignty as a contested idea and experience in Australia. It is also written, as part of this collection, as a demonstration of a particular Australian scholarly tradition. Scholarship in this tradition seeks to decentre the European entry points for writing about sovereignty (statecraft, moral imperative, and critique). Instead, it makes central the contests of sovereignty in Australia. This includes Indigenous ways of knowing and speaking about Indigenous and non-Indigenous sovereignty. These 'ways' (Behrendt 2003; Black 2010; McMillan 2014; Watson 2014, 2017) are about conducts of lawful relations between peoples, organised around obligations of rule, role, and designated responsibilities to land. Beginning this chapter with an acknowledgement of these guides is important for two reasons. It marks an intention to describe how laws and histories that think with sovereignty encounter each other in place (in and on country), and how sovereign thinking grounds practices in the past and about the future that are relevant to contemporary Australian life. It also guides the chapter's framing argument, that non-Indigenous scholars (in Australia) have obligations to locate commensurate political and jurisprudential thinking about rule, role, responsibility in their own traditions, and to identify how these can be drawn from as resources. We understand this task as both jurisprudential and historical. We write this chapter as scholars trained in the academic disciplines of law (McVeigh, Genovese) and/or history (Cruickshank, Evans, Genovese, McKinnon). We also write from our standpoints as Yamatji (McKinnon) and non-Indigenous (Cruickshank, Evans, Genovese, McVeigh) people living on Kulin Nation lands. As such, beginning with this acknowledgement is not offered as a redemptive act for Anglo-Australian, European, British, and international law and statecraft, or a form of instruction. Rather, it is a way to make plain that any writing about non-Indigenous sovereignty, in our case in Australia, is written in the shadow and presence of Indigenous sovereignty, where there are then continuing contests and negotiations of Indigenous and non-Indigenous sovereignty that require acknowledgement and attention in form as well as content.

At the time of writing – 2021 – these contests are institutionally circumscribed by the Australian state, in terms of political movements for constitutional recognition of Indigenous Australians as First Nations peoples, and a legislatively embedded voice for Indigenous nations in representative government. These contests are also found in the many formulations of land rights, agreements, and treaties between Indigenous and non-Indigenous polities.[1] Indigenous sovereignty and self-determination are both present, and disavowed or avoided, by the representative bodies of the state in each frame of these contests (Moreton-Robinson 2020). For many, such a situation is characteristic of a sovereignty 'impasse' (Gover 2011), in which the Australian state can neither recognise nor completely deny Indigenous sovereignty. This might be recast as a continuing contest, based on understanding (and misunderstanding) of sovereignty as rulership, relationship, and responsibility.

In the Australian context, then, any discussion of non-Indigenous sovereignty has to offer accounts of Indigenous and non-Indigenous sovereignties and relations between them. Those who talk of non-Indigenous sovereignty must address two concerns: first, the internal formation of sovereign authority and its relation to tradition; and second, relations between sovereigns (Falk & Martin 2020). As noted, we address these concerns through the histories and jurisprudence of rulership, relationship, and responsibility from a located perspective, and a self-consciousness about placement, to describe some practices of sovereignty that have shaped, and shape, thinking with sovereignty in Australia. Describing these practices to make them visible (rather than only positioning them as a basis for critique) matters. This is because the continual disavowal of Indigenous sovereignty by the Australian state is oppressive. Furthermore, it limits the understanding of the Australian state, and non-Indigenous Australians, as to what it means to take responsibility for the relations between peoples and laws, as it does not pay close enough attention to the specific histories of sovereign encounters in particular (Indigenous) nations and places.

This chapter, then, presents a case for writing about sovereignty that pays attention to joining the legal, archival, and experiential details of those located contests and meetings. This is an exercise of historiography and jurisprudence that makes visible and meaningful the writing about contest and lived relations of sovereignty in time and place. This activity we describe as 'thinking with sovereignty …', to address how contemporary accounts of Indigenous and non-Indigenous

---

[1] *Agreements, Treaties and Negotiated Settlements* website, www.atns.net.au.

sovereignty are crafted. A key aspect of that contemporary project, which we would suggest is methodological as well as political, is to pay close attention to how any account of contemporary lawful and sovereign relations is already diverse and carries weight and experience. We understand this 'thinking with' as a matter of ethos or orientation, as much as a method for encompassing the practical conduct of sovereign relations (Genovese 2013).

This chapter offers examples of the historiographic and jurisprudential engagement of 'thinking with sovereignty' and writing about 'sovereign relationships'. In offering a series of examples, in and over time, we link thinking with sovereignty to the practice of lawful and lawless relations between Indigenous and non-Indigenous peoples.

In our first section, we redescribe the traditional, legal language of sovereignty by animating concerns of rulership, relationship, and responsibility in Australia across different traditions of sovereignty writing. This is to show patterns and resources in how sovereign relations are connected. By engaging in redescription as technique, the argument in this section is not to assert the political truth of sovereignty (although this can also be done), but to delineate how sovereign thinking organises practices. The short report we offer on some traditions of sovereign writing draws out how historians and legal scholars and practitioners ('law people') work with plural concepts of sovereignty in ways that make the shadow of contemporary contests visible. The challenge for non-Indigenous scholars' own practice, we suggest, is to be conscious of how the writing we do and writing we use is already part of a constant re-working of a conflict. The second and third sections of the chapter address these (and other) resources for 'thinking with sovereignty' in relation to historic and contemporary examples. Our second example addresses archival resources for considering the scope and scale of sovereign conduct. What we follow is the conduct of Kulin Nation peoples in the context of settler invasion in the colony (later state) of Victoria. We identify the continuing insistence of Kulin Nation peoples on lawful conduct in relating to the invaders from the 1850s, focusing particularly on an 1881 government inquiry into the management of Coranderrk Reserve, where many Kulin Nations people had come to live. In the third and fourth sections, we draw these together, and examine contemporary discussions about treaty and citizenship status – in order to address the responsibilities of contemporary patterns of sovereign relations.

Together, these examples introduce a protocol: to the effect that any account of non-Indigenous sovereignty must include an account of sovereign relations. For us, that means giving accounts of the quality of relations of law, to respond to the question of how to make a point of engagements and comparison of sovereignties. We argue that what can be gained in attending to the forms and quality of relationship between 'peoples of law' is a public acknowledgement of how such practices themselves both authorise lawful relations and provide a way of exercising (and contesting) authority.

In giving our examples, we do not (as noted) engage with some of the prominent discourses of sovereignty in political science, and political and legal theory. We have limited our engagement here to formulations of historians and jurisprudents writing within the university. As a consequence, we do not offer a legitimation of the exercise of sovereignty as a form of public authority, or a direct critique of it. We take it as understood that the British Imperial and colonial relations and their Australian inheritance have been largely lawless in relation to Indigenous peoples and law. (In a strong sense this continues to be shaped by the legal forms and historical practice of colonial engagement.) It is also the case that Indigenous law and life can be lived without formulation in terms of a state-directed understanding of authority and law or life (Graham 2008; Black 2010; Moreton-Robinson 2016; Watego 2021).

Writing about sovereignty/sovereign relations

In this section we examine how history writing and jurisprudence writing are bound into concerns of law and of rightful or lawful relationship. The jurisprudence writing we consider below relates to British, international, and Indigenous sovereignty, to draw out the sense in which 'thinking with' sovereign relations is (at least) two-sided, and continuous. Our presentation here is schematic in the sense that it is designed to do no more than offer a reminder of the entwining of the different roles of historians and legal scholars and of the ways in which history writing draws on legal thought and theory to shape its subject, as well as, more obviously, legal thought draws on assumptions about history and history writing.

British colonial sovereignty

The claim of sovereignty – as something like the authority (and the right) to rule through arms and law – has been a central topic of government and legal scholarship. Within legal thought, such assertions of sovereignty have long been engaged within national and international arrangements. Our first comment is to note that the ways in which sovereignty and rulership (or governorship) are understood shape how they are written about by both historians and jurists.

If, for a moment, the key formulations of British, and then Australian, sovereignty are treated as 'projects', then it is possible to see that the contests and arguments about sovereignty form a part of British colonial administrative, and then Australian, state formation projects. The intellectual resources used in British colonisation were varied. For jurists, these included the political writings of 17th-century civil (state) jurists such as Samuel Pufendorf, Jean Bodin, and Thomas Hobbes (Tuck 2016: 63–120) as well as the institutional writings of leading jurists such as William Blackstone. The writings of civil jurisprudence equate political and legal sovereignty with a civil sovereign that should be distinguished from government, administration, and adjudication. Ideologically, at least, these formulations were central to the elaboration of the project of European state formation. This project has often been given emblematic form in the Treaty of Westphalia (1648) (Cutler 2001). This tradition of sovereign thinking was also taken up by English jurists such as William Blackstone and John Austin (Fitzmaurice 2014: 229–39).

In the British Empire, colonial enterprises proceeded juridically, at least, through customary consent and occupation (possession) – even if relations of government were by no means regular (or well-ordered) (Benton & Ford 2016: 78–80). The important practical and conceptual distinctions of authority were shaped between *potestas* and *violentia* (right and might). Within juristic and political literatures, the alignment of political right and force became entwined with the central formulations of sovereignty as absolute, or ultimate, authority. The law that arrived alongside the First Fleet with Captain Philip in 1788 was British Imperial law, penal law and common law, and the assertion and assumption of sovereignty presented by the Crown was British sovereignty.

Presented as a matter of sovereign relations between non-Indigenous and Indigenous peoples, the characterisation of sovereignty as absolute is most easily understood from within the administrative offices of Imperial institutions (Attwood 2020. In this context, absolute sovereignty of the jurists finds expression in the disposition of the practices of government, and the understanding that the colonisation of the peoples and land of Australia was done with little acknowledgement of Indigenous peoples, as we will describe in this chapter relation to the colony of Victoria).

Within the colonies, and as part of a practice of settlement, sovereignty was understood in terms of government and jurisdiction (Dorsett 2019). Prior to the 1830s, the claim of sovereignty over a large proportion of the east of Australia was shaped by the sense that the Crown had little administrative or military control over that area. Authority and jurisdiction rested more on personal status than the administration of a defined body of land and the government of a population. The expression of sovereignty in law was shaped through personal status – the common law applied to settlers because of their status as subjects. The reasons it might not apply to Indigenous Australians was also because of status. It was not until the *Murrell* case that Aborigines were deemed subjects of British colonial law because of their presence in British territory (*R v Murrell and Bummaree* (1836) 1 Legge 72; Dorsett & McVeigh 2012: 100–4). However, until the 1860s it was not uncommon in proceedings involving Aboriginal defendants to contest the jurisdiction of the court and effectively claim that another law applied.

Despite many changes in the political and juridical understanding of relations between Indigenous and non-Indigenous people in Australia, the assertion of sovereignty as shaped by territorial jurisdiction remains largely unchanged. Even the seminal case of *Mabo v State of Queensland (No 2)* (1992) 175 CLR 1, in which the High Court of Australia judicially recognised traditional laws acknowledged and customs observed by the Indigenous peoples of a territory and the existence of

Aboriginal and Torres Straits Islander law, traditions still maintained an account of absolute sovereignty and territorial jurisdiction. The conceptions of absolute sovereignty upheld by the High Court establish a significant impasse to thinking with sovereignty (Mansell 2016). While this situation is a common legacy of the British colonial system, each state has its own particular formulation.

For groups of jurists and historians, the complexity of asserting sovereign relations has been shaped by accounts of absolute sovereignty and territorial jurisdiction and by genres of history writing that stay close to the archival sources of the offices of the state (Attwood 2020). If we pluralise these sources and address the relations of peoples and laws, British and now Australian sovereignty take on a different inflection.

International

'Westphalian' accounts of absolute sovereignty were not the only accounts of sovereignty and the law of nations that circulated in 18th-century Europe. They displaced nominally older accounts of civil authority associated with Aristotelian thinking. Where juristic accounts of sovereignty, influenced by Bodin and Hobbes, emphasise the relation between sovereignty and government, Hugo Grotius, for example, emphasised the way that sovereignty embraced both legislative (constitutional) and deliberative (magisterial and judicial) tasks (Brett 2020). In *The Law of War and Peace*, Grotius drew attention to the way that sovereignty should be understood as an attribute of an office fulfilled by appropriate public conduct (*materia moralis*) (Brett 2020: 623). The division of the tasks of the sovereign into offices (functions or roles) also allowed for the division of sovereignty. Such formulations and their reiteration were established in the treaties of the Law of Nations. In this account, rather than a supreme point of political power, civil power is viewed as a moral faculty that governs a political community. This had three aspects: government of the polity; deliberation on common affairs; and the responsibility for public justice. In Brett's reading of Grotius, one that we follow here, this formulation provides a way of drawing out a moral science of practical reasoning that is not identical to thinking of sovereignty as *summa potestas* (highest authority) or *imperium* (empire, sovereignty). Grotius directs attention to ways of thinking across state and national regimes, one that provides a way of negotiating aspects of the interlocking polities of 17th-century Europe. In particular, it allowed Grotius to consider mixed or divided sovereignty as the proper subject of a moral jurisprudence (Brett 2020: 642). For historians of early modern Europe, such as Lauren Benton (2010), Grotius' normative theory also provides a useful description of 'inter-political' relations. It also provides the register of authority of the analysis of the international law of occupation and the analysis of the British colonisation of Australia, whether it be by conquest, settlement or cessation (Simpson 1993). The plural discourses of sovereignty that circulated in the 17th and 18th centuries serve as a reminder that there were, and still are, multiple ways of engaging sovereignty from the standpoint of moral science and international law (Reynolds 2021).

We would identify three points of engagement that currently resonate in contemporary Australian legal thought. The first observation is that the kind of moral science and legal thought promoted by Grotius can render quite different accounts of the significance of domestic sovereignty. While emphasising relations between polities as the proper place for thinking of sovereignty and peace, it treats sovereignty as an incidence of the law of nations (Brett 2020: 622; Eslava and Pahuja 2020). Second, Grotius' way of elaborating an international domain shaped by a moral jurisprudence (which addresses offices, statuses, duties, rights, powers, and so forth) has allowed jurists and historians to elaborate relations between different forms of polities. Indigenous peoples and nations have long used international institutions to press claims for sovereignty and political, cultural, and economic rights (de Costa 2006). The United Nations Declaration of the Rights of Indigenous Peoples is now the primary international document framing the status of Indigenous peoples.[2] It develops an extensive statement of rights, protections, and aspirations of Indigenous peoples, and the right to self-determination is framed in distinction to the duties and rights of sovereign states.

Third, whilst not using the language of sovereignty, the Declaration does address many of the incidents of sovereignty in the form of rulership and self-determination, administration and adjudication, and the maintenance of lawful relations to land and culture. It is this understanding of self-determination – held by culture and governance – that established the repertoire of rights which provides the public language of many contemporary debates about Indigenous sovereignty in the United Nations and in Australia. However, as Ravi de Costa has made clear, alongside the rights of Indigenous peoples within the domains of international law, there are also many forms of Indigenous transnationalism and internationalism where relations between nations are related through Indigenous law and life (de Costa 2006; McMillan & Rigney 2016). In these domains, Australian sovereignty, if it is acknowledged, is patterned into forms of Indigenous law, knowledge, and sovereignty (Borrows 2010).

Indigenous sovereignties

In taking up the modern idiom of sovereignty, Indigenous people have emphasised that their sovereignty must be understood in radically different ways from western models. Many Indigenous scholars have articulated the ways that Indigenous sovereignty is distinctly different to non-Indigenous sovereignty. One of the key ways is that it is first derived from land and Country. Kombumerri/Munaljahlai scholar

---

[2] See www.un.org/development/desa/indigenouspeoples/declaration-on-the-rights-of-indigenous-peoples.html.

Christine Black (2010) has argued that Aboriginal law derives not from Aboriginal culture or people, but from the land itself. Yamatji scholar Crystal McKinnon (2018: 9) writes that:

> Indigenous sovereignty ... is about relationships to family, to ancestors and to kin. It is about the land, territory and country. It is about our rights and our obligations to each other. It is about our knowledges and our understandings of ourselves and of others. It is about our spiritual and religious beliefs and our creators. It is also about our place within our country, our stars and our worlds. It encompasses everything about who we are as Indigenous people. It is the past, the present and Indigenous futures.

Goenpul theorist Aileen Moreton-Robinson (2016) defined Aboriginal sovereignty as:

> being connected, what it means to have bloodline to Country – sharing the life force with the ancestors that created our lands. That life force is in every Aboriginal person. It's in the land, of the land, and cannot be killed, even if they annihilated us tomorrow, they cannot kill our sovereignty. That is why it can never be ceded.

Here, Moreton-Robinson describes a sovereignty that is very different from non-Indigenous conceptions of sovereignty; it is something that has always existed and will always exist. It derives from traditions much older and longer than non-Indigenous sovereignty, and each Indigenous nation has its own sovereignty through peoples' bloodlines to that country, waters, and territory. Palyku scholar Ambellin Kwaymullina (2020: 2) writes that:

> There is not one Indigenous sovereignty
>
> there are many
>
> all the Aboriginal and Torres Strait Islander nations
>
> are sovereign in their homelands.

The plurality of Indigenous sovereignties means that generalisations about Indigenous sovereignty should be avoided. However, Indigenous scholars have identified a number of elements that are common to Indigenous sovereignties. Moreton-Robinson (2020: 2) writes that 'Our sovereignty is embodied, it is ontological (our being) and epistemological (our way of knowing), and it is grounded within complex relations derived from the intersubstantiation of ancestral beings, humans and land.'

Wiradjuri academic Wendy Brady (2020: 143) articulates the expression of this interdependent relationship in the exercise of authority and models of governance:

> The sovereign Indigenous nation is formed through the ancestral and communal relationship. Unlike the sovereign of the European nation, authority does not reside in one figurehead and is not exercised downwards through layers of ever-declining levels of power. In the Indigenous nation, each individual is part of the fabric of both authority and power that is interdependent on the other. Although elders retain authority and the administration of law, it is a communal exercise, carried by those who are designated to carry particular forms of authority derived from ancestral and kinship relationships. There is a common engagement in the governance of the sovereign nation.

Speaking of the contemporary context, Koori scholar Tony Birch (2020: 107) expands Brady's argument, writing that 'sovereignty within Indigenous communities ... is maintained through pre-existing, pre-European models of governance. ... It is also enacted in the daily struggles of Indigenous people striving to maintain autonomous lifestyles'.

Indigenous people, each from distinct Indigenous nations, practice and live within their laws, which are derived from each nation's sovereignty. Consequently, when we speak of lawful relations, this must first take into account different Indigenous nations, which have been conducting themselves lawfully and meeting lawfully with each other long before they encountered non-Indigenous peoples. Indigenous nations also have histories of lawful relations with non-Indigenous peoples prior to European invasion, such as long-standing trading relations with neighbouring peoples (Macknight 1976).

With regards to non-Indigenous and Indigenous lawful relations, Indigenous legal scholars and law experts have together led much of the theorising about ways that non-Indigenous legal systems can recognise Indigenous sovereignty, and act in relation to that knowledge. Kamillaroi scholar Larissa Behrendt describes sovereignty as 'a set of political, economic, social and cultural aspirations that are achievable, that fit well within our current understanding of basic human rights'. She has also written that

> the recognition of sovereignty is a device by which other rights can be achieved. Rather than being the aim of political advocacy, it is a starting point for recognition of rights and inclusion in democratic processes. It is seen as a footing, a recognition, from which to demand those rights and transference of power from the Australian state, not a footing from which to separate from it.
>
> (Behrendt 2003: 99)

Some of the ways this can be seen are through arguments about constitutional recognition and in the ongoing treaty discussions, which are taking place at a state and territory level.

For many Indigenous scholars, whether or not the Australian state and its non-Indigenous sovereignty recognises Indigenous sovereignty does not matter. Cobble Cobble scholar Megan Davis and George Williams (2021) argue that sovereignty in legal cases like *Mabo* 'does not affect how Aboriginal people view their own sovereignty. As a result, it does not prevent them from asserting their own independence and the continuing validity of their laws and customs'. For some, too, non-Indigenous sovereignty cannot meet Indigenous sovereignty. Moreton-Robinson has argued that the two different sovereignties are incommensurable. She writes that:

> As a regime of power, it is a juridical omnipresent with ontological roots in a monotheistic religion. A sovereignty that is narcissistic, self-interested, possessive and self-serving. This is incommensurate with how Indigenous sovereignties originated, how we, and our non-human relatives, came to be and to which lands we belong as peoples of the earth. Our sovereignties are in and of the earth.
>
> (Moreton-Robinson 2020: 267)

Lastly, it is important to be reminded that, as Tanganekald, Meintangk, Boandik scholar Irene Watson (2017: 88) asserts, Aboriginal sovereignty is inherent and 'First Nations' status as sovereign and independent peoples cannot be given to us by the colonial states'.

Conduct of lawful relations

In this section we address sovereignty in the context of historical encounters between Indigenous and non-Indigenous peoples, focusing on the lawful conduct of Indigenous sovereigns and the response of European invaders. To do so we focus on the conduct of Kulin Nation peoples, whose traditional territories surround the bay where the city of Melbourne is now located. The Kulin Nation is an alliance of five language groups: the Woiwurrung, Boon Wurrung, Taungurung, Dja Dja Wurrung, and Wathaurung peoples. The languages of these five groups are related, and the peoples were connected by trade, marriage, ceremonies, and shared responsibilities for some sites (Presland 2002). In 1788, Captain Arthur Phillip claimed Kulin lands for Britain, as part of the much wider territory of the penal colony of New South Wales. Until the 1830s, however, settler authorities restricted settlement in the southern part of the colony, which they named the 'Port Phillip District'. After a period of rapid settler invasion, in 1839 a Superintendent of the District was appointed. In 1851, the Port Phillip District became the self-governing colony of Victoria, which in turn became a state of the new Commonwealth of Australia in 1901 (Boyce 2011).

In the following analysis, we focus on events that occurred between the 1830s and the 1880s. We focus particularly on the creation of a government reserve, named Coranderrk Aboriginal Reserve, where many Kulin Nation peoples lived. These events have received significant attention from historians, including authors of this chapter (Barwick 1998; Nanni & James 2014; Cruickshank & Grimshaw 2015; Evans & Nanni 2015; Curthoys & Mitchell 2018). Here, however, we tell this story in terms of the conduct of lawful relations. We consider, first, the conduct of settler (and imperial) authorities who had responsibility for relations with Kulin Nation peoples. We then provide an account of the continuing lawful conduct of Kulin Nation peoples.

Settler disavowals

On Kulin country, as elsewhere on the continent, British colonists failed to seek treaties or lawful agreements with the peoples whose country they were invading. One possible exception proved the rule. In June 1835, a colonist named John Batman, acting on behalf of a group calling themselves the Port Phillip Association, claimed to have met and signed a private treaty with a number of Kulin elders. Among this group were a Woiwurrung *ngurungaeta*, or senior man, Billibellary, and a child named Barak, who as an adult would recall his elders' meeting with Batman. On the basis of this 'treaty', Batman claimed to have gained rights for the Association to occupy over 200,000 hectares of Kulin land. This was land that was already included within the British Crown's claim to territory. Batman had a history of murder and fraud, and his interpretation of any agreement he had made with the Kulin was undoubtedly spurious. Kulin leaders would never have agreed to give up responsibility for their country in this way. In seeking to present such an agreement as the basis of a land claim, however, the Association forced an open discussion among imperial and settler authorities about lawful relations and the basis of the British claim to Indigenous lands.

The Port Phillip Association argued that Kulin people had the authority to make such an agreement with colonists, because they retained rights to the land. '[I]t is undoubted fact', the Association stated, 'that these Tribes are the actual possessors of the soil, and that although the land is situated within the limits of the British Territory of New Holland, yet it is without the jurisdiction of New South Wales, or any other British settlement'.[3] In London, there was acknowledgement that such arguments might be lawful. Attorney-General Alfred Stephen advised the Colonial Secretary at the end of 1934 that while it was 'a matter of history that the English government has possessed itself of New Holland', he could not state how far these claims to possession 'may be insisted on, to deprive the Aboriginal Inhabitants of the power of selling any part of the Territory'.[4] In spite of this acknowledgement, the Batman treaty was almost immediately declared void by Governor Bourke in Sydney, and this was reinforced by Lord Glenelg, the Colonial Secretary. In April 1836, Glenelg wrote to Bourke that to recognise the claimed agreement between Batman and Kulin peoples would 'subvert the foundation of which all proprietary rights in New South Wales currently exist' (Glenelg, 13 April 1836).

The Port Phillip Association's attempt to secure land by claiming to have made a treaty with Kulin peoples – and the responses that their claim evoked from colonial and imperial authorities – demonstrate a pattern of disavowal which would be repeated throughout the late 19th century and beyond (Moreton-Robinson 2020). Settlers would describe, refer to, draw upon, and otherwise show awareness of aspects of Kulin sovereignty while simultaneously refusing to conduct themselves lawfully in relation to these aspects.

While the Colonial Office refused to accept the Batman Treaty, Batman's actions nonetheless led to the rapid invasion of Kulin lands, as settlers accompanied by vast flocks of sheep and cattle streamed north from Van Diemen's Land and south from Sydney (Boyce 2011: 147–63). In London, evangelical humanitarians pressured the Colonial Office to provide some check to settler violence. In 1838, therefore,

---

[3] J. Batman to G. Mercer (27 June 1835) Port Phillip Association Papers, SLV, quoted in Attwood (2020: 46).
[4] A. Stephen to Colonial Secretary (3 November 1834) SLV M5082, Box 52/2 (3), quoted in Boyce (2011: 61).

Lord Glenelg appointed a Chief Protector and four Assistant Protectors to the Port Phillip District. The Protectors, who were each allocated an extensive territory, were expected to travel with Aboriginal people, learn their languages, establish schools for their children and act as advocates for them in settler courts. From the start, there was considerable settler hostility towards the Protectors, and over ten years the Protectorate was gradually defunded and then abolished in 1849. Two of the Assistant Protectors – William Thomas and Edward Parker – remained living among the clans with whom they had been working. Thomas, who had developed some knowledge of the Woi Wurrung and Boon Wurrung languages, was appointed to the largely powerless position of 'Guardian of Aborigines'. Pastoralists, magistrates, and missionaries were appointed as local guardians throughout the colony, with few duties other than distributing an annual supply of blankets to Aboriginal people in their vicinity.

The pattern of disavowal was repeated in the findings of the Select Committee of the Legislative Council on the Aborigines, which was formed in 1858 to investigate the conditions of those Aboriginal people who had survived invasion. The Committee consulted a range of settler 'experts' through interviews and an ethnographic questionnaire.[5] No Aboriginal people were consulted by the Committee. The resulting report stated that 'a great injustice' had been done to Aboriginal people, arguing 'that, when the Government of the Colony found it necessary to take from them their hunting grounds and their means of living, proper provision should have been made for them'. It was, the Committee members concluded, a matter of 'duty' that efforts should be made to provide for and also convert those 'whose country God's Providence has given to the British Crown, and whose amelioration and happiness he has confided to British Christian benevolence' (*Select Committee Report* 1859: iv). In this account, the assertion of British sovereignty, understood as authority over both territory and people, was explained as the result of both the necessary exercise of state power and the working of God's Providence. The Committee did not question the lawfulness of British dispossession of Aboriginal people, but they claimed that it had created a responsibility to provide for those who had been dispossessed.

The settlers who were questioned by the Committee were unreliable witnesses of Aboriginal conduct and culture. Other than William Thomas, the majority had no capacity to speak or understand Aboriginal languages and had limited experience with Aboriginal people. Collectively, they were the beneficiaries of Aboriginal dispossession, with a vested interest in denying Aboriginal sovereignty. Nonetheless, their testimony included detailed descriptions of Aboriginal laws, forms of governance, and relationship to country and other nations. In response to a series of questions about Aboriginal government and laws, the

---

[5] *Report of the Select Committee of the Legislative Council on the Aborigines, 1858–1859* (1859), available at https://aiatsis.gov.au/sites/default/files/docs/digitised_collections/remove/92768.pdf (henceforth '*Select Committee Report* 1859').

respondents largely agreed that government in Aboriginal clans was 'democratic', with collective decision-making led by senior men who had been chosen by the community. These leaders, William Thomas explained, 'serve the community, without even the least burden to the state', as each person worked for their daily food. While the respondents disagreed about the source of Aboriginal laws, they agreed that these laws were never 'modified' and were 'implicitly obeyed'. Thomas identified them as 'natural laws, like the Medes and the Persians'. The respondents agreed that all 'trials' were public and overseen by the senior men (*Select Committee Report* 1859: 64–6).

In answer to questions about geography, all the settler respondents also testified that different tribes had clearly demarcated territories, whose boundaries were known and defended (*Select Committee Report* 1859: 66). The Select Committee paid careful attention to the question of how Aboriginal people related to these territories, because many of the Committee members had initially supported the idea of establishing a single, large reserve, to which all Aboriginal people in the colony could be confined. This idea was repeatedly criticised as impractical by the more knowledgeable of the respondents, including William Thomas. One missionary stated in his testimony that 'it would not do to take them away from their hunting grounds, they are too much attached to them, and they would pine away, I am sure' (*Select Committee Report* 1859: 6). Edward Parker, a magistrate and another former Assistant Protector, recommended that the location of any potential reserves should be selected based on Aboriginal peoples' 'previous associations and alliances' (*Select Committee Report* 1859: 21).

The ethnographic knowledge reproduced in the Select Committee Report is evidence that settler authorities were aware of the structures of governance within Aboriginal communities, Aboriginal law giving, and the responsibilities that Aboriginal nations took for land and each other. Yet the Committee's recommendations ignored the possibility of any relation with these aspects of Aboriginal sovereignty. The one exception to this, based on the advice of many of the Committee's informants, was the recommendation that multiple reserves be established, corresponding to the traditional territories of different tribes. This recommendation was represented as a pragmatic and humanitarian decision, made necessary by the superstitions of Aboriginal people, rather than as a matter of lawful relations (*Select Committee Report* 1859: v).

As a consequence of the recommendations of the Select Committee, six Aboriginal reserves were eventually established and placed under the oversight of a 'Central Board to Watch over the Interests of the Aborigines'. In 1869, after extended lobbying by the Board, the Victorian Legislative Assembly passed an Act to Provide for the Protection and Management of the Aboriginal Natives of Victoria (henceforth Aborigines Act). This Act gave the Board – now renamed the Board for Protection of the Aborigines (BPA) – direct powers over Aboriginal people's employment, earnings, children and place of residence. As the Minister for Justice assured his fellow members of Parliament, the legislation would allow the BPA to 'act *in loco parentis* to the aborigines'.[6] This Act was the basis for ongoing relations between settler authorities and Aboriginal nations. In determining that the settler government would relate to Aboriginal people through an unelected body that faced very minimal oversight and by forming no relationship with the traditions, engagements of governance or territorial responsibilities of Aboriginal nations, the Act represented a comprehensive disavowal of lawful relations.

Kulin insistence

In response to the ongoing disavowal of Kulin sovereignty, which began with the British invasion, leaders of the Kulin Nation peoples insistently called on colonial officials to stabilise the immediate upheaval that was being visited upon their peoples and to engage meaningfully with them.

In the aftermath of the first wave of settler invasion that followed the Batman 'treaty', the leaders of different Kulin clans sought government agreement to select land in their particular countries on which displaced and distressed peoples could begin to rebuild their lives and cultures and safeguard their futures. As early as 1843, Billibellary, the aforementioned *ngurungaeta* of the Wurundjeri clan of the Woiwurrung people, approached William Thomas to promote their wish to secure land with the higher colonial authorities (Nanni & James 2014: 7). While the government rejected that request, the nature and quality of the relation established between Thomas and Billibellary, and eventually with Billibellary's sons Simon Wonga and Tommy Munnering, underpinned later campaigns for land.

Different clan groups within the Kulin Nation drew on their traditional alliances to form deputations and negotiate land grants. In 1859, Wonga, Munnering, and five Taungerong men approached Thomas for assistance in pressing their case with Crown lands officials. Wonga informed Thomas that 'They want a block of land in the country where they may sit down, plant corn, potatoes … and work like white men'.[7] A deputation to Melbourne was successful in having land reserved within their chosen boundaries in Taungerong country. Taungerong people moved quickly to establish crops and fencing at Acheron Station, but within a year the government handed over their selection to settler farmers, and forced residents to relocate to an inhospitable site it had allocated to them at Mohican (Curthoys & Mitchell 2018: 274–8). Thomas protested to the newly established Central Board, conveying the views of Taungerong 'that it is not the Country they selected, it is too cold and blackfellows soon die there'.[8]

---

[6] J.J. Casey (19 August 1869), *Victorian Parliamentary Debates* (1869): 1726, quoted in Boucher (2015: 65).

[7] W. Thomas to R. Barry (21 October 1861), William Thomas Papers, MS214/17–18, Mitchell Library NSW, cited in Nanni & James (2014: 6).

[8] W. Thomas to R. Brough Smyth (5 October 1860), quoted in Curthoys & Mitchell (2018: 277).

Facing further incursions into their ancestral lands, Wurundjeri and Taungerong sought to fortify their political and economic positions in the colony. The recommendations of the Select Committee, discussed above, provided some opportunity for Kulin peoples to seek land for a reserve. With his cousin and future *ngurungaeta* William Barak, Wonga once again called on his long-standing relationship with Thomas to help them acquire a grant of designated land beside the Coranderrk Creek in the Yarra ranges of Wurundjeri country. By this time, too, Wurundjeri were able to rely on the support of a Presbyterian lay preacher, John Green, and his wife Mary, who for some time had lived and worked respectfully alongside them, holding church services and providing schooling for the children. By 1861, Green was able to use his new appointment as Inspector for the Board to foster both clans' quest for a permanent location to set up a farming community (Nanni & James 2014: 6–8).

Further, when a reception was held by Governor Barkly in honour of Queen Victoria in May 1863, Wonga and Barak asked Thomas to join a delegation of Taungerong, Wurundjeri, and Boon Wurrung people to Melbourne to present a written and illustrated statement of loyalty to the sovereign. Thomas witnessed the offering of ceremonial gifts to be forwarded to different members of the royal family and translated Wonga's spoken address, which was delivered in Woiwurrung (Curthoys & Mitchell 2018: 280–3). The event was reported by the Board as a gratifying spectacle: 'The conduct of the Aborigines was grave and dignified; and Wonga, the principal man of the Yarra tribe, addressed His Excellency with becoming modesty, and yet with earnestness.'[9] When Kulin were later informed of the Secretary of State's letter describing the Queen's pleasure with their gifts and vows of loyalty, the Board observed that 'they appeared to be sensible of the kindness and favour shown to them'.[10]

In June 1863, 2300 acres were reserved for Wurundjeri and Taungerong people at Coranderrk and placed under the management of John Green. While there is no evidence, from the colonial archive, of any direct relationship between the delegation, the Queen's response, and the granting of land, Coranderrk leaders and residents subsequently spoke of the reserve as being authorised by the British sovereign herself (Curthoys & Mitchell 2018: 280–3). The encounter was interpreted as an encounter in which the British sovereign had responded to the Kulin delegation, who had conducted themselves according to their own traditions of authority and relationship.

Within three years the Coranderrk community had grown to around 100 as other displaced people – particularly other Kulin Nation peoples such as Dja Dja Wurrung families – came to reside there. During this period, the amount of reserved

---

[9] *Third Report of the Central Board Appointed to Watch Over the Interests of the Aborigines in the Colony of Victoria* (1863) (Melbourne, John Ferres), cited in Curthoys & Mitchell (2018: 281).

[10] *Fourth Report of the Central Board Appointed to Watch Over the Interests of the Aborigines in the Colony of Victoria* (1864) (Melbourne, John Ferres), cited in Curthoys & Mitchell (2018: 283).

land had been doubled, and housing, fencing, grazing, and cropping were well underway. Residents had agreed to Green's appointment as 'manager', given his understanding of the nature and scope of his authority and – within the limits of his Christian faith – his commitment to the appropriate observance of Aboriginal laws and modes of conduct, both within and beyond the settlement. Green was forthright with outside officials that Aboriginal people should be allowed 'to rule themselves as far as possible'.[11] He would later claim that he made laws on the reserve only 'with [the residents'] own sanction. If the aboriginal [sic] is put into the question, he will strive to keep his own law'[12] (*Report of the Board* 1881: 136).

The terms on which Kulin and other Aboriginal nations across the colony were able to acquire such land – as secular or mission-style reserves placed under government control – severely compromised their sovereign claims (McLisky *et al.* 2015). In addition, from 1869, as noted, the Aborigines Act gave the BPA substantial new powers over Aboriginal people. Nevertheless, for the residents of Coranderrk, their immediate quest for a land base on which to reclaim some internal autonomy was making fragile progress.

By the early 1870s, however, it became evident that the BPA intended to support settler demands to take over the valuable Coranderrk land. Plans were afoot to break up the reserve, sell off the improved land, and remove residents to northern regions of the colony. The Greens opposed this plan and were openly critical of the BPA's disrespectful, authoritarian style of management. In response, the BPA pressured Green into resigning as manager in 1874. From 1875, the Kulin leaders repeatedly addressed the settler authorities through letters, petitions, and deputations, criticising the management of Coranderrk and seeking confirmation of their right to remain at the reserve. William Barak, now Wurundjeri *ngurungaeta*, worked closely with Taungerong clan head Thomas Bamfield, as well as a younger Wurundjeri man Robert Wandon, who would later succeed Barak as *ngurungaeta*. A younger Dja Dja Wurrung man, Thomas Dunolly, wrote many of the letters and petitions. The majority of men and women signed the petitions, while Barak walked with groups of men to Melbourne to deliver petitions and address the Chief Secretary directly, much to the fury of the BPA (Nanni & James 2014: 106–7).

The repeated efforts of the Kulin people at Coranderrk, supported by some sympathetic settlers and publicised by the colony's newspapers, led in 1877 to a Royal Commission, established 'to inquire into the present condition of the Aborigines in this colony, and to advise as to the best means of caring for, and dealing with them, in future'. The Commission failed almost entirely to relate directly to the people at

---

[11] J. Green to R. Broughton Smyth (5 May 1862), B312 (Correspondence Files of the Central Board for the Protection of the Aborigines), item 6 National Archives of Australia, cited in Nanni & James (2014: 10).

[12] Report of the Board Appointed to Inquire into and Report upon the Present Condition and Management of the Coranderrk Aboriginal Station Along with the Minutes of Evidence (1881) (Melbourne, John Ferres), 135-6. Available at http://www.minutesofevidence.com.au/static/media/uploads/coranderrk_moe_digitized.pdf

Coranderrk, only interviewing four men from the reserve who were not leaders of the main Kulin clans and had not been involved in the petitions or deputations.[13] Following the Commission, the BPA heightened its efforts to close the reserve, and in response, Barak led two further deputations to Melbourne, while the community wrote repeated letters to the newspapers and members of Parliament. The manager at Coranderrk wrote to the Secretary of the BPA, stating 'the men are in a state of revolt, they say they are waiting to hear if they are to have the place to themselves, that the Board in Melbourne is to be done away with, that I am to go about my business, that you will not be required'.[14]

In September 1881, as a result of the ongoing insistence of the people at Coranderrk, the Chief Secretary established a Parliamentary Inquiry to 'Enquire into, and Report upon, the Present Condition and Management of the Coranderrk Aboriginal Station'. The Inquiry was held over three months and summoned 69 witnesses, including 22 Aboriginal people from Coranderrk. In response to the questions of the Commissioners, the residents made a wide range of complaints about the management of the reserve. They claimed that Rev. Strickland and his wife were disrespectful to residents and did not properly provide for their material needs; that Rev. Strickland used physical violence against Aboriginal children and was prone to drunkenness; that Mrs Strickland refused to pay Aboriginal women who worked for her; and that the BPA had repeatedly failed to maintain the reserve or engage rightly with the residents (*Report of the Board* 1881: 8–10, 60–1, 71, 98–9). At the end of the Inquiry, the residents submitted a petition, in which they stated their central demands:

> We want the Board and the Inspector, Captain Page, to be no longer over us. We want only one man here, and that is Mr John Green, and the station to be under the Chief Secretary, then we will show the country that the station could self-support itself.
> (Report of the Board 1881: 98)

We read this statement as addressing both the exercise of authority and its relation to law within the Coranderrk community and the conduct of relations between this community and the settler authorities. The people of Coranderrk asserted both their desire for autonomy and their determination to conduct relations with settler authorities on their own terms, using a trusted settler as manager and relating directly to Parliament.

The Coranderrk Inquiry resulted in a report that was highly critical of the BPA. Yet although a number of Commissioners recommended that the central demands

---

[13] *Report of the Commissioners Appointed to Inquire into the Present Condition of the Aborigines in this Colony and to Advise as to the Best Means of Caring for, and Dealing with them in the Future* (1877) (Melbourne, John Ferres), available at https://aiatsis.gov.au/sites/default/files/catalogue_resources/92914.pdf.

[14] Rev. Strickland to Capt. Page (10 October 1881), VPRS 1226 (Chief Secretary: Inward Registered Correspondence), Unit 4/Item 81/U9612, Public Records Office Victoria, reproduced in Nanni & James (2014: 38).

of the residents be met, Parliament was not willing to restrict the power of the BPA. While the Inquiry put a halt to the plan to sell off the reserve, the BPA continued to lobby for greater powers over Aboriginal people throughout the colony (Nanni & James 2014: 177–83). In 1886, their lobbying led to the passing of further legislation, which has come to be known colloquially as 'the Half-Caste Act'.[15] This Act extended the powers of the BPA and forced all Aboriginal adults identified as being of mixed descent off the reserves. Enforcement of the 1886 Act radically disrupted the internal structures of Kulin Nations people and undermined their capacity to collectively address settler authorities. On the one hand, the Act meant that Parliament was fundamentally refusing responsibility for Aboriginal people whom they no longer recognised as Aboriginal. On the other hand, the sovereign autonomy of those people still recognised as Aboriginal was further disavowed, as they were subjected to increasingly paternalistic controls.

In giving this account of settler and Kulin conduct between the 1830s and the 1880s, we have described the repeated failure of British and settler authorities to acknowledge the law and sovereign life of Indigenous nations and people. However, our main focus has been on Kulin conduct, which we have identified as a repeated insistence on lawful relations. The claims that Billibellary, Wonga, Barak, Thomas Bamfield, and others made – on behalf of and alongside other members of their nations – related to place, self-government, and the desire for autonomy. In modern idiom, these claims were an assertion of sovereignty. These claims were at times presented using non-Indigenous forms such as petitions, but the way in which they were presented clearly reflected Indigenous models of governance.

In our analysis of these events, we have suggested that the insistence on lawful relations should be understood as an aspect of sovereign relations. This might be contrasted with some recent historical accounts of sovereignty, referenced above. There, sovereignty was sometimes viewed as a specific political, legal, and/or administrative activity of the British sovereign and its various offices (Attwood 2020). In such an account, the historian's task is to identify and describe the actors engaged in the political and institutional arrangement of events. From this perspective, sovereignty is concerned with Euro-American states and not Indigenous nations and their law. A second version draws attention to the legality of the assertion of British sovereignty over Australia (Reynolds 2021). Reynolds gives emphasis to historical and ethical accounts of unlawful relations as framed by international law. By contrast, in focusing on lawfulness as a quality of relations, we have emphasised a concern with authority and conduct. While the content of the Kulin petitions did not include explicit claims to live life according to Indigenous law and knowledge, we can see in these encounters the patterning of British legal forms into an Indigenous ordering of law and life.

---

[15] An Act to Amend an Act Intituled 'An Act to Provide for the Protection and Management of Aboriginal Natives of Victoria' (1886), available at www.austlii.edu.au/au/legis/vic/hist_act/tapa1886265.pdf.

'Working through ...'

This final section returns briefly to contemporary legal formulations of sovereignty in Australia since the 1990s. While the patterns of sovereignty and relationship, we argue, repeat earlier forms, the contest of forms and the redescription of sovereignty has had effects for both Indigenous and non-Indigenous peoples in the conduct of sovereignty and of lawful relations. We want here to follow the quality of relationship and some links between sovereignty and responsibility.

The patterning of laws we take up forms part of a concerted political assertion of Indigenous sovereignty through the Australian Courts. This engagement itself forms a small part of the engagement of Indigenous and non-Indigenous concerns with forms of sovereignty. Here, we look at the pattern of responsibility for the consequences of Australian state and common law jurisprudence as framing Indigenous and non-Indigenous sovereignties as an impasse.

Our first gloss or reading of contemporary Australian jurisprudence develops the way in which the disavowal of sovereign relations with Indigenous nations and peoples of Australia shapes accounts of lawful relations. In many respects, the legal understanding of the indivisible sovereignty of the Australian state has not changed its formal account of sovereignty. In this respect, at least, the Australian state has not elaborated a postcolonial account of its own sovereignty, let alone fully elaborated its relation to the sovereign relations of Indigenous peoples. Any direct contestation of the indivisible sovereignty of the Commonwealth of Australia remains non-justiciable.

The formulation of the relationship that has emerged, one that we consider here as an aspect of sovereignty, remains broadly concerned with links between self-government and participation in public administration. This can be seen in the complex understanding of 'Native Title' that has emerged in a series of Australian High Court decisions, starting with *Mabo v Queensland (No 2)* in 1992 and culminating in *Members of the Yorta Yorta Community v Victoria* in 2002 (194 ALR 538). In these cases, the High Court of Australia established the forms of conduct of relations between the common law of Australia and the 'laws, customs and traditions' of Aboriginal peoples. In *Mabo (No 2)*, the High Court declared that Eddie Mabo could inherit family land under the laws of Mer. In doing so, the High Court attempted to settle Indigenous and non-Indigenous laws by reviving a doctrine of 'Native Title' that provided an account of the recognition, under certain circumstances, of Aboriginal laws and customs that had continued after settlement (Evans et al, 2013; Attwood 2020). For us, these cases, and the Native Title Act 1993 (Cth), can be understood as shaping what a meeting of peoples and laws might require from the standpoint of the Australian state. In this situation Aboriginal laws, traditions and customs are addressed as fact rather than law.

Whilst the majority of the justices of the High Court in *Mabo (No 2)* acknowledged the continuing efficacy of the laws, customs and traditions of Aboriginal Australians, the Court has avoided acknowledging Indigenous sovereignty. In the case of *Members of the Yorta Yorta* (2002), the High Court formulated the meeting of laws as of two 'normative systems': Aboriginal laws and traditions, on the one hand, and common law, on the other. The High Court also asserted that the sovereignty of the British (and now Australian) Crown 'necessarily entailed' that thereafter there could be 'no parallel law-making system in the territory over which it asserted sovereignty'. Evidence of Aboriginal law and custom is evidence of a continuing relation to a law that was sovereign prior to the assertion of British, and then Australian, sovereignty.

Yet such formulations also facilitate relations of government and law. In *Mabo (No 2)*, Justice Brennan stated that 'the antecedent rights and interests in land possessed by the [I]ndigenous inhabitants of the territory survived the change in sovereignty' (57–8). Importantly, Justice Gummow in *Wik Peoples v Queensland* observed that the High Court in *Mabo (No 2)* 'declared the content of the common law upon a particular view which now was taken of past historical events'[16]. In the comments, the High Court states that this judgment changed the understanding of sovereignty and the justness of settlement. Professor Marcia Langton (Yiman and Bidjara nations) has argued that with this altered historical view comes more than continuation of interests in land; it must also mean that 'Aboriginal government under the full body of Aboriginal customary laws' also survived (Langton 2001: 15–19).

In the more recent case of *Love-Thoms v the Commonwealth*, the High Court addressed the relationship of laws in more substantive terms. In this case two Aboriginal men who were not citizens were seeking to overturn the Commonwealth's decision to cancel the visas that gave a right to residence in Australia. The plaintiffs had separately been convicted of criminal offences, which resulted in the cancellation of their visas under the Migration Act 1958. As a consequence, they would be subject to deportation from Australia. The plaintiffs contested the power of the power (authority) of the state to do so. They claimed that the power to exclude 'aliens' under section 51 (xix) of the Constitution did not apply to them. Their Aboriginal status meant that they should be treated as 'non-alien'. The majority of the High Court agreed with the plaintiffs and held that they must establish that they are recognised as a member of a particular people. This vests decision-making authority in recognised Aboriginal Elders. In recognising this authority to decide, the High Court is also, arguably, recognising the presence of an Aboriginal law and custom, albeit controlling the status of who decides (membership of a tribe, clan, or people) in the sense that the authority to decide can be reviewed by the Commonwealth. The provisional conclusion from this discussion might be that the High Court will recognise some of the incidence of sovereignty or at least a certain judicial self-restraint.

This account has followed some of the attempts to acknowledge and give governmental form to Indigenous nations, peoples, and laws within an Australian polity.

---

[16] The Wik Peoples v The State of Queensland & Ors; The Thayorre People v The State of Queensland & Ors [1996] HCA 40: 179.

These attempts recognise neither the national nor international status of Indigenous peoples as sovereign peoples. Sometimes this path follows national or state law; at other times it follows non-Indigenous international law.

Outside the context of the High Court, there are also various contemporary movements toward agreement-making between Indigenous and non-Indigenous people, in which questions of sovereignty and lawful relations are addressed. In 2017, a Constitutional Convention made up of representatives from a number of Aboriginal nations produced the Statement from the Heart. The Statement was delivered to the Australian people, and by extension to the Commonwealth of Australia. It affirms the spiritual and material understanding of Aboriginal sovereign existence and continuing obligations to country. It invites people of the common law tradition to participate in (transnational) lawful relations amongst peoples of law, within 'Australia'.

In the state of Victoria, the government has been engaged in a treaty process with Aboriginal people since 2018. The First Peoples' Assembly, the elected body that will represent Aboriginal communities in treaty discussions, has repeatedly stated that Aboriginal sovereignty was never ceded. However, the Advancing the Treaty Process with Aboriginal Victorians Act (2018) states only that 'Victorian traditional owners maintain that their sovereignty has never been ceded'. The Act does not state that the Victorian government accepts this claim and speaks instead of 'advancing self-determination'. How questions of sovereignty will be addressed in the treaty process – and what consequences this will have for non-Indigenous understandings of sovereignty – is unclear at the time of writing.

These examples provide instances of contemporary attempts to bring Indigenous and non-Indigenous laws and sovereignties into relation. For many Indigenous people, however, this remains a secondary or impossible task. Professor Aileen Moreton-Robinson (2016), Goenpul woman and scholar, has warned Aboriginal people against 'shaping things according to the alien sovereignty'. She continues:

> I'm not really interested in negotiating with the State over a treaty. What I want to start thinking about is how we nation build as Indigenous people and how we treaty with each other. How is it that Yuggera [and] Turrbal talk to one another? How is it that Quandamooka talks to Gumbaynggirr? How is it that we as nation peoples talk to one another?

This task of building lawful relations between Indigenous sovereigns is, in Moreton-Robinson's view, the way in which lawful relations can best be conducted on these lands.

Conclusion

Our analysis of sovereignty in Australia has followed the work of historians and jurisprudents in addressing Indigenous and non-Indigenous sovereignty. Taking a cue from thinking of sovereignty relationally, we have linked our accounts of sovereignty and Australia to particular engagements of lawful relations. In this way we have presented our accounts as commentaries and reports on existing practice. In doing so we have kept our accounts apart from the major political and constitutional understanding of sovereignty. This has the drawback of not engaging closely with questions of public authority, the task of securing forms of political authority that can accommodate more than one law, and a concern with the development of institutional arrangements. However, holding back a little from such engagement has, we think, allowed us to foreground a concern with lawful relationships as a concern with the conduct of authority. In doing so, we have tried to make visible and meaningful the different ways in which obligations for the conduct of sovereign and lawful relations have been taken up.

References

Attwood, B. (2020), *Empire and the Making of Native Title: Sovereignty, Property and Indigenous People* (Cambridge, Cambridge University Press).
Barwick, D. (1998), *Rebellion at Coranderrk* (Canberra, Aboriginal History).
Birch, T. (2020), 'The Invisible Fire: Indigenous Sovereignty, History and Responsibility', in Moreton-Robinson (2020), 104–17.
Behrendt, L. (2003), *Achieving Social Justice: Indigenous Rights and Australia's Future* (Annandale, N.S.W.).
Benton, L. & Ford, L. (2016), *The Rage for Order: The British Empire and the Origins of International Law, 1800–1850* (Cambridge MA, Harvard University Press).
Benton, L. (2010), *A Search for Sovereignty: Law and Geography in European Empires, 1400–1900* (Cambridge, Cambridge University Press).
Black, C. (2010), *The Land Is the Source of the Law: A Dialogic Encounter with Indigenous Jurisprudence* (New York, Routledge).
Borrows, J. (2010), *Canada's Indigenous Constitution* (Toronto, University of Toronto Press)
Boucher, L. (2015), 'The 1869 Aborigines Protection Act: Vernacular Ethnography and the Governance of Aboriginal Subjects', in Boucher & Russell (2015), 63–94.
Boyce, J. (2011), *1835: The Founding of Melbourne and the Conquest of Australia* (Melbourne, Black Inc.).
Brady, W. (2020), 'That Sovereign Being: History Matters', in Moreton-Robinson (2020), 140–51.
Brett, A. (2020), 'The Subject of Sovereignty: Law, Politics and Moral Reasoning in Hugo Grotius', *Modern Intellectual History*, 17.3: 619–45.
Cruickshank, J. & Grimshaw, P. (2015), 'Indigenous Land Loss, Justice and Race: Anne Bon and the Contradictions of Settler Humanitarianism', in Z. Laidlaw & A. Lester (eds), *Indigenous Communities and Settler Colonialism: Land Holding, Loss and Survival in an Interconnected World* (Basingstoke, Palgrave), 45–61.
Curthoys, A. & Mitchell, J. (2018), *Taking Liberty: Indigenous Rights and Settler Self-Government in Colonial Australia, 1830–1890* (Cambridge, Cambridge University Press).
Cutler, C. (2001), 'Critical Reflections on the Westphalian Assumptions of International Law and Organization: A Crisis of Legitimacy', *Review of International Studies*, 27.2: 133–50.

Davis, M. & Williams, G. (2021), *Everything You Need to Know about the Uluru Statement from the Heart* (Sydney, New South Publishing).
de Costa, R. (2006), *A High Authority: Indigenous Transnationalism and Australia* (Sydney, NSW Publishing).
Dorsett, S. (2019), 'Proceduaral Reform in the Nineteenth Century British Empire: The Failure of Barron Field in Gibraltar', *Comparative Legal History*, 7.2: 130–56.
Dorsett, S. & McVeigh, S. (2012), 'Conduct of Laws: Native Title, Responsibility, and Some Limits of Jurisdictional Thinking', *Melbourne University Law Review*, 36: 470–93.
Eslava, L. & Pahuja, S. (2020), 'The State and International Law: A Reading from the Global South', *Humanity: An International Journal of Human Rights, Humanitarianism & Development*, 11.1: 118–38.
Evans, J., Genovese, A., Reilly, A., & Wolfe, P. (2013), *Sovereignty: Frontiers of Possibility* (Honolulu, University of Hawai'i Press).
Evans, J. & Nanni, G. (2015), 'Re-imagining Settler Sovereignty: The Call to Law at the Coranderrk Aboriginal Reserve, Victoria 1881 (and Beyond)', in Z. Laidlaw & A. Lester (eds), *Indigenous Communities and Settler Colonialism: Land Holding, Loss and Survival in an Interconnected World* (Basingstoke, Palgrave), 24–44.
Falk, P. & Martin, G. (2020), 'Misconstruing Indigenous Sovereignty: Maintaining the Fabric of Australian Law', in Moreton-Robinson (2020), 33–45.
Fitzmaurice, A. (2014), *Sovereignty, Property and Empire, 1500–2000* (Cambridge: Cambridge University Press).
Genovese, A. (2013), 'Inheriting and Inhabiting the Pleasures and Duties of Our Own Existence: The Second Sex and Feminist Jurisprudence', *Australian Feminist Law Journal*, 38: 41–57.
Gover, K. (2011), *Tribal Constitutionalism: States, Tribes, and the Governance of Membership* (Oxford, Oxford University Press).
Graham, M. (2008), 'Some Thoughts on the Philosophical Underpinnings of Aboriginal Worldviews', *Australian Humanities Review*, 45: 181–94.
Kwaymullina, A. (2020), *Living on Stolen Land* (Broome, Magabala Books).
Langton, M. (2001), 'Dominion and Dishonour: A Treaty between Our Nations?', *Postcolonial Studies: Culture, Politics, Economy*, 4.1: 13–26.
McKinnon, C. (2018), 'Expressing Indigenous Sovereignty: The Production of Embodied Texts in Social Protest and the Arts' (PhD thesis, La Trobe University).
Macknight, C.C. (1976), *The Voyage to Marege: Macassan Trepangers in Northern Australia* (Melbourne, Melbourne University Press).
McLisky, C., Boucher, L. & Russell, L. (2015), 'Managing Mission Life, 1869–1886', in L. Boucher & L. Russell (eds), *Settler Colonial Governance in Nineteenth-Century Victoria* (Canberra, ANU Press), 117–38.
McMillan, M. (2014), '*Koowarta* and the Rival Indigenous International: Our Place as Indigenous Peoples in the International', *Griffith Law Review*, 23: 110–26.
McMillan, M. & Rigney, S. (2016), 'The Place of the First Peoples in the International Sphere: A Necessary Starting Point for Justice for Indigenous Peoples', *Melbourne University Law Review*, 39.3: 981–1002.
Mansell, M. (2016), *Treaty and Statehood: Aboriginal Self-Determination* (Leichardt, NSW, Federation Press).
Moreton-Robinson, A. (2016), 'Sovereignty X', Clancestry Conversations 3, Queensland Performing Arts Centre, accessed 2 June 2022, www.youtube.com/watch?v=RdjBMQ-0FPQ.
Moreton-Robinson, A. (ed.) (2020), *Sovereign Subjects: Indigenous Sovereignty Matters* (New York, Routledge).

Nanni, G. & James, A. (2014), *Coranderrk: We Will Show the Country* (Canberra, Aboriginal Studies Press).
Presland, G. (2002), 'People, Land, Spirit: Koorie Life on the Yarra Yarra', *Victorian Historical Journal*, 73.1: 21–33.
Reynolds, H. (2021), *Truth-Telling: History, Sovereignty and the Uluru Statement* (Sydney, New South Publishing).
Simpson, G. (1993), 'Mabo, International Law, Terra Nullius and the Stories of Settlement: An Unresolved Jurispridence', *Melbourne University Law Review*, 19: 195–210.
Tuck, R. (2016), *The Sleeping Sovereign: The Invention of Modern Democracy* (Cambridge, Cambridge University Press).
Watego, C. (2021), *Another Day in the Colony* (St Lucia, University of Queensland Press).
Watson, I. (2014), *Aboriginal Peoples, Colonialism and International Law: Raw Law* (London: Routledge).
Watson, I. (2017), 'Aboriginal Treaties: For the Past, Present and Future', *ILA Reporter*, accessed 2 June 2022, http://ilareporter.org.au/2018/08/aboriginal-treaties-for-the-past-present-and-future.

7

Scalar, Spectacular, and Subaltern Sovereignty: Colonial Autocracy, Democracy, and Interwar India

STEPHEN LEGG*

Introduction

THIS CHAPTER REFLECTS on the global question of sovereignty from two perspectives. The first relates to discipline (political and historical geography); the second relates to period and region (South Asia in the late colonial period). While lacking political philosophical depth, the *Oxford English Dictionary* entry for sovereignty ('the quality or condition of being sovereign') offers a useful hierarchy of definitions. This etymology charts a gradual grounding of the concept, from an ancient quality, through power and rule, to an earthlier geography:

> Sovereignty, n.
> 1. Supremacy or pre-eminence in respect of **excellence** or efficacy.
> 2. Supremacy in respect of **power**, domination, or rank; supreme dominion, authority, or rule.
> 3a. spec. The position, rank, or power of a supreme **ruler** or monarch; royal authority or dominion.
> 3b. transf. The supreme controlling power in communities not under monarchical government; absolute and independent **authority**.
> 4. A **territory** under the rule of a sovereign, or existing as an independent state.
> (*Oxford English Dictionary* 1989, emphasis added)

---

* This research was supported by AHRC grant AH/M008142/1. I would like to thank Mike Heffernan, Jake Hodder, and Ben Thorpe, my fellow investigators on the grant, for their support throughout. Special thanks to Christopher Smith for his invitation to the 'Sovereignty: A Global Perspective' conference and his generous editing of this chapter.

For geographers, this fourth definition has been a staple concern, exploring how sovereignty has been expressed over and through space. Defined as a 'claim to final and ultimate authority over a political community' (Flint 2009b: 706), the geographies of sovereignty are most apparent through both external relations (the mutual recognition of states) and internal control (the lack of external interference). This internal function has a very particular impact on space. The space over which sovereignty is enacted is not simply that of land (a property category) or landscape (a perspective, and land that is remade to fit it); it is not the terrain (a strategic view of space) nor is it a collection of places (locations of meaning and human association) (Elden 2010). In his epic exploration of the concept of territory, Stuart Elden (2013: 329) concluded that after millennia of experimentation, by the mid-18th century the western definition of territory had finally settled upon a firm association with the exercise of sovereignty:

> To be in the territory is to be subject to sovereignty; you are subject to sovereignty while in the territory, and not beyond; and territory is the space within which sovereignty is exercised: it is the spatial extent of sovereignty. Sovereignty, then, is exercised over territory: territory is that over which sovereignty is exercised.

Even in the 18th century, however, it was clear that sovereignty was also exerted in less pure spaces than that of a clearly bounded, demarcated, and mutually recognised territory. Modern forms of sovereignty, and the theories that emerged from and for them, emerged within a Europe where the authority of the church and the state were only slowly separating, and within which it took centuries to demarcate sovereign territories (Sheehan 2006). In a world of encroaching colonial empires, sovereignty expanded in anticipation of, and created, formal territorial acquisition. The legal historian Lauren Benton (2010) has shown how imperial sovereignty expanded inland up rivers, experimented upon islands, and tentatively ascended mountains in search of spaces to claim for a distant sovereign. These geographies are necessarily regionally specific, and our approaches to telling these stories depend upon our theorisations of sovereignty (see Beverley 2020). The section that follows explains how South Asian scholarship has contributed to broader understandings of sovereignty through reflecting on the sources of sovereign authority and on the connections between larger and smaller scales, violence and aesthetics, and elite and subaltern groups.

South Asian sovereignty

Supreme and popular Indian sovereignty

A useful way to approach the tailoring of western theories of sovereignty to India is to consider it through a classic fissure in western theories themselves. Mathew Coleman (2009) has summarised this (undoubtedly complex and contradictory) divide as that between theories which see sovereignty as 'supreme command'

and those which envisage it as 'political authority'. The former category sees sovereignty 'as a sort of transcendent command or injunction to obey' (Coleman 2009: 256), a trait identified in texts from the early modern period to the present day. It can be found in Jean Bodin's (1955 [1576]) description of sovereignty as the unfettered power to make laws and exact obedience, limited only by natural and divine law. It can be found in Thomas Hobbes' (1967 [1651]) *Leviathan* from 1651, advocating a powerful sovereignty resolving states of nature via the social contract. It can also be seen in Carl Schmitt's (1976 [1932]) avocation, drawing upon Hobbes, of a strong sovereign who can work through emergency powers, within and beyond the constitution, to protect the public sphere.

In opposition are those theories which oppose absolutist definitions of sovereignty with concepts of 'popular sovereignty', defining sovereignty as the 'political authority' of a sovereign to act for the people. John Locke (2016 [1689]) argued for a decentralised sovereignty, which was located in the people and only bestowed upon rulers for a period of time, from whom it was always (theoretically) revocable. Jean-Jacques Rousseau (2012 [1762]) argued that the social contract was not an instrument of the sovereign that could be detached from the popular sovereignty of the people. In the 20th century, Hans Kelsen opposed Schmitt's vision through arguing for advanced constitutional defences domestically, and a fortified legal order internationally.

The question for scholars of South Asia, however, regards regional and colonial difference (Heath & Legg 2018). The similarities, or not, of pre-colonial South Asian and European forms of sovereignty will be alluded to briefly but are largely beyond the scope of this chapter. The question of the impact of colonial sovereignty is vital to understanding the development of the countries that would gain independence as India and Pakistan in 1947. This question of difference must be posed both in relation to the colonial sovereign and the colonial people.

In terms of 'supreme command', the English East India Company established itself up-country beyond the trading ports of Bombay (Mumbai), Madras (Chennai), and Calcutta (Kolkata) between 1770 and 1830, 'articulating an expatriate sovereignty, civilization, and polity' (Sen 2002: xxix). The trading company soon after assumed the functions of a proselytising state in the mid-19th century (Stokes 1959). If, as Sheehan (2006) suggests, territorial borders and orders of sovereignty were slow to evolve and change in Europe, the East India Company expanded its territories with, at times, reckless speed (Sen 2002: xxiv). The uprising of 1857 (denounced by the British as the 'Sepoy Mutiny') was in part a reaction against this hasty proto-state, but actually led directly to the creation of a highly centralised bureaucratic state, via the Government of India Act of 1858. From the outset, this state had to contend with the ambiguity emanating from colonial sovereignty existing within a supposedly liberal-imperial global frame: 'Colonial sovereignty, one could say, was a contradiction in terms. British colonial rule in the years 1858–1947 was a political arrangement that, by definition, denied to Indians the principle of popular sovereignty. Indians were subjects, not citizens' (Chakrabarty 2007: 41).

To understand the nature and tensions between colonial sovereignty and liberal political thought, Dipesh Chakrabarty turned to Hobbes' *Leviathan*. Complicating a common reading of the *Leviathan* as a justification of authoritarian and unchecked sovereignty, Hobbes was situated within the liberal tradition; the sovereign was not a master of domination or slavery. Hobbes introduced instead a distinction between two types of sovereignty: acquired and instituted. While acquired (or constituent) sovereignty emerged through conquest and force, instituted (or constituted) sovereignty was willingly given to representatives by the people. While acquired sovereignty was premised on the people's fear of the sovereign, instituted sovereignty was premised on the people's fear of each other. While in the former obedience arose from submission, in the latter it emerged from the social contract. However, even acquired sovereignty required that the people accept the conqueror. Without it, there would be domination but not sovereignty.

Chakrabarty argues that colonial sovereignty in India, at best, approximated to acquired sovereignty. It was in the latter half of the 19th century that he considers the British victors of 1857 got closest to the assent of their colonial subjects and approached a form of sovereignty. However, any challenge to this sovereignty was met with the threat or use of force. In the language of Chakrabarty's mentor, what the British had in India was *Dominance without Hegemony* (Guha 1997). In response to the disproportionate use of force, and the denial of liberal reforms, a powerful nationalist movement emerged in interwar India and made demands for popular sovereignty (Mantena 2016). The Indian *demos* increasingly withdrew their sanction from the government, bringing colonial sovereignty back closer to colonial domination: 'Unwilling obedience ... made the exercise of sovereignty precarious. Colonial sovereignty in the age of nationalism, in other words, always risked becoming domination and could never approximate even the Hobbesian model of acquired sovereignty' (Chakrabarty 2007: 47). The sections that follow explore late colonial acquired sovereignty in the context of an emergent anti-colonial nationalism via the three lenses of scale, spectacle, and the subaltern.

Scale and the divisibility of sovereignty

> *Sovereignty* is obviously a political concept, but unlike political concepts such as *democracy* or *monarchy*, it is not about the location of power (the sovereign, Hobbes wrote, can be 'the one or the many'); unlike *parliament* or *bureaucracy*, it does not describe institutions that exercise power; and unlike *order* or *justice*, it does not define the purposes of power. The concept of sovereignty has to do with the relationship of political power to other forms of authority.
>
> (Sheehan 2006: 2, emphasis in original)

Sheehan explains the nature of sovereignty's relationship to other forms of authority through it being both distinct (for instance, from the family, economy, or religion, though clearly not being separate) and never subordinate (the international equal of over sovereigns, and the master domestically). While this works conceptually, in practice sovereignty proves less singular, and much more divisible, than much theory would suggest. One way of approaching these divisions is to think about scale (Legg 2009). A central, coordinating scale of sovereignty might present the image of unity and monopoly, while simultaneously dividing and devolving sovereign powers to distant and smaller units. This raises the questions: at what scale can we comprehend sovereignty? And does sovereignty mean the same thing at the scale of empire, nation, or city? These questions have recurred throughout South Asian history.

As Sudipta Sen (2002: xxiv) has said of late Mughal and early Company India, the question of sovereignty remained an 'enigma', resulting in the 'riddle of "British India"'. The latter consisted of East India Company acquisitions before the uprising of 1857. These had been forcibly acquired over two centuries from an already heterogeneous landscape of sovereign units. Thomas Blom Hansen (2005) has summarised the still partial literature on this expansive field, covering early tributary states in south India, Hindu theories of the priest-king, and the emergence (from within India as much as being imported from Central Asia) of a Mughal Empire which united much of north and central India under a Muslim bureaucracy.

Surveying this vast historical scope, Lloyd and Susanne Rudolph (2010: 558) detect a long-standing pattern of divided sovereignty. This was a feature of both regional kingdoms and periodic sub-continental empires, such as the Mauryan (320–185 BCE), Gupta (320–497 CE), Tughlaq (1320–1413), or Mughal (1526–1857). Regional identities and bureaucratic institutions formed the foundational units of these empires and survived them, which the Rudolphs read as an abiding spirit of 'parcellated sovereignty' in Indian history.

It was into the fissures of the Mughal Empire and the remaining Hindu kingdoms that the East India Company spread in the 18th century. Imperial gazetteers and geography textbooks made much of this internal disunity of India. That 'India' had not existed until the British created it was a staple justification for the almost-acquired sovereignty of the Raj, and cartography was used to represent the divided sovereign landscape into which the East India Company had spread (see Figure 7.1). The Government of India Act (1858) guaranteed the qualified sovereignty of those parts of the sub-continent which had retained their independence up to that point. This independence had often come at the price of hefty tributes, which had helped fund the expansion of the East India Company itself (Datla 2015), forging a compact that would last into the 20th century. From 1858 these territories were known as the 'Indian', or 'Princely', States, while ex-East India Company areas would be known as 'British India' (yellow and pink respectively in Figure 7.2). As such, rather than a colony, India would be an empire within the British Empire. British India would be directly administered, while the Indian States would have technical independence on most matters but would be overseen by a British Resident and would have no voice in international affairs. The Princely States were ruled indirectly, allowing many to stand as geographical and social expressions of Indian

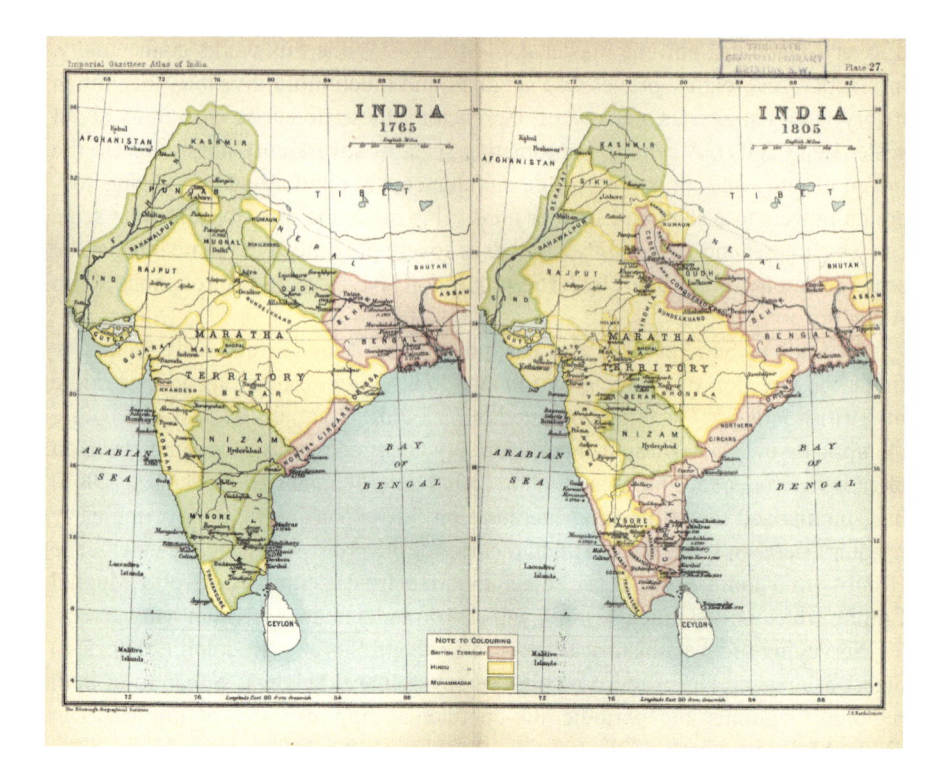

Figure 7.1 Historical maps of India, 1765 and 1805. From *Imperial Gazetteer of India*, v. 26, Atlas 1931 edition, Historical Map (1765) and Historical Map (1805), p. 28, accessed 29 April 2019, http://dsal.uchicago.edu/reference/gaz_atlas_1931/pager.php?object=35.

Source: The maps of 'India 1765' and 'India 1805' are provided courtesy of the Digital South Asia Library at the University of Chicago (http://dsal.uchicago.edu/).

'tradition', while others could demonstrate the benevolent British patronage and support for provincial experiments with modernity. The 526 Princely States listed in 1929 ranged from the large and wealthy territories of Hyderabad, Kashmir, and Mysore to dozens of small, hereditary-ruled territories (Ramusack 2004).

British India was also riven by internal divisions. The East India Company had divided its territories into the three Presidencies of Bombay, Bengal, and Madras, which coordinated the affairs of provinces that the Company acquired. In response to demands made during the First World War for democratic reforms, and in reward for India's participation, a series of promises were made that India would be set on the path to 'responsible government' (Legg 2016a). Quite what this meant was the subject of fervent debate, but the result was the Government of India Act (1919). This explicitly aimed to break the stranglehold of the heavily centralised colonial autocratic government by devolving powers to the provinces and placing some of these subjects into ministries run by elected Indian officials. That is to

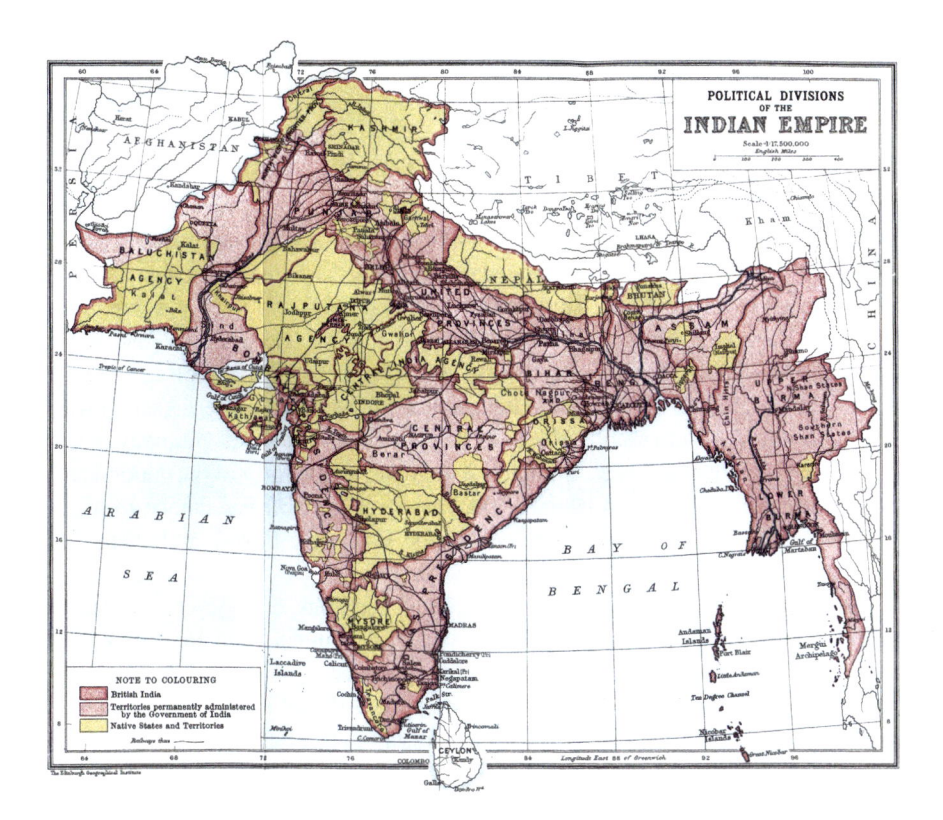

SCALAR, SPECTACULAR, AND SUBALTERN SOVEREIGNTY   153

Figure 7.2 Political divisions of the Indian Empire. From *Imperial Gazetteer of India*, v. 26, Atlas 1931 edition, Political Divisions, p. 21, accessed 29 April 2019, http://dsal.uchicago.edu/reference/gaz_atlas_1931/pager.php?object=28.

Source: The map is the frontispiece to R.V. Russell, *The Tribes and Castes of the Central Provinces of India*, London, 1916; it was adapted from the Imperial Gazetteer of India. Atlas, Vol. 26, Oxford, 1909, map 20 (https://www.gutenberg.org/files/20583/20583-h/20583-h.htm).

say, the central autocratic colonial state oversaw a wilfully divided geography of sovereignty.

This internal division was not, however, always apparent to the outside world. 'India' was represented in the British government by its own Secretary of State for India who sat alongside the Secretary of State for the Colonies in the British cabinet. 'India' functioned internationally with a coherence that it did not possess internally. This was a process that had gained traction during the 19th century as India secured representation at international congresses and conferences (Legg 2014). Having attended Imperial and War Conferences and cabinets between 1914 and 1918, India secured an invitation to the Paris Peace Conference, going on to sign the Treaty of Versailles. This made it a founding member of the League of

Nations and its only ever non-self-governing member. This raised questions about India's international status just as the internal structure of the state was coming into question and being re-designed.

As shown above, early modern Europe saw the development of both sovereign states and state-sponsored theories of sovereignty that naturalised these forms. A prominent alternative to the nation-state form of sovereignty, however, was that of the federation of states and peoples. Such federations have international legal personalities, their own public legal orders, and internal legislative capacities, yet their internal relations are not informed by classic interpretations of sovereignty (i.e. legal hierarchy, supremacy, comprehensive control, and political rule by the centre; Cohen 2018). Sovereignty is not absent; rather, the locus of sovereignty remains undecided. In the 18th and 19th centuries federal systems emerged in what would become the Netherlands, the United States of America, and Germany. These federal experiments, however, ultimately capitulated to the form of the nation-state. The dominance of the nation-state has been replicated in political theory, in which historical and viable federal alternatives to the state have been largely forgotten (Smolenski 2016).

Olivier Beaud (2018) suggests that states, federations, and empires constitute the three great political forms, and that they cannot be understood apart from each other. Both empires and federations are more pluralistic than nation-states, being political forms resulting from the concepts and processes of imperialism and federalism (Beaud 2018: 1202). But they also differ in interesting ways. Empires bring together different polities by force yet remain relatively heterogeneous; federations come together by consent but tend to homogenise their component parts. Subsidiary units in federations tend to have decentralised powers, while in colonies power tends to remain centralised.

While Beaud compares and contrasts empires and federations, he does not consider how the forms have intersected. One hybrid was imperial, such as the campaign led by the 'Round Table' movement from 1909 (Bosco & May 1997). The movement scored some notable successes, including the Imperial War Cabinet of 1917 and the influence of Round Table acolyte Lionel Curtis in implementing constitutional reform in India (Legg 2016a). But in the face of growing anti-colonial nationalist movements demanding popular sovereignty, a different federal hybrid came into prominence that sought to promote collaborationists so as to maintain and extend colonial influence during decolonisation (Collins 2013: 24). While Collins focused on the British creation of federations in central Africa in the 1940 and 1950s as a 'federal moment', Frederick Cooper (2014) has outlined a broader discussion of federation in French West Africa between 1945 and 1960 as a way of thinking of such federations as a political bridge between colonialism and postcolonialism.

In India, federation had been experimented with in the interwar period but as a means of re-forming the colonial state (Rudolph & Rudolph 2010). For the British, the object was to dampen nationalism and prolong colonial rule; for nationalists the object was to bring India closer to responsible government (Purushotham 2020a). Rather than being parallel or stadial forms, the Indian Empire provided the foundations for Indian federation. For Rudolph and Rudolph (2010: 560), in organising the territories it was acquiring into Presidencies, the East India Company had created 'a federal way of thinking'. The devolutions and reservations of the 1919 reforms infuriated nationalists, who boycotted and campaigned against them throughout the 1920s as part of an upsurge in both non-violent and violent anti-colonial nationalism. The British in India had used scale as a mechanism of reform in the hope of stymying anti-colonial nationalism. Nationalists had, however, proved adept at mobilising on international and provincial scales while making continual claims that only they could establish constituted, popular sovereignty at the national scale. The following section explores the spectacular forms of sovereignty the British deployed to cling on to power.

A violent and dazzling spectacle

The 21st-century turn to analyses of 'sovereign power' can, in part, be explained by the recrudescence of forms of violence in the post-9/11 world. The New York attacks, the invasions of Iraq and Afghanistan, the emergence of drone warfare, the establishment and decline of Islamic State, and the Syrian civil war have compelled critical scholars to explain how contests over territories and contests over bodies constitute each other: 'The concept is a challenge to established ideas of sovereignty that concentrate upon political authority over territory. Sovereign power focuses attention to the scale of the body, the authority to classify individuals in a particular way to grant them life or death' (Flint 2009a: 705). Giorgio Agamben's re-reading of Michel Foucault provided, for some, a route towards an explanation.

Foucault (1979: 133–59) had differentiated his analysis of modern forms of power, which focused on disciplining abnormal individuals or securing the productivity of the population, from the more ancient practices of sovereign power. This power was characterised by its extractive nature: taking taxes, taking property, and taking life. This was a public form of power, and it functioned as much through spectacle as through direct action. Were a subject to be executed, it would be done as publicly and as violently as possible (see the now famous description of the punishment of Damiens for his attempted regicide which opens Foucault 1977) As central as the role of ceremony is for sovereignty, this was the spectacular force of the sovereign. While Foucault acknowledged that sovereign power imbricated itself with bio-power in modern governmentalities, Agamben (1998) insisted that bio-power was also ancient, and that sovereignty had always worked to strip citizens down to subjects and expose them to violence as 'bare life'.

An easy application of these insights to the colonial past would be to declare all colonies as states of exception in which subjects not only did not approach citizenship but were forced to live either at or on the border of total exposure to the sovereign right to kill, or to 'let die'. Achille Mbembe's (2003) subtle reading of Carl Schmitt, Agamben, Foucault, and others refuses such generalisations, but does insist that in many colonies, especially in Africa, states of exception and technologies of violence were used so regularly as to denote not a biopolitics but a necropolitics. Violence began with brute force, but this sovereign power went on to structure colonial society beyond the moment of acquiring (in Hobbes' and Chakrabarty's usage) sovereignty, which Mbembe (2001: 25) terms 'founding violence'.[1] Violence also 'legitimised' its own usage, and that of the state, as well as structuring the 'imaginary' of colonial society, how its subjects were encouraged to relate to each other, and to the state. Violence functioned as much through spectacle and fear as through bodily contact and wounding.

In more putatively liberal colonial contexts like India, the prevalence of necropolitical acts and policies sat uneasily alongside claims for *Pax Britannica*. As Chakrabarty (2007) has it, having never achieved instituted sovereignty, even acquired sovereignty was denied when the people rejected colonial acquisition. The bloodletting in retribution for the uprising of 1857 and the violent putting down of largely peaceful protests in 1919 are cases in point, the latter 'spectacle of violence' resurfacing fears of a rerun of the former (Wagner 2016). Challenges to the claim of state sovereignty therefore were met with displays of violent force, which brought the colonial state perilously close to the acts of uncivilised violence that it often cited as the justification *for* the imperial project: 'The exigencies of governing the colonized ultimately produced uncomfortable similarities between the so-called barbarism of native practices and the acts of terror and violence used to contain them' (Rao & Pierce 2006: 2).

One type of sovereign spectacle was, therefore, violent. But colonial society was also marked by a more mundane and theatrical form of spectacle. It was the expression of that facet of sovereignty best understood as 'a set of claims made by those seeking or wielding power, claims about the superiority and autonomy of their authority' (Sheehan 2006: 3) As Hansen & Stepputat (2005: 4) have put it, 'Colonial forms of sovereignty were more fragmented and complex, more reliant on spectacles and ceremony and demonstrative and excessive violence, than the forms of sovereign power that emerged in Europe after several centuries of centralising efforts'. Just as with Mbembe's classifications of necropolitical violence, ceremonies and spectacles were used to both found and continually legitimate colonial rule. Sen (2002: xiii) has shown how, in the late 18th and early 19th centuries, the ascendant East India Company gradually reduced its symbolic subservience to the Mughal Empire: cutting its tributes; refusing permission for the Emperor to address Britain's King-Emperor on equal terms; and eventually removing the keys to palace gates in Delhi within which the last Mughal Emperors were effective confined.

The Raj, established after the exile of the last Mughal Emperor and the founding of the Government of India, is renowned for its attachment to ceremony and theatricality. Without exaggeration, this attachment to spectacular performances of sovereign authority can be directly related to the fragmented and divided sovereignties

---

[1] See also Fontein, this volume, for use of Mbembe.

of supreme command. In a subcontinent of *c.* 330 million subjects governed by a ruling class numbering in the thousands, strong spectacle was as important as a strong state bureaucracy in sustaining Britain's almost-acquired sovereignty.

David Cannadine (2002) has shown how 'ornamentation' and spectacle was used to combine the sovereignty regimes of the British and Indian systems. Especially regarding the Princes, military and aristocratic iconographic traditions were combined into a symbolic chain linking India's direct and indirect rulers. Indian history was cherry-picked for symbols that could be incorporated into new spectacles of Anglo-Indian society. Hence, Queen Victoria was proclaimed Queen-Empress of India in 1876, which was declared in India at a great 'durbar' in 1877, a ceremony adapted from Mughal tradition and upscaled to a spectacle of high imperial pomp, held at the ancient capital of Delhi. Further Delhi durbars were held in 1903, to celebrate the succession of Edward VII, and in 1911, to welcome George V to Delhi itself. These ceremonies located sovereignty in a person and a place. Anti-colonial activism at the time and subaltern studies since the 1980s have contested the body politics and political geography of the theatrics of sovereignty.

The subaltern

From the perspective of the sovereign, the difference of colonial sovereignty from western sovereignty was that it was an almost-acquired sovereignty, at constant risk of lapsing into mere domination. From the perspective of the people subject to this colonial sovereignty, the question of difference has also been raised. The Indian people were, as Chakrabarty pointed out, subjects not citizens, although this could also be said about the disenfranchised masses in Britain at the time. Yet, as Chakrabarty, Guha and others have pointed out, the majority of the Indian population were also 'subaltern'. In Guha's (1982) founding work of the Subaltern Studies Collective, the subaltern was defined as the non-elite part of the population who were written-off as pre-political by colonial, nationalist, and Marxist elites alike. In response, Guha and the collective set out to read the colonial archive for evidence of subaltern political agency and mobilisation beyond the norms of liberal society.

These efforts met, however, with early and transformative critiques regarding the model of the presumed political subject that was being sought out. Both Gayatri Spivak (1985) and Rosalind O'Hanlon (1988) pointed out the similarities between the political subaltern that was emerging through the Collective's research and the constituting subject of classical liberal theory. This subject conformed to universalist humanist traditions, had their acts of resistance categorised as politics, and was objectified into a subject lacking differentiation in terms of class, caste, sexuality, and, especially, gender:

> At the very moment of this assault upon western historicism, the classical figure of western humanism – the self-originating, self-determining individual, who is at once a subject in his possession of sovereign consciousness whose defining quality is reason, and an agent in his power of freedom – is readmitted through the back door in the

figure of the subaltern himself, as he is restored to history in the reconstructions of the Subaltern project.

(O'Hanlon 1988: 191)

The response of the Collective was to adopt a more hermeneutic approach to colonial texts, questioning our ability to read against the archival grain, and to pay attention to the significant difference of the colonial subaltern subject, a difference which went way beyond being a non-citizen. Spivak's work, in particular, emphasised the impossibility of retrieving a true representation of the subaltern. Rather, the colonial archive abounded with evidence of representations that spoke not only 'of' but 'for' the subaltern, rendering them silent even when they were portrayed as displaying agency (Spivak 2000 [1988]). While a pessimistic conclusion, Spivak insists that we must attempt to hear the subaltern, and to use this quest to reflect on our own positionality, our privilege, and the postcolonial afterlives of subaltern subjectivity (Legg 2016b).

With the founding of an instituted form of sovereignty after independence in 1947, both India and Pakistan would continue to face the difference between their subaltern populations and the liberal traditions that informed their new constitutions (Chatterjee 1997). Subaltern studies continue to provoke scholars of South Asia to think harder about questions of popular and state sovereignty, and have also contributed to debates about scale and spectacle in the functioning of colonial sovereignty. I will turn next to these approaches through examining an intense political event at which sovereignty was addressed square and centre.

The Round Table Conference

The dyarchy reforms of 1919 had launched a bold and unprecedented constitutional experiment regarding the divisibility of colonial sovereignty. They attempted to reconcile autocracy and democracy through a bureaucratic machinery combining devolution, expanded franchise, and emergency imperial powers. The 1919 Government of India Act had provided for a decadal review of dyarchy's functioning, but the Act was so unpopular that the review was brought forward, concluding its investigations in 1929 and publishing its report the following year. The all-white 'Simon Commission' had been largely boycotted by the Indian public, and its recommendations were widely considered too conservative, confining responsible government to the provinces. A rival report launched by the Indian National Congress (INC), the Nehru Report, demanded Dominion Status for India, meaning responsible government internally and equality with the white settler colonies of the Empire externally. It was Britain's rejection of this demand that ultimately led to Congress launching the 1930 Civil Disobedience movement, which was in full swing during the next stage of constitutional debate.

In response to the deteriorating political situation in India, the British Labour government decided to hold a Round Table Conference (RTC) in London. The INC boycotted the first session (November 1930–January 1931) of the conference due to its failure to consider a full range of options (including Dominion Status, or even complete independence), but was represented by MK ('Mahatma') Gandhi at the second session (September–December 1931). Gandhi failed to resolve a deadlock between Hindu and Muslim delegates at the conference and was arrested on his return to India. The last session (November–December 1932) finalised the proposals which provided the basis for the Government of India Act of 1935. The limited existing literature on the conference tends to focus on its political manoeuvrings, emphasising in general its failures to reconcile Indian and British opinion (Moore 1974). This chapter does not aim to recuperate or defend the conference, or its politics. Rather, it uses the conference as a way of examining how spectacular, scalar, and subaltern sovereignty was negotiated.

A spectacular event

Before the constitutional work began, the delegates were assembled in the Royal Gallery of the Palace of Westminster for the official opening of the conference, on 12 November 1930, by King-Emperor George V. Intensive preparation went into staging this inauguration, which was reported in great detail in the United Kingdom, in India, and across the Empire. The ceremony took place in the geographical and symbolic centre of British sovereignty, but there was also a delicately spatial and deeply theatrical choreography of Britain's two sovereigns at play. In the terms of the *Oxford English Dictionary*'s definitions of sovereignty, this was an interplay between 3a ('a supreme ruler or monarch': King-Emperor George V) and 3b ('absolute and independent authority': Prime Minister Ramsay MacDonald). Being a constitutional monarchy, the monarch was not supreme, and the premier was not absolutely independent. While the King-Emperor had little direct input into the running of the conference, it was within his power to confer an aura of regal splendour to the proceedings, before ceding to his democratic representative. The performance of this ritual was laid out with military exactitude. The Prime Minister (PM) was to await the King-Emperor in the Norman Porch of the Palace of Westminster at 11.45am. The Prime Minister's assistant, Sir Stuart Brown, explained that on entering:

> The Prime Minister will walk on the left of the King along the broad avenue between the seats to the Throne. His chair is immediately on the right of and close to the Throne. I will bring a plan with me to show the Prime Minister when I come tomorrow morning.
>
> Assembly will raise and stand during speech. After King has left PM will resume seat to right of Throne, while [the Maharaja of] Patiala and [the Aga] Khan make their speeches. As soon as the motion is accepted, the Throne will be removed from the central position and a chair placed for the Prime Minister to take its place.[2]

[2] British Library, London, India Office Records, European Manuscripts D712/20.

Photographs from the opening ceremony show MacDonald chairing the remainder of the session sat in a humble chair, with the throne looming behind him.[3] The King-Emperor went on to host social events for the delegates, and especially the visiting Princes and their wives, but took no further part in proceedings. For the British government this was, however, just the beginning of a first conference session that lasted over two months. In addition to formal work in St James's Palace, the conference social secretaries laid on private functions and fieldtrips for the delegates, while the Princes laid on lavish dinners. The press, especially those with picture supplements, lavished their full attention on these spectacular demonstrations of the coming together of the British and Indian sovereign regimes.[4]

While demonstrating the hospitality of both Indian and British elites, the spectacle of consumption on such a lavish scale was not universally appreciated. For many the hospitality barely masked the naked display of power and patronage that these events embodied. The constant barrage of spectacle to which the delegates were exposed (inaugurations, teas at Buckingham Palace, dinners at the finest hotels, field trips to military academies) worked to reinforce the spectacular might from which many of the delegates were attempting to demand concessions.[5] For some of the less well-off delegates the expenditure was a constant source of comment. The Hindu delegate Dr BS Moonje noted in his diary on 28 November 1930:

> 8.15 with Tambe to Savoy Hotel to join bday dinner given by Maharaja Darbhanga. 200 people. Three or four kinds of wine including champagne were served. The menu too was pretty large. I am sure the charges per head must have come to £2, that means about Rs7000 spent on one dinner.[6]

Such profligacy was also reported in the Indian press, during the Civil Disobedience movement, which had resulted in most of the Congress leadership and thousands of members of the public being imprisoned. The *Pratap* newspaper in India's United Provinces reported on 22 November 1930:

> How much do the representatives who are taking part in the London Conference care for India? They are comfortably lodged in hotels. They get delicious food, keep themselves engaged in sports and pastimes and have totally forgotten that those Indians who still possess some self-respect, have still some heat in their blood and feel the chains of slavery irksome at every moment are carrying on an unprecedented struggle for freedom.[7]

---

[3] For the throne, see https://spacesofinternationalism.omeka.net/exhibits/show/1/scales/props-technology, accessed 28 January 2021.

[4] For example, 'An Indian Prince's Birthday', *The Graphic*, 6 December 1930; 'A Maharaja's Anniversary Banquet', *The Graphic*, 27 December 1930, available at www.nottingham.ac.uk/research/groups/conferencing-the-international/representations/candid-camera.aspx, accessed 28 January 2021.

[5] On previous Indian travellers' awe at the technological might and displays of imperial power, see Majeed (2007).

[6] Nehru Memorial Museum and Library, New Delhi, BS Moonje Papers Microfilm Roll 1. £2 in 1930 had £91 worth of purchasing power in 2017, from www.nationalarchives.gov.uk/currency-converter, accessed 12 June 2020.

[7] National Archives of India, New Delhi (NA), Report on Native Newspapers, UP of Agra, Oudh 1930.

The government received weekly briefings regarding coverage of the conference in India, which was resoundingly negative in much of the press for the first and third sessions, which Congress did not attend. While claiming to speak for the people, Indian journalists were mostly part of the educated elite and spoke for a very particular public. This chapter will conclude by seeking out evidence of any subaltern voice at the conference, after considering how sovereignty in India was being reworked at the conference itself.

Federation

The Princes were a key fixture in the spectacle of the RTC. They featured heavily in the opening ceremony and were rarely absent from media coverage of the conference. But the Princes are also the key to understanding why federalism emerged as the proposed solution to the constitutional enigma of Indian sovereignty. Although only a footnote in Rudolph & Rudolph's (2010: 570 n. 59) account of federalism in India, they were pivotal (Purushotham 2020b). Alongside the Simon Commission, which reviewed the functioning of dyarchy in British India, the Butler Commission had been exploring the future of the Princely States. The RTC brought delegates of both sovereign units of the Indian Empire to London (Copland 1997: 73–112).

Congress was increasingly hostile to the Princely States, seeing them as a feudal and anti-democratic hangover, whilst also propping up the current British Empire in India (Mantena 2018; Mantena & Mantena 2018). While this was true, in the 1920s the Government of India had increasingly emphasised the Princely State's subservience to the Viceroy, as the King-Emperor's sovereign representative in India. Faced with a twofold threat from both supreme (British) and popular (Congress) sovereignty, at the opening sessions of the RTC the Princes took many by surprise by coming out in favour of an Indian federation that would unite British and Princely India. The Princes supported provincial autonomy (full devolution to elected ministers in British India) but a less responsible centre. This would rule out the possibility of a Congress-elected federal government interfering in the federated Indian states. However, this also risked unbalancing the finely tuned relationships between the paramount British power and their Princely rulers.

Although the Princes agreed with the Viceroy directly, at a July 1930 conference in India, not to use the conference to question the paramountcy of the Viceroy over them, they were certainly going into the conferences ready to fight their corner. The Nizam of Hyderabad, for instance, represented the Princely State with the largest population (14.4 million in 1931), which, though mostly Hindu, had a sizeable Muslim minority. On 29 September 1930, the British resident in the Hyderabad court passed on the Nizam's instructions to his delegates to the first RTC. In his view the most important issues to be addressed at the conference were:

1. The adjustment of future relations of the Indian States and British India.

2. The obligations of the British Government in respect of the protection of Hyderabad from external aggression and maintenance of peace and order within its borders.

3. Position of Berar in new Indian policy and the preservation of my sovereignty in that area.
4. Future economic and financial relations British India and Hyderabad.[8]

Berar was a cotton-growing region which had been claimed by the Nizam after the fall of a Maratha ruler in 1803 (Beverley 2015: 67). There had been petitions from Berar to be granted separate status from Hyderabad in a new constitution, which was dismissed out of hand by the Nizam, demonstrating that the Princes themselves had their own battles to fight over internal divisions of sovereignty. The main struggle, however, regarding the preservation of Princely sovereignty concerned the paramountcy of the Viceroy. The Nizam made clear his calculated ambivalence on the reforms, leaving his delegates a free hand to work in London while maintaining a tight grip on the core principles of his state sovereignty:

> Towards an All-India Federation the attitude of my Delegation should be one of sympathy, but also of wise caution. While on the one hand, the Delegation must be careful not to give its support to any scheme that may threaten the continuance of my relationship with the British Crown or may jeopardise the interests of the Empire and my State, it will, on the other, if the deliberations of the Round Table Conference should show that the welfare of the States as well as of British India lies in that direction, use its influence towards securing for British India a constitution that will facilitate an All-India Federation when the moment for it is ripe. … My Delegation should realise that I am not at present disposed to declare for immediate entry into any federal union that does not fully preserve the position of Hyderabad as the Premier Indian State.[9]

What the Nizam was highlighting was the imbalance of sovereign positionality of the two sets of delegates at the conference. While British India only stood to gain sovereignty, with increased devolution of powers to the provinces, the Princely States only stood to lose sovereignty (see Mantena 2018: 50). Working hard to craft a federation that would preserve Princely sovereignty and prevent a strong central government, which could be taken over by Congress in the future, the Princes worked in tandem with the British government. The Government of India Act (1935), which the RTC ultimately led to, provided for immediate provincial autonomy for British India but could only invite the Princes to join a federation with British India, given that they were not subject to British Acts of Parliament. Only when Princely States who were entitled to fill not less than half of the 104 seats of the Council of State and having subjects not less than 39,490,956 acceded would the federation be born (Keith 1936: 327). This did not happen before the outbreak of war in 1939 so the colonial Indian federation remained a virtual federation.

Acknowledging the politics of the second RTC session, attended by MK Gandhi, Congress rejected the proposed federation. It henceforth campaigned for a constituent assembly to draw up a new constitution on the basis of popular sovereignty,

---

[8] National Archives of India (henceforth NA)/Reforms/1930/154/30-R.
[9] NA/Reforms/1930/154/30-R.

not one devised through a conference dominated by India's two sovereigns of supreme command, the British and the Princes.

Subaltern voice?

If the spectacle of the RTC highlighted displays of 'supreme command' sovereign powers, and the emerging plans for a federation redrew India's divisions of sovereignty, how did the conference make space for those who authorised Indian sovereignty (or withheld their consent)? Was there any trace of subaltern voice at the conference? Being an elite gathering in imperial Britain, the ultimate answer is 'no'. But we can examine petitions as a possibility of subaltern representation, if only to see how they failed.

In the spring of 1930, the Government of India had announced that the British government would be inviting Indian representatives to London. The government was inundated over the following months with correspondents offering their services and their advice. In addition, petitions were received from individuals and public bodies, making the case for their concerns to be addressed, or for them to be invited to London themselves. While few, if any, of the petitions were acceded to, such petitions raise at least the possibility of recording subaltern voice and evidence of mobilisation (see De & Travers 2019). The Government of India collected a series of petitions that were received in Delhi, many of which had been addressed to provincial governments and passed on to the central government. While some of the petitions claimed to speak for larger demographics, if present at all here the subaltern was certainly being spoken 'for'.

Some petitions made few if any concessions to non-elitist concerns. The Government of Burma passed on an application by Princess Teik Su Myat Paya Gale, the fourth daughter of the ex-King of Burma, who had written on 19 May 1930 requesting permission to attend the RTC.[10] The Princess requested funds to cover her return travel to the conference and expenses while in London, as well as those of her six children, an interpreter, and a private secretary. Her presumption was that 'the British Government is convening this Conference to consider sympathetically the rightful claims and aspirations of the people' and thus that they would support her attempt to 'represent our just claims at this Conference'.[11] The Burmese Government considered that the Princess 'cannot be considered as in any way representative of the people of Burma' and recommended the refusal of her request.

The tone of other communications was free of any over-due reverence for the colonial state. A communication from the high-caste Brahmin Sabha (society) of Tanjore District in Madras Presidency, on 21 May 1930, asked that the final settlement of the RTC be delayed until their organisation had had its own provincial

---

[10] NA/Reforms Department/1930 29/30-R(Pt II).
[11] NA/Reforms Department/1930 29/30-R(Pt II).

conference and passed on its resolutions. The Bharat Dharma Mahamandal orthodox Hindu association of Benares (Varanasi) also petitioned on 16 July for the non-interference of the British state in Hindu matters and to not cooperate with anti-orthodox Indian reformers.

Other organisations offered support to the government in their conflict with Congress (Civil Disobedience had been started in April 1930), speaking on behalf of Indian workers. The Hon. Lieutentant Rao Bahadur Chaudhri Lal Chand, of Rohtak division in the Punjab, wrote to the Reforms Office in New Delhi on 2 July advocating a strong voice for rural communities in government affairs: 'Men with strong rural views will be able to give effective replies to agitators if they could get fair representation at the Round Table Conference.'[12] Chand submitted his recent self-published leaflet, *A Plea for Rural Classes in India*, in which he argued that the representation of rural (subaltern) populations was imperative because:

> rural classes do not possess their own Press nor are they sufficiently organised to make themselves heard from the Platform. But their silence should not be mis-construed into their consent, or incapacity. They are no longer content to have either the Government or the urban classes as their spokesman. For, it is only men of rural extraction and bias who can represent their real grievances.[13]

In the recent disturbances against the government, it was claimed that rural populations had stayed loyal to Viceroy Irwin and that giving rural groups representation at the RTC would be the best way to guarantee such behaviour in the future. The government replied that the Simon Commission showed that rural views were not being overlooked.

At exactly the same time, the Reforms Office also received a letter from Mr Nawle, the editor and manager of the *Dinbandhoo* (Brother of the People) newspaper, based in Poona city in Bombay Presidency. It claimed that while political parties were to be represented at the RTC the 'major portion of the nation viz the agricultural class is forgotten in this conference'.[14] This class was said to supply the government with men and taxes and to stand aloof from anti-government protests. Invoking a caste metaphor, the government were said to be prioritising the stomach and the head over the hands and feet of the nation. This was also a geographical reading, in which the urban 10 per cent of the population was represented but the rural 90 per cent was not. The conclusion of this petition was that Mr Nawle, who had met the Secretary of State for India in 1917 and had attended the Labour Conference at Scarborough in 1920, should represent the rural classes at the RTC.

Both Chand and Nawle spoke 'of' the rural subaltern and clearly wanted to speak 'for' them too. While marginal groups often used their limited resources to hire lawyers or petition makers on their behalf, the representational logic of the archive often suggests that the more detailed the archival trace of the subaltern is,

---

[12] NA/Reforms Department/1930 29/30-R(Pt II).
[13] NA/Reforms Department/1930 29/30-R(Pt II).
[14] NA/Reforms Department/1930 29/30-R(Pt II).

the more heavily mediated the subaltern voice will be. A short set of resolutions were received by the central government which had been passed between 4 and 5 May at Azamgarh in the United Provinces by the Abi Hindu Depressed Classes Society, requesting representation at the RTC according to the size of their population: 'If our rights are not granted to us we shall be obliged to make propaganda and agitate the masses in the same way and in the same manner as the other communities do.'[15] The implicit threat in the resolution hints at the quantitative majority of subaltern populations as well as their willingness to consider the tactics of Congress should they not secure adequate representation in the constitution to be devised in London. The depressed classes ('untouchables') were actually represented at the RTC, by BR Ambedkar, a member of that caste but also the holder of a doctorate from the University of Chicago. Ambedkar famously clashed with Gandhi over the latter's ability to speak for the untouchables. When Ramsay Macdonald's communal settlement (awarded in March 1932 in an attempt to break the deadlock resulting from the second session of the RTC) awarded untouchables separate electorates, Gandhi went on a fast to the death until the settlement was amended. For many, at the time and since, Gandhi's use of sovereign power against his own body in order to reclaim his right to speak for *harijans* (children of god, his term for those known as untouchables) marked a spectacular (both aesthetic and violent) assertion of elite over subaltern sovereignty.

This hints at the complex intersections at play here, between command and popular sovereignty; between acquired sovereignty, domination, and resistance; and between scalar, spectacular, and subaltern sovereignty. These intersections are specific to period and place but alert us to some of the analytical turns that may help us further explore the geographies of global sovereignty.

References

Agamben, G. (1998), *Homo Sacer: Sovereign Power and Bare Life*, trans. Daniel Heller-Roazen (Stanford, Stanford University Press).
Beaud, O. (2018), 'Federation and Empire: About a Conceptual Distinction of Political Forms', *International Journal of Constitutional Law*, 16: 1199–206.
Benton, L. (2010), *A Search for Sovereignty: Law and Geography in European Empires 1400–1900* (Cambridge, Cambridge University Press).
Beverley, E.L. (2015), *Hyderabad, British India, and the World: Muslim Networks and Minor Sovereignty, c.1850–1950* (Cambridge, Cambridge University Press).
Beverley, E.L. (2020), 'Introduction: Rethinking Sovereingty, Colonial Empires, and Nation-States in South Asia and Beyond', *Comparative Studies of South Asia, Africa and the Middle East*, 40: 407–20.
Bodin, J. (1955 [1576]), *Six Books of the Commonwealth*, abridged and translated by M.J. Tooley (London, Blackwell).

---

[15] NA/Reforms Department/1930 29/30-R(Pt II).

Bosco, A. & May, A.C. (1997), *The 'Round Table': The Empire-Commonwealth and British Foreign Policy* (London, Lothian Foundation Press).
Cannadine, D. (2002), *Ornamentalism: How the British Saw their Empire* (Oxford, Oxford University Press).
Chakrabarty, D. (2007), '"In the Name of Politics": Democracy and the Power of the Multitude in India', *Public Culture*, 19: 35–57.
Chatterjee, P. (1997), *A Possible India: Essays in Political Criticism* (New Delhi, Oxford University Press).
Cohen, J.L. (2018), 'Federation', in J.M. Bernstein, A. Ophir, & A.L. Stoler (eds), *Political Concepts: A Critical Lexicon* (New York, Fordham University Press), 145–58.
Coleman, M. (2009), 'Sovereignty', in N. Thrift & R. Kitchen (eds), *International Encyclopaedia of Human Geography* (Amsterdam, Elsevier Science), 255–61.
Collins, M. (2013), 'Decolonisation and the "Federal Moment"', *Diplomacy & Statecraft*, 24: 21–40.
Cooper, F. (2014), *Citizenship between Empire and Nation: Remaking France and French Africa, 1945–1960* (Princeton, Princeton University Press).
Copland, I. (1997), *The Princes of India in the Endgame of Empire, 1917–1947* (Cambridge, Cambridge University Press).
Datla, K.S. (2015), 'The Origins of Indirect Rule in India: Hyderabad and the British Imperial Order', *Law and History Review*, 33: 321–50.
De, R. & Travers, R. (2019), 'Petitioning and Political Cultures in South Asia: Introduction', *Modern Asian Studies*, 53: 1–20.
Elden, S. (2010), 'Land, Terrain, Territory', *Progress in Human Geography*, 34: 799–817.
Elden, S. (2013), *The Birth of Territory* (Chicago, University of Chicago Press).
Flint, C. (2009a), 'Sovereign Power', in R. Johnston, D. Gregory, G. Pratt, & M. Watts (eds), *Dictionary of Human Geography*, 5th edn (Oxford, Blackwell), 705–6.
Flint, C. (2009b), 'Sovereignty', in R. Johnston, D. Gregory, G. Pratt, & M. Watts (eds), *Dictionary of Human Geography*, 5th edn (Oxford, Blackwell), 706–7.
Foucault, M. (1977), *Discipline and Punish: The Birth of the Prison*, trans. Alan Sheridan (Harmondsworth, Penguin).
Foucault, M. (1979), *The History of Sexuality*, vol. i: *The Will to Knowledge*, trans. Robert Hurley (London, Allen Lane).
Guha, R. (1982), 'On Some Aspects of the Historiography of Colonial India', in R. Guha (ed.), *Subaltern Studies I* (Delhi, Oxford University Press), 1–8.
Guha, R. (1997), *Dominance without Hegemony: History and Power in Colonial India* (Cambridge MA & London, Harvard University Press).
Hansen, T.B. (2005), 'Sovereigns beyond the State: On Legality and Authority in Urban India', in T.B. Hansen & F. Stepputat (eds), *Sovereign Bodies: Citizens, Migrants, and States in the Postcolonial World* (Princeton & Oxford, Princeton University Press), 169–91.
Hansen, T.B. & Stepputat, F. (2005), 'Introduction', in T.B. Hansen & F. Stepputat (eds), *Sovereign Bodies: Citizens, Migrants, and States in the Postcolonial World* (Princeton & Oxford, Princeton University Press), 1–36.
Heath, D. & Legg, S. (2018), 'Introducing South Asian Governmentalities', in S. Legg & D. Heath (eds), *South Asian Governmentalities: Michel Foucault and the Question of Postcolonial Orderings* (New Delhi, Cambridge University Press), 1–36.
Hobbes, T. (1967 [1651]), *Hobbes's Leviathan, Reprinted from the Edition of 1651* (Oxford, Clarendon Press).
Keith, A.B. (1936), *A Constitutional History of India 1600–1935* (London, Metheun & Co.).

Legg, S. (2009), 'Of Scales, Networks and Assemblages: The League of Nations Apparatus and the Scalar Sovereignty of the Government of India', *Transactions of the Institute of British Geographers NS*, 34: 234–53.
Legg, S. (2014), 'An International Anomaly? Sovereignty, the League of Nations, and India's Princely Geographies', *Journal of Historical Geography*, 43: 96–110.
Legg, S. (2016a), 'Dyarchy: Democracy, Autocracy and the Scalar Sovereignty of Interwar India', *Comparative Studies in South Asia, Africa and the Middle East*, 36: 44–65.
Legg, S. (2016b), 'Empirical and Analytical Subaltern Space? Ashrams, Brothels and Trafficking in Colonial Delhi', *Cultural Studies*, 30: 793–815.
Locke, J. (2016 [1689]), *Two Treatises of Government* (Indianapolis, Focus).
Majeed, J. (2007), *Autobiography, Travel and Postnational Identity: Gandhi, Nehru and Iqbal* (London, Palgrave Macmillan).
Mantena, K. (2016), 'Popular Sovereignty and Anti-Colonialism', in R. Bourke and Q. Skinner (eds), *Popular Sovereignty in Historical Perspective* (Cambridge, Cambridge University Press), 297–319.
Mantena, K. & Mantena, R.S. (2018), 'Introduction: Political Imaginaries at the End of Empire', *Ab Imperio*, 3: 31–5.
Mantena, R.S. (2018), 'Anticolonialism and Federation in Colonial India', *Ab Imperio*, 3: 36–62.
Mbembe, A. (2001), *On the Postcolony* (Berkeley, Los Angeles & London, University of California Press).
Mbembe, A. (2003), 'Necropolitics', *Public Culture*, 15: 11–40.
Moore, R.J. (1974), *The Crisis of Indian Unity, 1917–1940* (Oxford, Clarendon Press).
O'Hanlon, R. (1988), 'Recovering the Subject: Subaltern Studies and Histories of Resistance in Colonial South Asia', *Modern Asian Studies*, 22: 189–224.
Purushotham, S. (2020a), 'Sovereignty, Federation, and Constituent Power in Interwar India, ca. 1917–39', *Comparative Studies of South Asia, Africa and the Middle East*, 40: 421–33.
Purushotham, S. (2020b), 'Federating the Raj: Hyderabad, Sovereign Kingship, and Partition', *Modern Asian Studies*, 54: 157–98.
Ramusack, B. (2004), *The Indian Princes and their States* (Cambridge, Cambridge University Press).
Rao, A. & Pierce, S. (2006), 'Discipline and the Other Body: Humanitarianism, Violence, and the Colonial Exception', in S. Pierce and A. Rao (eds), *Discipline and the Other Body: Correction, Corporeality, Colonialism* (Durham NC, Duke University Press), 1–35.
Rousseau, J.-J. (2012 [1762]), *Of the Social Contract and Other Political Writings*, trans. Q. Hoare (London, Penguin).
Rudolph, L.I. & Rudolph, S.H. (2010), 'Federalism as State Formation in India: A Theory of Shared and Negotiated Sovereignty', *International Political Science Review*, 31: 553–72.
Schmitt, C. (1976 [1932]), *The Concept of the Political*, trans. G. Schwab (New Brunswick, Rutgers University Press).
Sen, S. (2002), *A Distant Sovereignty: National Imperialism and the Origins of British India* (London, Taylor & Francis).
Sheehan, J.J. (2006), 'The Problem of Sovereignty in European History', *The American Historical Review*, 111: 1–15.
Smolenski, J. (2016), 'Challenging the Sovereign: Three Types of Early Modern Federal Theory', *Politik*, 19: 8–29.

Spivak, G.C. (1985), 'Subaltern Studies: Deconstructing Historiography', in R. Guha (ed.), *Subaltern Studies IV* (Delhi, Oxford University Press), 330–63.

Spivak, G.C. (2000 [1988]), 'Can the Subaltern Speak?', in D. Brydon (ed.), *Postcolonialism: Critical Concepts in Literary and Cultural Studies* (London, Routledge), 1427–77.

Stokes, E. (1959), *The English Utilitarians and India* (Oxford, Clarendon Press).

Wagner, K.A. (2016), '"Calculated to Strike Terror": The Amritsar Massacre and the Spectacle of Colonial Violence', *Past & Present*, 233: 185–225.

Part III

Sovereign Technologies

Introduction

THE FIRST HALF of this book has been historical in approach; the second half looks at contemporary challenges. We examine in this section how sovereignty is deployed as a technique of power, and then, in the final section, how it fares under pressure and in crisis. The complexity of the modern world, especially with the globalised interdependencies of trade and commerce, stretches the meaning of sovereignty and also creates new arenas in which more traditional power games are played out.

We begin by picking up the thread of Chinese sovereignty. Jones and Zhang show how China has used western notions of sovereignty against the west and added its own layers of subtlety. The five principles of peaceful coexistence in some ways offer a brilliant encapsulation of a normative argument emerging from a strong notion of territorial sovereignty, cloaked with moral language such as the responsibility of good global citizenship, and used ruthlessly in areas of contest and dispute.

Similarly, Costa Buranelli shows how in Central Asia the long experience of external interference and imposition of normative frameworks has led to the development of local versions of sovereignty which underpin the authoritarian attempts to overturn a postcolonial order in favour of a revised and reinforced conception of the nation-state, and one which, albeit with the reversal of fortunes of individual leaders, commands significant popular support. Just as Lundgreen argued that external recognition and internal capacity went hand in hand in antiquity, so here we see a profound linkage of ever sharper external borders and ever strengthened internal control. This is a challenging narrative, especially at a time when even liberal democratic states are in retreat from policies of open borders.

The next pair of chapters look at two areas where states have endeavoured to manage the realities of looking beyond themselves to create broader regulatory frameworks. It should be said that this is not wholly divorced from the experiences we have discussed – for instance in Central Asia, there are agreements which mutually reinforce individual autonomy. However, Sahr and Müller tackle head on one of the most intriguing modern attempts to create a supervening body that exists over nation-states, that of the European Union. They do this through the very specific lens of monetary sovereignty. This is the most explicitly 'economic' chapter in the volume, but it serves to reflect on the critical issue of the financial realities of sovereignty. China too uses ties of economic interdependence to underpin its claims, and arguably part of the settlement of India was a complex scheme of hierarchical financial as well as political and administrative organisation, again to support a cautious devolution of limited sovereign authority.

What Sahr and Müller demonstrate through their exploration of monetary agency is the extent to which the European Union stepped above the nation-state in its desire to create the mechanisms for enhanced collaboration. Their analysis shows a deliberately limited intention, underpinned by a cautious assessment that the nation-state would always reclaim power in crisis. This has turned out to be less clear than expected, and the realities of the euro as effectively almost a foreign currency required greater central intervention – and the other side of this particular coin was the role of non-state private investors and creditors. So the 2008/9 debt crisis, and the 2020/1 pandemic crisis, which at the time of writing is far from over, has driven the experiment to further lengths, expanding the notion of monetary sovereignty but also forcing greater recognition of its demands.

It is precisely this push and pull of negotiating the opportunities of supranational jurisdiction and understanding the payoffs that interests St John in her account, based in part on her own experiences, of contemporary investment law. The existence of a place where states set rules makes her argument intersect in part with Sahr and Müller's conundrum over the importance of private actors. Her observation of the performance of negotiation reminds us that what a state is in this context is often a group of officials operating at quite an individual level, which returns us to some of the performativity we saw in Legg and Cruickshank *et al.*'s accounts of spectacle and judgement. Unsuprisingly, this is a forum where equality is in tension with realpolitik. And finally, as St John notes, and in negotiation more than anywhere, sovereignty is relational. We return again to the idea we have seen throughout that 'sovereignty-language' is situational. In the book's last section, we then turn to examples where sovereignty as a functional concept is stretched to its limit.

8

Chinese World Order, Sovereignty, and International Practice

CATHERINE JONES AND CHI ZHANG

Introduction

As CHINA'S ECONOMIC growth has become an embedded fundamental feature of the global political economy, other related aspects of China's rise have received global attention. Scholars and commentators alike have focused their attention on what China's rise means for the rules-based international order, whether in the realm of maritime security, economic order, or implications for global institutions.

In parallel, we have also seen the emergence and greater emphasis of academics in China in focusing on what this rise means for 'what China wants' and whether it is well positioned to achieve these goals. These internal debates in China have been manifested in debates on whether China has an alternative world order or alternative theory for international relations that it could seek to promote, or whether it has a fundamentally different way of approaching great power relations. These debates have been encapsulated in the drive towards developing a Chinese School of international relations (IR). Scholars seeking to develop a 'Chinese School' explore whether China can, and will, draw on its 2000 years of history, and the lessons and processes developed under the traditional Chinese World Order, in developing its approach to current international relations.

In evaluating the emergence of this endeavour, according to Kristensen & Nielsen (2013: 20), the motivation of intellectuals has been in 'seeking attention and prominence, rather than through the macro-lenses of power transition and counter-hegemony'. But it has become clearer under Xi Jinping's government that there is a policy drive to develop a 'new type of great power relations' (Xi 2012; also Lampton 2016; Zeng 2016), and in analysis of his policy speeches and foreign policy actions there is an emphasis on whether there are overtones and a harking back to themes of the traditional Chinese world (e.g. Li & Zhangxi 2018).

In the context of these evolving debates, this chapter highlights and illustrates a tension between the tendency to draw on the traditional Chinese World Order in theory and the Chinese foreign policy practice of evoking and supporting a traditional 'Westphalian' approach to sovereignty (for discussion of what constitutes this form of sovereignty see, for example, Alston's Chapter 3 and Habberstad's Chapter 5). In the traditional Chinese World Order, the term sovereignty is an incongruous term and concept. Relations between the middle kingdom and its tributaries were variously based on trade and deference rather than respect for legitimate governance over a given population and territory (Zhang 2009; Kang 2010; Zhao 2015). Ostensibly, this tension presents a puzzling relationship between the developments of a Chinese School of IR, statements by the Chinese leadership and how we understand them, and China's international practice and rhetoric. The use and application of sovereignty is at the heart of this puzzle. This chapter then asks the question: what is the relationship between China's emerging theory and its practice in relation to the concept of sovereignty?

At its base, sovereignty is a fundamental feature of the current international society, in that it determines what entities can be members of that society, and which basic behavioural expectations underpin relations between those members. But, despite the provision of this base line, sovereignty does not have a fixed definition (see St John's Chapter 11 and Habberstad's Chapter 5). Instead, how we understand sovereignty is linked to a particular distribution of power between members and a distribution and levels of acceptance of common ideas between those members. As Philpott (2001: 4) puts it: 'Revolutions in sovereignty result from prior revolutions in ideas about justice and political authority.' He goes on to emphasise the point that changes in power are insufficient to produce revolutions in sovereignty ideas, and a shift in (collective) ideas are paramount.

As a result, merely indicating that China is rising is insufficient to claim or suggest there could be a change in our understanding of sovereignty. Following from Philpott, it is necessary to separate this objective into three parts. First, there is a 'prior revolution in ideas' that can be seen as emerging from new or rediscovered understandings of the traditional Chinese World Order. Second, we must ask whether China holds sufficient authority (and credibility) to translate these new understandings into practice. Third, noting Reus-Smit's (2001: 538) argument that sovereignty should be treated as 'a variable, practically constituted institution, its precise content and political implications varying with time and context', how can we distil the effects of Chinese practice from other forces changing our understanding of sovereignty? If we can identify a change in practice and implementation, is this sufficient to imply a nudging of the interpretation of the norm as being the result of this particular practice, and that the practice connects to the ideas from the traditional Chinese World Order?

Separating out this process allows us to make the argument in this chapter that there is an internal contradiction in China's approach towards sovereignty – between its ideas and its practice. Its practice regarding Taiwan and the South and

East China seas demonstrates that this could be a two-level dialectic game. On one level, China indicates acceptance and compliance with concepts of sovereignty and is adopting and justifying its actions in relation to the expectations of legitimacy as determined by international society standards – albeit its own interpretation of those standards, though this is insufficient in Philpott's terms to produce a revolution in sovereignty. At the second level, utilising international practices literature, China adopts approaches that would have been consistent with the traditional Chinese World Order, wherein there is a clear hierarchy underpinned by social norms where there is an acceptance of the performance of deference and acknowledgement of Chinese centrality rather than direct rule. This practice then creates a new reality for other states to accept. The result, or at least the potential hope, of this two-level game is that by developing a new reality accepted or acquiesced to by neighbouring states China also begins to adjust what is meant by international concepts and legal standards. The result of these adjustments is that China is gently nudging the international community towards a new interpretation of sovereignty and practice of interaction rather than presenting a whole new schema through the lens of theory.

In making this argument the chapter is organised into four parts. First, it sets out a rudimentary understanding of the traditional Chinese World Order, highlighting its central features. Second, it outlines the current literatures and approaches to understanding Chinese interpretations of sovereignty and China's presentation of these approaches in the United Nations Security Council (UNSC). Third, it considers China's actions in relation to the South China Sea and Taiwan (also known as the Republic of China) as examples relating to reinterpreting international concepts. Finally, the chapter concludes with some scenarios as to how this approach could evolve.

Traditional Chinese World Order

The concept of the traditional Chinese World Order is derived from a process of systemising and simplifying 2000 years of Chinese history encompassing the rule of 13 dynasties.[1] During this time, the geographical space known as 'China' varied considerably. At various times this space was so expansive it encompassed Mongolia, but at times when it was more geographically limited it only included spaces within the Great Wall. As a result, it would be impossible to do justice here to the huge variety of governance structures, conflicts, processes and patterns of deference and subordination within this chapter. Indeed, as rightly noted by some authors (e.g. Fairbank & Reischauer 1978; Zhang 2009; Zhang & Buzan 2012), the Chinese World Order is not a homogeneous description of how China governed its internal and external affairs for 2000 years. Instead, under different dynasties

---

[1] See Habberstad, this volume, for a detailed account of early transformations of sovereignty.

the practice of the Chinese empire contained significant variation, and the current debate drawing on this approach cherry-picks the most positive or 'harmonious' elements and periods as being emblematic.

This diversity aside, there are some elements that were consistently present in the social order (Zhang & Buzan 2012: 12), if not consistently important: in particular, hierarchy and Sino-centrism maintained through economic relations of dependence. Within these elements, the tributary system (as described by Fairbank & Reischauer 1978) is viewed as a framework for understanding the social relations between political entities. In the literature, there is a vibrant debate about how these connections should be viewed. Zhang & Buzan (2012: 10) focus on the constitutional elements of the system whereby the system prescribes behaviours between members, and grants privileges and duties among them. According to Zhang's (2009) reading of Fairbank, he viewed the system as a framework and set of ideas that enabled the continuation of Chinese primacy over centuries. Kang (2010), however, indicates that among the member entities there were differing degrees of acceptance of these ideas, potentially showing that it was not the ideas but the structure that was significant for the maintenance of the Sino-centric order. Zhang (2009), on the other hand, notes the importance of the bureaucracy as a central element of the order. Among these elements and the hotly contested nature of these debates, it becomes clear that it is the practice of China rather than the theory that gives contents or meaning to the order, but in maintaining itself two features are essential: hierarchy and Sino-centrism.

Within these practices, the traditional Chinese World Order projects an international system in which hierarchy leads to stability and order (Qin 2006: 33). This hierarchical order, seeking centrality rather than dominance, is distinctive from Realist assumptions about an anarchical 'state of nature' wherein individuals compete with each other to survive. This hierarchical structure, evident in the tributary system, does not advocate equality between actors, but ideally relies on benevolent governance to ensure stability.

This traditional world view experienced an abrupt shock when China was forced out of isolation by the First Opium War in 1840. The experience of humiliation felt by the Chinese people and their political elites was brought about by a traumatising loss of geographic integrity and an inability to determine their own territory. This experience is considered a crucial factor in understanding the respect for traditional sovereignty held by the current Chinese Communist Party (CCP) leadership. Yet this insistence would be in contradiction to the experience and practice of the tributary system under the traditional Chinese World Order and therefore the approach that modern-day China could advocate were it not for the century of humiliation. However, what the humiliation thesis fails to explain is why, after one-and-a-half centuries, China is still 'celebrating', in Callahan's (2004a) words, its humiliation. Can the trauma be so profound that even today, when China no longer faces the kind of threat it faced back in 1840, it is still clinging to the principle of non-interference?

We argue that China's insistence on sovereignty today is driven, to a larger extent, by practical considerations – as a useful mechanism to achieve a Sino-centric hierarchy – rather than by a normative commitment to respect the territory or internal governance of neighbouring cultural entities. As a result, in pursuit of this practice-based approach, China will gradually develop new practices of implementing the norm of sovereignty, rather than developing a new theory to underpin or replace sovereignty. In this sense it mimics the Traditional World Order that was premised on practice rather than ideology or theory.

Xi Jinping and the practice of the Traditional Chinese World Order

In December 2018, Xi Jinping made the claim that China will not seek to dominate the world. His approach to leadership both domestically and internationally has been explained as being 'Xi Jinping's thought', which has (as of 2019) been inserted into the state constitution. In speeches, Xi regularly draws on China's centuries of humiliation and points to the significant differences in China's historical conduct of foreign relations. In this, Xi is in line with his predecessors, who throughout their presidencies also affirmed that China would never seek hegemony. In making these claims they also invoked history by claiming that even when China was a great civilisation and empire, it was never a dominating or hegemonic state; rather it developed peaceful trading routes with the peoples and states on its borders.

Before Xi became president, he started to use the phrase 'new great power relations' (see Jones 2019b), through which he sought to argue that China does not have a history of the same type of wars of conquest and land-grabbing that western states do, and indeed that it may be able to develop peaceful great power relations precisely because of its different mentality and history. As a result, the theories of IR – particularly Realism – that are the result of reflection on western history and particularly conflict are not relevant to understanding China. Although this has long been acknowledged, and scholars of the English School have sought to incorporate it (see e.g. Zhang 2009; Zhang & Buzan 2012), other academics, including Qin (2016) and Zhao (2009), have then used this argument to promote the need for China's history to inform a new IR theory.

The development of a Chinese School of IR is an attempt to build a more extensive theory based on these claims that China can be different in how it interacts with other states and global entities. As Acharya (2011) points out, the close ties between power and knowledge are particularly evident in China, where scholarly practices became an extension of the state's efforts to create theoretical bases for China's peaceful rise. As a result, we have reasons to raise questions about the links between the academic and the theoretical debates about a Chinese School of IR that draws on China's history and Confucian beliefs, on the one hand, and the foreign policies developed and practised by the current leadership, on the other.

However, just as there are a multiplicity of different approaches to understanding what the traditional Chinese World Order was, there are also many different interpretations of how the Traditional World Order and the phrases used by the CCP are related, in particular because the meanings of phrases such as 'new great power relations' are in themselves contested. For example, Zeng and Breslin's (2016: 780) analysis based on 141 Chinese-language articles shows that although the Chinese School did not have a consensus on what the 'new type of Great Power relations' is, it has been made clear that it is different from the western version that 'involves power struggles, conflict and a zero-sum game'. As a result, seeking to understand the relationship between these contested terms from a theoretical or academic position may not be fruitful, especially as what these terms mean may only be revealed in their praxis.

Chinese approaches to sovereignty

This section could not possibility do justice to the plethora of sources and stimuli for the Chinese interpretations of sovereignty. Indeed, it is not necessary to do this here. Rather, this section aims at teasing out the main points of contention between Chinese and liberal interpretations of sovereignty (see e.g. Carlson 2005; Wu 2007; Glanville 2010).

The prevailing view among commentators up to the early 2010s was that China clung to a Westphalian interpretation of sovereignty, seeking to continue to uphold respect for sovereignty and non-interference (see He 2003). This view was supported by statements from Mao in 1959 that presented:

> According to the principle of sovereignty, a state has the power, in accordance with its own will, to decide its own form of state, political system, and social economic system, and intervention by other states in those matters is absolutely not permissible. What particularly should be carried out, and what should be reformed in internal affairs are matters concerning a state's own affairs. Intervention by other states in those matters is absolutely not permissible.
>
> (Cited in Carlson 2005: 42)

While Mao's understanding of China's position in the world is largely built on Marxism, Marxism has been appropriated by Lenin and Mao to serve their respective poltical visions. The Sinicisation of Marxism has integrated this foreign school of thought into the indegenous Chinese approach.

The importance of state sovereignty and non-interference is also enshrined in the Five Principles of Peaceful Coexistence[2] that guide Chinese foreign-policy making.

---

[2] The Five Principles of Peaceful Coexistence were first articulated in 1954 by Zhou Enlai but have been repeated ever since. They are 'mutual respect for sovereignty and territorial integrity, mutual non-aggression, non-interference in each other's internal affairs, equality and mutual benefit and peaceful coexistence'; Foreign Ministry of the People's Republic of China, 'Carrying Forward the Five Principles of Peaceful Coexistence in the Promotion of Peace and Development', speech by Wen Jiabao, 28 June 2004, available online at www.fmprc.gov.cn/eng/topics/seminaronfiveprinciples/t140777.htm, accessed 4 November 2011.

Furthermore, in the debates on peacekeeping and sovereignty in the UNSC in the 1990s, Chinese delegations also restated this view, most notably in the Chinese statement on the Agenda for Peace, 'First, the principle of respect for State sovereignty and non-interference in a country's internal affairs must always be observed. The United Nations is an intergovernmental organisation composed of sovereign States rather than a world government' (S/PV.3492, 18 January 1995: 13). As a result, there is a plethora of evidence that demonstrates the continued commitment to a Westphalian approach to sovereignty (see also Jones, 2019a: 178).

However, there are also challenges to this view, as Carlson (2002: 18) notes in relation to non-interference:

> Even the most trenchant Chinese analysts accepted that the United Nations occasionally has a right, indeed an obligation, to intervene in the affairs of some of its member states. In other words, the Chinese most strenuously objected to the looseness with which some in the west referred to humanitarian crises, the selective way in which the term was appropriated by western governments, and the application of the concept – not the concept of intervention itself.

This view is now becoming common in respect to China's interpretation of the norms of sovereignty – in particular in the discourses on China's engagement with peacekeeping practices where the focus is on non-interference (不干预) rather than non-intervention (不干涉) (see Kent 2009; Foot and Walter 2010; Hirono 2011: 339; Lanteigne 2011: 314; Teitt 2011; Jones 2019a). This discussion then focuses on how Chinese interpretations of sovereignty are connected to the ideas found in the traditional Chinese World Order.

From the outline of the traditional Chinese World Order, one potential view is that China would seek to create its own hierarchy, akin to the tributary system, wherein the order becomes China-centric, rather than 'liberal', western, or US-centric. However, there is a keen distinction here that centrality does not automatically assume hierarchy. Indeed, Loke (2019) argues that it is centrality rather than dominance that China seeks. Indeed, from Chinese foreign policy statements, the Chinese-preferred interpretation of this aspect of sovereignty advocates international relations based around the equality between states (FMPRC no date; Jiang 2000; S/PV.3046, 31 January 1992). The advocacy of this position can be seen as a reaction to China's 'century of humiliation' at the hand of the western (liberal) powers; on that interpretation of history, China, previously a respected and powerful empire, was subjugated to being an occupied territory and was exploited by other powers.[3]

There is a balancing act to be played out here: there are calls within China to re-emerge on the world stage with the power and glory of the past. This view has been stated by some sections of the People's Liberation Army (PLA). For example, in an address to the United States War College, Lieutenant General Li Jijun stated

---

[3] For a brief account of the century of humiliation and its lasting effects on China in the 20th and 21st centuries, see Ropp (2010: 135–55).

that 'For the Chinese government and people issues concerning our national sovereignty are not subject to reconciliation or negotiation' (Li 2007: 5) after stating earlier that it is because of the century of humiliation that 'the people of China show such strong emotions in matters concerning our national independence, unity, integrity of territory, and sovereignty' (Li 2007: 3). Alistair Iain Johnston (1998) refers to this attitude in the PLA as 'hyper-sovereignty': 'Hyper-sovereignty values are still a central driver of Chinese foreign policy. A *realpolitik* strategic culture still colours the world-views of many of China's senior security policy decision makers.'

Yet there are also calls for China to recall the lessons of Confucian thinkers that emphasised the responsibilities that China has towards other powers (Glanville 2010), and this is where we also see the selection of peaceful periods of history from within the traditional Chinese World Order, in the current rhetoric of Xi Jinping and previously Hu Jintao (in, for example, the harmonious world narrative). It is clear from the statements and speeches to a variety of international audiences that the leadership within China is mindful of the need of balance.

Whilst it would be naïve to think that China's conception of sovereignty would not produce a hierarchy over time, the conclusion of Rosemary Foot and Andrew Walter (2010: 300) states that China 'has not yet readily embraced a leadership role in relation to global order problems. Neither, however, does its conservatism form a basis for a radical rewriting of the rules of global order'. This suggests that China could appeal to a previous understanding of the norm in order to give it greater international legitimacy. The expectation of the behaviour corresponding to this interpretation would be an attempt to diminish the credibility of the group of states most supportive of this liberal interpretation (those at the top of a hierarchy), as well as highlighting the contradictions in the application of its 'supporting act', the pursuit of human rights, and the rule of law. This is evident from Beijing's manoeuvring in mobilising 37 countries to sign a UN letter defending China's Xinjiang policy – its own interpretation of human rights – against the criticism by a group of 22 western states (Miles 2019). Three months later the number of supporting countries increased to 54 (Permanent Mission of the People's Republic of China to the UN 2019) before some Mulsim-majority countries quietly withdrew their support in 2020 (Zhang 2022).

This position has been restated both during and after the debates on sovereignty in the UN throughout the 1990s.[4] In 1992, the Security Council commissioned the Secretary General to produce a report to provide an 'analysis and recommendations on ways of strengthening and making more efficient within the framework and provisions of the Charter the capacity of the United Nations for preventive diplomacy, for peacemaking and for peace-keeping' (Agenda for Peace 1995). The

---

[4] See for example UNSC 1992 Summit Meeting, S/PV.3046 of 31 January 1992; FOCAC Beijing Declaration of the Forum on China–Africa Cooperation, 10–12 October 2000, available online at www.fmprc.gov.cn/zflt/eng/zyzl/hywj/t157833.htm, accessed 17 August 2021.

outcome, published in 1995, was called 'An Agenda for Peace'. In the Chinese response there is evidence of the same interpretation of the relationship between sovereignty and human rights and the implications for the Security Council's responsibilities.

In looking at China's approach to territorial integrity, there is another clear distinction between the liberal interpretation and China's. In stark contrast to the liberal interpretation of territorial integrity being of diminishing importance relative to other norms of sovereignty (He 2003), for China and indeed for many developing states, territorial integrity and the corresponding norm of non-interference remain at the core of their understandings of sovereignty (ASEAN n.d.; 2005). The advance of scholarship on sovereignty in China at the turn of the century is driven by events associated with territorial integrity, such as the handover of Hong Kong and Macau in 1997 and 1999, respectively, and NATO airstrikes against Yugoslavia in 1999 (Wang 2004).

Finally, China's approach to the demands of sovereignty on sovereign states is also clear. These states should engage with each other peacefully, whilst at all times respecting the Five Principles of Peaceful Coexistence, and the UN Charter. Peacekeeping is an important tool of international society, but in order to maintain the integrity of sovereign states it should only be applied with the host country's consent and following approval from a legitimate authority. The concept of coercive (non-consensual) peacekeeping activities to uphold (contested) liberal principles cannot be reconciled with a Chinese interpretation of the norms of sovereignty.

Sovereignty, Chinese World Order, and territorial disputes

China's approach to sovereignty is often the focus of discussion in relation to its engagement with UN peacekeeping operations. Yet, the thornier issue related to China's interpretation of sovereignty is over the territorial disputes in the South China Sea and Taiwan. In these areas the connection between sovereignty and Chinese World Order becomes apparent.

South China Sea

The territorial disputes along the South China Sea involves numerous countries in Southeast Asia. China (initially the Republic of China, later the People's Republic of China) claims to enjoy sovereignty over most of the South China Sea, which is in conflict with the exclusive-economic-zone claims of other countries in this region. China's efforts in land reclamation to build military and other facilities in the Spratly Islands exacerbated the tensions between China and other Southeast Asian countries, which culminated in July 2016 when the arbitral tribunal constituted under Annex VII to the 1982 UN Convention on the Law of the Sea ruled in favour of the Philippines. China refused to participate in the arbitration and rejected the authority of the arbitral tribunal: 'The essence of the subject-matter of the arbitration is the territorial sovereignty over several maritime features in the South China Sea, which is beyond the scope of the Convention and does not concern the interpretation or application of the Convention' (Ministry of Foreign Affairs of the People's Republic of China 2014). The arbitration award was made in the absence of China's consent, and the legality of the arbitral procedure was questioned by China (Pinto 2018). Thirty-one countries supported Beijing's claim that the ruling was invalid, and 40 endorsed the legality of the arbitration and called on both parties to respect it (Amti Leadership 2021).

The difficulty of moving the arbitration forward is partly due to the dynamics within the Philippines. Since Rodrigo Duterte assumed the presidency on 30 June 2016, there has been a policy shift towards realignment with China in the context of deteriorating relations with the United States, partly due to American criticism of Duterte's war on drugs (Blanchard 2016). Duterte was reluctant to jeopardise his 'new commercial alliance', with US$13.5 billion in deals with China to be signed by raising the arbitral ruling (Blanchard 2016; Lim 2016). China took over the status as the largest investor in the Philippines from the United States with considerable investment in agriculture and infrastructure (Bloomberg 2016). Duterte's pivot to China indeed brought a boost in banana exports, which demonstrated the benefit of not bringing up the South China Sea issue (Peel and Ramos 2017).

In a broader context, Beijing's efforts in silencing Duterte on the issue of sovereignty disputes is in line with China's outward reaching economic strategy in the context of 'new normal'. At the Business 20 Summit on 3 September 2016, Xi Jinping used the phrase 'new normal' to characterise China's economic development strategy (*China Daily* 2017): 'This is a starting point for China to develop a comprehensively deepening reform, to continuously push forward economic and social development, to adjust to new normal by transforming development mode, to continuously be open to and have an in-depth interaction with the world.' This 'new normal' is powered by major economic strategies, including the Belt and Road Initiative and the Asian Infrastructure Investment Bank (AIIB), both of which enhance China's infrastructure links with Southeast Asia, among other regions. This does not only have effects on the Philippines; it effectively keeps other Southeast Asian countries occupied so they cannot focus on territorial disputes. In September 2015, China signed a US$5.5 billion deal with Indonesian state-owned companies to build the first high-speed railway in Indonesia (Soeriaatmadja 2015). The isolationist and protectionist foreign policy that the Trump administration pursued left Southeast Asia a battleground for competition between China and Japan. China's reach into Southeast Asia, notably in the form of the AIIB, is considered as an attempt to re-establish its centrality in the region, which has been seen as 'overly U.S.-centric' (Loke 2019: 51; see also Zhao 2019: 566).

As China's economic power grows, it naturally wishes to have a greater say in the global economic system (Ren 2016: 436). China's dissatisfaction with either the slow pace or lack of progress in reforming existing institutions has now made it inevitable that China will seek to create new international institutions that more closely align to its global priorities. China has been developing an alternative framework to present China's 'peaceful development' and counter-act the threatening rhetoric of the 'rise of China' (Loke 2019: 50). Rather than being converted by the UN and Association of Southeast Asian Nations (ASEAN) to their models of international relations, William Callahan (2004b: 77) argues that conversion can work another way around: China converting other countries to its own model of world politics, in other words a Chinese World Order.

However, in China's efforts to develop its own approach to development and engaging with developing states, it has also been heavily criticised for engaging in 'debt-trap diplomacy'. Certainly, China's different experiences in investing in African states will have a bearing on how successful China may be in bringing states on board with its approaches to development. However, as Oqubay and Lin (2019: 313) note, it would be wrong to assume that China's approaches are 'uniform'; instead it should be noted that they exhibit 'unevenness, diversity and dynamic trends'. As Taylor (2019: 98) puts it, 'policy coherence is fragmentary at best and in fact often contradictory in practice as policies are arbitrated by numerous Chinese actors'. Hence, even in the continent where China's economic footprint appears to be clearest and most deliberate, it appears that practice is driving China's actions, rather than an overarching policy agenda.

In practice, then, this Chinese World Order has been developed to address concerns about China's rising influence. For example, although the initial design of the AIIB projects a China-dominated revisionist institution, its eventual design did address some of these concerns reducing the ability for China to act as the single *mens rea* within the organisation. For example, China's veto power was reduced, and they had to increase the nationalities represented by the members of the board of directors (Hameiri & Jones 2018: 575). Similarly, although the bank is headquartered in Beijing, it is open to appointing a non-Chinese individual as its president, which is meant to epitomise China's intention of seeking centrality rather than dominance (Ren 2016: 439).

Taiwan

Taiwan's self-perception and foreign policy agenda changed dramatically after it was replaced by the People's Republic as the legitimate government of China in the UN. However, despite lacking international recognition as the legitimate government of China (by all but 14 UN member states, plus the Holy See):[5]

---

[5] In 2021 Taiwan was recognised as being the legitimate government of China by 14 states: Paraguay; Belize; Guatemala; Haiti; Honduras; Nicaragua; Saint Lucia; Saint Vincent and the Grenadines; Saint Kitts; the Marshall Islands; Nauru; Palau; Tuvalu; and Swaziland; it is also recognised by the Holy See. The Dominican Republic switched recognition to the People's Republic on 1 May 2018 and El Salvador switched in August 2018. In 2019, Kirbati and the Solomon Islands switched recognition away.

> Taiwan has been able to maintain informal international recognition and a degree of autonomy in its external affairs. It has achieved this through a mixture of cultural, economic, and informal relationships, often relying on crafting pragmatic work-arounds to satisfy the One China Policy. As a result, Taiwan has maintained a claim to de facto rather than de jure independent status, akin to sovereignty.[6]
>
> (Jones, 2020: 62)

This makes Taiwan a key obstacle to Xi Jinping's vision of the 'China dream' – a country that regains its full sovereignty and territorial integrity within his reign.

Beijing is aware of the practical difficulties in annexing a de facto independent political entity, especially considering its strategic importance to the United States and its emerging democratic political structure. Beijing and Taipei had maintained a precarious balance between the de jure independence and reunification, based on the 1992 consensus, before Tsai Ing-wen (president of Taiwan) began to harden Taipei's positions. Beijing was willing to acquiesce to Taiwan's de facto independence, especially when pro-China Ma Ying-jeou was the president. During this period, despite the absence of international recognition, Taiwan was able to sustain its economic growth 'because of the advanced level of its exports, its own patterns of business development, and a lack of institutionalised regional economic governance. ... Its economy continued to grow and flourish (Winkler 2008)' (Jones 2020: 68–9). Yu-long Ling (2011: 25) describes cross-strait relations under Ma Ying-jeou as a cautious balance whereby both parties did not seek to relinquish sovereignty but neither did they exercise it. Ma's 'status-quo approach' – no independence, no unification – won Taiwan the time to focus on developing economic ties in the region (Ling 2011: 28).

Taiwan joined the World Trade Organization in 2002. This gave it an informal recognition as an autonomous economy from the mainland. However, the expectation that this recognition would lead to greater engagement for the island in the global economic order was not realised. According to Winkler (2008: 483), the reason for the absence of further opportunities for Taiwan to be recognised was because it conflicted with the claims the People's Republic made in respect of the island. In 2010, China and Taiwan signed the Economic Cooperation Framework Agreement (ECFA), which reduced the likelihood of military confrontation (Ling 2011: 27).

In the ongoing 2020/1 global public health crisis, the rejection of Taiwan's sovereign status was another source of collision. Taiwan was successful in keeping the public health situation under control. As the outbreak in mainland China started to settle down, the pandemic became another platform for Beijing–Taipei wrestling: as Taipei took this opportunity to lobby to join the World Health Organization (WHO), Beijing was consolidating its position in the WHO by defending Tedros

---

[6] Taiwan maintains informal cultural offices and diplomatic relations with a number of states that formally recognise the PRC as the legitimate government. These states include the United States and the United Kingdom. Taiwan has also been able to achieve institutional recognition as an 'economy' at both the World Trade Organization and within the Asia Pacific Economic Cooperation forum (APEC). Furthermore, it is able to compete at the Olympic Games as 'Chinese Taipei', through the approval of the International Olympic Committee.

Adhanom Ghebreyesus, the WHO Director-General, against the Taiwanese call for his immediate resignation due to his handling of the pandemic.

Another key event was the Sunflower Student Movement against the Cross-Strait Service Trade Agreement (CSSTA), initially designed to bring the two economies closer by opening industries in both parties to market liberalisation. The Taiwan Solidarity Union vowed to block the trade pact as it would 'subject local business to fierce competition' and harm 'small and medium-sized enterprises and workers in Taiwan' (Shih 2013). J. Michael Cole, a journalist from the *Diplomat*, speculated that the CSSTA was used to pave the way for a reunification (Hsieh and Weigel 2014). On 30 March 2014, 500,000 Taiwanese protested against the hasty ratification of the CSSTA (Fan 2014). The obstruction to the CSSTA also undermined Taiwan's efforts to join the Trans-Pacific Partnership and the Regional Comprehensive Economic Partnership (RCEP) (*Taiwan News* 2014; Zhu 2015: 254).

Things have changed dramatically since Tsai Ing-wen, leader of the Democratic Progressive Party, came to power in Taipei. Ma's 'status-quo approach' was seen as a good strategy at the time, but it could only serve as a transitional strategy, which was bound to end at the point when voters were no longer content with the status quo (Ling 2011: 28). Tsai Ing-wen dismissed the 1992 consensus[7] in an interview with the *Washington Post*, which is significant because it is an explicit pro-independence statement made by the Taiwan authority to denounce China's claim of sovereignty (Hsu 2016). Xi's recent statement that 'We make no promise to renounce the use of force and reserve the option of taking all necessary means' elevated cross-strait tensions to a new level (Xi 2019). Threatening as this statement may be, it is, in fact, not fundamentally different from China's Taiwan policy under previous leaders, that is, 'China would not relinquish its authority to use force in the event that Taiwan did declare independence' (Ling 2011: 27).

To ensure China's centrality, Beijing has been seeking to marginalise Taiwan in the political realm. Since Tsai Ing-wen came into office, Beijing has sought to diminish Taiwan's presence in various fora, such as the WHO and the International Civil Aviation Organization (Lampert & Wu 2016; Agence France-Presse 2018). Beijing also committed a huge amount of resources to facilitate its COVID-19 diplomacy (including providing personal protective equipment or in providing vaccines to developing states), a strategy Taipei has also been pursuing during the pandemic. A more assertive foreign policy under Xi placed increasing emphasis on the 'near-abroad', making it difficult for Taiwan to maintain its trade autonomy. Furthermore, Taiwan is continuing to lose diplomatic allies, including Panama (Haas 2017), Burkina Faso, El Salvador, the Dominican Republic (BBC 2018), the Solomon Islands, and Kiribati (Lyons 2019).

---

[7] The 1992 consensus refers to the outcome of the meeting in 1992 between the representatives of the People's Republic of China and the Republic of China, which had been the diplomatic basis for semi-official cross-strait relations.

Conclusion

This chapter makes a crucial claim: China's approach to sovereignty is informed by its practical experience more than its theoretical preferences. Indeed, China is seeking to reconcile practice disunities in relation to sovereignty through conceptual gymnastics. Through the examples of the South China Sea and Taiwan, it is clear that China's attitude towards sovereignty is not as inflexible as many would assume from referenes to a traditional Chinese World Order, or recourse to interpretations of Westphalian soveriegnty. This chapter has demonstrated that there are at least two elements to China's approaches to sovereignty: on the one hand its international practice and on the other hand its domestic interpretations of sovereignty, derived from domestic narratives to regain past glories and the need to assume its international responsibilities. These two-handed approaches are essentially different from the liberal interpretations often adopted by Western liberal states that emphasise human rights that seem to more clearly adopt a teleological end that is desirable and then experiment with practical means through which to achieve those outcomes.

In this context, China has adopted and reinterpreted the concept of sovereignty as a useful mechanism towards a Chinese World Order, a Sino-centric hierarchy maintained through economic interdependence. This approach is almost a retrospective means to justify and explain its actions as a purposeful objective driven action, rather than a praxis-led approach. An interesting question that arises from this analysis is: why is China seeking to create a logical story arch to explain its sovereignty engagements?

References

Acharya, A. (2011), 'Dialogue and Discovery: In Search of International Relations Theories Beyond the West', *Millennium: Journal of International Studies*, 39: 619–37.

Agence France-Presse (2018), 'Taiwan Accuses World Health Organisation of Bowing to Beijing over Invitation to Top Health Meeting', *South China Morning Post* (8 May), accessed 17 October 2019, www.scmp.com/news/china/policies-politics/article/2145129/taiwan-accuses-world-health-organisation-bowing-beijing.

Agenda for Peace (1995), accessed 9 April 2020, www.un.org/ruleoflaw/blog/document/an-agenda-for-peace-preventive-diplomacy-peacemaking-and-peace-keeping-report-of-the-secretary-general/.

Amti Leadership (2021), 'Arbitration Support Tracker', Asia Maritime Transparency Initiative, accessed 16 August 2021, https://amti.csis.org/arbitration-support-tracker/.

ASEAN (n.d.), 'The ASEAN Charter', accessed 17 October 2011, http://www.aseansec.org/publications/ASEAN-Charter.pdf.

BBC (2018), 'Taiwan Loses Diplomatic Ally as Dominican Republic Switches Ties to China', *BBC* (1 May), accessed 16 August 2021, www.bbc.co.uk/news/world-asia-china-43958849.

Blanchard, B. (2016), 'Duterte Aligns Philippines with China, Says U.S. Has Lost', *Reuters* (20 October), accessed 10 September 2019, www.reuters.com/article/us-china-philippines/duterte-aligns-philippines-with-china-says-u-s-has-lost-idUSKCN12K0AS.

Bloomberg (2016), 'China Embraces Southeast Asia with Renewed Trade, Investment Push as US Turns Inward', *South China Morning Post* (12 December), accessed 16 October 2019, www.scmp.com/news/china/diplomacy-defence/article/2053920/china-embraces-southeast-asia-renewed-trade-investment.

Callahan, W.A. (2004a), 'National Insecurities: Humiliation, Salvation, and Chinese Nationalism', *Alternatives: Global, Local, Political*, 29: 199–218.

Callahan, W.A. (2004b), *Contingent States: Greater China and Transnational Relations* (Minneapolis & London, University of Minnesota Press).

Carlson, A. (2002), 'Protecting Sovereignty, Accepting Intervention: The Dilemma of Chinese Foreign Relations in the 1990's', *China Policy Series* No. 18 (New York: National Committee on US–China Relations).

Carlson, A. (2005), *Unifying China, Integrating with the World: Securing Chinese Sovereignty in the Reform Era* (Stanford, Stanford University Press).

China Daily (2017), 'New Normal in Economic Development', *China Daily* (5 October), accessed 17 October 2019, www.chinadaily.com.cn/china/19thcpcnationalcongress/2017-10/05/content_32869258.htm.

Fairbank, J.K. & Reischauer, E.O. (1978), *East Asia: Tradition & Transformation* (Boston, Houghton Mifflin).

Fan, J. (2014), 'The Economics of the Cross-Strait Services Agreement', *Brookings* (18 April), accessed 19 October 2019, www.brookings.edu/opinions/the-economics-of-the-cross-strait-services-agreement/.

FMPRC (n.d.), 'China's Independent Foreign Policy of Peace', accessed 9 April 2020, http://www.china-un.ch/eng/zgbd/zgwjzc/t85889.htm.

Foot, R. & Walter, A. (2010), *China, the United States and Global Order* (New York, Cambridge University Press).

Glanville, L. (2010), 'Retaining the Mandate of Heaven: Sovereign Accountability in Ancient China', *Millennium: Journal of International Studies*, 39.2: 323–43.

Haas, B. (2017), 'Panama Cuts Formal Ties with Taiwan in Favour of China', *The Guardian* (13 June), accessed 19 October 2019, www.theguardian.com/world/2017/jun/13/panama-cuts-diplomatic-ties-with-taiwan-in-favour-of-china.

Hameiri, S. & Jones, L. (2018), 'China Challenges Global Governance? Chinese International Development Finance and the AIIB', *International Affairs*, 94: 573–93.

He, B. (2003). 'Chinese Sovereignty: Challenges and Adaptation', *East Asia Institute Working Papers Series*, No. 104 (23 September).

Hirono, M. (2011), 'China's Charm Offensive and Peacekeeping: The Lessons of Cambodia – What Now for Sudan?', *International Peacekeeping*, 18.3: 328–43.

Hsieh, Y.-Y. & Weigel, M. (2014), '324: Dispatches from Taipei', *n+1* (27 March), accessed 19 October 2019, https://nplusonemag.com/online-only/foreign-affairs/324-dispatches-from-taipei/.

Hsu, S. (2016), 'Tsai Cites Public's Will over "Consensus"', *Taipei Times* (23 July), accessed 16 October 2019, www.taipeitimes.com/News/front/archives/2016/07/23/2003651597/1.

Johnston, A.I. (1998), 'China's Militarized Interstate Dispute Behaviour 1949–1992: A First Cut at the Data', *China Quarterly*, 153: 1–30.

Jones, C. (2019a), *China's Challenge to Liberal Norms* (Basingstoke, Palgrave).

Jones, C. (2019b), 'China's Middle-Power Practices with Great-Power Outcomes', *Asia Policy* 26.3: 61–77.

Jones, C. (2020), 'Regional Architects: Defining Taiwan Out?', *Contemporary Politics*, 26.1: 60–83.

Kang, D. (2010), *East Asia before the West: Five Centuries of Trade and Tribute* (New York, Columbia University Press).

Kent, A.E. (2009), *Beyond Compliance: China, International Organizations, and Global Security* (Stanford, Stanford University Press).

Kristensen, P.M. & Nielsen, R.T. (2013), 'Constructing a Chinese International Relations Theory: A Sociological Approach to Intellectual Innovation', *International Political Sociology*, 7.1: 19–40.

Lampert, A. & Wu, J.R. (2016), 'U.N. Agency Snubs Taiwan, Recognizing Beijing's "One China"', *Reuters* (23 September), accessed 17 October 2019, www.reuters.com/article/us-taiwan-china-idUSKCN11T08P.

Lampton, D.M. (2016), 'A New Type of Major-Power Relationship: Seeking a Durable Foundation for U.S.–China Ties', *Asia Policy*, 16: 51–68.

Lanteigne, M. (2011), 'A Change in Perspective: China's Engagement in East Timor UN Peacekeeping Operations', *International Peacekeeping*, 18.3: 313–27.

Li, J. (Lieutenant General) (2007), 'Traditional Military Thinking and the Defensive Strategy of China', address given on 29 August, published as Letort Paper No.1, accessed 7 November 2011, http://www.fas.org/nuke/guide/china/doctrine/china-li.pdf.

Li, X. & Cheng, Z. (2018), 'What Might a Chinese World Order Look Like?', *The Diplomat* (13 April), accessed 6 April 2020, https://thediplomat.com/2018/04/what-might-a-chinese-world-order-look-like/.

Lim, B.K. (2016), 'Philippines' Duterte Says South China Sea Arbitration Case to Take "Back Seat"', *Reuters* (19 October), accessed 14 October 2019, www.reuters.com/article/us-china-philippines-idUSKCN12J10S.

Ling, Y. (2011), 'Cross-Strait Relations under Ma's Administration and the Prospect of a Peaceful Settlement', *American Journal of Chinese Studies*, 18: 25–33.

Loke, B. (2019), 'China's Rise and U.S. Hegemony: Navigating Great-Power Management in East Asia', *Asia Policy*, 26: 41–60.

Lyons, K. (2019), 'Taiwan Loses Second Ally in a Week as Kiribati Switches to China', *The Guardian* (20 September), accessed 18 October 2019, www.theguardian.com/world/2019/sep/20/taiwan-loses-second-ally-in-a-week-as-kiribati-switches-to-china.

Miles, T. (2019), 'Saudi Arabia and Russia among 37 States Backing China's Xinjiang Policy', *Reuters* (12 July), accessed 16 August 2021, https://uk.reuters.com/article/uk-china-xinjiang-rights-idUKKCN1U721L.

Ministry of Foreign Affairs of the People's Republic of China (2014), Position Paper of the Government of the People's Republic of China on the Matter of Jurisdiction in the South China Sea Arbitration Initiated by the Republic of the Philippines.

Oqubay, A. & Lin, J.Y. (2019), 'The Future of China–Africa Economic Ties', in A. Oqubay & J.Y. Lin (eds), *China-Africa and an Economic Transformation* (Oxford, Oxford University Press), 310–24.

Peel, M. & Ramos, G. (2017), 'Philippine Banana Bonanza Sparks Debate on Shift to China', *Financial Times* (14 March), accessed 21 October 2019, www.ft.com/content/3f6df338-056b-11e7-ace0-1ce02ef0def9.

Permanent Mission of the People's Republic of China to the UN (2019), 'Joint Statement on Xinjiang at Third Committee Made by Belarus on Behalf of 54 Countries', 29 October 2019. http://www.china-un.org/eng/hyyfy/t1711761.htm.

Philpott, D. (2001), *Revolutions in Sovereignty: How Ideas Shaped Modern International Relations* (Princeton & Oxford, Princeton University Press).

Pinto, M.C.W. (2018), 'Arbitration of the Philippine Claim against China', *Asian Journal of International Law*, 8: 1–11.

Qin, Y. (2006), 'The Chinese School of International Relations Theory: Possibility and Necessity [国际关系理论中国学派的可能与必然]', *Global Review*, 534: 32–3.

Qin, Y. (2016), 'A Relational Theory of World Politics', *International Studies Review* 18.1: 33–47.
Ren, X. (2016), 'China as an Institution-Builder: The Case of the AIIB', *The Pacific Review*, 29: 435–42.
Reus-Smit, C. (2001), 'Human Rights and the Social Construction of Sovereignty', *Review of International Studies*, 27.4: 519–38.
Ropp, P.S. (2010), *China in World History* (Oxford, Oxford University Press).
Shih, H. (2013), 'Services Pact: TSU Knocks Cross-Strait Service Trade Agreement', *Taipei Times* (23 June), accessed 19 October 2019, www.taipeitimes.com/News/front/archives/2013/06/23/2003565441.
Soeriaatmadja, W. (2015), 'Indonesia, China Sign $7.6 Billion High-Speed Rail Deal', *The Straits Times* (17 October), accessed 16 October 2019, www.straitstimes.com/asia/se-asia/indonesia-china-sign-76-billion-high-speed-rail-deal.
Taiwan News (2014), 'Chang Chia-juch: Delay of CSSTA Threatens TPP, RCEP Chances', *Taiwan News* (7 April), accessed 19 October 2019, www.taiwannews.com.tw/en/news/2453632.
Taylor, I. (2019), 'The Institutional Framework of China–Africa Relations', in A. Oqubay & J.Y. Lin (eds), *China-Africa and an Economic Transformation* (Oxford, Oxford University Press), 98–125.
Teitt, S. (2011), 'The Responsibility to Protect and China's Peacekeeping Policy', *International Peacekeeping*, 18.3: 298–312.
UNSC (1992), Summit Meeting, S/PV.3046, 31 January 1992.
Wang, J. (2004), 'A Review of the Scholarship on State Sovereignty in China [国内国家主权问题研究综述]', *International Forum*, 6.3: 1–25.
Winkler, S. (2008), 'Can Trade Make a Sovereign? Taiwan–China–EU Relations in the WTO', *Asia Europe Journal*, 6.3: 467–85.
Wu, G. (2007), 'Identity, Sovereignty, and Economic Penetration: Beijing's Responses to Offshore Chinese Democracies', *Journal of Contemporary China*, 16.51: 295–313.
Xi, J. (2012), 'Xi Jinping (address at a luncheon co-hosted by the National Committee and the U.S.-China Business Council, Washington, D.C., February 15, 2012)', accessed 6 April 2020, https://www.ncuscr.org/content/video-vice-president-xi-jinping-policy-address.
Xi, J. (2019). 'Strive for the Great Rejuvenation of the Nation and Promote Peaceful Reunification of the Motherland [为实现民族伟人复兴 推进祖国和平统一而共同奋斗]' [online], Xinhua, accessed 18 October 2019, http://www.xinhuanet.com/politics/2019-01/02/c_1123937757.htm.
Zeng, J. (2016). 'Constructing a "New Type of Great Power Relations": The State of Debate in China (1998–2014)', *British Journal of Politics and International Relations*, 18.2: 422–42.
Zeng, J. & Breslin, S. (2016), 'China's "New Type of Great Power Relations": A G2 with Chinese Characteristics?', *International Affairs*, 92: 773–94.
Zhang, C. (2022), 'Fighting Tigers or Flies? Towards Effective Counter-Radicalisation Narratives in China', in X. Zhang & C. Schultz (eds), *China and the World in the 21st Century: Communication and Relationship Building* (London, Routledge).
Zhang, F. (2009), 'Rethinking the Tribute System: Broadening the Conceptual Horizon of Historical East Asia Politics', *Chinese Journal of International Politics*, 2: 545–74.
Zhang, Y. & Buzan, B. (2012), 'The Tributary System as International Society in Theory and Practice', *Chinese Journal of International Politics*, 5.1: 3–36.
Zhao, H. (2019), 'China–Japan Compete for Infrastructure Investment in Southeast Asia: Geopolitical Rivalry or Healthy Competition?', *Journal of Contemporary China*, 28: 558–74.

Zhao, S. (2015), 'Rethinking the Chinese World Order: The Imperial Cycle and the Rise of China', *Journal of Contemporary China*, 24.96: 983–1001.

Zhao, T. (2009), 'A Political World Philosophy in Terms of All-Under-Heaven (Tian-xia)', *Diogenes*, 56.1: 5–18.

Zhu, W. (2015), 'An Assessment of the Political Situation in Taiwan and the Status of Cross-Strait Relations', in Institute for Strategic Studies, National Defense, University of People's Liberation Army, China (ed.), *International Strategic Relations and China's National Security, National Defense University Blue Paper* (Singapore, World Scientific), 235–62.

9

The Institution of Sovereignty in Central Asia

FILIPPO COSTA BURANELLI

Introduction

THE CURRENT POLITICAL, historical, and cultural *Zeitgeist* is centred on a reconsideration of the role of sovereignty in international relations. As former US President Donald Trump has recently argued (2019), and with him several other politicians in the west as well as in the east and the Global South, 'the future belongs to patriots, and not to globalists', and it is easy to see what the role of sovereignty is in this renewed defence and praise for the *patria*.[1]

Until recently, and more specifically until the late 1990s, sovereignty was understood by many scholars and pundits as an institutional relic of an old international political architecture. Increased technological and infrastructural interconnectivity between peoples, states and private firms, stronger penetration of international organisations advocating market economy principles into domestic economies worldwide, surges in foreign humanitarian operations, and the creation of ad hoc international tribunals in different parts of the world all led several scholars to speak of the 'end' of sovereignty and of the emergence of a new, more complex principle of political organisation, sometimes described as 'neo-medievalist' (for an overview, see Camilleri & Falk 1992; Christiansen & Centre 1994; Calabrese 1999, Ward 2002; Eaton 2006; Jacobsen 2016).

Yet contemporary nationalist movements across the whole world have recently reaffirmed the *sacrosanctitas* of sovereignty, often linking it to religion, indigenous culture, and ethnicity. This all has been happening at a time when Mario Draghi, former Head of the European Central Bank and now prime minister of Italy, argued

---

[1] D. Trump, 'Remarks by President Trump to the 74th Session of the United Nations General Assembly', 25 September 2019, accessed 30 September 2019, https://trumpwhitehouse.archives.gov/briefings-statements/remarks-president-trump-74th-session-united-nations-general-assembly/.

that a country is authentically sovereign only when sovereign prerogatives are pooled and shared with others in a spirit of cooperation and solidarity. In his words:

> True sovereignty is reflected not in the power of making laws – as a legal definition would have it – but in the ability to control outcomes and respond to the fundamental needs of the people: what John Locke defines as their 'peace, safety, and public good'. The ability to make independent decisions does not guarantee countries such control. In other words, independence does not guarantee sovereignty. Countries that are completely shut off from the global economy, to take an extreme but instructive example, are independent but not sovereign in any meaningful sense – often relying on external food aid to feed their people.
>
> (Draghi 2019)

In theoretical and conceptual terms, sovereignty has often been thought of as a universal attribute of states, especially after the 'expansion of international society' that occurred in the second half of the past millennium. In the course of that period, European states and empires exported, often through coercion, colonisation, and violent imposition, the basic rules of European international law to achieve three goals. First, to entrench their economic and military primacy; second, to ensure predictability in the growing web of international trade that was being set up; and third, to narrow the perceived gap present in the mind of European chanceries and ideologues between an inside international society, constituted by civilised, sovereign nations, and an outside, the realm of 'savagery', 'barbarity', 'backwardness', and 'inequality' (Bull & Watson 1984; Gong 1984; Dunne & Reus-Smit 2017; Costa Buranelli 2020a).

Although the 'export' of sovereignty meant the imposition of a European principle of territorial political organisation and the suppression of local alternatives, after the decolonisation processes and the numerous struggles for independence that marked the second half of the 20th century, the legacy and path-dependent nature of that normative imposition is still visible in that sovereignty has now risen to the status of 'minimal benchmark' to be admitted to the society of nations. Those polities and would-be states that want to participate, so to say, in the game of international politics must define themselves as 'sovereign' and, equally if not more importantly, *be recognised as such* by other sovereign states in the international system.

Even if poorly working, or not working at all, in terms of provision of internal governance and ability to engage in external relations with other peers, states can still be part of international society if they manage to get full recognition as 'sovereign' by other governments – Robert Jackson (2000) called these polities 'quasi-states'. This would imply that sovereignty, despite having a European origin, is a concept that is now believed to have a universal meaning, equally applicable to all states in the world, that 'being sovereign' means the same thing at all latitudes and longitudes – to be *superiorem non recognoscens*.

However, the concept of sovereignty, once relatively uncontested, especially in the field of International Relations (IR) theory,[2] has recently become a major topic

---

[2] Following the common convention in the field, I refer to 'International Relations' (capitalised) to describe the discipline that seeks to study international politics, and to 'international relations' (lower case) as a synonym for 'international politics', that is, the subject of the discipline.

for reflection and further theorisation. Rather than presupposing that the concept of sovereignty has a timeless or universal meaning, more recent scholarship has focused on the changing meanings thereof across a variety of historical and political contexts (Sørensen 1999; Bartelson 2006; Costa Buranelli 2015).

This recent retheorisation and problematisation of sovereignty in IR theory has been prompted by several trends in international politics, all revolving around discourses and practices of sovereignty – a backlash against the so-called 'Responsibility to Protect' and its problems with 'preventive humanitarian interventions' (Paris 2014); alleged interference and selective bias of some supranational institutions, such as the International Criminal Court (Imoedemhe 2015); and the fact that different regions are reconfiguring their own discourses and practices of sovereignty more in line with historical experiences, pre-existing normative contexts, and local needs and understandings, thus creating a proliferation of subtle, yet meaningful, different interpretations (Acharya 2014; Costa Buranelli 2019). Thus, we require an analysis of how sovereignty gets localised in different socio-cultural contexts, especially outside the European domain where pre- and postcolonial traditions and practices of political power may intertwine with sovereignty.

For example, recent events in Eurasia, especially pertaining to the annexation of Crimea by the Russian Federation and its encroachment in several frozen conflicts in the region, as well as the current war in Ukraine, have led scholars to pay attention to the increasingly contested nature of sovereignty in the region (Navari 2014; Deyermond 2016; Allison 2017). Especially in the last decade, Russia's actions and discourses in Eurasia have put the Central Asian republics on a heightened guard, with the intention to tackle discursively, pragmatically, and normatively the former patron's revisionism (Tskhay & Costa Buranelli 2020). In June 2020, Russian President Vladimir Putin argued that the sovereignty and territory of several successor states to the USSR benefited from 'gifts' from Moscow, allegedly referring to Ukraine and other states and hinting at the threat of revanchism in the future.[3]

The Central Asian states, which in this chapter are understood as the republics of Kazakhstan, Kyrgyzstan, Tajikistan, Turkmenistan, and Uzbekistan, entered international society in 1991, when they became independent from the USSR, and had immediately to learn the language and the practice of sovereignty in a post-unitary regional complex surrounded by nuclear great powers. More precisely, they entered a western-shaped international system in a condition of postcoloniality and, perhaps more accurately, post-imperialism. Furthermore, they rapidly, if not immediately, all established authoritarian traits of government and governance. This

---

[3] RFE/RL's Russian Service, 'Kremlin Denies Eyeing Territorial Claims after Putin's Comments in Documentary', *Radio Free Europe / Radio Liberty* (22 June 2020), accessed 24 June 2020, www.rferl.org/a/kremlin-denies-eyeing-territorial-claims-after-putin-s-comments-in-documentary/30684797.html.

means that the alleged universal meaning and practices of sovereignty had to be learnt and localised in a postcolonial, increasingly authoritarian context.

In the light of the considerations offered above, this chapter discusses the nature of sovereignty in Central Asia, as well as its interpretation and practice. In doing so, two main questions will be considered. First, to what extent is sovereignty in Central Asia interpreted and practised along the lines of western legal traditions, rather than presenting indigenous traits? Second, how does the postcolonial condition of the region, and its general authoritarian governance, impact on the interpretation and the practice of sovereignty?

From a methodological perspective, in order to carry out this study, the chapter adopts a qualitative methodology utilising discourse analysis of primary sources such as speeches, declarations, press conferences, and documents found on the internet, in the archives in Central Asia during the period 2013–18 and on specific databases such as LexisNexis. Furthermore, the chapter's argument benefits from elite interviews that underpin the narrative, serving as background knowledge. These interviews were conducted in the region with diplomats, officials, experts, and policymakers in the period 2013–19, so as to shed an even brighter light on the conceptualisation of sovereignty in the region.

The chapter proceeds as follows. The next section briefly discusses sovereignty from a conceptual standpoint and clarifies as well as justifies the theoretical position taken in this chapter to make sense of sovereignty. The following section discusses Central Asia's entry into international society, while the subsequent one reflects on the relationship between sovereignty, authoritarianism, and postcolonialism in the region. The final section sums up the argument and indicates some possible avenues for further research.

The concept of sovereignty in IR

Talking about sovereignty in IR is like playing with fire, as this concept is indeed one of the most polysemic in the discipline (for an overview, see Krasner 1999). For most realists and liberalists, especially in their neo-structural form, sovereignty is a legal attribute of a state, it is legal condition to enter into agreements with other states, it is monopoly of power over a given territory and people and within certain boundaries. For constructivists, sovereignty is a set of recurrent and durable practices, and therefore something performed and enacted over time. In this way, as the name of the theory suggests, sovereignty is something 'constructed', and therefore its meaning and practice changes over time. For English School thinkers, sovereignty is not just a 'constructed' practice, but a practice imbued with normative content. That is to say, sovereignty is an *institution*, if not *the institution*, of international society. It is a practice that must be recognised as valid and conforming to the social context in which actors operate and live (here the system of states) in order to be accepted. Thus, its adoption defines the legitimate actors in the international system and regulates their interactions.

Whatever one's theoretical preference, two aspects are worth noting with respect to sovereignty. First, in order to understand sovereignty, we need history. While it is true that sovereignty is mostly associated to states (Thomson 1995, 220), for the very concept of sovereignty becomes an organisational principle only in a world of states (Ruggie 1983; 1993; Ashley 1984), it is crucial to remember that the story of sovereignty is not the story of states, but is the story of an idea. Second, the institution of sovereignty is, at least conceptually, inseparable from international law, as the two are the product of a relationship of co-constitution – a state is sovereign following an act of international law, and international law applies to sovereign states only.

So, what exactly does sovereignty *mean*? Conscious that this question may very well open a Pandora's box, I prefer to introduce this concept by adhering to a minimal definition of it which originated in western political and philosophical thought thanks to Bodin and Hobbes, that of being *superiorem non recognoscens* or, in the words of Charles Manning (1962; see also James 1993), 'constitutionally insular'. This means that a state, when sovereign, is not dictated both internal and foreign policy options by any other states. This is the basic condition for speaking of an anarchic system of states, one in which all states are at least legally equal and enjoy the same legal rights and obligations.

At the same time, Cynthia Weber reminds us that sovereignty is not something which should be thought of as having an ontological content. Rather, it has a function. In international relations, 'sovereignty's function is to demarcate the inside from the outside, the domestic from the international, so that they appear to be self-evident, not discursively constructed through complex interworkings of power and knowledge' (Weber 1997: 228; see also Walker 1993).

Yet, as discussed in the Introduction, this function does not come out of nowhere but is the specific understanding of the western conception of sovereignty as it evolved over centuries in Europe before being exported throughout the world, until it was challenged by the rising solidarism of international society in the early 1990s, when not just constitutional insularity, but also, and especially, human rights and human development began to be the defining criteria of responsible sovereignty. As it has been aptly put, 'traditional things [associated to sovereignty] like respecting borders have been joined by democracy, free markets, and human rights' (Thomson 1995: 228).

Some theorists push this argument even further, arguing that the very *attributes* of sovereignty (coinage, weaponry, monopoly of violence, flags, and so forth) have over the past 20 years been replaced by discourses and practices of good-governance, benchmarking, and conditionality over the *content* of sovereignty itself. In the words of Jens Bartelson, sovereignty is no longer a constitutive attribute of states, or an inalienable right whose ultimate source is to be found within the state. 'Sovereignty is ... rather a grant contingent upon its responsible exercise in accordance with the principles of international law under the supervision of a host of global governance institutions and non-governmental actors' (quoted in Holm & Sending 2018: 841).

This means that, as will be discussed in the next section, the Central Asian states became such in a world where concepts are being reframed and renegotiated. This is the main complexity of the theme under consideration – that sovereignty cannot be studied as detached from the historical context in which it is formulated and practiced. And by doing so, the implication is that by studying how sovereignty is used in a particular context, we contribute to perpetuating its framing and its legitimacy. In the words of Bartelson (2006: 464):

> the very moment that scholars decided that the meaning of sovereignty lies very much in what we make of it through our linguistic conventions and rhetorical practices, they also opened up a new field of inquiry within which this concept could survive and thrive, albeit now as an object of inquiry rather than as its uncontested foundation.

As pre-empted in the Introduction, this chapter addresses two questions. First, to what extent is 'sovereignty' in Central Asia interpreted and practised along the lines of western legal traditions, rather than presenting indigenous traits? Second, how do the postcolonial condition of the region and its general authoritarian governance impact on the interpretation and the practice of sovereignty? In order to answer these questions, or at least to provide some preliminary insights on them, this chapter makes use of the conceptual apparatus and jargon of the English School of International Relations (hereafter ES), according to which the international system is not a mechanic action–reaction realm where states interact blindly and simply following power dynamics, but is better conceived as an international society in which norms and rules of coexistence are established, observed, and acknowledged when broken or contested. Most famously theorised by Hedley Bull (1977: 13):

> A society of states (or international society) exists when a group of states, conscious of certain common interests and common values, form a society in the sense that they conceive themselves to be bound by a common set of rules in their relation with one another, and share in the working of common institutions.

In this theoretical framework, sovereignty is looked at not as an attribute, or as something 'possessed' or 'owned', but rather as a practice, as an array of discourses, norms, and principles, in other words, as discussed earlier, as an *institution*, meant as a set of durable (but not eternal) practices and discourses that guide and direct the actions of members of a given social context, and define its identity (Buzan 2004; Holsti 2004) by an act of socialisation, understood as the process by which states internalise norms originating elsewhere in the international system (Alderson 2001: 417).

Moreover, for the purpose of this chapter, this ES approach to sovereignty is then complemented by what the scholar Mohammed Ayoob has called 'subaltern realism', which takes into account the condition of postcolonial states at the moment of entrance into the international system. In other words, socialisation and admission into the society of states

> must be combined with a judicious interpretation of the current domestic and external, normative and practical predicaments facing the postcolonial states. The latter task is essential because it is these problems, many of them related to early state making

and late entry into the states system, that generate most conflicts in the international system, as well as determine the external and domestic behavior of most states.

(Ayoob 2002: 39)

Specifically, Ayoob (2002: 44) warns us that, as shall be evident later in the chapter, 'the geopolitical contours of states [in the Global South] were established largely by outside forces. Postcolonial state elites were left with the task of mobilizing human and material resources to effectively administer territories encompassed by colonially crafted boundaries'.[4]

Having reviewed, if rather briefly, the main theoretical and conceptual contours of sovereignty as understood in this chapter, and the theoretical basis for the present work, the next section moves on to see how the Central Asian states have incorporated and adapted the institution of sovereignty within their boundaries. Two caveats must be stated, though. First, the analysis will attempt to trace broad, general similarities among Central Asian states' understandings of sovereignty, and will seek to identify a 'family resemblance' among the potentially different interpretations of sovereignty that each Central Asian state may have. In other words, I am very aware that every country in the region has its own specific understanding and practice(s) of sovereignty, and this should not surprise anyone – yet, if sovereignty is an institution that socialises different actors around its content and legitimacy, it means that shared understandings and common traits are present, too. This is what has been recently called, quite aptly, theorisation 'from high altitudes' (Holsti 2018). Second, I acknowledge that my analysis will be prevalently state-centric and elite-focused. Due to space constraints, an analysis of how intellectuals, scholars, activists, and other political subjects in Central Asia conceptualise sovereignty cannot be offered, and I am conscious of the limitations and trade-offs that my statist, ontological commitment forces me into. Yet, as argued in the Conclusions, I strongly invite further research exactly on these potential alternative understandings of sovereignty, which are crucial if we are to identify glimpses of future changes of the institution in the region.

Legal sovereignty in Central Asia

In 1991, the five Central Asian republics became formally independent. Kazakhstan declared itself independent on 16 December 1991; Kyrgyzstan on 31 August 1991; Tajikistan on 9 September 1991; Turkmenistan on 27 October 1991; and Uzbekistan on 1 September 1991. The era in which they were part of the larger whole that was the Soviet Union was finally over. Administrative borders suddenly became borders to be defined by international law, and the capacity to interact with other states in international society through diplomacy and foreign policy as subjects of international law became available.

---

[4] Crucially, there are aspects of 'subaltern realism theory' that are less convincing, such as lumping all postcolonial experiences in a monolithic 'Third World' category, or the rather tenuous and problematic distinction between state repression for consolidating state authority and the purely predatory activities of self-seeking rulers. For a more detailed critique, see Michael Barnett's (2002) rejoinder.

Following the theorisation of 'subaltern realism' (Ayoob 2002), according to which newly independent states interpret international law in the strictest way possible to balance potential great powers' revisionism and to gain international legitimacy and validation for playing 'according to the rules' (which, it is worth remembering, they did *not* contribute to developing), the Central Asian states immediately adopted the principles of *uti possidetis* (Latin for 'as you possess'), non-interference, non-intervention, and sovereign equality in all their legal (constitutional) documents pertaining to internal and external acts of the states.

Even a cursory glance at the constitutions of all five Central Asian states reveals that the institution of sovereignty in its meaning as absolute control over a defined territory, the protection of its integrity, inviolability, and inalienability, and its legitimacy deriving from the population insisting on it has been fully legitimised: in Kazakhstan this is visible in the Preamble, as well as in articles 2 and 10-1; in Kyrgyzstan in the Preamble and in articles 1, 2, and 88; in Tajikistan we can find references to sovereignty in the Preamble and in articles 1, 6, 7, and 11; in Turkmenistan's constitution sovereignty is mentioned in the Preamble as well as in articles 1, 2, 3, 20, and 22; and in Uzbekistan, sovereignty is featured even more prominently – not only is it mentioned in the Preamble and in several articles (1, 17, 57, 93, and 125), but the Uzbek constitution even features a whole chapter (Chapter 1) titled 'State Sovereignty'.[5]

Other than this, the fact that sovereignty has been internalised is visible in the fact that the Central Asian elites have, over the years, become more confident and more aware of the content and the implications of the norms informing the institution. As the Central Asian republics were new to an already established system of norms underpinning international society, full familiarisation with sovereignty was a learning process.[6]

This is visible, for example, during the first decade of independence in the numerous incidents and skirmishes in areas where Central Asian states, such as Uzbekistan and Kyrgyzstan, share a border, as well as in the exceptionality of the civil war in Tajikistan (1993–7), in the course of which Russian and Uzbek troops as well as United Nations forces were deployed to support the government of Emomali Rahmon and the conclusion of a peace agreement between the belligerent factions, and in the episode of Batken (Kyrgyzstan, 1999), when Uzbek

---

[5] In the Uzbek constitution there is also Article 70 that mentions sovereignty, referring to the Republic of Karakalpakstan, the sovereignty of which 'shall be protected by the Republic of Uzbekistan'. In early July 2022 there were violent deadly clashes in Karakalpakstan over a proposed constitutional reform that would have revoked the region's right to secede from Uzbekistan through a referendum and curbed its autonomy significantly. As such clashes took place when proofs for this chapter were being finalised, and the analysis presented here could not take those events into account. Yet, once again this shows the contemporary relevance for sovereignty and its normative justifications, as well as competing logics, in Central Asia.

[6] The ideas of 'familiarisation' and 'learning' were present in several interviews with experts, officials and diplomats I conducted in Kazakhstan, Kyrgyzstan, Tajikistan, and Uzbekistan between 2013 and 2019.

troops entered Kyrgyz territory through Tajikistan to quell a terrorist group who kidnapped a group of tourists. All these instances, which pertain to what one may call 'territorial international law', were marked by diplomatic reactions and counter-initiatives to reaffirm the inviolability of sovereignty, thus signalling the existence of a norm and its importance. For example, in November 1998 President Emomali Rahmon accused neighbouring Uzbekistan of training Tajik rebels and aiding in anti-government raids, claiming that 'it is an aggression on the part of a neighbouring state. ... Uzbekistan has been interfering in our internal affairs for six years now. We have enough facts and proof to appeal to international organizations'. Uzbek authorities denied the allegations (Nardiev 1998).

With respect to the aforementioned episode of Batken, Tajik Foreign Minister Talbak Nazarov handed over a diplomatic note to the Uzbek ambassador to Tajikistan, Bakhtiyor Erjafhev, in Dushanbe on Monday 16 August 1999 in connection with the Uzbek air force raid. The head of the Tajik Foreign Ministry's Information Department, Igor Sattarov, speaking of 'bewilderment' for an 'unprecedented fact', said that during the conversation, which had taken place behind closed doors, the Tajik side expressed its surprise at 'this action by the Uzbek air force which cannot be justified by anything' and demanded that 'Tashkent take urgent steps to prevent such things from taking place in the future since they were at variance with principles and nature of relations that have developed between the two countries and in the region'.[7] The incident was then solved diplomatically, and the language used evidently showed a growing internalisation of the prescription of the norms informing the institution of sovereignty.

Over the years, such instances have been decreasing, and the complete inviolability of sovereignty, associated to non-interference and non-intervention, was codified in the charter of the Central Asian Cooperation Organisation (2002–5), and has been included in the founding document of the Shanghai Cooperation Organisation (SCO) (founded in the period 2001–5), and has been reaffirmed at the three recent, informal, consultative meetings of the Central Asian Heads of States in Astana (now Nur-Sultan), Tashkent, and Avaza (March 2018, November 2019, and August 2021, respectively). In territorial terms, a clear and unconditional understanding of *uti possidetis*, paired with a strong conceptualisation of sovereignty, has contributed to preventing territorial disputes and claims – such as those in Western Kazakhstan and the Ferghana Valley in the late 1980s, those on the Uzbek–Turkmen border in the early 2000s, as well as those pertaining to Bukhara and Samarkand, cities that historically have been inhabited by Tajiks but that after 1991 ended up being part of sovereign Uzbekistan (Allworth 1994: 574–6) – from materialising into conflict and open war. This is in line with the theoretical framework outlined in the previous section, for 'the twentieth-century state system showed much more acute sensitivity than earlier Central Asian ages to the

---

[7] 'Tajikistan Accuses Uzbekistan of Carrying Out Air Raids', *BBC* (19 August 1999), accessed through LexisNexis on 20 March 2019.

recognition and precision of certain state borders' (Allworth 1994: 598) in a period, that of the 1990s, that observed the rise of new nationalisms and irredentism in the region.

The legal interpretation of sovereignty in Central Asia, based on the idea of 'constitutional insularity' and on the 'inside/outside' dichotomy (Walker 1993), is interpreted rigidly and instrumentally also to enhance and entrench the insulation of the executive power from civil society and opposition forces as well as from encroaching great powers,[8] something that will be analysed more in depth in the next section. A case from Kyrgyzstan, for example, is quite famous. In 2016, President Almazbek Atambaev said parts of Kyrgyzstan's constitution were 'undermining Kyrgyzstan's sovereignty' and had to be amended. His remarks came after his aide, Busurmankul Taabaldiev, had harshly criticised a call by the United Nations Commission on Human Rights (UNCHR) to revise a ruling by Kyrgyzstan's Supreme Court against jailed human rights activist Azimjan Askarov. Taabaldiev said the UNCHR's call interfered in Kyrgyzstan's internal affairs while forgetting that Kyrgyzstan's constitution allows its citizens to call upon international courts to protect their rights, and it requires that Kyrgyz authorities comply with decisions made by such institutions.[9] Recently, the new president of Kazakhstan, Kassym-Jomart Tokaev, has made similar arguments, stating that citizens financed by some international human rights organisations are destabilising society, 'when what is needed is in fact a prosperous and sovereign Kazakhstan'.[10]

A similar logic is followed by Kazakhstan with respect to processes of Eurasia integration between Russia, Belarus, Kyrgyzstan, and Armenia. Adopting a very strict view of sovereignty as 'constitutional insularity' and as a legal bulwark against potential great power encroachment, former President Nursultan Nazarbayev argued that as soon as economic integration based on intergovernmentalism would evolve into political integration based on the creation of decision-making *supranational* institutions, Kazakhstan would exercise its right to withdraw from the Eurasian Economic Union (EAEU).[11] The new president, Tokaev, has recently reiterated these concerns, arguing in a viral interview to the popular Kazakh newspaper *Ana Tili* that in an era of turbulent geopolitical confrontation between great powers and potential revisionism at the regional level, 'Kazakhstan is obliged to take care of its national interests', emphasising at the EAEU summit on 19 May

---

[8] Interview with Central Asian international lawyer, February 2019.
[9] 'President Wants to Amend Laws Undermining Kyrgyzstan's Sovereignty', *States News Service* (5 May 2016), accessed through LexisNexis on 19 March 2019.
[10] 'Касым-Жомарт Токаев: Судьба казахского народа находится на весах истории' ('The Fate of the Kazakh People Is on the Scales of History'), interview by Zhanarbek Ashimzhan, *Kazinform*, 25 June 2020, accessed 1 July 2020, www.inform.kz/ru/kasym-zhomart-tokaev-sud-ba-kazahskogo-naroda-nah oditsya-na-vesah-istorii_a3665771.
[11] 'Kazakhstan to Give Up on Eurasian Economic Union if it Threatens Sovereignty – Nazarbayev', *AKI Press* (25 August 2014), accessed 1 July 2020, https://akipress.com/news:546355:Kazakhstan_to_give_up_on_Eurasian_Economic_Union_if_it_threatens_sovereignty_-_Nazarbayev/.

2020 that 'integration will be supported ... until it does not harm the sovereignty of Kazakhstan'.[12] Analogous remarks were offered a few months earlier by the Tajik government, too. A Tajik government official, in an interview with the media on condition of anonymity, maintained that the experience of Kyrgyzstan and Armenia shows that, 'if integrated, Tajikistan will lose some of its political and economic sovereignty'.[13]

This, again, signals that in Central Asia sovereignty as interpreted today is something that is not divisible, is not subject to compromise, and cannot infringe on the political decision-making of regional states. By using the metaphor of sovereignty as a 'fortress' (Luong & Weinthal 2002), the late Uzbek President Islam Karimov was even more categorical, rhetorically asking whether it was possible to have political sovereignty without economic sovereignty in an implicit criticism of Kazakhstan opening its market to Russia, although this seems to be changing under the new rule of Shavkat Mirziyoyev.

To recap – in Central Asia, sovereignty is an inalienable, indisputable right to constitutional insularity that independent states possess by virtue of an act of international law; it is not divisible; it is about power, control, and authority; and it is very much linked to the territorial nature of the state (*uti possidetis*, non-interference, non-intervention). Cosmopolitan calls to relax notions of sovereignty in favour of market economy principles, human rights, human security, and responsible governance are rejected as impositions and unilateral understandings of the bedrock institution of international society. This, again, is in line with a subaltern realist reading of the ES, for 'the road map for weak states is not to transcend the Westphalian state and adopt post-Westphalian characteristics (whatever that may mean for polities struggling to establish themselves), but to create political structures that approximate to a much greater degree than at present the Westphalian ideal type' (Ayoob 2002: 40) and set this Westphalian ideal as 'the norm' and 'the standard' to then receive from it legitimacy and equality.

Yet, to fully understand how this legal understanding of sovereignty has become so entrenched in Central Asia, we have to turn to the postcolonial nature of Central Asian statehood and the authoritarian character of regional governance. As a matter of fact, despite emphasis on territorial and juridical sovereignty, economic and geopolitical pressures deriving from regional and global trends as well as from old core–periphery patterns with Russia have characterised the specific nuances of the politics of Central Asian states, evidencing in some respects 'neither their full sovereignty nor the complete independence of their domains from foreign interference' (Allworth 1994: 605).

---

[12] 'Tokayev: The Development and Prosperity of Kazakhstan is in Our Hands [Promoted content]', *EurActiv.com* (29 June 2020), accessed 2 July 2020, www.euractiv.com/section/europe-s-east/interview/tokayev-the-development-and-prosperity-of-kazakhstan-is-in-our-hands/.
[13] 'Dushanbe Does not Hurry to Join the Eurasian Union', *Defense and Security* (7 February 2020), accessed through LexisNexis on 1 July 2020.

Sovereignty, authoritarianism, and postcolonialism

As Cummings and Hinnebusch (2011) have recently argued, it is impossible to understand how the Central Asian states have entered the society of states, and their norms and institutions, without an understanding of their previous experiences of rule and the imperial legacies associated with them – in other words, its postcolonial and post-imperial nature. In this respect, as this section will show, postcoloniality and authoritarianism are inextricably linked, as the former often serves as an *instrumental* precondition for the justification of the latter when performing sovereignty and the political control of 'the life' inside states.

The rigid interpretation of sovereignty in Central Asia is, on the one hand, linked to the specific authoritarian traits of the region which, rooted in the Soviet practice of personalistic cadre politics, reinforces a patrimonial, territorial understanding of sovereignty – sovereignty from the sovereign, through the sovereign, for the sovereign, despite sovereignty being described as belonging to 'the people' in the regional states' constitutions. On the other hand, the link between the authoritarian and the territorial understandings of sovereignty is provided by a specific postcolonial interpretation of sovereignty, what Sørensen (2016) calls 'the post-colonial sovereign game', which is about the consolidation of statehood and the control of violence within the territory of the state and the resistance to excessive intrusion from the great powers, using narratives of sovereignty in a modified version of the balance of power, similar to Ayoob's (2002) 'subaltern realism'. Indeed, one may argue that this postcolonial sovereign game played by the elites 'takes into account the impact of the international normative framework on state making and nation building in the Third World, as well as the Third World states' insistence on maintaining the essential norms of the Westphalian system to protect themselves from unwanted external intervention' (Ayoob 2002: 48) and, one may add, internal opposition.

As David Lewis (2011) argues, the nature of sovereignty that emerged in the post-Soviet period in Central Asia owes much to the attitudes of Soviet-era national elites towards the borders of the Soviet republics in the region, which emerged partly as a result of deep involvement in the bureaucratic politics of resources in the Soviet period. This, in turn, contributed to the emergence of a type of authoritarian regime that reflected this particular understanding of sovereignty. Moreover, the nature of authoritarianism in Central Asia – its neo-patrimonialism in particular – stems in part from the informal structures of social organisations and resource distribution that developed in Soviet Central Asia in the 1970s and 1980s. At the same time, despite calls for a united Central Asia under the name of Turkestan in the early 1990s (that is how the region was called during Tsarist domination in the 19th century), such federalist or supranational projects were very much resisted by state leaders coming from old Soviet nomenklatura, arguing that a system of sovereign states was the only one able to guarantee the newly independent states prosperity, development, and security (Allworth 1994; Costa Buranelli 2018).

Thus, the result of this form of colonial elite creation is a very particular understanding of sovereignty, which emerges primarily from the workings of party and state bureaucracy within republican boundaries over many years. As a result, post-Soviet Central Asian concepts of sovereignty did not emerge from an intellectual project, or as a result of a popular, nationalist struggle rooted in an ethnic version of history. Such projects were indeed in evidence in the late 1980s and early 1990s, when many Central Asian intellectuals were motivated by alternative visions of sovereignty informed by language issues, ethnic nationalism, and irredentism, but these were suppressed by state elites (Lewis 2011: 183; see also Allworth 1994: 584, 598).

This is perhaps the greatest difference between the western conceptualisation of sovereignty, mostly linked to popular will and nationalism, and the discourse/practice of sovereignty in Central Asia. Western-inspired nationalism failed to mobilise mass support to compete with informal networks of power and their leaders. Instead, such nationalist visions – almost all of which were based on rather mythical views of ethnicity and history – were swiftly defeated and in fact appropriated by Soviet-era elites in the early 1990s in Uzbekistan, Kazakhstan, and Turkmenistan, and eventually in Tajikistan later in the decade. To make things more complicated, as mentioned in the Introduction, the understanding of sovereignty in part of the west is now evolving through greater stress on the pooling of resources and accountability towards people, while in other parts of the world and in Central Asia in particular the understanding of the concept is still very much linked to principles of non-interference and absolute control.

Because of the stability of leadership, and the need for continuity with the past to ensure order in the process of transition to independence, post-Soviet sovereignty had no need for a democratic mandate; it did not rely on the populist impulses of ethnic nationalism from below and was wary of appealing too strongly to mass nationalist sentiment. Instead, it has been reliant on an authoritarian style of government, partially to counter the alternative concepts of sovereignty, linked to ethnicity or pan-Islamic ideals, advanced by its political opponents (Lewis 2011). As Diana Kudaibergenova (2016: 917) has maintained, in Central Asia the 'intersection of current discourses of nationalism and postcolonial rhetoric was appropriated by the ruling elites and, in the absence of major intellectual debates, theirs had become the dominant understanding of postcoloniality'.

In a full logic of norm localisation (Acharya 2004), it may then be argued that the institution of sovereignty, extended by international society to Central Asia, very much favoured local imperatives, goals, and strategies, however authoritarian. An international set of norms was therefore successfully and aptly localised to fulfil local imperatives and political goals – those of achieving a peaceful transition to independence – and to maintain political power over territory and resources in a condition of fragile statehood and reconfiguration of regional order in the phase immediately after independence. The process of localisation of the institution of sovereignty has then been fed back into international society through the reiteration of the importance of sovereignty and its inviolability at the international stage through a process of norm subsidiarity at the international level (Acharya 2011). The crucial importance of sovereignty, linked to political stability and regime resilience, has been used, for example, as part of a discursive 'Shanghai spirit' under the umbrella of the SCO to legitimise strong rule and to push back any sort of democratic norm that may penetrate the region (Ambrosio 2008; Aris 2011).

At the same time, the legitimacy that authoritarianism finds in the region is very much linked to its alleged ability to protect and shield sovereignty from *all* excessive external interference, be it the western democratic one or the Russian one at the regional level. From 1991 onward, sovereignty has been one of the most frequent norms and institutions advocated by the Central Asian representatives at the United Nations General Assembly, showing high degrees of voting-convergence every time a resolution pertaining to sovereignty is voted on (Costa Buranelli 2014), precisely to resist, at least discursively and normatively, the tensions and hierarchy present in the region due to postcolonial historical legacies.

Especially after the de facto annexation of Crimea by Russia, the Central Asian republics have become more vocal, locally and internationally, about their insistence on the principle of sovereignty. It is not by chance that, a few days after violence erupted in Crimea, the Minister of Foreign Affairs of Kazakhstan flew to the UN headquarters in New York to submit an official declaration reiterating the inviolability of Kazakhstan's sovereignty and territory, and, in 2015, the Ukrainian President Poroshenko and Nursultan Nazarbayev produced a joint statement reaffirming the inviolability of sovereignty and territorial integrity as foundational principles of international order.[14]

This problematic aspect of Russo-Kazakh bilateral relations was revamped recently, when Tokayev stated that:

> confrontation between big states is growing, and regional conflicts are escalating. This is a negative trend for Kazakhstan as a regional state. [Because of this,] the inviolability of our state border is the most important [principle]. Formalisation and delimitation of Kazakhstan's border with Russia, China, and Central Asian states has a truly historic significance. We can see the horrid, irreparable consequences of the lack of border agreements.[15]

A similar underpinning worry was recently seen in how both the Tajik and Kyrgyz governments rejected, with a diplomatic note, Moscow's offer to provide mediation and good offices to resolve border disputes between the two Central Asian states.[16]

---

[14] 'Joint Statement by President of Ukraine Petro Poroshenko and President of Kazakhstan Nursultan Nazarbayev', *Ukrainian Government News* (9 October 2015), accessed through LexisNexis on 12 July 2020.
[15] 'Kazakhstan to Support Integration as Long as its Sovereignty Is Unharmed – President', *Russia & CIS General Newswire* (25 June 2020), accessed through LexisNexis on 12 July 2020.
[16] 'Tajikistan Sends Note to Russian Foreign Ministry on Lavrov's Statement about Tajik-Kyrgyz Border', *AKI Press* (1 June 2020), accessed 10 June 2020, https://akipress.com/news:642621:Tajikistan_sends_note_to_Russian_Foreign_Ministry_on_Lavrov%E2%80%99s_statement_about_Tajik-Kyrgyz_border/.

Another area in which the tension between sovereignty and postcolonial relations with the former patron are visible is that of state language and related issues pertaining to alphabets and Latinisation of Cyrillic script (du Boulay & du Boulay 2021). Since 1991, the Central Asian states have tried to strike a balance between ensuring the development and predominance of local native languages over Russian, seen as a necessary step to ensure the consolidation and full achievement of sovereignty, while at the same time maintaining good political and diplomatic relations with the former patron. Focusing on the Kazakh case, Kudaibergenova (2016: 923) has also noted that 'political postcoloniality is defined precisely by the elites' inability to openly react against the former colonising regime, even in the setting of political agendas and of clear, "concrete" projects that aim to develop the state Kazakh language', which has potentially profound implications for the sovereignty of the country. This is evident in the most recent comments of Tokayev, who stated that:

> the language issues have a great political significance and, if handled carelessly, *can have implications on sovereignty and security*. We have seen how it unfolded in Ukraine. Attempting a frontal attack to raise the status of the state language and force the expansion of its use is counterproductive and can trigger interethnic tensions. Besides, we should take into account the geopolitical background, *including the world's longest land border with Russia*.[17]

This well encapsulates the delicate and Janus-faced relations between Russia and Central Asian states, which oscillate between 'strategic partnerships' and 'historical friendship' and feelings of oppression and subjugation. In the words of Sergei Abashin (2014: 87), 'criticism of the USSR is an important and inescapable element of modern national narratives in the region. The idea that the nation has taken the place of the previous unjust system, liberating people from it and overcoming its inadequacies, lies at the heart of political apparatus of the new states'.

Nazarbayev once referred to 'our grandfathers fighting for Kazakhstan's independence and sovereignty, the "most precious asset"' (Strokan 2014). In Kyrgyzstan, the postcolonial lexicon of struggle and conquest is also also visible, almost in mythical terms. 'Today is the day of rejoice for your people who realized their cherished dream and achieved sovereignty', President Sooronbai Jeenbekov said in his address at the celebrations of the Independence Day of Kyrgyzstan at Ala-Too central square in Bishkek in 2018. 'On this day we raised the flag of our independence and told the whole world that a new independent country appeared. ... Freedom can't be gifted, it should be earned in a continuous struggle. Many our sons [*sic*] and daughters of our people sacrificed their lives for this goal', the President said. Jeenbekov also recalled that 'the epic of Manas [the national epic of Kyrgyzstan] says that even in the most tragic minutes of historical fate the ability

---

[17] 'Forceful Approach to Raising Status of State Language Counterproductive – Tokayev', *Kazakhstan General Newswire* (25 June 2020), accessed through LexisNexis on 1 July 2020, emphasis added.

of revival was always peculiar to our people. The tougher the strokes of misfortune were, the stronger the will to live'.[18]

These narratives, again imbued with postcolonial understandings of sovereignty, have often contributed to escalating interethnic tensions and to threating the coexistence of different groups within Central Asian states, as the comments of Tokayev on the state language showed. For example, in Kyrgyzstan, during the clashes between Kyrgyz and Uzbeks in the south of the country, some politicians, such as parliamentary deputy Adakhan Madumarov, went as far as to say that the Kyrgyz, being the majority or 'titular' ethnic group of the country, 'are the masters of the house, the others [nations and peoples] only renters' (quoted in Laruelle 2021: 88). Building on Lev Gumilev's concept of titular nations, the first Kyrgyz president, Askar Akaev, 'adopted these ideas to claim that Kyrgyz ancestors had strived and fought for statehood and how it was maintained, even when the Kyrgyz were under the Russian Empire and Soviet Union' (Gullette & Heathershaw 2015: 131). These ideas then echoed in the discourses and actions of Osh's mayor, Melis Myrzakamatov,

> who traced his genealogy to the land and declared that his ancestors have always been prominent in the Fergana Valley. Thus, he presented himself as protecting the 'sovereignty' of the Kyrgyz people against intervention by separatists from minority ethnic groups. Shortly after the events, speaking to a correspondent from a Russian daily paper, Myrzakmatov echoed these sentiments, stating that 'Uzbeks had encroached on Kyrgyzstan's sovereignty. But, we repulsed them'.
> (Quoted in Gullette & Heathershaw 2015: 127)

Once again, it is visible here how the postcolonial condition of regional politics, especially as far as territories, borders, enclaves, and exclaves are concerned, leads to what has been aptly called the 'affective' nature of sovereignty in Central Asia, with an emphasis on 'how the emotional, the physical, and the psychological shape inter-ethnic relations, the elite politics of nationalism, and debates about international intervention' (Gullette & Heathershaw 2015: 135). And exactly because of the 'affection' of sovereignty, the autocrat, the leader, the president becomes the embodiment of the sovereign nature of the state, not so dissimilarly from the Leviathan, and presents himself as a guide that has led the people to the obtainment of the most precious gift – sovereignty.[19]

In what seems to be an excellent example of socialisation in Aldersonian terms, as discussed in the Introduction, Tajik President Rahmon is on the path of an even more increasing personalisation of power, for example, by becoming 'Leader of the Nation' in late 2015, following the example of 'Elbasi' in Kazakhstan and 'Turkmenbashi' and 'Arkadag' ('Protector') in Turkmenistan, and getting lifelong

---

[18] 'People of Kyrgyzstan Made their Cherished Dream Come True and Achieved Sovereignty – Jeenbekov', *Central Asian News Service* (31 August 2018), accessed through LexisNexis on 13 July 2020.

[19] References to Hobbes' Leviathan were actually discussed in the course of several interviews with Kazakh, Kyrgyz, and Uzbek experts.

immunity. This, importantly, has happened in the aftermath of talks with his regional peers over 'stability' and 'security' in the region in general and in Tajikistan in particular, with particular emphasis on the preservation of sovereignty, stressing the elements of struggle, liberation, and fight.[20]

Conclusions

In this chapter, I have offered some reflections on how the institution of sovereignty has been localised and interpreted in Central Asia since 1991. Far from providing a fine-grained analysis of how each state in the region interprets sovereignty, the narrative has focused more on the main general shared aspects of this institution, taking into account two main questions – whether the understanding of sovereignty in Central Asia follows Westphalian, western lines, and what role authoritarianism and postcolonial narratives play in substantiating such an understanding. The argument advanced is that a strictly legal and territorial understanding of sovereignty is the one prevalent in Central Asia, supported by an authoritarian form of governance intertwined with postcolonial discourses and processes of state- and nation-building. This, as discussed throughout the chapter, does nonetheless mean that such shared understanding prevents occasional conflict from arising. Recent violence on the Kyrgyz–Tajik border, in which dozens of people lost their lives and thousands were displaced, shows that contestations over disputed sovereignty are still happening in Central Asia. Yet, it is crucial to note that sovereignty and the norms associated to it still constitute the only acceptable framework for resolution of disagreements between the regional states (Costa Buranelli 2021).

By means of a conclusion, I would like to offer three suggestions for further research. First, it would be interesting to explore alternative conceptions of sovereignty in Central Asia, relying on alternative interpretations of current global norms or insisting on pre-colonial understandings of political power. As admitted in the course of the narrative, this piece of research focused predominantly on state elites and adopted a statist ontology, and so more is needed to go beyond state-centrism. Second, further research should consider the evolution of political regimes in Central Asia. The attitudes of the Uzbek government towards sovereignty, for example, are changing if compared to five years ago, and a more relaxed and permissive understanding of sovereignty, especially from an economic and trade viewpoint, seems to be materialising. At the same time, with time passing and older generations coming to the fore, nationalism may also increase or decrease. How and whether this will change in other parts of Central Asia, and whether changes

---

[20] Costa Buranelli (2020b). RFE/RL's Tajik Service, 'Teflon Rahmon: Tajik President Getting "Leader" Title, Lifelong Immunity', *Radio Free Europe / Radio Liberty* (10 December 2015), accessed 2 July 2020, www.rferl.org/a/tajikistan-rahmon-lifelong-immunity/27419474.html.

inside regional states will define a new regional understanding of the institution, is yet to be seen. Third, more research is needed in future on the impact of (de)globalisation and increasing systemic pressure coming from neighbouring great powers on the region. The current war in Ukraine is a case in point.[21] In particular, research is needed on the continuation of old, and the potential creation of new, imperial practices that may lead to a progressive hierarchisation of the regional environment and a constant erosion of territorial and economic sovereignty in the form of land concessions, remittances, financial and military dependence, and delocalisation of productivity (Schlichte 2017).

The ways in which the Central Asian states have localised and interpreted this institution shows that, far from being outdated and superseded, sovereignty has proved to be durable and persistent, although not fixed. How this will evolve in the future depends on a complex interaction of global, regional, state, and human dynamics, and most crucially on what discourses, narratives, and practices will be legitimised – by whom, and for whom.

References

Abashin, S. (2014), 'Nations and Post-Colonialism in Central Asia: Twenty Years Later', in C. Mouradian & S. Hohmann (eds), *Development in Central Asia and the Caucasus: Migration, Democratisation and Inequality in the Post-Soviet Era* (London, I.B.Tauris), 64–76.

Acharya, A. (2004), 'How Ideas Spread: Whose Norms Matter? Norm Localization and Institutional Change in Asian Regionalism', *International Organization*, 58.2: 239–75.

Acharya, A. (2011), 'Norm Subsidiarity and Regional Orders: Sovereignty, Regionalism, and Rule-Making in the Third World', *International Studies Quarterly*, 55: 95–123.

Acharya, A. (2014), 'Global International Relations (IR) and Regional Worlds: A New Agenda for International Studies', *International Studies Quarterly*, 58.4: 647–59.

Alderson, K. (2001), 'Making Sense of State Socialization', *Review of International Studies*, 27.3: 415–33.

Allison, R. (2017), 'Russia and the Post-2014 International Legal Order: Revisionism and Realpolitik', *International Affairs*, 93.3: 519–43.

Allworth, E. (ed.) (1994), *Central Asia: 130 Years of Russian Dominance* (Durham NC, Duke University Press).

Ambrosio, T. (2008), 'Catching the "Shanghai Spirit": How the Shanghai Cooperation Organization Promotes Authoritarian Norms in Central Asia', *Europe-Asia Studies*, 60.8: 1321–44.

Aris, S. (2011), *Eurasian Regionalism: The Shanghai Cooperation Organisation* (London, Palgrave Macmillan).

Ashley, R.K. (1984), 'The Poverty of Neorealism', *International Organization*, 38.2: 225–86.

---

[21] The intervention of the Russia-led Collective Security Treaty Organisation in Kazakhstan (6–19 January) and the Russian invasion of Ukraine (24 February 2022–ongoing) happened when this chapter was already at the proofreading stage. Unfortunately, this means that a thorough analysis of it and its relevance for sovereignty in Central Asia was not undertaken, but the reader will hopefully see the relevance of what is discussed here for the contemporary events. For a synopsis, see Costa Buranelli (2022).

Ayoob, M. (2002), 'Inequality and Theorizing in International Relations: The Case for Subaltern Realism', *International Studies Review*, 4.3: 27–48.
Barnett, M. (2002), 'Radical Chic? Subaltern Realism: A Rejoinder', *International Studies Review*, 4.3: 49–62.
Bartelson, J. (2006), 'The Concept of Sovereignty Revisited', *European Journal of International Law*, 17.2: 463–74.
Bull, H. (1977), *The Anarchical Society* (London, Macmillan).
Bull, H. & Watson, A. (1984), *The Expansion of International Society* (Oxford, Clarendon Press).
Buzan, B. (2004), *From International to World Society? English School Theory and the Social Structure of Globalisation* (Cambridge, Cambridge University Press).
Calabrese, A. (1999), 'Communication and the End of Sovereignty?', *info*, 1.4: 313–26.
Camilleri, J.A. & Falk, J. (1992), *The End of Sovereignty? The Politics of a Shrinking and Fragmenting World* (Aldershot & Brookfield, Edward Elgar).
Christiansen, T. & Centre, R.S. (1994), 'European Integration between Political Science and International Relations Theory: The End of Sovereignty', Robert Schuman Centre Working Paper No. RSC 94/4 (Florence, European University Institute).
Costa Buranelli, F. (2014), 'May We Have a Say? Central Asian States in the UN General Assembly', *Journal of Eurasian Studies*, 5.2: 131–44.
Costa Buranelli, F. (2015), 'Do You Know What I Mean? Not Exactly! Global International Society, Regional International Societies and the Polysemy of Institutions', *Global Discourse: An Interdisciplinary Journal of Current Affairs and Applied Contemporary Thought*, 5.3: 499–514.
Costa Buranelli, F. (2018), 'World Society as a Shared Ethnos and the Limits of World Society in Central Asia', *International Politics*, 55.1: 1–16.
Costa Buranelli, F. (2019), 'Global International Society, Regional International Societies and Regional International Organizations: A Dataset of Primary Institutions', in C. Navari & T.B. Knudsen (eds), *International Organisations in the Anarchical Society* (London, Palgrave Macmillan), 233–63.
Costa Buranelli, F. (2020a), 'Standard of Civilization, Nomadism and Territoriality in Nineteenth Century International Society', in J. Levin (ed.), *Nomad–State Relationships in International Relations: Before and After Borders* (London, Palgrave Macmillan), 77–99.
Costa Buranelli, F. (2020b), 'Authoritarianism as an Institution? The Case of Central Asia', *International Studies Quarterly*, 64.4: 1005–16.
Costa Buranelli, F. (2021), 'Conflict in the Kyrgyz–Tajik Border: A Potential Turning Point for Central Asia', *The CACI Analyst* (5 May), accessed 1 September 2021, www.caci analyst.org/publications/analytical-articles/item/13672-conflict-in-the-kyrgyz-tajik-border-%E2%80%93-a-potential turning-point-for-central-asia.html.
Costa Buranelli, F. (2022), 'The CSTO Intervention in Kazakhstan: Implications for Regional and World Order', *Baku Dialogues*, 5.3: 26–39.
Cummings, S.N. & Hinnebusch, R. (2011), *Sovereignty after Empire: Comparing the Middle East and Central Asia* (Edinburgh, Edinburgh University Press).
Deyermond, R. (2016), 'The Uses of Sovereignty in Twenty-First Century Russian Foreign Policy', *Europe-Asia Studies*, 68.6: 957–84.
Draghi, M. (2019), 'Speech by Mario Draghi, President of the ECB, on the Award of Laurea Honoris Causa in Law from Universita degli Studi di Bologna', *European Central Bank* (22 February), accessed 12 October 2019, www.ecb.europa.eu/press/key/date/2019/html/ecb.sp190222~fc5501c1b1.en.html.

du Boulay, S. & du Boulay, H. (2021), 'New Alphabets, Old Rules: Latinization, Legacy, and Liberation in Central Asia', *Problems of Post-Communism*, 68.2: 135–40.
Dunne, T. & Reus-Smit, C. (eds) (2017), *The Globalization of International Society* (Oxford & New York, Oxford University Press).
Eaton, D. (ed.) (2006), *The End of Sovereignty? A Transatlantic Perspective* (Münster, LIT Verlag).
Gong, G.W. (1984), *The Standard of Civilization in International Society* (Oxford & New York, Oxford University Press).
Gullette, D. & Heathershaw, J. (2015), 'The Affective Politics of Sovereignty: Reflecting on the 2010 Conflict in Kyrgyzstan', *Nationalities Papers*, 43.1: 122–39.
Holm, M. & Sending, O.J. (2018), 'States before Relations: On Misrecognition and the Bifurcated Regime of Sovereignty', *Review of International Studies*, 44.5: 829–47.
Holsti, K.J. (2004), *Taming the Sovereigns: Institutional Change in International Politics* (Cambridge, Cambridge University Press).
Holsti, K.J. (2018), 'Change in International Politics: The View from High Altitude', *International Studies Review*, 20.2: 186–94.
Imoedemhe, O. (2015), 'Unpacking the Tension between the African Union and the International Criminal Court: The Way Forward', *African Journal of International and Comparative Law*, 23.1: 74–105.
Jackson, R.H. (2000), *The Global Covenant: Human Conduct in a World of States* (New York, Oxford University Press).
Jacobsen, T. (2016), *Re-envisioning Sovereignty: The End of Westphalia?* (London, Routledge).
James, A. (1993), *States in a Changing World: A Contemporary Analysis* (Oxford, Clarendon Press).
Kazakhstan General Newswire (2020), 'Forceful Approach to Raising Status of State Language Counterproductive – Tokayev', accessed through LexisNexis on 1 July 2020.
Krasner, S.D. (1999), *Sovereignty: Organized Hypocrisy* (Princeton, Princeton University Press).
Kudaibergenova, D.T. (2016), 'The Use and Abuse of Postcolonial Discourses in Post-Independent Kazakhstan', *Europe-Asia Studies*, 68.5: 917–35.
Laruelle, M. (2021), *Central Peripheries* (London, UCL Press).
Lewis, D. (2011), 'Sovereignty after Empire: The Colonial Roots of Central Asian Authoritarianism', in S.N. Cummings & R. Hinnebusch (eds), *Sovereignty after Empire: Comparing the Middle East and Central Asia* (Edinburgh, Edinburgh University Press), 178–96.
Luong, P.J. & Weinthal, E. (2002), 'New Friends, New Fears in Central Asia', *Foreign Affairs*, 81.2: 61–70.
Manning, C.A.W. (1962), *The Nature of International Society* (London, London School of Economics and Political Science).
Navari, C. (2014), 'Territoriality, Self-Determination and Crimea after Badinter', *International Affairs*, 90.6: 1299–318.
Nardiev, E. (1998), 'Tajikistan Accused Uzbekistan of Training, Aiding Rebels', *Associated Press International* (12 November), accessed through LexisNexis on 20 October 2019.
Paris, R. (2014), 'The "Responsibility to Protect" and the Structural Problems of Preventive Humanitarian Intervention', *International Peacekeeping*, 21.5: 569–603.
Ruggie, J.G. (1983), 'Continuity and Transformation in the World Polity: Toward a Neorealist Synthesis', *World Politics*, 35.2: 261–85.

Ruggie, J.G. (1993), 'Territoriality and Beyond: Problematizing Modernity in International Relations', *International Organization*, 47.1: 139–74.

Schlichte, K. (2017), 'The International State: Comparing Statehood in Central Asia and Sub-Saharan Africa', in E. Schatz & J. Heathershaw (eds), *Paradox of Power* (Pittsburgh, Pittsburgh University Press), 105–19.

Sørensen, G. (1999), 'Sovereignty: Change and Continuity in a Fundamental Institution', *Political Studies*, 47.3: 590–604.

Sørensen, G. (2016), *Rethinking the New World Order* (London, Palgrave Macmillan).

Strokan, S. (2014), 'Nazarbayev Stands for Sovereignty', *What the Papers Say (Russia)* (1 September), accessed through LexisNexis on 20 October 2019.

Thomson, J.E. (1995), 'State Sovereignty in International Relations: Bridging the Gap between Theory and Empirical Research', *International Studies Quarterly*, 39.2: 213–33.

Tskhay, A. & Costa Buranelli, F. (2020), 'Accommodating Revisionism through Balancing Regionalism: The Case of Central Asia', *Europe-Asia Studies*, 72.6: 1033–52.

Walker, R.B.J. (1993), *Inside/Outside: International Relations as Political Theory* (Cambridge, Cambridge University Press).

Ward, I. (2002), 'The End of Sovereignty and the New Humanism', *Stanford Law Review*, 55.5: 2091–112.

Weber, C. (1997), '*A Genealogy of Sovereignty*. By Jens Bartelson. Cambridge: Cambridge University Press, 1995', *American Political Science Review*, 91.1: 228–9.

10

Contested Privatisation: On the State of Monetary Sovereignty in the Euro Zone

AARON SAHR AND CAROLIN MÜLLER

Introduction

IN 2019, SOCIAL media giant Facebook announced that it would introduce its own currency, together with partners from the financial and digital industries.[1] 'Libra', they declared, would soon be available as a means of payment via Facebook's messenger services (which include WhatsApp and Instagram). The aim was to create Facebook's own currency area, in which Libra would fulfil all the classic monetary functions, that is, become a unit of account, a store of value, and a medium of exchange. The announcement provoked disquiet in the economic policy discourse of the euro zone. German Finance Minister Olaf Scholz announced that the production of money was a sovereign right of states and thus reserved for them (Karth *et al.* 2020a; 2020c). Other politicians echoed this framing of Libra as a private challenge to state sovereignty. The French finance minister explained that what was endangered by the Facebook initiative was specifically the 'monetary sovereignty' of nation-states (e.g. Le Maire 2019; cf. Koning 2019). On Twitter, the head of the Libra Group defended the plan without contradicting the framing of the debate as one about monetary sovereignty itself: with regard to 'monetary sovereign nations vs. Libra', David Marcus (2019) wrote, the monetary sovereignty of nation-states was in fact not at stake. In particular, he argued, the right to create money would not be affected by the new digital currency: 'there's no new money creation, which will strictly remain the province of sovereign nations'. It was precisely this understanding of monetary sovereignty as the sovereignty over money creation that had previously also been addressed by Olaf Scholz (Karth *et al.* 2020a; 2020b).

---

[1] Libra Association (2019). On 1 December 2020, Libra and the Libra Association were renamed to 'Diem' and the 'Diem Association'. Since we are referring here mainly to debates from 2019, we continue to use the term 'Libra' in what follows.

This chapter will explore this entanglement of monetary sovereignty and money creation. But rather than considering the planned Facebook currency, it will focus on the common European currency that has been forcefully defended by its public representatives against this (alleged) attack by a private company. In light of the Libra challenge, euro-area politicians rushed to claim an intact monetary sovereignty in the hands of the member states against what was perceived as a presumptuous attack from the private sector. In December 2019, the European Council announced that no such 'initiative [that] has the potential to reach a global scale' should 'come into operation', as it would be considered to entail 'potential risks to monetary sovereignty' (European Council 2019). These clearly articulated defence manoeuvres are confusing, however, and not only because such (rapid) consensus about the need to oppose the power of private firms is surprising by European standards. Rather, they are remarkable because the euro area is already in itself a project that deconstructs monetary sovereignty and empowers private actors. '[T]he euro zone is the first instance of a group of independently powerful sovereign states voluntarily and formally undertaking to … relinquish a good deal of their monetary sovereignty', as sociologist Geoffrey Ingham (2004: 188) has written. However, this abandonment of nation-state monetary sovereignty was not replaced by the establishment of a comparable supranational or 'communitised' sovereignty, at least not with respect to money. Rather, room for national monetary decision-making, which was commonly referred to as monetary sovereignty, was transferred to the private sector. Thus, in the euro zone, monetary sovereignty was shared with private actors in crucial ways long before Facebook's initiative.

Our aim is to highlight this privatisation of monetary sovereignty in the euro zone and discuss it in the context of recent developments. The fierce reactions to Libra serve here merely as a jumping off point for our analysis. Our point of reference is the cascade of payment crises that have occurred since 2008 and the resulting impacts on the (yet to be defined) context of monetary sovereignty in the euro area. Indeed, the financial crisis of 2008, which according to the popular but not unproblematic narrative has been replaced by a euro or sovereign debt crisis, and the COVID-19 crisis beginning in 2020 both challenge the monetary arrangement called the 'euro'. The precise nature of this challenge can only be successfully identified, or so we argue, if one follows the Libra critics in framing monetary sovereignty as, at its core, referring to money creation. Conventional definitions of monetary sovereignty, however, neglect this core and instead use the concept as implying authority over the function of a medium of exchange within a territory; more precisely, its internal and external exchange value in a currency area. Recent critical debates, however, bring into play an alternative to the territorial definition of monetary sovereignty. The alternative concept of monetary sovereignty refers to an agency specific to modern monetary economies, that is, a high degree of autonomy regarding one's own ability to pay. We call this an *agential* understanding of monetary sovereignty. Here, 'monetarily sovereign' means someone who can pay according to his or her own will without having to resort to already existing means of payment. In the next section, we will distinguish between the two understandings of the concept – monetary sovereignty as *territorial control* and as an *autonomous monetary agency*. Since our agential definition of monetary sovereignty as an autonomous monetary agency refers to a scope for action which only arises in so-called modern monetary orders, the third section will call up the basic principles of these orders. The fourth section outlines the 'constitution' (Desan 2014) of monetary sovereignty in the euro zone and characterises the euro as a privatised foreign currency. We then recall, albeit succinctly for reasons of space, the tensions that the recent crises have created in this constitution, followed by concluding remarks.

What is monetary sovereignty?

As central as the concept of sovereignty is in debates on international politics, law, and global economic relations, it is used in a variety of ways and in a disparate manner. Since Bodin (1962 [1606]), a distinction has been made between two dimensions of sovereignty that are mutually dependent. Internal sovereignty refers to the characteristic of an 'authoritative decision-making structure within a political entity' (Krasner 2007: 1). It legitimises a hierarchical organisation of politics and the ability of a decision-maker to formulate and enforce rules. This internal sovereignty of a decision-making structure (usually a state) is simultaneously conditioned by its external claim to be recognised as an autonomous entity and to be able to negotiate as an equal with other political entities. Understood in this way, the central aspect of sovereignty is thus the distinction between a hierarchical, rule-led system internally and, externally, a non-hierarchical interaction of equals, independent of the size, power, and resources of the political entity. Since the Peace of Westphalia, the international state order has been largely constituted by these principles of 'non-dominance' and 'self-governance' (Bellamy 2017) within certain territories. Frequently, sovereignty is conceived as a legal claim, 'as a political entity's externally recognized right to exercise final authority over its affairs' (Biersteker & Weber 1996: 2). In the field of international relations analysis, as well, there is a widespread assumption that sovereign states exist in an international context of anarchy (Milner 1991).

This view of sovereignty as a more-or-less static claim has changed in recent decades. Under the impression of globalising economic and financial relations, interdependence and regime theories, for example, relativise this disorder between sovereign units by emphasising the dependencies of states on other actors such as global companies and international organisations, which increasingly erode national sovereignty in the Westphalian sense (Keohane & Nye 1977). At the core of such debates on sovereignty are always questions about the absoluteness and transferability of sovereignty claims and about whether the concept of sovereignty needs to be abandoned (e.g. MacCormick 1999) or changed (e.g. Sassen 1996; Krasner

1999) in the context of global dependencies, in order to retain analytical explanatory power. Social constructivist approaches argue in contrast that sovereignty has always been a historically specific, changing framework of legitimacy for claims to power (Biersteker & Weber 1996; Adler-Nissen & Gammeltoft-Hansen 2008). Thus, in place of earlier notions of a static, monolithic status inherent in political entities, a dynamic, power-oriented view of sovereignty is emerging. In this perspective, sovereignty is constituted as a continuous process, from which certain capacities for action and specific restrictions arise.

As a supranational community of states, the European Union is a central object of such debates on sovereignty. Some see it as entailing a fundamental loss of core competences of nation-state sovereignty (e.g. Wallace 1999). Others argue instead that there has been a gain or a shift in sovereignty, asserting that member states have not given up their sovereignty under international law but have used it to create supranational institutions. The EU is considered a 'pooling' of individual control in specific areas (such as monetary policy) to gain sovereignty at the collective level in dealing with global interdependencies (e.g. Sassen 1996; Krasner 2010: 102). Other authors hold that the EU can be seen as an example of a fundamental shift towards a post-sovereign liberal world order, in which individual autonomy replaces nation-state sovereignty (e.g. MacCormick 1999).

Territorial control over means of payment

Monetary sovereignty is traditionally understood as an element of state sovereignty in the sense of non-dominated self-governance of a territory, as mentioned above. This territory then becomes a currency area. Following Pistor (2017), we can speak here of a *territorial understanding* of monetary sovereignty that corresponds to the general use of the term 'sovereignty'.[2] Early on, Bodin (1962 [1606]) included the decision on what is to be considered as currency within the national territory, that is, the determination of the monetary value as well as the disposition of the composition of coins, among the sovereign rights of the state. Many contributions see the regulation of monetary issues by the state as an indispensable element in the creation of territorial unity in the course of the emergence of nation-states (Helleiner 1999; Herrmann 2008; Zimmermann 2013). With the expansion of the Westphalian model, that is, a political order based on the fundamental idea of a (peaceful) coexistence of sovereign nation-states, the principle of 'one nation/one money' has become increasingly important. Sovereign nation-states claim the right to provide

---

[2] Pistor (2017: 507ff.), however, refers to the subordination of the concept of monetary sovereignty to a generally territorial concept of sovereignty, which she considers problematic for modern monetary orders.

their territory with a means of payment without interference from other actors. In public international law, the right to coin money (*ius cudendae monetae*) has been recognised as a national right to issue and regulate currency (Herrmann 2008: 66).

To this day, the core of this regulatory claim has remained the same as outlined by Bodin in *The Six Bookes of a Commonweale* (1962 [1606]). Admittedly, in times of fiat money without substance, decisions on the composition of coins are no longer relevant. However, the power to determine the metal content of coins can be read as a cipher for the power to reach decisions about money and to control its quality, that is, its value in relation to traded goods and other currencies. The state has the right to treat its territory as a currency area, in which it supplies money, and to influence the price of this means of payment. Zimmermann (2013: 3) sums up common definitions of monetary sovereignty accordingly: 'The right to create money via the issuance of currency and the right to conduct independent exchange rate and monetary policies emerges as the lowest common denominator from the existing literature' (cf. van't Klooster & Murau 2020).

In economic sociology and political economy, the internal and external price of money is regarded as the result of social power struggles.[3] Actors and interest groups within an economy form preferences related to inflation levels (the internal price of money) and exchange rates (the external price of money). Dominant preferences condense into national cultural patterns and political strategies. A popular example is the inflation aversion and obsession with hard currency in Germany. If states can pursue different national strategies with their own currencies, those states that enjoy a high degree of monetary sovereignty in a territorial sense can opt to revalue or devalue their own currency. While the right of sovereign states to implement monetary policy with respect to the internal or external value of their currency is undisputed, their capacities to do so are unevenly distributed. Structurally, economists assume that, at best, one of the two prices of money can be adequately addressed: 'in practice, setting macroeconomic policies to assure domestic price stability implies a loss of control over the exchange rate, and vice versa' (Kirshner 2003: 648).

With regard to monetary sovereignty as price control, the euro zone is considered a structural disempowerment of nation-states (e.g. Streeck 2015; Höpner & Lutter 2018; Höpner & Spielau 2018; Scharpf 2018). The member states of the euro area have given up their right to undertake exchange rate adjustments between the (former) national currencies. However, the differences between the national

---

[3] Kirshner (2003: 647), for example, characterises money as a genuinely political institution, which above all institutionalises a conflict over exchange values: 'At bottom, there are two questions at the heart of all monetary matters. ... The two questions are about 1) The price (and variability of the price) of money in the home market (i.e. the inflation rate); 2) The price (and variability of the price) of money outside the home market (the exchange rate).'

economies in terms of productivity, key industries, and wages continue to exist, as the euro zone has renounced economic policy integration. Under the umbrella of the single ('one size fits all') monetary policy of the European Central Bank (ECB), all member states are now affected by a unified monetary policy strategy. Differences in trade and the balance of payments can no longer be countered by adjusting the exchange rate. As a result, and due to a stable euro and low wage increases, the export-oriented German economy, for example, was able to outdo its competitors with its cheaper products and without opportunities for other EU economies to maintain or enhance their competitiveness by adjusting their exchange rates accordingly (Streeck 2015).

We refer here to these results of research on the German example because they show the potential of a territorial interpretation of monetary sovereignty. However, the limits of such an interpretation become apparent when it is applied to contemporary developments and the state's monopoly on issuing money, the second element of the territorial interpretation. As we have seen, claims to this monopoly were vehemently renewed in the reactions to Facebook's Libra. This second element of the classical territorial understanding of monetary sovereignty plays a secondary role in such studies of the political economy of European integration – and for good reasons. Indeed, if monetary sovereignty is equated with the right to or a monopoly on issuing the means of exchange (cf. Herrmann 2008: 67; Zimmermann 2013), the very emergence of modern (or capitalist) monetary orders in the 18th century appears as a loss of monetary sovereignty. After all, in so-called modern monetary orders, which have become the worldwide standard of official currencies since the 18th century, the right to create money is not only granted to state institutions but also to private companies (Ingham 2004). The 'hybrid' architecture (Weber 2018: 47) of modern money has been undermining the ability of states to control the amount of money in their territory since its beginnings in the late Middle Ages. Since then, money creation has been a practice of political and private actors who, with the emergence of modern monetary orders, combine to form a resilient 'public–private partnership' (Ingham 2004; 2020; Koddenbrock 2019).

As early as the 12th and 13th centuries, European merchants began issuing their own money. These bills of exchange, bearer notes, or similar instruments were the preforms of bank accounts and banknotes. While the issuing of banknotes was at some point nationalised, today we rely all the more heavily on accounts with private companies for our payments, that is, on bank accounts. The sums of money in the accounts of private banks are also produced by them, that is, by private firms, in the process of lending. The cycles of this private money creation are not, as many believe, dictated by central banks but follow their own pace. At least in stable economic environments, private banks enjoy a great deal of autonomy regarding their capacity to issue money (e.g. Ryan-Collins *et al.* 2014; Bundesbank 2017; Huber 2017; Pettifor 2017; Sahr 2017). Accordingly, private money creation has accompanied the state's issuing of money since the early days of modern economics. It is virtually the defining feature of modern monetary 'design' that the right to create money is shared between central banks and private commercial banks, thus making the latter something like franchisees of money creation.[4]

It is therefore no wonder that research applying the concept of monetary sovereignty has mainly studied state options for controlling money prices. Monetary sovereignty in the sense of a territorial monopoly on money creation, as, for instance, the German finance minister assumed in his criticism of Libra mentioned above (Karth *et al.* 2020a), has gradually disappeared with the rise of modern nation-states. Modern monetary orders rely on a 'rejection of absolutist monetary sovereignty' (Ingham 2004: 128), that is, a hybridisation of the issuance of a territory's means of payment. There is, however, another understanding of the concept, which in turn allows us to address a different aspect of public and private money creation and to do so with an eye to recent transformations.

Autonomous monetary agency

An alternative understanding of monetary sovereignty focuses on the creation of money. This is not because it asserts a state monopoly where none exists but instead because it conceptualises monetary sovereignty in terms of action theory. This alternative understanding is therefore not necessarily referring to a part of the catalogue of rights that a state can traditionally claim for the independent administration of its territory. Rather, we define sovereignty as an extreme form of agency. Monetary economies are characterised by the fact that actors are forced to constantly reproduce their liquidity (ability to pay) to survive economically. In money economies, an ability to pay equals an ability to act. Actors can reproduce their ability to pay by four means, whereby private households are usually only (legally) given the first two options: (1) one can obtain money from others, through market exchange or as a gift; (2) one can borrow money; (3) one can take it from someone else or impose a payment obligation on others; or (4) one can produce money. Income (through exchange or gift), loans, appropriation through coercion, or money creation can make actors liquid, that is, give them the ability to pay their bills. In varying situations, different actors will have dissimilar opportunities to renew their liquidity. We would like to call varying degrees of the capacity for action in the reproduction of one's own liquidity *monetary agency*. Every actor has a higher or lower level of monetary agency in a given situation and structural context. What we call an agential understanding of monetary sovereignty refers to this particular form of agency and to (a degree of) autonomy from other actors regarding the reproduction of an actor's ability to pay.

---

[4] Hockett & Omarova (2017). Sometimes a nominalistic approach is applied here that defines only central bank money (of which cash is a part) as 'currency'. Private commercial banks then create 'money' but not 'currency' (e.g. Kelton 2020). This may be coherent in terms of definition, but it is a semantic trick that disguises the money-creation privilege of private banks. We ignore it here intentionally.

Monetary autonomy with respect to one's own economic actions in a money economy is ultimately only available to those who can create new money, that is, who can *pay* without being dependent on existing means of exchange. Anyone who seriously wants to claim monetary sovereignty must, therefore, have access to capacities for money creation. Those who cannot create new money run the risk of consuming their budget and thus exhausting their ability to pay. They must then take in new money, earn it, or borrow it in order to restore their own ability to pay. In concrete terms: their monetary agency is dependent on others. Although states can require that their citizens relinquish money to the state in the form of taxes, this also means taking it from others, that is (in monetary terms), being dependent. Those who can, on the other hand, issue new money, have an ability to pay that exists independently of the already existing capacity of others to pay, which would have to be ceded to them. The concept of monetary sovereignty thus refers to a form of access to liquidity that is independent of the liquidity of other actors.[5] *Monetarily sovereign are those who can dispose of their own liquidity*, and this can, ceteris paribus, only be done by those who *are* liquid when they *want* to be liquid, because they are able to pay with newly created money.

The power to implement money creation is perhaps not a sufficient but certainly a necessary condition of monetary sovereignty. Monetary sovereignty, as the ability to *choose* to be able to pay, of course only exists as a relative capacity. Monetary sovereignty is one end of a 'spectrum' between (absolute) dependence and (absolute) autonomy (Bonizzi *et al.* 2019; Kelton 2020). It is within this spectrum that we want to locate the member states of the euro zone.[6] Before we do so, however, we must first outline the emergence of this monetary room for manoeuvre. Within the action-theoretical framework, monetary sovereignty does not appear to be a capacity that was *lost* with the emergence of modern monetary orders and public–private sharing of the competence for money creation; rather, it *arises* thanks to the emergence of these phenomena.[7]

The modern money franchise

Key features of modern monetary orders

In the 18th century, an institutional architecture was established in England that was to become the blueprint for modern monetary orders (Ingham 2004). The economic and political dominance of the British (and then American) Empire, but also

---

[5] In this understanding of monetary sovereignty, it is irrelevant at first whether someone else can create money, too.
[6] We also limit ourselves here to discussing liquidity within a state's own currency.
[7] For another approach that develops the territorial definition of monetary sovereignty with respect to the modern monetary system, see van 't Klooster & Murau (2020).

the functionality of this 'design' (Desan 2014), determined its global adaptation. Today all official national and supranational currencies are based on this institutional architecture. The modern monetary design has four aspects.

First, modern money is legally constituted as claims against banks. The money in bank accounts is not a real asset; it does not constitute ownership like possessing a house or a car. Rather, it is a debt contract. It is accounted for as an asset by the beneficiary of the account (the one who 'has' the money) and as a liability by the bank itself. This is most obvious for money held as deposits, but even cash is recorded as a liability in the banking system and only enters the economy because it is registered as bank debt. Today, any amount of money belonging to the official euro, pound or dollar money supply is registered as a liability in a bank balance sheet. Money in private bank accounts is registered as a liability of private banks, while cash and those sums held by banks and governments in central bank accounts appear as liabilities in the central bank balance sheet, in the same way as private bank accounts. All (official) money is bank debt, either of public institutions (central banks) or private firms (commercial banks). Studies that choose this legal constitution of money as an item in bank balance sheets (rather than the function of money for its users) as the starting point for their analysis are accordingly referred to as applying the 'constitutional approach' (Desan 2017), 'balance sheet approach' (Ehnts 2017), or 'accounting view on money' (Bezemer 2016).

Second, public and private bank debts are hierarchically ordered. Customer payments with commercial bank balances generate debit and credit differences between commercial banks, which cannot be settled with private bank liabilities but only with central bank debts. So, while private banks in a sense still owe their customers something, namely money from the central bank, their debt no longer refers to anything else; central bank debts are 'irredeemable claims' (Quinn & Roberds 2014: 283). With modern money we are dealing with a franchise system of claims that refer to nothing more than other claims. The hierarchy between these claims translates to an international scale; for example, US Federal Reserve liabilities are much more likely to be able to make payments in world markets than bank claims in other currencies.

Third, modern money resembles a huge structure rather than a mere aggregate of means of payments, as claims used as money are 'backed' or offset by even more claims (Ingham 2004). As noted above, modern money consists of claims against banks, which can only be used to pay off other debts because they are part of this hierarchical system of debt relationships. Furthermore, they exist as claims on banks' balance sheets only because these balance sheets are in turn offset by other claims, now acting as assets of the banks. Banks can only offer their own debts as money because they also have assets, but these assets are usually the debts of others, such as loans, central bank deposits, bonds, or securities. Sociologically, this is interesting, because it leads to a further specification of the concept of modern money: a single asset can only be used as money as a dependent part of a network or network of debts. Perry Mehrling (2017: 138) refers to this network of mutually enabling and hierarchically structured claims as the 'money grid'. From this perspective, contemporary economic sociology no longer refers to modern money as a set or aggregate of singular assets serving as means of payments (nor as a pure function, such as the medium of exchange) but instead as a global entity – the money grid.

Fourth, the legal constitution of money refers to the specific mechanism by which it is produced. Since sums of money are debts in bank balance sheets, new money can only be created by entering new debts in the balance sheet of a bank. The bank's balance sheet must simply continue to function, that is, remain in balance; assets and liabilities must be in equilibrium. Private actors such as households or companies can offer a bank their own debts (for example as IOUs or claims against themselves) at any time and receive new money in return. This process is also called 'credit creation' and is the normal mode of production of new money in the modern money grid. In economic terms, money creation is an exchange of two claims, one of which is money, a 'swap of IOUs' (Mehrling 2020: 1). If a bank approves a loan application, new money is created on the borrower's account as a claim against the bank. In return, the bank receives a claim against the borrower, that is, the loan itself as a credit. Modern money is created in accounting terms by simultaneously writing assets (credit) and liabilities (deposit) of the same amount on the balance sheet. Banks do not have to collect money first to lend it elsewhere. They create these funds themselves, by simply posting them to the account.

Elasticity spaces

Within the money grid, liquidity can arise at any time when a bank posts a new liability on its balance sheet and thus creates money. The prerequisite is that it can simultaneously book a corresponding credit (a loan) as an asset. This keeps the bank balance sheet in equilibrium.[8] This modern mode of money creation gives various private and public actors varying degrees of opportunity to renew their liquidity through credit creation. In other words, actors may have different opportunities to access the basically unlimited capacities for money creation, depending on how attractive their promises to pay (IOUs) are for the banking sector. This attractiveness influences what we have called their monetary agency. Murau (2020) calls these different levels of monetary agency 'elasticity spaces'. The accessibility

---

[8] Private commercial banks' autonomy is very high, especially in stable economic phases. In the stability phase before the global financial crisis of 2008, also known as 'the great moderation', private money creation expanded accordingly. Commercial banks were able to meet the lucrative demand for new money more or less at their own discretion. However, especially in times of crisis, banks are dependent on the supply of hierarchically higher-ranking central bank money if there is no longer sufficient demand for credible and lucrative loans. At least in times of crisis, the dependence of private liquidity on public commitments comes into play, either in the form of loans from central banks or of loans from the state, which ensure stability in the money grid as *safe assets* and *safe havens*.

of money creation as a swap of IOUs is determined by the attractiveness of the debt offered to the central or commercial banks. If, for example, a private household with no income applies for a consumer loan, the IOU offered by the household is highly risky for a private bank. On the other hand, an investment loan to an established and profitable company is more attractive, because it is safer and more lucrative. Private households without income and successful companies therefore have different opportunities to exchange their own debts for newly created money; in other words, their monetary agency is characterised by elasticity spaces of different dimensions. Most governments' bonds are particularly attractive to the banking sector because they are very safe and can be used for benchmarks and refinancing transactions with central banks. In this sense, 'elasticity space' refers to a single actor's chances of accessing the money creation capacity of the banking sector in order to reproduce liquidity.[9]

Following Murau (2020), we assume that elasticity spaces are determined by three factors. First, other actors must be interested in accepting your debts as assets in their balance sheets and express a desire to do so. This could be for various reasons, for example, because these debts are profitable or, as in the case of many public debts, particularly secure. As a 'super safe asset', many bonds fulfil the function of stabilising portfolios. Second, elasticity spaces are influenced by regulatory requirements. Actors may be allowed or denied opportunities to expand their balance sheets in certain ways. Third and finally, the expectation of support from higher-ranking institutions affects the elasticity spaces of actors present in the field. This support (usually) boils down to the capacity and willingness of the central bank to use its balance sheet to support a faltering system.[10] To put it simply: the elasticity space of an actor is determined by the banking sector's willingness to accept its debt, this debt's regulatory embeddedness, and the expected support in case of an impending default.

According to the gradual definition of monetary sovereignty as a spectrum that marks the margins of monetary agency, one actor would be more sovereign than others if that actor's debt were more coveted by the banking sector, in other words, if it were easy for him to get new money through a swap of IOUs. A wide elasticity space would render the monetary agency of an actor gradually more autonomous, that is, less dependent on already existing money held by others. One could then speak of 'monetary sovereignty' as an extreme situation, in which an

---

[9] Murau's concept is in fact broader in scope and refers to the general possibility of extending one's own balance sheet by means of financial assets. We focus here on our question about the state of monetary sovereignty in the euro area, in terms of liquidity in one's own currency.

[10] Murau also speaks of 'contingent assets and liabilities' because these are measures that have not yet been realised but are potential measures that can be recorded in balance sheets as assets or liabilities: 'Each institution has its own respective *elasticity space* for balance sheet expansion that depends on available counterparties, stipulations for allowed on-balance-sheet activities and available contingent assets and liabilities which are provided by higher-ranking institutions and only become real once a crisis hits' (Murau 2020: vi).

actor's elasticity space would be independent of the approval of a second balance sheet, that is, if the actor could (basically) swap IOUs with themselves. This is precisely the option open to some states, which was voluntarily relinquished by the countries of the euro zone. Instead, the legal architecture of the euro zone stipulated that the final decision on member states' liquidity should be taken by private actors. This experiment has been challenged by the payment crises of the last decade.

The euro zone experiment

On a state's ability to pay

How does a state pay? With respect to the euro zone, a comparison with a country like Canada has proved useful (Ehnts 2017: 103–6; Lavoie 2019). The Canadian Ministry of Finance handles government payments. To do so, it maintains an account with the Bank of Canada. Nation-states therefore pay with central bank money. Whenever the government pays its bills, this account is debited by the central bank, which credits central bank money to the commercial bank of the beneficiary (a government employee, an infrastructure contractor, etc.). The recipient receives in return new deposits from his bank. This works even if the account is not funded, that is, in the Canadian case, if the Canadian government is not actually liquid. Like any bank, the central bank of Canada can credit the deposit of its 'customer' (the Canadian government) with the amount needed; all it has to do is balance its new obligation (the new credit balance created for the payment) with an asset. The balance sheet must remain in balance under the double-entry accounting regime. To achieve this, the Bank of Canada books a government bond on its balance sheet; the central bank of Canada is obliged to do so. In other words, the central bank of Canada issues a claim against itself (central bank money) by 'funding' it with a claim against the government to pay money (government bond).

This process of directly generating a central bank liability (money) while recording a liability of the government to which the central bank belongs (government bond) is known as *direct monetisation* of government bonds. Not only does Canadian government spending bring new money into circulation, Canada's promises to pay are absolutely safe, as long as they are denominated in the unit of account of the national currency. The Bank of Canada can and will pay every debt of the Canadian government, that is, convert the claim against the government into a claim against itself, that is, money. Therefore, the Canadian government's elasticity space is maximised with regard to payments in its own currency, because for regulatory reasons, government debt *must* be 'attractive' to the central bank. The Canadian government is therefore able to pay in its own currency when it wants to be liquid.

In many other countries, including the euro area, this direct monetisation of government expenditure is not allowed. The regulatory embedding of government debt here is thus different, and this affects the member states' elasticity spaces. The German treasury (*Deutsche Finanzagentur*, to be more precise) is obliged to sell claims against the government (bonds) to the market, that is, to private investors, when the government lacks sufficient ability to pay. Article 123 of the Treaty on the Functioning of the European Union (TFEU) prohibits the use of national central banks or the ECB to finance government expenditure. Therefore, government debt will not be payed directly by the central bank, as in the Canadian case, but government bonds must be sold by finance ministries to private investors in all euro zone countries. Those primary investors can then swap this IOU of a government with the ECB to get a new amount of money on their deposits at the central bank. This is called the 'secondary market'. In this way, bonds initiate the creation of new money as well, but first and foremost in the accounts of private actors.

The German Ministry of Finance manages the so-called 'central account of the Federal Government' (*Zentralkonto des Bundes*) at the Bundesbank on behalf of the German Federal Government. If the Federal Government wants to (further) overdraw this account, it needs, in other words, additional liquidity of its own, that is, it must instruct the *Deutsche Finanzagentur* to find buyers for a new bond. A group of selected investors called the *Bietergruppe Bundesemissionen*, which consists of 36 private companies, then bids for such a bond as in an auction. The members pay with money from their own accounts at the Bundesbank. New money is only created when they deposit the purchased bonds with the central bank to borrow new central bank money (which, ultimately, is comparable to Canada). Such an exchange of privately held government debt for central bank debt (i.e. for new money) can also be called an *indirect monetisation* of government debt.

Even where direct financing is prohibited, the banking sector is generally very willing to record government debt as an asset on its own balance sheet. One reason for this is the regulatory importance of bonds, such as their privileged status under capital adequacy rules or their eligibility for refinancing operations with the central bank. Government debt is thus generally regarded as a safe investment, even without the possibility of direct monetisation. This makes government debt essential for the stabilisation of investment portfolios everywhere in the economy, a function referred to as 'safe assets' or, in times of distress, 'safe havens'. This security is based on the expected existence of contingent assets and liabilities, that is, the expectation of support by the central banks in the event of a crisis. These expectations broaden the elasticity space of many governments. Creditors of most developed industrialised countries generally assume that the debts of many countries do not have a pure credit default risk because the central bank guarantees repayment through money creation. They are therefore considered 'risk-free' assets. The money-creating capacity of their central bank in the background prevents states from exposing themselves to the risk of becoming illiquid, at least with regard to obligations which – and here lies the crux of the matter – they can and must settle *in their own currency*. The bankruptcies of Argentina and Russia in the recent past were due to debts denominated in foreign currencies (Mellios & Paget-Blanc 2011: 326). Despite the ban on direct monetisation of government spending, many states therefore enjoy a high degree of autonomy regarding their ability to pay in their national currency, because their monetary agency is embedded in a robust and broad elasticity space.

A privatised foreign currency

The euro-area treaties explicitly prohibit the ECB from taking monetary policy decisions with regard to the financing of member states' budgetary policies. As a result, another twist is added to the regime of indirect monetisation of government bonds. The ECB is only permitted to exchange government bonds for money with private investors if such transactions serve its narrowly defined monetary policy objectives, more specifically, the maintenance of price stability. For this reason, and in precisely this sense, the power to decide whether new liquidity should be generated by the central bank lies with private actors. In structural terms, the German state is thus monetarily dependent on the willingness of private bidders to provide it with liquidity. What can render government bonds 'attractive' to the ECB is not the fact that a government needs to remain able to pay (and not its *budgetary* policy goals in general), but solely the bank's *monetary* policy goals. In practice, however, the incentives for private actors to swap their bonds with the ECB are manifold. Nevertheless, it is important to be aware of the structural limitations of the state's elasticity space that is no longer secured by a legal mandate to support the government's monetary agencies.

The scope of this restriction became clear during the euro crisis. The impacts of the collapse of US investment bank Lehman Brothers in 2008 and rising government debts in Europe revealed to holders of euro zone government bonds that the prohibition of direct monetisation of government bonds *indeed* implied a lack of support. It revealed, in other words, that the contingent assets and liabilities (the at least indirect guarantees of a government's monetary agency by its own central bank) had been *substantially* dismantled. As it became clear that the ban on (at least) indirect monetisation aiming at a restoration of state liquidity would not be lifted at the first sign of financial turbulence, the euro area experienced a 'sovereignty vacuum' (Ingham 2004: 195) induced by its creditors. This can be seen in the empirical data indicating the default risk associated with individual member states, that is, the valuation 'risk premiums' by investors of government bonds. After the introduction of the euro, the market valuations of risk premiums of all member countries had initially settled at the same level. This was a clear sign that investors were assuming the same probability of default for the various bonds. The fact that Greek and German bonds were considered to be *equally* risk free reveals that those who subscribed to such bonds apparently assumed that the ECB would hedge them. They were firmly convinced that, in an emergency, the euro states would resolutely claim monetary sovereignty for themselves. However, when the financial crisis suddenly raised the economic and political possibility that some crisis countries might leave the euro system, meaning that the default of some debt securities could no longer be ruled out because of Article 125 of the TFEU (the much-cited 'no-bailout paragraph'), which explicitly prohibits any financial assistance among the member states, market valuations diverged drastically and rapidly. Suddenly, it became a de facto option that states would become illiquid *in their own currency*.

Without the guarantee of government bonds – at least implicitly – by the tandem of national treasuries and their central banks, which could swap new money for government bonds at any time, the relationship of the euro countries to the euro became like that of a single country to a foreign currency. The situation of the member states is thus similar to that of countries borrowing in US dollars to finance imports without themselves producing US dollars. It is generally thought that such foreign currency debt is riskier than debt in an economy's national currency, because the supply of currency can (at least in theory) be adjusted more flexibly to any bottlenecks that may arise. High foreign-currency debt is therefore also referred to as 'original sin' and identified as a problem above all for the so-called Global South (Eichengreen & Hausmann 1999). Accordingly, the euro area is also referred to as 'Europe's Original Sin' (Papadimitriou & Wray 2012). At least according to the constitution of the Eurosystem, the states in the euro zone have *only* foreign currency available to finance their expenditures: 'For the nations who have adopted the Euro', writes economist Randall Wray (2012: 171), monetary dependence is the self-inflicted reality: '[it] is as if they had adopted a foreign currency' (see also Ehnts 2017; Mitchell & Fazi 2017; Kelton 2020).

The euro was designed to function as a privately managed foreign currency for the member countries. The Eurosystem, which is composed of the national central banks of the euro countries and the ECB, not only excludes direct monetisation, but limits indirect monetarisation, which may only be used as a monetary policy tool, that is, it may not be used to bail out a member state that has run into payment difficulties. Consequently, the option of indirect monetisation of government bonds lacks the kind of guarantee promise that is part of the practice of indirect monetisation in other countries such as the United States. Moreover, the euro-area countries have set themselves contractual ceilings for new and total debt in the Stability and Growth Pact, thereby imposing further restrictions on their monetary agency. The package of these rules and measures destabilises the liquidity of the euro-area countries because it is de facto dependent on the ability and willingness of private investors to pay. Euro-area countries must first collect what they want to spend or borrow the corresponding sums. They must do this not from their own bank, where they can expect a formalised privileged access, but through debt auctions on transnational financial markets. In this respect, the construction principles of the euro area have placed the member countries in a position of budgetary dependency that is otherwise only common among private sector actors.

From the financial crisis to the COVID-19 crisis

The financial crisis

Before the crisis, the monetary agency of the euro-area states was characterised by a more-or-less homogeneous elasticity space.[11] One indicator of this was the adjusted interest rates, the 'risk premiums' mentioned above. Apparently, it was assumed that states would be able to fall back on implicit backstops in the event of a payment crisis. During the turbulent times after 2008, the willingness to hold some (e.g. Greek) government bonds declined. Other bonds, such as Germany's, remained attractive. With the low regulatory and financial barriers to substituting debt instruments among euro-area member states, investors' willingness to hold government bonds from individual states drifted apart quickly and dramatically. In other words, the elasticity space of states like Greece shrank, rendering their monetary space more dependent on income streams. This was partly due to the regulatory framework of the euro zone elasticity spaces in general. In 2005, the ECB made its transactions in government bonds entirely dependent on the ratings of private rating agencies, which is why bonds from an increasing number of member states also could not be used for central bank transactions.

This fragmentation into different elasticity spaces (some intact, some shrinking) provoked various reactions. Because some euro countries lacked the monetary instruments needed for measures aimed at tackling the 2008 financial crisis without massively jeopardising the positive assessment of their creditworthiness on the markets, the ECB increasingly assumed the role of a policymaker. The accelerated transformation of the global banking crisis into a sovereign debt crisis triggered a downward spiral in the assessment of sovereign liquidity, which the markets were able to counter by relying on the ECB's credible assertion that it would provide unlimited liquidity if necessary. Only the equally unequivocal and famous proclamation by the then-ECB President Mario Draghi that his authority would do everything to preserve the euro – 'Whatever it takes' – was able to slow the sell-off of government bonds and thus the loss of confidence in the ability of some countries to service their debts (Germain & Schwartz 2014: 1108). The announcement that contingent assets would be introduced to (more or less) stabilise the member states' monetary agency restored the investors' faith; contingent assets stabilised and homogenised the elasticity space of euro-area countries.

This support structure has been codified in regulatory terms, for example with the instrument called Outright Monetary Transactions (OMT). Since September 2012, in the event of a crisis, the ECB has thus been granted the authority to buy

---

[11] Again, note that in contrast to Murau (2020) we are referring to the attractiveness of one's own debts for the banking sector, that is, the opportunity to renew one's liquidity with newly created money. Murau's much broader understanding of the concept is by no means called into question here but has been simplified pragmatically for the specific purpose of this chapter.

short-term government bonds issued by an individual member state on the secondary market in a targeted manner and without quantitative limits. This was a measure that, thanks to its mere availability as an explicit contingent asset, had an impact on the markets without ever actually having been implemented. From 2015 onwards, the ECB launched a huge programme of public debt purchases as part of its so-called *unconventional measures*. Until 2018, bonds with a value equivalent to up to 80 billion newly created euros were monetised monthly. In contrast to the OMT, however, the purchases follow a fixed country key, so that all member states rather than just one are taken into account. Thus, this expansion of the elasticity spaces still does *not* depend on the individual needs of the monetary agency of individual euro-area members.

The COVID-19 crisis

The economic effects of the COVID-19 pandemic and the political reactions to it in Europe have once again highlighted the limited and unequal monetary agency of the euro area member states. A country like Italy, which was initially particularly hard hit by COVID-19, had significantly less opportunities to support its economy than Germany, for example, whose debt instruments are in particularly high demand in times of crisis, because they function as safe assets. The European Commission initially reacted to the looming financing bottlenecks in April 2020 with three liquidity support measures. Through the European Stability Mechanism (ESM), which was introduced in response to the financial crisis, the European Investment Bank (EIB), and a new instrument for mitigation of unemployment risk (SURE), grants and loans were made available to member states based on jointly guaranteed European debt (EIB 2020; ESM 2020; European Commission 2020). Before the financial crisis, the monetary capacity to act at the EU level was still largely inflexible. New support structures for crisis situations, such as the ESM, have now been expanded and made permanent in the wake of COVID-19. To ensure that these European funds could also be used by national governments, the Stability and Growth Pact, one of the most central European regulations for limiting the elasticity space of the member states, was suspended. Governments are now able to spend beyond a new deficit of 3 per cent of their gross domestic product (GDP) without sanctions.

As the COVID-19 pandemic hit those countries particularly hard that already had a comparatively low fiscal framework and less access to the money creation capacity of the banking sector, calls for further European solutions to prevent further drifting apart of the euro-area economies were voiced. On 18 May, German Chancellor Angela Merkel and French President Emmanuel Macron made a proposal for a European recovery plan based on joint borrowing by the European Commission (Bundesregierung 2020). The Next Generation EU Recovery and Resilience Facility adopted on 21 July builds on this proposal. It provides for an increase of the EU budget by 750 billion euros between 2021 and 2024. Of this amount, 390 billion euros are grants which do not have to be paid back to the EU by the nation-states. These funds will be raised on the financial markets as a collective debt (European Council 2020). This means that the European Commission will issue EU bonds on the international financial markets. This is not the first time that the Commission has taken on debt. However, the scale and the fact that the corresponding funds are being used as a macroeconomic instrument for crisis management make this different from previous EU debt. Until now, the EU's budgetary balance has been virtually inelastic. Exceptions have been made mainly through the EIB and the ESM, but with Murau (2020: 29) they can be understood as 'off-balance-sheet fiscal agencies'. The activities of the EIB and ESM are not implemented directly through the EU budget. The recovery plan, however, is a clear deviation from the rule that the EU budget cannot be expanded through borrowing.[12] After the limited elasticity spaces of the euro-area member states again became a problem in the COVID-19 crisis, the monetary agency of the nation-states was indirectly enlarged by extending the elasticity of the EU treasury.

At the beginning of March 2020, the willingness to hold government bonds of euro area member states declined for some bonds, which was reflected in diverging interest rates. These 'spreads' are crucial, because, as the case of Greece during the euro crisis has shown, doubts that spread on the financial markets about the creditworthiness of a euro country quickly generate a self-reinforcing dynamic.[13] It was therefore necessary to enhance the willingness of financial-market players to accept the respective government bonds in their bank balance sheets. The corresponding demand for such bonds was again provided by the ECB. On 18 March, it announced that it would buy up private and public bonds valued at 750 billion euros under the Pandemic Emergency Purchase Programme (PEPP), that is, include them in its own balance sheet (ECB 2020a). The capital key of the national central banks will continue to apply, that is, bonds cannot simply be bought according to national financing needs but only in relation to each member state's total population and GDP. However, unlike other programmes, the ECB's PEPP allows for a little more flexibility by not excluding fluctuations in the distribution of purchases over time, across asset classes, and between countries. In fact, the announcement had a direct impact on the risk premiums of European government bonds and thus on governments' financing conditions. Both after the first announcement of the PEPP on 18 March and after its extension on 4 June (ECB 2020d), not only the yields on euro-area government bonds as a whole fell but also the spreads in particular.

As mentioned above, in 2005 the ECB specified in its collateral framework that it will only accept those government bonds that are rated 'investment grade' by rating agencies. The decision on access to the central bank as a *liquidity provider of last resort* was thus further privatised, which had a significant impact

---

[12] For an example of the debates on the legality of the recovery plan, see Kauranen (2020).
[13] These spreads are measured against the European safe asset, the German federal bond. In this crisis, the comparison with Italian government bonds is particularly significant (https://ycharts.com/indicators/italygermany_10_year_bond_spread, accessed 20 August 2021).

on the elasticity space of the member states. Together with the announcement of the PEPP, the ECB relaxed this collateral framework (ECB 2020b). For the duration of the PEPP, a lower quality of bonds from a larger group of borrowers will be accepted. This includes, for the first time since the debt crisis, Greek bonds, which has already had a significant impact on their valuation. In addition, the ECB made itself additionally independent of private credit ratings by not allowing major deviations in private credit ratings during the COVID-19 crisis to influence its own decisions on the creditworthiness of government bonds. Moreover, the ECB lifted the ceiling for the purchase of government bonds. Previously, the ECB had committed itself to holding a maximum of one-third of the government bonds of a state in total and per issue (ECB 2020c). By abolishing this rule, the ECB can intervene even more decisively and potentially without limits in the pricing of government bonds. It now offers a near-guarantee of government debt, at least for the duration of the crisis. The PEPP programme has also been called 'Lagarde's whatever it takes moment', following Mario Draghi's proclamation in 2012 to do everything possible to stabilise the euro area. Indeed, the current support structures are in effect a confirmation and extension of the contingent liquidity backstops after the financial crisis.

Both the ECB's government bond purchase programmes under the PEPP and the Asset Purchase Programme (APP) and the Commission's Recovery Fund can be seen as attempts to prevent the spreads in the euro zone from drifting apart and to ensure member states' liquidity. In other words, both the European Commission and the ECB have once again exerted influence on the elasticity spaces of the member states and are trying to align them. This has harmonised and expanded the monetary agency of the individual nations, which have gained a heightened capacity to act within the spectrum of monetary sovereignty. However, the euro remains, in structural terms, a 'privately managed foreign currency'. Public liquidity is still only established through the private banking sector. The euro countries are dependent on the decisions of private actors to exchange IOUs with them. Only if private actors are willing to engage in such exchanges will the euro states be able to reproduce their liquidity independent of already existing sums of money. Moreover, a single elasticity space has not been created in the euro area as a reaction to the crises (as would be the case with a complete switch to eurobonds), nor can governments themselves decide to monetise their debts. There are still no ECB guarantees for government debt in the form of indirect monetarisation through regulatory measures; at best, there are contingency policies for such cases. The elasticity spaces of the member states are therefore still dependent on the approval of other actors. However, the room for manoeuvre within these dependencies has been expanded, as we have shown here. In particular, the willingness of the European Central Bank to step in in the event of a crisis and effectively finance government bonds as a 'contingent asset' by purchasing them on secondary markets was again confirmed in the COVID-19 pandemic.

Conclusion

Monetary sovereignty is usually understood as national authority over the means of payment. We have called this a territorial notion of monetary sovereignty. It implies that a sovereign state can claim to determine what acts (and functions) as a means of payment within its territory. This includes, first, the authority to determine what is considered legal tender; second, the authority to issue these means of payment; and third, the authority to determine the functionality of the means of payment, that is, to influence the internal and external value of money. The territorial interpretation is suitable, for example, for the study of power relations within the euro zone. However, its analytical power is limited when it comes to money creation. After all, sharing authority over money creation is one of the basic principles of modern monetary orders. Modern nation-states never had a true (de facto) monopoly over the issuance of means of payment.

In this chapter we have referred to an agential understanding of the term 'monetary sovereignty'. This concept is related to a specific agency that is constitutive for money economies. We have called this agency *monetary agency*. All actors in a money-mediated economy must strive to remain liquid, that is, able to pay. Monetary agency refers to the scope they have in reproducing their ability to pay. The monetary agency of each actor (not only that of states, to which the territorial notion is exclusively applied) covers a spectrum ranging from monetary dependence to monetary sovereignty. Absolute monetary dependence would describe an actor only able to pay thanks to the decision of others to supply money; such actors have neither assets to exchange for money nor (formal or informal) claims to payments. Absolute monetary sovereignty, on the other hand, would mean that an actor can simply *decide* to be able to pay and would, therefore, be independent of the liquidity of others.

In modern monetary orders, the supply of liquidity becomes hyper-elastic, because bank debts are used as a means of payment. Liabilities of the banking system act as liquidity for the creditors of this debt. New money can always be created when a bank extends its balance sheet. The new money (its liability) and a credit (its assets) are simultaneously booked into the banks' balance sheet. To create money, a bank must be willing (for whatever reason) to accept the debt of another actor as a credit (in the broadest sense) on its balance sheet. In modern monetary orders, money is thus created by an exchange of two debts ('swap of IOUs') – the new money as a liability of the bank and the debt of the borrower, which the bank records as assets. There is obviously no physical limit to this process. The monetary agency of each actor is therefore codetermined by his chances of accessing this hyper-elastic supply. And this chance depends on how attractive a claim against the actor is as an asset for the banking sector.

The attractiveness of one's own debt as an asset for the banking sector creates an 'elasticity space' for each actor, that is, a potential for restoring one's own ability to pay through the issuance of new money (a swap of IOUs with the banking sector).

By virtue of this possibility, the monetary agency of those actors with particularly attractive debts can slide on the spectrum from monetary dependency to monetary sovereignty towards the sovereignty pole. Actors with attractive debts have considerable opportunities for restoring their ability to pay by accessing money that is not taken away from anyone but is instead newly created in exchange for a loan. They thus become less dependent on liquidity already present in the system.

A sovereign country's ability to pay in its own currency is usually guaranteed directly or indirectly by its central bank. Its monetary agency becomes backed up by the possibility of swapping debts with the central bank or the central bank's promise to guarantee those debts. Although many economies are dependent on the world market and thus on foreign currencies, they can usually claim a high degree of sovereignty in their own means of payment. In this respect, the euro zone is an experiment in privatisation. The ECB is only permitted to use its balance sheet to create *private* liquidity. In terms of money creation, the euro countries' monetary agency is, therefore, dependent on the provision of liquidity initially produced for the private sector. This is remarkable, not least against the background of resistance against Facebook's own currency, Libra. Politicians from the euro zone argued explicitly that the issuing of money was an indispensable part of a state's sovereign rights and should be a protected part of its domain.

Turbulences in the financial markets after 2008 challenged this experiment. The ECB was forced to safeguard the euro countries' monetary agency but remained within its mandate. It still does not provide them with their own elasticity space, that is, it cannot swap debts with national treasuries. The ECB's money-creating capacities remain open only to the private sector. By making massive use of these capacities, it tried to secure private elasticity spaces, hoping to relieve member state's monetary agency. This assignment of contingent assets for the private sector was again substantially underpinned in the COVID-19 crisis. The euro zone experiment, as the establishment of a 'depoliticized' (Issing 2008: 234) common currency with its empowerment of private actors and the formal restriction of nation-state monetary agencies, has not been changed *structurally* by the financial crises of the last decade and policy responses to them.

The ability to pay is a crucial capacity for action in modern societies. This also applies to social groups or collectives that become agents through the establishment of statehood. States must also be able to act in a monetary economy, which means they must be able to access liquidity. Thus, the constitution (and any restriction) of their monetary agency has general implications in terms of theories of statehood, political theory, and, above all, theories of democracy. Regarding this last aspect, some critics of the euro zone experiment criticise the lack of democratic legitimacy for the common currency, a critique that is distinct from general criticisms of the political architecture of the European Union. Indeed, or so they argue, if public institutions can only reproduce their liquidity (even in an emergency situation) with the consent of private investors, as is still the case after the changes brought about by the crises, then the lack of monetary sovereignty can be identified as a lack of democratic sovereignty (Ingham 2004; Wray 2012; Ehnts 2017; Mitchell & Fazi 2017). With the help of the agential interpretation of the concept of monetary sovereignty that we have presented here, the privatisation of monetary sovereignty in the euro zone as part of a contested experiment can thus be linked to a broader debate on claims, capacities, and deficits of sovereignty.

References

Adler-Nissen, R. & Gammeltoft-Hansen, T. (eds) (2008), *Sovereignty Games: Instrumentalizing State Sovereignty in Europe and Beyond* (New York, Palgrave Macmillan).

Bellamy, R. (2017), 'A European Republic of Sovereign States: Sovereignty, Republicanism and the European Union', *European Journal of Political Theory*, 16.2: 188–209.

Bezemer, D.J. (2016), 'Towards an "Accounting View" on Money, Banking and the Macroeconomy: History, Empirics, Theory', *Cambridge Journal of Economics*, 40.5: 1275–95.

Biersteker, T.J. & Weber, C. (1996), 'The Social Construction of State Sovereignty', in T.J. Biersteker & C. Weber (eds), *State Sovereignty as Social Construct* (Cambridge, Cambridge University Press), 1–21.

Bodin, J. (1962 [1606]), *The Six Bookes of a Commonweale: A Facsimile Reprint of the English Translation of 1606. Corrected and Supplemented in the Light of a New Comparison with the French and Latin Texts*, ed. K.D. McRae (Cambridge, MA, Harvard University Press).

Bonizzi, B., Kaltenbrunner, A., & Michell, J. (2019), 'Monetary Sovereignty is a Spectrum: Modern Monetary Theory and Developing Countries', *Real-World Economic Review*, 89: 46–61.

Bundesbank (2017), 'Monthly Report 69.4, April 2017', accessed 20 August 2021, www.bundesbank.de/resource/blob/667334/e0e505cef22a8d0bbe8da812f4c634ff/mL/2017-04-monatsbericht-data.pdf.

Bundesregierung (2020), 'A French–German Initiative for the European Recovery from the Coronavirus Crisis', Press Release 173/20, 18 May 2020, accessed 20 August 2021, www.bundesregierung.de/breg-en/news/dt-franz-initiative-1753890.

Desan, C. (2014), *Making Money: Coin, Currency, and the Coming of Capitalism* (Oxford, Oxford University Press).

Desan, C. (2017), 'The Constitutional Approach to Money', in N. Bandelj, F.F. Wherry, & V. Zelizer (eds), *Money Talks: Explaining How Money Really Works* (Princeton, Princeton University Press), 109–30.

Ehnts, D. (2017), *Modern Monetary Theory and European Macroeconomics* (London, Routledge).

Eichengreen, B. & Hausmann, R. (1999), 'Exchange Rates and Financial Fragility', paper presented at Federal Reserve Bank of Kansas City symposium, New Challenges for Monetary Policy, 26–28 August, Jackson Hole, Wyoming, accessed 20 August 2021, www.nber.org/papers/w7418.

European Central Bank (ECB) (2020a), 'ECB Announces €750 Billion Pandemic Emergency Purchase Programme (PEPP)', Press Release, 18 March 2020, accessed 20 August 2021, https://www.ecb.europa.eu/press/pr/date/2020/html/ecb.pr200318_1~3949d6f266.en.html.

European Central Bank (ECB) (2020b), 'ECB Announces Package of Temporary Collateral Easing Measures', Press Release, 7 April 2020, accessed 20 August 2021, https://www.ecb.europa.eu/press/pr/date/2020/html/ecb.pr200407~2472a8ccda.en.html.

European Central Bank (ECB) (2020c), 'ECB Takes Steps to Mitigate Impact of Possible Rating Downgrades on Collateral Availability', Press Release, 22 April 2020, accessed 20 August 2021, https://www.ecb.europa.eu/press/pr/date/2020/html/ecb.pr200422_1~95e0f62a2b.en.html.

European Central Bank (ECB) (2020d), 'Monetary Policy Decisions', Press Release, 4 June 2020, accessed 20 August 2021, https://www.ecb.europa.eu/press/pr/date/2020/html/ecb.mp200604~a307d3429c.en.html.

European Commission (2020), 'Proposal for a Council Regulation on the Establishment of a European Instrument for Temporary Support to Mitigate Unemployment Risks in an Emergency (SURE) Following the COVID-19 Outbreak', accessed 20 August 2021, https://eur-lex.europa.eu/legal-content/EN/TXT/PDF/?uri=CELEX:52020PC0139&from=EN.

European Council (2019), 'Joint Statement by the Council and the Commission on "Stablecoins"', accessed 20 August 2021, https://www.consilium.europa.eu/en/press/press-releases/2019/12/05/joint-statement-by-the-council-and-the-commission-on-stablecoins/.

European Council (2020), 'Special Meeting of the European Council (17, 18, 19, 20 and 21 July 2020) – Conclusions', accessed 20 August 2021, https://www.consilium.europa.eu/media/45109/210720-euco-final-conclusions-en.pdf.

European Investment Bank (EIB) (2020), 'EIB Board Approves €25 Billion Pan-European Guarantee Fund in Response to COVID-19 Crisis', accessed 20 August 2021, https://www.eib.org/en/press/all/2020-126-eib-board-approves-eur-25-billion-pan-european-guarantee-fund-to-respond-to-covid-19-crisis.htm.

European Stability Mechanism (ESM) (2020), 'ESM Board of Governors Backs Pandemic Crisis Support', Press Release, 15 May 2020, accessed 20 August 2021, https://www.esm.europa.eu/press-releases/esm-board-governors-backs-pandemic-crisis-support.

Germain, R. & Schwartz, H. (2014), 'The Political Economy of Failure: The Euro as an International Currency', *Review of International Political Economy*, 21.5: 1095–122.

Helleiner, E. (1999), 'Sovereignty, Territoriality and the Globalization of Finance', in D.A. Smith, D.J. Solinger, & S.C. Topik (eds), *States and Sovereignty in the Global Economy* (London, Routledge), 138–57.

Herrmann, C.W. (2008), 'Play Money? Contemporary Perspectives on Monetary Sovereignty', in Adler-Nissen & Gammeltoft-Hansen (2008), 63–80.

Hockett, R.C. & Omarova, S.T. (2017), 'The Finance Franchise', *Cornell Law Review*, 102: 1143–218.

Höpner, M. & Lutter, M. (2018), 'The Diversity of Wage Regimes: Why the Euro Zone Is Too Heterogeneous for the Euro', *European Political Science Review*, 10.1: 71–96.

Höpner, M. & Spielau, A. (2018), 'Better than the Euro? The European Monetary System (1979–1998)', *New Political Economy*, 23.2: 160–73.

Huber, J. (2017), *Sovereign Money: Beyond Reserve Banking* (Cham, Springer International Publishing).

Ingham, G. (2004), *The Nature of Money* (Cambridge, Polity).

Ingham, G. (2020), *Money* (Medford MA, Polity).

Issing, O. (2008), *The Birth of the Euro* (Leiden, Cambridge University Press).

Karth, F., Müller, C. & Sahr, A. (2020a), 'Geld in privaten Händen: Missverständnisse und Missverhältnisse monetärer Souveränität in Europa (I)', accessed 20 August 2021, https://soziopolis.de/beobachten/wirtschaft/artikel/geld-in-privaten-haenden/.

Karth, F., Müller, C. & Sahr, A. (2020b), 'Staatliche Zahlungs(un)fähigkeit: Missverständnisse und Missverhältnisse monetärer Souveränität in Europa (II)', accessed 20 August 2021, https://soziopolis.de/beobachten/wirtschaft/artikel/staatliche-zahlungsunfaehigkeit/.

Karth, F., Müller, C. & Sahr, A. (2020c), 'Geldschöpfungspolitik: Missverständnisse und Missverhältnisse monetärer Souveränität in Europa (III)', accessed 20 August 2021, https://soziopolis.de/beobachten/politik/artikel/geldschoepfungspolitik/.

Kauranen, A. (2020), 'Finland's Parliament Questions Legality of EU Recovery Plan', accessed 20 August 2021, https://www.reuters.com/article/us-finland-parliament-eu-recovery-idUSKBN23J1SS.

Kelton, S. (2020), *The Deficit Myth: Modern Monetary Theory and the Birth of the People's Economy* (New York, Public Affairs).

Keohane, R.O. & Nye, J.S. (1977), *Power and Interdependence: World Politics in Transition* (Boston, Little, Brown).

Kirshner, J. (2003), 'Money is Politics', *Review of International Political Economy*, 10.4: 645–60.

Koddenbrock, K. (2019), 'Money and Moneyness: Thoughts on the Nature and Distributional Power of the "Backbone" of Capitalist Political Economy', *Journal of Cultural Economy*, 12.2: 101–18.

Koning, J.P. (2019), 'Does Libra Threaten Monetary Sovereignty?', accessed 20 August 2021, https://www.aier.org/article/sound-money-project/does-libra-threaten-monetary-sovereignty.

Krasner, S.D. (1999), *Sovereignty: Organized Hypocrisy* (Princeton & Chichester, Princeton University Press).

Krasner, S.D. (2007), 'Sovereignty', in G. Ritzer (ed.), *The Blackwell Encyclopedia of Sociology* (New York, Blackwell Publishing).

Krasner, S.D. (2010), 'The Durability of Organized Hypocrisy', in H. Kalmo & Q. Skinner (eds), *Sovereignty Infragments: The Past, Present and Future of a Contested Concept* (Cambridge, Cambridge University Press), 96–113.

Lavoie, M. (2019), 'A System with Zero Reserves and with Clearing Outside of the Central Bank: The Canadian Case', *Review of Political Economy*, 31.2: 145–58.

Le Maire, B. (2019), 'Discours de Bruno Le Maire, minister de l'Economie et des Finances', accessed 20 August 2021, https://minefi.hosting.augure.com/Augure_Minefi/r/ContenuEnLigne/Download?id=7403AE72-0571-4BEE-8E78-8E678BD8F3E7&filename=1412%20-%20Discours%20de%20Bruno%20Le%20Maire%20-%20Forum%20mondial%20de%20l%27OCDE%20sur%20la%20blockchain.pdf.

Libra Association (2019), 'White Paper', accessed 17 December 2020, https://www.diem.com/en-us/white-paper/?noredirect=de-de.

MacCormick, N. (1999), *Questioning Sovereignty: Law, State, and Nation in the European Commonwealth* (Oxford, Oxford University Press).

Marcus, D. (2019), tweet of the twitter account @davidmarcus on 16 September 2019, accessed 20 August 2021, https://twitter.com/davidmarcus/status/1173566572721389568.

Mehrling, P. (2017), 'Financialization and its Discontents', *Finance and Society*, 2.2: 138–50.

Mehrling, P. (2020), 'Payment vs. Funding: The Law of Reflux for Today', Institute for New Economic Thinking Working Paper Series, accessed 20 August 2021, https://www.ineteconomics.org/uploads/papers/WP_113-Mehrling-Payment-vs-Funding.pdf.

Mellios, C. & Paget-Blanc, E. (2011), 'The Impact of Economic and Political Factors on Sovereign Credit Ratings', in R. Kolb (eds), *Sovereign Debt: From Safety to Default* (Hoboken, Wiley), 325–33.

Milner, H. (1991), 'The Assumption of Anarchy in International Relations Theory: A Critique', *Review of International Studies*, 17.1: 67–85.

Mitchell, W. & Fazi, T. (2017), *Reclaiming the State: A Progressive Vision of Sovereignty for a Post-Neoliberal World* (London, Pluto Press).

Murau, S. (2020), 'A Macro-Financial Model of the Euro Zone Architecture Embedded in the Global Offshore US-Dollar System', *Global Economic Governance Initiative (GEGI) Working Paper* (Boston, Global Development Policy Center).

Papadimitriou, D. & Wray, L.R. (2012), 'Euroland's Original Sin', *Levy Economics Institute Policy Note*, 8: 1–5.

Pettifor, A. (2017), *The Production of Money: How to Break the Power of Bankers* (London, Verso).

Pistor, K. (2017), 'From Territorial to Monetary Sovereignty', *Theoretical Inquiries in Law*, 18.2: 491–517.

Quinn, S. & Roberds, W. (2014), 'The Bank of Amsterdam through the Lens of Monetary Competition', in P. Bernholz & R. Vaubel (eds), *Explaining Monetary and Financial Innovation: A Historical Analysis* (Wiesbaden, Springer), 283–300.

Ryan-Collins, J., Greenham, T., Werner, R. & Jackson, A.(2014), *Where Does Money Come From? A Guide to the UK Monetary and Banking System* (London, New Economics Foundation).

Sahr, A. (2017), *Das Versprechen des Geldes: Eine Praxistheorie des Kredits* (Hamburg, Hamburger Edition).

Sassen, S. (1996), *Losing Control: Sovereignty in an Age of Globalization* (New York, Columbia University Press).

Scharpf, F.W. (2018), 'There is an Alternative: A Two-Tier European Currency Community', MPIfG Discussion Paper 18/7 (Cologne, Max Planck Institute for the Study of Societies).

Streeck, W. (2015), 'Why the Euro Divides Europe', *New Left Review*, 95: 5–26.

van't Klooster, J. & Murau, S. (2020), 'Rethinking Monetary Sovereignty: The Global Credit Money System and the State', accessed 10 December 2020, https://doi.org/10.31235/osf.io/k9qm8.

Wallace, W. (1999), 'The Sharing of Sovereignty: The European Paradox', *Political Studies*, 47.3: 503–21.

Weber, B. (2018), *Democratizing Money: Debating Legitimacy in Monetary Reform Proposals* (Cambridge, Cambridge University Press).

Wray, L.R. (2012), *Modern Money Theory: A Primer on Macroeconomics for Sovereign Monetary Systems* (Basingstoke, Palgrave Macmillan).

Zimmermann, C.D. (2013), *A Contemporary Concept of Monetary Sovereignty* (Oxford, Oxford University Press).

11

Three Conceptions of Sovereignty in Contemporary Investment Law

TAYLOR ST JOHN[*]

Introduction

CONTEMPORARY INVESTMENT LAW is often regarded as the embodiment of runaway globalisation, a field in which transnational corporations and other private actors float freely above territorially bound, constrained states. This perception did not emerge without reason: investment treaties provide foreign corporations and individuals with the standing to bring legal claims against states. The state and the individual are equals when they stand before an arbitration tribunal constituted to hear the dispute. The arbitration tribunal is composed of three individuals who sit in their personal capacity, often in Paris or Washington or Singapore, and may award compensation to the investor if they see fit. If the state does not pay the award, then the investor may begin proceedings in various national courts in order to be given the right to seize state assets. For instance, if British investors have secured an arbitration award against the Russian Federation, they may ask German courts to seize Russian state assets in Germany.

The growth of investment law empowers corporations, law firms, arbitrators, and other private actors while curtailing the power of states hosting foreign investors in a range of ways. A specialised field of international law in which national governments have ceded (or lost) control of policymaking to shadowy private actors, and in which large sums of tax money are redirected to pay foreign corporations, is easily cast as a villain. So easily cast, in fact, that a storyline in which states 'take back control' from arbitration makes for an intuitive and compelling headline. It resonates with wider fears and currents of discontent about

---

[*] I would like to thank conference participants for stimulating discussions, Christopher Smith for excellent editorial guidance, and Isabella Cuervo-Lorens for superb research assistance.

runaway globalisation. It is easy to believe that this headline story is the only story of sovereignty in contemporary investment law.

Sovereignty, however, is part of multiple stories in investment law; as a concept sovereignty has both continuity and elasticity. It is a composite term with layers of meaning from earlier eras stacked like sediment, and how those layers appear varies depending on where individuals sit; the associations that individuals make depend on their perspective. When state officials hear the term sovereignty, as they often do in discussions at the United Nations about investment law reform, what does it mean to them? What resonances does it have?

This chapter draws out three conceptions of sovereignty and how they manifest in investment law today. These conceptions emerged at different times, and the prominence of any one conception ebbs or flows over time, but all of them are present today. In fact, all of them are present within a single room. Week-long negotiations at the United Nations about investment law reform occurred every six months between fall 2017 and spring 2020, bringing together expert officials from roughly 120 countries. As an academic observer of these negotiations, I listened to these officials from the back of the room and listened to how the term sovereignty was used as well as how sovereignty was present or absent even when the term was not spoken.

Each of the three conceptions ties sovereignty to a particular set of associations and memories. These associations can be shared, for instance when an official invokes the term sovereignty pointedly to bring decolonisation or sovereign equality to the surface, knowing that their meaning will be understood widely. Alternatively, associations and memories can be unique to a particular state's experience or even to an individual. Since these are sophisticated, multilingual officials, they also often understand one another's meaning even if the 'sovereignty talk' in their own national context is different. For instance, the official from Lesotho would understand the domestic political drivers if an American official began to emphasise sovereignty more and use it alongside terms like security and investment screening, even though domestic debates over sovereignty in Lesotho have different associations.

The first conception is sovereignty as control, and a sense that to be sovereign is to be the supreme authority within a defined territory. In contemporary investment law, this conception emerges in concerns that economic globalisation has eroded the ability of states to make economic, social, or environmental policy. Concerns about an erosion in public 'policy space' are accompanied by concerns about rising private power.

The second conception is sovereignty as eligibility, and a sense that to be sovereign is to be recognised as eligible to participate in intergovernmental deliberations. This conception is associated with recognition by the other states, decolonisation, and sovereign equality. Visually, it means having a placard with the country's name in the room at the United Nations. Even in an age of large, powerful transnational corporations, certain tasks and recognitions remain for states alone. States are the only actors eligible to reform investment law formally; while other actors can offer views, only states are able to vote on reform decisions that emerge during negotiations or sign whatever treaty might result from the negotiations.

The third conception is sovereignty as capability, and a sense that to be sovereign is to be able to participate meaningfully in intergovernmental deliberations. This conception is associated with disparities in resources and informal hierarchies; whereas all governments are eligible to participate in reforming investment law, their actual participation varies. While some governments send ten delegates, other governments are not able to send even one delegate; visually, this conception of sovereignty is an empty chair behind the state's placard.

The chapter concludes with a few observations on the persistence of sovereignty as a concept. Why do officials continue to use the term sovereignty? Beyond diplomatic symbolism, sovereignty serves as a bridge to enduring questions about representation and rulemaking. These enduring questions take new forms as more economic globalisation means more rulemaking occurs at the global level: should private actors participate in rulemaking? Should all states, or just some states, participate in rulemaking? Sovereignty is a composite, with layers of meaning from earlier eras, a bridge to fundamental questions about who should participate in rulemaking, and a carrier for aspirations.

Sovereignty as control

A stylised image of European states after the Peace of Westphalia has cast a long shadow over thinking about sovereignty in International Relations and International Law.[1] Even as scholars demonstrate that this imagined Westphalian state system was more mythical than real, and probe the historicity of sovereignty's emergence, the stylised image continues to influence visions of sovereignty (De Carvalho *et al.* 2011; Glanville 2013; Costa Lopez *et al.* 2018; Herzog 2020). The stylised Westphalian image has internal and external dimensions. Internally, within defined territorial boundaries, the sovereign possesses supreme authority.[2] Given their authority internally, the sovereign could interact externally as an equal of other sovereigns, interactions that occur in an anarchic environment (Philpott 1995).

---

[1] For an example of how Westphalia appears in classic texts, see Hans Morgenthau's (1985 [1948]: 254) declaration that 'the Treaty of Westphalia brought the religious wars to an end and made the territorial state the cornerstone of the modern states system'.

[2] Philpott (2001); Costa Lopez *et al.* (2018: 491). Jean Bodin's (1992 [1576]: 1) definition of sovereignty as 'supreme and absolute power over citizens and subjects' still echoes here. Drawing a connection to Bodin is a way to highlight the historical specificity of this definition of sovereignty; rather than being universal, it emerged in Europe, in a particular moment. Reflecting on non-Eurocentric sovereignty and sovereignty in earlier eras (as contributions to this volume do) can help to develop a richer and more global picture of sovereignty (Zarakol in the Costa Lopez *et al.* [2018] forum; see also Zhang 2003; Kang 2010).

While the internal dimensions of sovereignty and the external dimensions of sovereignty are intrinsically linked, their different emphases give rise to two sets of concerns, which this chapter considers separately. Internal dimensions of sovereignty feed directly into concerns about control (or lack of control) over domestic policymaking, which are discussed in this section, while external dimensions lead to a focus on eligibility to participate on the world stage, discussed in the next section.

Concerns about a loss of control over domestic policymaking due to economic globalisation pervade contemporary politics in many states.[3] Rallying cries to 'take back control' in the United Kingdom and political speeches calling for a return to an imagined past in the United States feel louder than ever before, but the underlying anxieties about economic globalisation that give them resonance are not new. Does the state still have room to move? That is, do national governments still have the autonomy to decide economic and social policies? Can there be varieties of capitalism, or do global markets dictate a particular policy recipe? These questions have long been asked by scholars and citizens.[4]

Each time economic globalisation advances, the relationship between states and markets comes under renewed scrutiny. Economic globalisation generates questions about state–market relations that cross national borders and state–market relations within those borders, like what rate of tax a transnational corporation ought to pay and to whom that tax ought to be paid. Questions about state–market relations are imbued with sovereignty concerns, whether asked transnationally or domestically. Questions about who regulates transnational corporations are a common source of sovereignty anxieties, including a latent sense that private actors are able to ignore borders when it suits them, for instance structuring their corporations through several jurisdictions to lessen or avoid taxes. If sovereignty means exercising supreme control within defined borders, and if transnational corporations are able to evade that authority or slip around those borders, then sovereignty has been compromised.

Yet transnational corporations are not natural, biological creatures – they are legal creatures. Laws, contracts, and legal entities like corporations transform

---

[3] Krasner (1999) and Thomson (1995) distinguish between control and authority. Both believe that even though states may lose 'control' over certain policies and transborder flows due to globalisation, they are still the sole holders of 'authority'. For them, authority is essential for sovereignty while control is not. Yet other scholars, notably liberal interdependence theorists within International Relations, measure sovereignty in terms of state control over policy and transborder flows (Thomson 1995: 216). Therefore, I call this first conception of sovereignty control to recognise that what gives rise to anxieties about globalisation is a perceived loss of control (or a perceived loss of policymaking autonomy, used as equivalents in this chapter).

[4] In International Relations, an influential wave of research exploring the consequences of economic interdependence for policymaking autonomy began in the 1970s (Morse 1969; 1976; Vernon 1971; Cooper 1972; Keohane & Nye 1977). Subsequently, these questions have generated a large and diverse literature on the topic of globalisation and the state, which continues to arrive in waves that reflect the anxieties of the day. For prominent examples from a later wave, see Hall & Soskice (2001); Mosley (2000); Rodrik (1997); Strange (1996).

assets into capital; the law and lawyers play a crucial role in the coding of capital (Pistor 2019). National and international law are required to create transnational corporations. These corporations can then generate or modify the rules of economic globalisation, including by creating new transnational legal regimes or relocating judicial authority to commercial arbitration tribunals, which Sassen (1996: 15–17) describes as 'basically a private justice system'. Yet laws made by public authorities enable these transnational relations. The role of the state is even larger in investment law, since disputes are resolved through investor–*state* arbitration and the main rules are contained in formal inter-*state* treaties. Law firms, arbitrators, and other private actors shape how these treaties are applied and interpreted, but ultimately, the rules are still made by public authorities.

Does it affect sovereignty when states or other public authorities make rules that constrain their policymaking autonomy and provide private actors with new rights or powers? Negotiating international law, even agreeing to limit one's own autonomy, can be viewed as an exercise of sovereignty. Advocates of this view emphasise that 'expressed consent is the traditional basis of international law' (Raustiala 2003: 846), and since governments have *chosen* to limit their freedom of action, economic globalisation and the legal edifice enabling it have not compromised the sovereignty of states. When states make similar policies domestically, their sovereignty has not been compromised, the state's authority is merely being deployed in the service of policies that empower private transnational actors. For instance, writing national law in a way that creates tax loopholes and permits transnational corporations to avoid tax reflects a choice made by the responsible government. Realist scholars have long argued that actions like this reflect the exercise of sovereignty, not its absence (Carr 2016 [1939]; Gilpin 1975; 1987). For Raustiala (2003: 844) and others, 'much of the contemporary debate over sovereignty conflates sovereignty with freedom of action'.

Stephen Krasner and others do not necessarily conflate sovereignty with freedom of action, however; Krasner distinguishes between four types of sovereignty, which provides language to describe how an exercise of *legal* sovereignty can compromise or limit *domestic* sovereignty.[5] Krasner (1999: 4) is explicit that 'the exercise of one kind of sovereignty – for instance, international legal sovereignty – can undermine another kind of sovereignty'. This is how he sees much of international economic law; rulers voluntarily compromise their domestic autonomy, and the extent to which Westphalian principles have been transgressed depends on relative bargaining power (Krasner 1999: 4, 149). Even contracts given with consent, like World Bank loan contracts, compromise sovereignty and 'violate the Westphalian model' because leaders 'compromise their domestic autonomy' for loans (Krasner 1999: 148). This is a point of disagreement with other scholars, who argue that contracts or treaties 'restrict the state's legal freedom of action, but

---

[5] Krasner's (1999) four types of sovereignty are international legal sovereignty, Westphalian sovereignty, domestic sovereignty, and interdependence sovereignty.

do not alter norms of sovereignty' (Philpott 1995: 368). Since international law depends on state consent, which can be withdrawn, international economic law does not impact sovereignty in this view.[6]

Reliance on consent papers over the reality that consent has not always been the basis for international law. Or if consent was expressed formally, it was a legal fiction papering over what participants experienced as relations of dominance and subjugation. Imperialism has shaped international legal discourse in many ways, some direct and some subtle (Anghie 2004; Gathii 2007); in investment law, the legacy of imperialism is especially pronounced and inescapable. The rules and practices developed in the 'informal empire', when investment was secured through treaty and not direct control, gave rise to investment law (Miles 2013). Treaties protecting investment first appeared between European states and were then exported outside Europe alongside trading firms like the Dutch East India Company (Lipson 1985: 38; Sornarajah 2004: 180; Miles 2013: 21–4). These 'unequal treaties' usually established direct consular control within a host state. Within these areas, foreign nationals and their property were not subject to local laws but remained within the jurisdiction of their home state – a blatant violation of host country sovereignty, except that these countries were not seen as sovereign.

Protecting investment could be the pretence for armed intervention. For instance, non-payment of a loan could justify armed intervention, or a nominally independent state could be invaded by a powerful state merely to signal dominance to another powerful state (Shea 1955: 14; Oliver 1975: 348). International law was advanced in the service of both armed invasion and freedom from interference. On the side of armed intervention, officials from capital-exporting states argued that the doctrine of diplomatic protection extended to cover disputes concerning the overseas property of their nationals (Brownlie 1979: 521; see generally Sornarajah 2004). For instance, in the 19th century, the British government asserted that it always had the right to intervene in disputes regarding its citizens' overseas property but chose not to in most instances (Miles 2013: 29).

Officials from capital-importing states had to fight for the principle of non-intervention to be recognised in international law. Venezuelan jurist Andrés Bello outlined a vision, later picked up by Carlos Calvo and others, to help weaker countries combat abusive diplomatic protection (Montt 2009: 40–5). What would eventually be known as the Calvo Doctrine emphasises that equality among nations is not a concept reserved solely for Europe; all sovereign states, being free and independent, enjoy the right to freedom from interference (Shea 1955: 18). It would take over a century for Bello's vision to become reality, for the idea of equality among states to become law. Even after decolonisation, when states pushed for

---

[6] Koskenniemi (2011: 62) makes this point about investment law: 'States are bound by the agreements they have made not as a derogation of their sovereignty but as an effect of it. They had been able to bind themselves because they were sovereigns. If they were not able to bind themselves – and thus receive the benefits they were looking for – well, then they could not really be sovereigns, could they?'

General Assembly declarations to enshrine non-intervention in international law – a principle of great significance to those who had been subject to predation by more powerful states – they faced American opposition (Krasner 1999: 21–2). From decolonisation onward, non-intervention was integrated into most conceptions of sovereignty, which Luke Glanville (2013) argues creates another myth about sovereignty, since it was the right to wage just war that defined sovereignty previously, not freedom from intervention.

Decolonisation and freedom from intervention marked turning points in sovereignty, but in investment law, past practices were not thrown off or radically revised. Instead, investment law underwent a soft rebranding to fit the new era of sovereign equality while providing continuity in investment protection. This reframing was clearest in dispute resolution.

During the 18th and 19th centuries, arbitration had not been a replacement for armed invasion or gunboat diplomacy: gunboats were used, as needed, to bring countries to arbitration. Diplomatic protection, force, and arbitration all played roles in dispute resolution. During the era of decolonisation, a new Convention was drafted that sets out a procedure for arbitrations between states and foreign investors. When a state ratifies the Convention, it formally recognises that individuals – natural or corporate – have the legal standing to bring a claim directly against a state. Although there are historical antecedents, for many governments around the world, the idea of equal standing between individual investors and states was radical.

When this Convention was introduced to states, a World Bank official argued that providing investors with access to arbitration would protect weaker states from armed invasion or coercive involvement by powerful states because they could now resolve disputes in legal settings (ICSID 1970: 303). Many states, especially those that had been areas of informal empire, found the new Convention unacceptable and spoke of the need to find a formula that 'respect[ed] the sovereignty of each country in accordance with the principles of international law and the constitutional rules of the country' (ICSID 1970: 301). Despite these misgivings, the Convention came into force in 1966 and now has wide membership. In addition, bilateral investment treaties began to spread from the 1960s onward, and today there are over 3000 such treaties in force. This network of treaties underpinned by investor–state arbitration constitutes contemporary investment law.

Arbitration cases heard under investment treaties have led to perceptions that investment law unduly constrains state autonomy. Initially cases were slow to appear, then the caseload grew exponentially in the 2000s, from one case a year to at least 70 known cases in 2018. These developments are often portrayed as a loss of sovereignty; states found themselves as respondents, having their policies challenged and often losing, while private actors – transnational law firms, arbitrators, and multinational corporations – set the agenda. The amounts of compensation claimed have increased dramatically, and large cases relating to public policies thrust investment law into a public spotlight. After tobacco multinational

Philip Morris brought a claim against Australia for plain packaging legislation, and again after energy company Vattenfall brought a claim against Germany for the way the government phased out nuclear energy after the Fukushima disaster, investor–state arbitration became an embodiment of runaway corporate globalisation.

As public criticism of investment law grew, it generated a 'legitimacy crisis' that became increasingly acute as wealthy democratic states like Australia, Canada, and Germany faced controversial cases (Waibel *et al.* 2010; Langford & Behn 2018). Widespread criticism does not necessarily generate reform, however: civil society groups and academics had been writing critically about investment law for many years, but reform had been slow and piecemeal. Only governments, speaking and acting on behalf of sovereign states, have the legal ability to reform and rewrite investment law. To do so, they rely on the second conception of sovereignty in this chapter: sovereignty as eligibility to act on the world stage.

Sovereignty as eligibility to act on the world stage

Eligibility to act on the world stage is central to most definitions of sovereignty within International Relations.[7] States are sovereign, in this view, because other states and international organisations recognise them as such. 'There is a rough and ready idea of sovereignty and non-sovereignty on the part of political leaders and other people who get involved in such practical questions', Robert Jackson (1999: 2) observes, and 'that idea usually comes down to recognition as an independent state'. Recognition bestows on a state the right to participate in international organisations or deliberations with other states.

This conception of sovereignty is associated with decolonisation and sovereign equality. Daniel Philpott (2001: 255) sees decolonisation as a second revolution in sovereignty, which extended the Westphalian vision of sovereign states to the entire globe. Extending the Westphalian vision did not necessarily change power asymmetries or perceived hierarchies, making it tempting to dismiss this conception of sovereignty as mere legality. Jackson (1999: 3) chafes at this dismissal: 'Of course it is legality. But legality, i.e., legal authority and right, is not something that is trivial or of little interest or concern to practical politicians. On the contrary, in the case of sovereignty it is of profound interest and concern.' Recognised eligibility to participate in intergovernmental deliberations is still vitally important today.

Sovereignty defines who has been eligible to participate in investment law reform – and while that may seem natural in retrospect, it was not obvious who

---

[7] For instance, Alan James (1986: 93) states that 'sovereignty is what makes a territorial entity eligible to participate in international relations'. Janice Thomson (1995: 219) notes that International Relations scholars emphasise the external dimension of sovereignty, and how external forces help constitute, define, and shape sovereignty: 'Interstate relations (or state practices) play as significant a role in constituting the sovereign state as do the relations between individual states and their societies.'

would participate or how eligibility would be determined when calls for reform first emerged. The legitimacy crisis of investment law swelled throughout the 2000s, with civil society mobilisation leading to large protests in several countries, often after controversial cases or during negotiations of investment treaties. In response to this discontent, officials around the world began rethinking their countries' investment law commitments, taking steps domestically or bilaterally to limit their exposure to claims (Peinhardt & Wellhausen 2016; Polanco 2019; Thompson et al. 2019). Reforms bubbled up in individual governments for many years, and continue to emerge, but it was not enough to quiet the discontent.

After particularly large protests in several European countries in 2014, the European Commission began to explore the idea of multilateral reform. It was not clear how multilateral reform could occur since investment law is decentralised traditionally; it is comprised of bilateral treaties and does not have a multilateral hub. There is no single judicial body that resolves investment law cases (there are many secretariats, some private, which compete to administer arbitrations), and there is no legislative body tasked with oversight of the regime as a whole. If there were to be reform discussions among a wide number of participants in investment law, where should these discussions be held? Who should be eligible to participate in these discussions?

These questions generated speculation among investment law observers because there were many plausible answers. Since perceived conflicts of interest and expansive decisions by arbitrators were a proximate cause of discontent, perhaps the International Bar Association, a private organisation of international legal practitioners, could gather these arbitrators together to write guidance about conflicts of interests and discuss how arbitrators might provide more consistency in their decisions? Since arbitral secretariats have a long-term interest in the legitimacy of investment law, perhaps these secretariats – two of which are public international organisations, the rest of which are private, commercial organisations – could co-host symposia to spur reflection on the legitimacy crisis and actions to address it? Since the beneficiaries of investment law are primarily transnational corporations and other investors, perhaps industry groups or chambers of commerce would work across borders to develop principles or guidelines to address issues exacerbating the legitimacy crisis? In fact, private actors did initiate many discussions in response to the legitimacy crisis and spur small changes in investment law. Could the discontent with investment law have been addressed fully by industry or private actor-led initiatives? It is impossible to say but seems unlikely since the perception that private actors had gained too much power relative to public authorities was a driver of discontent.

Even among investment law observers who saw public authorities – that is, states – as the most appropriate actors to lead reform discussions, there were many open questions. Most fundamentally, which states should participate? There is almost no tradition of substantive negotiations in investment law occurring between a global group of states, since investment law has long been an area of 'acute controversy' (Brownlie 1979: 522). The substance of investment law is contained in bilateral or regional treaties, and in 2014, as the idea of multilateral reform emerged, the main focal points in investment law were 'mega-regional' trade and investment treaties like the Trans-Pacific Partnership or Transatlantic Trade and Investment Partnership, then under negotiation. These treaties were expected to set new standards for investment law, which would then slowly spread around the world.

Therefore, when an initial, exploratory intergovernmental discussion on investment law reform was held in December 2016, co-hosted by the European Commission and Canada, they easily could have decided to pursue reform as a small club. The Organisation for Economic Co-operation and Development in Paris, an international organisation with 37 state members (wealthier and more democratic than other states), had provided a home for such discussions in investment previously and still provided a ready home for such discussions in 2016. Yet this time, the small club strategy was not selected.

Instead, the European Commission, Canada, and other governments decided to pursue reform in a global forum. Yet even here, there was a choice to be made among several possible organisations. Perhaps the World Trade Organization, which has 164 member states and has previously hosted negotiations related to some aspects of investment law, would be chosen? Perhaps the World Bank, which has 189 member states and has an arm dedicated to the resolution of disputes between foreign investors and states, would be chosen? Perhaps the United Nations Conference on Trade and Development, which has 195 member states and has long advised developing countries on investment law? Each of these international organisations works in a different way, and these operating procedures have direct repercussions for sovereignty, in that they determine who is eligible to participate and the voting rules through which decisions are taken.

Ultimately, states decided to task the United Nations Commission on International Trade Law (UNCITRAL) with the reform mandate. UNCITRAL is a subsidiary body of the General Assembly, which means all United Nations member states can participate, and its working groups had previously drafted model laws and conventions related to arbitration.[8] UNCITRAL working groups traditionally operate as relatively technocratic exercises in which texts are drafted to harmonise international trade law. It is not a place of high politics or controversy, and for most governments most of the time, discussions at UNCITRAL are not a top priority. Yet, even at this stage, after UNCITRAL had been selected as the venue for the reform negotiations, questions about who should be eligible to participate emerged.

---

[8] Formally, states rotate on and off the Commission: at any one time, 60 states are members of the Commission (elected for terms of six years) while other states participate as observers, until they are elected again. During discussions, the views of states that are currently observers of the Commission are taken into account so the difference between members and observers, while formally important, does not often seem meaningful.

Negotiations at UNCITRAL, due in part to their expert nature, traditionally include practitioners. In their study of UNCITRAL as a site of global lawmaking, Block-Lieb & Halliday (2017) emphasise that a handful of states dominated discussions, with other states not attending or sending someone from their embassy to take notes but without authorisation to speak. Some of the individuals that spoke were government officials, but others were not – they were private practitioners speaking on behalf of states. States that spoke frequently were particularly likely to have private practitioners in their delegation. For instance, behind Switzerland's placard, and making interventions on behalf of the Swiss government, would be an arbitration lawyer in private practice. This was not seen as particularly problematic since discussions at UNCITRAL were technocratic. Yet could this practice of letting private actors speak for states be used for reform negotiations that had been triggered by a legitimacy crisis fuelled by perceptions that private actors had gained too much power and influence relative to public authorities? The answer reached, perhaps unsurprisingly, was no.

The reform negotiations would be 'conspicuously government-led', it was decided, ideally with expert officials from national capitals sitting in the chairs behind their countries' placards (Peterson 2017). In the diplomatic phrasing of the formal report, a new balance between representation and expertise would be struck: 'while benefiting from the widest possible breadth of available expertise from all stakeholders, [the negotiations] would be government-led with high-level input from all governments, consensus-based and be fully transparent' (UNCITRAL 2017: 3). The words 'government-led with high-level input from all governments' may sound routine, but they mark a radical departure from existing practice in investment law.

In theory, with the principle of sovereign equality enshrined in the United Nations, one might assume that the default setting for negotiation is government-led deliberations among 193 states. Yet this setting is traditionally the exception in investment law, just as it is exceptional for most of the rulemaking that enables contemporary economic globalisation. Several obstacles had to be overcome to construct a setting in which government-led deliberations among all governments could even be contemplated. There was also vociferous opposition; even making UNCITRAL into more of an intergovernmental space generated fury from some private actors (Brower & Ahmad 2017). Government-led, global deliberations are the exception rather than the rule today, and take work to create and sustain, but they are possible.

Observing this episode in which states reasserted their primacy is a reminder that states are the masters of their treaties. Even though these investment treaties endow individuals with rights, states can revoke those rights; states can modify or take away what they create. For several decades, states were viewed primarily, or only, as respondents, as passive actors responding to legal claims brought by private firms and paying legal awards written by private arbitrators. Yet states have always been more than respondents to claims, they have always had dual roles as both treaty parties and disputing parties in investment law (Roberts 2010). As treaty parties, states are eligible to reclaim lost policy autonomy or negotiate a balance of rights and obligations vis-à-vis private investors that their citizens like better. Governments – all governments – are formally eligible to renegotiate or reform investment law. To what extent are all governments actually able to pursue their reform options and take their place in the reform debate? This question leads to the third conception of sovereignty.

Sovereignty as the capability to act on the world stage

Capabilities are present but implicit in how most classic International Relations scholarship views sovereignty. For instance, Kenneth Waltz's (1979: 96) claim that the essence of sovereignty is that the state 'decides for itself how it will cope with its internal and external problems' suggests that capabilities are central, as Janice Thomson (1995: 220) points out.

Many scholars have addressed the challenges to sovereignty that stem from the differences in states' capabilities. Alan James (1986), for instance, refers to 'permeated' states, while Robert Jackson (1990) uses the term 'quasi-states' for those whose sovereignty is more juridical than empirical. Jackson (1990) draws a parallel distinction between 'positive sovereignty' and 'negative sovereignty': the capabilities of states and their societies provide the basis for positive sovereignty, while the external recognition of other states provides the basis for negative sovereignty.

When sovereignty is defined as capability, it is something to be measured, rather than assumed. This understanding of sovereignty fits with newer scholarship on hierarchies in international relations, which does not take sovereignty as a hard given, but instead highlights the 'softness of sovereignty – its contingency and porousness' (Bially Mattern & Zarakol 2016: 624). The first and third conceptions of sovereignty in this chapter are contingent and depend on concrete capabilities. While the first conception of sovereignty measures a state's ability to make policy internally, this third conception of sovereignty measures a state's ability to make policy externally. What is required for a state to be able to make external policy, that is, to participate meaningfully in international negotiations? Is there some set of traits or capabilities that is necessary to be sovereign, such that 'once a particular threshold of capabilities is crossed, sovereignty is achieved' (Thomson 1995: 224)? Or is it relative, so that what matters is if a state has certain capabilities relative to other states?

For constructivist theorists, sovereignty is relative since it is an inherently social concept, not something possessed but something that is made and remade through interactions and practices. 'Rather than proceeding from the assumption that all states are sovereign', Thomas Biersteker and Cynthia Weber (1996: 11) are interested in 'considering the variety of ways in which states are constantly negotiating their sovereignty'. For them, sovereignty is a set of practices and interactions – it can be studied empirically, is constantly undergoing change and transformation, and is mutually constituted with state identities (Biersteker & Weber 1996: 11–12).

Who has sovereignty and what does it look like if it is a set of practices and interactions rather than something possessed automatically by all states with a seat at the United Nations? There are many linguistic practices and interactions at UNCITRAL that create and recreate impressions of sovereignty, but the most telling occurs before anyone speaks, as the chairs in the room are filled or not filled. While every member state of the General Assembly is eligible to have a chair reserved for them in these discussions, which states actually take their seats? Around 100 out of 193 eligible states take their seats in Working Group III, the body tasked with investment law reform.

Nearly 50 per cent of states are absent, and this is in a process where inclusivity and multilateralism have been prioritised from the start. In these negotiations, powerful governments have strategic reasons to push inclusivity and foster wide participation. This means that unusually large resources have been dedicated towards supporting the participation of officials from the least developed countries in these negotiations, compared with other multilateral negotiations. There is a United Nations-administered travel fund, which is replenished by donor governments specifically to enable travel to these negotiations. An expert think tank runs trainings for officials from developing countries attending their first negotiating round the weekend before the negotiations. The Secretariat makes special efforts to help first-time officials navigate the negotiations. In other words, conditions for meaningful participation are relatively auspicious in these negotiations; several aspects of the setting make it more conducive to participation by the least developed countries than most multilateral negotiations.

Yet the asymmetries that appear even in a context that is conducive to participation by least developed countries reveals just how far the ideal of sovereign equality is from reality. Empty chairs and missing placards make the asymmetries physically apparent, even in a room that is organised to create impressions of sovereign equality: a room in which seating is organised alphabetically, in which all states have two seats behind a placard, in which every formal message is translated simultaneously in the six languages of the United Nations.

Beyond the asymmetries that are physically apparent are a range of practices and interactions through which officials recognise each other as meaningful players in the room. A preliminary question that officials use to assess a new official is if that official is a generalist from the embassy or an expert from the capital. Sending a specialised expert is often seen by other officials as a preliminary requirement for meaningful participation. If the official is a generalist from the embassy, it suggests either that the government does not prioritise the subject or that the government lacks the resources or capacity to send officials from the capital. The first reason, that a certain topic is not a priority, does not necessarily reflect diminished sovereignty, but is likely to go hand-in-hand with limited capabilities because when a government faces more intense constraints, they are able to follow fewer topics.

Government ministries often face budget pressures, and officials face many competing pressures for their time; these pressures are more intense in some countries than in others. Reforming investment law is not inherently high-priority since an arbitration case is a relatively low-probability risk. It may not be easy to convince a minister with a broad portfolio to prioritise investment law reform over other reforms. Government officials may have other issues that are more urgent priorities, perhaps where reforms seem likely to offer more benefit and less cost. Even if the multilateral travel fund covers some of the costs of flying an official to New York twice a year and two weeks of hotel accommodation, there are still visas to procure and other hurdles, and every minute an official spends on this takes their time away from other issues. Additionally, when weighing costs and benefits, an official might ask themselves: coming from a country that is generally a rule-taker rather than a rulemaker in multilateral negotiations, am I really going to make a difference to what emerges? Or perhaps an official knows that they want to prioritise one or two issues within investment law, so given their constraints, they only attend when those issues are discussed. In these small, practical ways, sovereignty when measured as meaningful participation is diminished.

Sovereignty, in the sense of ability to participate meaningfully in international negotiations, is also shaped by government staffing procedures, even if governments are able to send experts from their national capitals. These disparities do not always align with size or wealth; it is possible for officials from a small, lower-middle income state to command respect for their expertise or thoughtful positions and have outsize influence.

Some governments are represented by officials who specialise in investment law and expect to spend their career within the field of investment law. This empowers these officials in several ways. First, by the time they speak for their country, these officials are truly expert. Their long experience also means that they command respect and may have reputations for knowledge or toughness that precede them in the room. They are also more likely to know other officials in the room; two officials who worked closely when their countries negotiated five years or ten years ago may be able to trust each other and work as a coalition in ways that officials new to the scene cannot. Other governments are represented by officials who rotate every few years, which means these governments lose technical expertise. Additionally, if the new official knows that they will rotate in three years, they have limited incentives to spend time developing expertise about investment law. A lack of specialised expertise and experience also leaves these governments particularly open to influence from lobbyists, academics, or other private actors outside of defined consultation processes.

The United Kingdom's presence in the negotiating room is an interesting point of departure from which to think through how the first conception of sovereignty, the ability to make policy domestically, and the third conception of sovereignty, the ability to make policy externally, relate to each other. If commerce is happening across borders, then rules need to cross borders too. Cross-border rules can take many forms, and in theory all options are on the table, but in practice a government's ability to realise their priorities (or save space for particular domestic arrangements) in negotiations varies widely. In some ways, then, domestic policy autonomy depends on external policymaking capabilities, that is, on negotiating prowess. What effect did leaving the European Union have on the United Kingdom's ability to influence these UNCITRAL negotiations?

The United Kingdom always sat behind its own placard at UNCITRAL because all European Union member states represent themselves at the United Nations. In addition, the European Commission sits as an observer; Commission negotiators speak often and help coordinate the interventions from European states. If Brexit had not occurred, British priorities would be represented by both British officials and the European Commission, as well as be echoed by 27 countries, who form a powerful bloc within the UNCITRAL room. Instead, British officials – coming from a high-rotation, generalist civil service overburdened with many complex negotiations – do not yet know who their allies are and find their ability to influence the negotiating agenda quite limited. China, the European Union, and the United States are the heavyweights in the room, and the United Kingdom does not negotiate with these countries as an equal (in this third sense of sovereignty, the ability to make policy externally); it negotiates as a much smaller state with less negotiating experience.

In putting forward her argument for a relational understanding of sovereignty, Helen Stacy (2003: 2043–4) observed that it does not follow from economic globalisation that the state has been superseded: 'Clearly, some nation states still matter. And some nation states clearly matter more than others.' Is the United Kingdom a state that matters on its own? Or is its sovereignty enlarged, as Stacy suggests it is for most states, through pooling it? She acknowledges that 'relational sovereignty turns the historical and political kaleidoscope a few notches' to argue that participation by the state in 'the full panoply of international institutions' is an extension of the sovereign's care for its own citizens (Stacy 2003: 2048). In other words, sovereignty, in the sense of domestic policymaking autonomy, may be best protected by pooling sovereignty when it comes to international negotiations. In a world with transborder commerce, there will be transborder rules. The question is: who writes them? Whose values and whose priorities do they reflect?

Conclusion

Even within one field of international law, even within one negotiating room, there are multiple conceptions of sovereignty. Given this indeterminacy, and the general conceptual stretching of sovereignty, why does it endure as an idea?

Sovereignty endures because of its elasticity, because it serves a bridge to many pasts and to many possible futures. Sovereignty is 'at once anachronism and aspiration, dead form and living project' (Kennedy 1992: 238). It is a rhetorical toolkit that actors can use to invoke hard-won progress, like enshrining the principle of non-intervention in international law or to invoke nationalist nostalgia for an imagined past. Sovereignty can carry the aspirations of many projects. Therefore, despite 'a thousand calls for [sovereignty's] elimination over the last hundred years, its death announced a thousand times in speeches and articles about the "new" interdependence, still it continues to structure our legal positions, our political alliances, our discipline's imagination' (Kennedy 1992: 238). Sovereignty clearly structures investment law negotiations at the United Nations: it is the main organising principle of the physical space and the trait that determines who is a full participant in the negotiations. Yet perhaps the design of rooms at the United Nations are anachronisms, monuments to mid-century idealism. What uses does sovereignty serve in the context of today's economic globalisation?

Sovereignty as a term recalls enduring questions about representation and rulemaking. Among its many associations, the concept of sovereignty is imbued with concerns about authority and social contracts between the ruled and the rulemakers. As transborder commerce and economic globalisation mean that more rulemaking occurs at the global level, the enduring question of 'who should participate in rulemaking?' takes new forms. Beneath today's sovereignty talk lie two forms of this question. First, should private actors participate in rulemaking? Second, which states should participate in rulemaking?

These questions are not outdated – they are the crux of rulemaking under contemporary economic globalisation. The answers to these questions can change over time, as seen in investment law – where reform-minded governments moved rulemaking to a forum in which states were the main actors and in which all states could participate. Will this move help improve societal perceptions of investment law's legitimacy? It is too soon to tell, but not too soon to observe that sovereignty in this context is both a composite, with layers of meaning from earlier eras, and a bridge, which connects us to fundamental questions about who should participate in rulemaking.

References

Anghie, A. (2004), *Imperialism, Sovereignty, and the Making of International Law* (Cambridge, Cambridge University Press).

Bially Mattern, J. & Zarakol, A. (2016), 'Hierarchies in World Politics', *International Organization*, 70: 623–54.

Biersteker, T. & Weber, C. (1996), 'The Social Construction of State Sovereignty', in T. Biersteker & C. Weber (eds), *State Sovereignty as Social Construct* (Cambridge, Cambridge University Press), 1–21.

Block-Lieb, S. & Halliday, T. (2017), *Global Lawmakers: International Organization in the Crafting of World Markets* (Cambridge, Cambridge University Press).
Bodin, J. (1992 [1576]), *On Sovereignty*, trans. J.H. Franklin (Cambridge, Cambridge University Press, 1992).
Brower, C.N. & Ahmad, J. (2017), 'Why the "Demolition Derby" that Seeks to Destroy Investor–State Arbitration?', *Southern California Law Review*, 91: 1139–96.
Brownlie, I. (1979), *Principles of Public International Law*, 3rd edn (Oxford, Clarendon Press).
Carr, E.H. (2016 [1939]), *The Twenty Years' Crisis, 1919–1939* (London, Palgrave Macmillan).
Cooper, R.N. (1972), 'Economic Interdependence and Foreign Policy in the Seventies', *World Politics*, 24: 159–81.
Costa Lopez, J., De Carvalho, B., Latham, A., Zarakol, A., Bartelson, J., & Holm, M. (2018), 'Forum: In the Beginning there Was No Word (for it): Terms, Concepts, and Early Sovereignty', *International Studies Review*, 20: 489–519.
De Carvalho, B., Leira, H., & Hobson, J. (2011), 'The Big Bangs of IR: The Myths that Your Teachers Still Tell You about 1648 and 1919', *Millennium: Journal of International Studies*, 39: 735–58.
Gathii, J.T. (2007), 'Imperialism, Colonialism and International Law', *Bufffalo Law Review*, 54: 1013–66.
Gilpin, R. (1975), *US Power and the Multinational Corporation: The Political Economy of Foreign Direct Investment* (New York, Basic Books).
Gilpin, R. (1987), *The Political Economy of International Relations* (Princeton, Princeton University Press).
Glanville, L. (2013), 'The Myth of "Traditional" Sovereignty', *International Studies Quarterly*, 57: 79–90.
Hall, P.A. & Soskice, D. (2001), *Varieties of Capitalism: The Institutional Foundations of Comparative Advantage* (Oxford, Oxford University Press).
Herzog, D. (2020), *Sovereignty, RIP* (New Haven, Yale University Press).
International Centre for Settlement of Investment Disputes (ICSID) (1970), *History of the Convention: Documents Concerning the Origin and the Formulation of the Convention in English* (Washington DC, ICSID).
Jackson, R. (1990), *Quasi-States: Sovereignty, International Relations and the Third World* (New York, Cambridge University Press).
Jackson, R. (1999), 'Sovereignty in World Politics: A Glance at the Conceptual and Historical Landscape', in R. Jackson (ed.), *Sovereignty at the Millennium* (Oxford, Blackwell Publishers), 9–34.
James, A. (1986), *Sovereign Statehood: The Basis of International Society* (London, Allen & Unwin).
Kang, D. (2010), *East Asia before the West: Five Centuries of Trade and Tribute* (New York, Columbia University Press).
Kennedy, D. (1992), 'Some Reflections on "The Role of Sovereignty in the New International Order"', in E.L. Hughes (ed.), *State Sovereignty: The Challenge of a Changing World* (Ottawa, Canadian Council of International Law), 237–45.
Keohane, R.O. & Nye, J. (1977), *Power and Interdependence: World Politics in Transition* (Boston, Little, Brown).
Koskenniemi, M. (2011), 'What Use for Sovereignty Today?', *Asian Journal of International Law*, 1: 61–70.

Krasner, S.D. (1999), *Sovereignty: Organized Hypocrisy* (Princeton, Princeton University Press).
Langford, M. & Behn, D. (2018), 'Managing Backlash: The Evolving Investment Treaty Arbitrator?', *European Journal of International Law*, 29: 551–80.
Lipson, C. (1985), *Standing Guard: Protecting Foreign Capital in the Nineteenth and Twentieth Centuries* (Berkeley, University of California Press).
Miles, K. (2013), *The Origins of International Investment Law: Empire, Environment, and the Safeguarding of Capital* (Cambridge, Cambridge University Press).
Montt, S. (2009), *State Liability in Investment Treaty Arbitration: Global Constitutional and Administrative Law in the BIT Generation* (Oxford, Hart Publishing).
Morgenthau, H.J. (1985 [1948]), *Politics among Nations* (New York, McGraw-Hill).
Morse, E.L. (1969), 'The Politics of Interdependence', *International Organization*, 23: 311–26.
Morse, E.L. (1976), *Modernization and the Transformation of International Relations* (New York, Free Press).
Mosley, L. (2000), 'Room to Move: International Financial Markets and National Welfare States', *International Organization*, 54: 737–73.
Oliver, R. (1975), *International Economic Co-operation and the World Bank* (London, Macmillian).
Peinhardt, C. & Wellhausen, R. (2016), 'Withdrawing from Investment Treaties but Protecting Investment', *Global Policy*, 7: 571–6.
Peterson, L.E. (2017), 'UNCITRAL Meetings on ISDS Reform Get Off to Bumpy Start, as Delegations Can't Come to Consensus on Who Should Chair Sensitive Process – Entailing a Rare Vote', *Investment Arbitration Reporter* (9 December), accessed 16 August 2021, https://www.iareporter.com/articles/uncitral-meetings-on-isds-reform-gets-off-to-bumpy-start-as-delegations-cant-come-to-consensus-on-who-should-chair-sensitive-process-entailing-a-rare-vote/.
Philpott, D. (1995), 'Sovereignty: An Introduction and Brief History', *Journal of International Affairs*, 48: 353–68.
Philpott, D. (2001), *Revolutions in Sovereignty: How Ideas Shaped Modern International Relations* (Princeton, Princeton University Press).
Pistor, K. (2019), *The Code of Capital: How the Law Creates Wealth and Inequality* (Princeton NJ, Princeton University Press).
Polanco, R. (2019), *The Return of the Home State to Investor–State Disputes: Bringing Back Diplomatic Protection?* (Cambridge, Cambridge University Press).
Raustiala, K. (2003), 'Rethinking the Sovereignty Debate in International Economic Law', *Journal of International Economic Law*, 6: 841–78.
Roberts, A. (2010), 'Power and Persuasion in Investment Treaty Interpretation: The Dual Role of States', *American Journal of International Law*, 104: 179–225.
Rodrik, D. (1997), *Has Globalization Gone Too Far?* (Washington DC, Peterson Institute for International Economics).
Sassen, S. (1996), *Losing Control: Sovereignty in the Age of Globalization* (New York, Columbia University Press).
Shea, D. (1955), *The Calvo Clause: A Problem of Inter-American and International Law and Diplomacy* (Minneapolis, University of Minnesota Press).
Sornarajah, M. (2004), *The International Law on Foreign Investment*, 2nd edn (Cambridge, Cambridge University Press).
Stacy, H. (2003), 'Relational Sovereignty', *Stanford Law Review*, 55: 2029–59.

Strange, S. (1996), *The Retreat of the State: The Diffusion of Power in the World Economy* (New York, Cambridge University Press).

Thomson, J.E. (1995), 'State Sovereignty in International Relations: Bridging the Gap between Theory and Empirical Research', *International Studies Quarterly*, 39: 213–33.

Thompson, A., Broude, T., & Haftel, Y.Z. (2019), 'Once Bitten, Twice Shy? Investment Disputes, State Sovereignty, and Change in Treaty Design', *International Organization*, 73: 859–80.

UNCITRAL (2017), Report of Working Group III (Investor–State Dispute Settlement Reform) on the Work of its Thirty-Fourth Session (Vienna, 27 November–1 December 2017) (New York, United Nations A//CN.9/930/Rev.1).

Vernon, R. (1971), *Sovereignty at Bay: The Multinational Spread of US Enterprises* (New York, Basic Books).

Waibel, M., Kaushal, A., Chung, K.H., & Balchin, C. (eds) (2010), *The Backlash against Investment Arbitration* (London, Kluwer Law International).

Waltz, K. (1979), *Theory of International Politics* (Reading MA, Addison-Wesley).

Zhang, Y. (2003), 'System, Empire and State in Chinese International Relations', *Review of International Studies*, 27: 43–63.

Part IV

Sovereignty on the Edge

Introduction

THIS VOLUME HAS traced the deep roots of competing and overlapping notions of sovereignty, from ancient expressions of external recognition and internal control, which, however fragile, contained within them the seeds of later evolutions, through the deployment of the western canon as a mechanism of imperial power and negation of non-western models; it has traced a long arc of Chinese versions of sovereignty, and introduced other non-western models, whilst at the same time seeing how the western model has itself flexed extraordinarily to seek competitive advantage in finance and international arbitration.

Sovereignty has proven to be durable as an aspiration, a language of power and a knowledge deployed in relations of dominance, but the challenges now are fierce. We have seen a pandemic upturn all our assumptions. Climate change and loss of biodiversity are recognised as existential threats. There are claims for retrospective justice, so that past dominance is now subject to claims of restitution, and current polluters look to countries who have created environmental and ecological problems to resolve them rather than prevent others from attaining their own prosperity through their natural resources.

This section looks at different ways in which sovereignty is located in spaces and times of profound crisis. Our argument is not so much that sovereignty is to be abandoned than that sovereignty must be seen not just relationally (as St John argues in the previous section) but as functioning towards recognition of non-state actors, and must become, through our understanding of its limitations and failures, a part of our work towards a better world.

We start in the slums of Nairobi, where Fontein worked during a climatic event that brought both flooding and cholera. Fontein argues the way water flows and is blocked both is metaphorical for, and literally shapes, the contorted and interrupted passages of power and authority, from administrative structures to religious figures to self-help groups. Interestingly, the worst of the problems came not from El Niño, as feared and anticipated, but from an unrelated flooding episode, and this sharpens the understanding that the crises and solutions happened at deeper levels of moral and social collapse and resilience. The question of the sovereignty of nature lurks in the background of faltering human endeavour.

What seems inevitable is that worsening climatic conditions will place additional stress on conditions of precarity, and heighten unrest. This will lead to dispossession and movement, as it always does, and thus the plight of the refugee in a sovereign political order will become even more acute. Two case studies illustrate the problem.

Isayev takes us back to the beginning of the book with her account of decision-making around when and whether to offer hospitality, starting with the Greeks. Isayev shows that with weaker claims to territorial integrity and stronger claims to responsibility, individuals acquired greater agency. It is only rarely today that such agency is permitted – Isayev reverts to a test case from Australia where Indigenous rights to restitution are beginning to find a voice (reverting to similar arguments that Cruickshank *et al.* raised). This direct comparison of ancient and modern shows that sovereignty could be constituted differently at least in its relations to individuals on the margins and in the interstices of society.

The challenge of finding a voice in statelessness preoccupied Hannah Arendt, who found in sovereignty something wholly antithetical to human flourishing. She did not readily see the capacity of modern states to accord dignity to humans precisely because of her own experience of exile and the horrendous consequences of nationalism; she saw the endpoint of the nationalist use of sovereignty we described in Part II. The drive to perverse mastery left non-spaces where the dispossessed were rendered voiceless and invisible. Arendt's understandable pessimism is, however, to a degree countered by her own advocacy, and it is not where the story ends. In the Palestinian camp of Baddawi, Stonebridge shows how poetry, specifically that of Yousif M. Qasmiyeh, creates a resistant and resilient voice, which insists on the visibility of the camp through witness and as archive. Being stateless here is given voice, at least partly through hosting, through private initiative. The interrupted and unexpected flows that Fontein identifies (both of support and of degradation), and the paradoxes of hosting, which Isayev describes, arrive at the profound experience of the refugee, the stateless person, struggling to find a voice.

If sovereignty is to have a future, and we might recall the comment of Leila Sansour from Open Bethlehem that closed the conference from which these papers emerge, and which was cited in the volume's Introduction, that no one should underestimate how hard it is to live without it, it clearly needs to be reconfigured. Our studies have shown that sovereignty has never been fixed and is always a contingent instrument and reflection of human society. Since it has been repeatedly reimagined, it can be reimagined again.

In our last chapter, which serves as a sort of epilogue, Rosa offers one diagnosis of how sovereignty has gone awry and one way to think about its reconfiguration. The relationality of sovereignty becomes central here, but not in terms of the relations between states, but in terms of our relationships with each other and with society. Many of the techniques of sovereignty described in Part III are in fact responses to the ever-quickening pace of modernity (the development of central currencies and accompanying political deficit, the attempts to regulate the rapidly escalating complexity of inter-state obligations). But where they fail, we find cholera and climate disaster, statelessness and endemic poverty, hopelessness and violence.

Rosa sets the bar high in arguing for a reconfigured sovereignty. He includes 'a *social axis* (which connects citizens to each other in a responsive mode), a *political axis* (which defines the relationship between citizens and the body politic as an institutional totality), an *environmental axis* (which defines the relationship between citizens and the natural and material world), a *temporal axis* (which connects the body politic to history, i.e. past and future), and finally an *external axis* (which defines the relationship between the body politic and its social "outside")'. In so doing, though, he sums up much of what this volume argues for in terms of a plural and contingent notion of sovereignty.

Our first encounter is with the common defence of the individual's goods, in Arena's discussion of the *res publica* or common weal. Politics has underpinned much of our discussion, but here also we see it operating at the level of biopolitics, the control of people's bodies and lives. Fontein reveals just one example of the intersections between sovereignty and the environment; Stonebridge shows us patterns of statelessness written again and again in the archive of the camp. At the end, we are returned to the dark paradox of sovereignty that Agamben identified so well, that it is a force for defining who (or in the case of natural resources which are daily depleted, what) does not belong. Only if we can turn that into a relationship of beneficial resonance can sovereignty find a role in the dynamic stabilisation of our world and our place within it.

12

El Niño, Cholera, and the Productive Uncertainties of Water in Nairobi

JOOST FONTEIN

Introduction: flows and blockages, making cities and bodies

LIKE BODIES, CITIES such as Nairobi can be seen as emerging from, transformed by, or constituted through the movement, blockages, control, regulation, containment, and stabilisation, or not, of in- and out-flows of materials, things, beings, and substances. Although there is a long debate, dating back to the 19th century, linking bodies and cities as analogous 'metabolic systems' – an approach which both endures in new forms and has come under sustained critique (Gandy 2004; 2005) – this chapter takes the position that if viewed through the lenses of materiality and corporeality, the relatedness of bodies and cities are not simply an analogy. Bodies and cities are directly related through these material processes. The constitution, flows, containment, and movement of bodies in Nairobi are deeply imbricated in the constitution, transformations, flows, and blockages of the city. This may be highly ordered, or not, defying all attempts at ordering. Although often the subject of idealised technocratic and architectural planning interventions, more often than not they emerge in piecemeal, incomplete, and fractured ways, reminding us of the resistance of the real, or the 'torque of materiality' (Pinney 2005: 270), that emergent human–thing relationalities are rarely 'smooth' and more often marked by disjunctures, fractures, and incoherence, and that cityscapes are never blank spaces simply awaiting the imposition of a totalising order. And like so much in the capricious city of Nairobi, it is always highly uneven and deeply differentiated, and differentiating. Structures of inequality and difference replicate themselves through these uneven flows and blockages.

The shape, layout, and architecture of Nairobi was planned from the very beginning to enable the movement of some bodies and the containment or exclusion of others (cf. Murunga 2012). At certain junctures in time, such as during tense election months, or the Mau Mau emergency of the 1950s, authorities intervene with dramatic, draconian, and sometimes violent measures to curtail the movement of some bodies, particularly those mobilised collectively in the pursuit of political ends, or even to enforce the evacuation of entire populations of bodies deemed undesirable or a security threat to other bodies. Conversely, efforts to resist such official measures of containment and control – stretching from legitimate forms of peaceful protest to the extremes of post-election violence – too often target geographies of movement, such as when makeshift road blocks of debris and burning tires create impromptu blockages impeding flows of people across parts of the city in ways that mirror police check points but are also supposed to defy them.[1]

Yet the differentially constrained, blocked, or enabled flows of bodies that shape the emerging city are only part of the story here. We can be even more literal in our understanding of how cities and bodies are related. We need to think about how the in- and out-flows, containments and obstructions of substances through the city (and the processes that enable, constrain, or seek to regulate them) constitute the very moving bodies that shape the city's emergence. Like cities, bodies don't just exist, they emerge, or are stabilised, transformed, and remade through such material flows and blockages which constitute, or threaten, corporeal existence; material processes that bind the becoming of the city with that of its bodies in diverse, uneven, emergent, and often exclusionary ways. There are many material in/outflows, blockages, and containments that co-constitute a city like Nairobi and the bodies within it, in all of their incomplete patchiness and emergent disjunctures. Think, for example, of the politics of rubbish at Dandora in the east of the city,[2] or the role that the accumulation of detritus plays in the making of late colonial housing projects, like Kaloleni (Smith 2018; 2020), or the recursive circulations of architectural materials – stone, wood, iron sheets, roof tiles – that make up both the very substance of the city, and the livelihoods and bodies that inhabit and enliven it (Fontein 2017). Or the vibrant trade in second-hand clothes (*mitumba*) which illustrates graphically how global circulations of stuff are part of the making of Nairobian bodies and subjectivities, not to mention abject informal livelihoods.[3]

But perhaps the most obvious and important place to start is water, the stuff of life itself, whose properties and flows link climate, geography, and urban topographies to the very vitality, health, and productivity of its bodies. Indeed, during the 19th- and early-20th-century emergence of modernist 'metabolic' urban planning in industrialising cities in Europe, it was safe domestic water provision and sanitation infrastructure which preoccupied urban planners and public health concerns (Gandy 2004). It is important, however, that we consider water and what it does in relation to all its properties, affordances, and effectivities, unconstrained by

---

[1] Gabrielle Lynch, 'Address Root Cause of Violent Protests to Curb their Frequency', *Daily Nation* (20 February 2015).
[2] Thieme (2013); 'Garbage Piles Up as Officials Pass the Buck', *Daily Nation* (30 December 2015).
[3] See, for example, Annie Njanja, 'Our Mitumba, Our Lives, Say Young Traders', *Nairobi News* (19 March 2014), accessed 5 July 2019, https://nairobinews.nation.co.ke/featured/our-mitumba-our-lives-say-young-traders.

normative frameworks that tend to isolate water's salience in terms of its qualities as a 'scarce natural resource', or as a public health concern, or indeed as a 'human right'. As I have argued elsewhere (Fontein 2015) (and discuss in more detail below) in relation to rain making, dam building, and the politics of water in Zimbabwe, water is interesting stuff exactly because it is ubiquitous and uncertain. The multiplicity of water's material properties and qualities means it matters in very different ways, and that it is therefore imbricated in very diverse registers of meaning and governance: both life enabling and threatening; for biopolitics and necropolitics; for demonstrations of capacity and sovereignty; in the constitution of legitimacy through performances and discourses of 'pastoral' and 'responsive' power; in scarcity (droughts) and excess (floods); in its flows (soil erosion, landslides); and in its essentiality for life (agriculture, food, hydration), as well as its medical dimensions and dangers (health, food, sickness). Water's material properties give it an uncertain and unclear ubiquity that crosses over and is implicated in many different regimes of meaning and rule encountered in urban contexts, governing (or not) its bodies, threatening or enabling (or not) some lives to thrive.

Focusing on the nexus of weather, sanitation, and disease in Nairobi's neglected slums, this chapter explores how material and corporal flows – and the processes that manage and contain, or not, such flows – are deeply imbricated in the production of different forms of privileged or precarious life, and different forms of sovereignty and legitimacy linked to them, across the city. It also shows how such flows cross vastly different scales of geography, how global and regional climate patterns and temporalities intertwine with the in/outflows of water and sanitation across a particular city, and in and out of particular bodies, and particular bodies of bodies, in highly variable ways. Access to safe, state-regulated controls over in/outflows of water, waste, and bodily substances are hugely differentiated across Nairobi, and the scarcity of toilets, safe drinking water, and sanitation in informal 'slum' areas like Mathare generates deep (sometimes life-threatening) deprivations, but also offers opportunities and potentiality for different emergent structures, practices and forms of power, authority and sovereignty, as 'reformed' gangs, community groups, non-governmental organisations (NGOs), and city authorities jostle to assert control over service provision and delivery.

This chapter links to the arguments in the chapters that follow, by focusing on the conundrum between, on the one hand, the way that state sovereignty both constitutes and is constituted by actions, happenings, and people defined as outside of its reach and who are yet subjected to it – an argument that echoes anthropological debates (cf. Das & Poole 2004) about how the state is constituted exactly on its margins and, conversely, how the whole of the state can be seen as a margin – and on the other, how those excluded places, happenings, and people themselves work to constitute other, often plural, and usually emergent forms of sovereignty that can look very like the very political formations from which they have been marginalised or excluded. While the chapters by Isayev (13) and Stonebridge (14) explore these questions through ancient Greece and the writings and experiences of Hannah Arendt in engagement with more recent Palestinian experiences and expression, respectively, my context through which to think about these questions comes from the experiences of 'slum' dwellers in contemporary Nairobi, and my focus is on how the material qualities and political potentialities of water enable, constrain, or otherwise shape how these contested sovereignties emerge in uncertain but often productive ways.

Water as an index of power

My interest is therefore in what water and its material qualities do or enable politically. Uncertainty is central to how we can understand water as an index of power, exactly because water reappears and has salience in so many coexistent but diverse forms and contexts. Water's many salient material qualities – its multiplicity, as rain or run-off, as essential for life, but also for sanitation, and in terms of the risks of floodings and disease, for example – speaks to both the profound uncertainties of stuff in general (this is what Pinney calls the 'torque of materiality', cited above), but also the kind of ambiguities and uncertainties which derive from the multiplicity of regimes of meaning and rule in which water, in particular, is intertwined. These two are of course entangled and interdependent. Water's diverse material qualities means it reappears across very diverse regimes of rule (rain, water supply, sanitation, run-off, erosion, irrigation etc.), and is therefore subject to political contestation in multiple ways and contexts. Although this might apply to all or many kinds of material – for example, human remains too, for their own reasons, are often peculiarly salient in very diverse ways (Filippucci *et al.* 2012; Fontein 2014; 2022) – the politics of water nevertheless seems unusually fraught and complex, due exactly to its ubiquitous, and multiple, uncertain salience.

What I mean by suggesting that water indexes power is that it indexes the nexus between both sovereignty and legitimacy which is central to all efforts to stabilise and substantiate authority. That is between, on the one hand, demonstrations of capacity, coercion, and violence (or 'necropolitics', the power to make dead), and on the other, the need for legitimacy through ideological or discursive 'buy-in' and pastoral responsivity to material needs (or 'biopolitics', the ability to provide life). If power is necessarily about the emergent, uncertain and never complete relationships and tensions between these two elements – sovereignty and legitimacy – then water often indexes these ongoing contests in multiple ways and contexts exactly because of the multiplicity of its material qualities and the diversity of its salience that derives therefrom. Importantly, this operates across the different scales and different contexts in which water is implicated, from, for example, minute contests between competing community groups, NGOs, and city authorities over the control of particular water points in Mathare, to larger contests between centralised governments and devolved county and city authorities over sanitation and disease control policies and interventions. Often different kinds of state authority are in competition with other localised groups, who themselves do what looks very much like what state authorities would do, such as 'reformed' urban gangs controlling water services in Nairobi's informal areas like Mathare, for example.

In previous research I explored how water acts as an index of power (of the tension between biopolitics and necropolitics) across different regimes of rule around Lake Mutirikwi, in rural southern Zimbabwe, between the late colonial, dam-building period of the mid-20th century and the politics of postcolonial land reform of the early 2000s (Fontein 2015). I argued that through these lenses, both 'traditionalist' rain making and 'modernist' dam building can look very similar because both involve demonstrations of 'sovereignty' (by showcasing the capacity to deliver water), but also the need to constitute 'legitimacy' through pastoral and productive forms of power that centralise responsivity to human needs for water. And importantly, both are subject to meteorological uncertainties. So, rains or drought, and the availability or not of water for industrial sugar production, or for local small-scale agriculture, had real effects in attempts to constitute sovereignty and legitimacy among spirit mediums, rain makers, and governments alike. Not wishing to over-exceptionalise or exoticise either rain making or dam building, I also explored how such an argument might be possible for 'more technocratic regimes' of water to do with the control of fishing, wildlife, and local irrigation around Lake Mutirikwi in the 2000s. In terms of the control of fishing and wildlife, National Parks' authority around the lake involves both profound demonstrations of sovereignty/capacity through (often extra-judicial) forms of coercion and violence – by killing 'poachers', for example – but also the production of legitimacy through bureaucratic regulatory regimes involving the measuring of fish and wildlife stock, and by catering for local livelihoods through participation in conservation regimes. Likewise, in the context of deepening food insecurity in the wake of radical land reform and recurring droughts in the early 2000s, both the central government's calls for, and the attempts of local chiefs to implement, small irrigation schemes around the lake could be seen as attempts to reassert developmentalist credentials. The government's calls ran parallel with its political strategy to buffer its 'traditionalist' credentials by promoting 'national *biras*', 'rain making ceremonies', and other 'ancestral events'. At the same time, for chiefs, spirit mediums, and other local traditionalists, the appearance of ambivalent *njuzu* ('water spirits') in dams embodied the complex entanglement of a politics of autochthony – in which the sovereignty of ancestors and the divinity *Mwari* were central – with the more 'modernist', technocratic aspirations and regimes of regulatory, productive, and legitimising power that are often intrinsic to irrigation schemes. As with the intersection of dam- and rain-making, the ambivalent presence of *njuzu* spirits in 'modern' irrigation schemes points to the contested interplay of multiple forms of sovereignty, legitimacy, and subjectivity in differing coexistent regimes of meaning and rule to do with water, which are enabled and gain traction exactly in relation to the potentialities of its material qualities.

In the end, everyone occupies unique positions between contingent, coexistent regimes of meaning and rule around Mutirikwi, and the material potentialities of water imbricated with them, and all of this revolves around the provision of livelihoods, of making life possible (bio-power), but also of the determination of death (necropolitics) and therefore sovereignty. In all regimes of rule over water, sovereignties and legitimacies are contested and intertwined. Dam building and rain making are both 'heroic' demonstrations of capacity and interventions responsive to demands, needs, and aspirations. And in the way that all regimes of sovereignty and legitimacy are politically productive, such entangled multiplicities forge complex subjectivities that defy normative distinctions between different forms and structures of meaning and authority. So, water indexes the complex play of sovereignties, legitimacies, and subjectivities in southern Zimbabwe in which everyone is implicated. And in this chapter, what I seek to consider is whether or how this argument might also have traction in a very different context, that is in the politics of water, sanitation, and disease in the informal 'slum' of Mathare, in Nairobi. Because water's uncertain and multiple material qualities, particularly in terms of rain – that is, meteorological uncertainties – are a material link between the politics of water in rural Zimbabwe and that taking place in urban East Africa, I take the growing anticipation across Nairobi in 2015 of the impending El Niño rains as my entry point into this discussion.

El Niño in Mathare[4]

The year 2015 was an El Niño year. In the months that preceded the first expected El Niño deluge in the 'short rains' of the October to December season, anticipation across Nairobi, Kenya and the region was high.[5] On 12 May 2015, *The Standard* carried an article entitled 'How to Predict and Prepare for El Niño', and the following month, the government issued warnings that 'El Niño rains are

---

[4] Ethnographic research for the material presented in this section was carried out in 2016 by a team of researchers consisting of Joost Fontein, Syokau Mutonga, Lucy Wairimu, and Hannah Bornstein.

[5] See, for example, Gatonye Gathura, 'Scientists Warn El Nino to Be Worse than 1997/98', *Standard* (20 September 2015), accessed 30 August 2021, https://www.standardmedia.co.ke/environment/article/2000176966/scientists-warn-el-nino-to-be-worse-than-1997-98. In fact, anxieties about an impending El Niño event were first raised in 2014, and were then firmly denied by Kenya's Meteorological Office; see 'Experts Predict Massive El Niño Weather from July', *Standard* (9 May 2014); 'As Another El Niño Looms, Africa Aims to Cut Hunger Threat', *Standard* (17 November 2014); 'There Is No Impending El-Nino, Kenya Meteorological Service Assures', *Standard* (11 June 2014). The following year, however, these anxieties were confirmed by the Meteorological Office, and by international reports, which often indicated that while the southern Africa region might face El Niño-related droughts ('Drought Affects 14 m in Southern Africa', *East African* [23 January 2016]), in East Africa El Niño is often associated with heavy rains, floods, and infrastructural damage ('El Niño: 60 m Africans Could Face Hunger', *East African* [10 October 2015]; 'El Niño Seen Strengthening, Maybe One of the Biggest since 1950 – World Meteorological Organisation', *Standard* [1 September 2015]; 'Weatherman Confirms El Niño Fears', *Standard* [2 September 2015]).

looming', urging authorities and citizens 'to be ready' (*Standard*, 8 June 2015). In August, the Meteorological Department warned that the 'country could experience the worst floods in 40 years during the short rains'.[6] Amid such government and Meteorological Office warnings, the National Disaster Management Unit (first set up after the El Niño floods in 1997) was mobilised, and government (and international) funds were assigned to counties, and within counties, to prepare for El Niño.[7] As Corrine Torre, from Medecine Sans Frontiere's (MSF) base in Nairobi's Eastlands, explained: 'Everybody was organising huge meetings. UN, the County, asking all the partners for their plans: are you ready for El Niño?'[8] The growing anticipation of the government, NGOs, and international organisations as the short rains of October 2015 approached was matched by, and perhaps stoked (or was stoked by), media reporting.[9] Nairobi's Capital FM radio station even started a twitter handle *@ElNinoWatch984*.

Many Nairobians, particularly in Mathare, remembered the devastating floods that followed El Niño in 1997.[10] Esther Wanjiru, a resident of the Kosovo area of western Mathare, recalled how houses next to Mathare river were swept away during the 1997 floods, when one of her friends was killed as he tried to retrieve

---

[6] 'Stormy Times in the Offing', *Daily Nation* (25 August 2015); 'Advisory on Development of El Niño', Kenya Meteorological Department (22 September 2015); 'Press Release: Short Rains Season October to December 2015', Ministry of Environment, Natural Resources & Regional Authorities (no date, est. September 2015); 'Participatory Scenario Planning Advisory, OND 2015', County Meteorological Office, Nairobi (no date).

[7] 'State to Adjust Budget Ahead of El Niño Rains', *Standard* (9 September 2015); 'Team: Government Needs 10.5bn for El Niño Rains', *Standard* (22 September 2015); 'Thousands Facing El Niño in Coastal City', *Standard* (11 September 2015); 'Kenyna Ministries, Counties and Donors on Spending Alert over El Niño', *Standard* (30 September 2015); 'Up to SH5 Billion Has Been Set Aside and 70,000 National Youth Service Personnel Are on Standby to Deal with Expected El Niño Rains. Do You Think Kenyans Are Well Prepared for these Rains?', Young Nation Facebook Page, *Daily Nation* (13 September 2015); 'Kenya Will Get Share of SH8.5bn El Niño Fund', *Daily Nation* (5 December 2015).

[8] Interview with Corrine Torre, MSF Eastlands, Nairobi (10 February 2016). See also 'El Niño Calls for Meticulous Multi-Sectoral Planning', *Standard* (21 September 2015).

[9] 'El Niño to Disrupt Rains, Cut Africa, E Asia Harvests, Scientists Say', *Standard* (4 June 2015); 'We're Ready for El Niño, Say Officials', *Daily Nation* (26 August 2019); 'Up to SH5 Billion Has Been Set Aside and 70,000 National Youth Service Personnel Are on Standby to Deal with Expected El Niño Rains. Do You Think Kenyans Are Well Prepared for these Rains?', Young Nation Facebook Page, *Daily Nation* (13 September 2015); 'Kwale: County readies itself for the El Niño Deluge' *Daily Nation* (15 September 2015); 'ZUQKA: Brace Yourselves ... The El Niño Rains Are on the Way', *Daily Nation* (25 September 2015); 'Lamu: Residents in Flood Zones Told to Leave before Rains', *Daily Nation* (28 September 2015); 'Murang'a: Assessment of Landslide Prone Villages Starts', *Daily Nation* (28 September 2015).

[10] 'Scientists Warn El Niño to Be Worse than 1997/98', *Standard* (20 September 2015); 'Warning of an Impending El Niño Revives Memories of the Untold Suffering', *Standard Media* (19 August 2015), accessed 12 January 2016, https://www.standardmedia.co.ke/ktnhome/video/watch/2000097153/warning-of-an-impending-el-nino-revives-memories-of-the-untold-suffering; 'Nairobi Residents Warned against Looming El Niño Rain', *Standard* (18 August 2015); 'Experts Warn El Niño Rains Are Looming, Let's Be Ready', *Standard* (8 June 2015); 'Boost Preparedness Ahead of El Niño Rains', *Standard* (16 September 2015).

a box of money from his house, and told another story of another young boy who lost his life when floods swept through a village known as Jamaica in the Mlango Kubwa area.[11] Indeed the El Niño-linked floods of 1997 were destructive across Kenya and are believed to have 'contributed to about 2000 deaths', through flooding and landslides.[12] Mathare was one of the areas of Nairobi that was worst affected by floods. It is therefore not at all surprising that for many people in Mathare, El Niño had become synonymous with the threat of flooding. However, flooding in parts of Nairobi is almost an annual occurrence, the effects of which are experienced in dramatically different ways in different parts of the city, affecting different lives and bodies unevenly. It is also important to note that there have been a series of El Niño years since 1997, none of which have entered Nairobians' imagination in the way that the 1997 floods did. It was to 1997 that the widespread warnings and discussions about the impending El Niño rains of late 2015 all referred.[13]

But in 2015 in Mathare (and elsewhere) concerns about the anticipated El Niño rains of that year were not only about flooding. They were also about cholera and other water-borne diseases.[14] This too was based on memories of the increased cases of malaria, Rift Valley fever and especially cholera that had accompanied the El Niño rains of 1997.[15] Esther Wanjiru described how in 1997 a young school boy in class five was infected by *kipindupindu* (Swahili for cholera) after eating an orange, and immediately started feeling a stomach pain, and then later died in hospital. She also remembered an old man who used to collect stones from the river,

---

[11] Interview with Esther Wanjiru (14 January 2016).
[12] 'Scientists Warn El Niño to Be Worse than 1997/98', *Standard* (20 September 2015); 'Devastation: El Niño Destroys Infrastructure', *Daily Nation* (27 January 1998); 'El Niño Rains Havoc Hits the SHS 1 B Mark' *East African* (24 January 1998); 'Devastated: Chaos Has Kenya Washed Out', *East African* (16 January 1998); 'More Perish in Floods', *East Africa Standard* (21 October 1997); 'Government Declares Coast Floods a National Disaster', *East Africa Standard* (25 October 1997).
[13] Even the official warning issued by James Kongoti, director of Kenya's Meteorological Department, made this explicit link to the 1997 El Niño, but he also advised that there had been subsequent El Niños in 2002/3, 2006/7, and 2009/10, but these 'went unnoticed' by many people 'because their impacts were not as that of 1997/98' ('Advisory on Development of El Niño', Kenya Meteorological Office [22 September 2015]). See also 'El Niño Deluge to Kenya this Week', *Daily Nation* (5 October 2015); 'Scientists Warn El Niño to Be Worse than 1997/98', *Standard* (20 September 2015).
[14] This was also included in official advisories: 'Advisory on Development of El Niño', Kenya Meteorological Department (22 September 2015); 'Press Release: Short Rains Season October to December 2015', Ministry of Environment, Natural Resources & Regional Authorities (no date, est. September 2015); 'Participatory Scenario Planning Advisory, OND 2015', County Meteorological Office, Nairobi (no date). See also: 'Improve Hygiene to Curb Cholera, Locals Urged', *Daily Nation* (28 September 2015); 'Scientists Warn El Niño to Be Worse than 1997/98', *Standard* (20 September 2015); 'Bad Water Risky to City Kids', *Star* (6 November 2015); 'When El Niño Strikes there Are More Cases of Diarrhoea', *Star* (9 November 2015).
[15] 'Cholera Claims 22 in City Slums', *East African Standard* (13 December 1997); 'Cholera Kills 26 People, Fresh Outbreak Reported', *East Africa Standard* (6 December 1997); 'Cholera Hotlines: State Acts to Stem Panic over Disease', *East Africa Standard* (18 December 1997); 'Malaria Cases Likely to Soar after Rains', *East African* (28 January 1998); 'Cholera Roll Continues to Rise in Many Areas', *East African* (17 January 1998); 'Rift Valley Fever Kills Four People on Wajir', *East African* (24 January 1998).

who contracted cholera but didn't make it to hospital, and died at home because 'there was no one to assist him'. She described the fear and stigma that cholera provoked in 1997, which meant that often people 'did not want it to be known' they had been infected, because other 'people would avoid shaking your hand to avoid infection'.[16]

Indeed, the 1997 cholera outbreak was Kenya's largest in recent memory and resulted in '26901 cases and 1362 deaths' (Mutonga *et al.* 2013). As with flooding, cholera is an experience and risk that is very unevenly distributed across the city, and the country. Anthropological accounts of cholera epidemics often point to their deeply racialised and class dynamics, as, for example, Briggs & Mantini-Briggs (2004) have discussed in relation to a devastating cholera outbreak in Venezuela in the early 1990s. Their account describes how that outbreak's extraordinarily high mortality rate was the result not only of inadequate treatment facilities and poor public information sharing, but also of the way that the disease was represented and linked to social inequalities, particular geographies, and prevalent stigma and racial and ethnic prejudices about Indigenous groups by politicians and public health officials, all of which had the effect of redirecting 'blame' from institutions and authorities to the sufferers themselves. A similar intersection of social, microbiotic, material, infrastructural, and discursive factors are in play in how cholera affects different people in different parts of Nairobi in different ways. A key part of the story here is the material and corporeal nature of cholera as a disease which affords (and is afforded by) particular social and economic inequalities, stigma and prejudice, which link geography, class, infrastructure, and bodies in particular ways.

Cholera is an infectious bacterial disease spread by contaminated water or food, which causes an acute gastrointestinal infection leading to severe vomiting and diarrhoea. Deaths from cholera are caused by extreme dehydration, and can happen very quickly, even within hours, but are preventable by the early administration of oral rehydration solution, antibiotics, and, in severe cases, intravenous drips. Vaccines are available but need two doses at least a week before, so are of limited use once an outbreak has been declared.[17] Timing is therefore key. Cholera outbreaks are frequently associated with high population densities and mobility.[18] They 'tend to occur where living conditions are poor: where there is over-crowding, inadequate access to safe drinking water or proper latrines, and insufficient rubbish collection'.[19] In February 2016, one clinical worker, Elizabeth, at a Cholera Treatment Unit (CTU) in Mathare North discussed the case of a school

---

[16] Interview with Esther Wanjiru (14 January 2016).
[17] 'Cholera', Medecins Sans Frontieres (MSF) International, website, accessed 20 February 2016, www.msf.org.za/cholera.
[18] 'Kenya: MSF Concerned with Rapid Spread of Cholera Outbreak', MSF (2 June 2015), accessed 30 August 2021, https://www.msf.org.za/news-and-resources/press-release/msf-concerned-rapid-spread-cholera-outbreak-kenya.
[19] 'Cholera', Medecins Sans Frontieres (MSF) International, website, accessed 20 February 2016, www.msf.org.za/cholera.

boy who got sick after eating a mango, and was rushed to hospital but died later the same day. We 'admitted several kids from the same school', she continued, explaining that:

> There are several schools in Mathare North and when kids come from school they like playing a lot on the road and you find that other kids help themselves on the road. In case it rains and kids play with mud on the road they may end up touching or stepping on waste from a cholera infected person and carry the bacteria to the house where they may end up getting infected.[20]

This, and numerous accounts like it, illustrate how cholera can result from the failure to contain and isolate flows of clean water, human waste, and food. Children are often particularly vulnerable. Christopher Angwenyi described how his children were taken to Mbagathi hospital suffering from cholera in 1997.[21] Once infected, cholera exacerbates failure to isolate clean and dirty substances by its effect of defying, dangerously, the corporeal containments and flows necessary for bodies to function normally, particularly through vomiting and extreme diarrhoea, which is often white and watery and therefore sometimes described as 'rice water'.[22] Suffering cholera is undoubtedly a very immediate, visceral, and corporeal experience. Esther Wanjiru told us of her own experience of cholera in 1997:

> [Y]es I remember … back in 1997–1998 there was an outbreak of cholera in Mathare … and my neighbour got infected. We never knew it was cholera, we used to call it diarrhoea water. Her lips were white and dry and we had to hold her by the side as she was in a bad state. We had no money to take a taxi and we took her by the road-side and remembered a hospital named Mathare North where we took her. She was put on drip and because it was free, we let her be admitted. Then we went home, and it was at that time that I felt pain in my stomach. And so I had to go to the toilet and there was an old man who was very tough there, as they were city council toilets which we had to pay one shilling to use. I was so scared by the way I diarrhoea-ed over the entire wall and had to rush home feeling very weak. I was told that I also had the same disease and was given a lot of water … one litre. The water had salt and sugar as it was heavy, and I was ordered to finish it.[23]

The speed with which an infection takes hold, and the uncontained flows and mixing of clean water and human waste that both causes and can result from infection, means CTUs need to be established very quickly once an outbreak is suspected, and they involve very strict sterilisation and infection control procedures in order to isolate leaky, infected bodies and contain their dangerous flows of bacteria. Likewise, outside of these units, official cholera response programmes often involve spraying and disinfecting the homes of cholera suffers, once they have been identified.[24] We

---

[20] Fieldnotes (Lucy Wairimu), 'Mathare North CTU Visit' (12 February 2016).
[21] Interview with Christopher Angwenyi, village elder (18 March 2016).
[22] Fieldnotes (Syokau Mutonga), 'CTU Visit – Mathare North' (12 February 2016).
[23] Interview with Esther Wanjiru (14 January 2016).
[24] In 2015–16, this work was carried out by the Red Cross, while MSF focused on managing and funding its CTU units; Fieldnotes (Lucy Wairimu), 'Mathare North CTU Visit' (12 February 2015).

visited one CTU in the grounds of Mathare North clinic in February 2016, and were struck by the disciplined and sanitised nature of the place, defying its makeshift, tented appearance. Movement in, out, and through different sections of the unit was strictly controlled by chorine solution sprays and hand washes. Different tents were divided and marked for triage, observation, isolation, and acute cases. The clinical staff who showed us around explained how all admitted patients are immediately stripped of their clothes, covered with issued blankets, and assigned a bed. The eerie, empty beds of the then soon-to-be-closed unit spoke to the intense corporeality of suffering cholera, which, the clinical staff agreed, often reinforces stigma around the disease 'in the community'. Each bed, with its own drip stand and two buckets, had 'ominous holes in the middle, to allow patient's shit to drip down and be collected in a bucket beneath'.[25]

In Mathare and other 'slums' and 'informal' areas of the city, the risk of flooding and that of water-borne diseases are deeply linked through the inadequacies, decay, or even non-existence of water infrastructure, particularly poor drainage, lack of sewerage, and inadequate clean water supply (MSJC 2018). In these circumstances, keeping flows of human waste separate from clean water supplies, avoiding the contamination of food, and keeping bodies clean can be very difficult. The threat of cholera and other water-borne diseases is therefore, in many respects, an infrastructural concern, and Nairobi's slums are decidedly marked by the lack of sufficient, or even any, state-provided water infrastructure, and this makes residents of these areas particularly vulnerable to diseases like cholera.

In the absence of adequate state provision of water and sanitation, other kinds of actors often become involved in providing these services. When the Kosovo area of Mathare was first occupied in the late 1990s, there was no water at all, until a water pipe from Thika Road was installed to a nearby school, by a nearby Catholic church, St Teresa's, which offered the water for free. During the 2000s, the water connections were taken over and controlled by Mungiki, a violent gang which took control over much of Mathare in the 2000s, who began charging people to use the water. They 'used to charge whatever they wanted – even 40,000ksh to connect to that water', Peter Otieno, the 'water chairman' for Kosovo, explained, until they were violently driven away by the police and other local gangs in 2007.[26] As this and other water sources across Mathare were inevitably inadequate for the rapidly growing areas, some people continued to draw water from Mathare's deeply polluted river. It is only since the late 2000s that Nairobi Water has provided more water points across much of Mathare, after being prompted into action by community groups working with a local NGO called Pamoja Trust, who raised funds and constructed the first water points in the Kosovo area.[27] Water supplies remain

---

[25] Fieldnotes (Joost Fontein), 'Visit to CTU at Mathare North Clinic' (12 February 2015).
[26] Interview with Peter Otieno, water chairman, Kosovo (22 January 2016); interview with 'Nicholas', Shantit area, Mathare (22 January 2016); interview with Father Mwaura Kamau, Ruku Parish (23 March 2016).
[27] Interview with Peter Otieno, water chairman, Kosovo (22 January 2016).

patchy and uneven, and are sometimes cut off completely. In some parts of Mathare these water points soon became subject to power struggles between competing 'community groups', so-called 'reformed gangs' or youth groups, and other forms of local 'authority' and 'sovereignty'. Still very few people have water piped into their homes, and many of those are illegal and unmetered connections.

Sanitation and sewerage provision is even worse, with a massive shortage of toilets allowing rudimentary private toilet providers to charge for the use of improvised toilets, the waste from which usually runs straight into Mathare river. When Esther Wanjiru first settled in the Kosovo area in the late 1990s, there were no toilets at all, and people would relieve themselves in the bush or behind their houses. Christopher Angwenyi described how 'they used to go to trenches famously known as *athara* (bush), where there were open spaces'.[28] 'Sanitation', Peter Otienio stressed, 'is for the community to organise'.[29] This absence of adequate toilet facilities have allowed common Nairobian jokes about 'flying toilets' to abound, even though these are very real hazards for residents of 'slums' like Kibera, Kangemi, and Mathare, to name only three. The threat that heavy rains and flooding pose in terms of water-borne diseases like cholera is that, in the context of poor drainage and a lack of sanitation infrastructure which is supposed to isolate, contain, and remove human waste, flows of clean water, food, and waste readily mix, causing outbreaks of cholera, typhoid, and other diseases. This is exacerbated when water supplies are cut off, which is not an infrequent occurrence in Mathare or surrounding areas. As Peter Otieno explained, it is very difficult to keep clean if you don't have clean water.[30] Therefore, 'all the criteria for cholera are here', as Corrine Torre put it. 'When I [first] came here', she continued, 'I kept asking myself why cholera had not broken out because the context was there. The waste. The water. They don't have toilets and the few that are there have to be paid for. I mean, how can you have one latrine for two thousand people?'[31]

In this context, it is not surprising that in the widely announced, central and county government preparations ahead of the anticipated El Niño deluge, huge financial resources were marshalled to the creation of 'El Niño preparation committees', whose function was to organise local youth and unemployed people into labour groups deployed to clear blocked drains across Mathare and elsewhere around the city. Funds were distributed across counties creating opportunities for (and suspicions of) graft, particularly later in 2015 when it became apparent large sums of money had gone missing from the National Youth Scheme.[32]

---

[28] Interview with Esther Wanjiru (14 Janary 2016); interview with Christopher Angwenyi, village elder (18 March 2016).
[29] Interview with Peter Otieno, water chairman, Kosovo (22 January 2016).
[30] Interview with Peter Otieno, water chairman, Kosovo (22 January 2016).
[31] Fieldnotes (Syokau Mutonga), 'Interview with Corrine Torre' (5 February 2016).
[32] 'Team Denies Inflating El Niño Budget', *Daily Nation* (19 October 2015); 'El Niño: A Cash Cow Milked by Counties', *Star* (14 October 2015); 'Counties Accused of Trying to Cash in on El Niño Rains', *Daily Nation* (7 October 2015); 'Exposed: Shame of Billions Wasted on CDF Projects', *Saturday Nation* (12 September 2015); 'Waiguru Acts on NYS Scandal', *Saturday Nation* (12 September 2015).

Simultaneously, a large Chinese-funded sewage project also began laying down plans, and demolishing houses, for the installation of sewage pipes across and along Mathare valley to isolate and channel away waste water and sewage, and attempt to address both the hazards of cholera and the deeply polluted waters of Mathare river.

Contesting sovereignty and legitimacy in Mathare

In the emerging literature on Mathare and other slum areas across Nairobi – often driven by NGO and human rights agendas – much emphasis has been placed on the long, continuing history of 'abandonment' and 'neglect' of these areas by city planners and authorities. The profound infrastructural inadequacies of these 'informal' residential areas are often linked in such accounts with the prevalence of extra-judicial killings, gang violence, physical insecurity, unemployment, and poverty in order to illustrate the extreme marginality of lives and bodies in Nairobi's large and numerous informal residential areas and slums (e.g. van Stapele 2015; Kimari 2017). Some of this literature utilises a lexicon of 'hustling to survive' (see e.g. Thieme 2013; Price *et al.* 2016; Thieme *et al.* 2021) – very common in everyday parlance across Nairobi – in a bid to identify and perhaps restore (or even celebrate) the 'agency' and creativity required of people living in such conditions to make live-able lives, what others might describe as extreme abjection. Whatever position one takes on these concerns about academic representation – and on what many Marxist-inclined scholars might frown upon as a neoliberal celebration of poverty and exclusion (e.g. Rizzo 2017) – it is clear that the marginality of areas like Mathare from state provision of basic services like water and sanitation has created opportunities (as well as deep deprivations) for different kinds of players, especially NGOs, community groups, churches and mosques, and gangs, each of whom have in different ways become involved in organising and controlling water-related services and infrastructure in Mathare. As a result, water infrastructure – both clean water provision and sanitation – have become sites of struggle between different kinds of 'local authority', which align, intertwine, and confront each other in complex, always shifting ways.

For example, as Peter Otieno explained, around 2008/9, following much community pressure, four 'water kiosks' or 'points' were established in the Kosovo area, paid for by a local NGO *Pamoja*.[33] Later, perhaps in recognition of the success or urgency of the project, Nairobi Water established similar water points all over Mathare. In Kosovo, unlike in Mathare's 11 other 'villages', there are also about 160 houses which have water taps and meters in their houses. Some 'landlords' in the area sell the water from the taps in their houses to other residents. The water chairman explained that his role as the 'local authority' over Kosovo's water points is, first, to ensure that no one gets water into their houses without meters. The

---

[33] Interview with Peter Otieno, water chairman, Kosovo (22 January 2015).

illegal tapping of water pipes (and electricity) is very common in the area. Second, to find out when water pipes have broken or been cut, and inform Nairobi Water so repairs can be made. And third, to collect water bills from Nairobi Water and ensure they are paid or distributed to those residents with their own meters. This combination of punitive and enforcer roles on the one hand, and his role as 'enabler' to ensure water infrastructure remains intact and water supplies are kept flowing, on the other, captures the tensions between sovereignty and legitimacy that may be common to many or all regimes of rule involving water (Fontein 2015: 78–138).

For Peter Otieno, being the 'water chairman' for Kosovo was a voluntary position, while he made a living from his work as a tailor. He also fulfilled other, similar community roles, such as being a 'community health worker' responsible for handing out tablets and calling MSF to rush patients to hospital during cholera outbreaks.[34] It remains a little bit unclear how he acquired his position as 'water chairman', whether appointed by Nairobi Water or elected by community members, or some combination thereof, so the question of where in local hierarchies his authority derived from remains unclear. Yet he very clearly distinguished the control of water points by 'legitimate community groups' such as in Kosovo and several other of Mathare's villages, from three other areas in Mathare – 3c, Bondeni, and Shantit – where what he described as 'illegal' groups (youth groups, sometimes known as 'reformed gangs')[35] had chased 'legal' community groups (like his *Munungano wa Vijiji* group) away, and taken control over water points themselves.[36]

Yet in speaking to youth group members in the Shantit area of Mabatini ward about their control of water points in that area, they spoke of their role in remarkably similar terms to the water chairman. Nicholas (a pseudonym), for example – who is also a community health worker ('I inform MSF to come and pick up the sick') – described how Nairobi Water built water points in Mabatini Ward with the help of 'local youth', in order to 'give them money and something to do'.[37] They registered formally as a 'youth group', and now manage three water points in the Shantit area, selling the water to residents and paying Nairobi Water's charges, and keeping the difference, while ensuring the water points and meters remain functional, and alerting Nairobi Water when repairs were necessary. The area's three water points are clearly marked with the graffiti 'tags' of the Shantit gang, identifying who controls them, because, as Nicholas put it 'when you take over somewhere, you must put your mark … you must be aggressive, nothing comes easy

---

[34] Interview with Peter Otieno, water chairman, Kosovo (22 January 2016).

[35] As Gacheke Gachii, a prominent human rights activist in Mathare reminded me (email correspondence, 20 January 2016), it is important to be careful with the lexicon used here, because although they are often described as 'reformed gangs', including by members themselves, such language contributes to the criminalisation of youth groups, which in the context of Nairobi's extreme problem with 'extra-judicial' killings by the police can be very dangerous for self-organised groups of young men running car washes, or water and sanitation services.

[36] Interview with Peter Otieno, water chairman, Kosovo (22 January 2016).

[37] Interview with 'Nicholas', Shantit area, Mathare (22 January 2015).

... blood, sweat and tears and you get what you want'.[38] But he also emphasised that they sell water to local residents very cheaply, at 5ksh for 20 litres, 'because it is in the ghetto, people are poor, you cannot ask for more, you must cry for them, they are yours'. 'We pay Nairobi water every month according to the meter', but 'we also have a car wash, and for that we charge differently', he explained. 'Every month' they collect about '150,000–200,000ksh, most goes to Nairobi water, the rest we share amongst ourselves'.[39]

Although Kosovo's water chairman emphasised the difference between 'legal' community groups and the so-called 'reformed gangs' controlling water points in different parts of Mathare, what they do and how they understand what they do appear rather similar. Both operate through a combination of coercion and enforcement, on the one hand, and legitimacy and responsiveness to people's needs, on the other. Furthermore, it was also clear that for both Nicholas and Peter Otieno, running water services or being a community health worker was part of their 'hustle', their daily livelihoods if you prefer, from which status, social connections, and maybe sometimes resources derive. At the same time, it would be mistaken to allow this to detract from their claims to good social intentions, which clearly mattered to both of them. However, it is also true that Nicholas's rather 'happy' narrative of relations between Nairobi Water and the local community facilitated through his registered 'youth group' did not really reflect whole situation. In February 2016, a week or two after talking to Nicholas, there were serious riots along Juja Road, on the side of Mathare near the Shantit area, after Nairobi Water confiscated car wash equipment from the group, claiming the youth were using illegal water connections to operate it.[40] At the same time, however, there was also a sense among some residents in Kosovo that they were unhappy with Peter Otieno's chairmanship of the water point in Kosovo, describing him as 'nasty', and implying he abused his position to 'sell water', or that he had dubious relationships with local authorities, like the MP, councillors, and the chief.[41] Some were also unhappy about the way in which water connections and meters had been issued to some local residents but not others, and used that to justify their own illegal connections and non-payment to Nairobi Water.[42]

What these local struggles over Mathare's relatively new water points illustrate is a larger, salient point about the entanglement of water as a particular kind of substance and 'resource', with material properties that afford or constrain

---

[38] Interview with 'Nicholas', Shantit area, Mathare (22 January 2015).
[39] Interview with 'Nicholas', Shantit area, Mathare (22 January 2015).
[40] 'Chaos in Mathare as Residents Protest Crackdown on Illegal Connections' *Daily Nation* (1 February 2016); 'Mathare Youth Protest Impound of Car Wash Machine', *Daily Nation* (1 February 2016).
[41] For an example of community action against perceived corrupt local authorities in Mathare, see also 'Corrupt Village Elder in Kosovo Is Now Gone!', Mathare Social Justice Centre (29 March 2016), accessed 29 March 2016, https://matharesocialjusticecentre.wordpress.com/2016/03/28/corrupt-village-elder-of-kosovo-is-now-gone/article-by-lokal-2-2/#main.
[42] Interview with Esther Wanjiru (14 January 2016).

particular corporeal necessities (and therefore also offer particular kinds of opportunity) in different contested and contingent structures, practices and forms of power, authority and sovereignty. Why else would 'reformed gangs' – normally associated (in Mathare and elsewhere) with controlling illegal trades in drugs and alcohol and protection rackets, or driven (and sponsored) by nefarious political or ethnic interests – concern themselves with water provision or sanitation? The entanglement of Mathare's and other slums' long history of infrastructural, social, and political marginalisation and neglect with water's corporeal necessities for life and livelihoods affords opportunities that generate complex, multi-layered contests and struggle. City authorities and planners may be historically responsible for the continued infrastructural neglect, and social, economic and political marginalisation that forms part of the backdrop here, but they are also, because of this history, only players in a much more emergent and fractured multiplicity of actors whose localised struggles centre on, and are afforded by, the entangled flows, blockages, and containments that link the materialities of bodies and the city.

So what did El Niño do?

Anticipation of El Niño in 2015 made all of this much more urgent, exactly because incomplete flows, blockages, and dangerous mixtures of clean and dirty water threaten the corporeal containment of bodies that life demands, as graphically illustrated by Esther Wanjiru's description of suffering cholera in 1997. As a result, funding was allocated to counties and to the National Youth Service (NYS) to fund 'El Niño committees' of local 'youth' to unblock drains that would allow dirty water and run-off to flow properly, and avoid contaminating water sources and food.[43] Public health warnings were issued, and authorities and landlords advised people residing close to Mathare river – where the cheapest accommodation is to be found – to leave their homes or risk being flooded out. In 1997, homes and lives were lost due to flooding in these areas, when bridges linking two sides of the valley were also washed away. In 2015, however, many residents near the river chose to stay put, against this advice, as they also did in Kibera and other slums across Nairobi and elsewhere, for fear of losing their homes to others, or to land-grabbers.[44]

---

[43] 'County Steps Up Efforts to Handle El Niño', *Star* (6 October 2015).
[44] 'Slum Residents Resign to Fate as El Niño Looms', *Sunday Nation* (6 September 2015); 'Nyeri: Residents Defy Order to Leave Village Ahead of Downpour', *Daily Nation* (7 October 2015); 'The El Niño Warning Has Gone Out for Kenya, but Is Anyone Listening?', *Standard* (5 October 2015); 'Most People Stay Put Despite El Niño Warning' *Standard* (7 October 2015); 'Bungoma Residents in Landslide-Prone Areas Ignore El Niño Threat', *Standard* (12 October 2015); 'Slum Residents in Nyeri Refuse to Relocate Ahead of El Niño Rains', *Star* (6 October 2015).

Nicholas explained how he had been drafted onto an El Niño committee, as well as into the planning and demarcation of houses to be demolished to make way for the new sewage pipe project funded by the Chinese. His involvement in both projects drew on his local know-how and connections and offered him a way to subsidise his weekly earnings. They were part of his 'hustle'. El Niño and the risks it brought clearly created opportunities for Nicholas and others like him, but also for others like the clinical workers employed by MSF to manage its CTUs,[45] as well as people located much higher up in the city's and county's hierarchies. Reports and rumours soon emerged of El Niño-related emergency funds allocated to counties being delayed, exaggerated, or misdirected, or going missing.[46] Rumours also emerged that equipment and resources marshalled and donated by MSF, such as the CTU's beds and other equipment, later went missing.[47] Cartoons carried in the press captured the mood well; for example the 'El Niño ATM' cartoon by Victor Ndula, published in *The Star* on 20 October 2015, which showed well-dressed pigs collecting bags of cash from an 'El Niño teller machine' under a dark cloud and heavy rain. Nicholas complained that after several weeks working on the El Niño committee, under very poor conditions and with inadequate equipment, their promised NYS payments did not come through, and so they stopped work.[48] It soon emerged that there had been a huge corruption scandal in the higher echelons of the NYS, and the money that had been made available for drain clearance and other infrastructural improvements ahead of El Niño had been looted higher up the chain.[49] This was one of a series of financial scandals that have rocked the NYS in recent years.[50] These blocked and misdirected flows of funding and other resources illustrate how the El Niño hype created opportunities, but they also threatened the containment and safe flows of dangerous water, thereby putting the corporeal containment of Mathare's bodies at further risk.

---

[45] Fieldnotes (Syokau Mutonga), 'CTU Visit – Mathare North' (12 February 2016).
[46] 'Team Denies Inflating El Niño Budget', *Daily Nation* (19 October 2015); 'El Niño: A Cash Cow Milked by Counties', *Star* (14 October 2015); 'Counties Accused of Trying to Cash in on El Niño Rains', *Daily Nation* (7 October 2015); 'Counties Impatient on El Niño Funding', *Daily Nation* (1 October 2015); 'Counties Ask State to Release El Niño Funds', *Daily Nation* (2 October 2015); 'Letters to the Editor: No Sign of the Billions for El Niño the Flood', *Daily Nation* (21 November 2015); 'We Need SH380 Million for El Niño, Says Bungoma Governor Ken Lusaka', *Standard* (16 October 2015).
[47] Interview with Corrine Torre, MSF Eastlands, Nairobi (10 February 2016).
[48] Interview with 'Nicholas', Shantit area, Mathare (22 January 2015).
[49] 'El Niño Rains Will not Wash Away Jubilee Scandals', *Daily Nation* (1 November 2015); interview with 'Nicholas', Shantit area, Mathare (22 January 2015).
[50] 'Exposed: Shame of Billions Wasted on CDF Projects', *Saturday Nation* (12 September 2015); 'Waiguru Acts on NYS Scandal', *Saturday Nation* (12 September 2015); 'Resign? Not Me, Says Waiguru as Fights Graft Claims in Her Ministry', *Daily Nation* (5 November 2015); 'Kenya: MP Says Waiguru Unlikely to Be Removed over Corruption Because of Powerful Protectors', *Star* (10 November 2015); 'Waiguru Denies Overspending at Devolution Ministry and Says More Corruption Elsewhere', *Star* (4 November 2015); 'Waiguru Finally Quits after Call to President Uhuru Kenyatta', *Daily Nation* (22 November 2015).

In the event, however, El Niño didn't really happen,[51] at least not in Nairobi. As Corrine Torre of MSF put it, 'El Niño never showedup'.[52] There was increased rainfall and some localised flooding, but there were no major floods during the El Niño period in Nairobi.[53] Those living by the river had won their gamble, or at least so it seemed. There were major floods, and loss of lives and homes, in other areas of the country,[54] but in Nairobi El Niño was mainly felt in the extension of the 'short rains' into January 2016.[55] In fact, the worst rains and floods that Nairobi, and Mathare in particular, experienced that year (2015–16) had nothing to do with El Niño. That came in April and May 2016, during the 'second' rainy season, the 'long rains', when there was an enormous deluge over Nairobi, and Mathare was terribly flooded.[56] Houses by the river were washed away and hundreds of people made homeless.[57] These floods happened all over Nairobi and much of the country, where roads and bridges were flooded and washed away. This was when, in Huruma, not far from Mathare, a building collapsed killing 51 people, and raising, again, concerns about poor quality construction, corruption, and the poor enforcement of building regulations.[58]

---

[51] 'El Niño Threat Has Turned Every Kenyan into a Weatherman but Where's the Rain?', *Standard*, accessed 30 August 2021, https://www.standardmedia.co.ke/entertainment/crazy-monday/2000180011/el-nino-threat-has-turned-every-kenyan-into-a-weatherman-but-wheres-the-rain; 'Narok MP Threatens to Sue to Kenya Meteorological Agency over El-Nino Rains', *Standard* (21 October 2015).

[52] Interview with Corrine Torre, MSF Eastlands, Nairobi (10 February 2016).

[53] 'No Death, Damage from City Floods', *Allafrica.com* (30 November 2015), accessed 30 August 2021, https://allafrica.com/stories/201511300304.html.

[54] 'Kenya: 53 killed and 70,000 Made Homeless in El Niño Fury', *Allafrica.com* (28 November 2015), accessed 30 August 2021, https://allafrica.com/stories/201511290106.html; 'Destruction and Fears of Humanitarian Crisis as Heavy Rains Pound the Country', *Daily Nation* (12 November 2015); 'Kenyans Paying Price for Ignoring Weatherman's Warning', *Daily Nation* (14 November 2015); '20 Perish as El Niño Rains Pound Most Parts of Kenya', *Daily Nation* (10 December 2015); 'El Niño Worsens Food Crisis in Eastern Africa, Says UN', *Daily Nation* (21 December 2015); 'Thousands Homeless as El Niño Floods Sweep Somalia', *Standard* (30 October 2015); '23 Houses Destroyed as Storm Hits Isiolo', *Standard* (5 November 2015); 'Kenya Starts Experiencing Heavy Rains', *Standard* (6 November 2015); '2 People Swept Away by Floods as Predicted El Niño Comes to Pass', *Standard* (10 November 2015); 'El Niño Is Here, Let's Step Up the Rescue Efforts', *Standard* (14 November 2015).

[55] 'El-Nino Rains Still With Us, Says Weatherman', *Sunday Nation* (17 January 2016); 'Brace for Severe El Niño Rains in December', *Standard* (30 October 2015).

[56] 'Heavy Rains Kill Four as Floods Hit Nairobi', *Standard* (29 April 2016); 'Address Perennial Floods Menace Once and For All', *Standard* (20 May 2016); 'I'm Tired of Waiting for a Saviour', *Standard* (3 May 2016).

[57] 'Floods Leave Hundreds Homeless in Mathare', *Ghetto Radio* (29 April 2016); 'Raging Floods Leave over 800 People Homeless', *Daily Nation* (3 May 2016), accessed 26 April 2018, https://www.nation.co.ke/news/Raging-floods-leave-over-800-people-homeless/1056-3186538-ogah3iz/index.html.

[58] 'National Disaster Management Unit Releases a Report on the Huruma Building Collapse Disaster', *Ebru Televison* (19 May 2016). For the report, see Ministry of Interior and Coordination of National Government Inter-Agency Report, Nairobi County, *Huruma (Ngei)Building Collapse Disaster Incident*, May 2016, p. 9, accessed 25 April 2018, http://www.disastermanagement.go.ke/downloads/. See also 'Uhuru Orders Arrest of Huruma Building Owner. Death Roll Rises to 8', *The Star* (30 April 2016), accessed 26 April 2018, https://www.the-star.co.ke/news/2016/04/30/uhuru-orders-arrest-of-huruma-building-owner-death-toll-rises-to-8_c1342371.

In terms of cholera, there was a large and serious cholera outbreak in Kenya in 2015–16, but it is unlikely that this was El Niño-related.[59] It began in Nairobi in December 2014, long before El Niño concerns were raised in mid-2015, and then spread rapidly across 21 other counties.[60] The outbreak peaked in February 2015,[61] and by June 2015, in Nairobi at least, had been contained,[62] although the short rains did precipitate a 'second wave' outbreak later in the year. It is possible that El Niño-linked floodings elsewhere 'aggravated' cholera outbreaks in other counties,[63] but it is clear that, unlike what was suggested by the media hype of later that year, cholera in Nairobi in 2015 was not an effect of El Niño.

Although the Director of Medical Services in Kenya had issued a 'cholera outbreak alert' on 3 February, Kenya's 2015 cholera outbreak went by largely unreported in the press or government announcements until a stakeholders meeting was called by the national government in May, and a communiqué was signed 'to stop cholera in the next 30 days as part of the government rapid responses initiatives'.[64] This general silence stood in marked contrast to the amount of publicity that El Niño received later in the year. Dr Stephen Wanjala, the MSF's Deputy Medical Coordinator in Kenya, explained that the delay 'in declaring the outbreak and responding appropriately' was 'because they were concerned it would cause shame and anxiety among the population'.[65] Corrine Torre of MSF, working in the Eastlands side of Nairobi, explained that after the outbreak was first identified in Mathare in late 2014, the city authorities were very reluctant and slow to grant permission for MSF to open Cholera Treatment Units in Nairobi for fear of raising adverse publicity. 'They didn't want to inform the population' and 'they delayed

---

[59] The World Health Organization has been careful about linking El Niño to cholera directly, noting that 'evidence for an association between cholera and sea surface temperatures is limited but suggestive'. However, attention was drawn to a possible link because of the several severe cholera outbreaks that occurred in East Africa in the context of the heavy El Niño rains of 1997, a result of which is that 'increased attention is again being paid to the environmental determinants of this disease' ('El Niño and Health', 1999, World Health Organization report, WHO/SDE/PHE/99.4, p. 24).
[60] 'Kenya: Cholera Outbreak', *Emergency Plan of Action, Operation Update*, International Federation of the Red Cross and Red Crescent Societies, issued 2 October 2015.
[61] George et al. (2016).
[62] Interview with Corrine Torre, MSF Eastlands, Nairobi (10 February 2016).
[63] 'Sh15 Billion Needed for El Niño Disasters as Cholera, Malnutrition Plague Region', *X News* (20 February 2016); George et al. (2016).
[64] 'Urgent Resolve to End Cholera Outbreak in Kenya', Report by World Health Organization, Regional Office for Africa (23 May 2015). Other UN and NGO reports followed in June ('Kenya: MSF Concerned with Rapid Spread of Cholera Outbreak', MSF [2 June 2015]), July ('Kenya: The Cholera Test and the Kenyan Health System Has Failed' by Dr Stephen Wanjala, Deputy Medical Coordinator, MSF, Kenya [27 July 2015]), October ('Kenya: Cholera Outbreak', *Emergency Plan of Action, Operation Update*, International Federation of the Red Cross and Red Crescent Societies, issued 2 October 2015), December ('Kenya: Cholera Outbreak Spreads to Dadaab Refugee Camp', MSF [17 December 2015]), and January (George et al. 2016).
[65] 'Kenya: The Cholera Test and the Kenyan Health System Has Failed', by Dr Stephen Wanjala, Deputy Medical Coordinator, MSF, Kenya (27 July 2015).

the response' for six weeks.[66] Eventually, in February 2015, three emergency CTUs were opened by MSF across the Eastlands area, including in Mathare North, which stayed open until August 2015.[67] They treated thousands of cases, and by February 2016, when we spoke to her, Corrine Torre estimated that 96 people in Mathare and the surrounding areas had died. We heard many stories of cholera deaths in 2015 from people in Mathare.[68]

The country-wide epidemic peaked in February 2015, but there were 'second wave' outbreaks in different counties throughout the rest of the year. Reports suggested that by January 2016 there had been 11,033 cases across the country, and 178 reported deaths, with a Case Fatality Rate (CFR) ranging between 0.5 and 13.[69] These figures are likely under-representations of actual numbers of cases and deaths. Both the recurring nature of some of the outbreaks (initial containment followed by 'second' and even 'third waves') in different counties and the variable and often high CFR figures suggest that capacity and coordination for treatment and containment of the outbreak was markedly uneven across different counties.

MSF's Nairobi CTUs were closed in August, after the initial outbreak was contained by June 2015; but amid the growing hype and anticipation surrounding the pending El Niño rains in late 2015, they were re-opened the following month, in September, and stayed open until early 2016. But by then the worst of the outbreak of that year had already passed, although there was a new smaller spike in cases after the onset of the 'short rains' late in the year. As Corrine Torre indicated, El Niño did not 'show up'; if it had done so, Nairobi's cholera outbreak might have been far worse. 'It would have been a disaster if El Niño had come', she agreed.[70] We visited the last CTU to remain open in February 2016, by which stage its beds were empty and the unit just about to close. A glance at that CTU's records indicated it alone had treated more than 1000 patients in 2015.

Therefore, the hype and anticipation that had been raised around the impending risks and dangers of El Niño in 2015 were for an event that did not really materialise. The cholera and flooding witnessed in Mathare that year were not directly El Niño related. The major cholera event of 2015 started long before El Niño, and the major floods took place afterwards. Both are already perennial and endemic problems in Mathare and across Nairobi's slums. What El Niño, and the hype around it, did do was create opportunities for other, extraordinary, distributions of national and international resources, opportunities that people higher up in city and government

---

[66] Interview with Corrine Torre, MSF Eastlands, Nairobi (10 February 2016).

[67] Four CTUs were set up by MSF across Nairobi ('Kenya: MSF Concerned with Rapid Spread of Cholera Outbreak', MSF [2 June 2015]) with three in the wider Eastlands area, at Mathare North Health Centre, at Lucy Kibaki Hospital and at Bahati Health Centre (interview with Corrine Torre, MSF Eastlands, Nairobi [10 February 2016]).

[68] Interview with 'Nicholas', Shantit area, Mathare (22 January 2015); interview with Peter Otieno, water chairman, Kosovo (22 January 2015); fieldnotes (Syokau Mutonga) 'CTU visit – Mathare North' (12 February 2015); interview with Christopher Angwenyi, village elder (18 March 2016).

[69] George et al. (2016).

[70] Fieldnotes (Syokau Mutonga), 'Interview with Corrine Torre' (5 February 2016).

hierarchies had better access to than others. El Niño's affects turned out to have had less to do with the dangers of flooding and water-borne disease (as these are insecurities that bodies and lives in Nairobi's slums already face), and much more to do with Mathare's 'productive marginality' on the frontier of different, contested and contingent, emergent and entangled, regimes of rule that circulate around the provision (or failed provision) of basic services like water supply, health care, drainage, and sanitation. This reflects the political materialities of water's uneven flows, blockages, and inadequate containment, upon which the making and unmaking of Nairobian bodies are predicated. It is possible to suggest that all the El Niño talk and publicity did bring Mathare's struggles for state services, at the intersection of corporeal and urban flows, to the fore and made them visible, if only for a short time. More likely, however, is that Mathare's struggles and neglect, its endemic and recurring problems with clean water provision, sanitation, and flood control, were hidden under the much-hyped anticipation of an 'exceptional' weather event.

Conclusions

This discussion of flooding and cholera in Mathare – and of the anticipation that preceded the (non) arrival of the El Niño rains in Nairobi in 2015 – illustrates in quite graphic ways how the politics of life and of death – of bio- and necro-politics (Mbembe 2003) – are firmly intertwined; and how struggles to establish authority, across very different scales and in diverse contexts, necessarily involve aspects of both sovereignty and legitimacy. It also shows how such emergent struggles are entangled with and gain traction exactly in the context of the productive uncertainties of the material flows and blockages that make up and link bodies in and of the city, literally and metaphorically. By focusing on the nexus of weather, sanitation, and disease in Mathare, I have tried to explore how material and corporeal flows – and the processes that manage and contain, or not, such flows – are deeply imbricated in the production, reproduction, and contestation of different forms of sovereignty and legitimacy in the city. There are both particular specificities and more broader resonating dynamics at play here. In Mathare, the productive potentialities of its long history of 'state neglect' in terms of clean water, drainage, and sanitation provision – engendering the kind of ongoing struggles between different emergent forms of power, legitimacy, and sovereignty that I have discussed here – intersect with a far less subtle politics of death as manifest in the proliferation of gang-related and extra-judicial killings by police (Mutahi 2011; van Stapele 2015; 2016; 2020; Price et al. 2016; Jones et al. 2017), for which Mathare is particularly infamous, but which I have not had space to discuss here. Suffice to say, however, that this is a kind of necropolitics that itself reveals (even as it constantly re-affirms) the deficiency of state legitimacy – that is, its biopolitics – in some parts of Nairobi. Elsewhere in the city, and in many diverse urban contexts beyond, in Kenya and across the region, the biopolitics of regulatory control of material and corporeal flows are likely to be more salient, pointing to greater efforts to establish governmental regimes of legitimacy, and yet, conversely, offering much less opportunity for other contested loci of power and authority to emerge. In the end, however, the way that water's many material qualities can index multiple, coexistent, and contested regimes of meaning and rule, shows how in struggles for authority the nexus of legitimacy and sovereignty is always, like water and weather, uncertain and incomplete.

References

Briggs, C.L. & Mantini-Briggs, C. (2004), *Stories in the Time of Cholera: Racial Profiling during a Medical Nightmare* (Berkeley, University of California Press).
Das, V. & Poole, D. (2004), *Anthropology in the Margins of the State* (Oxford, James Currey).
Filippucci, P., Harries, J., Fontein, J., & Krmpotich, K. (2012), 'Encountering the Past: Unearthing Remnants of Humans in Archaeology and Anthropology', in D. Shankland (ed.), *Archaeology and Anthropology: Past, Present and Future* (London, Berghahn Books), 197–218.
Fontein, J. (2014), 'Remaking the Dead, Uncertainty and the Torque of Human Materials in Northern Zimbabwe', in F. Stepputtat (ed.), *Governing the Dead: Sovereignty and the Politics of Dead Bodies* (Manchester, Manchester University Press), 114–40.
Fontein, J. (2015), *Remaking Mutirikwi: Landscape, Water & Belonging in Southern Zimbabwe* (Woodbridge, James Currey).
Fontein, J. (2017), 'Demolition', installation at the exhibition, *Sensing Nairobi: Remains, Waste & Metonymy II*, at the British Institute in Eastern Africa, February 2017, and at the Nairobi National Museum, June 2017.
Fontein, J. (2022), *The Politics of the Dead in Zimbabwe 2000–2020: Bones, Rumours & Spirits* (Woodbridge, James Currey).
Gandy, M. (2004), 'Rethinking Urban Metabolism: Water, Space and the Modern City', *City*, 8.3: 363–79.
Gandy, M. (2005), 'Cyborg Urbanisation: Complexity and Monstrosity in the Contemporary City', *International Journal of Urban and Regional Research*, 29.1: 26–49.
George, G., Rotich, J., Kigen, H., Kiama, C., Waweru, B., Boru, W., Galgalo, T., Githuku, J., Obonyo, M., Curran, K., Narra, R., Crowe, S.J., O'Reilly, C.E., Macharia, D., Montgomery, J., Neatherlin, J., De Cock, K.M., Lowther, S., Gura, Z., Langat, D., Njeru, I., Kioko, J., & Muraguri, N. (2016), 'Notes from the Field: Ongoing Cholera Outbreak: Kenya 2014–2016', *MMWR Morb Mortal Weekly Report*, 65: 68–9, www.cdc.gov/mmwr/volumes/65/wr/mm6503a7.htm.
Jones, P., Kimari, W., & Ramakrishnan, K. (2017), '"Only the People Can Defend this Struggle": The Politics of the Everyday, Extrajudicial Executions and Civil Society in Mathare, Kenya', *Review of African Political Economy*, 44.154: 559–76.
Kimari, W. (2017), '"Nai-Rob-Me", "Nai-Beg-Me", "Nai-Shanty": Historicizing Space-Subjectivity Connections in Nairobi from its Ruins' (unpublished PhD thesis, York University, Toronto).
Mbembe, A. (2003), 'Necropolitics', *Public Culture*, 15.1: 11–40.
MSJC (Mathare Social Justice Centre) (2018), 'Maji Ni Uhai Maji Ni Haki. Eastlands Residents Demand Their Right To Water: A Participatory Report', accessed 5 July 2019, https://www.matharesocialjustice.org/wp-content/uploads/2019/02/MajiNiHaki_Report_MSJCFinal_Web.pdf.

Murunga, G.R. (2012), 'The Cosmopolitan Tradition and Fissures in Segregationist Town Planning in Nairobi, 1915–23', *Journal of Eastern African Studies*, 6.3: 463–86.

Mutahi, P. (2011), 'Between Illegality and Legality: (In)security, Crime, and Gangs in Nairobi's Informal Settlements', *South African Crime Quarterly*, 37: 11–18.

Mutonga, D., Langat, D., Mwangi, D., Tonui, J., Njeru, M., Abade, A., Zephania, I., Njeru, I., & Dahlke, M. (2013), 'National Surveillance Data on Epidemiology of Cholera in Kenya, 1997–2010', *Journal of Infectious Diseases*, 208.1: S55–S61.

Pinney, C. (2005), 'Things Happen: Or, From Which Moment Does That Object Come?', in D. Miller (ed.), *Materiality* (Durham NC, Duke University Press), 256–72.

Price, M., Albrecht, P., Colona, F., Denney, L., & Kimari, W. (2016), 'Hustling for Security: Managing Plural Security in Nairobi's Poor Urban Settlements', Rift Valley Forum, report, accessed 5 July 2019, http://riftvalley.net/event/hustling-security-managing-plural-security-nairobi's-poor-urban-settlements#.XR8D7C2Q3_8.

Rizzo, M. (2017), *Taken for a Ride: Grounding Neoliberalism, Precarious Labour and Public Transport in an African Metropolis* (Oxford, Oxford University Press).

Smith, C.R. (2018), 'Accumulating History: Dirt, Remains and Urban Decay in Nairobi', *Social Dynamics*, 44.1: 107–27.

Smith, C.R. (2020), *Nairobi in the Making: Landscapes of Time and Urban Belonging* (Woodbridge, James Currey).

Thieme, T. (2013), 'The "Hustle" amongst Youth Entrepreneurs in Mathare's Informal Waste Economy', *Journal of Eastern African Studies*, 7.3: 389–412.

Thieme, T., Ference, M.E., & van Stapele, N. (2021), 'Harnessing the "Hustle": Struggle, Solidarities and Narratives of Work in Nairobi and Beyond: Introduction', *Africa*, 91.1 (special issue, 'Harnessing the Hustle'): 1–15.

van Stapele, N. (2015), 'Respectable "Illegality": Gangs, Masculinities and Belonging in a Nairobi Ghetto' (unpublished PhD thesis, University of Amsterdam).

van Stapele, N. (2016), '"We Are Not Kenyans": Extra-Judicial Killings, Manhood and Citizenship in Mathare, a Nairobi Ghetto', *Conflict, Security and Development*, 16.4: 301–25.

van Stapele, N. (2020), 'Police Killings and the Vicissitudes of Borders and Bounding Orders in Mathare, Nairobi', *Environment and Planning D: Society and Space*, 38.3: 417–35.

13

Hosts and Higher Powers: Asylum Requests and Sovereignty

ELENA ISAYEV

Introduction

ASYLUM APPEALS, BY their nature, initiate encounters that demarcate the hosting body by pointing to the existence of those who are positioned external to it. They make visible the skin or membrane of the host's jurisdiction, articulating its coherence and independence from other entities. The host is thus brought into being through the refuge seeker's appeal to their power of protection and their ability to make autonomous decisions on whether to provide hospitality (or not). This idea is encapsulated in the emphatic address to the king of Argos by the Danaids, the suppliant women of Aeschylus' 2500-year-old Greek tragedy: 'You are the city, I tell you, you are the people! A head of state, not subject to judgement.'[1] Ancient literature's exploration of the discourse surrounding appeals for refuge and supplication appears at crucial junctures, such as the 5th-century BCE experimentation with polis (city-state) democracy. This shows a deep interest of how authorities, in exercising their power, struggle to balance their responsibility and obligation to the people (*demos*), the asylum seekers, and the gods.

By focusing on ancient appeals for asylum and repatriation of exiles (at times also enforced), this inquiry draws on the evidence of encounters in the east Mediterranean of the 5th and 4th centuries BCE as an entry-point into the enduring perplexities of sovereignty. It seeks to show that, whether historical or of the present day, the request for asylum serves as a catalyst for the practice of sovereignty, invokes its power, and thus becomes a form of recognition, through deference, of the potential host as sovereign. At the same time, the appeals for refuge and negotiations that follow expose the ambiguity of who the host actually is, or with whom

---

[1] Aeschylus, *Suppliant Women*, 365–75. All translations of Aeschylus, *Suppliant Women*, unless stated otherwise, from Sommerstein (2009).

sovereignty rests. Furthermore, they test the potential for sovereign action through exposing the constraints imposed on it by such factors as internal society structures; the geopolitical positioning amongst other sovereign entities; their mutual relations and interdependence; and the presence of higher powers – whether kings or polities with overarching authority, the gods, or supra-state protocols and organisations such as today's United Nations (UN). The root causes of displacement will not be considered here directly, but their diversity within and across time is fully recognised, not least the extent to which current 21st-century migration trends are in part the result of colonial legacies, and that the majority of forced displacement takes place within state borders, resulting from climate change and the disasters associated with it.[2]

Displaced groups and individuals have a key role within sovereignty discourse. Their engagement with potential hosts and polities does more than expose the workings of sovereignty; it also reveals those who are displaced as agents bearing the tools of its articulation. As will be argued here, people who are forced into such conditions are facilitators of the way sovereign power is recognised, invoked, deemed interdependent, and constrained by external pressures and obligations. It demonstrates the forms of pressure on sovereignty in practice that come into conflict with its ideals of freedom (ἐλευθερία), autonomy (αὐτονομία; ἑκών), and power (δυναστεία; δύναμαι) – the central conceptions to which ancient Greeks appealed in articulating what today we term sovereignty.[3]

Territorialities of sovereignty

Hospitality decision-making marks the boundary between civic society and the international community, confronting the space between civil rights and human rights. It is here that the perplexities of sovereignty are revealed, not only for the host, but for the citizen-strangers, those deemed stateless, or people with non-effective citizenship, whose existence lies seemingly beyond the possibilities of sovereign action. Within the context of today's system of territorial nation-states, individuals who are forced to endure the condition resulting from displacement become a counter to a world-order so defined (further discussion by Haddad 2003: esp. 300;

---

[2] In 2019 the *Internal Displacement Monitoring Centre* reported a worldwide total of 33.4 million displaced individuals, of whom 24.9 million were displaced due to 'natural' disasters: https://www.internal-displacement.org/global-report/grid2020/ (accessed 14 July 2021).
[3] The following are examples where these terms appear in ancient texts:
ἐλευθερία – free, freedom of yourselves: Euripides, *Children of Herakles*, 287; Isocrates, *Plataicus*, 14.17; Isocrates, *Panegyricus*, 4.117.
αὐτονομία – living independently under own laws, of one's free will, autonomously: Isocrates, *Plataicus*, 14.17; Isocrates, *Panegyricus*, 4.117.
ἑκών – willing, of free will: Isocrates, *Plataicus*, 14.12–13.
δύναμαι – to be able, strong enough, powerful enough, mighty: Isocrates, *Panegyricus*, 4.56–7.
δυναστεία – exercise political power, sovereignty, lordship: Isocrates, *Panegyricus*, 4.22.

Luoma-aho 2004). At the same time, this condition reifies the national imaginary of coherently constituted entities of the world-order, in the gaps of which, those who are displaced ostensibly exist. This modern paradox – the technical impossibility of such gaps since all territory is assigned to political entities (with a few exceptions, as at the North and South Poles) – will not be confronted here directly.[4] This paradox is less evident in the ancient context where status, citizenship, and notional rights were not determined through territory,[5] although land belonging to sanctuaries, while not in itself sovereign, was sacred and therefore did have certain protective powers, as we will see.

Territory does not come into play in articulating the sovereign entity in the ancient context. Land and space mattered but in different ways.[6] Of interest for our purposes is the transformation of the site from which supplication was made. Prior to the emergence of the polis, ancient narratives position requests for refuge – expressed as hospitality (*xenia*) – at the threshold or the hearth of the head of the household, who alone made the decision to grant it, or not. Homer's protagonist Odysseus is the Mediterranean archetype of such in/hospitable encounters, around which the epic *Odyssey* is constructed. Several hundred years later, in the world of city-states with democratic institutions from the 5th century BCE on, the responsibilities and obligations become less clear, and those seeking refuge make their appeals not at domestic thresholds, but at other liminal places, such as altars and sanctuaries, where their wellbeing was protected by the gods. It is from such altars that Aeschylus' suppliant Danaids make their appeal to Pelasgos, king of Argos. Within these sacred precincts – the primary purpose of which was to host worshippers and festival goers during religious celebrations – accommodating asylum seekers was so common that the ancient Greek historian Herodotus likened their presence to that of nesting birds (*The Histories*, 1.159.3). There is also evidence that provisions for additional lodgings at sanctuaries were at times necessary for that purpose (Sinn 1993; Chaniotis 1996: 69). The shift of focus on the site of appeal from the private threshold to a space that is under a different jurisdiction, which can be defined as both belonging to the community and being under the wider-reaching protection of the gods, makes the position of the host more ambiguous. It is no longer just the individual but the community which is appealed to. Such diffusion of responsibility to provide hospitality directly touches on issues of sovereign practice, and the ancient tragedians use it to question where authority

---

[4] This critical difference of territoriality, as the basis for determining citizenship, rights and protection, was a fundamental point already addressed by Arendt (1943) when considering the predicament of refugees of the past and in our own time, with critical engagement in relation to the ancient world by Gray (2018) and discussion in Isayev (2021).

[5] Some argue that while there was no conception of 'rights' in ancient Greece, there was still an understanding of the need for, and attempts to secure, individual liberty. For discussion in relation to Isaiah Berlin's (1958) 'negative liberty': Cartledge & Matt (2009), who argue that ancient Greece was less concerned with rights per se, as much as liberty.

[6] For ancient perceptions of spatiality, see: Isayev (2017a: chapters 10 and 11).

lies. In Aeschylus' *Suppliant Women*, the ambivalent position of the king, which is exposed through the suppliants' appeal, becomes central – is he operating as the ultimate authority, as a head of a household, or as an intermediary representative of the common will? Whatever his jurisdiction, it is not defined by territorial extent. The supplicant appeals may have been made from the liminal space of the sacred altars on the shore, but their ability to request refuge was not determined by any border belonging to a state.

In the ancient civic context, it was not the territorial boundaries that constituted communities, and which were difficult to cross, but those of status, especially between the position of slave and free, or non-citizen and citizen. In granting refuge, the hosts could distinguish between accessing the land and accessing the membership privileges of the community that occupied that land. This allowed for the possibility of gaining the status of *metic* (resident alien), which in 5th-century Athens provided certain privileges and duties but without citizenship.[7] This status was the likely outcome of the successful plea by the suppliant women in Aeschylus' tragedy (Bakewell 2013: 58, 103–5, 121–5). Centuries later, the Roman statesman Cicero, in his *De Officiis* (3.11.47), expressed the distinction more explicitly, by stating that while 'it is right not to permit the rights of citizenship to one who is not a citizen … to debar foreigners from using the city is clearly inhuman'.[8] Such a distinction would become difficult to articulate with the advent of the nation-state from the 17th century onwards – once territory and membership overlapped. Even then, this need not have been a foregone conclusion; its development emerged in tandem with 17th-century discourse centred on cosmopolitanism and the values associated with free movement (Benhabib 2004). Within it, justifications of mobility, in terms of colonial ventures and expanding empire, developed alongside sovereign entities' exclusionary policies, which saw the right of access become the exception. Samuel von Pufendorf's writings reveal a turning point: for him the admission of foreigners became determined by the host states' own interest and granted as a favour (von Pufendorf 1749 [1672]: book 3 at 3.251–2; Chetail 2016: 911). The position of exclusionary territoriality became further consolidated by such views as those of Christian von Wolff, who approved the states' discretion to admit outsiders to be enforced by criminal sanctions. The view was based on his belief that 'in a state of nature there is no right to emigrate' (von Wolff 1934 [1749]: vol. 2 at 3.83.154; Chetail 2016: 911).

More recently, in their controversial proposals for addressing the current 'refugee crisis', Betts and Collier (2017: 132) reiterated a 21st-century version of these early modern claims: that while those seeking refuge have the right to migrate insofar as they need to reach a safe haven, this is not an unqualified right to move. They stress that refugees are entitled to expect rescue and pathways to autonomy with an

---

[7] Kennedy (2014: 26–67); Sosin (2016). For an in-depth extensive study of the figure of the *metic* as a site of discourse, see Kasimis (2018).
[8] Translation by the author, adapted from the translation in Miller (1928).

eventual route out of limbo, but not a pathway to migration per se. They also indicate that refugees' access to autonomy was originally a key intention of the refugee regime, and that almost half of the Refugee Convention focuses on socio-economic rights, including the right to work and freedom of movement. However, these rights are not currently implemented, in part due to the shift in policy to encampment in the 1980s (Betts & Collier 2017: 155–6, chapter 6). The paradoxical legacy they try to address is the result of the 'old trinity' of state–people–territory, as Hannah Arendt (1968 [1951]: 358) referred to it, that created a particular form of statelessness (Gundogdu 2015: 2–5), in which the dimension of physical placedness became part of the difficulty in accessing human rights. The perplexity of human rights that Arendt (1968 [1951]) confronted in her work was that while promising equality irrespective of citizenship status, and despite advances in the institutionalisation and universalisation of human rights norms, they are still confined by state-centric international law.[9] Even in seeing the state as a project of international law (rather than the reverse), Eslava and Pahuja (2020) demonstrate how the maintenance of the sovereign territorial state system is a primary aim of the international legal order. Therefore, the UN is necessary in Macklem's (2015: 3) view, precisely as a way to counteract the negative consequences of such sovereignty: the central 'purpose of international human rights law is to identify and mitigate adverse effects of the structure and operation of the international legal order' – a palliative response for the shortcomings of the international legal order. But to what extent can the UN, and the directives it oversees, act as a counter? Since the UN Charter is founded on respect for state sovereignty, it gives precedence to the right to decide whether to grant asylum over the right to receive it (Heuser 1997; Haddad 2003).

These shortcomings of the global order of nation-states are borne out of a particular framing of sovereignty that emerged from the crucial 17th-century discourse – as did the term itself. Whether it is even appropriate to talk about sovereignty prior to this period is an issue addressed by other contributors to this volume, and will not be confronted here directly. The premise of what follows is that the concept of sovereignty is never independent of its time and circumstances, and that it existed in different guises prior to the appearance of the term itself. Hence, as Smith (2020: 173) reflects, 'the prehistory of sovereignty underlines the possibility for it to have a different future'. In addition, as demonstrated by Cruickshank *et al.* in this volume, when focusing on indigenous knowledge systems and practices, sovereignty continues to exist in different guises simultaneously. Of the key aspects that define today's nation-state sovereignty – territory, population, authority, and recognition – it is the last three, and particularly that of recognition that will be of most interest here. Krasner's (1999; 2001: 1–23) four ways of understanding sovereignty, that define these further, reveal how ancient cases encourage diverse

---

[9] See Article 2.1 of the International Covenant on Civil and Political Rights and Article 14 of the Universal Declaration of Human Rights. For discussion directly on these issues, engaging with Hannah Arendt's writings, see Gundogdu (2015); Stonebridge, this volume.

meanings of sovereignty that are less constrained (see also Lundgreen, this volume). First, internal sovereignty, or what Krasner terms 'domestic sovereignty' – the internal organisation of authority that controls the polity within – forms a particular interest within ancient discourse of power and responsibility of emerging *polis* society. Second, Krasner's category of 'international legal sovereignty' – the mechanism of recognition by other states that allows a sovereign state to come into being – concerns the constitution of a sovereign entity through external prerogative. The issue of recognition, by whom and of whom, will be a key point of entry into the ancient discourse, by confronting first the modern notion that technically only juridically independent territorial entities can be recognised as sovereign, and only by other equal sovereigns. Third, Krasner's 'Westphalian sovereignty' is less a reference to the Treaty or Peace of Westphalia than a reflection on the autonomy of domestic governing structures, and the extent to which they are free from external authoritative pressure and interference. Fourth, Krasner's final category of 'interdependence' also concerns external sovereignty, with specific reference to a government's ability to regulate movement of goods, capital, people, and ideas across its borders. This narrow configuration of interdependence, aside from the lack of hard borders in the ancient world, is where the historic context provides most potential to expand our understanding of sovereignty, by showcasing the extent of interconnectivity not only across space but in time, and an interdependence that affects sovereignty beyond that of equally constituted polities.

Recognition

An outsider's request for protection, in the first instance, acts as a recognition of the 'insider' as an entity capable of autonomous decision-making and with the power to carry it out – as sovereign. The bold statement by Aeschylus' suppliant women to the king of Argos is one rendering of this, which we will return to below. Displaced persons such as refugees become a particular form of the outsider – the 'other'. It is not an 'otherness' constituted through any claims to a specific ethnicity or place of origin, but resulting from the condition of displacement itself. This outside perspective through displacement activates a kind of contingent agency (Isayev 2017b), which demarcates that which is on the inside and makes it tangible. There are similarities between the demarcation of sovereignty and identity – they are both relational and oppositional. Where they differ is that identity may be self-defined or *emic*, but sovereignty cannot be claimed without external endorsement. To have meaning, sovereignty as a claim needs to be technically recognised by equally defined others. As Wallerstein (2004: 44) indicates: 'Sovereignty is more than anything else a matter of legitimacy … [that] requires reciprocal recognition. Sovereignty is a hypothetical trade, in which two potentially conflicting sides, respecting *de facto* realities of power, exchange such recognitions as their least costly strategy.' In the context of nation-states, which this statement refers to, it becomes questionable whether meaningful recognition of sovereignty can originate from a source other than another sovereign state, and hence also by definition prevent any possibility of sovereign existence to that which is not recognised as a state.

Yet even within a narrow state-centred definition, recognition by other sovereign states is not self-evident. To be deemed sovereign, the recognition need not be unanimous by all existing states, and moreover recognition by a majority of states (even for example those that hold UN membership) does not necessarily lead to the right for a polity to claim sovereign status. Recognition may be one of the four pillars that define contemporary sovereignty, yet its foundation remains unstable. There is persistent ambiguity not only concerning whose polity is allowed to be recognised as sovereign, how and by whom, but also in the differential value of those doing the recognising, even among de jure sovereign states. The following examples from the present day briefly expose how some have more sovereign weight than others. They also provide an opening for diverse configurations of sovereignty, precisely because of its unresolved complexities. It is this opening which the investigation will then turn to examine within the Greek past, by zeroing in on several episodes to expose the wider, more expansive possibilities of imagining de facto sovereignty, and diverse approaches to it in the ancient world.

One of the most acute cases in point is that of modern Palestine. Following its Declaration of Independence in November 1988, it submitted a request to be so recognised to the UN General Assembly. The summary of the voting is contained in a statement of a few months later as part of *The Request for the Admission of the State of Palestine to UNESCO*: 'On 15 December 1988, the General Assembly adopted, by 138 votes in favour, 2 against and 2 abstentions, resolution 43/177, in the first paragraph of which it "*acknowledges the proclamation of the State of Palestine by the Palestine National Council on 15 November 1988*".'[10] This resolution was a significant achievement, but not enough for Palestine to be able to practice full sovereignty – as it did not receive enough backing from certain states, namely of the group encompassing among others Israel, the United States, Switzerland, Canada,

---

[10] United Nations Resolution of the General Assembly: A/RES/43/177, 15 December 1988: 'Question of Palestine', accessed 10 May 2021, https://unispal.un.org/UNISPAL.NSF/0/146E6838D505833F8 52560D600471E25. Executive Board, 131st, 1989 [69], 12 May 1989: 'Request for the Admission of the State of Palestine to UNESCO as a Member State' (Document code: 131 EX/43 + ADD + CORR. 1 & 2), Section V.2, accessed 10 May 2021, https://unesdoc.unesco.org/ark:/48223/pf0000082711_eng. NB: The total number of countries that had acknowledged the State of Palestine, was in fact 137 in the end, as the attached 'Corrigendum', dated 25 May 1989, states that: 'Austria should be deleted from the list of countries that have recognized the State of Palestine, as set out in Annex II'. Accompanying documents: United Nations General Assembly, Security Council: A/43/827, S/20278, 'Letter Dated 18 November 1988 from the Permanent Representative of Jordan to the United Nations Addressed to the Secretary-General', accessed 10 May 2021, https://unispal.un.org/UNISPAL.NSF/4f35dda09 69b398885256c940075d006/6eb54a389e2da6c6852560de0070e392?OpenDocument. The subject of recognition as concerns the state of Palestine also has a detailed entry on Wikipedia under the title 'International Recognition of the State of Palestine', accessed 10 May 2021, https://en.wikipedia.org/wiki/International_recognition_of_the_State_of_Palestine.

Japan, South Korea, Mexico, Australia, New Zealand, and most of the European Union – none of which had acknowledged the State of Palestine.

Another case of the incongruities of recognition is that of the Aboriginal Tent Embassy in Australia.[11] It relates to the themes addressed in this volume by Cruickshank *et al.* in their powerful discourse on rethinking sovereign practice in terms of lawful relations, by drawing on indigenous knowledge systems. The Tent Embassy was set up in front of the Australian Parliament in Canberra in 1972 as a call for land, rights, and self-determination and as a declaration that the Aboriginal peoples were treated as foreigners in their own country. It was recognised immediately by Aboriginal peoples across Australia, and to this day continues in its mission. Across the front of the embassy is inscribed the word SOVEREIGNTY. It is a demand for recognition and a rejection of the attempt of the Australian government to incorporate the Australian aboriginal polities within the constitution, where due to being subsumed they would not be represented, since the aboriginal people now makes up only 5 per cent of Australia's population. This led to the paradoxical, if not criminal, situation that Australia's High Court considered whether an Indigenous person can be deemed an 'alien' under the Australian Constitution, and therefore can be technically deported.[12] That the High Court had to resort to working within these categories of exile and the outsider shows a failure of the sovereign imagination. It is precisely such failings that Cruickshank *et al.* try to remedy in their study by foregrounding alternative possibilities for expressions of sovereignty and relations between its diverse systems. The case of the Aboriginal Tent Embassy leaves us with the question of how much recognition is enough? Or rather, recognition by whom is enough? Even in a seemingly strictly defined global sovereign-state system, what emerges is a spectrum of sovereignty in relation to states' external facing role and position within international conglomerates. It is a spectrum on which there is acknowledgement of the existence of non-state polities, who have de facto capacity to recognise and be recognised. This sovereignty spectrum also incorporates people who are displaced and stateless, as people in such conditions also affect the balance of power and expose the interdependence of polities. There is a further dimension, although beyond the scope of this chapter, that needs to be recognised in the case of Australian aboriginal polities, as well as that

---

[11] Maldoon & Schaap (2012); Foley *et al.* (2014); Howell & Schaap (2014). The Embassy was recognised as a site of outstanding heritage value, of national significance to all Australians, when it was listed on the Register of the National Estate in its own right in 1995. https://www.environment.gov.au/cgi-bin/ahdb/search.pl?mode=place_detail;search=place_name%3Dtent%2520embassy%3Bkeyword_PD%3D0%3Bkeyword_SS%3D0%3Bkeyword_PH%3D0;place_id=105836 (accessed 10 May 2021).

[12] 'High Court Will Decide if Indigenous People without Citizenship Can Be Deported', NITV News (12 April 2019), accessed 10 May 2021, https://www.sbs.com.au/nitv/article/2019/04/12/high-court-will-decide-if-indigenous-people-without-citizenship-can-be-deported. The case continues: 'Disrespectful and wrong': lawyers slam Coalition's push to restore power to deport Aboriginal non-citizens', *The Guardian* (11 March 2022), accessed 30 March 2022, https://www.theguardian.com/australia-news/2022/mar/12/disrespectful-and-wrong-lawyers-slam-coalitions-push-to-restore-power-to-deport-aboriginal-non-citizens.

of Palestine, in that they have both suffered settler colonialism and dispossession by those who set up the officially recognised sovereign state, within the territory of which they live.

Turning to the ancient world we witness the power of the asylum request that is at the core of such ancient Greek tragedies as Aeschylus' *Suppliant Women* and Euripides' *Children of Herakles*; the plays' actions are contingent on it. These two productions were created a generation apart (circa 463 and 430, respectively), during a crucial period in the making of the Athenian polis. Internally, forces at the time of Pericles in the mid-5th century BCE engendered the experiment of democracy that necessarily required a re-articulation of the responsibilities and obligations that lie between state and citizen, questioning the balance of power and the true place of decision-making. Externally, the looming conflict with Sparta meant Athens was sensitive to intrusions on sovereignty – its own by others and, as itself a growing imperialist, on others – a sentiment that is vividly captured in the Melian dialogue of Thucydides' *History of the Peloponnesian War* (5.84–116), which we will return to later in this chapter.

The potential force of the request for refuge pervades the action of the *Suppliant Women*. The play is the remaining part of Aeschylus' trilogy, which was performed in the 460s BCE but is set in the mythical past of the Bronze Age (*c.* 3000–1000 BCE). It tells the story of 50 Danaids, the daughters of Danaus (brother of a mythical Egyptian king), who have fled Egypt with their father to find refuge in the land of the Argives. Their flight is to escape marriage being forced on them by their suitor cousins, who are in pursuit. As the play opens, we find the women on the shores of a liminal space between the sea and the city, clinging to the altars of a sanctuary. From here they supplicate Pelasgos, king of Argos, to provide them with refuge, thus recognising him as sovereign and on that basis invoking him into action. The king's reply, however, instead of addressing their plea, focuses on the issue of who is being invoked (Aeschylus, *Suppliant Women*, 365–8): 'You are not sitting at the hearth of my house. If the city as a whole is threatened with pollution, it must be the concern of the people as a whole to work out a cure.' Is it the king or the people who have the capacity for sovereign action? Which of them is the host? Who is it that carries the ultimate responsibility for the safety of the suppliants in the eyes of the gods to whom they are sacred? The king's response is greeted with the forceful reply from the women – which we have already encountered (Aeschylus, *Suppliant Women*, 370–2): 'You are the city, I tell you, you are the people! A head of state, not subject to judgement, you control the altar, the hearth of the city.'

As the play progresses, the Danaids are made to realise that their appeal, made from the sanctuary of the public shrines, has positioned them as suppliants not of an individual, King Pelasgos, but of the Argive state – *polis*. The intermediary between them is the god who is invoked as protector and the altar which guarantees this protection. Hence, the request for refuge establishes a relationship between the asylum seeker, the host, and also a higher power with the capacity of holding the host to account. In the context of this tragedy, this ultimate authority is divine will, but it could also be that of ancestral custom or international law. In ancient literature, at least, the possibility of punishment for not addressing suppliant appeals is taken seriously. The threat of pollution, which the king mentions, is a reference to the punishment by the gods if the pleas of the guests and suppliants they protect are ignored, and the potential host's action leads to their harm or death.

Unsympathetic treatment of those who come to seek refuge always has moralistic undertones in ancient literature, with numerous legends of catastrophes, which have their roots in divine retribution for crimes against suppliants (Belfiore 1998: 143–4; Sinn 1993: 71). Natural disasters that affected ancient Sparta, Sybaris, Metapontum, Croton, Aegina, and a number of other *poleis* are traced back to the mistreatment of such groups (Sinn 1993: Appendix III). The earthquake and tidal wave that buried the ancient Achaean city of Helike in 373 BCE were explained as divine anger for the city's crime against the suppliants sheltering in its sanctuary of Poseidon.[13] In Aeschylus' tragedy the decision of the Argive king Pelasgos on whether to help the Danaids took account of the potential anger of Zeus Hikesios, the protector of suppliants, which the king reflects is one of the greatest fears a mortal can have (Aeschylus, *Suppliant Women*, 347, 427–9). The stories may have symbolic power, but they are also examples that such power is not a deterrent to ignoring appeals for refuge. The question then concerning the gods, as with the UN today, is whether the pressure that they exert is based on grounded authority and action which can keep potential hosts to account.

The current policies on refugees and asylum seekers, in such states as the United Kingdom, United States, and Australia, for example, suggest there is little weight to any pressure from such higher powers as the UN. Nevertheless, it is evident that some power remains, paradoxically, in the great pains that states take to follow the letter of the law when it comes to human rights, in the search for legal loopholes to reduce the number of refugees they would have to support. In the ancient world, one of the avoidance tactics was to prevent asylum seekers from reaching the safety of the sanctuary in the first place, for example by prohibiting foreigners' entry into the sacred precincts, where they would be under the protection of the gods (Chaniotis 1996: 73). Today's creative approaches to avoiding responsibility owed to those who seek refuge have led some states to declare their airport arrival areas and other border entry points not part of their territory for purposes of asylum (Carens 2013: 198–200). In relation to what is expected of the sovereign, the protection of the UN differs, at least de facto, from the protection anticipated from the gods. As these examples show, both ancient and modern polities have tried to find loopholes to avoid their responsibilities as hosts. Yet, in the ancient context, it was precisely the positioning of an entity as sovereign that brought with it the duty to acknowledge suppliant requests. The ability to provide the securest refuge is part of Isocrates' praise of Athens' greatness in his *Panegyric* (4.42). Sovereignty was not

---

[13] Pausanias 7.25.1. In addition, the Spartan earthquake is blamed on their ejection of Helots from the Poseidon Sanctuary in 464 BCE: Thucydides 1.128.1.

a reason for a state to relinquish its duty, but seemingly the opposite. As we go on to consider, in Euripides' tragedy, the inability to provide refuge could be used to signal weakness and the result of sovereignty under threat.

Invocation

Decisions about how to respond to suppliants seeking refuge frames a wider discourse on the positioning of sovereign entities within the inter-state system. Suppliant transactions may be considered as one of the earliest forms of foreign relations (Zeitlin 1992: 211), as these challenge the potential host to demonstrate the strength of their sovereignty in practice. The challenge is encapsulated in the tragedy of Euripides, *Children of Herakles*, performed *c.* 430 BCE, which is in part about the community tensions that result from having to make such decisions. These show the pressures on both internal and external sovereignty. Within this mythical story, Argos is positioned as the aggressor with the Argives in pursuit of Herakles' children. The suppliant children with their grandmother Alcmene, under the care of Herakles' friend Iolaus, appeal to Athens and its king, Demophon, from their sanctuary at the altar of Zeus. They seek Athenian protection in their escape from Eurystheus, king of Argos, who demands their return as they are his subjects. The play, therefore, begins with an act of infringement on Athenian sovereignty by the Argives' attempt, through their herald, to force Athens to give up the suppliants. This includes Argives trying to physically remove them from the protection of the sanctuary, claiming they have the right to punish Herakles' children. The Chorus of Old Men, who represent the will of the Athenian people (*demos*), remind the herald of Athens' sovereignty – here expressed as freedom – and the herald's behaviour as interference and a challenge to it (Euripides, *Children of Herakles*, 110–15). In so doing, they defy the Argives' attempt to apply their own laws within Athenian jurisdiction. Athens will not be like other polities who were unable to withstand the challenges to their sovereignty and protect the suppliants, thus giving into the Argive threat (Burnett 1976). The Athenian king Demophon's response to the herald is clear (Euripides, *Children of Herakles*, 284–7): 'Clear off! I am not afraid of your Argos. You were not going to remove these suppliants from Athens and disgrace me. The city that I rule is not Argos' subject but free (ἐλεύθερος)'.[14]

The infringement attempted by the Argives is not specifically of the territorial boundary of the community – as ancient sovereignty was not determined

---

[14] All translations are adapted from Kovacs (1995).

Δημοφῶν
φθείρου· τὸ σὸν γὰρ Ἄργος οὐ δέδοικ' ἐγώ.
ἐνθένδε δ' οὐκ ἔμελλες αἰσχύνας ἐμὲ
ἄξειν βίᾳ τούσδ'· οὐ γὰρ Ἀργείων πόλιν
ὑπήκοον τήνδ' ἀλλ' ἐλευθέραν ἔχω.

by territorial coherence and integrity. It is the sacred protective boundary of a sanctuary that was being threatened. The Athenians would be held responsible for suppliants' wellbeing, not so much because the sanctuary *belongs* to the polis – technically the sanctuary belongs to the gods – but rather because the request was made to the *polis* as host, represented by the king. Despite the threat of war, there is resistance to giving up the suppliants, who would likely be killed by the Argive king Eurystheus. Ultimately, the Athenian decision is to provide refuge, but it was hardly unanimous, and Demophon is left with the possibility of both a civil and an external war (Euripides, *Children of Herakles*, 415–17): 'Now you will see crowded assemblies being held, with some maintaining that it was right to protect strangers who are suppliants, while others accuse me of folly. If I do as I am bidden, civil war will break out.'

The anxiety of the citizens is not rooted in resistance to outsiders, but in the threat of external aggression. Their internal deliberations concern the priority of obligations. What measures is the community expected to take in adhering to: the will of the gods, its fellow citizens, and the suppliants? The Chorus of Old Men, in preparation for the ensuing war with the Argives, reveal the burdens of sovereignty in accepting the challenge of providing protection (Euripides, *Children of Herakles*, 750–70):

> I pray, and raise your shout to heaven, to the throne of Zeus and in the house of grey-eyed Athena! For we are about to cut a path through danger with the sword of grey iron on behalf of our fatherland, on behalf of our homes, since we have taken the suppliants in. But it is cowardly, O my city, if we hand over suppliant strangers at the behest of Argos. Zeus is my ally, I have no fear, Zeus is justly grateful to me: never shall I show the gods to be inferior to men.

In such mytho-historical accounts, the Athenians prided themselves on not giving into external pressure to give up their asylum seekers or deny them shelter. It is an attitude which seems to echo the spirit of today's non-refoulement clause, in Article 33 of the UN's 1951 Geneva Convention on Refugees. However, their emphasis on being protectors of the weak and destitute, as echoed in the play by the Chorus of Old Men, is also – or perhaps primarily – a political claim (Euripides, *Children of Herakles*, 329–32): 'It is always the will of this land (γαῖα) to side with custom/justice and help the weak/those without means. Therefore, she has borne countless toils on behalf of friends, and now too I see another such struggle coming upon us.' The play uses the suppliant request to position Athens in a heroic role, and her decisions on the side of justice, adhering to the will of the gods through a democratic process that reflects the will of the people. It shows itself strong enough to take on the challenges of sovereignty: internally – to make difficult decisions that represent the people's will; and externally – to stand up to pressure of outside interference.

The historical context of the play's performance in the second year of the Peloponnesian War is relevant here. Athens' role is presented as the antithesis to that of its enemy Sparta. It may be a comment on Athens' reassertion of sovereignty in the face of Spartan aggression, where the ability to grant asylum becomes a statement of state power and autonomy. Or, conversely, it may be foreshadowing the appraisal of Athens' treatment of autonomous entities as the war progressed. Thucydides, in his not uncritical account of the war (Morley 2020), exposes the disparity between Athenian adherence to democratic principles in conducting internal affairs and acting akin to a tyrant in external dealings, at times forcing autonomous states into submission. This is captured in Book 5 (84–116) of his *Peloponnesian War*, in his stark dramatisation of the dialogue between the men of Melos, a neutral state, and the Athenians who were poised to destroy it in 416 BCE. In justifying their actions, the Athenians resort to outlining the reality of the power relations of the two states, implicitly acknowledging that autonomy and freedom – de jure sovereignty – are not enough to be allowed to act independently, or be de facto sovereign (Thucydides, *Peloponnesian War*, 5.89): 'You know as well as we know that what is just is arrived at in human arguments only when the necessity on both sides is equal, and that the powerful exact what they can, while the weak yield what they must.'

The Athenians of Thucydides' historical narrative have taken on the role of the tyrannical Argives in the tragedy of Euripides' *Children of Herakles*. It is they, the Athenians, who are in the role of the outsiders, arriving not as suppliants but as the uninvited, imperially sanctioned 'raiders', who demand allegiance and resources. It is their aggression that leads to people fleeing and seeking refuge from others. In light of the historical backdrop against which the play is performed, with Athens' imperialist attitude in its external relations, what is it that Euripides' play is about? Is it a showcasing of Athens' heroism through an assertion of its sovereignty and its legendary hospitality of offering refuge to suppliants despite the danger to themselves? Or is it a critical comment on the irony of Athens' sovereign role in creating the very suppliants it later rejects?

Interdependence

Requests for asylum challenge the host to enact sovereignty in deciding on the response. Yet at the same time they reveal the extent to which polities are interdependent, and hence the limits on independent sovereign action – no polity operates in a vacuum. The nature of interdependence apparent from ancient sources is more encompassing than what is found in inter-state diplomatic negotiations and treaties, and more wide-reaching than Krasner's narrowly defined interdependence, which primarily concerns cross-border movements of goods, capital, people, and ideas. A significant component of ancient requests for asylum was to foreground interconnectivity across time – past, present, and future – not only between similarly constituted polities, but also groups beyond and in-between them, as well as higher powers, represented by the gods or customs and traditions. This is traceable not only in the discourse of narratives such as the Homeric epics and the tragedies, but also in the more historical cases, as that of the failed plea by the Plataeans to the Athenians, which is expounded in Isocrates' 14th speech, *Plataicus*. The Plataean predicament was the result of the Theban takeover of their home in the 370s BCE, which forced the city's population to seek refuge and assistance from Athens for a second time (as they had been in a similar situation 80 years prior). In Isocrates' version of their plea to the Athenian assembly in 373 (Isocrates, *Plataicus*, 14.11–14, 46–8), interconnectivity – their own and that of Athens more broadly – is the core element through which they attempt to position themselves on a more equal footing, despite being displaced and lacking the ability to practice sovereignty in their own right as a polity. The Plataean case in many respects is a model of the way that interdependence across space and time could be used strategically to persuade the potential host to provide protection and refuge, even if in this instance it is not successful.

The Plataeans begin their case with an outline of their interconnected past by pointing to their shared experience of exile; the Athenians too had suffered in their own former wars and had taken shelter among willing hosts (Isocrates, *Plataicus*, 14.50, 57). They appeal to reciprocity, at the base of which is trust. This recalling of a different past is also a reminder that the Plataeans too are free people who are not enslaved, and who carry citizenship, even one that is not currently effective. In this way, it becomes an anticipation into a different future, beyond their current predicament. The Plataean case furthermore employs claims of kinship, reminding the Athenians of their joint family ties through intermarriage (Isocrates, *Plataicus*, 14.51–2). These date back to the preceding century (Thucydides, *Peloponnesian War*, 2.2; 2.71; 3.20), when Athens had taken in Plataean refugees who had escaped the previous takeover of their city by Thebes in 428/427 BCE (Isocrates, *Plataicus*, 14.51–2, trans. Norlin 1980):

> For indeed we are not aliens to you; on the contrary, all of us are akin to you in our loyalty and most of us in blood also; for by the right of intermarriage granted to us we are born of mothers who were of your city. You cannot, therefore, be indifferent to the pleas we have come to make.

The recourse to kinship, which also pervades the mythical narratives, is one of the most robust claims that can be made, as it infers an ancestral right to hospitality. In Aeschylus' *Suppliant Women*, the Danaids, as part of their request for refuge, appeal to their descent from Io, a priestess of Hera who originated from Argos but was eventually driven to Egypt. Such kinship claims are part of the diplomatic tool-kit used throughout the centuries, and embedded in the discourse of the right of return, which requires a separate investigation that is beyond our present scope.[15] The Plataeans also appeal to another key criteria for claiming asylum, based on past and potential future services provided by those seeking refuge. The Plataeans,

---

[15] For the way in which right of return is operationalised in the case of the ancient world: Ma (2004); Luraghi (2008); Isayev (2021). For a more contemporary discourse on return: Black & Koser (1999); Ramadan (2013); Hilal & Petti (2018: esp. 44–5, 141–2).

drawing on their former alliances and loyalty to the Athenians, indicate that they would continue to support them in any forthcoming military ventures. It was they, after all, who had fought alongside Athens against the Persians at Marathon in the 5th century BCE (Isocrates, *Plataicus*, 14.45–7, 57). They remind the Athenians that the precious sovereignty which they now possess is in part thanks to the people who are currently requesting them to enact it, and by its prerogative give them refuge. The reminders of historic service, and hence potential future joint action, turn into a warning that the Athenian response to their plea will affect the balance of international diplomatic relations and alliances (Isocrates, *Plataicus*, 14.11–18). If Athens should not meet their request, it risks losing allies to Sparta.

Underpinning the case made by the Plataeans – which is expressed primarily through past, present, and future diplomatic relations – is also the notion of reciprocity. It has its roots in the pre-state ancient society that depended on such exchanges of guest-friendship tied into networks of obligation that were overseen by the gods.[16] A system based on the anticipation of reciprocal hospitality underpinned any decision and action of whether to allow the stranger in and provide hospitality or asylum. That anticipation may be described as the Law that there is an expectation to adhere to, which goes beyond international relations that form part of Krasner's definition of interdependence. It is not about direct or perfect reciprocity, but rather trust – a negotiation of social relationships – along the lines that Smith (2020: 164–5) articulates in his discourse on Mauss' (2016 [1923–4]) *The Gift*. The Law encapsulates the way sovereign entities are co-located within a meshwork of interdependence. Something of this seems to have been lost in the world of 21st-century states. Those from the 'Global North' may not consider that their citizens would need to appeal to states in the 'Global South' for asylum. But such an attitude requires a kind of amnesia. It was not so long ago that Europeans were fleeing the ravages of the Second World War in their millions, and some, such as the parents of the theatre director Stefan Kaegi, found refuge in Morocco; others relied on the Middle East Relief and Refugee Administration (MERRA), established by the British in 1942, which placed around 40,000 Europeans in camps set up in Syria, Egypt, and Palestine.[17] These actions bring into view other

---

[16] For hospitality – *Xenia* – as part of ancient discourse on the measure of society, see Isayev (2018).

[17] The remembering of this episode has been coming to the surface and public consciousness in the last few years; see for example articles and summaries on the following diverse media sites (all accessed 22 April 2019):
- *The National*, 17 August 2016, 'When a Refugee Fled in the Other Direction', by Rym Ghazal: https://www.thenational.ae/world/when-a-refugee-fled-in-the-other-direction-1.138760.
- *Public Radio International (PRI)*, 26 April 2016, 'During WWII, European Refugees Fled to Syria: Here's what the Camps were Like', by Evan Taparata and Kuang Keng Kuek Ser: https://www.pri.org/stories/2016-04-26/what-it-s-inside-refugee-camp-europeans-who-fled-syria-egypt-and-palestine-during
- *Anadolou Agency*, 11 January 2019, 'Syria Hosted European Refugees during World War II: Civilians from Europe and the Balkans Sought Refuge in Middle East to Escape Nazi and Soviet Occupation', by Selen Temizer and Sena Guler: https://www.aa.com.tr/en/europe/syria-hosted-european-refugees-during-world-war-ii/1362254.

complexities around sovereignty and colonialism – by the machinations of which these refugees were dispersed to what were then British protectorates, a topic that requires its own investigation, beyond our current scope.

Reciprocity can encompass sovereignty and interdependence and need not only be attributable to ancient world contexts. Rather, it reveals the potential for expansive ways of understanding sovereign actions that exist beyond, and in spite of, territorially defined sovereign entities. The following 21st-century example of the Acehnese fishermen reflects the possibilities of moving beyond the narrow definitions of understanding sovereignty. The story of a small Acehnese fishing community in Indonesia (Aceh), which rescued the Rohingya who were stranded in the Andaman Sea, is detailed in a study by McNevin and Missbach (2018). This community chose to act despite the deliberate inaction by the national and international community, and despite the threats from their own state authorities should they respond to Rohingyan appeals. In their reflections on what drove their actions, the fishermen drew on the culture of rescue prescribed by customary maritime law (*hukum adat laot*). Breaching that code of conduct would place all seafarers at risk, including the fishermen themselves. They could imagine themselves in scenarios where they could shift from rescuer to rescued, which informed their sense of obligation to rescue and provide refuge. It sprang from moral codes and bonds of solidarity, the Law of the Sea, that for them superseded what state-law might technically demand or minimally require: 'The rescue of the Rohingya by Acehnese fishermen stands in stark contrast to the non-entrée strategies increasingly deployed by states that are signatories to the 1951 International Refugee Convention and its 1967 Protocol' (McNevin and Missbach 2018: 303). The action of the fishermen was sovereign: the request came to them – and they had a duty to act in that capacity. This they were able to do, at least in the short term, prompting a national and international response to provide further aid to the Rohingyan refugees.

Interference

Individuals who are out of place of rights and protection – asylum seekers, refugees, exiles, and even those who manage to gain some form of reprieve through temporary or partial forms of hospitality, protection, and settledness – are distinctly more vulnerable than those who carry fully functioning forms of state membership or other equivalent status. This means that people in such conditions of displacement can be more easily moved or used for political ends or weaponised in inter-state relations and power struggles. In the ancient period we are concerned with, an individual's condition of displacement could become instrumentalised through actions such as the directive for states to recall their exiles, such as that issued by Alexander the Great in 324 BCE, which we consider below. Such episodes demonstrate forms of infringement and threat that can be carried through non-militarised bodies and actions, to challenge or constrain the sovereign practices of some entities, while extending or securing the influence and jurisdiction of others.

Exiles in particular, whether as groups or individuals, appear prominently in our sources from the late 5th and especially the 4th centuries BCE, throughout the Mediterranean region. They are the protagonists in oratorical and forensic treatises, and the focus of decrees; their names along with those of their exilic hosts are inscribed on honourary stelae.[18] We know of the predicament and precarity of their lives through detailed exegesis in philosophical and other writings, especially those focusing on prominent exiles, such as the mercenary general and writer Xenophon and Diogenes the Cynic. Emerging from this rich record are clear signals that although exiles are not always able to achieve a return, or full status elsewhere, still there are possibilities for subverting their condition to move towards their own goals and ambitions (Isayev 2021). Some exiles, precisely because of their circumstances of banishment – resulting from challenges to governing authorities or incoming usurpers – are treated as-if allies by rival polities. In the midst of the shifting power struggles between Athens, Sparta, and Thebes in the 4th century BCE, orators tell of how Athens supported the Theban exiles who had helped to recapture Thebes from the Spartan hold (Dinarchus, *Against Demosthenes*, 1.37–9; Lysias, *On Behalf of Pherenicus over the Estate of Androclides* [fr. 286] = Dionysius of Halicarnassus 6 [Fr. 3.a]). In this case in particular, which would have involved elite exiles with some authority, we need to envisage them bargaining around mutual interests with their Athenian hosts, resulting in a sort of 'alliance' that served both ends. Even underlying the deployment of exiles in the way Alexander the Great strove to do through his directives, we need to imagine wide-ranging negotiations that, although between unequal partners, would have integrated the interests of those in exile.

Enforced restoration of exiles was an exhibition of power through overt interference in state sovereignty. The mechanics of its execution we can glimpse from inscriptions, which record the responsibilities of states for reintegrating the recalled exiles. These inscriptions prescribe the necessary steps for the restoration of property and legislation to ensure a peaceful return.[19] In their detailed outline there is an underlying expectation of tension that such situations engender, especially when the initial act of exile was the result of clashes between political factions that culminated in *stasis* (στάσις) – akin to a civil-war scenario – which was relieved through expulsion (Gray 2015). The following excerpts are from a decree of 324/ 323 BCE, concerning the restoration of exiles to Tegea. It survives as a copy on an inscription from the sanctuary at Delphi (*GHI* 101), which was presumably

---

[18] A substantial collection is included in *IG* XII, 6.1.17–41. They are also discussed in detail by Engen (2010), Gray (2015), and Rubinstein (2018). I am very grateful to Darel Engen for sending me parts of his book while all the libraries were closed.

[19] See, for example, the restoration of exiles in the second half of the 4th century BCE: to Chios – *GHI* 84; to Mytilene – *GHI* 85; and to Tegea – *GHI* 101.

deposited there as a guarantee of rights granted to the returnees, and to ensure the decree's enforcement by Tegean authorities:[20]

[Lines 1–3]:

– – – With reference to the things about which the city sent the envoys and King Alexander sent back his judgement to us, the transcript [*diagramma*] shall be written according to the corrections made by the city of what was spoken against in the transcript.

[Lines 4–6]

The exiles who are returning shall recover their paternal possessions from which they went into exile, or their maternal possessions, i.e. in cases when women were not remarried and held their property and did not possess brothers ...

[Lines 9–11]

With reference to the houses, each [*sc.* returned exile] shall have one in accordance with the transcript. If a house has a garden adjacent to it, let him not take another ...

[Lines 18–20]

The city shall discharge the money [for the compensation](?), and shall not exempt from taxation (?) either the exiles or those previously living at home as citizens ...

[Lines 24–36]

The foreign court shall give judgment for sixty days. As many as are not adjudicated in the sixty days, it shall not be possible for them to go to law in the foreign court with reference to property, but always in the city's court. ... If any return later, when the foreign court is no longer in existence, let him register the property with the *strategoi* in sixty days, and if there is any defence against him the court shall be Mantinea; and, if it is not adjudicated in these days, it shall no longer be possible for him to go to law ...

[Lines 57–60]

I swear by Zeus, Athena, Apollo, Poseidon, that I shall show good will to those who have returned whom the city resolved to receive back, and I shall not harbour grudges against any of them for what he may have plotted (?) from the day on which I have sworn the oath, nor shall I hinder the safety of those who have returned, neither in the – – – nor in the community of the city ...

This inscription preserves one of the texts linked to Alexander's directive of 324 BCE for the restoration of exiles, shortly before his death. According to the later historian Diodorus Siculus (17.109.1; 18.8.4–5), it was announced at the Olympic Games, where some 20,000 exiles had gathered for the festival. Alexander's message, which was to have been conveyed by the herald, reads as follows:[21]

King Alexander to the exiles from the Greek cities. We have not been the cause of your exile, but, save for those of you who are under a curse, we shall be the cause of your return to your own native cities. We have written to Antipater about this to the end that if any cities are not willing to restore you, he may constrain them.

[20] For the text and discussion, with preceding bibliography, see *GHI* 101 (pp. 526–33).
[21] Diodorus Siculus: 18.8.4. All translations from Geer (1947).

Diodorus goes on to describe the jubilant response by the exiles and the anger with which this proclamation was met by some, such as the Aetolians and the Athenians, who were at the sharp end of the decree. It was not long before the king's will was implemented, as we can see from the preceding text, which was inscribed soon after the announcement, either in the same year or in the following one. Alexander's presence pervades the text, highlighting his direct interest in the cases of individual states, and expectation that decisions would be deferred to him if any changes were necessary. They also position him as the patron acting in the interests of the exiles to be restored. That he became widely known for such positioning may be exemplified through the fact that knowledge of it was widespread enough for it to be subverted. In a famous legendary encounter between Diogenes the Cynic of Sinope and Alexander, who standing in front of the exiled philosopher, casting his shadow, is said to have asked whether there was anything he could do – Diogenes allegedly replied that he 'can move out of his light' (Diogenes Laertius 6.38 = *TGF* 88.F.4). Whether there is any truth to this apocryphal story or not, it is unlikely that Alexander's acts arose out of concern for the exiles' condition, but as a way for him to secure further fame and power. By reinstalling exiles into their home communities, Alexander could ensure a committed and widely distributed support base, which in its loyalty would monitor any resistance to his power. As Diodorus reports: 'Alexander decided to restore all the exiles in the Greek cities, partly for the sake of gaining fame, and partly wishing to secure many devoted personal followers in each city to counter the revolutionary movements and seditions of the Greeks' (18.8.1–2). It was a way of constraining individual states' sovereignty, not only by interfering in the inner workings of internal civic practices, but through an implicit submission to his overarching power beyond that wielded by any single polity, which furthermore affected their external inter-state relations.

That the enforced restoration of exiles was a widespread tool for exerting power is evident from counter clauses in decrees explicitly stating that the communities would *not* be subject to such restorations without their consent.[22] One example is the decree issued by Athens (*GHI* 18; *c.* 387/6 BCE) in relation to Clazomenae, off the coast of Asia Minor, which was won for Athens by Thrasybulus in his Aegean campaigns of 390 BCE (Xenophophon, *Hellenica*, 4.8.25–30). Part of the generous terms of the decree include a statement concerning exiles (*GHI* 18):

[Lines 10–12]

... it shall not be permitted to the people of Athens either to restore the exiles without the consent of the people of Clazomenae or to remove any of those who have remained.

These may be read as moments of reinstitution, or recognition and reaffirmation of the sovereignty of one state by another – or at least some elements of it – between what are clearly unequal partners.

---

[22] See for example *GHI* 17 – concerning Erythrae; and *GHI* 18 – concerning Clazomenae. Prevention of restoration of exiles, causing them distress, is noted by Aeschines, *On the Embassy*, 2.142–8.

Whether the exiles had an option of whether to return or not is harder to ascertain. Most of the surviving evidence suggests they would have been happy for the restoration, as in the writings of such exiles as Xenophon, who painfully charts the loss and striving for a return to his Athenian home in the *Anabasis*. We also have remains of stelae set up by returnees to honour their hosts during their time of exile. A prominent selection of these survive from the Heraion of Samos, which point to the multiplicity of destinations where exiles were hosted during 4th-century BCE conflicts.[23] The following Samian honorary decree for Batichos of Kos (*IG* XII, 6.1.18), dating to circa 320 BCE, is a typical example from this group, which outlines the honours to be given and reveals the ties and networks that such reciprocity engendered. It also charts how private or individual acts of hospitality and protection intertwine with state-sponsored acts and honours, which affect status and inter-community relations:[24]

1. (document) of Batichos from Kos.
2. Decision of the council and the people,
3. Pamphilos S. d. Critodemos applied: Since
4. Batichos S. d. Sonikos from Kos was useful in his time in exile
5. and benevolent at all times to the
6. Samian people and privately helped petitioners
7. always in a loyal manner; and now
8. announces that he will effect good (also in the future), as far as it is in
9. his power, for the Samian people, so will
10. Council and people decide: to give praise to
11. Batichos S. d. Sonikos for the benevolence and commitment,
12. which he always has for the Samians;
13. and that he should be a Proxenus and a Benefactor
14. of the Samian people; that should be due to him
15. also free entry and exit in peace and
16. in war, undisturbed and without a contract, as well
17. as access to the council and the people about whatever
18. he covets, equally after what concerns religion and king;
19. that one also give him the citizenship with full
20. equality in rights, him and his descendants,
21. and assign him by lot in (the) phyle and
22. thousands and hundreds and genos
23. and add him to the genos,
24. whom he chose by lot, as well as other citizens;
25. that care should be taken for the entry
26. by the (commission) elected for the census.

More difficult to track are the conditions of exiles who did not necessarily want to return but preferred to continue living elsewhere, even if that meant not having full

---

[23] See in particular the set of inscriptions from the Samos Heraion honouring those who helped their citizens while in exile: *IG* XII, 6.1.17–41. Some of the sites where the honourands were from, and where it seems the exiles were helped, include Iasus, Kardia, Elis, Cyrene and Miletus, among others.
[24] *IG* XII, 6.1.18. English translation with the help of Staffan Müller-Wille, adapted from the German translation of Klaus Hallof (editor of *IG* XII).

citizenship status, such as that of a *metic*. Safety, among other motivations, would have been a major concern. Reading through the directives for returnees, as in the treatises noted above, it is evident they were designed to reduce any enduring hostilities between those who stayed and those who left. If a volatile seditious environment continued, it may have been safer not to go back. That individuals, even those trapped in conflict situations abroad, may have chosen to go elsewhere other than their 'home' can be gleaned from an episode during the campaigns of Lysander, the Spartan general whose successes brought victory over Athens during the Peloponnesian War in the late 5th century BCE. The episode that is of particular interest for our purposes is the one noted by Xenophon in his *Hellenica* (2.2.1). He describes how as part of Lysander's military operations against Byzantium and Calchedon, instead of just driving out the Athenian garrison there, 'every other Athenian whom he saw anywhere, Lysander sent home to Athens, giving them safe conduct if they sailed to that one place and not if they went to any other; for he knew that the more people were collected in the city and Piraeus, the more quickly there would be a scarcity of provisions'.[25] It is unclear what the position of these 'other' Athenians was, and there is no indication that they were exiled or displaced, but they were mobile. Lysander was able to instrumentalise their volatile and untethered condition to harm Sparta's enemy directly, not just through their expulsion but by directing their movements towards Athens so as to undermine her power base through depletion of resources.

These few examples of deploying those who are exiled to undermine the practices of sovereignty by independent states expose the politicisation and weaponisation of the forcibly displaced. The cases also signal that people in such volatile conditions are not mere instruments but can potentially form part of negotiations that help to affect their own ambitions from within the exiled state. Using individuals in conditions of displacement to test or unbalance power is a practice that continues well into the present day. In the spring of 2021, this was visible through such actions as the state-induced push-backs of refuge seekers between Turkey and Greece in the states' ongoing Mediterranean contestations over sea borders and resources, or the positioning of asylum grants as an infringement and disrespect of sovereignty, as has flared up between China and the UK.[26] Notable in these two situations is that in the former there is no mention of the names of the people who are pushed back – they are presented as boat-loads tossed across the sea. The latter is focused on a single prominent individual – Nathan Law – whose back story in politics and activism, which necessitated his flight from Hong Kong, is well known. While it is beyond the scope of this investigation, it

---

[25] Xenophon, *Hellenica* 2.2.1. Translation from Brownson (1918–21).

[26] See, for example, on Greek–Turkish push-backs, Michael Varaklas, 'Greece Accuses Turkey of Trying to Provoke it with Migrant Boats', *Al Jazeera* (3 April 2021), accessed 10 April 2021, https://www.aljazeera.com/news/2021/4/3/greece-accuses-turkey-of-trying-to-provoke-it-with-migrant-boats; on UK granting of asylum to Nathan Law, see Helen Davidson, 'China Blasts UK for Granting Asylum to Hong Kong Activist Nathan Law', *The Guardian* (9 April 2021), accessed 10 April 2021, https://www.theguardian.com/world/2021/apr/09/china-blasts-uk-asylum-hong-kong-nathan-law.

is worth recognising that in sovereignty discourse and negotiations those who are nameless in displacement and those who are named have a different role, which in turn affects the prospects for their return to a state of protection, settledness, and rights.

Conclusion

The aim of this investigation has been to showcase the ways in which individuals who are displaced form part of sovereignty discourse – ancient and modern – by focusing on those elements of sovereign practice that concern recognition, invocation, interdependence, and interference. A select number of cases have been used to highlight how in the presence and engagement of seekers of refuge and exiles there is agency and potential to affect the sovereign positioning of hosts and their external relations. These cases have also served to expose how authorities, whether in the form of states or kings, use people who are displaced to buttress and showcase their capacity for sovereign action, as well as constraining that of others. They also bring into view the relation of all parties to higher powers – the gods, ancestral customs, or supra-state directives and organisations such as the UN – which serve as intermediaries and guarantors. Whether such entities and protocols are able in the end to hold polities to account, for example in honouring their duty to provide refuge and protection, has only been touched on here, and remains to be fully explored. The way in which such higher powers, as that of Alexander, are seen to infringe on or bolster sovereign action is another subject that needs attention. Looking at such practices of sovereignty from a period in which the term itself did not exist, and where key elements of sovereignty today – such as territorial integrity – did not have the same relevance, allows for diverse configurations of sovereignty to emerge. It gives presence to those whose sovereign practices – even if they are transient – are not recognised as such, whether it is local actors, such as the Acehnese fishermen, or people who have been forcibly displaced. Through their actions they expose the permeability and volatility of the sovereign position, as well as expansive forms of its understanding. In so doing they question whether sovereign practice is only in the remit of the state. A different approach to the subject may have been to ask how the meaning of sovereignty changes if perceived from within displacement and its sites, and thus to probe the potential for sovereign practice from within the protracted condition of permanent temporariness (Hilal & Petti 2018). Such a condition can no longer be considered a state of exception, but rather part of the experience of numerous individuals and communities, including some who technically have citizenship, but are not treated with equal rights. Along with finding alternative modes of sovereignty these actors also make and unmake the sovereign from the systemic edge.[27]

---

[27] Sassen (2014: 211) uses 'systemic edge' to articulate the way 'the extreme character of conditions at the edge makes visible larger trends that are less extreme and hence more difficult to capture'. For context and further discussion in relation ancient wandering and permanent temporariness, see Isayev (2021).

References

Arendt, H. (1943), 'We Refugees', *Menorah Journal*, 31: 69–77.
Arendt, H. (1968 [1951]), *The Origins of Totalitarianism* (New York, Harcourt).
Bakewell, G.W. (2013), *Aeschylus's Suppliant Women: The Tragedy of Immigration* (Madison, University of Wisconsin Press).
Belfiore, E. (1998), 'Harming Friends: Problematic Reciprocity in Greek Tragedy', in C. Gill, N. Postlethwaite, & R. Seaford (eds), *Reciprocity in Ancient Greece* (Oxford, Clarendon Press), 139–58.
Benhabib, S. (2004), *The Rights of Others: Aliens, Residents, and Citizens* (Cambridge, Cambridge University Press).
Berlin, I. (1958), 'Two Concepts of Liberty', in H. Hardy (ed.), *Liberty* (Oxford, Oxford University Press, 2002), 166–217.
Betts, A. & Collier, P. (2017), *Refuge: Transforming a Broken Refugee System* (London, Allen Lane, Penguin Random House).
Black, R. & Koser, K. (eds) (1999), *The End of the Refugee Cycle? Refugee Repatriation and Reconstruction* (Oxford, Berghahn).
Brownson, C.L. (trans.) (1918–21), *Xenophon in Seven Volumes, vols 1 and 2* (Cambridge MA, Harvard University Press).
Burnett, A. (1976), 'Tribe and City, Custom and Decree in *Children of Heracles*', *Classical Philology*, 71.1: 4–26.
Carens, J.H. (2013), *The Ethics of Immigration* (New York, Oxford University Press).
Cartledge, P. & Matt, E. (2009), '"Rights", Individuals, and Communities in Ancient Greece', in R.K. Balot (ed.), *A Companion to Greek and Roman Political Thought* (Malden MA, Wiley-Blackwell), 149–63.
Chaniotis, A. (1996), 'Conflicting Authorities: *Asylia* between Secular and Divine Law in the Classical and Hellenistic Poleis', *Kernos*, 1: 65–86.
Chetail, V. (2016), 'Sovereignty and Migration in the Doctrine of the Law of Nations: An Intellectual History of Hospitality from Vitoria to Vattel', *The European Journal of International Law*, 27.4: 901–22.
Engen, D.T. (2010), *Honor and Profit: Athenian Trade Policy and the Economy and Society of Greece, 415–307 BCE* (Ann Arbor, University of Michigan Press).
Eslava, L. & Pahuja, S. (2020), 'The State and International Law: A Reading from the Global South', *Humanity: An International Journal of Human Rights, Humanitarianism & Development*, 11.1: 118–38.
Foley, G., Howell, E., & Schaap, A. (eds) (2014), *The Aboriginal Tent Embassy: Sovereignty, Black Power, Land Rights and the State* (London, Routledge).
Geer, R.M. (trans.) (1947), Diodorus Siculus's *Library of History, Volume IX: Books 18–19.65* (Cambridge MA, Harvard University Press).
GHI – Rhodes, P.J. & Osborne, R. (eds) (2007), *Greek Historical Inscriptions 404–323 BC* (Oxford, Oxford University Press).
Gray, B. (2015), *Stasis and Stability: Exile, the Polis, and Political Thought, c. 404–146 BC* (Oxford, Oxford University Press).
Gray, B. (2018), 'Citizenship as Barrier and Opportunity for Ancient Greek and Modern Refugees', in E. Isayev & E. Jewell (eds), *Displacement and the Humanities*, special edition of *Humanities*, 7.3: 72.
Gundogdu, A. (2015), *Rightlessness in an Age of Rights* (Oxford, Oxford University Press).
Haddad, E. (2003), 'The Refugee: The Individual between Sovereigns', *Global Society*, 17.3: 297–322.

Heuser, B. (1997), 'Sovereignty, Self-Determination and Security: New World Orders in the 20th Century', in S. Hashmi (ed.), *State Sovereignty: Change and Persistence in International Relations* (Philadelphia, Pennsylvania University Press), 81–104.

Hilal, S. & Petti, A. (2018), *Permanent Temporariness* (Stockholm, Art and Theory Publishing).

Howell, E. & Schaap, A. (2014), 'The Aboriginal Tent Embassy and Australian Citizenship', in E.F. Isin & P. Nyers (eds), *Routledge Handbook of Global Citizenship Studies* (New York & London, Routledge), 569–80.

IG XII.6 – *Inscriptiones Graecae: Inscriptiones Chii et Sami cum Corassiis Icariaque*, eds K. Haloff & A.P. Mattahiou (Berlin & New York, Berlin-Brandenburgische Akademie der Wissenschaften, 2000).

Isayev, E. (2017a), *Migration, Mobility and Place in Ancient Italy* (Cambridge, Cambridge University Press).

Isayev, E. (2017b), 'Between Hospitality and Asylum: A Historical Perspective on Agency', *International Review of the Red Cross, Migration and Displacement*, 99.904: 1–24.

Isayev, E. (2018), 'Hospitality: A Timeless Measure of Who We Are?', in M. Berg & E. Fiddian Qasmiyeh (eds), *Hospitality and Hostility Towards Migrants: Global Perspectives*, special issue of *Migration & Society: Advances in Research*, 1: 7–21.

Isayev, E. (2021), 'Ancient Wandering and Permanent Temporariness', in E. Isayev & E. Jewell (eds), *Displacement and the Humanities*, special issue of *Humanities*, 10: 91–124.

Kasimis, D. (2018), *The Perpetual Immigrant and the Limits of Athenian Democracy* (Cambridge, Cambridge University Press).

Kennedy, R.F. (2014), *Immigrant Women in Athens: Gender, Ethnicity, and Citizenship in the Classical City* (New York, Routledge).

Kovacs, D. (ed. & trans.) (1995), Euripides's *Children of Heracles. Hippolytus. Andromache. Hecuba* (Cambridge MA, Harvard University Press).

Krasner, S.D. (1999), *Sovereignty: Organized Hypocrisy* (Princeton, Princeton University Press).

Krasner, S.D. (2001), *Problematic Sovereignty: Contested Rules and Political Possibilities* (New York, Columbia University Press).

Luoma-aho, M. (2004), 'Carl Schmitt and the Transformation of the Political Subject', *The European Legacy*, 5.5: 703–16.

Luraghi, N. (2008), *The Ancient Messenians: Constructions of Ethnicity and Memory* (Cambridge, Cambridge University Press).

Ma, J. (2004), 'You Can't Go Home Again: Displacement and Identity in Xenophon's Anabasis', in R. Lane Fox (ed.), *The Long March: Xenophon and the Ten Thousand* (New Haven & London, Yale University Press), 330–45.

Macklem, P. (2015), *The Sovereignty of Human Rights* (New York, Oxford University Press).

McNevin, A. & Missbach, A. (2018), 'Hospitality as a Horizon of Aspiration (or, What the International Refugee Regime Can Learn from Acehnese Fishermen)', *Journal of Refugee Studies*, 31.3: 292–313.

Maldoon, P. & Schaap, A. (2012), 'Aboriginal Sovereignty and the Politics of Reconciliation: The Constituent Power of the Aboriginal Embassy in Australia', *Environment and Planning D: Society and Space*, 30: 534–50.

Mauss, M. (2016 [1923–4]), *The Gift: Expanded Edition*, selected, annotated and translated by Jane I. Guyer (Chicago, Chicago University Press).

Miller, W. (trans.) (1928), Cicero's *De Officiis* (Cambridge MA: Harvard University Press).

Morley, N.D.G. (2020), *Thucydides and the Idea of History* (London, I.B. Tauris).

Norlin, G. (trans.) (1980), *Isocrates* (Cambridge MA, Harvard University Press).

Pufendorf, S. von (1749 [1672]), *The Law of Nature and Nations or a General System of the Most Important Principles of Morality, Jurisprudence and Politics*, trans. Basil Kennet (London: J. and J. Bonwicke *et al.*).

Ramadan, A. (2013), 'Spatialising the Refugee Camp', *Transactions of the Institute of British Geographers*, 38.1: 65–77.

Rubinstein, L. (2018), 'Immigration and Refugee Crises in Fourth-Century Greece: An Athenian Perspective', *The European Legacy*, 23: 5–24.

Sassen, S. (2014), *Expulsions: Brutality and Complexity in the Global Economy* (Cambridge MA, Harvard University Press).

Sinn, U. (1993), 'Greek Sanctuaries as Places of Refuge', in N. Marinatos & R. Hagg (eds), *Greek Sanctuaries: New Approaches* (London, Routledge), 67–84.

Smith, C. (2020), 'The Gift of Sovereignty: Kings from Mauss to Sahlins and Graeber', *Politica Antica. Rivista di prassi e cultura politica nel mondo greco e romano*, 10: 157–77.

Sommerstein, A.H. (trans.) (2009), Aeschylus's *Suppliant Women* (Cambridge MA: Harvard University Press).

Sosin, J. (2016), 'A Metic was a Metic', *Historia: Zeitschrift für Alte Geschichte*, 65.1: 2–13.

TGF – Snell, B., Kannicht, R., & Radt, S. (eds) (1971–85), *Tragicorum Graecorum Fragmenta*, 4 vols (Göttingen, Vandenhoeck & Ruprecht).

Wallerstein, I. (2004), *World-Systems Analysis: An Introduction* (Durham NC & London, Duke University Press).

Wolff, Christian C. von (1934 [1749]). *Jus Gentium Methodo Scientifica Pertractatum*, trans. J.H. Drake, 2 vols (New York, Oceana).

Zeitlin, F. (1992), 'The Politics of Eros in the Danaid Trilogy of Aeschylus', in R. Hexter & D. Seldon (eds), *Innovations of Antiquity* (London, Routledge), 203–52.

14

'The Definite Is the Shadow and not the Owner': Hannah Arendt in the Shadows of Sovereignty

LYNDSEY STONEBRIDGE[*]

Introduction

> Necessarily, the camp is the border.
>   We wait before the place never to claim the seen but to count the eyes of which we dream.
>   Come to the camp to remember what will never come.
>   The definite is the shadow and not the owner.
>   Those feet are the creator of time.
>   'Necessarily, the Camp is the Border', Yousif M. Qasmiyeh[1]

REFUGEE, 'ILLEGAL EMIGRANT' (her words), and stateless person: perhaps few mid-century European thinkers were as well placed to understand sovereignty's failures as Hannah Arendt.[2] The chaotic decline of the European nation-state, in her now famous account, had exposed the lethal frailty of Westphalian conceptions of

---

[*] This chapter derives from my collaboration with Yousif M. Qasmiyeh as part of the AHRC/ESRC-funded project, Refugee Hosts, https://refugeehosts.org (AH/P005438/1), led by Elena Fiddian-Qasmiyeh. I'm indebted to Yousif's thoughtfulness, creativity, and generosity. I presented earlier versions at 'We Refugees: 75 Years Later', *Leibniz-Zentrum für Literatur-und Kulturforschung*, Berlin, March 2018; 'Archives of Resistance', Leeds, UK, June 2018; the IHR Intellectual History Seminar, London, January 2018; the Cambridge Seminar in Contemporary Political Thought, February 2018; the 'We the People' workshop, Durham, UK, March 2019; and 'Sovereignty: A Global Perspective', University of St Andrews, April 2019. Thanks for these invitations, and for generous interventions, readings, and conversations are due to: Duncan Bell, Homi K. Bhabha, Hannah Dawson, Daniel Hartley, Humeira Iqtidar, Henry Jones, Thomas Keenan, Itamar Mann, Mezna Qato, Michael Rothberg, Leila Sansour, Christopher Smith, and Sigrid Weigel.
[1] Yousif M. Qasmiyeh, 'Necessarily, the Camp is the Border,'in Qasmiyeh (2021): 83-85.
[2] Arendt described herself as an 'illegal emigrant' in an interview with Günter Gaus in 1964. See Hannah Arendt, 'Zur Person': https://www.youtube.com/watch?v=dsoImQfVsO4 (accessed 25 September

sovereignty. Nor did she believe that post-war global forms of interrelated sovereign power promised much better. Sovereignty was a political trap, Arendt argued, to be resisted and out-thought. Her alternative was a political plurality sustained by action – action that was always beginning, and so also always the first step towards another politics: 'as in the Greek word *archein*, "to begin", "to lead", and eventually "to rule"', she wrote in *The Human Condition* (1958).[3]

In search of these new political beginnings, she raided the archives of dispossession, exile, and innovation, and looked to Greece, Rome, and the forgotten radicalism of the American Revolution. Where she did not look, at least not after the question of Palestine 'marked a point of crystallization' for her politics in the 1940s, was to the ongoing histories and narratives of statelessness and political struggle that continued after the Second World War, in Palestine, Lebanon, Jordan, and elsewhere, even as many of her concerns with 'pre-political' terms for co-living – co-suffering, givenness, love, compassion – continued to bear traces of refugee history, and of a life lived in the shadows of sovereign power.[4]

In this chapter I suggest that Arendt's critique of sovereignty can, at least in part, be situated in the modern refugee history that she herself lived and chronicled so eloquently. That history, as she argued, was never just about mass displacement, wretchedness, and bare life. It was the story of how the modern nation-state was crippled and finally, if temporarily, undone by nationalism, racism, imperialism, and a deathly bureaucratic colonialism that boomeranged back to Europe in the 20th century. It was out of the ruins of her own moment that Arendt sought to think politics anew. What became plurality in her thinking, I suggest, also began as a question of survival for a historically new kind of people – the 'we' of her famous essay, 'We Refugees', a people who both exist beyond sovereign protection and are utterly subject to sovereign rule.

A refugee politics was not the direction of travel that Arendt, or anybody else for that matter, wanted to take in the late 20th century. And for good reason: the lesson she took from her experience of statelessness was that all peoples must have the right to have their say, to live, appear, speak, and determine their lives together in a bounded space made possible by politics. What political form that space could take was up for debate, but Arendt was in no doubt that a people deprived of a homeland could never be free, even as she pushed against conventional understandings

---

2021). Arendt's repudiation of sovereignty as an attack on plurality was constant and implacable: in particular, her discussion of Rousseau in *On Revolution* (1963: 68–9). See also see Dana Villa's (1995: 82–6) excellent reading of non-sovereignty in Arendt.

[3] Arendt (1998 [1958]: 177). Patchen Markell (2010) has helpfully elaborated the vital connections between *archē*, political authority, and new forms of democracy for Arendt, which I am indebted to here.

[4] Young-Bruehl (1982: 178). Since the publication of *The Jewish Writings* in 2007, Arendt's alternatives to nation-state sovereignty have received new critical attention as political roads less travelled, such as her commitment to bi- and multi-national polities in the case of Palestine. See Butler (2012: 114–80); Raz-Krakotzkin (2011); Ghanim (2011).

of national sovereignty. For many since, such a homeland has been a long time coming.

The refugee history out of which her commitment to the political realm emerged did not end with Arendt's new life as an émigré political theorist in Cold War America. In the final part of this chapter, I turn to the recent writing of the Palestinian poet, Yousif M. Qasmiyeh. In a sequence of poems about his home-camp, Baddawi, in Northern Lebanon, Qasmiyeh explores the long-times of Palestinian refugee history as it is experienced in the camp today. Writing of the 'plurality of lives' (his phrasing) that exist in Baddawi Camp, Qasmiyeh picks up from where Arendt stopped: with the question of how to both survive and begin again in the shadows of sovereignty.[5] At once conserving lives and memories otherwise lost to statelessness, and at the same time challenging the terms of that loss, in his poetry plurality does not converge neatly around conventional understandings of sovereignty – which, as Arendt understood, at least for those who have been failed by those understandings, may well be the point.

'We Refugees'

The 'sovereignty of the nation state ended in absurdity', Arendt wrote shortly after she arrived, stateless, in New York in 1941, 'when it began to decide who was a citizen and who not', and left 'hundreds and thousands' to the 'sovereign and arbitrary decisions of other nations'.[6] Expelling those you deem undesirable doesn't simply create a refugee problem for your neighbours and a humanitarian problem for the world, it exposes how dependent your sovereignty is on that of others – which is to say, probably not quite so sovereign as you had imagined. In Arendt's argument, in this sense, 20th-century nationalist ideologies, with their fantasies of origin, ethnic unity, and entitlement, were the woodworm in the scaffolding of European sovereignty (Ben-Dor Benite *et al.* 2017). 'If one regards European history as the development of the European nation-state, not as the development of European peoples into nation-states', she wrote in the blisteringly hot summer of 1940, as she attempted to escape occupied France, 'then … the stateless, are the most important product of recent history'.[7]

If the stateless are obviously not the '*il faut une volunté UNE*' – the identification of one with all, or the 'will of the one people' – of European nationalist sovereignty, then who are they? One answer is a people awaiting their return to a homeland or arrival in a new home. Before that, however, are the refugees who, for Arendt in the late 1930s and 1940s, were a category of people whose defining

---

[5] Yousif M. Qasmiyeh, 'The Camp Is Time', accessed 11 March 2019, https://refugeehosts.org/2017/01/15/the-camp-is-time/. Qasmiyeh's poems are now collected in Qasmiyeh (2021).
[6] Hannah Arendt, 'Active Patience' (1941), in Arendt (2007: 140).
[7] Hannah Arendt, 'The Minority Question' (1940), in Arendt (2007: 128).

characteristic was to survive partly by refusing the categorisations given to them by sovereign power. 'In the first place, we do not like to be called refugees' is the memorable first line of her now classic 1943 essay, 'We Refugees'.[8] It is a brilliant rhetorical opening to an essay that performs the disentitlements of refugeedom in the ironic ventriloquism of its doubled voice. In the first place, 'we' do not like be called refugees, say the parvenus in the essay, such as the hapless chameleon, Mr Cohen, desperate to assimilate and thus escape the label of 'refugee'. Yet, as I have argued elsewhere, it is by ironically mimicking the voice of the parvenu that Arendt brings the historical novelty of the modern refugee into view: 'Apparently nobody wants to know that contemporary history has created a new kind of human beings – the kind that are put in concentration camps by their foes and in internment camps by their friends', she writes.[9] Sovereign power does not want to know about those who suffer in its name. Nonetheless, the stateless undeniably speak through Arendt's writing, and the essay that begins with a negation, ends with a provocative affirmation of the critical agency of refugees:

> Those few refugees who insist upon telling the truth, even to the point of 'indecency', get in exchange for their unpopularity one priceless advantage: history is no longer a closed book to them and politics is no longer the privilege of gentiles. They know that the outlawing of the Jewish people in Europe has been followed closely by the outlawing of most European nations. Refugees driven from country to country represent the vanguard of their peoples – if they keep their identity.[10]

'We Refugees' negates one category of the refugee, the helpless parvenu, so as to smuggle in another kind of refugee, the pariah, who refuses either to be consigned to the shadows of sovereignty or to abide by its terms.

Keeping your identity as a Jew for Arendt in the 1930s and 1940s was, among other things, an uncompromising avowal of the indecent truth of politicised racism: I am a refugee, not because of bad luck, but because of who I am and a racist political ideology that wants me to vanish from the earth. Committed to Jewish existence, a hazardous enough faith to have in 1943, but not to a Jewish-only sovereign state, note how Arendt insists that it is the 'refugees driven from country to country' – not simply 'the Jews' – who are the vanguard of their peoples. Arendt was the first thinker to give the modern category of 'the refugee' a collective pronoun – a 'we' that demands the right to exist, but yet is constituted outside of conventional sovereignty. She was also one of the first to recognise that the history of statelessness had not ended with the conclusion of the Second World War, but had just begun. The formation of Israel did not solve what the world persisted in thinking of as the 'Jewish problem', she noted in 1949, but 'merely produced a new category of refugees, the Arabs, thereby increasing the number of stateless and rightless by another 700,000 to 800,00 people' (Arendt 2004 [1951]: 68).

---

[8] Hannah Arendt, 'We Refugees' (1943), in Arendt (2007: 274).
[9] Arendt, 'We Refugees' (1943), in Arendt (2007: 265); Stonebridge (2011: 101–18).
[10] Arendt, 'We Refugees' (1943), in Arendt (2007: 274).

As Amnon Raz-Krakotzkin (2001: 169; see also n. 3 above) has noted, Arendt's warnings about erecting a Jewish sovereign state on the same nationalist model which had made the case for a Jewish homeland necessary in the first place became irrelevant at the very moment when, for much of the world, the sovereign existence of Israel appeared a *fait accompli*.

Experimenting with different forms of political governance was not a luxury many had in the last part of the 20th century. Just as Arendt predicted, the creation of new nation-states, often made from old colonial maps, produced new generations of refugees and stateless people, leaving millions more to the arbitrary decisions of other nations. In 1955, the same year that Baddawi refugee camp was 'established', the Bandung Conference stepped in line and asserted in its final Communiqué that self-determination and independence were best fostered through mutual respect for the integrity of territorial sovereignty. Palestine, then a non-territorial sovereignty, was not represented at the conference, although the Communiqué supported United Nations resolutions on Palestinian claims.[11] Whilst national and territorial sovereignty were the currency of post-war internationalism, including the governance of decolonisation by new human rights regimes, 'humanitarian reason' was the small change left to those with little, or no, purchasing power (see Fassin 2012; Stonebridge 2017). Baddawi Camp, along with other refugee settlements and camps that came under United Nations jurisdiction in this period, were largely Bandung's forgotten cousins.

As postcolonial nations quickly discovered, in terms of sovereignty the post-war global leviathan turned out be something of a slippery eel when it came to jurisdiction. 'The acquisition of sovereignty by the Third World was an extraordinarily significant event', Antony Anghie (2004: 2) has dryly observed of this period, 'and yet, various limitations and disadvantages appeared to be somehow peculiarly connected with that sovereignty'. Sovereignty for decolonising nations turned out to mean both national self-determination and subjection to the new world order. Grand claims for sovereignty often try to disguise the paradox that in order to gain some freedom, you need to give some up. Postcolonial sovereignty also mandated – and Anghie's 'peculiarly' is just the right word here – that you also had to give up something you never had for the sake of something that the powers of the world were, in practice, reluctant to share with you.

At first glance, the post-war reassertion of national and territorial sovereignty would appear to put Arendt's commitment to non-sovereign forms of political being out of time with prevailing political winds. Writing in 1960, just five years after Bandung, in the essay that would become 'What Is Freedom?', Arendt delivered

---

[11] As Nahed Samour (2017: 596) has argued, the awkward absence of Palestine at Bandung demonstrates the extent to which the commitment to nation-state sovereignty in the name of 'universal' human rights clouded political horizons: 'The Palestine Question highlights the predicament of how Bandung was defined, and limited, by a state-centric perspective which excluded Palestinians, who were not invited, and adopted a universalist legal rhetoric as a solution, with the United Nations as key reference.'

perhaps her most unequivocal statement about what she saw as the moral and political zero-sum game of sovereignty:

> The freedom of one man, or a group, or a body politic can be purchased only at the price of the freedom, i.e., the sovereignty, of all others. Where men wish to be sovereign, as individuals or as organised groups, they must submit to the oppression of the will, be this the individual will with which I force myself, or the 'general will' of an organised group. If men wish to be free, it is precisely sovereignty they must renounce.[12]

Even as the slipperiness of post-war sovereignty was becoming apparent, Arendt's uncompromising conclusion – 'If men wish to be free, it is precisely sovereignty they must renounce' – would have sounded, if not unintelligible, certainly otherworldly to many for whom the struggle for sovereignty appeared, with justification, to be the only political option in 1960. There is no great surprise in the narrowness of worldly vision here; more often than not, Arendt had one eye shut when it came to understanding the stakes of postcolonial struggle. Just ten years later, she would sweepingly reject the politics of Third World solidarity on the grounds that it was simply one more example of questionable absolutist sovereign dreaming ('The Third World is not a reality but an ideology', she snapped in *On Violence* [1970]).[13]

If her arguments about politics and freedom might as well have been Greek to much of the world, this is because, on the one hand, that is exactly what they were. Without a body politic in which our actions and interactions can be recognised, there simply is no freedom, she argues in 'What Is Freedom?' The *polis* is where freedom is created in the busy *interesse* between actors. By contrast, in communities driven by necessity and survival, in the household (*oikos*), in despotic regimes, and, many would assume, in camps and communities of the stateless and rightless, however much it is dreamt of, freedom simply cannot exist.

But as so often in Arendt's writing of this period, apparent endpoints are also beginnings; the pre-political, and sometimes even the seemingly anti-political, are the points from which another kind of politics might emerge (see Esposito 2017). Freedom, famously, begins with action for Arendt. But whereas the consensus was that post-war bids for political agency should fit into existing models of sovereignty, Arendt wanted to begin this action elsewhere, in another time, and in another place, thereby breaking the assumption that there could be no freedom with sovereignty. 'The question which then arises', she writes provocatively in *The Human Condition* (1998: 236), 'is whether our [conventional] notion that freedom and non-sovereignty are mutually exclusive is not defeated by reality, or to put it another way, whether the capacity for action does not harbor within it certain potentialities

---

[12] Hannah Arendt, 'What Is Freedom?' (1960), in Arendt (1993 [1961]: 143–71, at 164–5).

[13] She continues: 'To think ... that there is such a thing as a "Unity of the Third World", to which one could address the new slogan in the era of decolonization "Natives of all the underdeveloped countries unite!" is to repeat Marx's worst illusion on a greatly enlarged scale and with considerably less justification. The Third World is not a reality but an ideology' (Arendt 1970: 21).

which enable it to survive the disabilities of non-sovereignty'. How can you possibly have freedom without sovereignty in a world entirely set up for sovereignty? Arendt's answer is that other kinds of political action have always been possible, and that to find these we need to look in *res gestae*, in the non-sovereign archive of history and human action – to the stories of Greece, Rome, the nascent American republic, the soviet councils before they were swept up into the Soviet Union, and to different kinds of political reality.

Political theory gave Arendt models to think with, but it is on the level of her own language – her writing and her style – that we can really glimpse her straining to articulate a state of political and historical being that exists but is yet to have a discrete imaginative form. Reality – things that have happened in the world – raises the question 'whether the capacity for action does not harbor within it certain potentialities which enable it to survive the disabilities of non-sovereignty', she writes. Yet, precisely what action might follow from these realities is peculiarly hidden in her wordiness in this passage and elsewhere in *The Human Condition*, Arendt's most stylistically complex yet hauntingly sparse text. The double-voiced denial as avowal style of 'We Refugees' persists here, but now less as controlled irony and more as a kind of gently insistent linguistic stammer: 'does not harbor within it certain potentialities which enable it to survive the disabilities of non-sovereignty'. Unpick this sentence and it becomes clear just how compacted, and as yet obscure, this potential for action is. Arendt writes only of a capacity, not yet a reality, for something itself which is only potential, as yet waiting in a blockaded harbour, like a ship of human cargo going nowhere – or, perhaps, a collective of people, thrown together, forced to act in order to survive and discovering in that work, sometimes, the potential for new forms of political being.

Whilst the idea of abandoning the struggle for political sovereignty would have sounded strange to many, the question of how to 'survive the disabilities of non-sovereignty' might sound more familiar to those who have endured the disabilities of non-sovereignty for generations. What if we read 'What Is Freedom?' as a belated response to 'We Refugees'? The association between surviving non-sovereignty and the 'we' of 'We Refugees' is not a connection Arendt makes, but is one, I would argue, that is latent in places in her post-war writing.

To be borderline, stateless, rightless, for Arendt, was unequivocally one of the worst things that could happen; without a political community to make sense of our actions, there can be no 'right to have rights' in her now well-known phrase. This is why statelessness, the life of the refugee, is worldless, in her view. Yet it is equally striking how nothing ever is simply passive in Arendt's writing, even when – actually *especially* when – she is describing life lived on the borders of the *polis*. 'The human sense of reality demands that men actualize the sheer passive givenness of their being, not in order to change it but in order to make articulate and call into full existence what otherwise they would have to suffer passively anyhow', runs another notably peculiar passage from *The Human Condition*, in which, yet again, Arendt's (1998 [1958]: 208) assemblage of near cognate words – 'sheer passive givenness' – has the uncanny effect of animating – actualising – what otherwise her own analysis would simply condemn to the shadows. Here, as elsewhere, it takes a lot of linguistic activity in order to present absolute passivity in her prose.

In the notoriously twisty passages that close the 'Decline of the Nation State and the End of the Rights of Man' chapter in *The Origins of Totalitarianism*, first published as a separate article in 1949, Arendt explains how the creation of political life makes this 'sheer passive givenness' appear strange and threatening because it reminds us of the limits of our capacity to make the world. This produces, she says, in one of her ill-chosen colonial metaphors, 'barbarians from its own midst by forcing millions of people into conditions which, despite all appearances, are the conditions of savages'.[14] Arendt's repudiation of non-political life could not be clearer. Yet again, however, the 'savage', in this case, is also clutching a representation of herself.[15]

Hauntingly present in these passages, to my ears at least, is Arendt's own position as one-time 'savage'. The exclusionary logic that makes mere human life so threatening is the same by which refugees are consigned to unqualified 'mere existence'. Here, and throughout much of her post-war writing, Arendt occupies both positions at once. Nowhere is this more poignant and unsettling than in this extraordinary passage, notable for the unexpected evocation of love that erupts towards its end:

> The human being who has lost his place in a community, his political status in the struggle of his time, and the legal personality which makes his actions and part of destiny as a consistent whole, is left with those qualities which usually can become articulate only in the sphere of private life and must remain unqualified, mere existence in all matters of public concern. This mere existence, that is, all that which is mysteriously given us by birth and includes the shapes of our bodies and the talents of our minds, can be adequately dealt with only by the unpredictable hazards of friendship and sympathy, or by the great and incalculable grace of love, which says with Augustine, '*Volo ut sis* [I want you to be]', without being able to give any particular reason for such supreme and unsurpassable affirmation. (Arendt 2004 [1951]: 382)

This 'mere existence' is not the 'bare life' of Agamben's 'liminal spectres' (in Homi Bhabha's pithy phrasing); or, at the least, it is not only that.[16] When sovereignty is no more, says Arendt, all you have left is your existence with others. But it is also at this precise point that we become neighbours, entangled with one another's

---

[14] Arendt (2004 [1951]: 384). For excellent critical discussion of the unhappy boomeranging of the language of race and colonialism in these passages, see Rothberg (2009: 33–65).

[15] I am borrowing here from Denise Riley's 'A Note on Sex and the Reclaiming of Language', a poem that understands the hazardous loops between essentialising colonial metaphors and writing the self beautifully, and with an ironic pathos that you sometimes also find in Arendt: 'The Savage weeps as, landing at the airport | she is asked to buy wood carvings, which represent herself' (Riley 1977: 1).

[16] Homi K. Bhabha, 'The Burdened Life: Reflections on Arendt's "We Refugees"', paper given at 'We Refugees: 75 Years Later', ZfL, Berlin, 15 March 2018. See Alston, this volume, for a fuller account of Agamben's work.

existence, beginning something new, however reluctantly, and however much – as for all refugees – we did not want to begin again in the first place.

Baddawi Camp

If it is in the intensities of her writing that Arendt begins to think about surviving in the shadows of sovereignty, then maybe it is in poetry that we might also discover how refugees negotiate the 'disabilities of non-sovereignty' today. This, at any rate, was one of the bold propositions underpinning an interdisciplinary research project, *Refugee Hosts*, created in 2016 by the migration and refugee studies scholar, Elena Fiddian-Qasmiyeh. The war in Syria, following the wars in Iraq, precipitated a new chapter of refugee history in the Middle East, and beyond. While some in Europe used the occasion to (yet again) conflate ethno-nationalism with some rather spongy arguments in favour of sovereignty, *Refugee Hosts* was concerned to uncover the larger refugee history across the Middle East and North Africa which gave context to this new chapter of refugee hosting, principally in Lebanon and Jordan. Poetry, in the form of workshops, analysis, and practice, joined more conventional ethnographic methods such as interviews and data collection, theology and critical theory. Poetry, we argued, can make present historical and emergent forms of historical, political, religious, and communal being in ways that other social and political languages do not. The now Oxford-based writer and translator, Yousif M. Qasmiyeh, was the project's poet-in-residence, and Baddawi, his home camp, was one of the sites focused on.

The major theme of the project was the changing nature of refugee hosting, often manifesting itself across generations, between not only citizens and refugees, but refugees who host other refugees. The neighbourliness which Arendt discovers in survival, to this extent, was a historical mainstay in Baddawi Camp and others like it long before western writers rediscovered the ambivalent legacies of hospitality when the end of the Cold War and the subsequent growth of the European Union, globalisation, and the Afghan and Iraq wars bought new visitors to Europe's borders. Like all Palestinian camps, Baddawi began with al-Nakba, but since then its refugee history has multiplied, accumulating layers of memory and grief, biography, resistance, political organisation, and community. The Six Day War or an-Naksah in 1967 brought a new group of refugees to the camp. The siege of Tel al Zaatar, another Palestinian camp, by Syrian-backed Phalangists in Beirut in 1976 ushered in more; those displaced during the War of the Camps (1985–8) in the Lebanese Civil War followed. In 2007, the destruction of nearby Nahr el Bared camp drove a further generation of refugees into what few remaining spaces were left for new buildings. Refugees not only from Syria, but also from Kurdistan and Iraq began arriving in the 2010s.

A history of hosting, of neighbourliness, love, and faith, has helped make all this work as well as it possibly can, and usually in appalling circumstances. But not unequivocally. In a piece written at the beginning of the project, Fiddian-Qasmiyeh and Qasmiyeh reminded us that, similar to Greco-Christian etymologies, whilst 'Qur'anically and according to the Sunnah, the term neighbour has a clear spatial and moral reading that is defined, reaffirmed and demarcated by proximity, neighbourhood and charity', at the same time, the concept can 'invoke antagonism, antonyms as well as organic clashes with the overarching religious canon'. According to *Lisan Al-Arab*, the authoritative Arabic dictionary, a neighbour is: 'The one whose house is next to yours, the stranger, the partner, the beneficiary, the ally, the supporter, the spouse, the intimate parts, the house that is closer to the coast, the good, the bad, the hypocrite, the changeable, the kind' (trans. Qasmiyeh, in Fiddian-Qasmiyeh & Qasmiyeh 2018). Such ambivalence is not only part of the genealogical inheritance of neighbourliness, but, as refugees once again remind us, a direct consequence of existing between often competing, and powerful, forms of sovereignty.

In the case of Baddawi Camp, as with other refugee camps and communities, the struggle to exist in the shadows of different kinds of sovereignty could not be clearer. The sovereign state of Israel, most obviously, produced the category of Palestinian refugees, the longest standing stateless people in modern history, in the first place. The refugees of Baddawi and other camps are also subject to the sovereign power of their host state, Lebanon, with which, to say the least, there has never been an easy relationship (Sayigh 2005: 17–19; 2015). One reason why so many Syrian, Kurdish, and Iraqi refugees went to Baddawi Camp and other Palestinian camps was because they felt safer there than under the protection of the Lebanese state alone. 'In this context, the Palestinian refugee camps are simultaneously "islands of insecurity" and "islands" that are in many ways separated from national Lebanese policies', note Fiddian-Qasmiyeh and Qasmiyeh (2018). Within the camp itself, the global sovereignty of the UNRWA (United Nations Relief and Works Agency for Palestinian Refugees in the Near East) and, more recently, the UNHCR (Office of United Nations High Commissioner for Refugees) makes itself felt in the few open schools and medical centres and the agencies' ubiquitous blue and white branding.

Picking up on Arendt's description of the 'human condition', Ilana Feldman (2018) has described how Palestinian camps exist in what she calls 'the humanitarian condition', whereby inhabitants are both subject to humanitarianism, yet always striving to make something human out of that condition. More recently, the different rights and rationing regimes of the two agencies have exacerbated tensions. Syrians and other refugees come under the more generous (relatively speaking) jurisdiction of the UNHCR, whereas the Palestinian population suffer under the rapidly dwindling aid governance of the UNWRA.

And then there is, most importantly, the sovereignty of the Palestinian people, both a sovereignty of continual political struggle in the present and also a sovereignty to come, always there, active, being worked through, pushed into new forms, archived, and begun again (see also Hammer & Schulz 2003; Ahmad

& Abu-Lughod 2007; Khalili 2007; Doumani 2009). In a recent essay, Qasmiyeh (2019: 321) has written of how political agency is made present in the camp as a form of archiving:

> whereby refugees themselves (consciously) narrate the camp in their daily presences in ways that not only instate their solitude but also in order to remember who they are. ... One might say that such processes are the only processes that remind the camp's inhabitants that it is their right to write what is deemed theirs in the spatial and territorial sense, even though such markers are never conspicuous, nor are they markers of permanence as such.

At this point it is worth going back to Arendt. First, to her suggestion that a refugee vanguard – a 'We Refugees' – might also be where the victims of nationalism, racism, and sovereign violence might politically identify themselves as a people – as Palestinians and Kurds, for example – within the historical, but not existential, category of refugeedom. And second, relatedly, to her description of non-sovereign political beginnings within such a collectivity: 'as in the Greek word *archein*, "to begin", "to lead", and eventually "to rule"', as she wrote in *The Human Condition* (Arendt 1998 [1958]: 177).

Archein shares its root with the word 'archive'. 'Only refugees can forever write the archive', Qasmiyeh writes in 'Writing the Camp Archive, Refugees are Dialectic Beings: Part One' (2017c):

> The camp owns the archive, not God.
>
> For the archive not to fall apart, it weds the camp unceremoniously.
>
> The question of a camp-archive is also the question of the camp's survival beyond
>
> speech.

Only refugees can write their own archive. Just because the camp is caught between different forms of sovereign power, it does not follow that there is no historical or political agency there. To survive 'beyond speech', as in Arendt's eloquent convolutions, for Qasmiyeh too is to keep enduring beyond known and conventional forms of existing: to be active within a historically designated passivity.[17]

This might be why the distinguishing features of Qasmiyeh's poetry are not, as we might presume, the loss of sovereignty, mourning for home, exile, loss, and powerless, but a sustained meditation on beginnings: on the differences revealed by new arrivals, on birth, natality, midwives, thresholds, re-origination, moving feet. Death is always present in Qasmiyeh's poetry, along with darkness and precarity,

---

[17] For more on how archives of resistance can be established in the shadows of sovereignty, see Azoulay (2013; 2017). Azoulay notes that, in the absence of state sovereignty, alternative archives survive only because of what 'we' – a necessarily non-sovereign collective of people – put in it: 'Not necessarily you or me personally, but you and me as those sharing our world with others. "We" beyond the borders of a certain time and place.' A 'we', we might add, that is not only out of time, and place, but actively, quietly, desperately, determinedly, archiving another time and place.

pain and suffering, but so too is movement, beginning: this is a poetry that creates the sense of activity out of mere existence. Here is his extraordinary poem 'Writing the Camp, Vis-à-Vis or a Camp' (Qasmiyeh 2016) in full[18]:

WRITING THE CAMP, VIS-À-VIS OR A CAMP

'To experience is to advance by navigating, to walk by traversing.'

Derrida, Points ..., p. 373

I

What makes a camp a camp? And what is the beginning of a camp if there is any? And do camps exist in order to die or exist forever?

II

Baddawi is my home camp, a small camp compared to other Palestinian camps in Lebanon. For many residents, it comprises two subcamps: the lower and the upper camps that converge at the old cemetery. As I was growing up, it was common for children to know their midwife. Ours, perhaps one of only two in the entire camp, was an elderly woman, who died tragically when a wall collapsed on top of her fragile body during a stormy day in the camp. The midwife was the woman who cut our umbilical cords and washed us for the first time. She lived by the main mosque – *Masjid al-Quds* – that overlooked the cemetery. She would always wait by the cemetery to stop those who she delivered en route to school, to give them a kiss and remind them that she was the one who made them.

III

The camp is never the same albeit with roughly the same area. New faces, new dialects, narrower alleys, newly-constructed and ever-expanding thresholds and doorsteps, intertwined clothing lines and electrical cables, well-shielded balconies, little oxygen and impenetrable silences are all amassed in this space. The shibboleth has never been clearer and more poignant than it is now.

IV

Refugees ask other refugees, who are we to come to you and who are you to come to us? Nobody answers. Palestinians, Syrians, Iraqis, Kurds share the camp, the same-different camp, the camp of a camp. They have all come to re-originate the beginning with their own hands and feet.

V

Now, in the camp, there are more mosques, more houses of God, while people continue to come and go, like the calls to prayer emanating at slightly varied times from all these mosques, supplementing, interrupting, transmuting, and augmenting the voice and the noise simultaneously.

---

[18] A slightly altered version of 'Writing the Camp, Vis-à-vis or a Camp' is also published in Qasmiyeh (2021: 59-60), and became the poem after which Qasmiyeh's *Writing the Camp* is titled.

VI

> Baddawi is a camp that lives and dies in our sight. It is destined to remain (not necessarily as itself) so long as time continues to be killed in its corners.

'They have all come to re-originate the beginning with their own hands and feet.' Or, to quote a more recent poem, in Baddawi Camp a 'plurality of lives', 'has traversed the place itself to become its own time' (Qasmiyeh 2017b).

For Arendt, those who live in the shadows of sovereign life appear 'different' to those with secure political citizenship; her rejection of sovereignty, at least in part, came from her endeavour to bring its victims back into the political light without reproducing its violence, even as her own writing often hovered uncomfortably on the very opposition between 'citizen' and 'refugee' that she historicised. Seventy years on, Baddawi Camp's refugees differ from one another, but share the spaces and meanings of the camp: 'Palestinians, Syrians, Iraqis, Kurds share the camp, the same-different camp, the camp of a camp.' As such, with the actions of their hands and feet, they are also beginning something new: 'They have all come to re-originate the beginning with their own hands and feet.'

In Baddawi Camp today it is not God, remember, Qasmiyeh writes, who owns the archive of rightlessness, but the refugee camp. 'Only refugees can forever write the archive.' The human feet are creating time. The 'we refugees' of Qasmiyeh's Baddawi are imagining (because they are living) what Arendt could not quite bring herself to. Even as she archived the experience of worldless coexistence in her postwar writing, she pushed back, or away, from the implication that is latent throughout her work, and which I have been teasing out throughout this chapter: that because action and enforced passivity are not necessarily mutually exclusive, it is perhaps to the stateless that we must look to understand the impasses – and possibly the future – of our politics.

Conclusion

There are two political 'foundation' narratives, Arendt argues towards the end of *On Revolution*. It is not coincidental that they are also both refugee narratives: the story of Exodus, and the story of Aeneas' journey after the fall of Troy. Both occupy a 'hiatus between the end of the old order and the beginning of the new' (Arendt 1963: 197). In such hiatuses, maybe it makes less sense to speak of sovereignty and non-sovereignty than of borders of political existence that are constantly defining and redefining their terms. Out of her own hiatus, Arendt evoked the 'right to have rights': the right to belong to a political community, a homeland. Out of Baddawi's compromised sovereignties, Qasmiyeh (2019) insists on the 'right to write what is deemed [the people of Baddawi] in the spatial and territorial sense, even though such markers are never conspicuous, nor they are they markers of permanence as such'. This is not simply poetry. The people of Baddawi may not own the land they live on, but as Nadya Hajj (2016) has demonstrated, over the years the spatial and territorial property of the camp has been worked into new forms of legality and rights. Out of *fouda* (chaos) new forms of political institution and new forms of co-living emerge.

In the end, this reality cannot change the fact that Baddawi was and continues to be made by sovereign violence. 'The famous sovereignty of political bodies has always been an illusion, which, moreover, can be maintained only by the instruments of violence, that is, with essentially nonpolitical means', Arendt wrote in 'What Is Freedom?'[19] 'Privileging death in the camp is the sacral of the refugee body', Qasmiyeh (2017c) writes in 'Writing the Camp-Archive':

> Without its death, the archive will never exist.
>
> In whose name is the camp a place?
>
> It is the truth and nothing else that for the camp to survive it must kill itself.

'*In whose name is the camp a place?*' Baddawi is a Palestinian refugee camp, but it is because of the sovereign state of Israel that the camp is a place at all. This is why it can only be when the camp kills itself – when it is no longer needed simply for people to exist – that the generations of refugees that have lived and passed through it can truly be said to have survived; only then will the archive exist, and only then can political beginnings ever truly be realised. In the meantime, there is the writing, the archiving for a future time. 'In writing about these events and others', Qasmiyeh (2017a) has said of his contemporary *res gestae* in an interview, 'we chase the camps as if we were chasing ourselves in details that are no longer there to be observed transiently but to be inscribed and re-inscribed to create a new archive, that of the upcoming and the future'. Arendt, I think, might have understood where he was coming from.

References

Ahmad, S.H. & Abu-Lughod, L. (eds) (2007), *Nakba Palestine, 1948, and the Claims of Memory* (New York, Columbia University Press).
Anghie, A. (2004), *Imperialism, Sovereignty and the Making of International Law* (Cambridge, Cambridge University Press).
Arendt, H. (1963), *On Revolution* (Harmondsworth, Penguin).
Arendt, H. (1970), *On Violence* (London, Harvest).
Arendt, H. (1993 [1961]), *Between Past and Future* (Harmondsworth, Penguin).
Arendt, H. (1998 [1958]), *The Human Condition* (Chicago, Chicago University Press).
Arendt, H. (2004 [1951]), *The Origins of Totalitarianism* (New York, Schocken Books).
Arendt, H. (2007), *The Jewish Writings*, ed. Jerome Kohn & Ron H. Feldman (New York, Schocken Books).

---

[19] Hannah Arendt, 'What Is Freedom?' (1960), in Arendt (1993 [1961]: 143–71, at 164).

Azoulay, A. (2013), 'Potential History: Thinking through Violence', *Critical Inquiry*, 39.3: 548–74.
Azoulay, A. (2017), 'Archive', *Political Concepts: A Critical Lexicon*, accessed 11 March 2018, http://www.politicalconcepts.org/archive-ariella-azoulay/.
Ben-Dor Benite, Z., Geroulanos, S., & Jerr, N. (eds) (2017), *The Scaffolding of Sovereignty: Global and Aesthetic Perspectives on the History of a Concept* (New York, Columbia University Press).
Butler, J. (2012), *Parting Ways: Jewishness and the Critique of Zionism* (New York, Columbia University Press).
Doumani, B. (2009), 'Archiving Palestine and the Palestinians', *Jerusalem Quarterly*, 36: 3–12.
Esposito, R. (2017), *The Origins of the Political: Hannah Arendt or Simone Weil?*, trans. Vincenzo Binetti & Gareth Williams (New York, Fordham University Press).
Fassin, D. (2012), *Humanitarian Reason: A Moral History of the Present* (Berkeley, University of California Press).
Feldman, I. (2018), *Life Lived in Relief: Humanitarian Predicaments and Palestinian Refugee Politics* (Berkeley, University of California Press).
Fiddian-Qasmiyeh, E. & Qasmiyeh, Y.M. (2018), 'Refugee Neighbours and Hospitality', *Refugee Hosts* (20 March), accessed 3 August 2021, https://refugeehosts.org/2018/03/20/refugee-neighbours-hostipitality/.
Ghanim, H. (2011), 'The Urgency of a New Beginning in Palestine: An Imagined Scenario by Mahmoud Darwish and Hannah Arendt', *College Literature*, 38.1: 75–94.
Hajj, N. (2016), *Protection amid Chaos: The Creation of Property Rights in Palestinian Refugee Camps* (New York, Columbia University Press).
Hammer, J. & Schulz, H. (2003), *The Palestinian Diaspora: Formation of Identities and the Politics of Homeland* (London, Routledge).
Khalili, L. (2007), *Heroes and Martyrs of Palestine: The Politics of National Commemoration* (Cambridge, Cambridge University Press).
Markell, P. (2010), 'The Rule of the People: Arendt, Archē and Democracy', in S. Benhabib (ed.), *Politics in Dark Times: Encounters with Hannah Arendt* (Cambridge, Cambridge University Press), 71–8.
Qasmiyeh, Y.M. (2016), 'Writing the Camp, Vis-à-Vis or a Camp', accessed 11 March 2019, https://refugeehosts.org/2016/09/30/writing-the-camp/.
Qasmiyeh, Y.M. (2017a), 'Yousif M. Qasmiyeh in Conversation with Theophilus Kwek: On *Language* and *Liminality*', *Asymptote Journal* (15 February), accessed 12 March 2019, https://www.asymptotejournal.com/blog/2017/02/15/in-conversation-yousif-m-qasmiyeh-on-language-and-liminality/.
Qasmiyeh, Y.M. (2017b), 'The Camp Is Time', accessed 11 March 2019, https://refugeehosts.org/2017/01/15/the-camp-is-time/.
Qasmiyeh, Y.M. (2017c) 'Writing the Camp Archive', accessed 12 April 2021, https://refugeehosts.org/2017/09/01/refugees-are-dialectical-beings-part-one/.
Qasmiyeh, Y.M. (2019), 'Writing the Camp: Death, Dying and Dialects', in E. Cox, S. Durant, D. Farrier, L. Stonebridge, & A. Woolley (eds), *Refugee Imaginaries: Research Across the Humanities* (Edinburgh, Edinburgh University Press), 311–29.
Qasmiyeh, Y.M. (2021), *Writing the Camp* (Talgarreg, Wales, Broken Sleep Books).
Raz-Krakotzkin, A. (2001), 'Binationalism and Jewish Identity', in S. Aschheim (ed.), *Hannah Arendt in Jerusalem* (Berkeley, University of California Press), 165–80.
Raz-Krakotzkin, A. (2011), 'Jewish Peoplehood, "Jewish Politics" and Jewish Responsibility – Arendt on Zionism and Partitions', *College Literature*, 38.1: 57–74.

Riley, D. (1977), *Marxism for Infants* (London, Reality Street Editions).
Rothberg, M. (2009), *Multidirectional Memory: Remembering the Holocaust in the Age of Decolonization* (Stanford, Stanford University Press).
Samour, N. (2017), 'Palestine at Bandung', in L. Eslava, M. Fakhri, & V. Nesiah (eds), *Bandung, Global History, and International Law: Critical Pasts and Pending Futures* (Cambridge, Cambridge University Press).
Sayigh, R. (2005), 'A House Is not a Home: Permanent Impermanence of Habitat for Palestinian Expellees in Lebanon', *Holy Land Studies*, 4.1: 17–39.
Sayigh, R. (2015), *Too Many Enemies: The Palestinian Experience in Lebanon* (Beirut, Al Mashriq).
Stonebridge, L. (2011), *The Judicial Imagination: Writing after Nuremberg* (Edinburgh, Edinburgh University Press).
Stonebridge, L. (2017), 'Humanitarianism Was Never Enough: Dorothy Thompson, *Sands of Sorrow*, and the Arabs of Palestine', *Humanity: An International Journal of Human Rights, Humanitarianism, and Development*, 8.3: 441–65.
Villa, D. (1995), *Arendt and Heidegger: The Fate of the Political* (Princeton, Princeton University Press).
Young-Bruehl, E. (1982), *Hannah Arendt: For the Love of the World* (New Haven, Yale University Press).

15

Resonant Sovereignty? The Challenge of Social Acceleration – and the Prospect of an Alternative Conception

HARTMUT ROSA

Introduction

TRADITIONALLY, CONCEPTIONS OF sovereignty are based on, and dependent on, the capacity to synchronise political decision-making with both the internal dynamics of social and economic life and the external speeds of global markets and technologies as well as environmental processes. Only as long as politics is capable of setting and/or following the pace of societal life does the idea of sovereignty appear to be plausible. Yet modern societies continue to operate in a mode of dynamic stabilisation, which means that they are persistently forced to grow, accelerate, and innovate in order to reproduce their structure and to preserve their institutional status quo. This leads to a form of social acceleration which threatens or even destroys this very capacity for synchronisation; it leads to serious forms of desynchronisation on all levels of social and political life (i.e. between citizens, between markets and politics, between states, as well as between social life and environmental temporalities). Hence, this chapter argues, what is needed is a different conception of 'soft sovereignty', which is not based on autonomy and instrumental control, but on *responsivity* on all those levels. This form of sovereignty, or of the common good, is realised when a body politic establishes 'axes of resonance' (a) between citizens, (b) between citizens and the 'body politic' as a whole, (c) towards the (natural and institutional) environment, (d) towards history, and (e) towards other political bodies beyond its borders. *Resonance* here signifies a form of relationship that consists of four elements: (1) *affectivity*, that is, the capacity to *listen* to the 'other'; (2) *responsivity*, that is, the capacity *to answer* (with a firm voice); (3) *transformativity*, that is, the capacity to be perpetually transformed without losing the ability for (1) or (2); and (4) *uncontrollability*, that is, the capacity to accept the loss of autonomous control over outcomes without losing the sense of self efficacy and self-determination. In this sense, the chapter argues, the core idea of sovereignty can be reinterpreted as centred around (2) *responsivity*, but it involves all four elements.

Sovereignty and the mode of dynamic stabilisation

In my understanding, the modern conceptions of political sovereignty and of (individual as well as collective) autonomy, or self-determination, are closely intertwined. To be sovereign means to be capable of making decisions and implementing them independently of, or against, the will of others, the precepts of tradition or history, and, to some extent, even of nature, etc. In modern societies, we find a close connection between the cultural preponderance of the value of, and desire for, autonomy, or sovereignty, in this sense, and the structural and institutional mode of what I call *dynamic stabilisation*. The deep-rooted desire for self-determination and, as Charles Taylor (1985: 277, cf. 267) calls it, 'spiritual independence' from nature, history, others, is one of the driving motors for a structural logic that requires incessant growth, acceleration, and innovation for the reproduction or preservation of the institutional status quo. Without a permanent increase in speed, output, and efficiency, the core spheres of societal life turn dysfunctional. The economy loses jobs, the state suffers a decline of tax-revenue and hence a budgetary deficit, the health system, the pension schemes, the universities and schools etc. are all going into decline, which, in turn, leads to a progressive loss of political agency, etc. Hence, modern societies are characterised by fundamental processes of *social acceleration*, that is, by a progressive transformation of their temporal fabric which can be understood as a consistent trend towards dynamisation and speed-up (Rosa & Scheuerman 2009; Rosa 2013). This trend implies that there is not just an ongoing technological acceleration in the speed of transport, communication, and the production of goods and services, but also a progressive decrease in the stability of social arrangements and practices, that is, a change in the rates of change themselves.

Of course, the speed-up of change and of the pace of social life itself is a largely unnoticed side-effect rather than a manifest objective of the process of modernisation. As Talcott Parsons (1971), Reinhart Koselleck (1985), Jürgen Habermas (1987), and many others have pointed out, the political project of modernity was propelled by the idea that human beings as citizens should themselves and collectively determine their own fate by shaping society independently of the demands of tradition, custom, or even nature. Self-determination thus appears to be the key promise of modernity, and social acceleration figured as a crucial means to break free from the inertia of tradition, custom, and convention, and to overcome natural scarcities and social barriers to true autonomy.

The principle of sovereignty thus lies at the heart of the modern form of *being-in-and-to-the-world*, and it is equivalent to a fivefold 'spiritual' declaration of independence: modern sovereignty is about (1) spatio-material, (2) temporal, (3) political, (4) social, and (5) existential independence at once. (1) First of all, any sovereign requires territorial sovereignty, that is, the exclusive control of a given 'Lebensraum' which is shaped socially as well as materially: sovereignty implies the right to autonomously use, shape, or destroy the natural resources of the given territory including its mountains, lakes, forests, plants, animals, etc. This induces an instrumental, manipulative, and 'accumulative' relationship towards nature, which, as Charles Taylor illuminatingly points out in his comprehensive analyses of modernity, should not be understood as a merely hedonistic attitude, but as a genuinely 'spiritual' disposition, because it is foundational for modernity's self-understanding. It is through this stance towards nature that modern subjects are constituted as autonomous, rational actors:

> Increasing production ... became a value in our civilization, against all the temptations to sloth, and all the blandishments of traditional ethics, because in producing we came to see ourselves as not just meeting our needs, but also realizing our status as autonomous, rational agents. Continued accumulation bespoke a consistent, disciplined maintenance of the instrumental stance to things; it was a realization of man's spiritual dimension. Far from being an obsession with things, an entrapment in them, as it might be stigmatized on a Platonic conception, it is an affirmation of our autonomy; that our purposes are not imposed on us by the supposed order of things. The instrumental stance towards nature is meant to be a spiritual declaration of independence from it. (Taylor 1985: 277)

(2) Alongside this spatio-material dimension of sovereignty, modernity is constituted by a temporal claim to self-determination which is pursued and defended with the same degree of persistence; this is the claim to sovereignty over history. A modern sovereign is characterised by the fact that he or she is not bound by or obliged to the past; quite to the contrary, sovereignty consists precisely in the capacity and will to break loose from traditions, conventions, and obligations and to shape the future anew in an autonomous, sovereign, and rational manner. In this way, the bond between the past and the future significantly changes its shape and meaning. There still is a vital connection between the past and the future, but this connection is narrated in the form of progress: the future will be *different* than the past; history gains a dynamic and a direction. In this transformation of the connection between the past and the future, there is certainly a spiritual element, too, because it is foundational for modernity's sense of history and temporality.[1]

(3) Obviously, the declaration of independence from history is closely interwoven with the claim to political autonomy. This claim involves sovereignty and self-determination over all the structures and institutions regulating the social and political life within the given territory, and hence the negation of all claims

---

[1] Many authors in social science and the humanities have identified this reconceptualisation of history as foundational for modern society and culture; see, for example, Koselleck (1985); Blumenberg (1985); Bauman (2000).

emanating from *other*, alien authorities or entities. This implies that the shape and substance of the socio-political life of a community in its essence is completely up to the sovereign's disposition, except for the limits set by the natural or material conditions or the (military) power of neighbouring sovereign entities.

(4) If we seek to understand modernity's basic cultural (or even 'spiritual') disposition, it is of crucial importance to realise that this conception of sovereignty is transferred to the individual actors' desire for autonomy. The main vehicle for this transfer is the institution of private property. Modern individuals encounter each other in the sense of independent 'sovereigns' reigning over individual partitions of space and things which are legally defined and protected. Thus, the institution of private property safeguards modern subjects' right to a 'sovereign' command over specific, individual segments of the world. Things in private possession may be used, commodified, sold, transferred, or destroyed at will, even though this right can be constrained by the political sovereign. Once again, this constitutes a specific cultural stance towards the world, and more than this, it constitutes a specific form of subjectivity and sociality, for on the one hand, as Hegel (2008 [1820]: 53–83) observed, it bestows a sense of self-efficacy and agency on the individuals. But on the other hand, as we know from Marx (1988 [1844]) and later on from MacPherson (1964), the sovereign market players meet each other as atomised competitors with aversion or indifference.

(5) Taken together, these dimensions of sovereignty are foundational for modernity's sense of being; they constitute its most basic form of relating to the world. If we read sovereignty as a spiritual declaration of independence from nature, life, history, and everything else that constitutes the 'world', we realise as its essence the negation of existential dependence and relatedness; sovereignty in this sense is the denial of sources of value, or of something 'sacred' or unimpeachable, or even of something (essentially) uncontrollable, beyond our will (Rosa 2020). True, in the course of history, we often find references to sacred or divine powers in order to *legitimate claims to sovereignty*, but these claims do not serve to essentially limit the sovereign's powers, or, at least, such limitations progressively lose their meaning and their force. Quite to the contrary, in modern society, the sacred and the inviolable is defined or created by the sovereign themselves, and thus is dependent on their will or respect. Therefore, sovereignty constitutes a complete and total form of being-in-the-world.

Now what I want to claim here is that scientific progress, technological acceleration, economic growth, political dynamisation, and cultural innovation were the cardinal tools by and through which this form of comprehensive sovereignty over nature, space, social life, and history has been pursued in the course of modernity. And no doubt, significant progress has been achieved in all the realms or dimensions of independence. But the *cultural* (or 'spiritual') disposition which can be called the paradigm of sovereignty gradually has been turned from a moral claim and value into an institutional requirement. By consequence, the social, technological, and economic world transforms itself at an ever-increasing pace. The reason for the almost 'blind' persistence of these patterns of speed-up from the 18th century onward is that acceleration and dynamisation by now have become a *structural necessity* for contemporary society. Looked at in structural terms, *a society should be called modern*, I suggest, *when its mode of stabilisation is dynamic*, that is to say, *when it systematically requires (economic) growth, (technological and social) acceleration and (increasing, cultural) innovation in order to reproduce its structures and to maintain its institutional status quo* (Rosa et al. 2017).

When we look at it historically, it turns out that the shift from an adaptive to a dynamic mode of stabilisation can be observed as a systematic transformation in all cardinal spheres of social life that occurs, despite some historic predecessors, mainly from the 18th century onwards, that is, in parallel with the evolution of the modern conception of sovereignty. Most obviously, of course, it can be found in the realm of economy. The accounts of both Max Weber and Karl Marx vividly focus on this transformation. In a capitalist economy, virtually all economic activity depends on the expectation and promise of an *increase* in the sense of profit of one sort or another. Money – Commodity – Money' (m-c-m') is the short formula for this, where the prime (') signifies the increased return. It is realised, of course, through innovation (of product or process) and through acceleration, mostly in the form of increased productivity: the latter can be defined as an increase in output (or value production) per unit of time, that is, as acceleration. I do not want to go into the details of economic theory here, which can show that the need for innovation, acceleration, and growth really is intrinsic to the logic of capitalist production, to the logic of competition, and even to the logic of the monetary and the credit systems. The net result of it is that without permanent growth, acceleration, and innovation, at least under late modern conditions of globalised economic and financial markets, capitalist economies cannot maintain their institutional structures: jobs are lost, companies close down, tax revenues decrease, while state expenditure (for welfare and infrastructural programmes) increases, which in turn tends to cause a severe budget deficit at first and then a delegitimation of the political system. All of this can be seen in the present crisis in Southern Europe, particularly in Greece and Spain, where the institutional structure of the health system, the educational system, the retirement schemes, the arts and sciences etc. are all in disarray or even decay due to the lack of economic growth. Thus, it is not just the economic system in a narrow sense that depends on the logic of escalation, which is the consequence of a mode of dynamic stabilisation, but also the welfare-state and the system of democratic politics. As Niklas Luhmann (1981) showed more than 30 years ago, the latter is based on the logic of dynamic stabilisation, too: not only has the rather static monarchic order – where kings or queens rule for a lifetime before being simply replaced by a dynastic succession that preserves order in an identical fashion – given way to a democratic system which requires dynamic stabilisation through repeated voting every four or five years, but, much more dramatically, elections can only be won on the basis of political programmes that promise an *increase* – an increase in income, or in jobs, or in universities, high school diplomas, hospital beds, etc.

There is a lot more to be said about this mode of dynamic stabilisation, which prevails not just in the economy and in politics, but also in the realms of science, the arts, and even everyday life. But for the purposes of the current investigation, it suffices to point out that it leads to serious problems of *synchronisation*. As we will see, the ensuing forms of desynchronisation undermine modernity's claims and aspirations to sovereignty thoroughly and on all counts.

Desynchronisation and the crisis of dynamic stabilisation

The argument I seek to develop in the following is, in short, this: the escalatory logic of dynamic stabilisation, apart from yielding impressive results in the process of striving for autonomy, that is, in the aspiration to overcome the limitations of nature, history, poverty, and social domination, at the late modern stage of speed-up leads to an aggravating problem of fundamental desynchronisation between the pace of democratic political-will formation and decision-making on the one hand and the speed of the markets, the media, and cultural life on the other. This, by consequence, undermines the possibility and the promise of sovereignty in our relationship towards nature, towards history, and towards 'others', too. In fact, all the dimensions of sovereignty or autonomy identified above appear to be terminally strained by desynchronisation. Let me explain.

Obviously, political temporality is closely linked to, and interacts with, the temporal structures, patterns, and horizons of other social spheres, such as the economy, and of society and culture at large, but also with the temporal patterns of what we call 'nature', or 'the environment'. Thus, the idea of comprehensive sovereignty, that is, that the overall basic shape or framework of society is politically (or democratically) controlled, includes most significant temporal presumptions about the synchronisation between the pace of democratic-will formation and decision-making on the one hand and the speed of social evolution and change on the other, or between the political, economic, scientific, cultural, and ecological subsystems of society. It is here that changes in society's temporal structures quite obviously impact on the opportunities and limits of democratic politics. These crucial temporal preconditions only came to be fulfilled in modern times, but they are at the verge of breaking away in late modernity. It is this latter aspect, I want to argue, that has not yet been adequately taken into account in contemporary approaches to democratic theory (Held 1993; 1996).

In my temporal account of modernity, democracy itself historically was a crucial element of social acceleration and dynamisation, since it enabled not only a fast-paced and regular succession of governments, but also a dynamic political sensitivity towards the evolving needs of society. Hence, after the French Revolution, and embedded in ideas of historical progress and a corresponding philosophy of history, politics quickly became a pacemaker and a driving force of social acceleration. Political language itself provides an accurate indicator for this: 'progressive' ('leftist') forms of politics tried to accelerate the course of history towards a desired and/or predetermined end, whereas 'conservative' ('rightist') politicians and parties tried to preserve as much as possible from the past into the future, and to possibly *slow down* change. As Reinhart Koselleck (1985) notes, this temporal index of progress and conservation quickly came to dominate the totality of modern political thinking, speaking, and acting, turning politics into the realm responsible for (accelerating or decelerating) social movement.

Now, such a conception of (democratic) politics appears to be possible and plausible only within certain 'speed-barriers' of social change. On the one hand, social change has to be *fast enough*, that is, societies have to be dynamic enough, for political projects and programmes to actually bear on them. Only if the effects of change are noticeable between the three generations simultaneously living together at a given point in time could ideas of a *political shaping* (and thus of a 'spiritual independence') of society become plausible. On the other hand, the speed of change, or the dynamics of society, have to be *slow enough* for (democratic and deliberative) political processes of will-formation and decision-making actually to be effective, or for politics actually to control (or steer) social developments and set the pace. Beyond a certain temporal threshold, the dynamic forces of society are too strong for (democratic) political *self-determination* – and thus for sovereignty to be exerted. Collective will-formation, deliberation, and action require a certain degree of centralisation, public stability, and political identity which might not be compatible with late modern degrees of dynamisation and speed.[2]

Perhaps we witness this very temporal threshold right now in what could be called the global crisis of democracy. This crisis appears, at least in part, to be caused by the widening temporal gap between the speed of proper democratic legislation and the temporal requirements made on this very legislation by faster social spheres or systems such as the markets, the media, or techno-scientific progress (cf. Schmitt 1950).

As I have argued at length elsewhere (Rosa 2013: 251–76), the current weakness of western-style democracy – which can be seen from both its unattractiveness for non-western states in Africa or Asia as well as the decline in support and credibility it receives in its core countries, where populists and demagoguery are on the rise (see e.g. Crouch 2004) – basically arises from the fact that the democratic processes of political will-formation, decision-making, and implementation are, by their very nature, inevitably time-consuming. In fact, the more pluralistic and post-conventionalist society gets, and the more complex its networks, chains of interaction, and contexts of action and decision-making become, the slower democracy – and hence legislation – proceeds. Thus, while the speed of cultural and

---

[2] 'How can a public be organized, we may ask, when literally it does not stay in place? Without abiding attachments, associations are too shifting and shaken to permit a public readily to locate and identify itself', John Dewey (1954: 140–1) asked already back in 1927.

economic life and technological change increases, the pace of democracy slows down – and hence, we can observe a frightening extent of desynchronisation between politics on the one side and the social systems it tries to control or steer on the other (Rosa 2005).

It is important to notice at this point that this has not always been the state of affairs. Legislation is not intrinsically slower than the rest of society – quite to the contrary: when society shifted to a mode of dynamic stabilisation in the 18th century, legislation was the prime political instrument through which this shift was achieved, and furthermore, it was the prime instrument to dynamise or speed-up social developments all through the 19th and most of the 20th century, the prime tool of social engineering. In this way, legislation and, if we think of supreme court decisions such as in the United States, adjudication, too, for a long time have been the pacemakers and drivers of social change and thus an engine of social acceleration.

By the 21st century, however, democracy no longer appears to be a pacemaker of social change; rather, it has shifted to a role of 'fire-extinguisher' and to a mode of 'muddling through', at best, reacting to the pressures created elsewhere rather than shaping the world (cf. Rosa & Scheuerman 2009; Francot & Mommers 2016). It is not just that new rules and regulations often take too long to be forged. Worse than this: when, possibly after years of deliberation and negotiation, a new law (for example on internet traffic or protection of intellectual property rights or genetic engineering) is finally passed, the chances are high that it is already anachronistic, that it has been outpaced and overtaken by new developments in that very sector. Nowhere could this be seen more clearly than in the recent financial crisis, when political decisions almost invariably came too late and too slow for the markets – and yet too fast for legislatures to even have a say. Parliaments, it seems, are reduced to ex-post-facto yea- or nay-sayers, and this leads to increasing frustration or alienation on the part of the voters, who (at least in some cases) are tempted to elect xenophobic or populist parties (or to adopt completely 'desynchronised' propsals, such as the Brexit Referendum by the British electorate in 2016) in response, or to abstain from voting altogether. Needless to say, this can be interpreted as, and is experienced as, a severe collective loss of political sovereignty. The desynchronisation between democratic politics through parliamentary legislation and the economy, or its markets, thus results in a state of affairs where citizens have lost faith in political self-efficacy; for them, political institutions no longer respond to their needs and aspirations.

If we look more closely, it turns out that *there are* in fact (legal) provisions against legal desynchronisation in the modern political system. For this system actually allows for three distinct patterns of temporality in the legal order (cf. Riescher 1994; Scheuerman 2004). In most countries, constitutional law (defended and interpreted often by the corresponding courts) serves as the infrastructural 'airport' so to speak, to safeguard against the eroding pressures of high-speed dynamics. It guarantees that lawmaking follows stable, predictable patterns and pathways even in turbulent times, and thus provides long-term stability, calculability, and predictability. It is extremely hard and time-consuming to change constitutional provisions. Parliamentary legislation, by contrast, also takes its time and includes a whole array of temporal regulations that ensure democratic deliberation and consultation on many levels and between different actors – with the notorious filibuster being just the most folkloristic element of it. Nevertheless, as I have pointed out, legislation is the instrument that turns democracies into dynamic societies, and it can well serve as a tool for comprehensive social acceleration. Finally, emergency laws and executive regulations allow for an additional speed-up of legislation in times of crisis, when speed is vital. As we have seen most vividly in the ongoing COVID-19 crisis, executive orders and decrees can be forged on short notice and within hours; they are the tools that allow for high-speed political action and reaction. Little wonder, therefore, that authors like Bill Scheuerman (2001: 57) observe a shift from legislative to executive policymaking, even before Trump- or Johnson-style politics arrived. Yet this obviously comes at a price that resembles the destruction of the airport: once executive decrees and orders become a regular element of politics, the calculability and predictability of the background conditions of action are on the decline – and thus, the speed game starts to undermine itself. Sovereignty cannot be preserved in this way.

But desynchronisation also lies at the heart of three other major crises of late modern societies in the 21st century. If we loosely follow a 'systems-theoretical' approach (cf. Reheis 1996), we can envision the 'social system' as being located between the overarching ecological system(s) and the individuals' psychosomatic systems. The acceleration of society places stress and pressures of desynchronisation on both these other systems. Furthermore, and perhaps most interestingly, there appears to be a rupture in the temporal fabric of society itself, that is, in the connection between its past, its present, and its future. This rupture shows in theories of an 'end of history' (Fukuyama 1992) or of the advent of 'timeless time' (Castells 2010: 460–99), but most obviously in the fading away of the experience of, and belief in, historical progress. Perhaps we can interpret this as a desynchronisation between social time and history. Let us take a brief look at those desynchronisation processes one by one.

Eco-crisis: the desynchronisation of nature

Virtually all aspects of what we call 'the ecological crisis' can be reinterpreted as a problem of desynchronisation. The temporality of many natural processes – or nature's proper time (Nowotny 1996) – obviously is out of sync with our socio-technical and socio-economic temporalities. For example, it is not a problem for nature per se if we cut down trees and catch fish – but it becomes a problem if we cut down the trees in the rainforest and catch the fish in the oceans at rates too high for the pace of natural reproduction. Obviously, the discrepancy vastly increases when we look at the rate at which we deplete oil and carbon-based energy supplies and the time needed for nature to reproduce them. Similarly, most of what is considered to be a 'poisoning' of the environment is only a problem because we produce these substances and emissions at speeds that are higher than nature's capability to dispose of them. Finally, even the problem of 'global warming' can be read as a form of physical and material desynchronisation: *heating up the atmosphere* literally means making the molecules in the corresponding layers of air *move faster*; thus, the physical heat produced through carbon-based acceleration on the ground leads to atmospheric acceleration in the skies. In other words, the process of material dynamisation driven by the consumption of physical energy leads to a 'desynchronisation' in the earth's atmosphere that results in its warming.

Psycho-crisis: burnout and the desynchronisation of the subject

If the mode of dynamic stabilisation entails the incessant acceleration of the material, social, and cultural reproduction of society, this cannot leave the structures of the individual psyche (and body) and the character of the human subject untouched (Sennett 1999). Thus, the question arises as to how much acceleration and dynamisation individuals can take before they 'break', so to speak. Here, the evidence for pathological forms of desynchronisation appears to be overwhelming as well. Thus, while the use of drugs that slow people down ('downers' like heroin, LSD, alcohol) are on the decline, 'speed', amphetamines, and other drugs that promise 'synchronisation' (like Ritalin, Taurin, Focus Factor, etc.) are on the rise (UNODC 2015). In fact, most forms of 'human enhancement' are concerned with increasing the accelerability of human bodies and minds – from 'fixing' those who are viewed as 'disabled' to transhumanist fantasies of reconciling the limited speed of social actors with the (unlimited) speed of digital technology through the fusion of bodies and machines. Signs of growing pathological desynchronisation in the form of burnout and depression are alarming. In fact, the World Health Organization now realises that – apart from COVID-19 and alongside other pathological stress-reactions like eating and sleeping disorders and chronic anxieties – depression and burnout are the fastest-growing health problems on a worldwide scale (cf. Stoppe *et al.* 2006). One of the most striking features of both burnout and depression is the resulting lack of dynamics. For those who fall into the trap of a burnout or depression, time stands still, the world and/or the self appear to be 'frozen', void of motion and significance. This has led researchers like Alain Ehrenberg (2010) to suppose that depression is a stress-induced reaction of a desynchronised psyche to the speed requirements of modern life. The fact that journals and magazines all over the world regularly double their sales by reporting on stress, burnout, depression, and exhausted selves on their cover-page can be read as the symptom of a growing cultural sensitivity to the threat of desynchronisation even by those who are sceptical of the diagnostic practices of our medical services.

Historical disconnection: the desynchronisation of past and future

Most interestingly, this temporal standstill, that is, the impression of 'frozen time', appears to be not just a symptom of pathological individual experience, but also a cultural reality in the 21st century. The perception of a singular, moving 'history' that connects the past to the future through a sense of historical direction (and progress), identified above as a crucial feature of modernity's aspiration to 'spiritual independence', seems to be lost; it is replaced by a temporal experience that resembles pre-modern perceptions of time. We can see this on two levels of cultural life. On the one hand, for the first time in modern history, in all highly industrialised societies from Europe to Northern America to Japan, the majority of parents are no longer driven by the ambition, hope, and desire for their kids to have a better, brighter future than themselves, but by the desperate attempt to enable them to *keep the standards they have achieved already*. This means that subjects feel they have to run faster and faster *just to stay in place*, not to make headway. This feeling resembles running uphill on a downward escalator: as soon as we relax, we are losing ground. The same holds true for collective political experience: political parties and programmes have turned defensive, in the sense that they justify reforms and projects as necessary adjustments to preserve what we have. I have called this the perception of a 'frenetic standstill' on the individual as well as the collective level (Rosa 2013: 299–322). But furthermore, the dominant perception of historical time can also be read from the fact that subjects (at least in the Global North) lose their sense of historical direction: while even in the 1990s, people were convinced that things like torture, piracy, or religious wars, even though they were always present on a global level, were essentially *things of the past*, whereas democracy, the welfare state, and the United Nations were essential ingredients of the time to come, by 2020, the situation has changed fundamentally. Now the latter might well appear as things of the past, while the former could be signs of the future to come. But it is not that past and future simply have inverted their places: it rather appears that all elements of socio-cultural life have become 'timeless' possibilities on an equal rank. In my analysis of social acceleration, I have interpreted this as the consequence of the acceleration of social change beyond the threshold of generational exchange, that is, as the consequence of an intra-generational pace of change (Rosa 2013: 259–76). However, for the purpose of this contribution, it suffices to realise that the modern attempt to achieve political autonomy, or sovereignty, vis-à-vis tradition, social forces, nature, and history, has thoroughly failed.

The broken promise of democratic sovereignty and the resonance conception of the common good

The claim I want to make in the remainder of this contribution is this: the promise and dream of political modernity, that 'we the people' can become the sovereign masters of our lives by achieving independence from and control over nature, history, tradition, and socio-political heteronomy, has been broken on all counts. The main reason for this is that individually as well as collectively, we have to run faster and faster just to keep our place, that is to say: we need to muster more and more physical, material, psychological, and political energy in order to keep the engines of growth, acceleration, and innovation – or optimisation – going. This certainly is not the posture of a sovereign; it rather is the situation of a prisoner. It is the imperatives of growth and acceleration which are the true 'sovereign' of social operations and of social change. Politics has become just a tool in the struggle for competitiveness; it is reduced to a question of strategy in the growth-and-speed game; the whole logic of politics is subjected to the requirements of dynamisation. By consequence, citizens encounter each other as competitors or opponents as well; the experience of an antagonistic social ontology, where politics is about friends and foes (Carl Schmitt) and essentially about irreconcilable conflict (Rancière 2013; Laclau & Mouffe 2014) prevails. Likewise, the dominant perception of our relationship to nature is not a perception of sovereignty but of ecological destruction and environmental disaster. And instead of sovereignty over history, it seems that the connection to a significant past and a meaningful future is lost altogether. Instead of moving in the direction of progress, that is, of a brighter future, it feels like the escalators of history are moving downwards. What the global *Fridays For Future* movement expresses very aptly is the fear that there might be no meaningful future at all: the future has died alongside the past, sucked up in the frenetic standstill of the present. We are not the sovereign masters of time, but slaves of acceleration. So the Pink Floyd- or Tolstoy-question inevitably arises once again: *what shall we do now?*

What I want to suggest in this situation is in essence an alternative version of sovereignty, or, put more aptly, a conception alternative to sovereignty as we know it. This is the conception of resonance. The core idea is that instead of seeking 'sovereignty' in the sense of dominance and control over time, nature, and politics, the *common good* should be envisioned *as a particular form of connection or relationship*. Let me explain.

The modern notion of political 'sovereignty' implicitly hinges on the assumption that it serves the common good. But since defining this elusive common good in substantive terms has turned out to be impossible, because it always implies ideological or particularistic assumptions, it has become an 'empty signifier' in social and political theory; it is considered to be nothing but an empty concept that is used as a strategic weapon in political conflict (Laclau & Mouffe 2014). If, however, we start to view the common good as a specific *type of relationship*, we can perhaps redefine it in a sense that requalifies sovereignty, too – or that replaces sovereignty by a concept which is based not on dominance and control but on responsivity. My thesis is that the idea of the common good can be reinvigorated only if we try to understand it in the sense of a specific way of relating to the *past and future* of a political community, to a lifeworld that is shared both materially and institutionally (and is thus always spatially constituted), as well as to other *members* of this community – and finally, to entities and people *outside* the particular community. This proposal is based on the conception of resonance (Rosa 2019). Using this concept as a regulatory idea, my suggestion is this: *the common good can be pursued and achieved only when and where a body politic succeeds in establishing relationships of resonance, or, more precisely: axes of resonance, first, between the members of the community, second, between those members and the institutional reality of the body politic as a whole, third, with the natural, spatial and material environment, fourth, with the past and the future, and finally, towards those living beyond its borders*. Then (and only then) can democracy's promise – in practice, as an ongoing process – be delivered. Thus, my proposition is that *the common good* should be *seen as a state of resonance*. But what could this mean?

In the history of political thought, from ancient times to very recently, scholars have repeatedly questioned what exactly it is that constitutes the 'social bond' between members of a community, or what is capable of creating such a bond. Recently, this question has been posed not only by communitarian-, republican-, or Neo-Durkheimian-minded thinkers (Internationale Convivialiste 2020), but also, and in fact in particular, by post-structuralist authors (Bedorf & Herrmann 2016). The theory of resonance provides us with the following response: the social bond does not evolve from a predetermined foundation – shared values, customs, traditions, or histories, for instance – but rather it is formed by a specific type of relationship between individuals, one that can be described as being based on the interactional process of *listening* and *responding*. Listening and responding are the two poles that constitute a resonant relationship. Such a relationship is characterised by four key qualities. First, the willingness and ability to allow ourselves to be affected and *moved* by the voices of others (or other voices). This implies that one of the first preconditions for the common good is the basic assumption and acknowledgement among citizens that when they encounter one another they both will *have something to say*. This prerequisite is undermined, for instance, when political actors mutually perceive each other as racists and fascists or as traitors and bloodsuckers and are not interested in *hearing anything the others might have to tell them*, instead attempting to shout them down or silence them. Second, the social bond in this understanding is not confined to pure receptiveness, but essentially also evolves as part of, and as a result of, the experience that everyone is able to make their voices heard and to contribute. This is the fundamental promise of democracy: everyone receives a voice, a vote, which they do not simply *hand over*, but use to *contribute* in a responsive, proactive, and reactive manner. To my mind, it is utter nonsense to see the casting of the vote as a *cost* incurred by each individual in their endeavour to pursue personal interests, as assumed by rational (or public) choice theorists, who then go on to wonder why people bother participating in elections at all (Wittman 1997; Caplan 2008). *Having a voice* by casting a vote provides citizens with an inimitable experience of political *self-efficacy*: their voice and vote connects them with others and with the community and enables them to participate in the collective shaping of the world. It is not simply a (very limited) tool that enables us to *achieve something* in the sense of asserting our own interests; it is an instrument (actually comparable to a musical instrument; see Love 2006), which we use to reach out to *others* with whom we then enter into a relationship. The second condition of the common good is thus that the political process is organised so as to permit and facilitate this experience of *self-efficacy*. Self-efficacy in this sense does not mean control and domination, but refers to the capability of reaching out and being heard.

Third, and I believe this to be of paramount importance, an inevitable consequence of *entering into a resonant relationship* is the *transformation* of the participating voices. Resonance means allowing ourselves to be 'called' or moved by one or several other individuals (or entities) in such a way that when we respond and react to those individuals, we are personally transformed (Rosa 2013: 164–74; Latour 2013: 456–7). Hence, resonance is a dialogical process of reciprocal, *transformative appropriation*, where participants do not remain the same people that they were before. This, in fact, has always been at the core of republican political thinking (Buchstein 2018): the common good is not conditional on citizens having shared specific values or goals all along, but rather it is contingent on them being accessible and open to one another, on them being able to transform themselves for the purpose of reaching common ground or achieving a joint project. The fact that the ensuing shared world also involves conflict and dispute, and is even based on and results from such conflict, is irrefutable and unavoidable. It is thus entirely wrong to define the concept of resonance simply as *consonance* or *harmony*. In fact, conceptually, resonance always requires *difference* and thus also *dissonance*, because it is only in their presence that an encounter with a genuine other and the accompanying self-transformation are possible.

Thus, it is of vital importance to realise that resonance lies right *between* identity and difference, between consonance and dissonance; it bridges the gap between these concepts via the principle of transformation (Rosa 2017). Accordingly, the third condition of the common good is the ability and willingness of a community and its members to substantively and continually transform. This ability is undermined when a priori stipulations outside the political process or socially constructed, naturalised practical constraints cause the structures of the community to reify or fossilise (cf. Sörensen 2016).

The fourth and final crucial quality of a resonant relationship is, however, its fundamental unpredictability and uncontrollability. This means that a relationship of resonance can never be enforced or guaranteed; it cannot be *engineered*, neither institutionally nor instrumentally. What is more, the *outcome* of a resonant encounter is impossible to predict, anticipate, or control (Rosa 2020). Resonance is essentially open-ended. By consequence, there is no possible way of guaranteeing democratic resonance institutionally. It is impossible to create constitutional, procedural, or other safeguards which could ensure that the political process will be implemented in a mode of resonance. Torpor, alienation, instrumentalisation, and reification as alternative modes of political relations are always a possibility and a risk. Having said that, much to the chagrin of authoritarian and totalitarian rulers, this non-engineerability and uncontrollability fortunately also has the flip side that there is no way to suppress or prevent for sure the emergence of political resonance in the democratic and transformative sense outlined here.

Yet, uncontrollability does not mean that it is impossible to use social, legal, and organisational means to create the dispositional, cultural, and institutional *conditions* for resonant relationships. Thus, the constitutional institutions of democratic participation and representation can be, and should be, used to establish and protect the lines of connection, if you will, or the *axes of resonance* along which vibrant, responsive relationships can develop. Given the elusive nature of resonance, the quality of democracy, or of the common good, can never be determined or measured by simply using predefined *output* criteria. The substantive outcome of processes of resonance is, by necessity, undetermined.

If it is plausible to use the notion of resonance in order to understand the common good as a *specific type of relationship between citizens (axis 1)*, this reconceptualisation of the common good gets all the more attractive by the fact that all four elements of this relationship can also be applied to the ways people relate to the institutional reality they live in as a whole (axis 2), to their natural and material environment (axis 3), and to the past and future of a community (axis 4). For what emerges (in the mode of transformation and accepted uncontrollability) is a shared world arising from joint political action, much in line with Hannah Arendt's conception of politics (Arendt 1958; see also Sörensen 2016).

People living in the modern world generally do not see themselves as being part of a cosmic totality inhabited by spirits or decreed by God ('the great chain of Being'; Taylor 1991: 3), but rather as placed in a world that has become more or less arbitrary and shaped by historical coincidences, a world which strikes them as the contingent result of countless historical conflicts of interest. Consequently, the rules and institutions and hence also the socio-material space of the lifeworld are primarily perceived as something external, something determined by others, something which limits them and subjects them to all manners of restrictions. And yet, this modern world, with its strategy of democratic representation and participation, provides people with a powerful instrument enabling them to *appropriate* this lifeworld in a way that is transformative. This encapsulates the fundamental idea of modern political republicanism and the key promise of democracy (Buchstein 2018): the joint shaping of the world is the instrument by means of which society and public space can become *a sphere of resonance* for the citizens, a world which *responds* to their desires, values, and needs and in which they recognise themselves. The socio-political system thus becomes a structure that *is their own*. Again, when I say a structure that *is their own*, this does not mean that this system is fully consistent or in total harmony with their desires, needs, and interests, but rather that there is a constitutive *responsiveness* between the citizens and the institutions and practices, spaces and buildings, rules and traditions they live by. Hence, opposition or conflict is an important and inevitable form of this response – without contradiction, there can be no transformation or encounter, without the opposition of an *other*, there can be no *experience of resonance*.

Interestingly, this conception of responsivity can also be applied to our relationship with the natural, spatial, and material worlds around us: those who treat the material (and especially the living) environment simply as a *resource* to be exploited, shaped, and processed cannot experience that environment as a sphere of resonance or a vibrant *other* that is in a lasting and responsive reciprocal relationship with us as human beings. The reverse also holds true: those with a stable resonant relationship with the natural world (whatever your definition of that might be) need not *force* themselves to protect or care for the environment. Rather, this is something they will automatically do in order to avoid rendering the voice of that 'other' inaudible and then losing their own voice in the process. Resonance in this sense inevitably implies a certain ethics of care towards the other, and *nature* as an 'other' which should be *listened to* appears to be a conception vital for modern culture in many respects anyway (Taylor 1989: 305–92; Rosa 2019: 268–79). It figures in the way modern culture approaches the mountains and the forest, the desert and the sea, for example, and even in our fascination with organic food or horoscopes. Treating nature as a sphere of resonance rather than a repository for resources might provide a vital way out of the environmental crisis which clearly cannot be solved by 'green technologies' alone. This, however and obviously, requires giving up the idea of a sovereign stance vis-à-vis nature.

Finally, from a temporal perspective, the common good is achieved when a *resonant relationship* to both the past and the future materialises. With regard to the past, this means that, as citizens, the history of the community we live in actually *concerns us* and *has something to tell us*, that we are in a *responsive relationship* with that community, or the body politic, and its history. In fact, the success of a democratic process where the common good is attained is contingent on this. It involves all four principles of a relationship of resonance. (1) Past events and experiences actually continue to affect or move us. By no means do we have to be moved in a positive or pleasant way, however. For instance, someone visiting a concentration camp museum or a holocaust memorial may well experience an existential obligation arising from this memory of the past brought to life by the location. (2) The individual may react with a 'never again!' response that is (3) transformative, one which affects who they are at present and how they will act in the future, even if (4) they might not be able to specify exactly *what* the obligation is that arises from this situation (unpredictability). Such resonance creates a strong link, or an *axis of resonance*, from the past through the present to the future. This holds, I want to claim, despite the fact that *a vibrant relationship to the past* of course always is in danger of being turned in to an 'echo-chamber' of antagonistic memory politics, in which past violence and suffering is used to create a strong sense of an exclusionary 'us vs. them'. In my conception, 'echo' should be strictly distinguished from 'resonance' in that the former denotes the amplification and conceptual 'purification' of a given identity through a sharp demarcation from everything or everyone conceived of as 'other', while resonance means the transformation of a given identity through encounter with the *other*. A resonant relationship to the past in this sense could be developed not through an *antagonistic*, but through an *agonistic* mode of remembering in the sense of Anna Cento Bull and Hans Lauge Hansen (2016).

Furthermore, once someone feels a vibrant and responsive connection not only with past but also with future generations, they have an immediate sense, as it were, both emotional and physical, of the relevance of their actions for those who come after them. The consideration of future needs and interests then stops being an irksome obligation or a cost that outweighs the benefits; instead, it creates an experience of *connection* and *transformative self-efficacy*. Here, once again, the element of *dispositional care* that is implied in any relationship of resonance does the trick. Therefore, I am convinced that the quality of a democratic system can be 'measured' by the quality of trans-historical connection: the common good tends to be achieved where there is a vibrant axis of resonance connecting the past with the future. This axis of resonance does *not* determine actions in the present but rather *inspires* and *motivates* those actions.

However, if we thus redefine the conceptual pairing of the common good and democracy as a multidimensional relationship of resonance, one fundamental problem of any notion of the common good at first glance appears to remain unchanged: *whose* good are we talking about when we talk of the *common* good; where are *the boundaries* of the community we are referring to, and how does this community relate to the outside social world? My thesis (and my hope) here is that a society cannot be unjust, violent, repressive, or destructive to the *outside world* if it wishes to maintain the capacity to be resonant *within*. If we define the common good in terms of resonance theory as a complex of responsive relationships, then resonance describes a way of relating to the world as a whole, a way of *being in the world*. Repression, violence, and suppression, however, force not just the victims but also and particularly *the perpetrators* into an objectifying, repulsive stance towards others. This stance is characterised by the habitual, or dispositional, suppression of resonant relations and reactions in oneself *and* in others, and by the ruthless obliteration of the corresponding impulses. Thus, repression and violence impose a relationship with the world in which the transformative *listening* to the voice of the (genuine) other is systematically impeded or rendered impossible, while the echo-like amplification of our own unvarying voice is systematically promoted or enforced. Colonial injustice and oppression, for example, therefore is intrinsically tied to the west's development of a cold, *mute*, instrumental stance towards the world as a whole, identified, for example, by Theodor W. Adorno & Max Horkheimer (1997).

Conclusion

In sum, I am proposing that we try to reconceptualise the common good as the creation of five axes of resonance which, in a way, replace the five dimensions of sovereignty identified in section two of the present contribution: a *social axis* (which connects citizens to each other in a responsive mode), a *political axis* (which defines the relationship between citizens and the body politic as an institutional totality), an *environmental axis* (which defines the relationship between citizens and the natural and material world), a *temporal axis* (which connects the body politic to history, i.e. past and future), and finally an *external axis* (which defines the relationship between the body politic and its social 'outside'). *The common good, then, is achieved when and where the social and material, temporal and spatial conditions allow the respective axes of resonance to be established and maintained.*

Of course, *it is not* the argument of this chapter that resonance could simply replace the idea and ideal of sovereignty in a world driven by the escalatory logic of dynamic stabilisation and hence by the imperatives of growth, increase, innovation, and acceleration which undermine the whole essence of that idea. Rather, it is my claim that the prevailing notion of political sovereignty and *spiritual independence* with its emphasis on control and domination is a cultural correlate and driving force of that fateful escalatory logic itself. Hence, replacing it conceptually with relationships of resonance and responsivity might be a constitutive and crucial first step towards establishing an *alternative mode of structural reproduction and stabilisation* – and an alternative form of *being in the world*. It might then well turn out that resonance is not so much an alternative to sovereignty per se, but rather an alternative to a one-sided or even perverted interpretation of it. Perhaps it could actually be claimed that resonance is a more adequate interpretation of sovereignty, or at least, that it preserves its core aspirations. Sovereignty, in that perspective, is the insistence on *self-efficacy* (as the second element of a resonant relationship with the world). It refers to the idea that it is vitally important *to have a (political) say* in the world – to have an *effective voice* with respect to history, tradition, nature, fellow citizens, and other political entities. Resonance, then, only adds the idea that it is just as important to have *ears* – to be receptive, responsive, and willing as well as capable to be transformed in a way beyond control and prediction. *Resonant Sovereignty*, then, would be the name of the game we are looking for.

References

Adorno, T.W. & Horkheimer, M. (1997), *Dialectic of Enlightenment* (London, Verso).
Arendt, H. (1958), *The Human Condition* (Chicago, Chicago University Press).
Bauman, Z. (2000), *Liquid Modernity* (Cambridge, Polity Press).
Bedorf, T. & Herrmann, S. (eds) (2016), *Das soziale Band: Geschichte und Gegenwart eines sozialetheoretischen Grundbegriffs* (Frankfurt am Main & New York, Campus).
Blumenberg, H. (1985), *The Legitimacy of the Modern Age* (Boston, MIT Press).
Buchstein, H. (2018), 'Auf dem Weg zur Postwachstumsgesellschaft – Von der Resonanztheorie zur aleatorischen Demokratie', *Berliner Journal für Soziologie*, 28: 209–36.
Bull, A.C. & Hansen, H.L. (2016), 'On Agonistic Memory', *Memory Studies*, 9: 390–404.
Caplan, B. (2008), *The Myth of the Rational Voter: Why Democracies Choose Bad Policies* (Princeton, Princeton University Press).

Castells, M. (2010), *The Rise of the Network Society (The Information Age, Vol. 1)*, 2nd edn (Chichester, Wiley-Blackwell).
Crouch, C. (2004), *Post-Democracy* (Cambridge, Polity).
Dewey, J. (1954), 'The Eclipse of the Public', in *The Public and its Problems* (Athens OH, Ohio University Press), 138–42.
Ehrenberg, A. (2010), *The Weariness of the Self: Diagnosing the History of Depression in the Contemporary Age* (Montreal, McGill-Queens University Press).
Francot, L. & Mommers, S. (2016), 'Picking Up the Pace: Legal Slowness and the Authority of the Judiciary in the Acceleration Society (a Dutch Case Study)', *International Journal of the Legal Profession*, 24.3: 1–19.
Fukuyama, F. (1992), *The End of History and the Last Man* (London, Hamish Hamilton).
Habermas, J. (1987), *The Philosophical Discourse of Modernity* (Cambridge MA, MIT Press).
Hegel, G.W.F. (2008 [1820]), *Outlines of the Philosophy of Right* (Oxford, Oxford University Press).
Held, D. (ed.) (1993), *Prospects for Democracy: North, South, East, West* (Cambridge, Polity Press).
Held, D. (1996), *Models of Democracy*, 2nd edn (Cambridge, Polity Press).
Internationale Convivialiste (2020), *Second manifeste convivialiste: pour un monde post-néolibéral* (Arles, Actes Sud).
Koselleck, R. (1985), *Future Past: On the Semantics of Historical Time* (Cambridge MA, MIT Press).
Laclau, E. & Mouffe, C. (2014), *Hegemony and Socialist Strategy: Towards a Radical Democratic Politics*, 2nd edn (London, Verso).
Latour, B. (2013), *An Inquiry into Modes of Existence: An Anthropology of the Moderns* (Cambridge MA, Harvard University Press).
Love, N.S. (2006), *Musical Democracy* (Albany, State University of New York Press).
Luhmann, N. (1981), *Politische Theorie im Wohlfahrtsstaat* (Munich, Olzoc).
MacPherson, C.B. (1964), *The Political Theory of Possessive Individualism: Hobbes to Locke* (Oxford, Clarendon Press).
Marx, K. (1988 [1844]), *Economic and Philosophic Manuscripts of 1844* (Buffalo, Promotheus).
Nowotny, H. (1996), *Time: The Modern and Postmodern Experience* (Cambridge & Malden MA, Polity).
Parsons, T. (1971), *The System of Modern Societies* (Englewood Cliffs, Prentice Hall).
Rancière, J. (2013), *Dissensus. On Politics and Aesthetics* (London, Bloomsbury).
Reheis, F. (1996), *Kreativität der Langsamkeit. Neuer Wohlstand durch Entschleunigung* (Darmstadt, Wissenschaftliche Buchgesellschaft).
Riescher, G. (1994), *Zeit und Politik. Zur institutionellen Bedeutung von Zeitstrukturen in parlamentarischen und präsidentiellen Regierungssystemen* (Baden-Baden, Nomos).
Rosa, H. (2005), 'The Speed of Global Flows and the Pace of Democratic Politics', *New Political Science*, 27: 445–59.
Rosa, H. (2013), *Social Acceleration: A New Theory of Modernity* (New York, Columbia University Press).
Rosa, H. (2017), 'Für eine affirmative Revolution. Eine Antwort auf meine Kritiker', in C.H. Peters & P. Schulz (eds), *Resonanzen und Dissonanzen. Hartmut Rosas kritische Theorie in der Diskussion* (Bielefeld: transcript), 311–30.
Rosa, H. (2019), *Resonance: A Sociology of Our Relationship to the World* (Cambridge & New York, Polity).

Rosa, H. (2020), *The Uncontrollability of the World* (Cambridge & New York, Polity Press).
Rosa, H. & Scheuerman, W. (eds) (2009), *High-Speed Society: Social Acceleration, Power and Modernity* (University Park, Pennsylvania State University Press).
Rosa, H., Dörre, K., & Lessenich, S.S. (2017), 'Appropriation, Activation and Acceleration: The Escalatory Logics of Capitalist Modernity and the Crisis of Dynamic Stabilization', *Theory, Culture and Society*, 34: 53–74.
Scheuerman, W. (2001), 'Liberal Democracy and the Empire of Speed', *Polity*, 34: 41–67.
Scheuerman, W. (2004), *Liberal Democracy and the Social Acceleration of Time* (Baltimore & London, Johns Hopkins University Press).
Schmitt, C. (1950), 'The Motorized Legislator', in Rosa & Scheuerman (2009), 65–75.
Sennett, R. (1999), *The Corrosion of Character* (New York, W.W. Norton & Company).
Sörensen, P. (2016), *Entfremdung als Schlüsselbegriff einer kritischen Theorie der Politik. Eine Systematisierung im Ausgang von Karl Marx, Hannah Arendt und Cornelius Castoriadis* (Baden-Baden, Nomos).
Stoppe, G., Bramesfeld, A., & Schwartz, F.-W. (eds) (2006), *Volkskrankheit Depression? Bestandsaufnahme und Perspektiven* (Heidelberg, Springer).
Taylor, C. (1985), 'Legitimation Crisis?', in *Philosophical Papers, vol. 2: Philosophy and the Human Sciences* (Cambridge, Cambridge University Press), 235–94.
Taylor, C. (1989), *Sources of the Self: The Making of the Modern Identity* (Cambridge MA, Harvard University Press).
Taylor, C. (1991), *The Ethics of Authenticity* (Cambridge MA, Harvard University Press).
UNODC (United Nations Office on Drugs and Crime) (2015), *World Drug Report 2015* (New York: United Nations Publication).
Wittman, D.A. (1997), *The Myth of Democratic Failure: Why Political Institutions Are Efficient* (Chicago, Chicago University Press).

Index

Aeschylus, *Suppliant Women* 290–1
Agamben, Giorgio 2, 82–3, 155, 257, 314
Ai, Chinese emperor 108
Akaev, Askar, President, Kyrgyzstan 204
Alexander the Great 297, 299, 300
Alfenus Varus, Publius, Roman writer 49, 52
Angwenyi, Christopher 268, 270
Anthropocene 2
Antigone 23
archives 317
Arena, Valentina 70
Arendt, Hannah 59, 262, 286, 307–20
Argentina, economy 223
Argos, ancient 282
Armenia 198
Association of Southeast Asian Nations (ASEAN) 181
asylum 292–4, 315
Atambaev, Almazbek, President, Kyrgyzstan 198
Athens, Athenians, ancient 23, 25, 29, 285, 290–6, 298, 300
Augustus, Roman emperor 72–4, 78–92; *Res Gestae* 85–8
Australia 123–44; Aboriginal Tent Embassy 289; contemporary formulations of sovereignty 141; Kulin nation 132–40; 'Statement from the Heart' 143
autonomy 283

Balbus, L. Cornelius, Roman writer 66
Bandung Conference 311
banks, banking 225–6
Barak, William, *ngurungaeta* of theWurundjeri clan 138
Batichos of Kos 301
Batman, John, British colonist 132
Belarus 198
Bello, Andrés, jurist 240
Benjamin, Walter 89
Bethlehem 5
Bhabha, Homi 314
Biden, Joseph, President, US 1
Billibellary, *ngurungaeta*, Wurundjeri clan, Kulin nation 136
Bodin, Jean 3, 17, 19, 23, 26–7, 79, 81–2, 88, 126, 128, 149, 193, 212–14
Boni, Giacomo 3
Bourke, British Governor 133

Brexit, Brexit referendum 1, 8, 249, 330
British empire 127
Burkina Faso 183

Caesar, G. Julius 64, 72–4, 84
Calvo, Carlos 240
Canada, economy 221
Carthage; Adherbal (Carthaginian general) 61
Chakrabarty, Dipesh 150
China 1; and AIIB 181; and Asian Infrastructure Investment Bank 180; and Belt and Road Initiative 180; calendars, early imperial 108; Chinese Communist Party 174; Chinese School of International Relations 171, 175; Chinese World Order 171–84; Cross-Strait Service Trade Agreement 183; early imperial 99–117; Economic Cooperation Framework Agreement 182; First Opium War, 1840 174; Five Principles of Peaceful Coexistence 176, 179; Han dynasty 114; modern 171–84; Qin dynasty 104–7; 'Rhapsody Criticising the World and Objecting to Evil' (Ci shi ji xie fu), mid 2nd century CE 112; Solitary Decisions (Du duan) c.189 CE 111; and South China Sea 181; and Taiwan 172, 181–3; Zhou dynasty 99–117
cholera 280
Cicero, Marcus Tullius 74, 79, 285
Clazomenae, ancient 300
climate change 331
Corinth 15, 20
COVID-19 182–3, 211, 226–8, 230, 331–2

Danaids, daughters of Danaos 290, 295
Decimus Brutus, Roman general 68
Deiotarus, Armenian general 64
Delphi, ancient 298
democracy 1, 23, 158, 193, 230, 328–30, 333, 335, 337, 339
desynchronisation 323–40
Diogenes the Cynic 298, 300
Dionysius, tyrant of Syracuse 53
Dominican Republic 183
Draghi, Mario, Head of the European Central Bank 189, 228
Duterte, Rodrigo, President, Philippines 180

East India Company 240
Egypt 296
El Nino 280
El Salvador 183
Eurasian Economic Union 198
Euripides, Children of Herakles 292–4
European Central Bank 1, 215, 222–3, 225–8, 230
European Commission 243
European Council 211
European Investment Bank 226
European Stability Mechanism 226
European Union 7, 28, 213
Exodus 319

Facebook 210, 215, 230
fascism 91
Fiddian-Qasmiyeh, Elena 315
financial crisis, 2009 226
Flamininus, T. Quinctius, Roman general 67
Foucault, Michel 82, 91, 155
Founding Fathers, America 117
Frazer, James George 3
free markets 193
freedom 283, 312
Freud, Sigmund 6
Fukuyama, Francis and the end of history 3

Gallus, Gaius Cornelius, Roman general 88
Gandhi, Mahatma 159, 162, 165
Genschel, P. 28
George V, King 159
Germany, economy 215, 222
Glenelg, Lord, British Colonial Secretary 133
globalisation 235, 238
Gortyn, ancient, lawcode 29
Gramsci, Antonio 91
Greece; ancient 15–30; modern 302, 327
Grimm, Dieter 17
Grotius, Hugo 128
Guangwu, Chinese emperor 108
Gumilev, Lev 204

Habermas, Jürgen 324
Hart, H.L.A. 24
Hegel, George 326
Herodotus 15, 20
Hobbes, Thomas 18, 19, 126, 128, 149–50, 156, 193
human rights 5, 7–8, 131, 178–9, 184, 193, 198–9, 271, 283, 286, 291, 311

India 147–65; East India Company 149, 151–2, 155–6; Government of India Act, 1858 151; Government of India Act, 1919 152, 158; Nehru report 158; regional kingdoms 151; Round Table Conference, 1930–1932 158; 'Sepoy Mutiny', 1857 149; Simon Commission 158
Indonesia 180, 297
International Bar Association 243
International Civil Aviation Organization 183
International Criminal Court (ICC) 18
Isocrates, Greek politician and orator 295
Israel 311, 316
Italy, economy 226

Japan 180
Johnson, Boris, Prime Minister, UK 1, 331
Jupiter 60

Karimov, Islam, President, Uzbekistan 199
Kazakhstan 189–206
Kelsen, Hans 149
Kenya, Meteorological Department 265
Kiribati 183
Koselleck, Reinhart 324, 329
Krasner, Stephen 4, 19, 21, 239, 286, 294, 296
Kyrgyzstan 189–206

Lanchester, John 6
Latour, Bruno 3
law of nations 129
League of Nations 153
Lebanon 307–20; Baddawi refugee camp 307–20
Lehman Brothers, US investment bank 223
Livy, Titus, Roman historian 58–74, 79
Locke, John 18, 149
Luhmann, Niklas 327
Lysander, Spartan general 302

Ma Ying-jeou, President, Taiwan 182
Mabo, Eddie, Australian aboriginal litigant 141
Macdonald, Ramsay, Prime Minister, UK 159, 165
Mao Zedong, President, China 176
Mark Antony, Roman general, politician 68–70, 84
Marx, Karl 326–7
Marxism 176
Mau Mau, rebellion, Kenya 1952–1960 259
May, Theresa, Prime Minister, UK 1
Médecins Sans Frontières 265, 277
Meier, Christian 23, 25
Melos 294
Merkel, Angela, Chancellor, Germany 226
Millar, Fergus 39
modernity 323–40

monetary agency 216
Mutina, ancient 68

Nairobi 259–80; Dandora 260; Eastlands 265; Jamaica 266; Kaloleni 260; Mathare 280
Nawle, V.M., editor of *Dinbandhoo* newspaper 164
Northern Ireland, protocol 1
Nyquist, Mary 2

Odysseus 284
Organisation for Economic Co-operation and Development (OECD) 244
Ostwald, Martin 25
Otieno, Peter 269–73
Ovid, P. Ovidius Naso, Roman poet 88

Palestine 288, 296, 308; al-Nakba 315
Panama 183
Paris Peace Conference 153
Parker, Edward, Assistant Protector, Australia 134, 135
Parsons, Talcott 324
Pelasgos, king of Argos 284, 290
Peloponnesian War 293
Periander 15, 27
Persia, ancient 20
Philip Morris, tobacco manufacturer 242
Philip, captain, British naval officer 127, 132
Philippines 180
Plataea, Plataeans, ancient 295–6
Polybius, Greek historian 24, 79
Pompey, Gn. Pompeius Magnus 64, 66
Poroshenko, Petro, President, Ukraine 202
Port Phillip Association 133
power 283
Pufendorf, Samuel 126, 285
Putin, Vladimir, President, Russia 1, 191

Qasmiyeh, Yousif M., poet 320
Quebec 4

Rabirius, Gaius Rabirius Postumus, Roman businessman 68
Rahmon, Emomali, President, Tajikistan 204
Rao Bahadur Chaudhri Lal Chand, Hon. Lieutenant, Punjab 164
Refugee Hosts, research project 315
'Responsibility to Protect' 191
Rhodes, ancient 64
Rome; Augustan restoration of Republic 85; condominium 62; *imperium* 59, 88; kings 2, 61; *maiestas populi Romani* 26, 38, 88; notion of *res publica* 38–54; *parricidium* 68; *patria potestas*, *paterfamilias* 2, 29, 62, 68, 74; penalties, punishment 46; *perduellio* 68; *persona* 63; popular sovereignty 38–54; *potestas* 59, 81; Republican 23, 25, 38–54, 58–74, 78–92; Roman empire 21, 78–92; Roman law 38–54; second triumvirate 84; *Senatus Consultum Ultimum* 24; tribunes of the plebs 22; and Veii 61
Rosa, Hartmut 9
'Round Table' movement 154
Rousseau, Jean-Jacques 149
Russia, Russian Federation 189–206, 223

Sallust, Gaius Sallustius Crispus, Roman historian 61
sanctuaries 284, 298
Saturninus, L. Appuleius, Roman politician 64
Schmitt, Carl 4, 5, 24, 59, 81, 84, 126, 285, 306
Scholz, Olaf, Finance Minister and Chancellor, Germany 210
Second World War 296, 310, 338
Select Committee of the Legislative Council on the Aborigines 134
Seneca, L. Annaeus, the Elder 67
Seneca, L. Annaeus, the younger 89
Serres, Michel 3
Six Day War 315
Skinner, Quentin 60, 67
slavery 2
Solomon Islands 183
Sophocles 23
South Africa 259–80
sovereign debt 1
sovereignty; and anthropology 280; and biopolitics 83; and 'bundles of rights' 8; and charisma 104, 107, 110; and colonialism 126; and contingency 191, 212; and decolonisation 241; and disease 259–80; and divisibility 190, 213; and fiction 60–3; as foundational authority 59; and God, religion 58; and hyper-sovereignty 178; and hypocrisy 4, 19; and imperialism 240; indigenous views of 144; inherited 110; and jurisprudence 126–9; and law 235–50; and the 'Mandate of Heaven' (China) 99–117; medieval 17; and merit 99–117; and monetary sovereignty 210–31; and myth 6, 150; and performance 6; and political authority 149; popular sovereignty 6, 25; and postcolonialism 189–206, and power 4; and reciprocity 297; and religion 102; and resonance 323–40; and scale 151; and sovereign assemblies 22; sovereigntism 3; and space, geography 148; and spectacle

159–63; and the state of exception 4; and the subaltern 157–8, 163–5; and supreme command 148; and territory 236; and Treaty of Westphalia 176, 199, 212, 237, 242, 287, 307
Sparta, Spartans 21, 290, 291, 293, 296, 298, 302
state, stateness, statehood 27, 30, 44, 47, 52, 53, 58, 59, 61, 67, 83, 90, 91, 92, 126, 131, 141, 158, 170, 176, 199, 214, 221, 229, 239, 240–2, 246, 249, 262, 286, 309
statelessness 307–20
Stephen, Alfred, British Attorney-General 133
Strickland, Rev. and Mrs, Coranderrk Aboriginal Station 139
Sulla, L. Cornelius, Roman general and politician 84
synchronisation 328
Syracuse, ancient 53
Syria 7, 296

Tacirtus, Publius Cornelius, Roman historian 79, 88, 89
Taiwan 1; Cross-Strait Service Trade Agreement 183; Economic Cooperation Framework Agreement 182
Tajikistan 189–206
Taylor, Charles 324, 325, 337
Tegea, ancient 298
Teik Su Myat Paya Gale, Princess, Burma 163
Thebes, Thebans, ancient 295, 298
Thomas, Edward, Assistant Protector 137
Thomas, William, Assistant Protector, Australia 134
Thucydides, Greek historian 20, 290, 293; Melian Dialogue 20
Tiberius, Roman emperor 88
Tokaev, Kassym-Jomart, President, Kazakhstan 198
Torre, Corinne, Nairobi 270, 276, 277
Transatlantic Trade and Investment Partnership 244
Trans-Pacific Partnership 244
Treaty of Westphalia 127
Tribunal Arbitral du Sport (TAS) 18
Trump, Donald, President, US 1, 189, 331
Tsai Ing-wen, President, Taiwan 183
Turkestan 200
Turkey 302
Turkmenistan 189–206

Ukraine 1, 7; Crimea 191, 202
United Nations 177, 178, 181, 202, 236, 265, 283, 286, 288, 311, 333; Conference on Trade and Development 244; High Commissioner for Refugees 316; Refugee Convention, 1951 286; Relief and Works Agency for Palestinian Refugees in the Near East 316
United Nations Commission on Human Rights 198
United Nations Commission on International Trade Law (UNCITRAL) 244, 247
United Nations Declaration of the Rights of Indigenous Peoples 129
urban planning 260
US Federal Reserve 218
Uzbekistan 189–206

vaccine sovereignty 1
Varro, M. Terentius, Roman writer 52
Vattenfall, energy company 242
Venezuela 267
Verres, Gaius, Roman general and politician 68
Victoria, Queen 157
von Wolff, Christian 285

Wang Mang, Chinese emperor 108
Wanjiru, Esther, Nairobi 265, 266, 268, 270, 274
Weber, Max 16, 63, 327
Wittgenstein, Ludwig 4, 16
Wonga, Simon, son of Billibellary 136
World Bank 239, 244
World Health Organization (WHO) 182, 183, 332
World Trade Organization 182, 244

Xenophon, Greek general and historian 298, 301, 302
Xi Jinping, President, China 171, 175, 178, 182

Yelle, Robert 116

Zangl, B. 28
Zimbabwe 263; Lake Mutirikwi 263